CompTIA®
Linux+™/LPIC-1

Training and Exam Preparation Guide

Exam Codes
LX0-103/101-400
LX0-104/102-400

First Edition

October 2017

Asghar Ghori

www.ingramspark.com

Technical Reviewer and Proof Reader: George Doumas
https://www.linkedin.com/in/george-doumas-2a104520/

Editors: FirstEditing.com
Cover Design: Rayan Syed

Printed in the USA, UK, France, Germany, Italy, Spain, and Australia.

ISBN: 978-1-7750621-0-3
Library of Congress Control Number: 2017911488

Printed and Distributed by: IngramSpark

To order in bulk at special quantity discounts for sales promotions or for use in training programs, please contact the author at *asghar_ghori2002@yahoo.com*

The following are registered trademarks in the U.S. and other countries:

Linux® is a registered trademark of Linus Torvalds.

CompTIA® is a registered trademark of CompTIA, Inc.

Linux+™ is a registered trademark of CompTIA, Inc.

LPI® is a registered trademark of Linux Professional Institute, Inc.

Oracle® is a registered trademark of Oracle Corporation, Inc.

Red Hat® is a registered trademark of Red Hat, Inc.

Ubuntu® and associated logos are registered trademarks of Canonical Ltd.

UNIX® is a registered trademark of The Open Group.

Microsoft® and Windows® are registered trademarks of Microsoft Corporation.

Intel® is the trademark or registered trademark of Intel Corporation or its subsidiaries.

All other trademarks, registered trademarks, and logos used in this book are the property of their respective owners.

The author has made his best efforts to prepare this book. The contents are based on CompTIA Linux+ Powered by LPI/LPIC-1 certification objectives version 4.0 for exam codes LX0-103/101-400 and LX0-104/102-400 published in January 2015, and are available on CompTIA's website at *https://certification.comptia.org/certifications/linux* and Linux Professional Institute's website at *http://www.lpi.org/our-certifications/lpic-1-overview*. The author makes no representation or warranties of any kind with regard to the completeness or accuracy of the contents herein and accepts no liability whatsoever including but not limited to merchantability, fitness for any particular purpose, or any losses or damages of any kind caused or allegedly caused directly or indirectly from this material. This book may be used to prepare for the CompTIA Linux+ Powered by LPI certification exams LX0-103 and LX0-104 (or LPI's LPIC-1 exam codes 101-400 and 102-400). Neither author nor publisher warrants that use of this publication will ensure passing the relevant exams or that the information contained herein is endorsed by CompTIA or Linux Professional Institute.

Preface

I wrote this book to create the most useful, effective, informative, and educational resource for readers who intend to learn Linux and want to prepare for the CompTIA Linux+/LPIC-1 certification exams, LX0-103/101-400 and LX0-104/102-400. I am confident that I have attained these objectives in this finished product.

In each chapter, I categorized the exam objectives according to the flow of the discussion and where they appeared to best support a convenient and logical learning path. I encourage readers to read each chapter chronologically, learn a concept, command, or topic, try it, ponder over the results, and move on to the next topic. Jumping around may result in confusion, frustration, and spending more time than required.

At the very outset in chapter 1, I furnished assistance to build a lab environment for practicing. Do not skip this chapter. As you read the book, please have your Linux lab systems up and running and switch user IDs or systems as depicted in the command prompt in order to get the most out of your time and effort. Each command demonstrated in this book was actually run on the indicated system and as the indicated user. Do not expect to see an identical output or behavior of a command or program on your lab system. Differences might occur due to variances in hardware configuration or software versions.

The CompTIA Linux+ Powered by LPI/LPIC-1 certification exams are distribution-neutral and vendor-neutral, which means that the exam objectives are not specific to any particular Linux distribution or vendor. However, a closer look at the objectives indicates that they are taken from two major distributions of Linux—Red Hat Enterprise Linux (RHEL) and Debian Linux—and they include topics from the distributions' latest as well as old versions. I, therefore, opted for CentOS Linux (a popular offshoot of RHEL) and Ubuntu Linux (a Debian Linux spinoff) to base the book material.

At the end of each chapter, I have provided an at-a-glance review of the entire chapter, which provides a one-sentence review of key topics discussed in that chapter. The two certification exams are multiple-choice and fill-in-the-blank, so I have provided one quiz per exam that contains sample questions with answers in the appendices. It is recommended to take the first quiz after you have completed Part One and the second quiz after finishing Part Two.

I maintain _www.getitcertify.com_ to support my readers with errata, additional exam information, and links to helpful resources. I have a YouTube channel— _https://www.youtube.com/channel/UCudp1t4z-W_OfsrGrE6uLiw_—where I upload useful videos on Linux. Visit my website and YouTube channel for updates.

I thank you for reading this book and hope that it serves you well. If you would like to ask any questions or send me some feedback, please email me at _asghar_ghori2002@yahoo.com_. We are all learners, and I am always open to suggestions for improvement and suggestions on what you would like to see different in the next edition.

Good luck in your endeavors.   Asghar Ghori / October, 2017 / Toronto, Canada

Acknowledgments

I am grateful to God who enabled me to write and publish this book successfully.

I would like to express my gratitude to my peers, students, friends, editors, YouTube channel subscribers, and readers of my previous books who offered support, provided comments, and aided in the layout, editing, and proofreading of this work. I am thankful to all of them for their generous assistance.

George Doumas, you deserve special kudos for your invaluable and productive feedback in minimizing the number of technical and grammatical errors and mistakes.

I want to express my special thanks to my wife and children who tolerated my mental absence as I sat right in front of them and worked on this project. I could not have accomplished it without their support.

Lastly, I would like to offer my very special tributes to my deceased parents and sister.

About The Author

Asghar Ghori is a seasoned Linux/UNIX consultant, trainer, and author. As a consultant, his experience ranges from IT infrastructure deployment, support, and administration to architecture, design, and consulting. As a trainer, Ghori has designed and delivered numerous training programs. He has six books on UNIX and Linux to his credit.

Ghori holds a bachelor of science in engineering. He is CompTIA Linux+ Powered by LPI/LPIC-1 Certified, RHCE, RHCSA, HP CSA, HP CSE, SCSA, IBM Certified Specialist for AIX, and CNE. He holds ITIL Foundation and PMP certifications as well.

Ghori lives in a small town near Toronto, Ontario, Canada with his wife and children. He can be reached via email at asghar_ghori2002@yahoo.com or on LinkedIn.

Previous publications of Asghar Ghori are:

1. RHCSA & RHCE Red Hat Enterprise Linux 7: Training and Exam Preparation Guide (EX200 and EX300), Third Edition (ISBN: 978-1495148200), published March 2015

2. Red Hat Certified System Administrator & Engineer: Training Guide and a Quick Deskside Reference (ISBN: 978-1467549400) (RHEL version 6), published December 2012

3. Red Hat Certified Technician & Engineer (RHCT and RHCE) Training Guide and Administrator's Reference (ISBN: 978-1615844302) (RHEL version 5), published August 2009

4. HP-UX: HP Certified Systems Administrator, Exam HP0-A01, Training Guide and Administrator's Reference (ISBN: 978-1606436547) (HP-UX 11iv3), published October 2008

5. HP Certified Systems Administrator, Exam HP0-095, Training Guide and Administrator's Reference (ISBN: 978-1424342310) (HP-UX 11iv2 and 11iv3), published August 2007

6. Certified System Administrator for HP-UX: Study Guide and Administrator's Reference (ISBN: 978-1419645938) (HP-UX 11iv1), published August 2006

Conventions Used In This Book

The following typographic and other conventions are used in this book:

Book Antiqua Italic 10 pt. is used to highlight new terms. For example:

> "The term *open source* is referred to the software with source code that is available to the public for download, duplication, amendment, repackaging, and re-sharing."

Times Roman Italic 10 pt. is used in text paragraphs to highlight names of commands, files, directories, service daemons, users, groups, hostnames, domains, and URLs. For example:

> "It has three additional hard links named *fsck.ext2*, *fsck.ext3*, and *fsck.ext4* (on *ubuntu14*, they are soft links under */sbin*)."

Times New Roman 9 pt. is used to segregate command output, contents of shell scripts and configuration files, and information expected to be entered in configuration files from surrounding text. This font and size is also used for text in tables.

Times Roman Bold 10 pt. is used to highlight commands within text paragraphs (example 1) and on the command line (example 2) that the user is expected to execute.

Example 1:

> "The *telinit* command is symlinked to *init* (run **ll /sbin/telinit** to verify), so it does not really matter which of the two you run, as both will have an identical effect."

Example 2:

> `[user1@centos73 ~]$` **ls >> ls.out**

`Consolas` 10 pt. is used for the command prompts, which identify the user account and the system where the user is expected to type and run a command. For instance, command prompts `[user1@centos73 ~]$` and `user1@ubuntu14:~$` indicate user1 running a command on centos73/ubuntu14 and the command prompt `[root@centos511 ~]#` represents the root user on centos511.

All headings and sub-headings are in California FB font, and are bolded.

Key sequences, such as `Ctrl+a` and `Ctrl+c`, imply that the user holds down the `Ctrl` key and then press the other key. `Courier New` 10 pt. is used to highlight such combinations. This font is also used for keystrokes, such as `Enter` and `Esc`.

. . . . Dotted lines represent truncated command output for brevity.

About CompTIA Linux+ Powered by LPI/ LPIC-1 Certification Exams

The CompTIA Linux+ Powered by LPI certification exams (LX0-103 and LX0-104) [also referred to as LPIC-1 exams 101-400 and 102-400] test a candidate's foundational knowledge of the Linux system. Each exam is 90 minutes in length and there is a mix of 60 single-response, multiple-response, and fill-in-the-blank type questions. During the exams, candidates do not have access to the Internet, a running Linux system, an electronic gadget, or to printed and electronic documentation, and they are not allowed to talk to other candidates taking the exam. Visit *https://certification.comptia.org/certifications/linux* or *http://www.lpi.org/our-certifications/lpic-1-overview* for up-to-date and in-depth information and exam policies.

The official exam objectives are grouped in 10 major categories (or topics)—4 for LX0-103/101-400 and 6 for LX0-104/102-400. Each major topic also indicates a percentage of its coverage. These 10 major topics and their percentages are:

LX0-103/101-400

Topic 101: System architecture	14%
Topic 102: Linux installation and package management	18%
Topic 103: GNU and Unix commands	43%
Topic 104: Devices, Linux File Systems, and Filesystem Hierarchy Standard	25%
	Total: 100%

LX0-104/102-400

Topic 105: Shells, Scripting, and Data Management	17%
Topic 106: User Interfaces and Desktops	8%
Topic 107: Administrative Tasks	20%
Topic 108: Essential System Services	17%
Topic 109: Networking Fundamentals	23%
Topic 110: Security	15%
	Total: 100%

Each major topic is divided into multiple sub-topics (or exam objectives). There are a total of 86 objectives for LX0-103/101-400 and 75 for LX0-104/102-400. Each objective provides a description, lists the knowledge areas, and highlights the files, key terms, and commands that are included in it.

Each objective has a "weight" associated with it, which designates the number of questions to expect on the exam from that objective. For instance, objective 101.1 with weight 2 implies that you expect to see 2 questions on the exam covering knowledge areas 1 to 8 and the listed files, terms, and utilities.

Based on the above explanation, here is the number of questions from each topic that you should expect to see on the certification exams:

LX0-103/101-400	%	?s
Topic 101: System architecture	14%	8
Topic 102: Linux installation and package management	18%	11
Topic 103: GNU and Unix commands	43%	26
Topic 104: Devices, Linux File Systems, and Filesystem Hierarchy Standard	25%	15
Total: 100%		**60**

LX0-104/102-400	%	?s
Topic 105: Shells, Scripting, and Data Management	17%	10
Topic 106: User Interfaces and Desktops	8%	4
Topic 107: Administrative Tasks	20%	12
Topic 108: Essential System Services	17%	11
Topic 109: Networking Fundamentals	23%	14
Topic 110: Security	15%	9
Total: 100%		**60**

For convenience, I have enumerated "key knowledge areas" under exam objectives and highlighted the chapter(s) where you can find them. I have also provided a description alongside each objective for assistance in locating them in the book. If an objective spans multiple chapters, apposite references are furnished. This information is furnished at the beginning of each chapter as well.

I have also summarized the exam objectives, chapters you can find them, associated weights, the number of questions to expect on the exam, and other useful information in a tabular format under "Summary of Exam Objectives and Relevant Details" following the detailed list of the exam objectives. This summary contains most of the information that I have already described here; however, the intent is to provide a quick and convenient reference.

LX0-103/101-400 Exam Objectives

Topic 101: System Architecture (14%)

101.1 Determine and configure hardware settings (weight 2) [this entire objective is covered in chapter 7]

Candidates should be able to determine and configure fundamental system hardware.

Key Knowledge Areas:
1. Enable and disable integrated peripherals
2. Configure systems with or without external peripherals such as keyboards
3. Differentiate between the various types of mass storage devices
4. Know the differences between coldplug and hotplug devices
5. Determine hardware resources for devices
6. Tools and utilities to list various hardware information (e.g. lsusb, lspci, etc.)
7. Tools and utilities to manipulate USB devices
8. Conceptual understanding of sysfs, udev, dbus

The following is a partial list of the used files, terms and utilities: /sys, /proc, /dev, modprobe, lsmod, lspci, lsusb

101.2 Boot the system (weight 3) [this entire objective is covered in chapter 6]

Candidates should be able to guide the system through the booting process.

Key Knowledge Areas:
9. Provide common commands to the bootloader and options to the kernel at boot time
10. Demonstrate knowledge of the boot sequence from BIOS to boot completion
11. Understanding of SysVinit and systemd
12. Awareness of Upstart
13. Check boot events in the log files

The following is a partial list of the used files, terms and utilities: dmesg, BIOS, bootloader, kernel, initramfs, init, SysVinit, system

101.3 Change runlevels / boot targets and shutdown or reboot system (weight 3) [this entire objective is covered in chapter 6]

Candidates should be able to manage the SysVinit runlevel or systemd boot target of the system. This objective includes changing to single user mode, shutdown or rebooting the system. Candidates should be able to alert users before switching runlevels / boot targets and properly terminate processes. This objective also includes setting the default SysVinit runlevel or systemd boot target. It also includes awareness of Upstart as an alternative to SysVinit or systemd.

Key Knowledge Areas:
14. Set the default runlevel or boot target
15. Change between runlevels / boot targets including single user mode
16. Shutdown and reboot from the command line
17. Alert users before switching runlevels / boot targets or other major system events

18. Properly terminate processes

The following is a partial list of the used files, terms and utilities: /etc/inittab, shutdown, init, /etc/init.d, telinit, system, systemctl, /etc/systemd/, /usr/lib/system/, wall

Topic 102: Linux Installation and Package Management (18%)

102.1 Design hard disk layout (weight 2) [this entire objective is covered in chapter 8]

Candidates should be able to design a disk partitioning scheme for a Linux system.

Key Knowledge Areas:
19. Allocate filesystems and swap space to separate partitions or disks
20. Tailor the design to the intended use of the system
21. Ensure the /boot partition conforms to the hardware architecture requirements for booting
22. Knowledge of basic features of LVM

The following is a partial list of the used files, terms and utilities: /(root) filesystem, /var filesystem, /home filesystem, /boot filesystem, swap space, mount points, partitions

102.2 Install a boot manager (weight 2) [this entire objective is covered in chapter 6]

Candidates should be able to select, install and configure a boot manager.

Key Knowledge Areas:
23. Providing alternative boot locations and backup boot options
24. Install and configure a bootloader such as GRUB Legacy
25. Perform basic configuration changes for GRUB 2
26. Interact with the bootloader

The following is a partial list of the used files, terms and utilities: menu.lst, grub.cfg and grub.conf; grub-install, grub-mkconfig, MBR

102.3 Manage shared libraries (weight 1) [this entire objective is covered in chapter 5]

Candidates should be able to determine the shared libraries that executable programs depend on and install them when necessary.

Key Knowledge Areas:
27. Identify shared libraries
28. Identify the typical locations of system libraries
29. Load shared libraries

The following is a partial list of the used files, terms and utilities: ldd, ldconfig, /etc/ld.so.conf, LD_LIBRARY_PATH

102.4 Use Debian package management (weight 3) [this entire objective is covered in chapter 5]

Candidates should be able to perform package management using the Debian package tools.

Key Knowledge Areas:
  30. Install, upgrade and uninstall Debian binary packages
  31. Find packages containing specific files or libraries which may or may not be installed
  32. Obtain package information like version, content, dependencies, package integrity and installation status (whether or not the package is installed)

The following is a partial list of the used files, terms and utilities: /etc/apt/sources.list, dpkg, dpkg-reconfigure, apt-get, apt-cache, aptitude

102.5 Use RPM and YUM package management (weight 3) [this entire objective is covered in chapter 5]

Candidates should be able to perform package management using RPM and YUM tools.

Key Knowledge Areas:
  33. Install, re-install, upgrade and remove packages using RPM and YUM
  34. Obtain information on RPM packages such as version, status, dependencies, integrity and signatures
  35. Determine what files a package provides, as well as find which package a specific file comes from

The following is a partial list of the used files, terms and utilities: rpm, rpm2cpio, /etc/yum.conf, /etc/yum.repos.d/, yum, yumdownloader

Topic 103: GNU and Unix Commands (43%)

103.1 Work on the command line (weight 4) [a part of this objective is covered in chapter 1 and the rest in chapter 4]

Candidates should be able to interact with shells and commands using the command line. The objective assumes the Bash shell.

Key Knowledge Areas:
  36. Use single shell commands and one line command sequences to perform basic tasks on the command line [chapter 1]
  37. Use and modify the shell environment including defining, referencing and exporting environment variables [chapter 4]
  38. Use and edit command history [chapter 4]
  39. Invoke commands inside and outside the defined path [chapter 4]

The following is a partial list of the used files, terms and utilities: [chapter 1: pwd, man, and uname], [chapter 4: bash, echo, env, export, set, unset, history, and .bash_history]

103.2 Process text streams using filters (weight 3) [a part of this objective is covered in chapter 2 and the rest in chapter 3]

Candidates should be able to apply filters to text streams.

Key Knowledge Areas:
  40. Send text files and output streams through text utility filters to modify the output using standard UNIX commands found in the GNU textutils package

The following is a partial list of the used files, terms and utilities: [chapter 2: head, tail, and less], [chapter 3: cat, cut, expand, fmt, od, join, nl, paste, pr, sed, sort, split, tr, unexpand, uniq, and wc]

103.3 Perform basic file management (weight 4) [most of this objective is covered in chapter 2, a part in chapter 4, and tar/cpio and dd commands in chapters 1 and 8, respectively]

Candidates should be able to use the basic Linux commands to manage files and directories.

Key Knowledge Areas:
  41. Copy, move and remove files and directories individually [chapter 2]
  42. Copy multiple files and directories recursively [chapter 2]
  43. Remove files and directories recursively [chapter 2]
  44. Use simple and advanced wildcard specifications in commands [chapter 4]
  45. Using find to locate and act on files based on type, size, or time [chapter 2]
  46. Usage of tar, cpio and dd [chapters 1 and 8]

The following is a partial list of the used files, terms and utilities: [chapter 1: tar, cpio, gzip, gunzip, bzip2, xz], [chapter 2: cp, find, mkdir, mv, ls, rm, rmdir, touch, file], [chapter 4: file globbing], [chapter 8: dd]

103.4 Use streams, pipes and redirects (weight 4) [a part of this objective is covered in chapter 2 and the rest in chapter 4]

Candidates should be able to redirect streams and connect them in order to efficiently process textual data. Tasks include redirecting standard input, standard output and standard error, piping the output of one command to the input of another command, using the output of one command as arguments to another command and sending output to both stdout and a file.

Key Knowledge Areas:
  47. Redirecting standard input, standard output and standard error [chapter 4]
  48. Pipe the output of one command to the input of another command [chapter 4]
  49. Use the output of one command as arguments to another command [chapter 2]
  50. Send output to both stdout and a file [chapter 4]

The following is a partial list of the used files, terms and utilities: [chapter 2: xargs] and [chapter 4: tee]

103.5 Create, monitor and kill processes (weight 4) [most of this objective is covered in chapter 4, with the exception of the uptime and free commands that are explained in chapters 1 and 8, respectively]

Candidates should be able to perform basic process management.

Key Knowledge Areas:
51. Run jobs in the foreground and background
52. Signal a program to continue running after logout
53. Monitor active processes
54. Select and sort processes for display
55. Send signals to processes

The following is a partial list of the used files, terms and utilities: [chapter 1: uptime], [chapter 4: &, bg, fg, jobs, kill, nohup, ps, top, pgrep, pkill, killall, screen], and [chapter 8: free]

103.6 Modify process execution priorities (weight 2) [this entire objective is covered in chapter 4]

Candidates should be able to manage process execution priorities.

Key Knowledge Areas:
56. Know the default priority of a job that is created
57. Run a program with higher or lower priority than the default
58. Change the priority of a running process

The following is a partial list of the used files, terms and utilities: nice, ps, renice, top

103.7 Search text files using regular expressions (weight 2) [this entire objective is covered in chapter 3]

Candidates should be able to manipulate files and text data using regular expressions. This objective includes creating simple regular expressions containing several notational elements. It also includes using regular expression tools to perform searches through a filesystem or file content.

Key Knowledge Areas:
59. Create simple regular expressions containing several notational elements
60. Use regular expression tools to perform searches through a filesystem or file content

The following is a partial list of the used files, terms and utilities: grep, egrep, fgrep, sed, regex(7)

103.8 Perform basic file editing operations using vi (weight 3) [this entire objective is covered in chapter 3]

Candidates should be able to edit text files using vi. This objective includes vi navigation, basic vi modes, inserting, editing, deleting, copying and finding text.

Key Knowledge Areas:
61. Navigate a document using vi
62. Use basic vi modes
63. Insert, edit, delete, copy and find text

The following is a partial list of the used files, terms and utilities: vi, /, ?, h, j, k, l, i, o, a, c, d, p, y, dd, yy, ZZ, :w!, :q!, :e!

Topic 104: Devices, Linux Filesystems, Filesystem Hierarchy Standard (25%)

104.1 Create partitions and filesystems (weight 2) [this entire objective is covered in chapter 8]

Candidates should be able to configure disk partitions and then create filesystems on media such as hard disks. This includes the handling of swap partitions.

Key Knowledge Areas:
  64. Manage MBR partition tables
  65. Use various mkfs commands to create various filesystems such as ext2/ext3/ext4, XFS, VFAT
  66. Awareness of ReiserFS and Btrfs
  67. Basic knowledge of gdisk and parted with GPT

The following is a partial list of the used files, terms and utilities: fdisk, gdisk, parted, mkfs, mkswap

104.2 Maintain the integrity of filesystems (weight 2) [this entire objective is covered in chapter 8]

Candidates should be able to maintain a standard filesystem, as well as the extra data associated with a journaling filesystem.

Key Knowledge Areas:
  68. Verify the integrity of filesystems
  69. Monitor free space and inodes
  70. Repair simple filesystem problems

The following is a partial list of the used files, terms and utilities: du, df, fsck, e2fsck, mke2fs, debugfs, dumpe2fs, tune2fs, xfs tools (such as xfs_metadump and xfs_info)

104.3 Control mounting and unmounting of filesystems (weight 3) [this entire objective is covered in chapter 8]

Candidates should be able to configure the mounting of a filesystem.

Key Knowledge Areas:
  71. Manually mount and unmount filesystems
  72. Configure filesystem mounting on bootup
  73. Configure user mountable removable filesystems

The following is a partial list of the used files, terms and utilities: /etc/fstab, /media, mount, umount

104.4 Manage disk quotas (weight 1) [this entire objective is covered in chapter 8]

Candidates should be able to manage disk quotas for users.

Key Knowledge Areas:
  74. Set up a disk quota for a filesystem
  75. Edit, check and generate user quota reports

The following is a partial list of the used files, terms and utilities: quota, edquota, repquota, quotaon

104.5 Manage file permissions and ownership (weight 3) [this entire objective is covered in chapter 2]

Candidates should be able to control file access through the proper use of permissions and ownerships.

Key Knowledge Areas:
   76. Manage access permissions on regular and special files as well as directories
   77. Use access modes such as suid, sgid and the sticky bit to maintain security
   78. Know how to change the file creation mask
   79. Use the group field to grant file access to group members

The following is a partial list of the used files, terms and utilities: chmod, umask, chown, chgrp

104.6 Create and change hard and symbolic links (weight 2) [this entire objective is covered in chapter 2]

Candidates should be able to create and manage hard and symbolic links to a file.

Key Knowledge Areas:
   80. Create links
   81. Identify hard and/or soft links
   82. Copying versus linking files
   83. Use links to support system administration tasks

The following is a partial list of the used files, terms and utilities: ln, ls

104.7 Find system files and place files in the correct location (weight 2) [this entire objective is covered in chapter 2]

Candidates should be thoroughly familiar with the Filesystem Hierarchy Standard (FHS), including typical file locations and directory classifications.

Key Knowledge Areas:
   84. Understand the correct locations of files under the FHS
   85. Find files and commands on a Linux system
   86. Know the location and purpose of important file and directories as defined in the FHS

The following is a partial list of the used files, terms and utilities: find, locate, updated, whereis, which, type, /etc/updated.conf

LX0-104/102-400 Exam Objectives

Topic 105: Shells, Scripting and Data Management (17%)

105.1 Customize and use the shell environment (weight 4) [a part of this objective is covered in chapter 9; most of it in chapter 10; and env, export, set, unset, alias, and lists commands/topics are explained in chapter 4]

Candidates should be able to customize shell environments to meet users' needs. Candidates should be able to modify global and user profiles.

Key Knowledge Areas:
1.   Set environment variables (e.g. PATH) at login or when spawning a new shell [chapter 10]
2.   Write Bash functions for frequently used sequences of commands [chapter 9]
3.   Maintain skeleton directories for new user accounts [chapter 10]
4.   Set command search path with the proper directory [chapter 10]

The following is a partial list of the used files, terms and utilities: [chapter 10: source, /etc/bash.bashrc, /etc/profile, ~/.bash_profile, ~/.bash_login, ~/.profile, ~/.bashrc, ~/.bash_logout], [chapter 4: env, export, set, and unset, alias, and lists], and [chapter 9: function]

105.2 Customize or write simple scripts (weight 4) [most of this objective is covered in chapter 9 and the rest in chapter 15]

Candidates should be able to customize existing scripts, or write simple new Bash scripts.

Key Knowledge Areas:
5.   Use standard sh syntax (loops, tests) [chapter 9]
6.   Use command substitution [chapter 9]
7.   Test return values for success or failure or other information provided by a command [chapter 9]
8.   Perform conditional mailing to the superuser [chapter 15]
9.   Correctly select the script interpreter through the shebang (#!) line [chapter 9]
10.   Manage the location, ownership, execution and suid-rights of scripts [chapter 9]

The following is a partial list of the used files, terms and utilities: [chapter 9: for, while, test, if, read, seq, exec]

105.3 SQL data management (weight 2) [this entire objective is covered in chapter 9]

Candidates should be able to query databases and manipulate data using basic SQL commands. This objective includes performing queries involving joining of 2 tables and/or subselects.

Key Knowledge Areas:
11.   Use of basic SQL commands
12.   Perform basic data manipulation

The following is a partial list of the used files, terms and utilities: insert, update, select, delete, from, where, group by, order by, join

Topic 106: User Interfaces and Desktops (8%)

106.1 Install and configure X11 (weight 2) [this entire objective is covered in chapter 13]

Candidates should be able to install and configure X11.

Key Knowledge Areas:
13. Verify that the video card and monitor are supported by an X server
14. Awareness of the X font server
15. Basic understanding and knowledge of the X Window configuration file

The following is a partial list of the used files, terms and utilities: /etc/X11/xorg/xorg.conf, xhost, DISPLAY, xwininfo, xdpyinfo, X

106.2 Setup a display manager (weight 1) [this entire objective is covered in chapter 13]

Candidates should be able to describe the basic features and configuration of the LightDM display manager. This objective covers awareness of the display managers XDM (X Display Manger), GDM (Gnome Display Manager) and KDM (KDE Display Manager).

Key Knowledge Areas:
16. Basic configuration of LightDM
17. Turn the display manager on or off
18. Change the display manager greeting
19. Awareness of XDM, KDM and GDM

The following is a partial list of the used files, terms and utilities: lightdm, /etc/lightdm

106.3 Accessibility (weight 1) [this entire objective is covered in chapter 13]

Demonstrate knowledge and awareness of accessibility technologies.

Key Knowledge Areas:

20. Basic knowledge of keyboard accessibility settings (AccessX)
21. Basic knowledge of visual settings and themes
22. Basic knowledge of assistive technology (ATs)

The following is a partial list of the used files, terms and utilities: Sticky/repeat keys, mouse keys, high contrast/large print desktop themes, screen reader, braille display, screen magnifier, on-screen keyboard, gestures (used at login, for example gdm), orca, GOK, emacspeak

Topic 107: Administrative Tasks (20%)

107.1 Manage user and group accounts and related system files (weight 5) [this entire objective is covered in chapter 10]

Candidates should be able to add, remove, suspend and change user accounts.

Key Knowledge Areas:
23. Add, modify and remove users and groups
24. Manage user/group info in password/group databases
25. Create and manage special purpose and limited accounts

The following is a partial list of the used files, terms and utilities: /etc/passwd, /etc/shadow, /etc/group, /etc/skel, chage, getent, groupadd, groupdel, groupmod, passwd, useradd, userdel, usermod

107.2 Automate system administration tasks by scheduling jobs (weight 4) [this entire objective is covered in chapter 14]

Candidates should be able to use cron or anacron to run jobs at regular intervals and to use at to run jobs at a specific time.

Key Knowledge Areas:
26. Manage cron and at jobs
27. Configure user access to cron and at services
28. Configure anacron

The following is a partial list of the used files, terms and utilities:
/etc/cron.{d,daily,hourly,monthly,weekly}, /etc/at.deny, /etc/at.allow, /etc/crontab, /etc/cron.allow, /etc/cron.deny, /var/spool/cron/*, crontab, at, atq, atrm, anacron, /etc/anacrontab

107.3 Localisation and internationalization (weight 3) [this entire objective is covered in chapter 12]

Candidates should be able to localize a system in a different language than English. As well, an understanding of why LANG=C is useful when scripting.

Key Knowledge Areas:
29. Configure locale settings and environment variables
30. Configure timezone settings and environment variables

The following is a partial list of the used files, terms and utilities: /etc/timezone, /etc/localtime, /usr/share/zoneinfo, environment variables (LC_*, LC_ALL, LANG, TZ), /usr/bin/locale, tzselect, tzconfig, date, iconv, UTF-8, ISO-8859, ASCII, unicode

Topic 108: Essential System Services (17%)

108.1 Maintain system time (weight 3) [this entire objective is covered in chapter 12]

Candidates should be able to properly maintain the system time and synchronize the clock via NTP.

Key Knowledge Areas:
31. Set the system date and time
32. Set the hardware clock to the correct time in UTC
33. Configure the correct timezone
34. Basic NTP configuration
35. Knowledge of using the pool.ntp.org service
36. Awareness of the ntpq command

The following is a partial list of the used files, terms and utilities: /usr/share/zoneinfo, /etc/timezone, /etc/localtime, /etc/ntp.conf, date, hwclock, ntpd, ntpdate, pool.ntp.org

108.2 System logging (weight 3) [this entire objective is covered in chapter 14]

Candidates should be able to configure the syslog daemon. This objective also includes configuring the logging daemon to send log output to a central log server or accept log output as a central log server. Use of the systemd journal subsystem is covered. Also, awareness of rsyslog and syslog-ng as alternative logging systems is included.

Key Knowledge Areas:
37. Configuration of the syslog daemon
38. Understanding of standard facilities, priorities and actions
39. Configuration of logrotate
40. Awareness of rsyslog and syslog-ng

The following is a partial list of the used files, terms and utilities: syslog.conf, syslogd, klogd, /var/log/, logger, logrotate, /etc/logrotate.conf, /etc/logrotate.d/, journalctl, /etc/systemd/journald.conf, /var/log/journal

108.3 Mail Transfer Agent (MTA) basics (weight 3) [this entire objective is covered in chapter 15]

Candidates should be aware of the commonly available MTA programs and be able to perform basic forward and alias configuration on a client host. Other configuration files are not covered.

Key Knowledge Areas:
41. Create e-mail aliases
42. Configure e-mail forwarding
43. Knowledge of commonly available MTA programs (postfix, sendmail, qmail, exim) (no configuration)

The following is a partial list of the used files, terms and utilities: ~/.forward, sendmail emulation layer commands, newaliases, mail, mailq, postfix, sendmail, exim, qmail

108.4 Manage printers and printing (weight 2) [this entire objective is covered in chapter 13]

Candidates should be able to manage print queues and user print jobs using CUPS and the LPD compatibility interface.

Key Knowledge Areas:
44. Basic CUPS configuration (for local and remote printers)
45. Manage user print queues
46. Troubleshoot general printing problems
47. Add and remove jobs from configured printer queues

The following is a partial list of the used files, terms and utilities: CUPS configuration files, tools and utilities; /etc/cups, lpd legacy interface (lpr, lprm, lpq)

Topic 109: Networking Fundamentals (23%)

109.1 Fundamentals of internet protocols (weight 4) [this entire objective is covered in chapter 11]

Candidates should demonstrate a proper understanding of TCP/IP network fundamentals.

Key Knowledge Areas:
48. Demonstrate an understanding of network masks and CIDR notation
49. Knowledge of the differences between private and public "dotted quad" IP addresses
50. Knowledge about common TCP and UDP ports and services (20, 21, 22, 23, 25, 53, 80, 110, 123, 139, 143, 161, 162, 389, 443, 465, 514, 636, 993, 995)
51. Knowledge about the differences and major features of UDP, TCP and ICMP
52. Knowledge of the major differences between IPv4 and IPv6
53. Knowledge of the basic features of IPv6

The following is a partial list of the used files, terms and utilities: /etc/services, IPv4, IPv6, subnetting, TCP, UDP, ICMP

109.2 Basic network configuration (weight 4) [this entire objective is covered in chapter 11, with the exception of the /etc/nsswitch.conf file that is explained in chapter 12]

Candidates should be able to view, change and verify configuration settings on client hosts.

Key Knowledge Areas:
54. Manually and automatically configure network interfaces
55. Basic TCP/IP host configuration
56. Setting a default route

The following is a partial list of the used files, terms and utilities: [chapter 11: /etc/hostname, /etc/hosts, ifconfig, ifup, ifdown, ip, route, ping] and [chapter 12: /etc/nsswitch.conf]

109.3 Basic network troubleshooting (weight 4) [this entire objective is covered in chapter 11, with the exception of the host and dig commands that are explained in chapter 12]

Candidates should be able to troubleshoot networking issues on client hosts.

Key Knowledge Areas:
57. Manually and automatically configure network interfaces and routing tables to include adding, starting, stopping, restarting, deleting or reconfiguring network interfaces
58. Change, view, or configure the routing table and correct an improperly set default route manually
59. Debug problems associated with the network configuration

The following is a partial list of the used files, terms and utilities: [chapter 11: ifconfig, ip, ifup, ifdown, route, hostname, netstat, ping, ping6, traceroute, traceroute6, tracepath, tracepath6, netcat] and [chapter 12: host, dig]

109.4 Configure client side DNS (weight 2) [this entire objective is covered in chapter 12]

Candidates should be able to configure DNS on a client host.

Key Knowledge Areas:
60. Query remote DNS servers
61. Configure local name resolution and use remote DNS servers
62. Modify the order in which name resolution is done

The following is a partial list of the used files, terms and utilities: /etc/hosts, /etc/resolv.conf, /etc/nsswitch.conf, host, dig, getent

Topic 110: Security (15%)

110.1 Perform security administration tasks (weight 3) [most of this objective is covered in chapter 10, and the rest is split between chapters 11 and 15]

Candidates should know how to review system configuration to ensure host security in accordance with local security policies.

Key Knowledge Areas:
63. Audit a system to find files with the suid/sgid bit set [chapter 15]
64. Set or change user passwords and password aging information [chapter 10]
65. Being able to use nmap and netstat to discover open ports on a system [chapter 11]
66. Set up limits on user logins, processes and memory usage [chapter 10]
67. Determine which users have logged in to the system or are currently logged in [chapter 10]
68. Basic sudo configuration and usage [chapter 10]

The following is a partial list of the used files, terms and utilities: [chapter 10: passwd, chage, sudo, /etc/sudoers, su, usermod, ulimit, who, w, and last], [chapter 11: nmap, netstat], and [chapter 15: find, fuser, and lsof]

110.2 Setup host security (weight 3) [this objective is split equally among chapters 10, 11, and 14; the /etc/inittab and /etc/init.d/* are explained in chapter 6]

Candidates should know how to set up a basic level of host security.

Key Knowledge Areas:
69. Awareness of shadow passwords and how they work [chapter 10]
70. Turn off network services not in use [chapter 11]
71. Understand the role of TCP wrappers [chapter 14]

The following is a partial list of the used files, terms and utilities: , [chapter 6: /etc/inittab, /etc/init.d/*], [chapter 10: /etc/nologin, /etc/passwd, /etc/shadow], [chapter 14: /etc/hosts.allow, /etc/hosts.deny], and [chapter 11: /etc/xinetd.d/*, /etc/xinetd.conf, /etc/inetd.d/*, /etc/inetd.conf]

110.3 Securing data with encryption (weight 3) [the entire objective is covered in chapter 15]

The candidate should be able to use public key techniques to secure data and communication.

Key Knowledge Areas:
  72. Perform basic OpenSSH 2 client configuration and usage
  73. Understand the role of OpenSSH 2 server host keys
  74. Perform basic GnuPG configuration, usage and revocation
  75. Understand SSH port tunnels (including X11 tunnels)

The following is a partial list of the used files, terms and utilities: ssh, ssh-keygen, ssh-agent, ssh-add, ~/.ssh/id_rsa and id_rsa.pub, ~/.ssh/id_dsa and id_dsa.pub, /etc/ssh/ssh_host_rsa_key and ssh_host_rsa_key.pub, /etc/ssh/ssh_host_dsa_key and ssh_host_dsa_key.pub, ~/.ssh/authorized_keys, /etc/ssh_known_hosts, gpg, and ~/.gnupg/*

Summary of Exam Objectives and Relevant Details

The following tables provide a summarized view of the exam objectives, chapters they are discussed in, associated weights, the number of questions to expect on the exam, and other useful information. This summary may be used as a quick and convenient reference.

Objective	Chapter(s)	Weight	LX0-103/ 101-400	LX0-104/ 102-400	Comments
PART ONE [Chapters 1 to 8]					
Topic 101: System Architecture (14%)					All objectives for exam LX0-103/ 101-400 are fully covered in Part ONE of the book. Some objectives are split into multiple chapters. Objectives 101.3 and 103.1 cover some Part TWO topics.
101.1	7	2	X		
101.2	6	3	X		
101.3	6	3	X	X	
Expect 8 questions from Topic 101 on the exam					
Topic 102: Linux Installation and Package Management (18%)					
102.1	8	2	X		
102.2	6	2	X		
102.3	5	1	X		
102.4	5	3	X		
102.5	5	3	X		
Expect 11 questions from Topic 102 on the exam					
Topic 103: GNU and Unix Commands (43%)					
103.1	1 and 4	4	X	X	
103.2	2 and 3	3	X		
103.3	1, 2, 4 and 8	4	X		
103.4	2 and 4	4	X		
103.5	1, 4 and 8	4	X		
103.6	4	2	X		
103.7	3	2	X		
103.8	3	3	X		
Expect 26 questions from Topic 103 on the exam					
Topic 104: Devices, Linux Filesystems, Filesystem Hierarchy Standard (25%)					
104.1	8	2	X		
104.2	8	2	X		
104.3	8	3	X		
104.4	8	1	X		
104.5	2	3	X		
104.6	2	2	X		
104.7	2	2	X		
Expect 15 questions from Topic 104 on the exam					

Objective	Chapter(s)	Weight	LX0-103/ 101-400	LX0-104/ 102-400	Comments
PART TWO [Chapters 9 to 15]					With the
Topic 105: Shells, Scripting and Data Management (17%)					exception of a
105.1	4, 9 and 10	4		X	handful of topics
105.2	9 and 15	4		X	discussed in
105.3	9	2		X	chapter 4 and
Expect 10 questions from Topic 105 on the exam					chapter 6 of Part
Topic 106: User Interface and Desktops (8%)					ONE, all other
106.1	13	2		X	objectives for
106.2	13	1		X	exam LX0-104/
106.3	13	1		X	102-400 are
Expect 4 questions from Topic 106 on the exam					fully covered in
Topic 107: Administrative Tasks (20%)					Part TWO of the
107.1	10	5		X	book. Some
107.2	14	4		X	objectives are
107.3	12	3		X	split into
Expect 12 questions from Topic 107 on the exam					multiple
Topic 108: Essential System Services (17%)					chapters.
108.1	12	3		X	
108.2	14	3		X	
108.3	15	3		X	
108.4	13	2		X	
Expect 11 questions from Topic 108 on the exam					
Topic 109: Networking Fundamentals (23%)					
109.1	11	4		X	
109.2	11 and 12	4		X	
109.3	11 and 12	4		X	
109.4	12	2		X	
Expect 14 questions from Topic 109 on the exam					
Topic 110: Security (15%)					
110.1	10, 11 and 15	3		X	
110.2	6, 10, 11 and 14	3		X	
110.3	15	3		X	
Expect 9 questions from Topic 110 on the exam					

Exam Fees and Registration Procedure

The fee for each of the two CompTIA Linux+ Powered by LPI/LPIC-1 certification exam is US$200 or equivalent in local currencies. To purchase an exam voucher, visit http://www.comptiastore.com/ProductDetails.asp?ProductCode=VWLNXLPI or http://www.lpimarketplace.com/category-s/1847.htm?searching=Y&sort=3&cat=1847&show=15&page=1&brand=LPI and follow the directions. To register for an exam, visit https://certification.comptia.org/testing/schedule-exam or http://www.vue.com/lpi/ and follow the instructions. The exams are administered by Pearson VUE.

About This Book

The focus of this book is to present the basics of Linux in an easy-to-understand manner while covering the objectives and preparing the readers for the certification exams. In order to study the nitty-gritties of Linux while preparing for the exams at the same time, I have provided guidance in chapter 1 on how to set up a lab environment. I have used CentOS 7.3, Ubuntu 14.04.5, and CentOS 5.11 for examples, demonstrations, and exercises throughout this book. I have chosen CentOS 7.3 to explain new concepts and additions, such as systemd and journald, introduced in the latest release of the official exam objectives; Ubuntu 14.04.5 to present Debian-specific tasks, such as APT package management system; and CentOS 5.11 to cover older stuff such as SysVinit and GRUB Legacy.

The book is organized in two parts. Each part covers the objectives for one exam. There are 15 chapters that are organized to learn and teach Linux in a progressive manner.

1. **Part ONE** (chapters 1 to 8) covers topics that will help readers learn Linux essentials and build certain system administration skills while preparing for exam LX0-103/101-400. Material presented includes CentOS and Ubuntu installations; general Linux concepts and basic commands; compression and archiving; online help; file system hierarchy concepts, and file and directory operations; file types, access permissions, and ownership; file linking, searching, and special permissions; text file editing and data manipulation with filter programs; regular expressions; Bash shell features and process manipulation; shared libraries, and Debian and rpm package administration; system boot and initialization; hardware management and kernel modules; disk partitioning and file system build and repair; and quota and swap administration.

2. **Part TWO** (chapters 9 to 15) covers additional topics on system administration and prepares readers for exam LX0-104/102-400. Material presented includes automation with shell scripts; SQL database management and query; users, groups, password aging, and shell startup files; networking fundamentals and network interface configuration; routing and Internet services; network connection testing and troubleshooting; Linux support for internationalization and localization; time synchronization and hostname resolution; X Window, desktops, and accessibility options; printer and print queue administration; task scheduling and local and remote message logging; TCP Wrappers and email; secure shell and GnuPG management; and miscellaneous topics on file searching for auditing, in-use file identification, and PID identification using a specific file.

Each chapter begins with highlights of major topics and relevant exam objectives covered and ends with a summary followed by an at-a-glance chapter review. Throughout the book, figures, tables, and screenshots have been furnished to support explanation. This book includes more or less 400 practice questions and answers for each exam in the appendices.

TABLE OF CONTENTS

Preface iv
Acknowledgments v
About The Author vi
Conventions Used In This Book vii
About CompTIA Linux+ Powered by LPI/ LPIC-1 Exams viii
LX0-103/101-400 Exam Objectives x
LX0-104/102-400 Exam Objectives xvii
Summary of Exam Objectives and Relevant Details xxiv
Exam Fees and Registration Procedure xxvi
About This Book xxvii

PART ONE

1. Installing Linux and Using Basic Commands 1

Linux and Open Source 3
  Popular Linux Distributions 4
  Enterprise Linux (Red Hat, Oracle Linux, CentOS, Scientific Linux, and Fedora) 4
  Debian Linux 4
  Ubuntu Linux 4
  SUSE and OpenSUSE Linux 4
LAB Setup for Practicing CompTIA Linux+ Powered by LPI/LPIC-1 Exam Objectives 5
Exercise 1-1: Installing CentOS Desktop 6
  Downloading CentOS 7.3 6
  Creating a Virtual Machine 6
  Initiating Installation 7
  Selecting Software for Installation 8
  Configuring Installation Destination 9
  Configuring Network and Hostname 10
  Beginning Installation 11
  Setting root User Password and Creating a User Account 11
  Finishing Installation 11
  Accepting the License 12
  Logging In 12
  Logging Out 13
Exercise 1-2: Installing Ubuntu Desktop 14
  Downloading Ubuntu 14.04.5 Desktop 14
  Creating a Virtual Machine 14
  Initiating Installation 14
  Preparing for Installation 15
  Selecting an Installation Type 15
  Configuring Locale 16
  Creating a User Account and Setting a Hostname 16
  Finishing Installation 16
  Logging In 16

Logging Out 17

Accessing the Linux Command Prompt 18

Common Linux Commands 19

Understanding the Command Syntax 19
Listing Files and Directories 20
Printing Working Directory 21
Changing Directories 21
Showing the Terminal File 22
Inspecting the System's Uptime 22
Viewing User Login Name 22
Examining User and Group Information 23
Viewing System Information 23
Displaying Hostname 24
Clearing the Screen 24

Compression Tools 24

Using gzip and gunzip 24
Using bzip2 and bunzip2 25
Differences between gzip and bzip2 25
Using xz and unxz 25

Archiving Tools 26

Using tar 26
Using cpio 28

Online Help 29

Accessing Manual Pages 29
Manual Sections 30
Searching by Keyword 30
Displaying Short Description 31

Chapter Summary 32

Chapter Review at a Glance 32

2. Working with Files and File Permissions 35

Filesystem Hierarchy Standard (FHS) 37

Static vs. Dynamic and Shareable vs. Non-Shareable 38
Common Directories Under / 38

File and Directory Operations 39

Creating Files and Directories 39
Listing Files and Directories 40
Displaying File Contents 41
Copying Files and Directories 42
Moving and Renaming Files and Directories 43
Removing Files and Directories 44

Common File Types 45

Regular Files 45
Directory Files 46
Executable Files 46
Symbolic Link Files 46
Device Files 46

File and Directory Access Permissions 47
    Determining Access Permissions 47
    Modifying Access Permissions 48
    Exercise 2-1: Modify File Permissions Using Symbolic Notation 48
    Exercise 2-2: Modify File Permissions Using Octal Notation 49
    Default Permissions 50
    Calculating Default Permissions 50
File Ownership and Owning Group 51
    Exercise 2-3: Modify File Ownership and Owning Group 52
Linking Files and Directories 52
    Hard Link 53
    Soft Link 54
    Differences between Copying and Linking 55
    Using Links to Support System Administration Tasks 55
Finding Files 56
    Using the find Command 57
    Using find with the -exec and -ok Options 58
    Using the xargs Command 59
    Using the locate Command 60
    Using the which, whereis, and type Commands 61
Special Permissions 61
    The setuid Bit on Binary Executable Files 61
    The setgid Bit on Binary Executable Files 62
    The setgid Bit on Shared Directories 63
    The Sticky Bit on Public-Writable Directories 63
Chapter Summary 64
Chapter Review at a Glance 65

3. Editing Text Files, Exploring Filters, and Using Regular Expressions 67
The vi Editor 69
    Modes of Operation 69
    Starting vi 69
    Inserting text 70
    Navigating within vi 70
    Searching for Text 71
    Copying and Pasting Text 71
    Changing Text 71
    Deleting Text 72
    Saving and Quitting vi 72
Exploring Filters 73
    Concatenating Files Using cat 73
    Extracting Columns of Data Using cut 73
    Converting Tabs to Spaces and Vice Versa Using expand and unexpand 74
    Formatting Text Using fmt 75
    Dumping Output in Different Formats Using od 75
    Joining Data Using join 75
    Numbering Output Lines Using nl 76
    Pasting Data Side-by-Side Using paste 76

Formatting Text for Printing Using pr 77
Filtering and Transforming Text Using sed 78
Sorting Input Using sort 79
Breaking Large Files into Smaller Files Using split 81
Deleting, Squeezing, or Translating Characters Using tr 82
Printing Unique or Identical Lines Using uniq 82
Counting Words, Lines, and Characters Using wc 83
Regular Expressions 83
Using grep for Pattern Matching 84
Using grep Variants for Pattern Matching 85
Using sed for Pattern Matching 85
Chapter Summary 86
Chapter Review at a Glance 86

4. Dealing with the Bash Shell and Processes 89
Introducing the BASH Shell 91
Internal and External Shell Commands 91
Shell and Environment Variables 92
Setting and Unsetting Variables 93
Command and Variable Substitution 94
Alias Substitution 94
Command History 96
Invoking Commands inside the Defined Path 97
Invoking Commands outside the Defined Path 98
Using Wildcard Characters in Filename Globbing 98
Redirecting Standard Input, Output, and Error Streams 100
Piping Output of One Command as Input to Another 102
Sending Output to Multiple Destinations Using tee 103
Using List Operators 103
Understanding and Manipulating Processes 104
Viewing and Monitoring Processes with ps 105
Viewing and Monitoring Processes with top 106
Process States 108
Listing a Specific Process 108
Listing Processes by User and Group Ownership 109
Understanding Process Niceness 109
Viewing and Changing Process Niceness 109
Renicing a Running Process 110
Controlling Processes with Signals 111
Signaling a Program to Continue Running after User Logout 112
Running and Controlling Jobs in Foreground and Background 113
Splitting a Terminal among Multiple Terminals using Screen 114
Chapter Summary 115
Chapter Review at a Glance 116

5. Managing Shared Libraries and Software Packages 119
Shared Libraries 121
Static vs. Shared Libraries 121
32-Bit and 64-Bit Library Versions and their Locations 122

Viewing Shared Library Dependencies 122
Adding Library Locations to the LD_LIBRARY_PATH Variable 123
Adding Shared Library Locations to the Cache 123

Debian Package Overview 124

Packages and Packaging 124
Package Naming 124
Package Dependency 125
Package Database 125
Debian Package Management Toolset 125

Managing Debian Packages with dpkg 125

The dpkg Command 125
Acquiring Package Information 126
Installing a Package 128
Reconfiguring an Installed Package 128
Verifying Package Integrity 128
Removing vs. Purging a Package 128

Managing Debian Packages with APT 129

Repository Configuration 129
The apt-get Command 130
Downloading a Package 130
Installing a Package 130
Updating the Package Database 131
Upgrading Packages 131
Removing a Package Without or With Configuration Files 132
Removing Transitory Packages 132
Cleaning the APT Cache 132
The apt-cache Command 132
Searching for a Package 133
Listing all Packages 133
Displaying Package Information 133
Listing Forward Dependencies 134
Listing Reverse Dependencies 134
Showing APT Cache Statistics 134
Viewing Unmet Dependencies 135
apt vs. apt-get and apt-cache 135
Understanding and Using aptitude 135

RPM Package Overview 137

Packages and Packaging 137
Package Naming 137
Package Dependency 138
Package Database 138
RPM Package Management Tools 138

Managing RPM Packages with rpm 138

The rpm Command 138
Querying Packages 139
Installing a Package 141
Upgrading a Package 141
Freshening a Package 141
Verifying Package Integrity 141
Removing a Package 142

     Extracting Files from an Installable Package 143

Managing RPM Packages with yum 143
    Yum Configuration File 143
    Yum Repository 144
    The yum Command 145
    Viewing Enabled Repositories 146
    Listing Packages 146
    Listing Package Dependencies and Providers 147
    Installing and Updating a Package 148
    Reinstalling a Package 149
    Displaying Package Information 149
    Determining What Provides 150
    Removing a Package 150
    Downloading a Package 151

Chapter Summary 151
Chapter Review at a Glance 152

6. Booting Linux and Initializing the System 153

The Linux Boot Process in a Nutshell 155
    The Firmware Phase (BIOS and UEFI) 155
    The Bootloader Phase 156
    The Kernel Phase 156
    The Initialization Phase (SysVinit, Upstart, and systemd) 156

The Bootloader Phase—GRUB Legacy 157
    Understanding GRUB Legacy Configuration File 158
    Interacting with GRUB Legacy 159
    Changing the Autoboot Timeout Value 161
    Installing a Corrupted Bootloader 161

The Bootloader Phase—GRUB2 162
    Understanding GRUB2 Configuration Files 162
    Interacting with GRUB2 164

The Kernel Phase 165
    Understanding Command Line Kernel Options 166

The System Initialization Phase—SysVinit 166
    Runlevels 167
    The /etc/inittab File 167
    Sequencer, Configuration, and Initialization Directories 168
    Examining Current and Previous System Runlevels 169
    Switching Runlevels and Modifying the Default Runlevel 169
    Managing SysVinit Services 171
    Exercise 6-1: List, Enable, and Disable Services 171
    Exercise 6-2: Start, Restart, and Check Status of Services 172
    Configuring Service Start and Stop via Text Interface 173

The System Initialization Phase—systemd 174
    Units 175
    Targets 176
    The systemctl Command 177
    Managing Units 177
    Managing Service Units 178

Managing Target Units 180
Viewing System Boot Messages 181
Chapter Summary 182
Chapter Review at a Glance 183

7. Understanding and Configuring Hardware and Kernel Modules 185

Computer Hardware 187
  Communication Channels 187
  PCI Express Devices 189
  Processors and Cores 190
  Mass Storage Devices 192
  Universal Serial Bus (USB) 195
  Hotplug and Coldplug Devices 196
  Probing and Managing Hardware Devices Dynamically with udev 196
System Runtime Information 197
  The Sysfs File System Mounted on /sys 198
  The Devices File System Mounted on /dev 198
  The Procfs File System Mounted on /proc 199
  D-Bus 200
Hardware Settings in the BIOS 200
Understanding and Managing Kernel Modules 202
  Determining Kernel Version 202
  Managing Kernel Modules 203
  Listing Loaded Modules 203
  Displaying Module Information 204
  Loading and Unloading Modules 204
Chapter Summary 205
Chapter Review at a Glance 206

8. Administering Partitions, File Systems, and Swap 209

MBR, GPT, and Partitions 212
  Master Boot Record (MBR) 212
  GUID Partition Table (GPT) 213
  Disk Partitions 213
  Disk Management Tools 214
Managing MBR Partitioning with fdisk 215
  Exercise 8-1: Create a Partition 216
  Exercise 8-2: Delete a Partition 217
Managing MBR and GPT Partitioning with parted 217
  Exercise 8-3: Create a Partition 218
  Exercise 8-4: Delete a Partition 219
Managing GPT Partitioning with gdisk 219
  Exercise 8-5: Create a Partition 220
  Exercise 8-6: Delete a Partition 222
Overview of Logical Volume Manager (LVM) 222
  Physical Volume 223

    Volume Group 223
    Logical Volume 223
    LVM Operations and Commands 224

Understanding File Systems and File System Types 224

    Extended File Systems 225
    XFS File System 225
    ISO9660 File System 226
    VFAT File System 226
    ReiserFS/Reiser4 File Systems 226
    Btrfs File System 226

Managing File Systems 226

    File System Administration Commands 227
    Mounting and Unmounting a File System 228
    Determining the UUID of a File System 229
    Labeling a File System 230
    Automatically Mounting a File System at Reboots 231
    Monitoring File System Usage 232
    Calculating Disk Usage 233
    Exercise 8-7: Create and Mount an Extended File System 233
    Exercise 8-8: Create and Mount an XFS File System 234
    Exercise 8-9: Create and Mount a VFAT File System 235
    Accessing File Systems in Removable Media 236

Disk Dumping and Backing up MBR 238

Inspecting and Repairing File Systems 239

    Analyzing and Repairing Extended File Systems 239
    Exercise 8-10: Restore a Corrupted Primary Superblock 241
    Debugging an Extended File System 241
    Examining and Repairing an XFS File System 242
    Dumping XFS File System Metadata to a File 243

Understanding, Configuring, Managing, and Reporting Quota 244

    Soft and Hard Quota Limits 244
    Activating Quota Support 245
    Initializing Quota Databases 245
    Enabling and Disabling Quota Enforcement 245
    Setting and Viewing User and Group Quotas 246
    Modifying Grace Period for Soft Limits 247
    Duplicating User and Group Quota Settings 248
    Activating Quota Automatically at System Reboots 248
    Reporting Quota Usage 248

Understanding and Managing Swap 249

    Determining Current Swap Usage 249
    Swap Space Administration Commands 251
    Exercise 8-11: Create a Swap Partition and Activate Swap 251
    Exercise 8-12: Deactivate and Remove Swap Space 251

Chapter Summary 252

Chapter Review at a Glance 252

PART TWO

9. Writing Shell Scripts and Managing a SQL Database 257

Shell Scripts 259

Displaying System Information—Script01 259
Executing a Script 260
A Word on SUID-Rights on Shell Scripts 261
Using Variable Substitution—Script02 262
Using Command Substitution—Script03 262
Understanding Shell Parameters 262
Using Special and Positional Parameters—Script04 263
Understanding Functions 263
Using Function—Script05 264
Writing Interactive Scripts—Script06 265
Generating Number Sequences 265
Replacing Current Shell Process with exec 266

Logical Statements or Conditionals 266

Exit Codes 266
Test Conditions 267
The if-then-fi Statement—Script07 268
The if-then-else-fi Statement—Script08 269
The if-then-elif-fi Statement—Script09 270

Looping Statements 271

Test Conditions 272
The for-do-done Loop—Script10 272
The while-do-done Loop—Script11 273
Controlling Loop Behavior 274

Understanding Databases, DBMS, and SQL 275

What is a Relational Database? 275
Understanding SQL 276

Managing and Querying a Database 276

Exercise 9-1: Install and Configure MariaDB 276
Starting the MariaDB Shell and Checking Connection Status 278
The mysql Command for Database and Table Operations 279
Exercise 9-2: Create a Database and Table, and Insert Records 279
Exercise 9-3: Perform Basic SQL Queries 282
Exercise 9-4: Perform Queries on Two Tables Using Join 283
Exercise 9-5: Update Records 284
Exercise 9-6: Delete Records 284
Exercise 9-7: Drop Tables and Database 285

Chapter Summary 285
Chapter Review at a Glance 285

10. Managing Users and Groups 287

Understanding User Authentication Files 289

The passwd File 289
The shadow File 291
The group File 292

The gshadow File 293
Activating and Deactivating Shadow Password Mechanism 294

Managing User Accounts and Password Aging 294

The useradd, usermod, and userdel Commands 295
The useradd and login.defs Files 296
Exercise 10-1: Create a User Account with Default Attributes 296
Exercise 10-2: Create a User Account with Custom Values 297
The passwd Command for Password Aging 298
The chage Command for Password Aging 298
Exercise 10-3: Set up Password Aging on User Accounts 299
The No-Login User Account 299
Exercise 10-4: Create a User Account with No-Login Access 300
Exercise 10-5: Modify a User Account 300
Exercise 10-6: Modify Password Aging and Delete a User Account 301
Listing Currently Logged-In Users 301
Viewing History of Successful User Login Attempts 302
Viewing History of Failed User Login Attempts 302
Switching (or Substituting) Users 303
Doing as Superuser 303
Displaying and Setting User Limits 305

Managing Group Accounts 306

The groupadd, groupmod, and groupdel Commands 306
Exercise 10-7: Create, Modify, and Delete Group Accounts 306

Getting Entries from Local Authentication Files 307

Shell Startup Files 308

System-wide Shell Startup Files 308
Per-user Shell Startup Files 309

Chapter Summary 310

Chapter Review at a Glance 310

11. **Understanding Networking and Administering Network Interfaces 313**

Networking Fundamentals 315

Introduction to OSI Reference Model 316
Layer 7: The Application Layer 316
Layer 6: The Presentation Layer 317
Layer 5: The Session Layer 317
Layer 4: The Transport Layer 317
Layer 3: The Network Layer 317
Layer 2: The Data Link Layer 317
Layer 1: The Physical Layer 317
Summary of OSI Layers 317
Encapsulation and De-encapsulation 318
Peer-to-Peer Model 319
Introduction to TCP/IP 319
TCP/IP Layers 319
Hardware Address 320
Address Resolution Protocol (ARP) 320
Hostname 320

IPv4 Address 321
Network Classes 321
Subnetting 322
Subnet Mask 323
Classless Inter-Domain Routing (CIDR) Notation 323
Protocol 324
TCP and UDP Protocols 324
Well-Known Ports 324
ICMP Protocol 325
IPv6 325
Major Differences between IPv4 and IPv6 326
Network Interfaces 326
Understanding Interface Configuration Files 326
Interface Administration Tools 328
Exercise 11-1: Configure and Activate a New Network Interface Non-Persistently and Persistently on centos73 328
Exercise 11-2: Configure and Activate a New Network Interface Non-Persistently and Persistently on ubuntu14 330
Exercise 11-3: Configure and Activate a New Network Interface Persistently on centos511 331
Understanding and Updating the Hosts Table 332
Routing 332
Routing Table 333
Managing Routes 334
Exercise 11-4: Add a Static Route Non-Persistently and Persistently 334
Exercise 11-5: Delete and Add the Default Route Non-Persistently and Persistently 335
Testing and Debugging Network Interfaces 336
Testing Network Connectivity with ping 336
Inspecting Network Interfaces with netstat 337
Exploring and Debugging Network Connections with netcat 337
Tracing Flow of Network Traffic with traceroute and tracepath 338
Scanning Networks with nmap 339
Manipulating the ARP Cache with arp 340
The Internet Services 340
Common Internet Services 341
/etc/xinetd.conf and /etc/xinetd.d 341
Enabling and Activating an xinetd-Controlled Service 342
Chapter Summary 343
Chapter Review at a Glance 343

12. Understanding Internationalization, and Configuring Localization, NTP, and DNS 345
Internationalization and Localization 347
Character Set and Character Encoding 347
Displaying Locale Information 348
Modifying System-Wide Locale 350
Modifying Per-User Locale 351
Converting Text from One Character Encoding to Another 351
Displaying Time Zone Information 351

Setting System-Wide Time Zone 352
Setting Per-User Time Zone 354

The Network Time Protocol 355
Time Sources 355
NTP Roles 356
Stratum Levels 356
NTP Packages and Utilities 357
NTP Configuration File 358
Exercise 12-1: Configure NTP Client 359
Querying NTP Servers 359
Updating System Clock Instantly 360
Displaying and Setting System Date and Time 360
Querying and Setting the Hardware Clock 361

DNS and Name Resolution 362
DNS Name Space and Domains 362
DNS Roles 362
Understanding Resolver Configuration File 363
Viewing and Adjusting Name Resolution Sources and Order 364
Performing Name Resolution with dig 364
Performing Name Resolution with host 365
Performing Name Resolution with nslookup 365
Performing Name Resolution with getent 366

Chapter Summary 366
Chapter Review at a Glance 367

13. Managing User Interfaces, Desktops, and Printers 369
X Server 371
Viewing X Configuration 371
Understanding X Configuration File and Rebuilding X Server 373
The startx and xinit Commands 375
Overview of the X Font Server 375

Working In a Graphical Environment 375
Display/Login Manager 375
Desktop Environment Manager 377
Window Manager 378
Changing Default Display Manager 378
Modifying GDM and XDM Greetings 378
Switching Display Manager On or Off 379
Customizing LightDM Interface 379
Remote X Sessions 380
Exercise 13-1: Run X Application Remotely 380

Accessibility Options 382
Keyboard Navigation 382
Onscreen Keyboard 383
Screen Readers and Speech Synthesizers 383
Screen Magnifiers and Resolution Adjustments 383
Mouse Cursors and Gestures 383
Visual and Audible Alerts 383
Accessibility Configuration in GDM and Unity 383

Understanding the Linux Printing System 385
  Types of Printer Setups 386
  CUPS Directory Hierarchy 386
Configuring and Managing Printers and Print Queues 387
  Managing the CUPS Service 387
  CUPS Management Tools 388
  Exercise 13-2: Add a Local Printer 389
  Exercise 13-3: Add Access to a Remote Printer 389
  Exercise 13-4: Add Access to a Network Printer 390
  Enabling and Disabling a Printer 390
  Accepting and Rejecting Print Requests 391
  Exercise 13-5: Remove a Printer 391
Submitting and Managing Print Requests 392
  Print Request Management Tools 392
  Submitting Print Requests 392
  Listing Queued Print Requests 393
  Removing Queued Print Requests 393
Troubleshooting General Printing Problems 393
Chapter Summary 395
Chapter Review at a Glance 395

14. Scheduling Tasks, Logging Messages, and Using TCP Wrappers 397
Understanding Job Scheduling 399
  Controlling Who Can Access 399
  Scheduler Log File 400
  Using at 400
  Exercise 14-1: Submit, View, List, and Remove an at Job 401
  Using crontab 402
  Syntax of User Crontab Files 402
  Exercise 14-2: Add, List, and Remove a Cron Job 403
  What is anacron? 404
System Logging 405
  The Syslog Configuration File 406
  Logging Custom Messages 407
  Logging System Messages Remotely 407
  Exercise 14-3: Configure a System as a Loghost 408
  Exercise 14-4: Configure a System as a Loghost Client 408
  Rotating Log Files 409
  What is syslog-ng? 410
Understanding the systemd Journal 411
  Viewing the Journal 411
TCP Wrappers 411
  Format of Access Control Files 412
Chapter Summary 413
Chapter Review at a Glance 413

15. Sending and Receiving Email and Securing Access with Secure Shell and GnuPG 415

SMTP and the Email System 417
Common Terms 417
How the Email System Works 418
Composing, Sending, Receiving, and Checking Mail 419
Redirecting User Mail 421

The OpenSSH Service 422
Basic Encryption Techniques 423
OpenSSH Versions and Algorithms 423
OpenSSH Server Daemon and Client Commands 423
System-Wide Server Configuration and HostKey Files 424
System-Wide Client Configuration and Per-User Key Files 424
Exercise 15-1: Configure Trusted Login on a Host 425
What is Authentication Agent? 426
Exercise 15-2: Configure Trusted Login with Authentication Agent 426
Copying Files Remotely Using scp 427
Understanding and Configuring SSH Port Tunneling 427

GNU Privacy Guard (GnuPG) 428
The gpg and gpg2 Commands 428
Generating and Listing Keys 429
Exporting and Sharing Public Key 430
Importing Public Key 431
Encrypting and Decrypting Files With or Without Signing 431
Generating Revocation Certificate 432

Miscellaneous Topics 432
Finding Files with Special Permission Bits for Auditing 432
Identifying Files Used by Processes (Listing Open Files) 433
Identifying and Terminating PIDs Using a Specific File 435

Chapter Summary 436
Chapter Review at a Glance 436

Appendix A: Sample LX0-103/ 101-400 Quiz 439

Appendix B: Answers to Sample LX0-103/101-400 Quiz 475

Appendix C: Sample LX0-104/ 102-400 Quiz 479

Appendix D: Answers to Sample LX0-104/102-400 Quiz 511

Glossary 517

Index 529

LIST OF FIGURES

Figure 1-1 VM Details 7
Figure 1-2 Boot Menu 7
Figure 1-3 Installation Summary 8
Figure 1-4 Installation Summary / Software Selection 9
Figure 1-5 Installation Summary / Installation Destination 9
Figure 1-6 Installation Summary / Network & Hostname 10
Figure 1-7 Installation Summary 11
Figure 1-8 Configuration / Create User 12
Figure 1-9 Sign In 12
Figure 1-10 GNOME Desktop 13
Figure 1-11 Log Out 13
Figure 1-12 Welcome Screen 14
Figure 1-13 Install Preparation 15
Figure 1-14 Installation Type 15
Figure 1-15 User Creation and Hostname Setting 16
Figure 1-16 Login Screen 17
Figure 1-17 Unity Desktop Environment 17
Figure 1-18 Log Out 18
Figure 1-19 Access Command Prompt (CentOS) 18
Figure 1-20 Access Command Prompt (Ubuntu) 19
Figure 2-1 Directory Tree 38
Figure 2-2 Permission Weights 48
Figure 2-3 Hard Link 53
Figure 2-4 Soft Link 54
Figure 2-5 Find Command Syntax 57
Figure 4-1 Process State Transition 108
Figure 5-1 aptitude Program Text Interface 136
Figure 6-1 GRUB Legacy Main Menu 160
Figure 6-2 GRUB Legacy Edit Menu 160
Figure 6-3 GRUB Legacy Kernel String 161
Figure 6-4 GRUB2 Kernel Edit 164
Figure 6-5 GRUB2 Commands 165
Figure 6-6 Service Start/Stop Management with ntsysv 173
Figure 7-1 BIOS Setup – Main Category 200
Figure 7-2 BIOS Setup – Advanced Category 201
Figure 7-3 BIOS Setup – Boot Category 202
Figure 7-4 Anatomy of a Kernel Version 203
Figure 8-1 LVM Structure 223
Figure 9-1 Special and Positional Parameters 263
Figure 9-2 The if-then-fi Construct 268
Figure 9-3 The if-then-else-fi Construct 269
Figure 9-4 The if-then-elif-fi Construct 270
Figure 9-5 The for-do-done Construct 272
Figure 9-6 The while-do-done Construct 273
Figure 9-7 Components of a Database Table 275
Figure 10-1 The /etc/passwd File 290
Figure 10-2 The /etc/shadow File 291
Figure 10-3 The /etc/group File 292
Figure 10-4 The /etc/gshadow File 293
Figure 11-1 The OSI Reference Model 316
Figure 11-2 Encapsulation and De-encapsulation 318
Figure 11-3 The TCP/IP Protocol Suite 319
Figure 12-1 NTP Stratum Levels 357
Figure 12-2 DNS Hierarchy 362
Figure 13-1 GNOME Display/Login Manager 376
Figure 13-2 LightDM Display/Login Manager 376

Figure 13-3 GNOME Desktop Environment Manager...377
Figure 13-4 Unity Desktop Environment Manager...377
Figure 13-5 LightDM Interface without Guest and User List 380
Figure 13-6 Accessibility Settings in GDM & Unity 384
Figure 13-7 Accessibility Settings in GDM & Unity | Typing Assist (AccessX)..385
Figure 13-8 Types of Printer Setups 386
Figure 14-1 Syntax of Crontables...403
Figure 15-1 Email – From Sender to Receiver 419

LIST OF TABLES

Table 1-1 tar Command Options 26
Table 1-2 tar with Compression Options 27
Table 1-3 cpio Command Options 28
Table 2-1 Navigating with less or more 42
Table 2-2 Octal Permission Notation 48
Table 2-3 Copying vs. Linking 55
Table 3-1 Inserting Text 70
Table 3-2 Navigating within vi 70
Table 3-3 Copying and Pasting Text 71
Table 3-4 Changing Text 72
Table 3-5 Deleting Text 72
Table 3-6 Saving and Quitting vi 72
Table 4-1 Common Pre-Defined Environment Variables 92
Table 4-2 Pre-Defined Command Aliases 95
Table 4-3 ps Command Output 106
Table 4-4 Control Signals 112
Table 4-5 Job Control 113
Table 4-6 Virtual Screen Control Sequences 115
Table 5-1 dpkg Command Options 126
Table 5-2 Common apt-get Operations 130
Table 5-3 Common apt-cache Operations 133
Table 5-4 Equivalent apt and apt-get/apt-cache Subcommands 135
Table 5-5 rpm Command Options 139
Table 5-6 Directives in /etc/yum.conf 144
Table 5-7 yum Subcommands 146
Table 6-1 GRUB2 Default Settings 162
Table 6-2 SysVinit Runlevels 167
Table 6-3 The /etc/inittab File 168
Table 6-4 systemd Targets 176
Table 6-5 systemctl Subcommands 177
Table 7-1 lspci Command Options 189
Table 8-1 File System Management Commands 227
Table 8-2 mount Command Options 229
Table 8-3 Quota Management Commands 244
Table 9-1 Test Conditions 267
Table 9-2 let Operators 272
Table 9-3 Database Administration Commands 279
Table 9-4 Data for use with Exercises 280
Table 9-5 Data for lx104 283
Table 10-1 Shadow Mechanism Control Commands 294
Table 10-2 useradd Command Options 295
Table 10-3 usermod Command Options 296
Table 10-4 passwd Command Options 298
Table 10-5 chage Command Options 299
Table 10-6 groupadd Command Options 306
Table 10-7 System-wide Startup Files 308
Table 10-8 Per-user Startup Files 309
Table 11-1 OSI Layer Summary 318
Table 11-2 IPv4 vs IPv6 326
Table 11-3 Network Interface Configuration File (CentOS) 327
Table 11-4 Network Interface Configuration File (Ubuntu) 328
Table 12-1 LC Variables 349
Table 12-2 Description of ntp.conf Directives 358
Table 12-3 The Resolver Configuration File 363
Table 12-4 Name Service Source and Order Determination 364
Table 13-1 CUPS Directory Hierarchy 387

Table 13-2 lpstat Options 389
Table 14-1 User Access Restrictions to Scheduling Tools 400
Table 14-2 Description of Crontable Syntax 403
Table 14-3 TCP Wrappers Access Control Files.. 412
Table 15-1 OpenSSH Client Commands.. 424
Table 15-2 gpg2 Options 428

PART ONE

LX0-103/101-400

Chapter 1

Installing Linux and Using Basic Commands

This chapter describes the following major topics:

- Overview of Linux, open source, and popular Linux distributions
- Obtain CentOS Linux, Ubuntu Linux, and Oracle VirtualBox software
- Create virtual machines and install CentOS and Ubuntu
- Access the new systems
- Access the command prompt
- General Linux commands and how to execute them
- Use basic compression and archiving tools
- Get Linux online help

This chapter covers the following objectives for LX0-103/101-400 Exam:

103.1 Work on the command line [a part of this objective is described in this chapter and the rest in chapter 4]

36. Use single shell commands and one line command sequences to perform basic tasks on the command line

The following is a partial list of the used files, terms and utilities: pwd, man, and uname

103.3 Perform basic file management [most of this objective is described in chapter 2, a part in chapter 4, the dd command in chapter 8, and the tar/cpio commands in this chapter]

46. Usage of tar and cpio

The following is a partial list of the used files, terms and utilities: tar, cpio, gzip, gunzip, bzip2, and xz

103.5 Create, monitor and kill processes [most of this objective is described in chapter 4, the uptime command in this chapter, and the free command in chapter 8]

The following is a partial list of the used files, terms and utilities: uptime

Linux has been around since 1991. It is a free operating system with source code that anyone—amateur and developers—can use for customization and redistribution. Companies such as Red Hat, SUSE, Canonical, and Oracle have tailored the source code and added features, enhancements, and bug fixes to make their Linux distributions stable, robust, and feature-rich for commercial use.

Linux distributions may be downloaded for learning as well as for practicing and preparing for Linux certification exams. This chapter sets up the foundation for learning the essentials of Linux and practicing the objectives for CompTIA Linux+ Powered by LPI/LPIC-1 certification exams as published on *www.comptia.org* and *www.lpi.org*.

Linux offers a variety of commands for users and system managers. User commands are general purpose that are intended for execution by any user on the system. However, system management commands require elevated privileges of the superuser. Knowledge of these tools is essential for productive usage and efficient administration of the system. This chapter provides an introduction to a number of user and administrative commands.

Users and administrators need help on command usage/syntax and on the format of configuration files. To assist users, Linux installs help in the form of manual pages, as part of software installation.

Linux and Open Source

Linux was originally developed in a collaborative effort by several developers who had the primary goal of creating a free, open-source operating system.

The term *open source* is referred to the software with source code that is available to the public for download, duplication, amendment, repackaging, and re-sharing. The open-source approach allows anyone to add enhancements and fix bugs for the larger global community benefit.

The development effort was called the GNU Project (*GNU's Not Unix*) and it included file system structure, tools, and utilities. In 1991, a piece of software called *kernel*, developed by Linus Torvalds, was integrated with the GNU software, which formed what is now referred to as *GNU/Linux, Linux operating system,* or simply *Linux*. Linux was initially released in 1991 under the GNU *General Public License* (GPL), which provided public access to its source code free of charge with full consent to amend and redistribute. The first major version 1.0 was released in 1994 followed by 2.0 in 1996, 3.0 in 2011, and the latest 4.0 in 2015. Each major version had plenty of minor releases. For instance, the 2.5 kernel had 75 minor releases, 2.6 had 39, 3.0 had 19, and 4.0 has had 9 so far. Each successive version/release saw bug fixes, new features, support for new hardware devices, enhancements, and security patches. At the time of this writing, version 4.9 is the latest Linux kernel.

Linux runs on an extensive range of computer hardware platforms, from laptop and desktop computers to massive mainframe and supercomputers. Linux also runs as the base operating system on a variety of networking, mass storage, and mobile devices. Numerous vendors including Red Hat, SUSE, Canonical, IBM, HP, Oracle, and Dell offer commercial support to Linux users worldwide.

The functionality, adaptability, portability, and cost-effectiveness that Linux offers has made it the main alternative to proprietary UNIX and Windows operating systems.

Linux is largely used in government agencies, corporate businesses, academic institutions, and scientific organizations, as well as on home computers. Linux deployment and usage has grown tremendously over the years. A number of companies are planning or executing a migration or have already migrated from UNIX to the Linux platform.

Popular Linux Distributions

There are over a hundred distributions of Linux available from various vendors, organizations, and individuals; however, only a handful of them gained popularity and wide acceptance amid user, developer, and corporate communities. Among these distributions are *Red Hat Enterprise Linux* (RHEL), Oracle Linux, CentOS (*Community Enterprise Operating System*), Scientific Linux, Fedora, Debian Linux, Ubuntu Linux, SUSE Linux, and OpenSUSE Linux.

Enterprise Linux (Red Hat, Oracle Linux, CentOS, Scientific Linux, and Fedora)

Of the list provided above, Red Hat and Oracle Linux are targeted for enterprise use and require paid subscription for support. CentOS and Scientific Linux are available for free and may be used for home and business purposes but without any official support. Fedora is a community-based project initiated, sponsored, and sustained by Red Hat as their test-bed for the development and testing of new features, enhancements, and bug fixes for inclusion in subsequent releases of RHEL. Oracle Linux, CentOS, and Scientific Linux branch off their releases from versions of RHEL. At the time of this writing, the latest version of RHEL, Oracle Linux, and CentOS is 7.3, Scientific Linux is 7.0, and Fedora is 25.

Debian Linux

Debian made its debut in 1993 as a community-powered project. Debian supports a number of different vendor hardware architectures including Intel/AMD processors, SPARC, PowerPC, and IBM mainframes.

Debian has three release types that are referred to as *unstable, testing,* and *stable.* An unstable release is the version that developers are currently working on, a testing release is in the testing phase, and a stable release is the one that is ready and available for use. At the time of this writing, the latest version of Debian Linux is 8.6.

Ubuntu Linux

Ubuntu is a spin-off of Debian. Ubuntu has two release types that are referred to as Ubuntu *Long Term Support* (LTS) and Ubuntu *standard.* The LTS version is stable, updated every six months, released every two years, and supported for five years. As of this writing, the latest Ubuntu LTS version is 16.04.1; however, for the purpose of this book, we use 14.04.5.

On the contrary, Ubuntu standard is released between six to twelve months and comes with a nine-month support. As of the writing of this book, the latest version of Ubuntu non-LTS is 16.10.

Ubuntu in comparison to Debian is more user-friendly and easier to use.

SUSE and OpenSUSE Linux

SUSE Linux was first released in 1994 and it is now a popular choice in the commercial space. OpenSUSE, on the other hand, is a community-driven project started when Novell owned SUSE in 2003. SUSE Linux Enterprise has two main versions: *SUSE Linux Enterprise Server* (SLES) and *SUSE Linux Enterprise Desktop* (SLED). At the time of this writing, the latest version of SLES and SLED is 12.2, and that of OpenSUSE is 42.2.

LAB Setup for Practicing CompTIA Linux+ Powered by LPI/LPIC-1 Exam Objectives

Beginning in this chapter and throughout this book, several topics on Linux system, networking, and security will be introduced and discussed, along with procedures on how to implement, administer, and use them. A number of exercises will be performed and commands presented and executed to support the learning in a practical environment. In order for a smooth and effective learning experience, I have summarized the lab setup that I have used to support my writing and I want you to use the same, if possible, for yourselves to avoid issues that might arise due to dissimilarities. Here is what I have used:

Linux software:	ISO images for CentOS 7.3, Ubuntu 14.04.5, and CentOS 5.11 attached to their respective virtual machines. A complete procedure is provided to help you download the images.
Virtualization software:	Oracle VM VirtualBox 5.1.18 on MS Windows 10. A link is provided on where to download the Oracle VM VirtualBox software.
Remote client connectivity software:	Binary SSH client file called putty.exe from https://www.chiark.greenend.org.uk/~sgtatham/putty/latest.html. Store this file on your Windows/Mac computer. You will need it to connect to the three Linux systems over the new network interfaces that you'll configure in Chapter 11.
Laptop architecture:	64-bit laptop with Intel Core i7 processor and 8GB of memory
Network interface:	1 WiFi network interface
Number of VMs:	3
Guest OS in VM1:	CentOS 7.3. This new OS version is included to expound on the exam objectives that require the knowledge and understanding of new concepts and procedures. This VM and OS is stood up in Chapter 1 and used throughout the book.
Guest OS in VM2:	Ubuntu 14.04.5. This new OS version is included to explicate the exam objectives that require the knowledge and understanding of concepts and procedures specific to Debian-based Linux systems. This VM and OS is stood up in Chapter 1 and used throughout the book.
Guest OS in VM3:	CentOS 5.11. This old OS version is included to support the exam objectives that require the knowledge and understanding of concepts and procedures specific to older Linux versions. This Linux system is needed in Chapter 6 and beyond. You need to build it yourselves; a procedure is not provided.
VM1:	Hostname *centos73*, 1 vCPU, 1024MB memory, 1 x 8GB virtual disk for CentOS 7.3, 3 x 200MB virtual disks for disk management exercises added and used in Chapter 8, and 1 virtual bridged network interface over WiFi with a DHCP-supplied IP address. A static IP address 192.168.0.100 will be applied to a new network interface in Chapter 11. Most tasks in the book are performed on this VM.
VM2:	Hostname *ubuntu14*, 1 vCPU, 1024MB memory, 1 x 8GB virtual disk for Ubuntu 14.04.5, and 1 virtual bridged network interface over WiFi with a DHCP-supplied IP address. A static IP address 192.168.0.101 will be applied to a new network interface in Chapter 11.
VM3:	Hostname *centos511*, 1 vCPU, 1024MB memory, 1 x 8GB virtual disk for CentOS 5.11, and 1 virtual bridged network interface over WiFi with a DHCP-supplied IP address. A static IP address 192.168.0.102 will be applied to a new network interface in Chapter 11.

If you prefer to continue to use IP addresses provided by your DHCP server (such as your home router) throughout this book, make sure that you keep a mapping between them and the ones provided above to avoid losing track.

Exercise 1-1: Installing CentOS Desktop

For the purpose of learning, practicing, and preparing for the exams, we have downloaded CentOS 7.3 to our MS Windows system and installed it in an Oracle VirtualBox virtual machine as directed in the following subsections. We use basic installation options, such as the default disk partitioning layout, and obtain IP assignments from the DHCP server that is running on our home router. We've named the system *centos73*.

Downloading CentOS 7.3

Installation images for CentOS are available in the ISO format for download on the official website at *www.centos.org*. Follow the instructions provided below to acquire a copy of the x86_64 version:

1. Go to *www.centos.org* and click "GET CENTOS" located at the top of the home page.
2. Click "DVD ISO" to list download locations for the image. The files should have 1611 version number embedded in their names.
3. Click any image from the list to download the software to your Windows desktop.

Creating a Virtual Machine

We use Oracle VirtualBox 5.1.10 to create a virtual machine (VM) to host CentOS. Download and install this software (or a closer version) from *www.virtualbox.org* on your Windows system. After the installation, launch the Oracle VM VirtualBox program and follow the steps provided below to create a VM:

1. Click New to begin the VM creation process.
2. Enter a name, such as *centos73*, for the VM and ensure Linux Red Hat (64-bit) is selected. Click Next.
3. Allocate 1024MB as the amount of memory and click Next.
4. Select "Create a virtual disk now" and click Create.
5. Choose "VDI (VirtualBox Disk Image)" as the type of virtual disk and click Next.
6. Select "Dynamically allocated" and click Next.
7. Choose the default disk size of 8GB and click Create.
8. Click "[Optical Drive] Empty" under Storage on the VM's Details page and select "Choose disk image...".
9. Browse to select the CentOS 7.3 ISO image (CentOS-7-x86_64-DVD-1611) that you just downloaded and click Open to attach the image to the VM.

This completes the steps to create a VM and attach an ISO image to it. The Details page of the VM will look similar to what is shown in Figure 1-1.

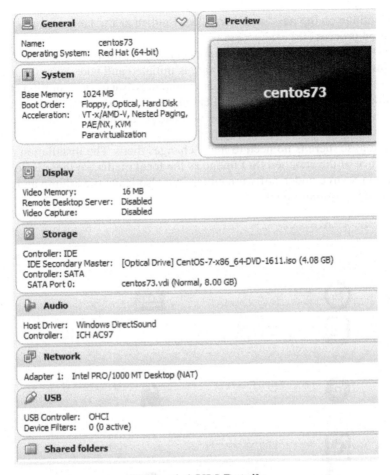

Figure 1-1 VM Details

You now have a VM ready for CentOS installation.

Initiating Installation

1. Power on the VM by highlighting it and then clicking Start. This will open a console window for the VM and start the boot program.
2. Highlight "Install CentOS Linux 7" and press Enter to begin installation.

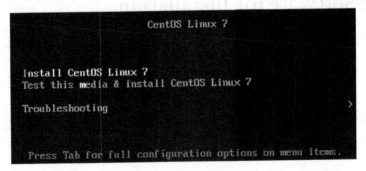

Figure 1-2 Boot Menu

3. Click Continue on the next screen to select English as the language to be used during the installation process.
4. The "Installation Summary" screen appears next, as shown in Figure 1-3. This is when the Linux installer program called *Anaconda* is initiated and takes over the installation process. Prior to starting the installation, you can make necessary configuration changes to localization (date, time, time zone, keyboard, and language), software (installation source and what to install), and system settings (disk selection and partitioning, kernel dump, network & hostname assignments, and security policy). For this exercise, we use the defaults for localization, so there is no need to make changes there. The installation program auto-detects the presence of the attached ISO image as the local media, so there is no need to modify Installation Source under Software either. We also leave the kdump and security policy settings under System intact.

Figure 1-3 Installation Summary

Selecting Software for Installation

5. The default software selected for installation is "Minimal Install" as displayed under Software Selection; however, for this exercise, click Software Selection and choose "GNOME Desktop" (Figure 1-4). Click Done in the top left-hand corner to return to the Installation Summary page.

GNOME is the default graphical desktop in numerous Linux distributions and it stands for (*GNU Network Object Model Environment*).

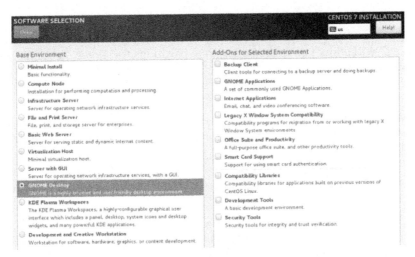

Figure 1-4 Installation Summary / Software Selection

Configuring Installation Destination

6. Choose a disk for installation and partitioning under Installation Destination. See Figure 1-5. By default, the installer selects "Automatic partitioning selected" as displayed on the Installation Summary page. However, you can either retain the automatic partitioning selection or configure your own scheme on the Installation Destination page. The 8GB disk that was added during the VM creation is visible here as *sda*.

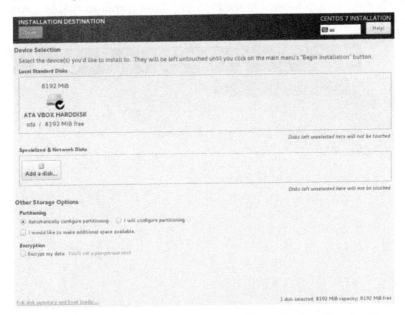

Figure 1-5 Installation Summary / Installation Destination

For this exercise, simply click the Done button to permit the installer to use the default automatic disk partitioning scheme. This will create a partition called */boot* for storing kernel and boot configuration files, and an LVM (*Logical Volume Manager*) volume group with two

---

partitions called / and swap. Together, the three partitions take up the entire disk capacity. Custom partitioning under the Other Storage Options by selecting "I will configure partitioning" will allow you to create separate partitions for *home*, *usr*, *var*, and *opt* with desired sizes.

LVM stands for Logical Volume Manager. It is a popular choice for disk partitioning and it is available in most Linux distributions. See Chapter 8 "Administering Partitions, File Systems, and Swap" for more details.

The installer program requires that three partitions: */boot*, /, and swap be created at a minimum.

The */boot* partition is created as a standard partition outside of LVM boundaries.

Configuring Network and Hostname

7. Assigning appropriate IP information and a hostname is essential for system functionality on the network. Click Network & Hostname on the Installation Summary page and a window similar to the one shown in Figure 1-6 will pop up. Anaconda automatically detects the network interface (represented as *enp0s3* here; however, it might be different on your system) and shows it in the left windowpane. It also shows the default hostname as *localhost.localdomain* in the bottom left side. You need to modify these assignments so that your system is able to communicate with other systems on the network. For this exercise, simply slide the switch located in the top right-hand corner to enable getting IP assignments automatically from DHCP.

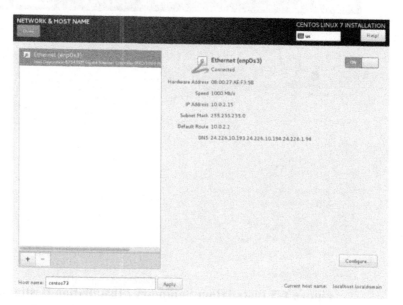

Figure 1-6 Installation Summary / Network & Hostname

Next, enter *centos73* in the Hostname field in the bottom left-hand corner and click Done to return to the Installation Summary page.

Beginning Installation

8. The Installation Summary page now looks like Figure 1-7. Click Begin Installation in the bottom right to begin the installation based on the configuration entered in the previous steps.

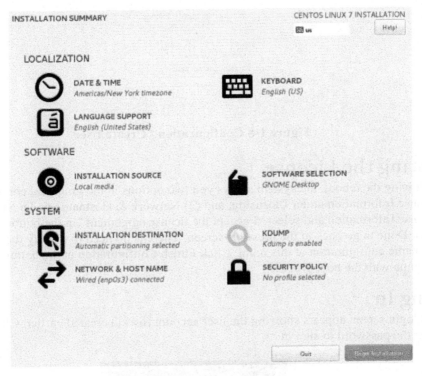

Figure 1-7 Installation Summary

The Begin Installation button is not visible until all required configuration is entered.

Setting root User Password and Creating a User Account

9. Once the installation has begun, a new screen appears that shows the installation progress. This screen also allows you to assign a password to the *root* user and create a normal user account.
10. While the installer continues with background configuration and software copy, click Root Password and enter a password for the *root* user. Click Done to return to the installation progress screen.
11. Next, click User Creation and create a user account called *user1* and assign a password of your choice. See Figure 1-8. Click Done to return.

Finishing Installation

12. When all software packages are installed, the Reboot button becomes active in the bottom right-hand corner of the screen. Click this button to reboot the new system.

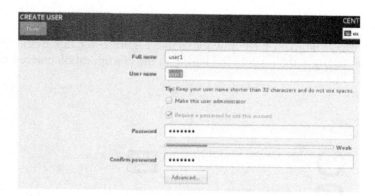

Figure 1-8 Configuration / Create User

Accepting the License

13. Following the reboot, the system shows you two options in the graphical console window: (1) License Information under Licensing, and (2) Network & Hostname under System. Click License Information and select "I accept the license agreement" in the bottom of the screen. Click Done to go back to the previous screen. There is no need to modify the network or hostname configuration at this point. Click Finish Configuration at the bottom right side to continue with the boot process.

Logging In

14. The login screen appears showing the user account (user1) created earlier. Click user1 and enter the password to sign in.

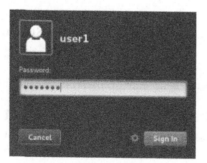

Figure 1-9 Sign In

15. Click Next on the Welcome screen and then click Next again to accept the selected keyboard layout.
16. Click Skip on Online Accounts and then click "Start using CentOS Linux."
17. Your system is now ready for use. The default graphical desktop called GNOME appears with Getting Started information (Figure 1-10). You should now be able to start using the system as *user1*.

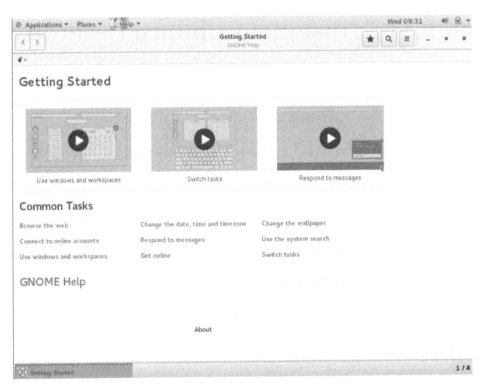

Figure 1-10 GNOME Desktop

Logging Out

18. After you are done navigating, click the down arrowhead at the top right-hand corner of the screen and then click the arrowhead beside user1. Click "Log Out" to log off the system.

Figure 1-11 Log Out

This completes the step-by-step procedure for installing CentOS 7.3 Desktop using the ISO image in a virtual machine.

 You need to press the right Ctrl key to release the mouse cursor.

Exercise 1-2: Installing Ubuntu Desktop

For the purpose of learning, practicing, and preparing for the exams, we have downloaded Ubuntu 14.04.5 Desktop to our MS Windows system and installed it in an Oracle VirtualBox virtual machine as directed in the following subsections. We use basic installation options such as the default disk partitioning layout and acquiring IP assignments from the DHCP server running on our home router. We've named the system *ubuntu14*.

Downloading Ubuntu 14.04.5 Desktop

Installation images for Ubuntu Linux are available in ISO format for download on the official website at *www.ubuntu.com*. Follow the instructions below to obtain a copy of the x86_64 version:

1. Go to *releases.ubuntu.com* and click "Ubuntu 14.04.5 LTS (Trusty Tahr)" under "Ubuntu Releases."
2. Click "64-bit PC (AMD64) desktop image" to download the image to your system.

Creating a Virtual Machine

Follow the instructions outlined in Exercise 1-1 to create a virtual machine (VM) using Oracle VirtualBox to host Ubuntu. Name the VM *ubuntu14* and attach the Ubuntu ISO image to the VM.

Initiating Installation

1. Power on the virtual machine by highlighting it and then clicking Start. This will open a console window and start the boot program.
2. Click "Install Ubuntu" on the Welcome screen to initiate the installation.

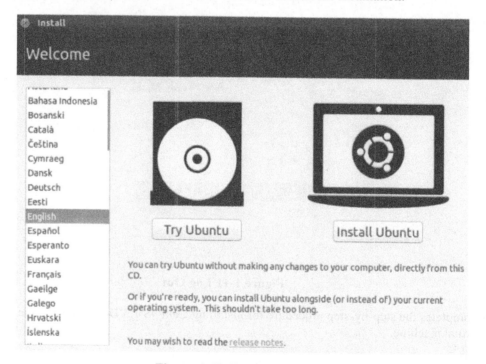

Figure 1-12 Welcome Screen

Preparing for Installation

3. The "Preparing to install Ubuntu" screen appears next, as shown in Figure 1-13.

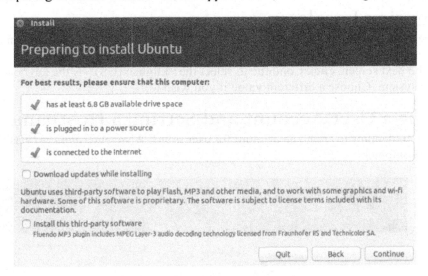

Figure 1-13 Install Preparation

The installer program shows the available drive space and whether the computer is plugged in to a power source. Click Continue while leaving the "Download updates while installing" and "Install this third-party software" options unselected.

Selecting an Installation Type

4. The installer detects the presence of the empty disk that had been added at the time of the VM creation and selects the option to erase the disk and use it for installing Ubuntu. For partitioning, choose "Use LVM with the new Ubuntu installation." Click "Install Now" to continue with the installation.

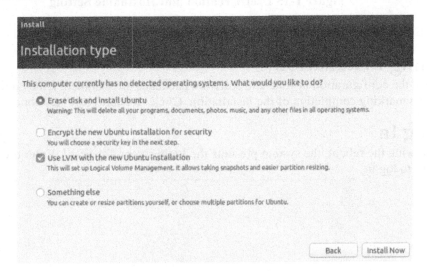

Figure 1-14 Installation Type

5. A pop-up screen prompts for confirmation to write the changes to the disk. Click Continue to confirm and proceed.

Configuring Locale

6. Type the name of your time zone (e.g., Eastern Standard Time; Mountain Time) and select an appropriate time zone from available choices. Click Continue.
7. On the next screen, click Continue to select the "English (US)" as the keyboard layout for your system. Choose a different value if you wish to.

Creating a User Account and Setting a Hostname

8. Enter credentials to create an account for user *user1*. Also, enter *ubuntu14* as the hostname for your computer.

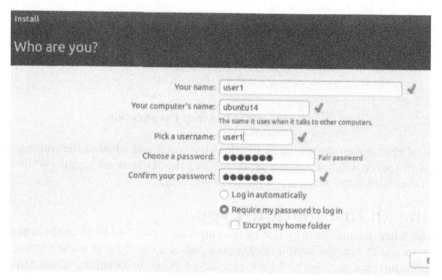

Figure 1-15 User Creation and Hostname Setting

Click Continue to complete the configuration steps and proceed with the installation.

Finishing Installation

9. When the configuration is done and software packages are installed, a message pops up on the screen marking completion of the installation. Click "Restart Now" to reboot the new system.

Logging In

10. Following the reboot, the system presents the login screen for *user1*. Enter the password for user1 to log in.

Figure 1-16 Login Screen

11. The default graphical desktop environment called *Unity* appears, allowing you to use the system as *user1*.

Figure 1-17 Unity Desktop Environment

Logging Out

12. After you are done navigating the system, click the little wheel icon at the top right-hand corner of the screen and choose Log Out to log off the system as *user1*.

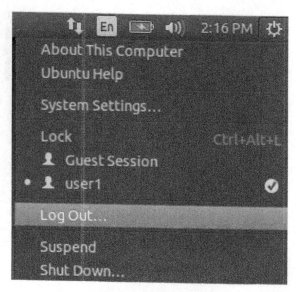

Figure 1-18 Log Out

This completes the step-by-step procedure for installing Ubuntu Desktop 14.04.5 in a virtual machine using the ISO image.

Accessing the Linux Command Prompt

To interact with the Linux shell and issue Linux commands, we must access the Linux command prompt. We can access the command prompt by re-logging as *user1* to both *centos73* and *ubuntu14*. Open a terminal session on *centos73* by clicking Applications in the top left-hand corner of the desktop screen and then selecting Favorites→Terminal. See Figure 1-19.

Figure 1-19 Access Command Prompt (CentOS)

The command prompt for *user1* will look similar to the following in the terminal window:

```
[user1@centos73 ~]$
```

On Ubuntu (Figure 1-20), click the Search icon at the top left-hand corner of the screen and type "terminal" in the search window that appears. Click the Terminal icon to get the command prompt.

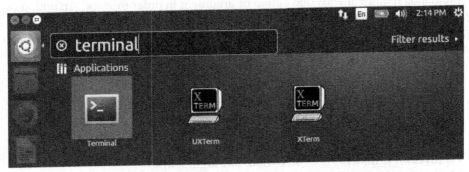

Figure 1-20 Access Command Prompt (Ubuntu)

The command prompt for *user1* will look similar to the following in the terminal window:

```
user1@ubuntu14:~$
```

 The font I have used for the command prompt is Consolas, and this representation is used throughout this book.

Notice the inclusion of the username and the Linux system name in the command prompts. The ~ (tilde) sign represents the user's home directory, and the $ sign is the default shell sign that identifies *user1* as a regular user. The CentOS command prompt appears slightly different because it is enclosed within square brackets ([]).

Common Linux Commands

Linux offers hundreds of commands for both privileged and non-privileged use. Privileged commands are for system management and intended solely for privileged users. Non-privileged commands do not require extra rights for execution and can be run with regular user rights.

These commands range from simple to complicated ones. Some of the commands only offer a few options, while others have as many as 70 options or more, which can be used to produce outputs of your choice. Knowledge of these commands is essential for proper use and efficient administration of the system. This section sheds some light on command syntax and then demonstrates the use of some common commands. Please note: the examples are run on *centos73* unless stated otherwise. In addition, we will show the output of a command where it's necessary for clarity. You should run each command and observe the output.

Understanding the Command Syntax

To practice the commands provided in this chapter, log in as *user1* on *centos73* and *ubuntu14* desktop consoles, run the commands, and observe their outputs. In most cases, the commands will yield the same or similar result on both Linux distributions.

The basic syntax of the Linux command is:

command option argument

You can specify zero or more options and arguments with a command. Some commands have default options and arguments that are used when executed, so you do not need to specify them. Other commands require at least one option or argument in order to work. An option (a.k.a. a *switch* or *flag*, and often preceded by the hyphen (-) character), modifies the behavior of the command, and an argument supplies a target on which to perform the command action. The following examples show some command structures. The text on the right states the number of options and arguments supplied:

$ ls	(no option, no argument; the default argument is the current directory name)
$ ls -l	(one option, no argument; the default argument is the current directory name)
$ ls directory_name	(no option, one argument)
$ ls -la directory_name	(two options, one argument)

Listing Files and Directories

The *ls* (*list*) command produces a list of files and directories and displays it on the screen. It supports several options such as -a, -h, -l, -d, -R, -t, and -r. The following examples describe the function of these options.

To list files in the current directory with the assumption that you are in the home directory */home/user1* for *user1*:

```
[user1@centos73 ~]$ ls
Desktop  Documents  Downloads  Music  Pictures  Public  Templates  Videos
```

To list files in the current directory with detailed information:

```
[user1@centos73 ~]$ ls -l
total 0
drwxr-xr-x. 2 user1  user1  6 Dec 21  09:28 Desktop
drwxr-xr-x. 2 user1  user1  6 Dec 21  09:28 Documents
drwxr-xr-x. 2 user1  user1  6 Dec 21  09:28 Downloads
drwxr-xr-x. 2 user1  user1  6 Dec 21  09:28 Music
drwxr-xr-x. 2 user1  user1  6 Dec 21  09:28 Pictures
drwxr-xr-x. 2 user1  user1  6 Dec 21  09:28 Public
drwxr-xr-x. 2 user1  user1  6 Dec 21  09:28 Templates
drwxr-xr-x. 2 user1  user1  6 Dec 21  09:28 Videos
```

As an alternative to using **ls -l**, you may use its shortcut **ll** to get the same result.

To list files under */home/user1* with hidden files and detailed information, use either **ll -a** or the following:

```
[user1@centos73 ~]$ ls -la
```

To list the listing of the *Desktop* directory without showing its contents:

```
[user1@centos73 ~]$ ls -ld Desktop
```

To list a file such as */etc/group*:

```
[user1@centos73 ~]$ ls -l /etc/group
```

To list files in the */boot* directory with detailed information and their sizes in human-readable format:

```
[user1@centos73 ~]$ ls -lh /boot
```

Replace -h with -t in the above example to list files sorted by date and time with the newest file first:

```
[user1@centos73 ~]$ ls -lt /boot
```

Add the -r option to the above command to list files in reverse chronological order:

```
[user1@centos73 ~]$ ls -ltr /boot
```

To list contents of the */etc* directory recursively:

```
[user1@centos73 ~]$ ls -R /etc
```

Printing Working Directory

The *pwd* (*print working directory*) command displays a user's current location in the directory tree. The following example shows that *user1* is presently in */home/user1*:

```
[user1@centos73 ~]$ pwd
/home/user1
```

Changing Directories

The *cd* (*change directory*) command is used to navigate the directory tree. Use the *pwd* command after each execution of *cd* to confirm the directory switch.

To change directory to */usr/bin*:

```
[user1@centos73 ~]$ cd /usr/bin
[user1@centos73 ~]$ pwd
/usr/bin
```

To go to the *Desktop* directory under the home directory of *user1*:

```
[user1@centos73 ~]$ cd ~/Desktop
```

 tilde (~) is used as an alternative to a user's home directory path.

To return to the home directory of *user1*, run either **cd** or **cd ~**.

To go to the home directory of user *sshd* from anywhere in the directory structure, use the ~ (tilde) character and specify the login name:

```
[user1@centos73 ~]$ cd ~sshd
[user1@centos73 ~]$ pwd
/var/empty/sshd
```

To go to the root directory, use the forward slash (/) character:

```
[user1@centos73 ~]$ cd /
```

To switch between the current and the previous directory, issue the *cd* command with a hyphen (-):

```
[user1@centos73 ~]$ cd -
```

To move one directory up to the parent directory, use the period (.) character twice:

```
[user1@centos73 ~]$ cd ..
```

Showing the Terminal File

This command displays the terminal name we are currently running the commands in:

```
[user1@centos73 ~]$ tty
/dev/pts/0
```

Inspecting the System's Uptime

The *uptime* command shows the system's current time, how long it has been up for, the number of users currently logged in, and the average number of processes over the past 1, 5, and 15 minutes:

```
[user1@centos73 ~]$ uptime
17:32:18 up 1:24, 4 users, load average: 0.00, 0.01, 0.05
```

The above output shows that the current system time is 5:32 p.m.; the system has been up for 1 hour and 24 minutes; there are four users currently logged in; and the system load averages over the past 1, 5, and 15 minutes are 0.00, 0.01, and 0.05, respectively.

Viewing User Login Name

The *whoami* (*who am i*) command displays the effective username of the person executing this command:

```
[user1@centos73 ~]$ whoami
user1
```

The *logname* (*login name*) command shows the name of the real user who originally logged in to the system:

```
[user1@centos73 ~]$ logname
user1
```

Examining User and Group Information

The *id* (*identifier*) command displays a user's UID (*user identifier*), username, GID (*group identifier*), group name, all secondary groups the user is a member of, and SELinux security context:

```
[user1@centos73 ~]$ id
uid=1000(user1) gid=1000(user1) groups=1000(user1)
context=unconfined_u:unconfined_r:unconfined_t:s0-s0:c0.c1023
```

Each user and group has a corresponding number (called UID and GID) for identification purposes. If you specify a username with the id command, the SELinux information will not be printed.

The *groups* command lists all groups a user is a member of:

```
[user1@centos73 ~]$ groups
user1
```

In case a user has membership of multiple groups, the first group listed will be the user's primary group and the rest will be the user's secondary (or supplementary) groups.

Viewing System Information

The *uname* command produces elementary information about the system and running kernel. The output will be different for different hardware types and Linux distributions and versions. Without any options, this command only displays the operating system name. You may use the -a option for details.

```
[user1@centos73 ~]$ uname
Linux
[user1@centos73 ~]$ uname -a
Linux centos73 3.10.0-514.el7.x86_64 #1 SMP Tue Nov 22 16:42:41 UTC 2016 x86_64 x86_64 x86_64
GNU/Linux
```

The information returned by the second command is:

Linux	Kernel name
Centos73	Hostname (or node name) of this system
3.10.0-514.el7.x86_64	Kernel release
#1 SMP Tue Nov 22 UTC 2016	Date and time of this kernel built
x86_64	Machine's hardware name
x86_64	Processor type
x86_64	Hardware platform
GNU/Linux	Operating system name

Try running this command with the -s (kernel name), -n (node name), -r (kernel release), -v (kernel build date), -m (hardware name), -p (processor type), -i (hardware platform), and -o (OS name) options separately to view specific information. Also run this command on *ubuntu14*.

Displaying Hostname

The *hostname* command can be used to view the system hostname. Run this command without any options to view the hostname of the system:

```
[user1@centos73 ~]$ hostname
centos73
```

Clearing the Screen

The *clear* command clears the terminal screen and places the cursor at the beginning of the screen. We can alternatively use the Ctrl+l key combination for this purpose.

```
[user1@centos73 ~]$ clear
```

Compression Tools

Compression tools are used to compress one or more files to conserve space. They may be used with archive commands, such as *tar*, to create a single compressed archive of hundreds of files and directories. Archiving is discussed in the next section. A compressed archive can then be copied to a remote system faster than a non-compressed archive. Linux offers a number of compression tools such as *gzip* (*gunzip*), *bzip2* (*bunzip2*), and *xz* that we can use for this purpose.

Using gzip and gunzip

The *gzip/gunzip* compression utility pair has been available in Linux for over two decades. The *gzip* command is used to create a compressed file of each of the specified files and it adds the *.gz* extension to each one of them for identification. This tool can be used with the -r option to compress an entire directory tree, and with the -l option to display compression information about a gzipped file. The -l option also instructs the command to display the filename that will be given to the file when it is uncompressed.

To compress the file *fstab* located in the */etc* directory, copy this file in *user1*'s home directory using the *cp* command and confirm with *ls*:

```
[user1@centos73 ~]$ pwd
/home/user1
[user1@centos73 ~]$ cp /etc/fstab .
[user1@centos73 ~]$ ls -l fstab
-rw-r--r--. 1 user1 user1 465 Dec 22 08:53 fstab
```

Now use the *gzip* command to compress this file and *ls* to confirm:

```
[user1@centos73 ~]$ gzip fstab
[user1@centos73 ~]$ ls -l fstab.gz
-rw-r--r--. 1 user1 user1 284 Dec 22 08:53 fstab.gz
```

Notice that the original file is compressed and it now has the .gz extension added to it. If you wish to view compression information for the file, run the command again with the -l option:

```
[user1@centos73 ~]$ gzip -l fstab.gz
    Compressed      uncompressed    ratio    uncompressed_name
         284               465      44.1%    fstab
```

To decompress this file, use the *gunzip* command. You may alternatively use the *gzip* command with the -d (decompress) option. Both will produce an identical result.

```
[user1@centos73 ~]$ gunzip fstab.gz
```

Check the file after the decompression with the *ls* command. It will be the exact same file with the exact same timestamp and other attributes.

Using bzip2 and bunzip2

The *bzip2/bunzip2* compression pair has been available in Linux for almost two decades. The *bzip2* command creates a compressed file of each of the specified files and it adds the *.bz2* extension to each one for identification.

To compress the *fstab* file again but this time with *bzip2*, issue the following and confirm with *ls*:

```
[user1@centos73 ~]$ bzip2 fstab
[user1@centos73 ~]$ ls -l fstab.bz2
-rw-r--r--. 1 user1 user1 318 Dec 22 08:53 fstab
```

Notice that the original file is compressed and it now has the .bz2 extension added to it. To decompress this file, use the *bunzip2* command. You may alternatively use the *bzip2* command with the -d option. Both will produce an identical result.

```
[user1@centos73 ~]$ bunzip2 fstab.bz2
```

Check the file after the decompression with the *ls* command. It will be the exact same file with the exact same timestamp and other attributes.

Differences between gzip and bzip2

The function of both *gzip* and *bzip2* is the same: to compress and decompress files. However, in terms of compression and decompression rate, *gzip* is faster with a compression ratio (smaller target file size) but not as good as *bzip2*'s. These differences are evident on fairly large files; on small files, you can use either *gzip* or *bzip2*. Both commands support several identical options.

Using xz and unxz

The *xz/unxz* compression pair may be used in place of *gzip* and *bzip2*. This tool is relatively new. It delivers a better compression ratio, but it is slower than *gzip* and *bzip2*. It adds the *.xz* extension to the compressed file for identification. You can use the -l option with the command to display compression information for an *xz*-compressed file. To uncompress, use either the *unxz* command or the -d option with *xz*.

To compress the *fstab* file again but this time with *xz*, issue the following and confirm with *ls*:

```
[user1@centos73 ~]$ xz fstab
```

```
[user1@centos73 ~]$ ls -l fstab.xz
-rw-r--r--. 1 user1 user1 340 Dec 22 09:27 fstab.xz
```

Notice that the original file is compressed and it now has the .xz extension added to it. If you wish to view compression information for the file, run the command again with the -l option:

```
[user1@centos73 ~]$ xz -l fstab.xz
Strms    Blocks  Compressed    Uncompressed  Ratio   Check   Filename
  1        1       340 B                465 B  0.731   CRC64   fstab.xz
```

To decompress this file, use the *unxz* command. You may alternatively use the *xz* command with the -d option. Both will produce an identical result.

```
[user1@centos73 ~]$ unxz fstab.xz
```

Check the file after the decompression with the *ls* command. It will be the same exact file with the exact same timestamp and other attributes.

Archiving Tools

Linux offers plenty of native tools that can be utilized to archive files for storage or distribution. These tools include *tar* and *cpio*, and both have the ability to preserve general file attributes such as ownership, owning group, and timestamp. The following subsections discuss the tools in detail.

Using tar

The *tar* (*tape archive*) command is used to create, append, update, list, and extract files or an entire directory tree to and from a single file, which is called a *tarball* or a *tar* file. This command can be instructed to also compress the tarball after it has been created.

tar supports several options such as those described in Table 1-1:

Option	Description
-c	Creates a tarball.
-f	Specifies the name of a tarball.
-r	Appends more files to an extant tarball.
-t	Lists contents of a tarball.
-u	Appends more files to an extant tarball provided the files being added are newer.
-v	Verbose mode.
-x	Extracts or restores from a tarball.

tar options

Table 1-1 tar Command Options

The -r and -u options do not support adding files to an existing compressed tarball.

A few examples are provided below to elucidate the use of *tar*. Note that the use of the hyphen (-) character with an option is not compulsory. Pay special attention to the syntax and options used in each command and observe the output.

To create a tarball called */tmp/home.tar* of the entire */home* directory, use the -v option for verbosity and the -f option to specify the name of the archive file with the command:

```
[user1@centos73 ~]$ tar -cvf /tmp/home.tar /home
tar: Removing leading `/' from member names
/home/
/home/user1/
/home/user/.mozilla/

. . . . . . . .
```

The resulting tarball will not include the leading forward slash (/) in the file paths as indicated on the first line of the output even though we supplied the full path of */home* for archival. This is the default behavior of the *tar* command, which gives us the flexibility to restore the files at any location of our choice without having to worry about the full pathnames. Use the -P option at the creation time to reverse this behavior.

To create a tarball called */tmp/files.tar* containing only a select few files (three files in this example) from the */etc* directory:

```
[user1@centos73 ~]$ tar -cvf /tmp/files.tar /etc/passwd /etc/yum.conf
```

To append files located in the */etc/yum.repos.d* directory to the existing tarball */tmp/home.tar*:

```
[user1@centos73 ~]$ tar -rvf /tmp/home.tar /etc/yum.repos.d
```

To list what files are included in the *home.tar* tarball:

```
[user1@centos73 ~]$ tar -tvf /tmp/home.tar
```

To restore all files from */tmp/files.tar* in */home/user1* and confirm the output with the *ls* command:

```
[user1@centos73 ~]$ cd
[user1@centos73 ~]$ tar -xvf /tmp/files.tar
[user1@centos73 ~]$ ls -l etc
```

tar also supports options to directly compress the target file while being archived using the *gzip*, *bzip2*, or *xz* command. These options are described in Table 1-2.

tar compression options

Option	Description
-J	Compresses a tarball with xz command.
-j	Compresses a tarball with bzip2 command.
-z	Compresses a tarball with gzip command.

Table 1-2 tar with Compression Options

Let's use these options in the following examples.

To create a tarball called */tmp/home.tar.gz* of the */home* directory and compress it with *gzip*:

```
[user1@centos73 ~]$ tar -czvf /tmp/home.tar.gz /home
```

To create a tarball called */tmp/home.tar.bz2* of the */home* directory and compress it with *bzip2*:

```
[user1@centos73 ~]$ tar -cvjf /tmp/home.tar.bz2 /home
```

Repeat either of the above two commands with -J to have the tarball compressed in xz format. Use */tmp/home.tar.xz* as the name for the compressed tarball.

To list the compressed gzip archive without actually uncompressing it (replace the -z option with -j for a bzip2 archive or -J for an xz archive):

```
[user1@centos73 ~]$ tar tzf /tmp/home.tar.gz
```

Replace -t with -x to extract files from the specified compressed tarball in the current directory.

To extract a tarball in a different directory location than the one you are currently positioned in, use the -C option:

```
[user1@centos73 ~]$ tar xvzf /tmp/home.tar.gz -C /tmp
```

Using cpio

The *cpio* (*copy in/out*) command is used to copy, list, and extract files to and from a single archive file. This command is commonly used with the *find* command to feed input. Details on the usage of *find* is available in Chapter 2 "Working with Files and File Permissions."

cpio supports a variety of options, some of which are summarized in Table 1-3. The *cpio* command requires that one of the -o, -i, or -p option be specified with every invocation.

Option	Description
-a	Resets access times on files after they have been copied.
-d	Creates destination directories during extraction if they do not already exist.
-i	Extracts or restores the contents of an archive.
-o	Creates an archive.
-p	Pass-through mode. Copies files directly from one directory to another without actually creating an archive file.
-t	Lists the contents of an archive.
-u	Overwrites the destination files even if they are newer than the files being restored.
-v	Verbose mode.

Table 1-3 cpio Command Options

The examples that follow elucidate the usage of this command. Pay special attention to the syntax and options used in each command and observe the output.

To create an archive called *home.cpio* of the */home* directory under */tmp*, use the output redirection symbol > to send the output to the specified file. We will discuss the redirection symbols (i.e., < and >) in Chapter 5 "Managing Shared Libraries and Software Packages." Also add the -v option for verbosity.

```
[user1@centos73 ~]$ find /home | cpio -ov > /tmp/home.cpio
/home
/home/user1
/home/user1/.mozilla
. . . . . . . .
```

To list what was included in the above archive, use the -i and -t options and instruct the command to read from */tmp/home.cpio* using the input redirection symbol <:

```
[user1@centos73 ~]$ cpio -itv < /tmp/home.cpio
```

To restore all files from */tmp/home.cpio*, remove the -t option to look like:

```
[user1@centos73 ~]$ cpio -iv < /tmp/home.cpio
```

To copy files directly from */home* into a new directory called *home.bkp* under */tmp*, use the pass-through (-p) option. Also use -d to ensure this directory is created, as it does not currently exist.

```
[user1@centos73 ~]$ find /home | cpio -pvd /tmp/home.bkp
```

To create an archive of */home* with file names without the default newline or other white-space characters, use the -print0 option with the *find* command and the corresponding --null option with *cpio*:

```
[user1@centos73 ~]$ find /home -print0 | cpio --null -o > /tmp/home.cpio
```

You may rerun the above by adding the -depth option to instruct the *find* command to list the child directory entries first and then the entries for their parent directories:

```
[user1@centos73 ~]$ find /home -depth -print0 | cpio --null -o > /tmp/home.cpio
```

 A sub-directory (a.k.a. a child directory) is located under another directory (a.k.a. a parent directory).

Online Help

While working on the system, you may need help to acquire information about a command, its usage, and available options. Linux offers online help via *man* (*manual*) pages. It also provides tools such as *apropos* and *whatis* to search through the manual pages.

Accessing Manual Pages

Manual (man) pages are user online documentation that provide details on commands, configuration files, etc. They are installed under the */usr/share/man* directory for tools and utilities when the associated software package is installed. The manual pages include the name, short description, synopsis, description, options, general notes, bugs, usage examples, writer information, and other information specific to the command. For configuration files, it also includes details on the syntax.

We can use the *man* command to view manual pages. This command uses the *less* command for displaying the manual pages. The following example shows how to check manual pages for the *passwd* command:

```
[user1@centos73 ~]$ man passwd
PASSWD(1)                   User utilities                   PASSWD(1)
NAME
      passwd - update user's authentication tokens
SYNOPSIS
      passwd [-k] [-l] [-u [-f]] [-d] [-e] [-n mindays] [-x maxdays]
      [-w warndays] [-i inactivedays] [-S] [--stdin] [username]
DESCRIPTION
      The passwd utility is used to update user's authentication token(s).
. . . . . . . .
Manual page passwd(1) line 1 (press h for help or q to quit)
```

The output shows the name of the command, the section of the manual pages it is documented in within the parentheses, and the type (User utilities) of the command on the very first line. It then shows a short description (NAME), the command's usage (SYNOPSIS), and a long description (DESCRIPTION), followed by a detailed explanation of each option that the command supports and other relevant data. The bottom line in the above output shows the total lines the manual pages contain and the line where you are. Press h to get help on how to navigate through the manual pages, press q to quit and return to the command prompt, use the Up and Down arrow keys to scroll up and down, and the Page Up and Page Down keys to scroll one page at a time.

For practice, open manual pages for the *passwd* command and navigate through to familiarize yourself.

Manual Sections

Depending on the type of information, the manual information is split in nine different sections. Key sections include: section 1, which contains help on general user commands; section 5, which describes system configuration files and their formats; and section 8, which contains help for the system administration commands designed for execution by the *root* user.

Some commands and configuration files have a common name. For instance, there is a command called *passwd* and there is a file also called *passwd*. If you want to look for help with the command passwd, you simply run **man passwd** and it will bring up the desired help for you. However, if you desire to peruse the format of the file *passwd*, you will have to specify the section number with the *man* command such as **man 5 passwd**.

Searching by Keyword

Sometimes you may need to use a command but do not know its name. Linux allows a keyword search on manual pages using the *man* command with the -k option, or the *apropos* command. Both commands search all sections of the manual pages and show a list of all entries matching the specified keyword in their names or descriptions. For instance, if you want to search the string "password," you can run either of the following:

```
[user1@centos73 ~]$ man -k password
```

```
[user1@centos73 ~]$ apropos password
chage (1)          - change user password expiry information
crypt_r (3)        - password and data encryption
endpwent (3)       - get password file entry
. . . . . . . .
```

Once you have identified the command you were looking for, you can either review that command's manual pages for usage, or use the --help or -? option with the command. These options instruct the command to only list options and their usage on the screen. For example, to get quick help on the *passwd* command, run either of the following:

```
[user1@centos73 ~]$ passwd --help
[user1@centos73 ~]$ passwd -?
Usage: passwd [OPTION...] <accountName>

. . . . . . . .
Help options:
```

 Some commands may not support the -? option.

Displaying Short Description

The *whatis* command provides a quick method for searching for a short description of the specified command or file in the manual database. It scans through the installed manual pages for the specified string and displays all matching entries. For instance, the following shows outputs of the command when run on *yum.conf* and *passwd* files:

```
[user1@centos73 ~]$ whatis yum.conf
yum.conf (5)       - Configuration file for yum(8).
[user1@centos73 ~]$ whatis passwd
passwd (1)          - update user's authentication tokens
sslpasswd (1ssl)   - compute password hashes
passwd (5)          - password file
```

The first output indicates that the specified file is a configuration file associated with the *yum* command, and the second output points to three entries for the *passwd* file (two commands and one password file).

You may also alternatively run the *man* command with the -f option to get identical results:

```
[user1@centos73 ~]$ man -f yum.conf
[user1@centos73 ~]$ man -f passwd
```
-f = same results as whatis

Look at the manual pages of all the commands that were presented in this chapter to make yourself accustomed to the use of manual pages and how information is formatted and presented in them. Going forward, referencing the manual pages of a command or configuration file that you need help with before trying an alternative source will be a good practice.

Chapter Summary

In this chapter, we looked at Linux history and defined open source. We explored popular Linux distributions and their popular derivatives. In Exercises 1-1 and 1-2, we downloaded the software for CentOS, Ubuntu, and Oracle VirtualBox, and created virtual machines to host Linux instances and performed installations. We logged in to the new systems as regular users and opened terminal sessions to access the command prompts. We analyzed the command prompts and highlighted the differences between them.

We looked at a variety of commands that were intended for use by both regular and super users. Those commands included basic viewing tools as well as compression and archiving utilities.

We learned how to access online help for commands and configuration files. We saw how to search through manual pages for desired text. Explanations regarding what commands to use were offered for additional help.

Chapter Review at a Glance

The following presents a one-sentence review of each key topic discussed in this chapter:

- Linux, as an operating system, is the result of efforts of several individuals with the core component, called kernel, developed by Linux Torvalds.

- Linux is an open-source operating system, which allows general public to download its source code, make copies, modify the source code and package it, and distribute the modified version for general access.

- Primarily, there are three major Linux distributions—Red Hat Enterprise Linux, Debian Linux, and SUSE Linux—all others are off-shoots of one of them; they all have many similarities and many differences.

- For learning and practice, download a free copy of Oracle VirtualBox software and copies of CentOS, Ubuntu, and OpenSUSE Linux, build VMs, and install the three Linux versions in the VMs.

- Linux includes hundreds of commands that are intended for either system administration (privileged commands) or general use (non-privileged commands).

- Majority of the Linux commands are the same across major distributions; however, subtle and key differences do exist.

- Some commands do not require any argument to be specified with them for their successful execution, while others do require at least one argument or exactly two.

- A command option is also referred to as a flag or switch, and it is normally preceded by the hyphen character.

- Compression is used to compress one or more files for disk space conservation and data transmission across the network.

- Archiving of files or entire directory structures is performed for various use cases including storage and network distribution.

- Linux comes standard with online manual pages and other documentation to help normal users and system administrators obtain assistance with command usage, file syntax, etc.

- Commands we learned in this chapter are: ls, pwd, cd, tty, uptime, whoami, logname, id, groups, uname, hostname, clear, gzip, gunzip, bzip2, bunzip2, xz, unxz, tar, cpio, man, apropos, and whatis.
- Files and directories we discussed in this chapter are: /usr/share/man/.

Chapter 2

Working with Files and File Permissions

This chapter describes the following major topics:

➢ Overview of the Filesystem Hierarchy Standard (FHS)
➢ Perform file and directory operations including creating, listing, displaying, copying, moving, renaming, and removing
➢ Overview of common file types
➢ Understand file access permissions
➢ Determine and modify file permissions with symbolic and octal notations
➢ Set default permissions for new files and directories
➢ Modify file ownership and owning group
➢ Understand and create file and directory links
➢ Key differences between file copying and file linking
➢ Search for files and commands using various searching tools and criteria
➢ Use the output of one command as an argument to another command
➢ Configure special permissions with setuid, setgid, and sticky bits
➢ Share files among group members

This chapter covers the following objectives for LX0-103/101-400 Exam:

103.2 Process text streams using filters [a part of this objective is described in this chapter and the rest in chapter 3]

40. Send text files and output streams through text utility filters to modify the output using standard UNIX commands found in the GNU textutils package

The following is a partial list of the used files, terms and utilities: head, tail, and less

103.3 Perform basic file management [most of this objective is described in this chapter, a part in chapter 4, the tar/cpio and dd commands in chapters 1 and 8, respectively]

41. Copy, move and remove files and directories individually
42. Copy multiple files and directories recursively
43. Remove files and directories recursively
45. Using find to locate and act on files based on type, size, or time

The following is a partial list of the used files, terms and utilities: cp, find, mkdir, mv, ls, rm, rmdir, touch, and file

103.4 Use streams, pipes and redirects [a part of this objective is described in this chapter and the rest in chapter 4]

49. Use the output of one command as arguments to another command

The following is a partial list of the used files, terms and utilities: xargs

104.5 Manage file permissions and ownership [this entire objective is described in this chapter]

76. Manage access permissions on regular and special files as well as directories
77. Use access modes such as suid, sgid and the sticky bit to maintain security
78. Know how to change the file creation mask
79. Use the group field to grant file access to group members

The following is a partial list of the used files, terms and utilities: chmod, umask, chown, and chrgp

104.6 Create and change hard and symbolic links [this entire objective is described in this chapter]

80. Create links
81. Identify hard and/or soft links
82. Copying versus linking files
83. Use links to support system administration tasks

The following is a partial list of the used files, terms and utilities: ln and ls

104.7 Find system files and place files in the correct location [this entire objective is described in this chapter]

84. Understand the correct locations of files under the FHS
85. Find files and commands on a Linux system
86. Know the location and purpose of important file and directories as defined in the FHS

The following is a partial list of the used files, terms and utilities: find, locate, updatedb, whereis, which, type, and /etc/updatedb.conf

Linux files are organized logically for ease of administration, and they are stored in hundreds of directories located in larger containers called file systems. Mainline Linux distributions follow the Filesystem Hierarchy Standard (FHS) for file organization, which describes names, locations, and permissions for many file types and directories. File systems are primarily of two types and they are used to retain permanent and runtime data.

There are a number of maintenance operations that can be performed on files and directories in addition to viewing their contents. Linux supports a variety of types of files, and the file type is based on the kind of data they store.

Permissions are set on files and directories to restrict their access to authorized users only. Users are grouped into three distinct categories. Each user category is then assigned required permissions. Permissions can be modified using one of two available methods. The user mask may be defined for individual users so that any new files and directories that are created always get preset permissions.

Every file in Linux has an owner and a group associated with it. There are tools available in the operating system that help in linking files and directories and in searching them using varying criteria. The OS offers three additional permission bits to control user access to certain executable files and shared directories.

Filesystem Hierarchy Standard (FHS)

Linux uses the conventional hierarchical directory structure based on the *Filesystem Hierarchy Standard* (FHS) document that outlines the specifics for the layout of the directories, the type of information they should store, and whether they should be shared. This standard helps store related information together in a logical fashion. Per the FHS, directories may contain both files and sub-directories. Sub-directories may further hold more files and sub-directories. A sub-directory, also referred to as a *child* directory, is a directory located under a *parent* directory. That parent directory is a sub-directory of some other higher-level directory. In other words, the Linux directory structure is similar to an inverted tree where the top of the tree is the root of the directory, and the branches and leaves are sub-directories and files, respectively. The root of the directory is represented by the forward slash (/) character, and this is the point where the entire structure is ultimately connected. The forward slash character is also used as a directory separator in a path, such as */etc/rc.d/init.d/network*. See Figure 2-1 (next page).

In the */etc/rc.d/init.d/network* path, the *etc* sub-directory is located under /, making *root* the parent of *etc* (which is a child). *rc.d* (child) is located under *etc* (parent), *init.d* (child) is located under *rc.d* (parent), and at the very bottom, *network* (leaf) is located under *init.d* (parent).

Each directory has a parent directory and a child directory, with the exception of the root and the lowest level directories. The root directory has no parent, and the lowest level sub-directory has no child. The term sub-directory is used for a directory that has a parent directory.

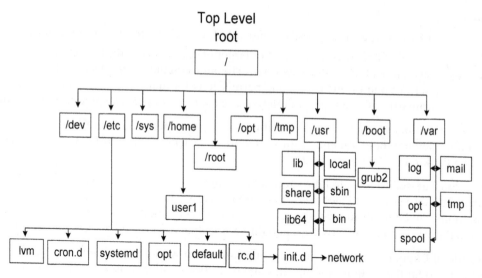

Figure 2-1 Directory Tree

Static vs. Dynamic and Shareable vs. Non-Shareable

Some of the directories, such as */usr*, */boot*, and */opt*, hold *static* data. These directories contain user commands, administrative commands, help files, and library files, as well as kernel and boot files. Static data is not usually modified. Other directories, such as */var*, */etc*, */tmp*, and */home*, contain *dynamic* (or *variable*) information. These directories hold log and spool files, configuration files, temporary files, and personal user files, respectively, that are modified and updated as required. Moreover, there are a few virtual file systems—*/dev*, */proc*, and */sys*—that hold runtime system information. They are created, maintained, and destroyed automatically by the kernel. These file systems are explained in Chapter 7 "Understanding and Configuring Hardware and Kernel Modules."

In addition to identifying which directories are supposed to hold static and dynamic data, FHS also describes which directories can or cannot be shared over the network based on the type of information they store. For this, there are four categories outlined in FHS: (1) static and shareable (e.g. */opt* and */usr*), (2) static and unshareable (e.g. */boot* and */etc*), (3) variable and shareable (e.g. */var/mail* and */var/opt*), and (4) variable and unshareable (e.g. */var/lock* and */run*).

Common Directories Under /

The root directory contains higher-level directories that hold specific information. This structure may vary among Linux distributions and among versions of the same distribution. For instance, the structure in CentOS version 7 is slightly different from the previous versions and from Debian as well. Some of the key directories are:

- */etc* (etcetera) to hold system configuration files
- */root* as the default home directory for the *root* user
- */media* (or */run/media*) to automatically mount removable media such as floppy, CD/DVD, and USB
- */mnt* to mount a file system temporarily
- */bin* and */usr/bin* to maintain user-level commands

- *sbin* and */usr/sbin* to store administrative commands, and
- */lib, /usr/lib, /lib64,* and */usr/lib64* to store 32- and 64-bit library routines that are needed by various commands and programs for successful execution.

On CentOS 7, */bin, /lib, /lib64,* and */sbin* are simply pointers (soft links) to the actual directories under */usr*; whereas, in CentOS 6 and earlier and in Debian, these directories exist directly under the top of the root file system as well as under */usr*. They have more files in */usr/bin* and */usr/sbin* as compared to */bin* and */sbin*. Run **ls -ld <dirname>** and **ls -l <dirname> | wc** on all these directories to explore them. Replace <dirname> with actual directory names.

File and Directory Operations

This section elaborates on various management operations that can be performed on files and directories. These operations include creating, listing, displaying contents of, copying, moving, renaming, and deleting files and directories. These common operations can be performed on files and directories by normal users who own or have appropriate permissions. The *root* user can perform these operations on any file or directory on the system, as it doesn't matter who owns it. In case of lack of user permissions, an error message is generated.

Creating Files and Directories

Files can be created in multiple ways using different commands as required; however, there is only one command to create directories. Let's look at them at the commands below.

Creating Empty Files Using the touch Command

The *touch* command creates an empty file and sets the modification and access times on the file to the time of its creation. If the file already exists, the *touch* command simply updates the timestamp on the file to match the current system date and time. Execute the following to create *file1* and then run *ll* to verify:

```
[user1@centos73 ~]$ touch file1
[user1@centos73 ~]$ ll file1
-rw-rw-r--. 1 user1 user1 0 Jan  4 08:03 file1
```

As expected, the fifth field (the size field) in the output is 0, meaning that *file1* is created with zero bytes in size. Now, if you re-run the *touch* command on this file after a minute or so, a new timestamp is placed on it:

```
[user1@centos73 ~]$ touch file1
[user1@centos73 ~]$ ll file1
-rw-rw-r--. 1 user1 user1 0 Jan  4 08:05 file1
```

The *touch* command has a few interesting options. The -d and -t options set a specific date and time on a file; the -a and -m options enable you to change only the access or the modification time on a file to the current system time; and the -r option sets the modification time on a file to that of the specified reference file's.

Creating Short Files Using the cat Command

The *cat* command allows you to create short text files. The ending angle bracket ">", as shown below, must be used to redirect the output to the specified file:

```
[user1@centos73 ~]$ cat > catfile1
```

Nothing is displayed when you execute the above, as the system is waiting for something to be input. Type some text. Press the Enter key to open a new line and continue typing. When you are done, press Ctrl+d to save the text in *catfile1* and return to the shell prompt. You can verify the file creation with the *ll* command.

Creating Files Using the vi (vim) Editor

You can use the vi editor to create and modify text files of any size. Refer to Chapter 3 "Editing Text Files, Exploring Filters, and Using Regular Expression" on how to use this tool.

Making Directories Using the mkdir Command

The *mkdir* command is used to make directories. This command shows an output if it is run with the -v option. The following example demonstrates the creation of a directory called *dir1*:

```
[user1@centos73 ~]$ mkdir dir1 -v
mkdir: created directory 'dir1'
```

You can create a hierarchy of sub-directories by specifying the -p option with *mkdir*. In the following example, *mkdir* is used to create the hierarchy *dir2/perl/perl5*. The -v option is added for prolixity.

```
[user1@centos73 ~]$ mkdir dir2/perl/perl5 -vp
mkdir: created directory 'dir2'
mkdir: created directory 'dir2/perl'
mkdir: created directory 'dir2/perl/perl5'
```

Listing Files and Directories

In chapter 1 "Installing Linux and Using Basic Commands," we looked at the *ls* command and how to use it with a number of common options to list files as desired. This is probably the most used command in Linux. The *ll* is the shortcut to **ls -l,** which is pre-defined on most Linux distributions. This command shows the details for each listed file in nine columns as depicted below:

```
-rw-rw-r--.   1   user1   user1   0   Jan   4   08:05   file1
drwxrwxr-x.   2   user1   user1   6   Jan   4   08:22   dir1
```

Each column in the output furnishes a unique piece of information about the file or directory:

Column 1: The first character (hyphen or d) divulges the file type and the next nine characters (rw-rw-r--) indicate permissions.
Column 2: Displays the number of links (links are explained later in this chapter).
Column 3: Shows the owner name.
Column 4: Displays the owning group name.
Column 5: Identifies the file size in bytes. For directories, this number reflects the number of blocks being used by the directory to hold information about its contents.
Columns 6, 7, and 8: Displays the month, day of the month, and time of creation or last modification.
Column 9: Indicates the name of the file or directory.

A grasp of the usage of this command and the output it produces is important. We will be using the shortcut *ll* throughout this book rather than the actual *ls -l* for brevity and convenience unless there is a specific need to use the actual.

Displaying File Contents

Linux offers a variety of tools for showing file contents. Directory contents are simply the files and sub-directories that it contains. Use *ll* as explained in Chapter 1 "Installing Linux and Using Basic Commands" to view directory contents.

For file viewing, you can use the *cat*, *less*, *more*, *head*, and *tail* commands. These tools are explained below.

Using the cat Command

cat displays the contents of a text file. It is typically used to view short files. It shows the entire file contents on the screen. In the example below, the *.bash_profile* file in *user1*'s home directory is displayed with the *cat* command:

```
[user1@centos73 ~]$ cat .bash_profile

# Get the aliases and functions
if [ -f ~/.bashrc ]; then
      . ~/.bashrc
fi

# User specific environment and startup programs

PATH=$PATH:$HOME/.local/bin:$HOME/bin

export PATH
```

You can add the -n option to the *cat* command to view line numbers as well.

Using the less and more Commands

Both *less* and *more* are text filters that are used for viewing long text files one page at a time, starting at the beginning. The *less* command is more capable than the *more* command, and it should be treated as a replacement for *more* going forward. *less* does not need to read the entire file before it starts to display its contents, thus making it faster. The *more* command is limited to forward text searching only, whereas, its counterpart is able to perform both forward and backward searches. Run **less /usr/bin/znew** and **more /usr/bin/znew** and use the keys from Table 2-1 to navigate.

Key	Purpose
Spacebar / f	Scrolls forward one screen
Enter	Scrolls forward one line
b	Scrolls backward one screen
d	Scrolls forward half a screen
h	Displays help
q	Quits and returns to the command prompt
/string	Searches forward for a string

Key	Purpose
?string	Searches backward for a string; only applies to the less command
n	Finds the next occurrence of a string
N	Finds the previous occurrence of a string; only applies to the less command

Table 2-1 Navigating with less or more

If */usr/bin/znew* file is unavailable, use */etc/profile* instead.

Using the head and tail Commands

head displays the starting few lines from the specified text file. By default, it shows the first ten lines. Run **head /etc/profile** and see the result. The output would include a few empty lines as well.

You can pass a numeral to the command as an argument to limit the output to that many lines. For example, run **head -3 /etc/profile** to view the first three lines only.

tail displays the ending ten lines from the specified file by default unless a numeral is passed as an argument to alter its behavior. Issue **tail /etc/services** and then **tail -3 /etc/services** to see the difference.

The *tail* command proves to be very useful when viewing a log file while it is being updated. The -f (follow) option enables this function. The following example shows how to view the system log file */var/log/messages* in real time. First, switch the user ID from *user1* to *root*, as *user1* will not have the permission to view this file being it is a normal user. Enter the *root* user password when prompted.

```
[user1@centos73 ~]$ su -
Password:
[root@centos73 ~]# tail -f /var/log/messages
```

You may have to wait for some time before you see an update. Press Ctrl+c to quit when you are done. Type the **exit** command to exit out of the *root* user account and return to *user1*.

Copying Files and Directories

The copy operation duplicates a file or directory. Linux provides the *cp* command for this purpose. This command has a variety of options available that may be used to get the desired results.

Copying Files

The *cp* command copies one or more files within a directory or to another directory. To duplicate a file in the same directory, you must give a different name to the target file. However, you may assign the same or a different file name if the copy is being made to a different directory. Consider the following examples:

To copy *file1* as *newfile1* in the same directory:

```
[user1@centos73 ~]$ cp file1 newfile1
```

To copy *file1* by the same name to an existing directory *dir1*:

```
[user1@centos73 ~]$ cp file1 dir1
```

By default, the copy operation overwrites the destination file if it exists without presenting a warning. To alter this behavior, use the -i (interactive) option to instruct *cp* to prompt for confirmation before overwriting:

```
[user1@centos73 ~]$ cp -i file1 dir1
cp: overwrite `dir1/file1'?
```

Press the Enter key after typing a "y" for yes or an "n" for no to proceed.

Some Linux systems, such as CentOS, has a pre-defined alias set for the root user to always use the -i option with the cp command.

You may add the -f option to *cp* to force it to overwrite a read-only destination file.

Copying Directories

The *cp* command with the -r or -R (recursive) option copies an entire directory tree to another location. In the following example, *dir1* is copied to *dir2* and then the directory contents of *dir2* are listed for validation:

```
[user1@centos73 ~]$ cp -r dir1 dir2
[user1@centos73 ~]$ ll dir2
drwxrwxr-x. 2 user1 user1 19 Jan  4 15:52 dir1
drwxrwxr-x. 3 user1 user1 19 Jan  4 08:45 perl
```

You may use the -i option for overwrite confirmation if the destination already has a matching file or directory.

Try running **ll dir2 -R** to view the entire hierarchy.

The *cp* command can also use -p, which is another useful option that can provide the ability to preserve the attributes (timestamp, permissions, ownership, etc.) of a file or directory being copied. Try running **cp -p file1 /tmp** and then use *ll* to compare the attributes on both files.

Moving and Renaming Files and Directories

A file or directory can be moved within the same file system or to another. Within the file system move, an entry is added to the target directory and the source entry is removed, which leaves the actual data intact. On the other hand, a move to a different file system physically moves the file or directory content to the new location and deletes the source.

A rename simply changes the name of a file or directory; data is not touched.

Moving and Renaming Files

The *mv* command is used to move or rename files. The -i option can be specified for user confirmation if a file already exists by the same name at destination. The following example moves *file1* to *dir1* and prompts for confirmation:

```
[user1@centos73 ~]$ mv -i file1 dir1
```
mv overwrite: dir1/file1? (y/n)

To rename *newfile1* as *newfile2*:

```
[user1@centos73 ~]$ mv newfile1 newfile2
```

You may add the -f option to *mv* to force the command to overwrite without prompting in case *newfile2* already exists. The behavior of the -f option is opposite to that of the -i option.

Moving and Renaming Directories

To move a directory along with its contents to elsewhere, or to simply change the name of a directory, use the *mv* command. For example, to move *dir1* under */tmp* (*/tmp* must exist, otherwise it will be a rename operation), issue the following:

```
[user1@centos73 ~]$ mv dir1 /tmp
```

To rename *dir2* as *dir20*:

```
[user1@centos73 ~]$ mv dir2 dir20
```

Removing Files and Directories

The remove operation deletes a file entry from the directory structure and marks its data space as free. For a directory, the remove operation weeds corresponding entries out from the file system structure.

Removing Files

You can remove a file using the *rm* command, which deletes one or more specified files. For example, to erase a file called *newfile1*, issue **rm newfile1** at the command prompt. You may add the -i and -v options to control accidental erasures and add verbosity, respectively.

By default, you do not need the -i option specified for a yes/no confirmation if you are *root*. There is a predefined alias "alias rm='rm -i'" in the *root* user's ~/.*bashrc* file that takes care of that. In this case you may use the -f (force) option with rm to override the behavior of -i.

The *rm* command can also be used to remove a file that has a wildcard character, such as an asterisk (*) or a question mark (?), embedded in its name. These characters have special meaning to the shell, and filenames containing them must be prepended with the backslash (\) character to instruct the shell to treat them as regular characters.

A careful use of the *rm* command is particularly important when you have administrative rights on the system.

For example, if a file exists by the name * under the */tmp/* directory (use **touch /tmp/*** to create it), you can remove it by executing **rm /tmp/***. If you mistakenly run **rm /tmp/*** instead, all files there will be deleted.

Wildcard characters are used in filename globbing and in commands where an action needs to occur on multiple files matching certain criteria. They are discussed in Chapter 4 "Dealing with the Bash Shell and Processes".

Removing Directories

The *rmdir* and *rm* commands are available to remove directories. The *rmdir* command is used to delete empty directories, while the *rm* command requires the -d option to accomplish the same. In addition, we can use the -r or -R (recursive) option with *rm* to remove a directory and all its contents. Both commands support the -v option for reporting what they are doing. Let's look at a few examples.

To erase an empty directory called *emptydir* (assuming *emptydir* exists), use either of the following:

```
[user1@centos73 ~]$ rmdir emptydir -v
[user1@centos73 ~]$ rm -dv emptydir
```

To remove *dir20* and all its contents recursively, use either -r or -R with the command:

```
[user1@centos73 ~]$ rm -r dir20
```

Both -i and -f options are supported for interactive and non-interactive deletions.

The same rules that apply on filenames with wildcard characters in their names, apply on directory names as well. See the previous topic for details.

Common File Types

Linux supports several different types of files such as regular files, directory files, executable files, symbolic link files, and device files. These file types are described in the following subsections. Linux does not require an extension to a file to identify its type. It provides two elementary commands called *file* and *stat* to ascertain the type of data that the file contain.

Regular Files

Regular files may contain text or binary data. These files may be shell scripts or commands in the binary form. When you list a directory, all line entries for files in the output that begin with the hyphen (-) character represent regular files:

```
[user1@centos73 ~]$ ll /usr/bin
. . . . . . . .
-rwxr-xr-x. 1 root root     5343 Jul 27  2015  znew
```

The *ll* command will produce a long list of files in the */usr/bin* directory; however, the output above only shows a single file called *znew*. Now, let's run the *file* and *stat* commands on this file and see what they report:

```
[user1@centos73 ~]$ file /usr/bin/znew
/usr/bin/znew: POSIX shell script, ASCII text executable
[user1@centos73 ~]$ stat /usr/bin/znew
  File: '/usr/bin/znew'
  Size: 5343        Blocks: 16        IO Block: 4096    regular file
```

The two commands report the file type differently as indicated by the bolded text in the above output. The first command shows the specific type of data that the file contains, whereas the latter command simply states that it is a regular file.

Directory Files

Directories are logical containers that are used to hold files and sub-directories. The following *ll* command output shows a few directories from */usr/bin*:

```
[user1@centos73 ~]$ ll /usr
dr-xr-xr-x.     2 root root 49152 Dec 21 09:13 bin
dr-xr-xr-x.    42 root root  4096 Dec 21 09:12 lib
dr-xr-xr-x.   139 root root 73728 Dec 21 09:13 lib64
dr-xr-xr-x.     2 root root 20480 Dec 21 09:13 sbin
drwxr-xr-x.  232 root root  8192 Dec 21 09:12 share
```

The letter "d" at the beginning of each line entry identifies the file as a directory. Try running the **file** and **stat** commands on */usr* and see what they report.

Executable Files

Executable files could be commands in the binary format or shell scripts. In other words, any file that can be run is an executable file. A file that has an "x" in the fourth, seventh, or the tenth field in the first column of the output of the *ll* command is executable. For instance, the file *whatis* located in the */usr/bin* directory is an executable file. It contains data in the binary form and it also has the "x" bit in the designated fields. Try running the following commands for validation:

```
[user1@centos73 ~]$ ll /usr/bin/whatis
[user1@centos73 ~]$ file /usr/bin/whatis
[user1@centos73 ~]$ stat /usr/bin/whatis
```

Symbolic Link Files

A *symbolic link* (a.k.a. a *soft link* or a *symlink*) may be considered a shortcut to another file or directory. When you issue *ll* on a symbolically linked file or directory, you will notice two things. One, the line entry begins with the letter l; and two, there is an arrow pointing to the target link. For example:

```
[user1@centos73 ~]$ ll /usr/sbin/vigr
lrwxrwxrwx. 1 root root 4 Dec 21 09:08 /usr/sbin/vigr -> vipw
```

Run the **file** and **stat** commands on */usr/sbin/vigr* for additional confirmation.

Device Files

Each piece of hardware in the system has an associated file in the */dev* directory that is used by the kernel to communicate with that device. This type of file is called a *device file*, and they are of two types: *character* (or *raw*) device files and *block* device files. The *ll* command distinguishes between the two with a "c" for character or a "b" for block in the first field of the first column as shown below for the console and hard disk device files:

```
[user1@centos73 ~]$ ll /dev/console
crw-------.  1 root root 5, 1 Jan  4 07:26 /dev/console
[user1@centos73 ~]$ ll /dev/sd*
brw-rw----. 1 root disk 8, 0 Jan  4 07:26 /dev/sda
brw-rw----. 1 root disk 8, 1 Jan  4 07:26 /dev/sda1
brw-rw----. 1 root disk 8, 2 Jan  4 07:26 /dev/sda2
```

Use the **file** and **stat** commands on */dev/console* and */dev/sda* for additional verification.

File and Directory Access Permissions

Linux is a multi-user operating system that allows hundreds of users the ability to log in and work concurrently. In addition, the operating system has hundreds of thousands of files and directories that it must maintain securely in order to warrant a successful system and application operation from a security standpoint. Given these factors, it is imperative to regulate user access to files and directories, and grant them appropriate rights to carry out their designated functions without jeopardizing system security. This control of permissions on files and directories for users may also be referred to as user *access rights*.

Determining Access Permissions

Access permissions on files and directories allow administrative control over which users (permission classes) can access them and to what level (permission types). File and directory permissions discussed in this section are referred to as *standard ugo/rwx permissions*.

Permission Classes

Users are categorized into three unique classes for maintaining file security through access rights. These classes are user (u), group (g), and other (o, also referred to as public), and represent the owner, the set of users with identical access requirement, and everyone else on the system.

Permission Types

Permissions control what actions can be performed on a file or directory and by whom. There are three types of permissions—read (r), write (w), and execute (x)—and they behave differently for files and directories. For files, the permissions allow viewing and copying (read), modifying (write), and running (execute). And in the case of directories, they allow listing contents with *ls* (read); creating, removing, and renaming files and sub-directories (write); and *cd* into it (execute).

If a read, write, or execute permission is not desired, the - sign is used to represent its absence.

Permission Modes

A permission mode is used to add (+), revoke (-), or assign (=) a permission type to a permission class.

We can view the permission settings on files and directories using the *ll* command. The following shows only the first column:

    - rwx rw- r--

The permission settings are enclosed in the first column of the command output. The first character (-) indicates the type of file, and the next nine characters (bolded)—three groups of three

---

characters—show read, write, and execute permissions for the three user classes, respectively. The hyphen (-) represents a permission denial for that level.

Modifying Access Permissions

Linux provides the *chmod* command to modify access rights. It works identically on files and directories. *chmod* can be used by *root* or the file owner, and can modify permissions specified in one of two ways: *symbolic* or *octal*. Symbolic notation uses a combination of letters and symbols to add, revoke, or assign permissions. The octal notation (a.k.a. the *absolute* notation) uses a three-digit numbering system ranging from 0 to 7 to express permissions for the three user classes. Octal values are given in Table 2-2.

Octal Value	Binary Notation	Symbolic Equivalent	Explanation
0	000	---	No permissions
1	001	--x	Execute permission only
2	010	-w-	Write permission only
3	011	-wx	Write and execute permissions
4	100	r--	Read permission only
5	101	r-x	Read and execute permissions
6	110	rw-	Read and write permissions
7	111	rwx	Read, write, and execute permissions

Table 2-2 Octal Permission Notation

In Table 2-2, each "1" corresponds to an r, w, or x, and each "0" corresponds to the hyphen (-) character for no permission at that level. Figure 2-2 shows weights associated with each digit position in the 3-digit octal numbering model.

Figure 2-2 Permission Weights

The right-most position has weight 1, the middle position carries weight 2, and the left-most position has weight 4. If we assign a permission of 6, for example, it would correspond to the two left-most digit positions. Similarly, a permission of 2 would point to the middle digit position only.

Exercise 2-1: Modify File Permissions Using Symbolic Notation

For this exercise, presume that a file called *file1* exists with read permission for the owner (*user1*), owning group (*user1*), and others, as shown below, and that you are logged in as *user1* (if the permissions vary, bring them to the desired state by executing **chmod 444 file1** as *user1* prior to starting the exercise).

    -r--r--r--. 1 user1 user1 0 Jan 03 08:21 file1

In this exercise, you will add the execute permission for the owner and the write permission for the group and public. You will then revoke the write permission from public and assign read, write, and execute permissions to the three user categories at the same time. Finally, you will assign read, write, and execute permissions to the owner, read and execute to the owning group, and read-only permission bit to the public. The *chmod* command accepts the -v option to display what it has changed. It is recommended to run *ll* after each command execution for additional verification.

1.   Add the execute permission bit for the owner:

     [user1@centos73 ~]$ chmod u+x file1 -v
     mode of 'file1' changed from 0444 (r--r--r--) to 0544 (r-xr--r--)

2.   Add the write permission for group members and public:

     [user1@centos73 ~]$ chmod go+w file1 -v

3.   Remove the write permission for the public:

     [user1@centos73 ~]$ chmod o-w file1 -v

4.   Assign read, write, and execute permissions to all three user categories:

     [user1@centos73 ~]$ chmod a=rwx file1 -v

5.   Assign all three permissions to the owner, read and execute to the owning group, and read-only to the public:

     [user1@centos73 ~]$ chmod u=rwx,g=rx,o=r file1

Exercise 2-2: Modify File Permissions Using Octal Notation

For this exercise, assume that a file called *file2* exists with permissions 444 and ownership belongs to *user1*, and that you are logged in as *user1*.

     -r--r--r--. 1 user1 user1 0 Jan 03 08:41 file2

In this exercise, you will add the execute permission for the owner and the write permission for the group and public. You will then revoke the write permission from public and assign read, write, and execute permissions to the three user categories at the same time. The *chmod* command accepts the -v option to display what it has done. It is recommended to run *ll* after each command execution for additional verification.

1.   Add the execute permission for the file owner:

     [user1@centos73 ~]$ chmod 544 file2 -v

2. Add the write permission for the group and public:

    [user1@centos73 ~]$ **chmod -v 566 file2**

3. Remove the write permission for the public:

    [user1@centos73 ~]$ **chmod 564 file2 -v**

4. Assign read, write, and execute permissions to all three user categories:

    [user1@centos73 ~]$ **chmod -v 777 file2**

Default Permissions

Linux assigns *default permissions* to a file or directory at the time of its creation. Default permissions are calculated based on the *umask* (user mask) permission value subtracted from a preset *initial* permissions value.

The umask is a three-digit octal value (also represented in symbolic notation) that refers to read/write/execute permissions for owner, group, and public. Its purpose is to set default permissions on new files and directories without touching the permissions on existing files and directories. The default umask value is set to 0022 for the *root* and other system users (in both CentOS and Debian) and 0002 (0022 in Debian) for all regular users with the bash shell assigned. Note that the left-most 0 has no significance. Run the *umask* command without any options and it will display the current umask value:

    [user1@centos73 ~]$ **umask**
    0002

Run the command again but with the -S option to display the umask in symbolic notation:

    [user1@centos73 ~]$ **umask -S**
    u=rwx,g=rwx,o=rx

The pre-defined initial permission values are 666 (rw-rw-rw-) for files and 777 (rwxrwxrwx) for directories. Even if the umask is set to 000, the new files will always get a maximum of 666 permissions; however, we can add the executable bits explicitly with the *chmod* command if desired.

Calculating Default Permissions

Consider the following example to calculate the default permission values on files for regular users:

Initial Permissions	666	
umask	− 002	(subtract)
================================		
Default Permissions	664	

This indicates that every new file created will have read and write permissions assigned to the owner and the owning group, and a read-only permission to others.

To calculate the default permission values on directories for regular users:

$$
\begin{array}{lll}
\text{Initial Permissions} & 777 & \\
\text{umask} & -\,002 & \text{(subtract)} \\
\hline
\text{Default Permissions} & 775 &
\end{array}
$$

This indicates that every new directory created will have read, write, and execute permissions assigned to the owner and the owning group, and read and execute permissions to everyone else.

To have different default permissions set on new files and directories, you will need to modify the umask. You first need to ascertain the desired default values. For instance, if you want all your new files and directories to get 640 and 750 permissions, respectively, you can set umask to 027 by running either **umask 027** or **umask u=rwx,g=rx,o=**.

The new value becomes effective right away, and it will only be applied to files and directories created thereafter. The existing files and directories will remain intact. Now create *file10* and *dir10* as *user1* under */home/user1* to test the effect of the new umask.

```
[user1@centos73 ~]$ touch file10
[user1@centos73 ~]$ ll file10
-rw-r-----. 1 user1 user1 0 Jan 4 09:48 file10
[user1@centos73 ~]$ mkdir dir10
[user1@centos73 ~]$ ll -d dir10
drwxr-x---. 2 user1 user1 6 Jan 4 09:48 dir10
```

The above examples show that the new file and directory were created with different permissions. The file got (666 – 027 = 640) and the directory (777 – 027 = 750) permissions.

File Ownership and Owning Group

In Linux, every file and directory has an owner. By default, the creator assumes the ownership, but this may be altered and allocated to a different user if required.

Similarly, every user is a member of one or more groups. A group is a collection of users with a common access requirement. By default, the owner's group is assigned to a file or directory.

The following *ll* command output shows the owner and the owning group for file *file10*:

```
[user1@centos73 ~]$ ll file10
-rw-r-----. 1 user1 user1 0 Jan 4 09:48 file10
```

The output indicates that the owner of *file10* is *user1* who belongs to group *user1*. If you wish to view the corresponding UID and GID instead, you can specify the -n option with *ll*:

```
[user1@centos73 ~]$ ll -n file10
-rw-r-----. 1 1000 1000 0 Jan 4 09:48 file10
```

Linux provides the *chown* and *chgrp* commands to alter ownership and owning group for files and directories; however, you must be *root* to make these modifications.

Exercise 2-3: Modify File Ownership and Owning Group

For this exercise, presume that *file10* and *dir10* with ownership and owning group set to *user1* exist, and that you are logged in as *root*.

```
-rw-r-----.  1 user1 user1 0 Jan 4 09:48 file10
drwxr-x---.  2 user1 user1 6 Jan 4 09:48 dir10
```

In this exercise, you will create a user account *user100* and change the ownership for *file10* to *user100*. You will then change the owning group to *user100* on this file. You will apply both ownership and owning group on *dir10* recursively to *user100* at the same time. Use *ll* after making ownership changes to view the results.

1. Create user account *user100*:

    ```
    [root@centos73 ~]# useradd user100
    ```

2. Change into the home directory of *user1* and modify the ownership on *file10* to *user100*:

    ```
    [root@centos73 ~]# cd /home/user1
    [root@centos73 ~]# chown user100 file10
    ```
    changed ownership of 'file10' from user1 to user100

3. Change the owning group to *user100* using either the following:

    ```
    [root@centos73 ~]# chgrp user100 file10 -v
    [root@centos73 ~]# chown :user100 file10 -v
    ```

4. Change both ownership and group membership to *user100* recursively on *dir10*:

    ```
    [root@centos73 ~]# chown -Rv user100:user100 dir10
    ```

Linking Files and Directories

Each file within a file system has a variety of attributes assigned to it at the time of creation. These attributes are collectively referred to as the file's *metadata*, and they change when the file is accessed or modified. A file's metadata includes several pieces of information, such as the file's type, size, permissions, owner's name, owning group name, last access/modification times, link count, number of blocks being used to store file's data, and so on. This metadata takes 128 bytes of space for each file. This tiny storage space is referred to as the file's *inode* (index node). An inode is assigned a unique numeric identifier that is used by the kernel for accessing, tracking, and managing the file. In order to access the inode and the data it points to, a filename is assigned to recognize it and access it. This mapping between an inode and a filename is referred to as a *link*. It is important to note that the inode does not store the file's name in its metadata; the file name and corresponding inode number mapping is maintained in the directory's metadata in which the file resides.

Linking files or directories creates additional instances of them, but all of them eventually point to the same physical data location in the directory tree. Linked files may or may not have identical inode numbers and metadata depending on how they are linked.

Linux has two ways for creating file and directory links, and they are referred to as hard links and soft links. An important point to note here is that links are created between files or between directories.

Hard Link

A *hard* link is a mapping between one or more filenames and an inode (or an inode number), making all hard-linked files indistinguishable from one another. This implies that all the hard-linked files will have identical metadata. Changes to the file content can be made by accessing any of these filenames. A hard link cannot cross a file system boundary, and it cannot be used to link directories because of the restrictions placed within Linux.

Figure 2-3 shows two filenames—*newfile2* and *newfile20*—and both are sharing the same inode number 1221. Each filename is a hard link pointing to the same inode.

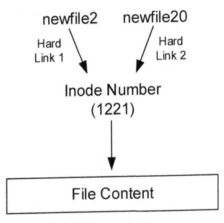

Figure 2-3 Hard Link

The following example uses the *ln* command to create a hard link for *newfile2* located under */home/user1* to *newfile20* in the same directory (create *newfile2* if it does not exist):

```
[user1@centos73 ~]$ ln newfile2 newfile20
```

After creating the link, run *ll* with the -i option:

```
[user1@centos73 ~]$ ll -i newfile2*
1221 -rw-rw-r--. 2 user1 user1 0 Jan 04 13:00 newfile2
1221 -rw-rw-r--. 2 user1 user1 0 Jan 04 13:00 newfile20
```

Look at the first and third columns. The first column indicates the shared inode number, and the third column provides a count (a.k.a. the link count) of the hard links that each file has. *newfile2* points to *newfile20*, and vice versa. If you remove the original file (*newfile2* in this example), you will still have access to the data through *newfile20*. Each time you add a hard link to an extant file, you will notice an increase in the number of inodes by 1. Similarly, if you delete a hard link, the number of the link count will reduce by 1 until you erase the last instance of it, which sets the link count to 0. The increase and decrease in the link count is reflected on all the hard linked files.

Soft Link

A *soft* link (a.k.a. a *symbolic* link or a *symlink*) makes it possible to associate one file with another. The concept is similar to that of the shortcut in MS Windows where the actual file is resident somewhere in the directory structure, but there may be one or more shortcuts (or pointers) with different names pointing to it. This allows accessing the file directly via the actual file name or any of the shortcuts. Each soft link has a unique inode number that simply stores the pathname to the file it is linked with. For a symlink, the link count does not increase or decrease, rather each symlinked file receives a new inode number. The pathname can be absolute or relative depending on what you specified at the time of its creation, and the size of the soft link is the number of characters in the pathname to the target.

Figure 2-4 shows the *newfile2* file with a soft link called *softfile1* pointing to it.

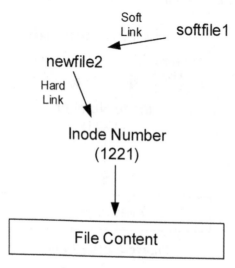

Figure 2-4 Soft Link

A soft link can cross a file system boundary and it can be used to link directories, as it simply uses the pathname of the destination object.

To create a soft link for *newfile3* as *newfile30* in the same directory, use the *ln* command with the -s switch:

    [user1@centos73 ~]$ ln -s newfile3 newfile30

where:

> *newfile3* is an existing file (create it if it does not exist)
> *newfile30* is soft-linked to *newfile3*

After you have created the link, issue *ll* with -i and notice the letter "l" as the first character in the second column of the output. Also notice the arrow that is pointing from the linked file to the original file. Both of these signs indicate that *newfile30* is merely a pointer to *newfile3*. The -i option displays associated inode numbers in the first column.

```
[user1@centos73 ~]$ ll -i newfile*
1219 -rw-rw-r--.   1 user1 user1 0 Jan 04 13:09  newfile3
1220 lrwxrwxrwx. 1 user1 user1 7 Jan 04 13:09  newfile30 -> newfile3
```

If you remove the original file (*newfile3* in this case), the link *newfile30* will become invalid.

CentOS 7 has four soft-linked directories under /. You can list them by running **ll /**. Here they are:

```
lrwxrwxrwx.  1  root  root   7 Dec 21 09:05  bin -> usr/bin
lrwxrwxrwx.  1  root  root   7 Dec 21 09:05  lib -> usr/lib
lrwxrwxrwx.  1  root  root   9 Dec 21 09:05  lib64 -> usr/lib64
lrwxrwxrwx.  1  root  root   8 Dec 21 09:05  sbin -> usr/sbin
```

The syntax for creating soft-linked directories is exactly the same as that for soft-linked files.

Differences between Copying and Linking

After looking closely at the copy and link operations in this chapter, let's look at the key differences between the two and see when we should use copy and when to opt for a soft or hard link. Table 2-3 highlights the main differences between the two:

Copy	Link
Creates a duplicate of the source file. If either file is modified, the other file will have no impact.	Creates a shortcut that points to the source file. The source can be accessed or modified using the name of either the source file or the link.
Each copied file stores its own data at a unique location.	All linked files point to the same data.
Each copied file has a unique inode number containing unique metadata.	**Hard Link:** All hard-linked files share the same inode number, and hence the metadata. **Symlink:** Each symlinked file has a unique inode number, but the inode number stores only the pathname to the source.
If a copy is moved, removed, or renamed, the source file will have no impact, and vice versa.	**Hard Link:** If the hard link is weeded out, the other file and the data will remain intact. **Symlink:** If the source is deleted, the soft link will be broken and become meaningless. If the soft link is removed, the source will have no impact.
Copy is used when the data is to be edited independent of the other.	Links are used when access to the same source is required from multiple locations.
Permissions on source and copy are managed independent of each other.	Permissions are managed on the source file.

Table 2-3 Copying vs. Linking

Keep these differences in mind when you need to decide whether to use copy or link.

Using Links to Support System Administration Tasks

Links are generally used for library files, startup scripts, and commands, as well as for device files in */dev* and virtual files in */proc*. A common example of files with multiple hard links is the *e2fsck* command, which is located in the */usr/sbin* directory. It has three additional hard links named *fsck.ext2*, *fsck.ext3*, and *fsck.ext4* (on *ubuntu14*, they are soft links under */sbin*). The following lists them:

```
[user1@centos73 ~]$ ll -i /usr/sbin/e2fsck /usr/sbin/fsck.ext*
508880 -rwxr-xr-x. 4 root root 256384 Nov 5 14:59 e2fsck
508880 -rwxr-xr-x. 4 root root 256384 Nov 5 14:59 fsck.ext2
508880 -rwxr-xr-x. 4 root root 256384 Nov 5 14:59 fsck.ext3
508880 -rwxr-xr-x. 4 root root 256384 Nov 5 14:59 fsck.ext4
```

All visible attributes for all the hard links are identical.

In comparison with the usage of hard links, the use of symlinks is more common given the benefits they have to offer. As an example, run the *ll* command on */usr/sbin* directory and look for filenames beginning with lv. You will see a number of symlinks that are all pointing to the *lvm* command, which is located in the same directory (for brevity, we have removed non-essential entries from the output):

```
[user1@centos73 ~]$ ll /usr/sbin/lv*
lrwxrwxrwx. 1 root root       3 Dec 21 09:09 /usr/sbin/lvchange -> lvm
lrwxrwxrwx. 1 root root       3 Dec 21 09:09 /usr/sbin/lvconvert -> lvm
lrwxrwxrwx. 1 root root       3 Dec 21 09:09 /usr/sbin/lvcreate -> lvm
lrwxrwxrwx. 1 root root       3 Dec 21 09:09 /usr/sbin/lvdisplay -> lvm
lrwxrwxrwx. 1 root root       3 Dec 21 09:09 /usr/sbin/lvextend -> lvm
-r-xr-xr-x. 1 root root 1775648 Nov 11 21:38 /usr/sbin/lvm
lrwxrwxrwx. 1 root root       3 Dec 21 09:09 /usr/sbin/lvmchange -> lvm
lrwxrwxrwx. 1 root root       3 Dec 21 09:09 /usr/sbin/lvmconfig -> lvm
lrwxrwxrwx. 1 root root       3 Dec 21 09:09 /usr/sbin/lvmdiskscan -> lvm
lrwxrwxrwx. 1 root root       3 Dec 21 09:09 /usr/sbin/lvmsadc -> lvm
lrwxrwxrwx. 1 root root       3 Dec 21 09:09 /usr/sbin/lvmsar -> lvm
lrwxrwxrwx. 1 root root       3 Dec 21 09:09 /usr/sbin/lvreduce -> lvm
lrwxrwxrwx. 1 root root       3 Dec 21 09:09 /usr/sbin/lvremove -> lvm
lrwxrwxrwx. 1 root root       3 Dec 21 09:09 /usr/sbin/lvrename -> lvm
lrwxrwxrwx. 1 root root       3 Dec 21 09:09 /usr/sbin/lvresize -> lvm
lrwxrwxrwx. 1 root root       3 Dec 21 09:09 /usr/sbin/lvs -> lvm
lrwxrwxrwx. 1 root root       3 Dec 21 09:09 /usr/sbin/lvscan -> lvm
```

All symlinks are three bytes in size (the fifth column) and they store the three-letter pathname "lvm," which is the name of the command they are pointing to.

Finding Files

A typical Linux system has a few hundred thousand files stored in various directories that are distributed across various file systems. At times, it is imperative to look for one or more files based on certain criteria. One example would be to find all files owned by employees who left the company over a year ago. Another example would be to search for all the files that have been modified in the past 20 days by a specific user. For such situations, Linux offers a command called *find*. You supply your search criteria and this command gets you the result. You can also instruct this utility to execute a command on the files as they are found. This command is expounded in the following subsection.

Using the find Command

The *find* command searches the directory tree recursively, finds files that match the specified criteria, and optionally performs an action on the files as they are discovered. This powerful tool can be tailored to look for files in a number of ways. The search criteria may include tracking files by name or part of the name, ownership, owning group, permissions, inode number, last access or modification time, size, and file type. Figure 2-5 shows the command syntax.

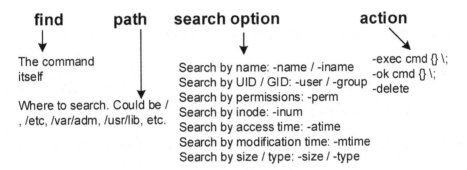

find	**path**	**search option**	**action**
The command itself	Where to search. Could be / , /etc, /var/adm, /usr/lib, etc.	Search by name: -name / -iname Search by UID / GID: -user / -group Search by permissions: -perm Search by inode: -inum Search by access time: -atime Search by modification time: -mtime Search by size / type: -size / -type	-exec cmd {} \; -ok cmd {} \; -delete

Figure 2-5 Find Command Syntax

With *find*, files that match the criteria are located and their full path is displayed. Let's look at a few examples to understand the usage.

To search for a file called *newfile1* by its name in *user1*'s home directory (assuming *newfile1* exists), run the *cd* command without any arguments to change into the *user1*'s home directory and then run *find*. The period (.) character represents the current directory, which is */home/user1* in this example.

```
[user1@centos73 ~]$ cd
[user1@centos73 ~]$ find . -name newfile1 -print
```

 -print is optional. *find* displays the results on the screen by default. You do not have to specify this option.

To perform a case-insensitive (the -iname option) search for files and directories in */dev* that begin with "usb" followed by any characters:

```
[user1@centos73 ~]$ find /dev -iname usb*
```

To find files smaller than 1MB (-1M) in size (-size) in *user1*'s home directory (~), run the following. You do not need to issue the command from this user's home directory. In fact, you can be anywhere in the directory tree.

```
[user1@centos73 ~]$ find ~ -size -1M
```

 The ~ (tilde) character represents a user's home directory.

To search for files larger than 40MB (+40M) in size (-size) in the /usr directory, run the following. You need to be *root* in order to be able to run this command successfully.

```
[root@centos73 ~]# find /usr -size +40M
```

To find files in the entire root file system (/) with ownership (-user) set to user *daemon* and owning group (-group) set to any group other than (-not or ! for negation) *user1*, use any of the following:

```
[root@centos73 ~]# find / -user daemon -not -group user1
[root@centos73 ~]# find / -user daemon ! -group user1
```

To search for directories (-type) by the name "src" (-name) in /usr at a maximum of two sub-directory levels below (-maxdepth):

```
[root@centos73 ~]# find /usr -maxdepth 2 -type d -name src
```

To run the above search but at least three sub-directory levels beneath /usr, substitute -maxdepth 2 with -mindepth 3.

To find files in the /etc directory that were modified (-mtime) more than (the + sign) 2000 days ago:

```
[root@centos73 ~]# find /etc -mtime +2000
```

To run the above search to find files that were modified exactly 12 days ago, switch "+2000" with "12". No + or - sign.

To search for block device files (-type) in the /dev directory with permissions (-perm) set to exactly (no + or - sign) 666 (octal notation):

```
[root@centos73 ~]# find /dev -type b -perm 666
```

To search for character device files (-type) in the /dev directory with at least (-222) world writable permissions. This example would ignore checking the write and execute permissions.

```
[root@centos73 ~]# find /dev -type c -perm -222
```

To search for symlinked files (-type) in /usr with permissions (-perm) set to read and write for the owner and owning group:

```
[root@centos73 ~]# find /usr -type l -perm -ug=rw
```

find is a useful powerful file-searching tool with numerous other options available to use with it. Refer to the command's manual pages, as there are a ton of examples there. Try some of them out.

Using find with the -exec and -ok Options

An advanced use of the *find* command is to perform an action on the files as they are found based on any criteria outlined in the previous subsection and in the command's manual pages. The action may include performing basic file management operations, such as copying, removing, renaming, changing ownership, or modifying permissions on each file found. This is done by using the -exec option available with the command. In the next subsection, we will look at another way to accomplish the same results with the help of the *find* and *xargs* command combination. Let's look at a couple of examples to understand the usage and construction.

To search for files by the name "core" (-name) in the entire directory tree and delete them (-exec) as they are discovered without prompting for user confirmation (-f):

[root@centos73 ~]# **find / -name *core* -exec rm -f {} \;**

The *find* command replaces {} for each filename as it is found. The ; character marks the termination of the command and it is escaped with the \.

In the following example, the *find* command uses the -ok option to prompt for confirmation before it copies each matched file in */etc* to */tmp*:

[root@centos73 ~]# **find /etc -name *.conf -ok cp {} /tmp \;**

In the above example, we specified the destination directory between {} and \;.

Using the xargs Command

The *xargs* command is a powerful tool that is used to execute a command on a number of supplied arguments. The supplied arguments may be obtained from the output of a command such as *find*, *grep*, or *ls*, or it can be read directly from a file. By default, the *xargs* command executes the *echo* command (a built-in shell command that is typically used to display text and variable values) on the input and treats the newline and blank characters as the delimiters. In order to understand the command's usage, let's create a file called *xargs.txt* with seven entries. Press Ctrl+d at the end of your typing to create the file.

```
[user1@centos73 ~]$ cat > xargs.txt
Toronto
Montreal
Ottawa
Calgary
Richmond
Saskatoon
Winnipeg
Ctrl+d
```

Each entry in the file is on a distinct line followed by a hidden newline character at the end. If we run the *xargs* command on this file, it will simply *echo* all seven entries on a single line:

```
[user1@centos73 ~]$ xargs < xargs.txt
Toronto Montreal Ottawa Calgary Richmond Saskatoon Winnipeg
```

By default, the *echo* command displays the entire list on a single line as shown above. We can specify the -n (--max-args) option to instruct the command to limit how many entries we want to see on one line. The following example will print not more than three entries per line:

```
[user1@centos73 ~]$ xargs -n3 < xargs.txt
```
Toronto Montreal Ottawa
Calgary Richmond Saskatoon
Winnipeg

Another option, -L (--max-lines) instructs the command to treat the specified number of lines as one argument. The following example will show a maximum of two consecutive lines from *xargs.txt* on each line:

```
[user1@centos73 ~]$ xargs -L 2 < xargs.txt
```
Toronto Montreal
Ottawa Calgary
Richmond Saskatoon
Winnipeg

Another example will read the */etc/passwd* file, cut the third field containing user IDs from each line using the colon (:) character as the delimiter, send the output to *xargs* to *echo* the entire list of user IDs on a single line:

```
[user1@centos73 ~]$ cut -f3 -d: /etc/passwd | xargs
```

Try the above example without "| xargs" and compare the outputs.

Now let's take a look at a more sophisticated and common use of *xargs*. This use is with the *find* command that feeds it with a list of arguments such as filenames. In Linux, a filename may contain blank and newline characters, which *xargs* treats as delimiters, resulting in an incorrect output. In order to avoid this behavior, we use the -0 option with *xargs* and the corresponding -print0 option with *find* to force both commands to use a null character as a delimiter in filenames with blanks or newlines. For example, the following *find* command searches for all files containing "core" (-name) in their names to a maximum of four directory levels (-maxdepth) below the / and sends the output to *xargs* through the | to determine the type of each file that's using the */usr/bin/file* command. This command example needs to be executed as *root*.

```
[root@centos73 ~]# find / -name "*core*" -maxdepth 4 -print0 | xargs -0 /usr/bin/file
```

Using the locate Command

The *locate* command is used to discover all occurrences of the specified string as they appear in file pathnames. It can also be used to locate files with certain extensions. Unlike the *find* command that performs a new search each time you run it, *locate* searches the */var/lib/mlocate/mlocate.db* database, finds matches, and displays them. This database is updated periodically when the */etc/cron.daily/mlocate* script is executed by the *cron* daemon based on a setting in the */etc/updatedb.conf* configuration file. Alternatively, it can be updated manually with the *updatedb* command. The output is the absolute path of files and directories for which the user has access permissions. Here are a few examples to explain the working of this command.

To locate all occurrences of the string "passwd":

```
[user1@centos73 ~]$ locate passwd
```

Use -n and specify the number of occurrences you wish to see:

    [user1@centos73 ~]$ locate -n 3 passwd

To locate all files with .sh extension and list only the first two of them:

    [user1@centos73 ~]$ locate -n 2 .sh

To view the number of files, directories, and size information retained in *mlocate.db*:

    [user1@centos73 ~]$ locate -S

Using the which, whereis, and type Commands

The *which, whereis,* and *type* commands print the entire path to the command that will be executed when you run that command without providing its full path. For instance, if you need to find out the path to the *cat* command that will run when you issue this command at the prompt, you can use any of the three commands as follows:

    [user1@centos73 ~]$ which cat
    /usr/bin/cat
    [user1@centos73 ~]$ whereis cat
    cat: /usr/bin/cat /usr/share/man/man1/cat.1.gz /usr/share/man/man1p/cat.1p.gz
    [user1@centos73 ~]$ type cat
    cat is /usr/bin/cat

As shown above, all three commands responded with an identical path location for the *cat* command which is */usr/bin/cat*. The *whereis* command also shows the path to the command's manual pages that are displayed when you run **man cat**.

Special Permissions

Linux offers three types of special permission bits that may be set on binary executable files or directories to allow them to respond differently to non-*root* users for certain operations. These permission bits are (1) *set user identifier* bit (commonly referred to as *setuid* or *suid*), (2) *set group identifier* bit (a.k.a. *setgid* or *sgid*), and (3) *sticky* bit.

The first two bits—setuid and setgid—may be defined on binary executable files to provide non-owners and non-group members the ability to run them with the privileges of the owner or the owning group, respectively. The setgid bit may also be set on shared directories for group collaboration. The third bit may be set on public directories for inhibiting file erasures by non-owners.

The use of the special bits should be regulated and monitored to evade potential security issues to system operation and applications.

The setuid Bit on Binary Executable Files

The setuid flag is set on binary executable files at the file owner level. With this bit set, the file is executed by non-owners with the same privileges as that of the file owner. A common example is

---

that of the *su* command that is owned by the *root* user. This command has the setuid bit enabled on it by default. See the highlighted "s" in the owner's permission class below:

```
[user1@centos73 ~]$ ll /usr/bin/su
-rwsr-xr-x. 1 root root 32088 Nov 5 18:27 /usr/bin/su
```

When a normal user executes this command, it will run as if *root* (the owner) is running it; therefore, the user is able to run it successfully and gets the expected result.

The *su* (switch user) command allows a user to switch to a different user account provided the user knows the password of the target user account.

Now, eliminate this bit from *su* and exchange it with the underlying execute attribute. You must be *root* in order to make this change. List the file with **ll /usr/bin/su** after making this modification for verification.

```
[root@centos73 ~]# chmod u-s /usr/bin/su
-rwxr-xr-x. 1 root root 32088 Nov 5 18:27 /usr/bin/su
```

The file is still executable by non-owners as indicated by the execute flag; however, it will prevent regular non-owning users from switching accounts, as they have lost that special elevated privilege. Here is what will happen when *user1* tries to switch into *root* with a valid password:

```
[user1@centos73 ~]$ su -
Password:
su: Authentication failure
```

user1 gets an "authentication failure" message even though they entered the correct login credentials.

To reset the setuid bit on *su* (or on any other file for that matter), use the following:

```
[root@centos73 ~]# chmod 4755 /usr/bin/su
```

When digit 4 is used with the *chmod* command in this manner, it enables setuid on the specified file. Alternatively, you can use the symbolic notation as follows:

```
[root@centos73 ~]# chmod u+s /usr/bin/su
```

If the file already has the "x" bit set for the owner, the ll command will show a lowercase "s", otherwise it will list it with an uppercase "S".

The setuid bit has no effect on directories.

The setgid Bit on Binary Executable Files

The setgid attribute is set on binary executable files at the group level. With this bit set, the file is executed by non-owners with the exact same privileges that the group members have. For instance, the *wall* command is owned by *root* with group membership set to *tty* and setgid enabled. See the highlighted "s" in the group's permission class below:

```
[user1@centos73 ~]$ ll /usr/bin/wall
-r-xr-sr-x. 1 root tty 15344 Jun 9 2014 /usr/bin/wall
```

The *wall* command allows users to broadcast a message to all logged-in users and print it on their terminal screens. By default, normal users are allowed this special elevated privilege because of the presence of the setgid flag on the file. To test, run the command and supply a message as an argument:

```
[user1@centos73 ~]$ wall Hello, this is to test the setgid flag set on the wall command
Broadcast message from user1@centos73 (pts/0) (Fri Jan 6 17:21:22 2017):
Hello, this is to test the setgid flag set on the wall command
```

Now, remove this bit from the *wall* command and replace it with the underlying execute flag. You must be *root* in order to make this change. List the file with **ll /usr/bin/wall** after making this modification for confirmation.

```
[root@centos73 ~]# chmod g-s /usr/bin/wall
-r-xr-sr-x. 1 root tty 15344 Jun 9 2014 /usr/bin/wall
```

The file is still executable by non-owners; however, it will prevent regular non-owning users from sending out messages, as they have lost that special elevated privilege.

To reset the setgid bit on *wall* (or on any other file for that matter), use the following:

```
[root@centos73 ~]# chmod 2555 /usr/bin/wall
```

When digit 2 is used with the *chmod* command in this manner, it sets the setgid attribute on the specified file. Alternatively, you can use the symbolic notation as follows:

```
[root@centos73 ~]# chmod g+s /usr/bin/wall
```

If the file already has the "x" bit set for the group, the ll command will show a lowercase "s", otherwise it lists it with an uppercase "S".

The setgid Bit on Shared Directories

The setgid bit can also be set on shared directories to allow files and sub-directories created underneath to automatically inherit the directory's owning group. This saves group members who are sharing the directory contents from changing the group ID for every new file and sub-directory that they create there. The standard behavior for new files and sub-directories is to always receive the creator's group.

The Sticky Bit on Public-Writable Directories

The sticky bit is set on public-writable directories (or other directories with rw permissions for everyone) to protect files and sub-directories owned by regular users from being deleted, unlinked, or moved by other regular users. This attribute is set on */tmp* and */var/tmp* directories by default as depicted below; however, it can be applied to any writable directory:

```
[user1@centos73 ~]$ ll -d /tmp /var/tmp
drwxrwxrwt. 24 root root 4096 Jan 6 08:33 /tmp
drwxrwxrwt. 15 root root 4096 Jan 6 06:17 /var/tmp
```

Notice the "t" in other's permissions, indicating the presence of this attribute on the two directories.

You can use the *chmod* command to set or unset the sticky bit. Add this flag to the */var* directory and then revoke it. Use the -v option for verbosity. The following lists the */var* directory, sets the bit on it, and then lists the directory again to confirm. This must be done as the *root* user.

```
[root@centos73 ~]# ll -d /var
drwxr-xr-x. 21 root root 4096 Jan 5 08:15 /var
[root@centos73 ~]# chmod 1755 /var -v
mode of '/var' changed from 0755 (rwxr-xr-x) to 1755 (rwxr-xr-t)
[root@centos73 ~]# ll -d /var
drwxr-xr-t. 21 root root 4096 Jan 5 08:15 /var
```

When digit 1 is used with the *chmod* command in this manner, it sets the sticky bit on the specified directory. Alternatively, you can use the symbolic notation to do the same:

```
[root@centos73 ~]# chmod o+t /var
```

To unset, use either of the following:

```
[root@centos73 ~]# chmod o-t /var
[root@centos73 ~]# chmod 755 /var
```

The sticky bit has no effect on files.

Chapter Summary

This chapter presented an overview of the Linux file system structure standard and significant higher-level sub-directories that consisted of static and variable files, and were grouped logically into lower-level sub-directories. We looked at several file and directory manipulation tools for creating, listing, displaying, copying, moving, renaming, and removing. The different types of files available in Linux were also discussed.

We studied topics related to file and directory permissions. We covered permission classes, types, and modes, and the first three exercises showed how to modify permissions using symbolic and octal notations. We looked at default permissions, how to set them up for new files and directories, and the role of the umask value in determining the new default permissions.

In addition, the chapter explained how to change the owner and owning group on files and directories, as well as soft and hard links and their use, and the comparison between copying and linking. Searching for files within the directory structure using specified criteria provided an understanding and explanation of the tools required to perform such tasks.

Finally, we learned how to gain privileged access on binary executable files and directories by using setuid and setgid permission bits, and prevent files located in public-writable directories from being deleted by non-owners by using the sticky bit.

Chapter Review at a Glance

The following presents a one-sentence review of each key topic discussed in this chapter:

- Linux directory structure follows the Filesystem Hierarchy Standard to ensure that the directory layout is consistent across major Linux distributions and versions, and that the directory contents are placed in directories based on their type and use.

- Every directory in Linux has a parent directory and a child directory with the exception of the top-level root (/) directory and the lowest-level child directory that have no parent or child, respectively.

- Static directories hold commands, kernel files, software binaries, library files, etc. that do not normally change; dynamic directories hold log files, spool files, process-related files, runtime system configuration data, temporary files, user files, configuration files, etc. that are frequently changed and updated.

- Directories may or may not be shared with other systems on the network, and that depends on the type of files and data they store.

- The root user is the superuser in Linux with full administrative powers on the system.

- File and directory operations include creating, listing, displaying contents of, copying, moving, and renaming them.

- Linux supports several types of files, such as regular files, directory files, executable files, symbolically linked files, and device files.

- Permissions management on files and directories ensures authorized users have appropriate access rights on the files that they need to accomplish their job successfully.

- Standard file permissions are based on permission classes (user, group, and public) with read, write, execute, or no access right (permission types).

- File permissions can be changed using either the symbolic or the octal format of permission allocation.

- Default permissions that new files and directories get are calculated by subtracting the user-configurable umask value from the initial value.

- Every file and directory in Linux has an owner and an owning group, which may be altered by the root user if required.

- A hard link is a mapping between a file name and its associated inode number, and this mapping can be extended to include multiple file names pointing to the same inode number.

- An inode number is a tiny area that is associated with a file to store the file's metadata, such as the file's size, owner name, owning group name, last access time, last modification time, number of links the file has, and pointers to where the file content's reside.

- A soft link is a shortcut that points to an actual file or a directory that exist somewhere on the system.

- A soft link only stores the path to the actual file or directory name in its assigned data block.

- A hard link may be used for files that reside within the boundaries of a file system; however, a soft link can be used for files or directories that may reside on other file systems.

- Files and directories of various types, varying permissions, and with different access and modifications times are stored in a number of different directories on the system.

- Files and directories may be searched in the entire directory structure or in a particular directory location by specifying one or more possible file attributes, and optionally be acted upon.

- There are three special permissions—setuid, setgid, and sticky bit—that may be set on files and directories.

- The setuid (suid) bit is set on executable files, such as the root-owned privileged commands, to allow non-owners the ability to execute the file with the owner's privileges.

- The setgid (sgid) bit is set on group-executable files, such as the root-owned privileged commands, to allow non-group owners the ability to execute the file with the owning group's privileges.

- The setgid (sgid) bit may also be set on group-shared directories to give group members identical rights on the directory contents.

- The sticky bit is set on public-writable directories to prevent file deletions by non-owners.

- Commands we learned in this chapter are: touch, cat, mkdir, less, more, head, tail, cp, mv, rm, file, stat, chmod, umask, chown, chgrp, ln, find, xargs, cut, locate, updated, which, whereis, and type.

- Files and directories we discussed in this chapter are: /, /root/, /usr/, /boot/, /opt/, /var/, /etc/, /tmp/, /home/, /dev/, /proc/, /sys/, /var/mail/, /var/opt/, /var/lock/, /run/, /media/, /mnt/, /bin/, /usr/bin/, /sbin/, /usr/sbin/, /lib/, /usr/lib/, /lib64/, /usr/lib64/, /etc/updatedb.conf.

Chapter 3

Editing Text Files, Exploring Filters, and Using Regular Expressions

This chapter describes the following major topics:

> ➤ Introduction to the vi editor
> ➤ Navigate and work with the vi editor
> ➤ Overview of Linux filter programs
> ➤ Use filters to concatenate files, extract desired data from output, convert text to spaces and vice versa, format text, dump output, join data, enumerate output, paste data side-by-side, format text for printing, transform text, sort output, split files, translate characters, display unique/identical lines, and count lines and words
> ➤ Understand regular expressions
> ➤ Employ regular expressions and their variants for pattern matching

This chapter covers the following objectives for LX0-103/101-400 Exam:

103.2 Process text streams using filters [a part of this objective is described in chapter 2 and the rest in this chapter]

40. Send text files and output streams through text utility filters to modify the output using standard UNIX commands found in the GNU textutils package

The following is a partial list of the used files, terms and utilities: cat, cut, expand, fmt, od, join, nl, paste, pr, sed, sort, split, tr, unexpand, uniq, and wc

103.7 Search text files using regular expressions [this entire objective is described in this chapter]

59. Create simple regular expressions containing several notational elements
60. Use regular expression tools to perform searches through a filesystem or file content

The following is a partial list of the used files, terms and utilities: grep, egrep, fgrep, sed, and regex(7)

103.8 Perform basic file editing operations using vi [this entire objective is described in this chapter]

61. Navigate a document using vi
62. Use basic vi modes
63. Insert, edit, delete, copy and find text

The following is a partial list of the used files, terms and utilities: vi, /, ?, h, j, k, l, i, o, a, c, d, p, y, dd, yy, ZZ, :w!, :q!, :e!

NORMAL and application users and database and system administrators all
need to edit text files on a regular basis as part of their job. Linux delivers several text
editors for this purpose, including an enhanced and improved version of vi called vim
(vi improved), which is popular within the Linux community. A sound, working
knowledge of this tool is essential for all these roles.

Filters are programs that transform input text for reporting or analysis. They may be used on
columns or rows of data. Linux supports many of them, including those that are used to concatenate,
count, enumerate, format, split, sort, or translate the input.

Regular expressions are text patterns for matching against an input provided in a search operation.
Text patterns may include any sequenced or arbitrary characters or character range. Linux offers a
powerful command to work with pattern matching.

The vi Editor

The vi editor is an interactive, full-screen *visual* text-editing tool that allows you to create and
modify text files. This tool, or its enhanced version called vim (*Vi IMproved*), is available as a
standard editor on all UNIX and Linux systems. All text editing within vi takes place in a *buffer* (a
small chunk of memory used to hold updates being done to the file). Changes can either be written
to the disk or discarded.

It is essential for system administrators and Linux users to master the vi editor skills. The following
subsections provide common information on how to use and interact with this tool.

See the manual pages of vi for details. Alternatively, you can run the *vimtutor* command to view the
vi tutorial.

Modes of Operation

The vi editor essentially has three modes of operation: the command mode, the edit mode, and the
last-line mode.

The *command* mode is the default mode of vi. The vi editor places you into the default mode when
you start it. While in the command mode, you can carry out tasks, such as copy, cut, paste, move,
remove, trade, change, and search on text, in addition to performing navigational operations. This
mode is also known as the *escape* mode because the Esc key is pressed to enter it.

In the *input* mode, anything typed at the keyboard is entered into the file as text. Commands cannot
be run in this mode. The input mode is also called the *edit* mode, or the *insert* mode. To return to
the command mode, press the Esc key.

While in the command mode, you may carry out advanced editing tasks on text by pressing the
colon (:) character, which places the cursor at the beginning of the last line of the screen, and hence
it is referred to as the *last-line* mode. This mode is considered a special type of command mode.

Starting vi

The vi editor may be started by typing the command *vi* at the command prompt, and it may
optionally follow an existing or a new filename as an argument. Without any filenames specified
with the command, it simply opens an empty screen where you can enter text from scratch. You can
later save the text in a file or discard using commands provided in subsequent subsections.

```
[user1@centos73 ~]$ vi
```

Alternatively, we can supply a filename as an argument to *vi*. This way, the *vi* command will open the specified file for editing if the file exists or create a file by that name if it does not exist.

```
[user1@centos73 ~]$ vi <filename>
```

There are options available that you may specify at the time of starting this editing tool.

Inserting text

Once vi is started, you have six commands available within vi to switch into the edit mode to begin entering text. These commands are simple lower and uppercase i, a, and o, and are described in Table 3-1.

Command	Action
i	Inserts text before the current cursor position
I	Inserts text at the beginning of the current line
a	Appends text after the current cursor position
A	Appends text to the end of the current line
o	Opens up a new line below the current line
O	Opens up a new line above the current line

Table 3-1 Inserting Text

Press the Esc key when finished in the edit mode to return to the command mode.

Navigating within vi

Navigational keys are equally helpful in editing small and large files. They allow you to make rapid moves in the file. There are a number of key sequences available within vi to control the cursor movement. Some of the elementary key strokes are elaborated in Table 3-2.

Command	Action
h	Moves backward one character
j	Moves downward one line
k	Moves upward one line
l	Moves forward one character
w	Moves to the start of the next word
b	Moves backward to the start of the preceding word
e	Moves to the ending character of the next word
$	Moves to the end of the current line
Enter	Moves to the beginning of the next line
Ctrl+f	Scrolls down to the next page
Ctrl+b	Scrolls up to the previous page

Table 3-2 Navigating within vi

We can precede any of the commands listed in Table 3-2 by a numeral to repeat the command action that many times in a row. For instance, 3h would move the cursor three places backward,

---

5Enter would move the cursor five lines downward, and 3Ctrl+f would move the cursor forward three screens.

In addition to these commands, you can use 0 (zero) to move to the beginning of the current line, [[to move to the first line of the file, and]] to move to the last line of the file.

Searching for Text

We can perform forward and reverse searches while in the vi command mode by using the / and ? characters followed by the string to be searched. For instance, in a file with numerous occurrences of the string "profile," we may run /profile or ?profile for a forward or reverse search.

We may press the "n" key followed by a forward or reverse string search to go to the next or the previous occurrence of the searched string.

Copying and Pasting Text

vi allows us to copy some text and paste it to the desired location within the file. We can copy (yank) a single character, word, or an entire line, and then paste it wherever we need it in that file. The copy function can be performed on multiple characters, words, or lines at a time as well. Table 3-3 describes the copy and paste commands.

Command	Action
yl	Yanks the current letter into the buffer
yw	Yanks the current word into the buffer
yy	Yanks the current line into the buffer
p	Pastes yanked data below the current line
P	Pastes yanked data above the current line

Table 3-3 Copying and Pasting Text

We can precede a number before any of the commands listed in Table 3-3 to perform the desired action that many times. For instance, 3yy would yank three lines into the buffer, and 2P would paste the yanked data twice above the current line.

Changing Text

We have numerous commands available within vi to change and modify text. Table 3-4 (next page) highlights a few of the basic ones. Some of these commands will switch into the edit mode, and you will need to press the Esc key to return to the command mode.

We can precede a number before any of the commands listed in Table 3-4 to perform that action that many times. For instance, 2cc would change the entire current and the next line, and 2r would replace the current character and the next character.

Command	Action
cl	Changes the letter at the current cursor location
cw	Changes the word (or part of the word) at the current cursor location to the end of the current word
cc	Changes the entire current line
C	Changes text at the current cursor position to the end of the current line
r	Replaces the character at the current cursor location with the character entered following this command
R	Overwrites the text on the current line
J	Joins the next line with the current line
xp	Switches the position of the character at the current cursor position with the character to the right of it
~	Changes the letter case (uppercase to lowercase, and vice versa) at the current cursor location

Table 3-4 Changing Text

Deleting Text

vi provides commands to perform delete actions. Some of the basic commands are described in Table 3-5.

Command	Action
x	Deletes the character at the current cursor position
X	Deletes the character before the current cursor location
dw	Deletes the word or part of the word to the right of the current cursor location
dd	Deletes the entire current line

Table 3-5 Deleting Text

We can precede a number before any of the commands listed in Table 3-5 to perform the command action that many times. For instance, 2X would delete two characters before the current cursor location, and 2dd would delete the current line and the line below it.

Saving and Quitting vi

When you are done with modifications in a file, you will either want to save or discard them. Use one of the commands listed in Table 3-6 as required.

Command	Action
:w	Writes changes to the file without quitting vi
:w file1	Writes changes to a file called *file1* without quitting vi
:e	Reloads the opened file to the last saved version
:e file1	Loads *file1* for editing
:wq or :x or ZZ	Writes changes to the file and quits vi
:q	Quits vi if no modifications were made. Add the ! sign to discard the changes and quit vi.

Table 3-6 Saving and Quitting vi

With any of the commands listed in Table 3-6 except for ZZ, we can use ! to override the write protection placed on the file for the owner.

Exploring Filters

A *filter* is a program that takes text input, transforms it, and displays the transformed data on the terminal screen or sends it to an alternate destination. There is a variety of filters available in Linux. Some of them have other uses as well. For instance, the *cat* command is a filter; however, it is a popular tool for text-file creation and viewing as covered in chapter 2. In this section, we are going to look at several text filtering commands—*cat, cut, expand/unexpand, fmt, od, join, nl, paste, pr, sed, sort, split, tr, uniq,* and *wc*—and their basic use. For more details and additional usage examples, refer to their manual pages.

Concatenating Files Using cat

As discussed in Chapter 2 "Working with Files and File Permissions," the *cat* command is a tool that is used to create and view text files. This command has another useful utility: to merge the contents of two or more text files into one. This feature is called *concatenation*, hence the name. We use the > symbol to write to the target file as shown below:

```
[user1@centos73 ~]$ cat .bash_profile .bash_logout > mergedfile
```

The *cat* command in this example will read the contents of *.bash_profile* and *.bash_logout* files and store them in a file called *mergedfile*. This file will be created if it does not exist or it will be overwritten if existed. Run the *cat* command on *mergedfile* to view the merged contents.

Another form of concatenation is to use the > symbol twice to instruct the command to append to an extant file. For instance, if you make changes in *mergedfile* and then re-run the above command, it will overwrite what was there in the file. To avoid this behavior, use >> to force an append operation rather than an overwrite. Try running the above command with >> and then *cat* to view the target file.

Extracting Columns of Data Using cut

The *cut* command is used as a filter to extract selected columns from the supplied input without modifying it. The default column separator used is the white space such as a tab. The following example command cuts out columns 1 and 3 from the */etc/group* file as specified with the -f option. The colon (:) character is used as the field separator.

```
[user1@centos73 ~]$ cat /etc/group
[user1@centos73 ~]$ cut -d: -f 1,3 /etc/group
root:0
bin:1
daemon:2
sys:3
. . . . . . . .
```

Ponder over the output of the *cut* command. Run *ll* again on */etc/group* and notice that there is no change in the timestamp on the file. *cut* does not alter the supplied input; it simply reads the input, filters it, and displays the output on the screen.

Converting Tabs to Spaces and Vice Versa Using expand and unexpand

The *expand* and *unexpand* pair is used to convert tabs to spaces and vice versa for formatting purposes. Create a file called *expfile1* in vi editor with tab-separated values as shown below:

expfile1

1	Toronto	Ontario
2	Calgary	Alberta
3	Montreal	Quebec
4	Victoria	BritishColumbia

Use the -t option with the *cat* command to show each occurrence of TAB with ^I without making any changes to *expfile1*:

```
[user1@centos73 ~]$ cat -t expfile1
1^IToronto^I^IOntario
2^ICalgary^I^IAlberta
3^IMontreal^IQuebec
4^IVictoria^IBritishColumbia
```

The output confirms the presence of TABs between values. Now, issue the *expand* command to convert the TABs into equal number of white spaces and store the output in a file called *expfile2*. We then verify with *cat* what was stored in *expfile2*.

```
[user1@centos73 ~]$ expand expfile1 > expfile2
[user1@centos73 ~]$ cat -t expfile2
1    Toronto    Ontario
2    Calgary    Alberta
3    Montreal   Quebec
4    Victoria   BritishColumbia
```

The original file *expfile1* is not affected with the execution of the *expand* command.

Now we run the *unexpand* command to convert all spaces (-a) back into TABs and store the output in a new file called *expfile3*. We confirm the conversion with the *cat* command.

```
[user1@centos73 ~]$ unexpand expfile2 -a > expfile3
[user1@centos73 ~]$ cat -t expfile3
1^IToronto^I^IOntario
2^ICalgary^I^IAlberta
3^IMontreal^IQuebec
4^IVictoria^IBritishColumbia
```

With either converter, we can use the -t option and specify the number of tab spaces we want.

Formatting Text Using fmt

fmt is an elementary text-formatting tool that may be used to set column width, add uniform spacing between words, add indentation to differentiate the first line in a paragraph, split long lines, and so on. Create a file called *fmtfile1* in vi editor and add two paragraphs of text to it as shown below:

fmtfile1

This file contains text   to explain the usage of the fmt command. It has a few lines of text in it. This command has   been available in Linux and Unix for a long time and it was originally used for formatting mail messages.

The file contains a few extra spaces between words. Try the *fmt* command and change the column width (-w) to 30 characters. Eliminate unnecessary spaces between words (-u), add indentation (-t), and split (-s) the text into multiple lines:

```
[user1@centos73 ~]$ fmt -w 30 fmtfile1
[user1@centos73 ~]$ fmt -uts fmtfile1
```

Dumping Output in Different Formats Using od

The *od* (*octal dump*) filter allows you to view a file in multiple formats. By default, it dumps the output to the screen in octal format, hence the name. As part of the dump, the filter also shows any unnecessary characters that the file or input supplied may contain; therefore, it may be used in fixing shell scripts. Let's run this command on the *fmtfile1* file, and see what it shows:

```
[user1@centos73 ~]$ od fmtfile1
```

od supports plenty of options to filter the output of which two options -A and -t are more common. With the -A switch, the command decides if the file offsets (the first column in the output) are to be displayed in decimal (d), hexadecimal (x), or octal (o, the default) format. We can specify "n" for no offset display. The -t switch allows us to choose an output format such as "a" for named characters (sp for space, nl for newline, etc.) and "c" for ASCII characters. We may skip -t and simply use -a or -c instead.

Try the following examples and observe the outputs:

```
[user1@centos73 ~]$ od -Ad fmtfile1 -tc
[user1@centos73 ~]$ od -a -An fmtfile1
```

The first example command would display the contents of *fmtfile1* in ASCII characters with file offsets (the first column) in decimal format. And the second example would use named characters in the output and will hide the offset column entirely. Note that the placement of options before and after the filename is acceptable.

Try this command with other options as explained above for more clarity. Refer to the manual pages of this filter to learn about the use of additional options.

Joining Data Using join

The *join* filter is used to join each corresponding line from two files if their join fields are identical. By default, this filter uses the first field as the join field. Consider the following two files—*joinfile1* and *joinfile2*—with first fields identical:

```
joinfile1    joinfile2
1 Toronto    1 Ontario
2 Calgary    2 Alberta
3 Montreal   3 Quebec
4 Victoria   4 BritishColumbia
```

Let's issue the *join* command on the two files and see what it does:

```
[user1@centos73 ~]$ join joinfile1 joinfile2
1 Toronto Ontario
2 Calgary Alberta
3 Montreal Quebec
4 Victoria BritishColumbia
```

The command validated the first fields for likeness and then it printed them on the screen followed by the text from the corresponding lines of each file.

 Create the two files using the vi editor for practice.

Here are some common options available with this filter that you can try: -i to ignore the letter case, and -j to perform the join on the specified field.

Numbering Output Lines Using nl

The *nl* filter is used to display the contents of a text file or supplied input. The following example enumerates the */etc/rsyslog.conf* file and shows only the first few lines:

```
[user1@centos73 ~]$ nl /etc/rsyslog.conf
    1  # rsyslog configuration file
    2  # For more information see /usr/share/doc/rsyslog-*/rsyslog_conf.html
    3  # If you experience problems, see http://www.rsyslog.com/doc/troubleshoot.html
    4  #### MODULES ####
    5  # The imjournal module bellow is now used as a message source instead of imuxsock.
```

The following example lists the contents of the */etc* directory and pipes the output to *nl* for numbering. Pipes are explained in Chapter 4 "Dealing with the Bash Shell and Processes."

```
[user1@centos73 ~]$ ll /etc | nl
    1  total 1392
    2  drwxr-xr-x. 3 root root     101 Dec 21 09:08 abrt
    3  -rw-r--r--. 1 root root      16 Dec 21 09:18 adjtime
    4  -rw-r--r--. 1 root root    1518 Jun  7 2013 aliases
    5  -rw-r--r--. 1 root root   12288 Dec 21 09:22 aliases.db
```

Pasting Data Side-by-Side Using paste

The *paste* filter is used to display lines consisting of sequentially corresponding lines from one or more specified files next to each other. By default, the data is separated with tabs and displayed in parallel; however, we can change these behaviors by using the -d option and specifying a delimiter of our choice, and using the -s option to display the output serially. Assuming we have the following two files—*pastefile1* and *pastefile2*—with the following contents:

pastefile1 **pastefile2**
Vancouver   BritishColumbia
Kingston   Ontario
Winnipeg   Manitoba
Saskatoon   Saskatchewan

 Create the two files using the vi editor for practice.

The following example runs the *paste* command on the two files to print their contents side by side. Notice it uses the TAB character as the delimiter.

```
[user1@centos73 ~]$ paste pastefile1 pastefile2
```
Vancouver   BritishColumbia
Kingston   Ontario
Winnipeg   Manitoba
Saskatoon   Saskatchewan

Now let's change the delimiter to the colon (:) character with the -d option:

```
[user1@centos73 ~]$ paste -d: pastefile1 pastefile2
```
Vancouver:BritishColumbia
Kingston:Ontario
Winnipeg:Manitoba
Saskatoon:Saskatchewan

The following will print all lines from *pastefile1* on one line, and all lines from *pastefile2* on the next, and use a single white space as the delimiter:

```
[user1@centos73 ~]$ paste -s pastefile1 pastefile2 -d " "
```
Vancouver Kingston Winnipeg Saskatoon
BritishColumbia Ontario Manitoba Saskatchewan

Formatting Text for Printing Using pr

The *pr* filter is used to format text files for printing. The output may be piped to a printer if one is configured. By default, *pr* prints a header, which includes the file name, date and time of printing, page numbers, and the file contents. It also prints a footer that contains two empty lines. The default page length is 66 lines. Let's run this command on *pastefile1* and observe the output:

```
[user1@centos73 ~]$ pr pastefile1
```

The filter delivers a number of options to alter the default behavior. For instance, we can use -d for adding double spacing between lines, -n for line enumeration, -h for adding a custom header name, -l for printing on a different length page, and -column for printing in multiple columns. The

---

following example prints *pastefile1* in two columns with double spacing between lines, the header title, "My PR Command Test", and the page length of 15 lines:

[user1@centos73 ~]$ **pr -2dh "My PR Command Test" -l 15 pastefile1 -m**

You can try the above command by limiting the options.

The *pr* filter also allows us to begin printing at a specific page number using the + sign followed by a page number. Try running **pr +2 /etc/profile** to view the file contents starting at page number 2.

If you want to print the contents of two files side by side, use the -m option with the command. For instance, **pr -m pastefile1 pastefile2** will print the two files in this manner.

Filtering and Transforming Text Using sed

sed is a powerful and versatile *stream editor* that is used for filtering and transforming text. It works on text rows, and accepts input from a file or command output. It does not modify the input provided; it merely reads it, processes it as required, and displays the outcome on the screen or redirects it to a file. It supports the use of regular expressions for search and replace operations. Regular expressions are covered in the next section.

Let's take a look at a few elementary examples to comprehend the usage of *sed*.

To search the */etc/nsswitch.conf* file for all lines containing the pattern "files" and hide those lines in the output, run the *sed* command example provided below. Note again that *sed* does not remove or modify anything in the input file. First, let's see what this file contains. The following shows a few rows from the beginning of this file:

```
[user1@centos73 ~]$  cat /etc/nsswitch.conf
#
# /etc/nsswitch.conf
#
# An example Name Service Switch config file. This file should be
# sorted with the most-used services at the beginning.
#
# The entry '[NOTFOUND=return]' means that the search for an
# entry should stop if the search in the previous entry turned
# up nothing. Note that if the search failed due to some other reason
# (like no NIS server responding) then the search continues with the
# next entry.
#
# Valid entries include:
#
#       nisplus         Use NIS+ (NIS version 3)
#       nis             Use NIS (NIS version 2), also called YP
#       dns             Use DNS (Domain Name Service)
#       files           Use the local files
#       db              Use the local database (.db) files
#       compat          Use NIS on compat mode
```

The /etc/nsswitch.conf file is explained in Chapter 12 "Understanding Internationalization, and Configuring Localization, NTP, and DNS".

Now run *sed* to get the desired result:

```
[user1@centos73 ~]$ sed /files/d /etc/nsswitch.conf
```

The /files portion tells *sed* to search for the pattern "files" and the /d part instructs the command to weed that pattern out from the output.

To delete all lines from the output of the *ll* command containing digit 4, run the following. Try this example on the home directory and also on */etc*.

```
[user1@centos73 ~]$ ll | sed /4/d
```

The above example used a shell feature called *pipe* (|). This feature allows a command (*ll* in this example) to send its output as input to another command (*sed* in this example). For details on the usage of this feature, refer to Chapter 4 "Dealing with the Bash Shell and Processes."

To weed out the second line from the output of the *ll* command, run **ll | sed 2d**. Try this command on the home directory.

To print all lines in duplicate from the */etc/nsswitch.conf* file that contain the pattern "files" and the rest of the lines one time, execute the following:

```
[user1@centos73 ~]$ sed /files/p /etc/nsswitch.conf
```

To print only those lines from the */etc/nsswitch.conf* file that contain the pattern "files," run either **cat /etc/nsswitch.conf | sed -n /files/p** or **sed -n /root/p /etc/nsswitch.conf**.

Consult the manual pages of *sed* for additional options and usage examples.

Sorting Input Using sort

Sorting arranges columns of text in a specified order. The *sort* command is used for this purpose and works on input provided via one or more files or a command. By default, it prints the result on the screen, which can alternatively be redirected to a file. We can sort the input in an alphabetic (default) or a numeric order.

Let's look at a few basic examples to understand the usage of *sort*.

Create a file called *sortfile1* using the vi editor in *user1*'s home directory with the following alphabetic and numeric values in two columns:

```
Maryland 667
Mississippi 662
Pennsylvania 445
Missouri 975
Florida 772
Montana 406
Massachusetts 339
```

To sort this file alphabetically:

```
[user1@centos73 ~]$ sort sortfile1
Florida 772
Maryland 667
Massachusetts 339
Mississippi 662
Missouri 975
Montana 406
Pennsylvania 445
```

To sort this file numerically (-n) on the second column (-k):

```
[user1@centos73 ~]$ sort -k 2 -n sortfile1
Massachusetts 339
Montana 406
Pennsylvania 445
Mississippi 662
Maryland 667
Florida 772
Missouri 975
```

To re-run the above command but in reverse order (-r):

```
[user1@centos73 ~]$ sort -k 2 -nr sortfile1
Missouri 975
Florida 772
Maryland 667
Mississippi 662
Pennsylvania 445
Montana 406
Massachusetts 339
```

To sort the output of the *ll* command, pipe it to the *sort* command as input:

```
[user1@centos73 ~]$ ll / | sort
```

To sort on the sixth column (month) of the *ll* command output:

```
[user1@centos73 ~]$ ll / | sort -k 6M
```

By default, the output of *sort* is displayed on the screen, but you can redirect it to a file by using the -o option. The example below saves the output in */tmp/sort.out* and does not display it on the screen:

```
[user1@centos73 ~]$ ll / | sort -k 6M -o /tmp/sort.out
```

To perform a multi-level sorting on the sixth column (month) and then on the seventh column (date) of the output of the *ll* command, try the following:

```
[user1@centos73 ~]$ ll / | sort -k 6M -k 7
```

There are numerous other options available with the *sort* command. Try them out for a better comprehension. Refer to the command's manual pages.

Breaking Large Files into Smaller Files Using split

The *split* filter is used to break a large file into smaller files for easy data transport. The resulting files are 1000 lines in length and named xa[a-z], xb[a-z], xc[a-z], and so on (prefixing x and suffixing with aa to az, ba to bz, ca to cz, and so on). Several options are available with the *split* command such as the following:

-a to set the suffix length
-b to specify file sizes in bytes
-d to define numeric suffixes instead of alphabetic
-l to set the number of lines

After transporting the small files to the desired location, we can use the *cat* command to merge them to reproduce the original.

In the following examples, we make a copy of the */etc/profile* file in *user1*'s home directory and then split it into files of size no more than 500 bytes. You can use the *wc* **command** after making a copy of the file to determine the number of lines in the file.

```
[user1@centos73 ~]$ cd
[user1@centos73 ~]$ cp /etc/profile .
[user1@centos73 ~]$ wc -l profile
1795 profile
[user1@centos73 ~]$ split -b 500 profile
```

Now run the *ll* command and you should be able to see four files: *xaa*, *xab*, *xac*, and *xad*:

```
[user1@centos73 ~]$ ll xa*
-rw-rw-r--. 1 user1 user1 500 Jan 16 09:17 xaa
-rw-rw-r--. 1 user1 user1 500 Jan 16 09:17 xab
-rw-rw-r--. 1 user1 user1 500 Jan 16 09:17 xac
-rw-rw-r--. 1 user1 user1 295 Jan 16 09:17 xad
```

The *profile* file is split into four short files, with the first three files exactly at the specified size, and the last file is composed of the rest of the bytes. Try the *wc* command also to determine the file sizes.

Now, let's remove the *profile* file from *user1*'s home directory and then recreate it using the concatenation feature of the *cat* command. Use the *ll* or *wc* command after the concatenation for confirmation.

```
[user1@centos73 ~]$ rm profile
[user1@centos73 ~]$ cat xaa xab xac xad > profile
[user1@centos73 ~]$ ll profile
```

Try splitting the file using the -a, -b, and -d options individually and in combination for practice. Check out the manual pages of the command for additional help.

Deleting, Squeezing, or Translating Characters Using tr

The *tr* filter is used to erase, squeeze, or translate input characters. This command displays the output on the screen and supports a few options that are used in the following examples.

Let's use the output of the *who* command and see how *tr* erases, squeezes, and translates characters. The *who* command is a simple tool that is used to display the list of all currently logged-in users on the system. Here is a sample output of this command and we will manipulate it with *tr*:

```
[user1@centos73 ~]$ who
root        :0       2017-01-16 08:57 (:0)
user1       pts/0    2017-01-16 08:57 (:1)
user1       :1       2017-01-16 08:58 (:1)
```

To delete (-d) all digits from the above output:

```
[user1@centos73 ~]$ who | tr -d [0-9]
```

Try the following to squeeze (-s) multiple white spaces between columns to one space. Notice a single white space between the quotation marks. You may instead use the double quotation marks (" "):

```
[user1@centos73 ~]$ who | tr -s ' '
```

Try the following to translate (-t) all lowercase letters into uppercase letters. Translation is the default feature for the *tr* command and therefore the inclusion of the -t option with the command is optional.

```
[user1@centos73 ~]$ who | tr [a-z] [A-Z]
```

The above should also work without enclosing the character ranges within square brackets. Try the above examples by replacing **who** with **cat /etc/profile**. Read the command's manual pages for more information.

Printing Unique or Identical Lines Using uniq

The *uniq* (*unique*) filter scans a text file or input provided for identical line entries appearing on adjacent lines. The duplication must be present on adjacent lines or the command will report them as unique. It is a good practice to sort a file or input before running the *uniq* command on it. Options such as the following can be used to change the command behavior:

-c to print a count of each line occurrence
-d to print the duplicate lines only
-i to ignore the letter case
-u to print the unique lines only

In order to observe the behavior of this filter, let's use these options with it and apply them on the */etc/passwd* file.

To peruse whether there are any identical (-d) entries appearing on successive lines in the file and how many (-c) times:

[user1@centos73 ~]$ **uniq -dc /etc/passwd**

To print all the unique (-u) lines appearing in the */etc/passwd* file and ignore (-i) the letter case in the comparison:

[user1@centos73 ~]$ **uniq -ui /etc/passwd**

There are a few additional options available with this filter. Check out the manual pages for this filter for more information.

Counting Words, Lines, and Characters Using wc

The *wc* (*word count*) command displays the number of lines, words, and characters (or bytes) contained in a text file or input supplied. For example, when you run this command on the */etc/profile* file, you will see output similar to the following:

[user1@centos73 ~]$ **wc /etc/profile**
76 252 1795 /etc/profile

The first column indicates the number of lines (76) in the file followed by the number of words (252), the number of characters (or bytes) (1795), and the file name (*/etc/profile*) in subsequent columns.

We can limit the output to what we want to see with the help of a few options available with this command. These options are -l, -w, -c, and -m, and in that sequence, they restrict the output to a count of lines, words, bytes, and characters.

The following example displays only the number of lines in */etc/profile*:

[user1@centos73 ~]$ **wc -l /etc/profile**
76 /etc/profile

Try running *wc* with the other options and observe the outcome.

Regular Expressions

A *regular expression*, also referred to as a *regexp* or simply *regex*, is a text pattern or an expression that is matched against a string of characters in a file or supplied input in a search operation. The pattern may include a single character, multiple random characters, range of characters, word, phrase, or an entire sentence. Any pattern containing one or more white spaces must be enclosed within quotes.

Linux provides a powerful tool called *grep* (*global regular expression print* or *get regular expression and print*) to work with pattern matching by using regular expressions. This tool searches the contents of one or more text files or input supplied for a match. If the expression is matched, *grep* prints every line containing that expression on the screen without changing the source content. *grep* has a number of options available with it and it accepts expressions in various forms.

In order to view additional options and usages available with *grep*, it is strongly suggested to consult this command's manual pages. To learn more about regex, issue **man 7 regex** in a terminal window.

Using grep for Pattern Matching

In order to comprehend the basic usage of the *grep* command, let's consider the following examples.

To search for the pattern "operator" in the */etc/passwd* file:

```
[user1@centos73 ~]$ grep operator /etc/passwd
operator:x:11:0:operator:/root:/sbin/nologin
```

To search for the pattern "nologin" in */etc/passwd* and exclude (-v) the lines in the output that contain this pattern. Add the -n option to show the line numbers associated with the lines that do not contain this pattern.

```
[user1@centos73 ~]$ grep -nv nologin /etc/passwd
1:root:x:0:0:root:/root:/bin/bash
6:sync:x:5:0:sync:/sbin:/bin/sync
7:shutdown:x:6:0:shutdown:/sbin:/sbin/shutdown
8:halt:x:7:0:halt:/sbin:/sbin/halt
43:user1:x:1000:1000:user1:/home/user1:/bin/bash
```

To search for all the lines in */etc/passwd* that begin with the pattern "root". The caret (^) sign is a special character that marks the beginning of a line or word. This is useful, for instance, if we need to know whether there are more than one users in the file by that name.

```
[user1@centos73 ~]$ grep ^root /etc/passwd
root:x:0:0:root:/root:/bin/bash
```

To list all the lines from */etc/passwd* that end with the pattern "bash". The dollar ($) sign is a special character that marks the end of a line or word. This is useful, for example, if we need to learn which users have their shells set to the bash shell.

```
[user1@centos73 ~]$ grep bash$ /etc/passwd
root:x:0:0:root:/root:/bin/bash
user1:x:1000:1000:user1:/home/user1:/bin/bash
```

To show all empty lines that exist in the */etc/login.defs* file:

```
[user1@centos73 ~]$ grep ^$ /etc/login.defs
```

To search for all the lines in */etc/passwd* that contain the pattern "root." The -i option instructs the command to perform a case-insensitive search. This is useful to establish if there are any *root* user accounts with a combination of lowercase and uppercase letters.

```
[user1@centos73 ~]$ grep -i root /etc/passwd
```

To print all the lines from the *etc/profile* file that contain an exact match for a word (-w). We can use a period (.) to match a position in the search string. The following example searches for any word in the *etc/profile* file that begins with letters "sb" followed by exactly any two characters:

```
[user1@centos73 ~]$ grep -w sb.. /etc/profile
    pathmunge /usr/sbin
    pathmunge /usr/local/sbin
    pathmunge /usr/local/sbin after
    pathmunge /usr/sbin after
```

Using grep Variants for Pattern Matching

egrep (*extended grep*) and *fgrep* (*fixed* or *fast grep*) are two variants of *grep* that may be used in advanced cases. The use of both variants is deprecated; however, Linux offers the -E and -F options with the *grep* command as their substitutes. The following will help understand the basic usages of the two variants.

Try the following to print all the lines from the *ll* output containing either the pattern "cron" or "conf". The pipe (|) character is used as an OR operator in this example, which means to match either pattern. This is referred to as *alternation*. Regex allows us to add more patterns to this set if desired. For instance, if we are to search for three patterns, we will use 'pattern1|pattern2|pattern3'. The patterns must be enclosed within single or double quotation marks. Here is what you will issue when you want to look for the patterns "cron" and "conf" in the *etc* directory listing:

```
[user1@centos73 ~]$ ll /etc | grep -E 'cron|conf'
```

Unlike grep and extended grep, the fixed grep is used to search for strings that include special characters such as *, $, |, etc. It interprets the special characters in literal terms, treating them just like any other normal character. The following example will help you understand the use of it.

To print all the lines from the *etc/profile* file that contain the string "$EUID" (including the double quotation marks), run the following. The string must be quoted.

```
[user1@centos73 ~]$ grep -F '"$EUID"' /etc/profile
```

Using sed for Pattern Matching

In addition to the use of the *sed* command as a filter, *sed* is also used in regular expressions for pattern matching. We will explain this use of *sed* with the help of a few simple examples.

To search for the hidden end-of-line character "$" and substitute each occurrence with the pattern "Linux" (a white space followed by Linux) in the output of the *ll* command:

```
[user1@centos73 ~]$ ll | sed 's/$/ Linux/'
```

To substitute all the occurrences of the pattern "files" in the *etc/nsswitch.conf* file with "FILES", use the following command; however, this will change only the first matching occurrence on a line. If you want to replace all the matching occurrences of this pattern that appear on the same line, use 's/files/FILES/g' (g for global) instead. Run both of the following and observe the differences:

```
[user1@centos73 ~]$ sed 's/files/FILES/' /etc/nsswitch.conf
[user1@centos73 ~]$ sed 's/files/FILES/g' /etc/nsswitch.conf
```

To perform multiple edits (-e) on /etc/nsswitch.conf where the first edit replaces all occurrences of the pattern "files" with "FILES" and the second one swaps the pattern "group" with "GROUP":

```
[user1@centos73 ~]$ sed -e 's/files/FILES/' -e 's/group/GROUP/' /etc/nsswitch.conf
```

Neither of the above two examples will modify the specified input file.

Chapter Summary

We learned about the vim editor, which creates and modifies files, and looked at its various modes of operations and how to switch between them. The basics of vim were discussed, including how to start and insert text, navigate and search for text, copy and paste text, change and delete text, save edits, and quit.

The next topic introduced the various common filter programs available in Linux. We covered a plethora of filter programs and understood their usages with some practical examples. Their proper understanding and usage knowledge is vital for both normal users as well as system administrators.

The last topic was related to regular expressions and how to employ them to find desired patterns within a text file or supplied input, and use the output for reporting, examination, or redirecting to some other program. We looked at a few *sed* command examples to experiment with its usage.

Chapter Review at a Glance

The following presents a one-sentence review of each key topic discussed in this chapter:

- The vi (vim) text file editor is available on virtually every Linux system and it has been the editor of choice for all users alike.

- There are three basic modes of operation for the vi editor—the command mode, the insert mode, and the last-line mode.

- The command mode provides several commands and ways for navigation and text manipulation, the insert mode allows entering text in the file, and the last-line mode is used to perform advanced search and edit operations.

- Linux furnishes a number of commands that are used for text filtering, such as concatenating files (cat), extracting data from output (cut), converting text to spaces (expand), converting spaces to text (unexpand), formatting text (fmt), dumping text output (od), joining data (join), enumerating output (nl), pasting data side-by-side (paste), formatting text for printing (pr), transforming text (sed), sorting output (sort), splitting large files into small files (split), translating characters (tr), displaying unique and identical lines (uniq), and counting lines and words (wc).

- The use of text filters is common in day-to-day system administration and in shell scripts.

- Regular expressions (a.k.a regex or regexp) are text patterns, which may contain a single character, multiple random characters, range of characters, word, phrase, or an entire sentence, that are used in search operations.

- A variety of advanced regex functions may be performed with variants of the standard grep command.

- Commands we learned in this chapter are: vi, vim, cat, cut, expand, unexpand, fmt, od, join, nl, paste, pr, sed, sort, split, tr, uniq, wc, grep, egrep, and fgrep.
- Files and directories we discussed in this chapter are: none.

Chapter 4

Dealing with the Bash Shell and Processes

This chapter describes the following major topics:

➢ Overview of the Bash shell, internal and external commands, and launching commands from inside and outside the defined paths
➢ Comprehend Bash shell features including variables; command, alias, and variable substitutions; command history; wildcarding and filename globbing; input, output, and error redirections; and piping output to one or more destinations
➢ Overview of list operators and how to use them
➢ Understand and show system- and user-executed processes
➢ View process states and priorities
➢ Process niceness and reniceness, and how to change process niceness
➢ Signals and their use
➢ Alert a program to continue to run after user logout
➢ Overview of foreground and background jobs and how to control them
➢ Split a terminal window into multiple sub-terminals

This chapter covers the following objectives for LX0-103/101-400 Exam:

103.1 Work on the command line [a part of this objective is described in chapter 1 and the rest in this chapter]

37. Use and modify the shell environment including defining, referencing and exporting environment variables
38. Use and edit command history
39. Invoke commands inside and outside the defined path

The following is a partial list of the used files, terms and utilities: bash, echo, env, export, set, unset, history, and .bash_history

103.3 Perform basic file management [most of this objective is described in chapter 2, a part in this chapter, the tar/cpio and dd commands in chapters 1 and 8, respectively]

44. Use simple and advanced wildcard specifications in commands

The following is a partial list of the used files, terms and utilities: file globbing

103.4 Use streams, pipes and redirects [a part of this objective is described in chapter 2 and the rest in this chapter]

47. Redirecting standard input, standard output and standard error
48. Pipe the output of one command to the input of another command
50. Send output to both stdout and a file

The following is a partial list of the used files, terms and utilities: tee

103.5 Create, monitor and kill processes [most of this objective is described in this chapter, the uptime command in chapter 1, and the free command in chapter 8]

51. Run jobs in the foreground and background
52. Signal a program to continue running after logout
53. Monitor active processes
54. Select and sort processes for display
55. Send signals to processes

The following is a partial list of the used files, terms and utilities: &, bg, fg, jobs, kill, nohup, ps, top, pgrep, pkill, killall, and screen

103.6 Modify process execution priorities [this entire objective is described in this chapter]

56. Know the default priority of a job that is created
57. Run a program with higher or lower priority than the default
58. Change the priority of a running process

The following is a partial list of the used files, terms and utilities: nice, ps, renice, and top

105.1 Customize and use the shell environment [a part of this objective is described in chapter 9; most of it in chapter 10; and env, export, set, unset, alias, and lists commands/topics are explained in this chapter]

The following is a partial list of the used files, terms and utilities: env, export, set, unset, alias and lists

Shells allow users to interact with the operating system for execution of their instructions through programs, commands, or applications. Linux supports a variety of shells of which the bash shell is the most common. It is also the default shell in many newer Linux distribution versions. The bash shell offers a variety of features that help users and administrators perform their job with ease and flexibility.

A process is any running program, command, or application. Every process has a unique numeric identifier and it is managed by the kernel through its entire lifespan. It may be viewed, listed, monitored, niced, and reniced. A process is in one of several states at any given time during its lifecycle. A process may be tied to the terminal window where it is launched, or it may run on the system as a service.

There are plenty of signals available that may be passed to a process to accomplish various actions. These actions include hard killing a process, soft terminating it, running it as a background job, bringing the background job back to the foreground, and forcing it to restart with the same identifier. A program or command may be run in a way that precludes termination by a hang-up signal such as the disconnection of the terminal session in which the program or command is running. A terminal screen may be split into two or more sub-screens, allowing users to run different programs in different screens.

Introducing the BASH Shell

A *shell* is referred to as the command interpreter, and it is the interface between a user and the Linux kernel. The shell accepts instructions (commands) from users (or scripts), interprets them, and passes them on to the kernel for processing. The kernel utilizes all hardware and software components required for a successful processing of the instructions. When concluded, it returns the results to the shell, which then displays them on the screen. The shell also shows appropriate error messages, if generated. In addition, the shell delivers a customizable environment to users.

A widely used shell by Linux users and administrators is the *bash* (*bourne again shell*) shell. Bash is a replacement for the older *Bourne* shell with numerous enhancements, and plenty of features incorporated from two other shells: Korn and C. It is the default shell in most popular Linux distributions and offers several features such as variable manipulation, command substitution, variable substitution, history substitution, input and output redirections, command line editing, tab completion, tilde substitution, filename globbing, metacharacters, command aliasing, conditional execution, flow control, and shell scripting. This section discusses only a few of these features.

The bash shell is identified by the dollar ($) sign for regular users and the number (#) sign for the *root* user. The bash shell is resident in the */usr/bin/bash* file on RHEL and its derivatives (or */bin/bash* on older versions) and */bin/bash* on Debian and its derivatives.

Internal and External Shell Commands

There are a number of commands that are built-in to the bash shell that are referred to as the internal commands. These include *cd, pwd, umask, alias/unalias, history, command,* . (dot), *export, exit, test, shift, set/unset, source, exec,* and *break*. Upon invocation, these commands are executed directly by the shell without creating a new process for them. Other commands located in various directories, such as */bin, /usr/bin, /sbin,* and */usr/sbin* are external to the shell, and the shell spawns a sub-shell (child shell) temporarily to run them.

Shell and Environment Variables

A *variable* is a temporary storage for data in memory. It retains information that is used for customizing the shell environment and referenced by many programs to function properly. The shell allows us to store a value in a variable. A variable value containing one or more white space characters must be enclosed within quotation marks.

There are two types of variables: *local* (or *shell*) and *environment*. A local variable is private to the shell in which it is created, and its value cannot be used by programs that are not started in that shell. This introduces the concept of *current* shell and *sub*-shell (or *child* shell). The current shell is where a program is executed, whereas a sub-shell is created within a shell to run a program. The value of a local variable is available only in the current shell, and not in any sub-shells. A local variable is also known as a shell variable.

The value of an environment variable, however, is inherited from the current shell to the sub-shell during the execution of a program. In other words, the value stored in an environment variable is accessible to the program, as well as any sub-programs that it spawns during its lifecycle. Any environment variable set in a sub-shell is, however, lost when the sub-shell terminates.

There are a number of pre-defined environment variables that are set for each user upon logging in. We can use the **env** (or the **printenv** or **set**) command to view their values. Run these commands on both *centos73* and *ubuntu14* systems as *user1* and observe the outputs. There are around 45 and 65 variables currently set on the two systems for *user1*. Some of the common pre-defined environment variables are described in Table 4-1.

Variable	Description
DISPLAY	Stores the hostname or IP address for graphical terminal sessions
HISTFILE	Defines the file for storing the history of executed commands
HISTSIZE	Defines the maximum size for the HISTFILE
HOME	Sets the home directory path
LOGNAME	Retains the login name
MAIL	Contains the path to the user mail directory
PATH	Defines a colon-separated (:) list of directories to be searched when executing a command
PPID	Holds the identifier number for the parent program
PS1	Defines the primary command prompt
PS2	Defines the secondary command prompt
PWD	Stores the current directory location
SHELL	Holds the absolute path to the primary shell file
TERM	Holds the terminal type
UID	Holds the logged in user's ID
USER	Retains the name of the logged-in user

Table 4-1 Common Pre-Defined Environment Variables

Linux provides us with the *echo* command to view the values stored in variables. For instance, to view the value for the PATH variable, run the *echo* command and ensure to prepend the variable name (PATH) with the dollar ($) sign:

```
[user1@centos73 ~]$ echo $PATH
/usr/local/bin:/usr/bin:/usr/local/sbin:/usr/sbin:/home/user1/.local/bin:/home/user1/bin
```

Try running **echo $HOME, echo $SHELL, echo $TERM, echo $PPID, echo $PS1**, and **echo $USER** and see what values they store.

We can also set custom environment variables at the command prompt or in scripts as required, and view them with *echo*.

Setting and Unsetting Variables

Shell and environment variables may be set or unset at the command prompt or via programs, and their values may be viewed and used as necessary. We define and undefine variables and view their values using built-in shell commands such as *export*, *unset*, and *echo*. It is recommended that you employ uppercase letters to name variables so as to circumvent any possible conflicts with a command, program, file, or directory name that exist somewhere on the system. To understand how variables are defined, viewed, made environment, and undefined, a few examples are presented below. We run the commands as *user1*.

To define a local variable called VR1:

    [user1@centos73 ~]$ **VR1=CentOS7**

To view the value stored in VR1:

    [user1@centos73 ~]$ **echo $VR1**

Now type **bash** at the command prompt to enter a sub-shell and then run **echo $VR1** there to see whether the variable is visible in the sub-shell. You will not find it there, as it was not an environment variable. Exit out of the sub-shell by typing **exit** to return.

To make this variable an environment variable, use the *export* command:

    [user1@centos73 ~]$ **export VR1**

Repeat the previous test by running the **bash** command and then the **echo $VR1**. You should be able to see the variable in the sub-shell, as it is now an environment variable. Exit out of the sub-shell with the **exit** command.

To undefine this variable and remove it from the shell environment:

    [user1@centos73 ~]$ **unset VR1**

To define a local variable that contains a value with one or more white spaces:

    [user1@centos73 ~]$ **VR2="I love CentOS"**

To define and make the variable an environment variable at the same time:

    [user1@centos73 ~]$ **export VR3="I love Ubuntu"**

We may also use the *set* or *export* command to view defined variables. The *set* command displays the values of both local and environment variables; whereas, the *export* command shows the

---

environment variables only, just like the *env* and *printenv* commands. Try running **set** and **export** without an argument and observe the outputs.

Command and Variable Substitution

The primary command prompt for the *root* user is the number (#) sign and for regular users it is the dollar ($) sign. Customizing the primary command prompt to display useful information, such as who you are, the system you are logged on to, and your current location in the directory tree, is a good practice. By default, this setting is already in place on both CentOS and Ubuntu through the PS1 environment variable, which defines the primary command prompt, and you can verify that by simply looking at the command prompt **[user1@centos73 ~]$** for CentOS and **user1@ubuntu14:~$** for Ubuntu.

We can also view the value stored in PS1 by issuing **echo $PS1**. The value is something similar to \u@\h \W. The \u translates into the logged-in username, \h represents the hostname of the system, and \W translates into your location in the directory tree.

Let's modify the command prompt for *user1* by altering the PS1 value. We will set the prompt to show hostname first, then the username, and then the directory location. While typing, make sure that spaces and special characters are entered correctly.

    [user1@centos73 ~]$ export PS1="< $(hostname):$LOGNAME \$PWD > "

The command prompt will change to:

    < centos73:user1 /home/user1 >

Running the command *hostname* and assigning its output to a variable is an example of a shell feature called *command substitution*. Note that the command whose output we want to assign to a variable must be enclosed within either backticks `hostname` or parentheses $(hostname).

The value of LOGNAME will display the user's login name.

And lastly, the value of the PWD variable will reflect the directory location in the prompt as *user1* navigates through the tree. This is an example of a shell feature called *variable substitution*. For instance, if *user1* moves to */usr/bin*, the prompt will change to:

    < centos73:user1 /usr/bin >

To revert to the original command prompt, simply exit out of the terminal window by issuing **exit** at the command prompt and opening a new terminal window session.

Alias Substitution

A *command alias*, or simply an *alias*, allows you to define a shortcut for a lengthy and complex command or a set of commands. Defining and using aliases saves time and saves you from typing. The shell executes the corresponding command or commandset when an alias is run.

The bash shell includes several pre-defined aliases that are set during user login. These aliases may be viewed with the *alias* command. The following shows all aliases that are currently set for *user1* on *centos73*:

```
[user1@centos73 ~]$ alias
alias egrep='egrep --color=auto'
alias fgrep='fgrep --color=auto'
alias grep='grep --color=auto'
alias l.='ls -d .* --color=auto'
alias ll='ls -l --color=auto'
alias ls='ls --color=auto'
alias vi='vim'
alias which='alias | /usr/bin/which --tty-only --read-alias --show-dot --show-tilde'
```

There are a number of pre-defined command aliases set for the user that are explained in Table 4-2.

Alias	Value	Definition
egrep /fgrep /grep	egrep --color=auto fgrep --color=auto grep --color=auto	Runs the *egrep*, *fgrep*, and *grep* commands and displays the matched expressions in color
l.	ls -d .* --color=tty	Runs the *ls* command with -d .* and shows hidden directories in color
ll	ls -l --color=tty	Runs the *ls* command with -l and shows files and directories in various colors
ls	ls --color=tty	Runs the *ls* command and shows files and directories in various colors
vi	vim	Runs the */usr/bin/vim* command instead of the old */usr/bin/vi*
which	alias	/usr/bin/which --tty-only -- read-alias --show-dot --show-tilde	Defines an alias for the *which* command with the specified options

Table 4-2 Pre-Defined Command Aliases

In addition to listing set aliases, the *alias* command is also used to define a new alias. The opposite function of unsetting an alias is performed with the *unalias* command. Both *alias* and *unalias* are internal shell commands. Let's look at a few examples.

Create an alias "f" to abbreviate the *find* command with several switches and arguments. Enclose the entire command within single or double quotation marks to ensure white spaces are taken care of. Do not leave any spaces before and after the equal (=) sign.

```
[user1@centos73 ~]$ alias f='find / -name core -exec rm {} \;'
```

Now, when you type the letter f at the command prompt and press the Enter key, the shell will trade the alias "f" with what is stored in it and will run it. Basically, you have created a shortcut to that lengthy command. This feature of shell is referred to as *alias substitution*.

Sometimes you create an alias by a name that matches the name of a system command. In this situation, the shell gives the execution precedence to the alias over the command. This means the shell will run the alias and not the command. For example, the *rm* command deletes a file without giving any warning. To prevent accidental deletion of files with *rm*, you may create an alias by the same name as the command but with the interactive option added, as shown below:

```
[user1@centos73 ~]$ alias rm='rm -i'
```

When you execute *rm* now, the shell will run what is stored in the *rm* alias and not the command *rm*. If you wish to run the *rm* command instead, run it by preceding a backslash (\) with it:

```
[user1@centos73 ~]$ \rm file1
```

We can use the *unalias* command to unset one or more specified aliases if they are no longer in need:

```
[user1@centos73 ~]$ unalias f rm
```

Command History

Command history is a time-saver bash shell feature that keeps a log of all commands or commandsets that you run at the command prompt in chronological order with one command or commandset per line. The history feature is enabled by default; however, you can disable and re-enable it if required. The bash shell stores command history in a file located in the user's home directory and in system memory. You may retrieve these commands, modify them at the command prompt, and re-run them.

There are three variables—HISTFILE, HISTSIZE, and HISTFILESIZE—that control the location and history storage. HISTFILE defines the name and location of the history file to be used to store command history, the default is *.bash_history* in the user's home directory. HISTSIZE dictates the maximum number of commands to be held in memory for the current session. HISTFILESIZE sets the maximum number of commands allowed for storage in the history file at the beginning of the current session and are written to the HISTFILE from memory at the end of the current terminal session. Usually, HISTSIZE and HISTFILESIZE are set to a common value. These variables and their values can be viewed with the *echo* command. The following shows the settings for *user1*:

```
[user1@centos73 ~]$ echo $HISTFILE
/home/user1/.bash_history
[user1@centos73 ~]$ echo $HISTSIZE
1000
[user1@centos73 ~]$ echo $HISTFILESIZE
1000
```

The values of any of these variables may be altered for individual users by editing the *.bashrc* or *.bash_profile* file in the user's home directory.

Linux provides us with the *history* command to display or re-run previously executed commands. This command gets the history data from the system memory as well as from the *.bash_history* file. By default, it shows all entries. Run this command at the prompt without any options and it will dump everything on the screen:

```
[user1@centos73 ~]$ history
```

The *history* command has some options that you may find useful. Let's use them and observe the impact on the output.

To display this command and the ten preceding entries:

```
[user1@centos73 ~]$ history 10
```

To re-execute a command by its line number (line 100 for example):

```
[user1@centos73 ~]$ !100
```

To re-execute the most recent occurrence of a command that started with a particular letter or series of letters (ch for example):

```
[user1@centos73 ~]$ !ch
```

To issue the most recent command that contained "grep":

```
[user1@centos73 ~]$ !?grep?
```

To repeat the last command executed:

```
[user1@centos73 ~]$ !!
```

To remove entry 74 from history:

```
[user1@centos73 ~]$ history -d 74
```

You may disable the shell's history expansion feature by issuing **set +o history** at the command prompt and re-enable it with **set -o history**. The *set* command is used in this way to enable or disable a bash shell feature.

Invoking Commands inside the Defined Path

Commands are located in various directories on the Linux system. These directories may include */bin, /usr/bin, /sbin, /usr/sbin,* and */usr/local/bin* and must be defined in a user's PATH environment variable in order for the user to be able to execute the commands located under these directories without specifying their full pathname. A full pathname always begins with a leading forward slash (/) character, and it is also referred to as an *absolute pathname* or a *fully qualified pathname*. When a user executes a command, the shell scans each pathname one after the other that is defined in the PATH variable to try to locate it. If it finds a match, it executes it, otherwise it produces an error that says that the command has not been found.

Here is what is currently defined in PATH for *user1* on *centos73*:

```
[user1@centos73 ~]$ echo $PATH
/usr/local/bin:/usr/bin:/usr/local/sbin:/usr/sbin:/bin:/sbin:/home/user1/.local/bin:/home/user1/bin
```

Linux gives us three commands—*which, whereis,* and *type* (*type* is a shell built-in command)—that print the absolute path to the command that is executed when you run that command without entering its full pathname. For instance, to view the path to the *cat* command, use any of the following:

```
[user1@centos73 ~]$ which cat
/usr/bin/cat
[user1@centos73 ~]$ whereis cat
cat: /usr/bin/cat /usr/share/man/man1/cat.1.gz /usr/share/man/man1p/cat.1p.gz
```

```
[user1@centos73 ~]$ type cat
cat is /usr/bin/cat
```

All three outputs indicate that the *cat* command will run from the */usr/bin* directory when it is executed without specifying its absolute path. Notice that the *whereis* command also shows the path to the command's manual pages.

Consult the manual pages for the *which*, *whereis*, and *type* commands and run them with a few simple options that are provided in their manual pages.

Invoking Commands outside the Defined Path

Commands that you want to run but are not in your defined PATH need to be specified at the command prompt either as a full pathname or as a *relative pathname*. Alternatively, you can modify your PATH variable and add or remove paths as desired. The PATH variable for a user is defined in the *.profile* (or *.bash_profile*) file located in the user's home directory. For a global path change that affects all users on the system, you need *root* privileges to modify the PATH that is set in the */etc/profile* file.

The choice of whether to use a full pathname or a relative pathname for command execution depends on the location of the command from your current location in the directory tree. You may invoke any command from anywhere by simply typing its full pathname such as */usr/local/bin/abcd*.

A relative pathname never begins with a forward slash (/); rather, it always begins in one of the three ways—with a solo period (.) character, dual period (..) characters, or a sub-directory name.

A single period (.) represents your current location in the directory tree. If you are logged in as *user1*, and you are in your home directory */home/user1* with an executable file called *script1*, you can run it as *./script1* with the leading period telling the shell the directory location of *script1*.

Dual periods (..) denote a *parent* directory, which is one level higher than your present directory. For example, if your current location is */home/user1*, then */home* will be your parent directory, and you can use **cd ..** to change into it.

A sub-directory name is used in relation to your current directory. Suppose you are in the */etc* directory and want to switch to the *X11/xinit* sub-directory, you will run **cd X11/xinit**.

Using Wildcard Characters in Filename Globbing

Wildcard characters are special characters that possess special meaning to the shell. They include asterisk *, question mark ?, and square brackets []. They are used in filename *globbing* and in commands where an action needs to be taken on multiple files matching certain criteria. Upon detection of a wildcard character, the shell resolves it to a list of matching patterns. Matching filename patterns using globbing is a bash shell feature, and it is also referred to as *filename expansion*.

Let's look at each of the three wildcard characters and their use in globbing.

The Asterisk (*) Character

The asterisk (*) matches zero to an unlimited number of any characters except for the leading period in a hidden filename. See the following examples on usage.

To list all files in the */etc* directory that begin with letters "ali" and followed by any characters:

```
[user1@centos73 ~]$ ls /etc/ali*
/etc/aliases  /etc/aliases.db
```

To list all hidden files (filenames beginning with the leading period) in */home/user1*:

```
[user1@centos73 ~]$ ls -d .*
.                   .bash_logout    .b.swp    .esd_auth       .local
..                  .bash_profile   .cache    .ICEauthority   .mozilla
.bash_history       .bashrc         .config   .lesshst        .viminfo
```

To list all files in the */var/log* directory that end in ".log":

```
[user1@centos73 ~]$ ls /var/log/*.log
/var/log/boot.log            /var/log/wpa_supplicant.log      /var/log/Xorg.9.log
/var/log/vmware-vmusr.log    /var/log/Xorg.0.log              /var/log/yum.log
```

The Question Mark (?) Character

The question mark (?) matches exactly one character except for the leading period in a hidden filename. See the following example to understand its usage.

To list all directories under */var/log* with exactly three characters in their names:

```
[user1@centos73 ~]$ ls -d /var/log/???
/var/log/gdm   /var/log/ppp
```

The Square Brackets ([]) Characters

The square brackets ([]) can be used to match either a set of characters or a range of characters for a single character position.

For a set of characters specified in this enclosure, the order in which they are listed has no importance. This means the shell will treat [xyz], [yxz], [xzy], and [zyx] alike during filename expansion. In the following example, two characters are enclosed within the square brackets. The output will include all files and directories that begin with either of the two characters and followed by any number of characters.

```
[user1@centos73 ~]$ ls /usr/sbin/[yw]*
/usr/sbin/weak-modules    /usr/sbin/wpa_passphrase          /usr/sbin/yumdb
/usr/sbin/wipefs          /usr/sbin/wpa_supplicant
/usr/sbin/wpa_cli         /usr/sbin/yum-complete-transaction
```

A range of characters must be specified in a proper sequence such as [a-z] or [0-9]. The following example matches all directory names that begin with any letter between m and o in the */etc/systemd/system* directory on our *centos73* system:

```
[user1@centos73 ~]$ ls -d /etc/systemd/system/[m-o]*
/etc/systemd/system/multi-user.target.wants
```

The shell allows us to use the exclamation mark (!) sign to inverse the matches. For instance, [!a-d]* would exclude all filenames that begin with any of the first four alphabets. The following example will produce the reverse of what the previous example did:

```
[user1@centos73 ~]$ ls -d /etc/systemd/system/[!m-o]*
```

The output will have several files printed.

For more information on globbing and wildcard characters, refer to globbing manual pages by issuing **man 7 glob**.

Redirecting Standard Input, Output, and Error Streams

Programs read input from the keyboard and write output to the terminal window where they are initiated. Any errors, if encountered, are printed on the terminal window too. This is the default behavior on Linux and other operating systems. Linux handles input, output, and errors as character streams. If you do not want input to come from the keyboard or output and error to go to the terminal screen, Linux shell gives you the flexibility to redirect input, output, and error messages to allow programs and commands to read input from a non-default source, and forward output and errors to one or more non-default destinations.

The default (or the standard) locations for input, output, and error streams are referred to as *standard input* (or *stdin*), *standard output* (or *stdout*), and *standard error* (or *stderr*), respectively. These locations may also be epitomized using the opening angle bracket (<) symbol for stdin and the closing angle bracket (>) symbol for both stdout and stderr. Alternatively, you may use the *file descriptors* (the digits 0, 1, and 2) to represent the three locations.

Redirecting Standard Input

Input redirection instructs a command to read input from an alternative source, such as a file, instead of the keyboard. The opening angle bracket (<) character is used for input redirection. For example, run the following to have the *cat* command read the */etc/redhat-release* file and display its contents on the standard output (terminal screen):

```
[user1@centos73 ~]$ cat < /etc/redhat-release
CentOS Linux release 7.3.1611 (Core)
```

Redirecting Standard Input Using here Document

A *here document* (or *heredoc*) is a type of input redirection that allows us to supply a list of commands, variables, or simple text as input to another command. This type of redirection can be used at the command line or in shell scripts to feed input rather than obtaining it from another file. A heredoc uses two << characters and a custom marker (such as EOF for End Of File) at the start and end of input. The syntax is illustrated in the following example that uses "LX0" as a marker to enclose the *pwd* command, the TERM environment variable, and a line of text. You must end the input with the same marker.

```
[user1@centos73 ~]$ cat << LX0
> pwd
> $TERM
> This is a simple heredoc example.
> LX0
pwd
xterm
This is a simple heredoc example.
```

In the above example, the shell reads the input provided between the two "LX0" markers and outputs it. It expands the environment variable and displays its value. All other text is displayed verbatim. If you wish to execute the *pwd* command and show its output as well, you need to enclose the command within back quotes (or as $(pwd)). In that case, the output will be:

```
[user1@centos73 ~]$ cat << LX0
> `pwd`
> $TERM
> This is a simple heredoc example.
> LX0
/home/user1
xterm
This is a simple heredoc example.
```

Redirecting Standard Input Using here String

A *here string* is a variant of heredoc. It uses three <<< characters. The syntax is illustrated in the following simple example that uses the PWD environment variable:

```
[user1@centos73 ~]$ cat <<< $PWD
/home/user1
```

In the above example, the shell reads the input provided, expands the variable, and displays its value. There is no need to use a marker in here strings to enclose the input.

We may modify the above heredoc example and use it as a here string to accomplish what we have just achieved with it. You need to detach the commands using the semicolon (;) command separator.

```
[user1@centos73 ~]$ cat <<< `pwd` ; echo $TERM ; echo This is a simple here string
example.
/home/user1
xterm
This is a simple here string example.
```

Redirecting Standard Output

Output redirection sends the output generated by a command to an alternative destination such as a file, instead of to the terminal window. The > sign is used for this purpose. For instance, we execute the following to direct the *ls* command output to a file called *ls.out*. This will overwrite the existing *ls.out* file if there is one that already exists; otherwise, a new file will be created.

```
[user1@centos73 ~]$ ls > ls.out
```

The above can also be run as **ls 1> ls.out**, where "1" represents the standard output location.

If you want to prevent an inadvertent overwriting of the output file, you can enable the shell's noclobber feature with the *set* command and confirm its activation by re-issuing the above redirection example:

```
[user1@centos73 ~]$ set -o noclobber
[user1@centos73 ~]$ ls > ls.out
-bash: ls.out: cannot overwrite existing file
```

You are denied the action.

 You can disable the noclobber option by running **set +o noclobber** at the command prompt.

To direct the *ls* command to append the output to the *ls.out* file instead of overwriting it, use the >> characters:

```
[user1@centos73 ~]$ ls >> ls.out
```

Again, the equivalent for the above is **ls 1>> ls.out**.

Redirecting Standard Error

Error redirection forwards any error messages generated to an alternative destination, such as a file, rather than to the terminal window. For example, the following directs the *find* command issued as a normal user to search for all occurrences of files by the name *core* in the entire directory tree and sends any error messages produced to */dev/null* (*/dev/null* is a special file that is used to discard data). This way only the useful output is displayed on the screen and errors are thrown away.

```
[user1@centos73 ~]$ find / -name core -print 2> /dev/null
```

Redirecting both Standard Output and Error

We may redirect both output and error to alternative locations as well. For instance, issue the following to forward them both to a file called *outerr.out*:

```
[user1@centos73 ~]$ ls /usr /cdr &> outerr.out
```

This example will produce a listing of the */usr* directory and save the result in *outerr.out*. At the same time, it will generate an error message complaining about the non-existence of */cdr*, and it will send it to the same file as well. You can exchange &> with &>> in the above example to append the information rather than overwriting.

 Another method to run the above command is by typing **ls /usr /cdr 1> outerr.out 2>&1**, which essentially means to redirect file descriptor 1 to file *outerr.out* as well as to file descriptor 2.

Piping Output of One Command as Input to Another

The *pipe*, represented by the vertical bar (|) and residing with the (\) on most keyboards, is a special character that is used to send the output of one command as input to the next. This character is also used to define alternations in regular expressions. You can use the pipe operator as many times in a command as you require.

The */etc* directory contains plenty of files, but they cannot fit on one terminal screen when we list them with the *ll* command. We can use the pipe operator with *ll* on */etc* to pipe the output to the *less* command in order to view the directory listing one screen at a time:

```
[user1@centos73 ~]$ ll /etc | less
```

In another example, the *who* command is run and its output is piped to the *nl* command to number each output line:

```
[user1@centos73 ~]$ who | nl
   1  (unknown)      :0        2017-01-18  09:41  (:0)
   2  root           pts/0     2017-01-18  10:21  (192.168.0.13)
   3  root           pts/3     2017-01-19  13:25  (:2)
```

The following example sends the output of *ll* to *grep* for the lines that do not contain the pattern "root". The new output is further piped for a case-insensitive selection of all lines that exclude the pattern "dec". The filtered output is numbered, and the final result is printed on the display one screen at a time.

```
[user1@centos73 ~]$ ll /proc | grep -v root | grep -vi dec | nl | less
```

A construct like the above with multiple pipes is referred to as a *pipeline*.

Sending Output to Multiple Destinations Using tee

The *tee* filter is used to send command output to more than one destination. This is particularly useful when you want the output displayed on the screen as well as recorded in a file. The *tee* command provides this facility when used with a pipe.

In the following example, the output from *ll* is numbered and captured in */tmp/ll.out* file. The output is also displayed on the screen.

```
[user1@centos73 ~]$ ll /etc | nl | tee /tmp/ll.out
```

Issue **cat /tmp/ll.out** and notice that the file contains the exact same information that was displayed on the screen when you executed the command.

By using the -a option with *tee*, the output may be appended to the file rather than overwriting the existing content. Here is an example:

```
[user1@centos73 ~]$ date | tee -a /tmp/ll.out
```

Run **cat /tmp/ll.out** again to confirm the above statement.

Using List Operators

The *list* operators in Bash shell are used to separate two commands from each other. There are three common operators: (1) the semicolon (;) character, (2) a pair of the ampersand (&&) character, and (3) a pair of the pipe (||) character—in this category.

The shell treats each command with a semicolon (;) in between as if it is typed and executed on a separate command line. It executes the first command, waits for its completion, and then runs the next command that follows the semicolon. For example, the following will run the *date* command first and print its output. It will then issue the next command *hostname* and display its result:

```
[user1@centos73 ~]$ date ; hostname
Tue Jul 11 17:25:37 EDT 2017
centos73
```

The ampersand pair performs a logical AND operation on two given commands. In this operation, the shell issues the first command in the sequence and checks for its success or failure status. If the result is a successful execution of the command, the shell executes the second command in the sequence; otherwise, it displays an error message on the screen and returns to the command prompt without even attempting to run the second command. Here is an example to prove its working. The following will run the *hostname* command only if the *date* command is successful:

```
[user1@centos73 ~]$ date && hostname
Tue Jul 11 17:26:07 EDT 2017
centos73
```

Replace "date" with "date1" and the result will be an error message. The shell will not run the *hostname* command. Next, replace "hostname" with "hostname1" and the result will be a successful execution of the *date* command with an error for hostname1.

The dual pipe characters perform a logical OR operation on two given commands. In this operation, the shell issues the first command in the sequence and checks for its success or failure status. If the result is a successful execution of the command, the shell ignores the second command in the sequence and returns to the command prompt. However, if the first command returns an unsuccessful result, the shell will execute the second command and display an output. Here is an example to prove its working. The following will ignore the *hostname* command if the *date* command runs successfully:

```
[user1@centos73 ~]$ date || hostname
Tue Jul 11 17:26:39 EDT 2017
```

Replace "date" with "date1" and the result will be an error message followed by a successful execution of the *hostname* command. Next, replace "hostname" with "hostname1" and the result will be a successful execution of the *date* command with "hostname1" ignored.

The use of the three list operators is common in Linux shell scripts. The semicolon list operator is a simple command separator, whereas, the other two evaluate the success or failure status of the first command and decide whether to proceed with the execution of the second command. They may be used in conditional and looping statements within shell scripts to make such decisions. Shell scripts are discussed in detail in Chapter 9 "Writing Shell Scripts and Managing a SQL Database".

Understanding and Manipulating Processes

A *process* is a unit for provisioning system resources. It is any program, application, or command that runs on the system. A process is created in memory when a program, application, or command is initiated. Processes are organized in a hierarchical fashion. Each process has a *parent process* (a.k.a. a *calling process*) that spawns it. A single parent process may have one or many *child processes* and passes several of its attributes to them at the time of their creation. Each process is assigned a unique identification number known as the *process identifier* (PID), which is used by the kernel to manage and control the process through its lifecycle. When a process completes its lifecycle or is terminated, this event is reported back to its parent process, and all the resources provisioned to it, such as cpu cycles, memory, etc., are then freed and the PID is removed from the system.

Plenty of processes are spawned at system boot, many of which sit in the memory and wait for an event to trigger a request to use their services. These background system processes are called *daemons* and are critical to system operation.

Viewing and Monitoring Processes with ps

An operational system may have hundreds or thousands of processes running concurrently depending on the purpose of the system. These processes may be viewed and monitored using various native tools such as *ps* (*process status*) and *top* (*table of processes*). The *ps* command offers several switches that influence its output, whereas *top* is used for real-time viewing and monitoring of processes and system resources.

Without any options or arguments, *ps* lists processes specific to the terminal where this command is issued:

```
[user1@centos73 ~]$ ps
  PID TTY       TIME CMD
 3442 pts/1  00:00:00 bash
 3818 pts/1  00:00:00 ps
```

The above output shows the elementary information about processes in four columns. These processes are tied to our current terminal window. It shows the PID, the terminal (TTY) the process spawned in, the cumulative time (TIME) the system CPU has given to the process, and the name of the actual command or program (CMD) being executed.

Some common options that can be used with the *ps* command to generate detailed reports include -e (every), -f (full-format), -F (extra full-format), and -l (long format). A combination of -e, -F, and -l (**ps -eFl**) produces a very thorough process report, however, that much detail may not be needed in most situations. Other common options such as --forest and -x will report the output in tree-like hierarchy and include the daemon processes. Check out the manual pages of the command for additional options and their usage.

The ps command can take options without a hyphen (BSD style), with a single hyphen (UNIX style), or with two hyphen characters (GNU style).

Here are a few sample lines from the beginning and end of the output when *ps* is executed with "e" and "f" options. You should see a similar output on your systems.

```
[user1@centos73 ~]$ ps -ef
UID         PID  PPID  C STIME TTY          TIME CMD
root          1     0  3 11:14 ?        00:00:01 /usr/lib/systemd/systemd --switc
root          2     0  0 11:14 ?        00:00:00 [kthreadd]
root          3     2  0 11:14 ?        00:00:00 [ksoftirqd/0]
root          4     2  0 11:14 ?        00:00:00 [kworker/0:0]
root          5     2  0 11:14 ?        00:00:00 [kworker/0:0H]
root          6     2  0 11:14 ?        00:00:00 [kworker/u4:0]
root          7     2  0 11:14 ?        00:00:00 [migration/0]
root          8     2  0 11:14 ?        00:00:00 [rcu_bh]
```

This output is spread across eight columns showing details about every process running on the system. Table 4-3 describes the content type of each column.

Column	Description
UID	User ID or name of the process owner
PID	Process ID of the process
PPID	Process ID of the parent process
C	CPU utilization for the process
STIME	Process start date or time
TTY	The controlling terminal the process was started on. "Console" represents the system console, and "?" represents a daemon process
TIME	Aggregated execution time for a process
CMD	The command or program name

Table 4-3 ps Command Output

The *ps* output above indicates the presence of several daemon processes running in the background. These processes have no association with any terminal, which is why there is a ? in the TTY column. Notice the PID and PPID numbers. The smaller the number, the earlier it is started. The process with PID 0 is started first at system boot, followed by the process with PID 1, and so on. Each PID has an associated PPID in the third column. The owner of each process is shown in the UID column along with the name of the command or program under CMD.

Information for each running process is recorded and maintained in the */proc* file system, which *ps* and many other commands reference to acquire desired data for our viewing.

The columns displayed in the output of the *ps* command can be customized if required. For instance, if we want to produce an output with the command name in the first column, PID in the second column, PPID in the third column, and owner name in the fourth column, we will run it as follows:

```
[user1@centos73 ~]$ ps -o comm,pid,ppid,user
```

Make sure the -o option is specified for user-defined format and there is no space before or after the column names. You can add or remove column names and switch positions as needed.

Another option to look at is -C (command list). This option is used to list only those processes that match the specified command name. For example, we can run **ps -C sshd** to view all *sshd* processes running on the system.

Viewing and Monitoring Processes with top

The other popular tool for viewing process information is the *top* command. This command displays the statistics in real-time and continuously, and may be helpful in identifying possible performance issues on the system. A sample default output screen from a running *top* session is shown below:

```
[user1@centos73 ~]$ top
top - 11:20:25 up 5 min,  2 users,  load average: 0.01, 0.12, 0.08
Tasks: 162 total,   1 running, 161 sleeping,   0 stopped,   0 zombie
%Cpu(s):  0.0 us,  0.2 sy,  0.0 ni, 99.8 id,  0.0 wa,  0.0 hi,  0.0 si,  0.0 st
KiB Mem :  1016344 total,   304620 free,   322324 used,   389400 buff/cache
KiB Swap:   918520 total,   918520 free,        0 used.   514376 avail Mem

  PID USER      PR  NI    VIRT    RES    SHR S  %CPU %MEM     TIME+ COMMAND
  103 root      20   0       0      0      0 S   0.3  0.0   0:00.16 kworker/0:3
  424 root      20   0       0      0      0 S   0.3  0.0   0:00.15 xfsaild/dm+
  741 root      20   0   19168   1180    960 S   0.3  0.1   0:00.02 irqbalance
 2877 user1     20   0  157712   2296   1560 R   0.3  0.2   0:00.23 top
    1 root      20   0  128092   6704   3956 S   0.0  0.7   0:01.92 systemd
    2 root      20   0       0      0      0 S   0.0  0.0   0:00.00 kthreadd
    3 root      20   0       0      0      0 S   0.0  0.0   0:00.14 ksoftirqd/0
    4 root      20   0       0      0      0 S   0.0  0.0   0:00.00 kworker/0:0
    5 root       0 -20       0      0      0 S   0.0  0.0   0:00.00 kworker/0:+
    7 root      rt   0       0      0      0 S   0.0  0.0   0:00.00 migration/0
```

Press q or Ctrl+c to quit *top*.

The default *top* screen output may be divided into two major portions: the summary portion and the tasks portion. The summary area spreads over the first five lines of the screen, and it shows the information as follows:

- Line 1: shows the system uptime, number of users logged in, and system load averages over the period of 1, 5, and 15 minutes.
- Line 2: displays the task (or process) information, which includes the total number of tasks running on the system and how many of them are in running, sleeping, stopped, and zombie states. See the next subsection for process state description.
- Line 3: shows processor usage that includes the CPU time in percentage spent in running user and system processes, in idling and waiting, and so on.
- Line 4: depicts memory utilization that includes the total amount of memory allocated to the system, and how much of it is free, in use, and allocated for use in buffering and caching.
- Line 5: displays swap (virtual memory) usage that includes the total amount of swap allocated to the system, and how much of it is free and in use. The "avail Mem" shows an estimate of the amount of memory available for starting new processes without using the swap.

The second major portion in the default output of the *top* command displays the details for each process in 12 columns as described below:

- Columns 1 and 2: indicate the process identifier (PID) and owner (USER).
- Columns 3 and 4: display the process priority (PR) and nice value (NI).
- Columns 5 and 6: depict amounts of virtual memory (VIRT) and non-swapped resident memory (RES) in use.
- Column 7: shows the amount of shareable memory available to the process (SHR).
- Column 8: represents the process status (S).
- Columns 9 and 10: express the CPU (%CPU) and memory (%MEM) utilization.
- Column 11: depicts the CPU time in hundredths of a second (TIME+).
- Column 12: identifies the process name (COMMAND).

While in *top*, you can press "o" to re-sequence the process list, "f" to add or remove fields, "F" to select the field to sort on, and "h" to obtain help. *top* is highly customizable. See the command's manual pages for details.

Process States

A process changes its operating state multiple times during its lifecycle. Factors such as load on the processor, availability of free memory, priority of the process, and response from other applications affect how often a process jumps from one operating state to another. It may be in a non-running condition for a while or waiting for some other process to feed it information so that it can continue to run. There are five basic process states, as illustrated in Figure 4-1.

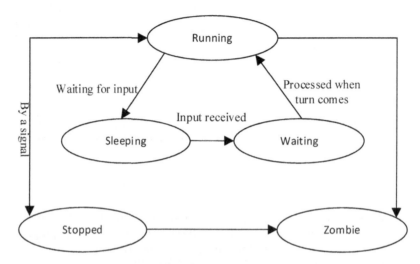

Figure 4-1 Process State Transition

Each process is in one state at any given time. These states are *running*, *sleeping*, *waiting*, *stopped*, and *zombie*, and are explained below:

Running: the process is being executed by the system CPU.

Sleeping: the process is waiting for input from a user or another process.

Waiting: the process has received the input it was awaiting and is now ready to run as soon as its turn arrives.

Stopped: the process is currently halted and will not run even when its turn comes unless a signal is sent to change its behavior. (Signals are explained later in this chapter.)

Zombie: the process is dead. A zombie process exists in the process table alongside other process entries, but it takes up no resources. Its entry is retained until its parent process permits it to die. A zombie process is also called a *defunct* process.

Listing a Specific Process

Though the tools discussed so far provide a lot of information about processes including their PIDs, Linux offers the *pidof* and *pgrep* commands to list only the PID of a specific process. These commands have a few switches available to modify their behavior; however, their most elementary use is to pass a process name as an argument to view its PID. For instance, to list the PID of the *rsyslogd* daemon, use either of the following:

```
[user1@centos73 ~]$ pidof rsyslogd
[user1@centos73 ~]$ pgrep rsyslogd
1035
```

Listing Processes by User and Group Ownership

A process can be listed by its ownership or owning group. We can use the *ps* command for this purpose. For example, to list all processes owned by *user1*, specify the -U (or -u) option with the command and then the username:

```
[user1@centos73 ~]$ ps -U user1
  PID  TTY TIME     CMD
2840  ?      00:00:01  sshd
2841  pts/0 00:00:00  bash
5332  pts/0 00:00:00  ps
```

The command lists the PID, TTY, TIME, and CMD name for all processes owned by *user1*. We can specify the -G (or -g) option instead and the name of an owning group to print processes associated with that group only:

```
[user1@centos73 ~]$ ps -G user1
  PID  TTY TIME     CMD
2840  ?      00:00:01  sshd
2841  pts/0 00:00:00  bash
5333  pts/0 00:00:00  ps
```

Understanding Process Niceness

A process is spawned at a certain priority, which is established at initiation based on a numeric value called *niceness* (a.k.a. a *nice* value). There are 40 niceness values, with -20 being the highest or the most favorable to the process, and +19 being the lowest or the least favorable to the process. Most system-started processes run at the default niceness of 0. A higher niceness lowers the execution priority of a process, and a lower niceness increases it. In other words, a process running at a higher priority gets more CPU attention. A child process inherits the niceness of its calling process in calculating its priority. Though we normally run programs at the default niceness, we may choose to initiate them at a different niceness to adjust their priority based on urgency and system load. As a regular user, you can only make your processes nicer; however, the *root* user can modify the niceness of any process.

Viewing and Changing Process Niceness

The current process priorities and niceness values can be viewed with the *ps* or the *top* command. With *ps*, add the -l option to the "ef" options and look for the priority (PRI, seventh column), which is calculated based on the niceness value (NI, eighth column):

```
[user1@centos73 ~]$ ps -efl
F S UID       PID PPID C PRI NI ADDR SZ WCHAN  STIME TTY         TIME CMD
4 S root        1    0 0  80  0 - 32023 ep_pol 11:14 ?       00:00:01 /usr/lib/systemd/sys
1 S root        2    0 0  80  0 -     0 kthrea 11:14 ?       00:00:00 [kthreadd]
1 S root        3    2 0  80  0 -     0 smpboo 11:14 ?       00:00:00 [ksoftirqd/0]
1 S root        4    2 0  80  0 -     0 worker 11:14 ?       00:00:00 [kworker/0:0]
1 S root        5    2 0  60 -20 -    0 worker 11:14 ?       00:00:00 [kworker/0:0H]
1 S root        7    2 0 -40  - -     0 smpboo 11:14 ?       00:00:00 [migration/0]
1 S root        8    2 0  80  0 -     0 rcu_gp 11:14 ?       00:00:00 [rcu_bh]
1 S root        9    2 0  80  0 -     0 rcu_gp 11:14 ?       00:00:00 [rcu_sched]
```

The above output indicates the use of the default niceness for the first three processes and the highest niceness of -20 for the fourth one. These values are used by the process scheduler to adjust their execution time on the CPU.

We can check the default niceness using the *nice* command:

```
[user1@centos73 ~]$ nice
0
```

A different niceness may be assigned to a program or command at its startup. For example, to run the *top* command at a lower priority with a nice value of +2, use any of the following:

```
[user1@centos73 ~]$ nice -2 top
[user1@centos73 ~]$ nice -n 2 top
[user1@centos73 ~]$ nice --adjustment 2 top
```

Open another terminal window and run the *ps* command to validate. Look for the priority and nice values in columns 7 and 8.

```
[user1@centos73 ~]$ ps -el | grep top
0  T  1000  7643 2841  0  82  2 - 38764  signal pts/0  00:00:00  top
```

To run the same program at a higher priority with a niceness of -10, specify the value with a pair of dashes. You must be *root* in order to run a program at a higher priority.

```
[root@centos73 ~]# nice --10 top
```

You may run the above as **nice -n -10 top** or **nice --adjustment -10 top**. Validate in the other window:

```
[root@centos73 ~]# ps -el | grep top
4  T  0  7784 7751  0  70 -10 - 38764  signal pts/0  00:00:00  top
```

As you can see, the process is running at a higher priority (70) with a nice value of -10.

Renicing a Running Process

The niceness of a running process may be altered using the *renice* command. This adjustment affects the priority at which the process is running. For example, to change the niceness of the running *top* session from -10 to +5, specify the PID (7784 from above) with the *renice* command:

```
[root@centos73 ~]# renice 5 7784 ; ps -l 7784
7784 (process ID) old priority -10, new priority 5
```

We can validate the above change with *ps* or *top*.

> The semicolon (;) character used in the example is a special character that serves the purpose of separating two or more independent commands on the same command line.

The *renice* command also allows us to alter the nice values of all the processes owned by a specific user or members of a particular group with the use of the -u or -g option. There are a few additional options available with this command. Refer to the command's manual pages for usage help.

Controlling Processes with Signals

As you know, a system may have hundreds or thousands of current processes running on it. Sometimes it becomes necessary to alert a process of an event. This is done by sending a control signal to the process. Processes may use signals to alert each other as well. The receiving process halts its execution as soon as it gets the signal and takes an appropriate action as per the instructions enclosed in the signal. The instructions may include terminating the process gracefully, killing it abruptly, or forcing it to re-read its configuration.

There are a number of signals available for use, but only a few are common. Each signal is associated with a unique numeric identifier, a name, and an action. A list of available signals can be viewed with the *kill* command using the -l option:

```
[user1@centos73 ~]$ kill -l
 1) SIGHUP       2) SIGINT       3) SIGQUIT      4) SIGILL       5) SIGTRAP
 6) SIGABRT      7) SIGBUS       8) SIGFPE       9) SIGKILL     10) SIGUSR1
11) SIGSEGV     12) SIGUSR2     13) SIGPIPE     14) SIGALRM     15) SIGTERM
16) SIGSTKFLT   17) SIGCHLD     18) SIGCONT     19) SIGSTOP     20) SIGTSTP
21) SIGTTIN     22) SIGTTOU     23) SIGURG      24) SIGXCPU     25) SIGXFSZ
26) SIGVTALRM   27) SIGPROF     28) SIGWINCH    29) SIGIO       30) SIGPWR
31) SIGSYS      34) SIGRTMIN    35) SIGRTMIN+1  36) SIGRTMIN+2  37) SIGRTMIN+3
38) SIGRTMIN+4  39) SIGRTMIN+5  40) SIGRTMIN+6  41) SIGRTMIN+7  42) SIGRTMIN+8
43) SIGRTMIN+9  44) SIGRTMIN+10 45) SIGRTMIN+11 46) SIGRTMIN+12 47) SIGRTMIN+13
48) SIGRTMIN+14 49) SIGRTMIN+15 50) SIGRTMAX-14 51) SIGRTMAX-13 52) SIGRTMAX-12
53) SIGRTMAX-11 54) SIGRTMAX-10 55) SIGRTMAX-9  56) SIGRTMAX-8  57) SIGRTMAX-7
58) SIGRTMAX-6  59) SIGRTMAX-5  60) SIGRTMAX-4  61) SIGRTMAX-3  62) SIGRTMAX-2
63) SIGRTMAX-1  64) SIGRTMAX
```

The output shows 64 signals available for process-to-process and user-to-process communication. Table 4-4 describes the control signals that are most often used.

Signal Number	Signal Name	Action
1	SIGHUP	Hang up signal causes a process to disconnect itself from a closed terminal that it was tied to. Also used to instruct a running daemon to re-read its configuration without a restart.
2	SIGINT	The ^c (Ctrl+c) signal issued on the controlling terminal to interrupt the execution of a process
9	SIGKILL	Terminates a process abruptly

Signal Number	Signal Name	Action
15	SIGTERM	Sends a soft termination signal to stop a process in an orderly fashion. This is the default signal if none is specified with the command.
18	SIGCONT	Same as using the bg command
19	SIGSTOP	Same as using Ctrl+z to suspend a job
20	SIGTSTP	Same as using the fg command

Table 4-4 Control Signals

The commands used to pass a signal to a process are *kill* and *pkill*. These commands are usually used to terminate a process. Ordinary users can kill processes that they own, while the *root* user can kill any process running on the system without caring about its ownership.

The *kill* command requires one or more PIDs, and the *pkill* command requires one or more process names to send a signal to. We may specify a non-default single name or number with either utility.

Let's look at a few examples to understand the usage of these tools.

To pass the soft termination signal to the *crond* daemon, use either of the following:

```
[root@centos73 ~]# pkill crond
[root@centos73 ~]# kill `pidof crond`
```

The *pidof* command in the above example was used to discover the PID of the *crond* process and was enclosed with its argument in backticks (you may also use the *pgrep* command to determine the PID of a process, as demonstrated in the next example). You can use **ps -ef | grep crond** to confirm the termination.

Using the *pkill* or *kill* command without specifying a signal name or number sends the default signal of 15 to the process. This signal may or not terminate the process. Some processes ignore this signal as they might be in a waiting state. Such processes may be terminated forcefully using signal 9 in any of the following ways:

```
[root@centos73 ~]# pkill -9 crond
[root@centos73 ~]# pkill -s SIGKILL crond
[root@centos73 ~]# kill -9 `pgrep crond`
```

You may run the *killall* command to terminate all processes that match a criterion. Here is how you can use this command to kill all *crond* processes (assuming there are many of them running):

```
[root@centos73 ~]# killall crond
```

There are plenty of options available with the *kill*, *killall*, *pkill*, *pgrep*, and *pidof* commands. Consult their manual pages for more details.

Signaling a Program to Continue Running after User Logout

When a command or program is executed, it ties itself to the terminal session where it is initiated and does not release the control to the shell until the command or program finishes execution.

During this time, if the terminal session is closed, terminated, or the user logs off, the command or program that was running is also terminated. Imagine if a large file transfer of hundreds of GBs is about to conclude when this unwanted termination occurs. This would be very frustrating.

To avoid such a situation, use the *nohup* (no hang up) command to execute commands or programs that need to run for extended periods without being interrupted or terminated. For example, to copy */usr/share* directory containing ~1.3GB of data (check the size with **du -sh /usr/share**) to */opt/data*, issue the *cp* command as the *root* user as follows:

```
[root@centos73 ~]# mkdir /opt/data ; nohup cp -rp /usr/share /opt/data &
```

The ampersand (&) sign is used to instruct the shell to run the copy in background. While the copy is running, exit and close the terminal screen, open another terminal and run **ps -ef | grep nohup**. You will see the process still running.

nohup also records the output and error messages generated during the execution of the specified command to a file called, by default, *nohup.out*. You may view the contents of this file during the command execution with **tail -f nohup.out**, or later with *cat*, *less*, or any other text file-viewing utility.

Running and Controlling Jobs in Foreground and Background

By default, any program or command we issue runs in the foreground and it ties itself to the terminal window where it is initiated. It can be moved to run in the background so that the associated terminal session is released for running additional commands or programs. A *job* is a process that is started in the background and controlled by the terminal where it is spawned. Just like any other process that is started on the system, a job is also assigned a PID by the kernel and, additionally, a job ID by the shell. Unlike a normal process, a job does not hold the terminal window where it is initiated. This enables us to run other programs from the same terminal window.

The shell allows running multiple jobs simultaneously, including transferring large amounts of data and running application programs in the background.

Jobs running in the background can be brought to foreground, taken to the background, suspended, or stopped. The management of several jobs within a shell environment is called *job control*.

The shell offers a few commands and control sequences for administering the jobs. See Table 4-5.

Command	Description
jobs	Shell built-in command to display jobs
bg	Shell built-in command to move a job to the background or restart a job in the background that was suspended with Ctrl+z
fg	Shell built-in command to move a job to the foreground
Ctrl+z	Suspends a foreground job and allows the terminal window to be used for other purposes

Table 4-5 Job Control

To run a job in the background, type the command at the command prompt followed by the ampersand (&) operator.

The examples below run commands *top* and *vi* in the background. The shell displays their assigned job IDs that are enclosed within square brackets and PIDs. The job IDs allow us to control the jobs and the PIDs are used by the kernel to manage the processes.

```
[user1@centos73 ~]$ top &
[1]  11508
[user1@centos73 ~]$ vi testfile1 &
[2]  11509
[1]+ Stopped          top
```

Issue the *jobs* command with the -l switch to view all running jobs:

```
[user1@centos73 ~]$ jobs -l
[1]- 11508  Stopped  (signal)      top
[2]+ 11509  Stopped  (tty output)  vim testfile1
```

The plus (+) sign indicates the current background job and the minus (-) sign signifies the previous job. "Stopped" indicates that the jobs are currently suspended and can be signaled to continue their execution in the background with the *bg* command or to bring them back to the foreground with using the *fg* command.

To bring job ID 1 to the foreground and start running it:

```
[user1@centos73 ~]$ fg %1
```

To suspend job ID 1, press ^z followed by **bg %1** to let it run the background.

To terminate job ID 1, supply its PID to the *kill* command:

```
[user1@centos73 ~]$ kill 11508
```

A message is displayed when a background job ends its execution:

```
[2] + Done vi testfile1 &
```

Splitting a Terminal among Multiple Terminals using Screen

Linux offers a tool called *screen* that allows us to split a terminal window into multiple virtual screens enabling us to run different programs in each one of them independent of one another. The *screen* program comes with a multitude of options and control sequences that we can use to manage and manipulate the virtual screens. It allows copy-and-paste text among screens, view and terminate screens, switch between screens, detach and re-attach screens, and so on.

If the screen program is not already installed on your system, you need to run **yum install -y screen** on centos73 or **sudo apt-get install screen** on ubuntu14 to install it. See Chapter 5 "Managing Shared Libraries and Software Packages" for help in case of issues.

Let's look at a few common control sequences summarized in Table 4-6 that will allow us to create, list, switch between, terminate, and attach/detach virtual screens. These default sequences begin with Ctrl+a (may also be represented as ^a or C-a; press Ctrl and a together and then release them) followed by another keystroke. The Ctrl key on the left-hand side of the keyboard works.

Sequence	Description
^ac	Creates a virtual screen, starts a shell process in it, and switches to it
^a?	Displays a list of available control sequences
^an	Switches to the next screen
^aBackSpace	Switches to the previous screen
^ad	Detaches the screen from the terminal
^aD	Detaches the screen from the terminal and log out
^ak	Kill the current screen
^a0...9	Switch to the selected screen
^aw	Lists active screens
^aS	Splits the current screen into two new ones

Table 4-6 Virtual Screen Control Sequences

To start the screen program and switch into it right away, type *screen* at the command prompt and press the Enter key. Then type **screen -list** to view a list of active screens on the system:

```
[user1@centos73 ~]$ screen
[user1@centos73 ~]$ screen -list
There is a screen on:
        21239.pts-0.centos73    (Attached)
1 Socket in /var/run/screen/S-user1.
```

The output shows that there is one screen program running on the system and it is attached to the terminal window where it was started. Now press ^ac and it should start a new screen with a shell program started in it. Type a simple command, such as **ls**. Press ^a0 and ^a1 (or ^an instead) to switch between screens 0 and 1. You will see the output of *ls* on one screen and nothing on the other one. Press ^aS to split the screen into two, and then use ^aTAB to switch to the new screen. While in the new screen, press ^ac to start the shell program. You can switch between the split screens using ^aTAB. Press ^ak and then "y" to kill the active screen or press ^d for screen termination.

Try a few other control sequences while you are in the screen program. It may be a little frustrating at the beginning, but you'll find it useful once you become accustomed to using it. It is recommended to view the manual pages of this program for more details.

Chapter Summary

In this chapter, we explored the bash shell, which has numerous features that are essential for users and administrators. These features included variable settings, command prompt customization using substitution techniques, command history, wildcarding in file globbing, I/O/E redirection, and sending a command's output to one or more specified destinations. Moreover, we looked at the difference between the shell's internal and external commands and how to invoke various commands that were located within or beyond a defined path.

In addition, we studied processes and their management. It is vital for users and administrators to have a strong understanding of running processes, resources they are consuming, process owners, process execution priorities, etc. Users and administrators should learn how to list processes in a variety of ways. We looked at the five process states, niceness and reniceness for increasing and decreasing a process's priority, and the signals and how they were passed to running processes to perform an action on them.

Finally, we reviewed how to initiate a program or command to continue to run even if the user who initiated it logs off and the associated terminal session is terminated. We examined how to split a user terminal into multiple virtual terminal screens to allow them to run a different program in each one of them.

Chapter Review at a Glance

The following presents a one-sentence review of each key topic discussed in this chapter:

- Users communicate with the operating system through one of many available shells, of which the Bash shell is the default in most major Linux distributions.

- The Bash shell presents a number of features—manipulating variables; substituting variables, commands, tilde, and history; redirecting input, output, and error streams from and to non-default locations; redirecting standard input using here document and here string; editing text at the command line; using special characters in file globbing; employing other metacharacters; setting aliases for lengthy commands; executing a block of commands one-time or continuously based on the success or failure of a condition; and writing shell scripts for task automation.

- Internal commands are part of the shell binary file and they are executed by the shell without invoking a sub-shell for them.

- External commands are stored in various directories—/usr/bin (or /bin) and /usr/sbin (or /sbin)—and the shell creates a sub-shell for their execution.

- A variable holds an assigned value in memory for use by commands, programs, and applications.

- The value of a local variable is available only in the current shell; the value of an environment variable is available in sub-shells of the invoking shell as well.

- Many environment variables are automatically set for users upon their logging in to the system through various system-wide (global) and per-user initialization files.

- Commands may be invoked without specifying their absolute pathnames from anywhere in the directory tree, provided the directory the commands are located in are defined in the PATH variable; commands that are not defined in the PATH must be executed using their full pathnames.

- The asterisk (*), question mark (?), and square brackets ([]) special characters are used in filename globbing to match all characters, one character, and a range (or any) of characters.

- A here document is an input redirection type that is used to feed input to a command.

- A here string is an input redirection type that is used to feed the output of one or more commands as input.

- The pipe (|) is a special character that allows the use of a command output as input by another command.

- The tee command is a Linux filter that is used to send the output of a command to two or more output destinations.

- The list operators are used to separate one command from the other by either using a simple semicolon (;) character or performing a logical AND or OR operation.

- A process is any command, program, or application that is running on the system.

- Every process running on the system is assigned a unique process identifier (PID), which is used throughout its lifecycle to handle it by the operating system.

- Daemon processes run in the background and they provide services to other server or client processes.

- A process is always held in one of the five operating states—running, sleeping, waiting, stopped, or zombie.

- A process niceness or nice value controls the execution priority of a process and it may be specified at the time of invoking the command (process) or changed during command execution.

- A control signal may be passed to a process to alert the process of an event, such as smooth or sudden termination, re-reading of its configuration file, etc.

- A user process can be started in a way to make it immune to certain termination signals.

- Commands and programs running on the system may be switched between foreground or background while continue to run.

- A Linux terminal screen can be divided into multiple virtual terminal screens to allow the execution of different programs in each screen independent of one another.

- Commands we learned in this chapter are: bash, echo, env, export, set, unset, alias, unalias, history, which, whereis, type, tee, ps, top, pidof, pgrep, nice, renice, kill, pkill, killall, nohup, jobs, fg, bg, and screen.

- Files and directories we discussed in this chapter are: ~/.bash_history and nohup.out.

Chapter 5

Managing Shared Libraries and Software Packages

This chapter describes the following major topics:

➢ Understand shared libraries, their versions, and where they are stored
➢ List shared library dependencies and add their storage locations to environment variable and cache
➢ Overview of Debian and Red Hat packages, their naming, dependencies, databases, and commandsets
➢ Perform package management tasks—query, install, reconfigure, verify, remove, and purge—with dpkg
➢ Comprehend software repository concepts and use available repositories – Debian
➢ Perform package management tasks—download, install, update, upgrade, remove, search, list, display info, and list dependencies—with APT toolset
➢ Compare apt, apt-get, and apt-cache commands
➢ Understand and use aptitude
➢ Perform package management tasks—query, install, upgrade, freshen, verify, remove, and extract files—with rpm
➢ Comprehend software repository concepts and use available repositories – Red Hat
➢ Perform package management tasks—list, install, update, reinstall, display info, query, remove, and download—with yum

102.3 Manage shared libraries [this entire objective is described in this chapter]

27. Identify shared libraries
28. Identify the typical locations of system libraries
29. Load shared libraries

The following is a partial list of the used files, terms and utilities: ldd, ldconfig,
/etc/ld.so.conf, LD_LIBRARY_PATH

102.4 Use Debian package management [this entire objective is described in this
chapter]

30. Install, upgrade and uninstall Debian binary packages
31. Find packages containing specific files or libraries which may or may not be
installed
32. Obtain package information like version, content, dependencies, package integrity
and installation status (whether or not the package is installed)

The following is a partial list of the used files, terms and utilities: /etc/apt/sources.list,
dpkg, dpkg-reconfigure, apt-get, apt-cache, and aptitude

102.5 Use RPM and YUM package management [this entire objective is described
in this chapter]

33. Install, re-install, upgrade and remove packages using RPM and YUM
34. Obtain information on RPM packages such as version, status, dependencies,
integrity and signatures
35. Determine what files a package provides, as well as find which package a specific
file comes from

The following is a partial list of the used files, terms and utilities: rpm, rpm2cpio,
/etc/yum.conf, /etc/yum.repos.d/, yum, and yumdownloader

A shared library is a file that contains compiled functions, and is loaded in memory. It is accessed and used by several programs and applications simultaneously and as required. Developers add links to shared libraries in their programs to take advantage of shared library code, which also helps lower the overall system memory utilization.

Linux is essentially a collection of thousands of compiled software packages that are bundled for distribution. These packages are signed, tested, and certified before dissemination. Debian and Red Hat, and their derivatives, follow a convention to name and identify their packages. Packages contain necessary files and metadata. They may be downloaded and saved locally, or on network shares for quick access, and they may require the presence of one or more other packages before they can be successfully installed. Once packages have been installed and their metadata stored in package database, each attempt to update the packages will also update their corresponding metadata. Package manipulation toolsets for both Debian and Red Hat (and their offshoots) are different; however, they perform the same or similar management operations. They both include a mechanism to take care of package dependencies automatically.

Shared Libraries

Shared libraries are software codes that programs, commands, and applications (collectively called *executables*) use for their successful installation or execution. They are stored in files and contain functions that executables may reference as and when they need them. Programmers, in their executables, reference specific functions in those shared libraries.

Every shared library has two names: a logical name and a real name. A *logical name*, also referred to as a *soname* (*shared object name*), contains the prefix "lib" to identify the file as a library file, a name, the ".so" (*shared object*) extension, a period, and a version number (in some cases the version number and extension are reversed). As an example, the following shows the listing of a soname called *libblkid.so.1* located in the */usr/lib64* directory on *centos73*:

```
[user1@centos73 ~]$ ll /usr/lib64/libblkid.so*
lrwxrwxrwx. 1 root root      17 Dec 21 09:06 libblkid.so.1 -> libblkid.so.1.1.0
-rwxr-xr-x. 1 root root 256960 Nov 5 18:27 libblkid.so.1.1.0
```

In this logical name, "lib" is the prefix, "blkid" is the library name, ".so" is the extension, and ".1" is the version number.

A *real name*, on the other hand, is the actual filename that stores the library code, and to which the soname points to. In the above *ll* command output, *libblkid.so.1.1.0* is the real name of the library file. Notice that it has a period, a minor number (1), another period, and a release number (0) appended to the soname. This granular information facilitates the co-existence of multiple versions of the same library on the system.

Static vs. Shared Libraries

There are two types of libraries: static and shared (or dynamic). A *static library* includes all the functions that an executable requires during its installation, build, or execution, and it is embedded in that executable. Such executables are complete and do not rely on external libraries to exist for their operation. These executables are larger in size, but they alleviate the need of installing additional libraries as pre-requisites. From a memory perspective, each executable that requires a

---

concurrent access to an identical or similar static library code loads that code into the memory, which results in an increased memory utilization.

A *shared library*, on the other hand, is referenced by executables for using specific functions embedded within it. It is also referred to as a *dynamic library*. The use of dynamic libraries help keep the executables smaller in size and are typically installed as pre-requisites. The other major benefit with using dynamic libraries is the fact that multiple executables can share the same copy of the library loaded in the memory, which results in less memory consumption. Given the benefits, dynamic libraries are more prevalent and their use is preferred.

An instance of a shared library file was listed earlier. We can confirm that this library is in fact a shared library by running the *file* command on it:

```
[user1@centos73 ~]$ file /usr/lib64/libblkid.so.1.1.0
/usr/lib64/libblkid.so.1.1.0: ELF 64-bit LSB shared object, x86-64, version 1 (SYSV), dynamically
linked, BuildID[sha1]=85971f50b0e6338ff3551f3cb0cfd9e834dfa2af, stripped
```

The bolded text verifies that it is a dynamic shared library.

32-Bit and 64-Bit Library Versions and their Locations

Libraries are available in both 32-bit and 64-bit versions. The 32-bit versions are stored in the */lib* or */usr/lib* directory, and the 64-bit versions are stored under */lib64* or */usr/lib64*. On newer Linux distributions, */lib* is a soft link to */usr/lib*, and */lib64* points to */usr/lib64*. Here is a listing of the standard directories that store library files:

```
[user1@centos73 ~]$ ls /lib
[user1@centos73 ~]$ ls /lib64
```

You may find additional library files located under */usr/libexec* and */usr/local*. These and any other paths may be added to the LD_LIBRARY_PATH environment variable or to the library cache discussed afterward. The standard locations (a.k.a. *trusted library locations*)—*/lib*, */usr/lib*, */lib64*, and */usr/lib64*—are always included in the library search path whether or not they are defined through this variable.

A typical 64-bit Linux system also has the required 32-bit libraries in addition to the 64-bit ones to support 32-bit executables.

Viewing Shared Library Dependencies

Linux allows us to list the libraries that are required by executables and other libraries to function properly. It provides us with the *ldd* (*list dynamic dependencies*) command to accomplish this purpose.

The *ldd* command shows us the dependencies for an executable or another library. The following example displays the libraries that the *who* command requires in order to work:

```
[user1@centos73 ~]$ ldd $(which who)
    linux-vdso.so.1 =>  (0x00007ffc85ffa000)
    libc.so.6 => /lib64/libc.so.6 (0x00007f27147bb000)
    /lib64/ld-linux-x86-64.so.2 (0x00007f2714b8f000)
```

The output indicates the soname and real names of the library files used by *who*. Repeat the above command but with the -v (verbose) option to see more details. You may also use the -u (unused) option to view unused direct dependencies.

The "$(which who)" in the above example is a preferred method of running a command (*who* in this case) when you're not sure of its exact path.

This command proves useful in determining the library names and locations for an executable that fails to run due to a missing or unavailable library, or an incorrect path. You may need to ascertain dependencies for each of these listed libraries as well in order to identify their dependencies and potential issues with them.

Adding Library Locations to the LD_LIBRARY_PATH Variable

The LD_LIBRARY_PATH environment variable contains a colon-separated list of directory paths that we want to be searched for shared libraries prior to exploring the ones recorded in the */etc/ld.so.cache* file. This may need to be done if we want an application such as Oracle DB to use a specific set of library files not located at standard directory locations. The following shows an example of setting this variable and specifying the libraries that are located, for instance, under */oracle/lib64* and */oracle/lib*:

```
[user1@centos73 ~]$ export LD_LIBRARY_PATH=/oracle/lib64:/oracle/lib
```

This variable is typically set through an application startup script to support a successful launch of the application or via a user initialization file created for the application. User initialization files are discussed in Chapter 8 "Administering Partitions, File Systems, and Swap." In either case, *root* privileges are not required to define this variable.

Notice the resemblance between the use and specification of this variable to that of the PATH variable. Both variables take a colon-separated list of directory paths; however, their purposes are different.

Adding Shared Library Locations to the Cache

An alternative approach to adding custom library locations to the search path is through one of the configuration files and then rebuilding the library cache. This is done automatically for applications and programs during their installation on the system. However, we can also accomplish this by following a simple two-step manual process for an existing shared library that is not located in a trusted library directory.

The first step in this process is to add the absolute path of the custom library location directly to the library configuration file */etc/ld.so.conf* or to one of the *.conf* files placed under the */etc/ld.so.conf.d* directory. Configuration files under this directory are processed as per the statement "include ld.so.conf.d/*.conf" present by default in *ld.so.conf*.

The second step is to run the **ldconfig** command without any options. This command uses the settings from all of these configuration files and update the cache file */etc/ld.so.cache* with the latest path and link information for all libraries.

The cache file stores the information in binary format allowing the referencing executables to search faster. The contents of this file can be read by running *ldconfig* with the -p switch:

```
[user1@centos73 ~]$ ldconfig -p
```

Depending on the number of libraries currently available on the system, the above output can be very long. You can pipe the output to the *grep* command to look for a specific library entry if needed.

The *ldconfig* command has other interesting switches available that you may explore. These options include: -v for detailed output; -n to use a custom directory path specified at the command line while ignoring the paths in the configuration files and to the trusted directories; -N to not rebuild the cache; -X to not update the links, and so on. Read the manual pages of this command for further details.

Debian Package Overview

Debian Linux and its derivatives are essentially a set of software packages grouped together to form an operating system. They are prepackaged for installation and assembled for various intended uses. They are built around the Linux kernel and include thousands of packages that are digitally signed, tested, and certified. There are plenty of concepts associated with packages and package management that are discussed in the following subsections.

Packages and Packaging

A *package* is a group of files organized in a directory structure along with metadata and intelligence that make up a software application. There are *binary* (or *installable*) and *source* packages. Binary packages are installation-ready and are bundled for distribution with the .deb extension. They contain install scripts, pre- and post-installation scripts, executables, configuration files, library files, and manual pages and other documentation.

The package metadata includes the package version, installation location, checksum values, and a list of included files. This metadata is exploited by package administration tools for package handling.

The package intelligence is used by package installation tools for a successful completion of the package installation process. It may include what pre-requisites to install, what user account to create and with what attributes, what directories to create, what soft links to create, and so on. The intelligence also includes the reverse of this process for uninstallation.

Source packages come with the original unmodified version of the software that may be unpacked, modified as desired, and repackaged in the binary format for installation or distribution. They usually include a compressed tarball, a patch file, and a .dsc file, which describes the source package and provides other useful information about the package.

Package Naming

Debian and derivatives follow a standard convention for naming their installable packages. Typically, there are four parts to a package name: (1) the package name, (2) the package version, (3) the Debian revision, and (4) the processor architecture that the package is built for. An installable package name always has the .deb extension; however, this extension is removed after the package has installed.

For example, if a package name is tar_1.27.1-2+b1_i386.deb, its installed name would be tar-1.27.1-2+b1.i386. Here is a description of each part of the package:

- ✓ **tar** – package name
- ✓ **1.27.1** – package version
- ✓ **2+b1** – Debian revision
- ✓ **i386** – processor architecture the package is produced for
- ✓ **.deb** – the extension

Package Dependency

An installable package may require the presence of one or more additional packages in order to be installed successfully. Likewise, a software package component may require the functionality provided by one or more other packages to exist in order to operate as expected. This is referred to as *package dependency*, where one package depends on one or more other packages for installation or execution.

Package Database

Metadata for installed packages is stored in the */var/lib/dpkg* directory. This directory location is referenced by package management tools to obtain details about installed and available packages for verifying dependencies and conflicts, upgrading and uninstalling existing packages, adding new packages, and performing other package manipulation tasks. This directory is referred to as the *administration directory*, as it contains more than just the package information.

Debian Package Management Toolset

The primary tool for package management on Debian Linux and its spinoffs is called *dpkg* (*debian packager*). This tool offers a number of options for easy software handling; however, one major drawback with using this tool is that it does not automatically fetch and install dependent software if there are any required. To overcome this deficiency, more sophisticated tools available in the APT (*Advanced Package Tool*) library are employed, which deliver a convenient way for manipulating software, and the tools are able to find, get, and install dependencies on their own.

For those who prefer to use graphical tools over command line and text interfaces, Debian offers a GUI program called *synaptic*. Graphical tools are not discussed in this book due to their exclusion from the exam objectives.

Managing Debian Packages with dpkg

The *dpkg* utility gives us the ability to perform a number of package management tasks: installing, upgrading, querying, and removing packages. One caveat with this command is that it does not automatically satisfy package dependencies, which may become a big nuisance in the software installation and upgrade process. There are a couple of *dpkg* command variants that will be used in the examples below.

The dpkg Command

Before getting into the details of the *dpkg* command, let's review some of its common options described in Table 5-1. Both short and long option formats are provided. You may use either of the two that you feel comfortable with.

Option	Description
-c (--contents)	Lists the contents of an installable package
-i (--install)	Installs a new package or upgrades an existing package
-I (--info)	Displays information about an installable package
-l (--list)	Lists all or the specified installed package(s)
-L (--listfiles)	Lists files for an installed package
-p (--print-avail)	Displays information for an installed package
-P (--purge)	Eliminates a package completely including its configuration files
-r (--remove)	Removes a package but leaves its configuration files intact to avoid reconfiguration if the package is later reinstalled
-s (--status)	Shows the status information for a package including installed/not-installed, install size, version, dependencies, etc.
-S (--search)	Searches the installed package the specified file belongs to
-V	Verifies the integrity of package files

Table 5-1 dpkg Command Options

Let's perform a few package administrations tasks on *ubuntu14* for practice. Attach the Ubuntu ISO 14.04.5 image to the VM in the Oracle VirtualBox console, and then make it available on the system using the *mount* command. Here is how to mount the image on */mnt* directory in read-only mode:

```
user1@ubuntu14:~$ sudo mount -o ro /dev/cdrom /mnt
```

You can use the *df* command to confirm the mount:

```
user1@ubuntu14:~$ df -h | grep mnt
/dev/sr0     1.1G     1.1G     0     100%     /mnt
```

The above output confirms that the ISO image is mounted and is available via */mnt*.

The behavior of the *dpkg* command can be controlled with the settings in the */etc/dpkg/dpkg.cfg* file. By default, the only uncommented directive in this file sets the logging location for this utility to */var/log/dpkg.log* file. This log file records all activities performed with the *dpkg* command.

Acquiring Package Information

Querying packages searches for the required information and displays it on the screen. The following are some examples.

To query all installed packages:

```
user1@ubuntu14:~$ dpkg -l
Desired=Unknown/Install/Remove/Purge/Hold
| Status=Not/Inst/Conf-files/Unpacked/halF-conf/Half-inst/trig-aWait/Trig-pend
|/ Err?=(none)/Reinst-required (Status,Err: uppercase=bad)
||/ Name                    Version                        Architecture     Description
+++-=====================================================================================
ii  account-plugin-aim      3.8.6-0ubuntu9.2               amd64    Messaging account ****
ii  account-plugin-facebook 0.11+14.04.20140409.1-0ubuntu2 all      GNOME Control ****
. . . . . . . .
```

To query whether the specified package is installed:

    user1@ubuntu14:~$ **dpkg -l tar**

To print a list of the files included in the specified installed package:

    user1@ubuntu14:~$ **dpkg -L tar**

To print a list of the files included in the specified installable package:

    user1@ubuntu14:~$ **dpkg -c /mnt/pool/main/s/shim/shim_0.8-0ubuntu2_amd64.deb**

To identify which package owns the specified file:

    user1@ubuntu14:~$ **dpkg -S /usr/bin/who**

To display a package's installation status, version, architecture, dependent packages, description, and other information:

```
user1@ubuntu14:~$ dpkg -s tar
Package: tar
Essential: yes
Status: install ok installed
Priority: required
Section: utils
Installed-Size: 784
Maintainer: Ubuntu Developers <ubuntu-devel-discuss@lists.ubuntu.com>
Architecture: amd64
Multi-Arch: foreign
Version: 1.27.1-1
Replaces: cpio (<< 2.4.2-39)
Pre-Depends: libacl1 (>= 2.2.51-8), libc6 (>= 2.17), libselinux1 (>= 1.32)
Suggests: bzip2, ncompress, xz-utils, tar-scripts
Breaks: dpkg-dev (<< 1.14.26)
Conflicts: cpio (<= 2.4.2-38)
Conffiles:
 /etc/rmt 3c58b7cd13da1085eff0acc6a00f43c7
Description: GNU version of the tar archiving utility
 . . . . . . . .
```

To print more details about a package that *dpkg* shows with -s:

    user1@ubuntu14:~$ **dpkg -p tar**

To display information about an installable package:

    user1@ubuntu14:~$ **dpkg -I /mnt/pool/main/s/shim/shim_0.8-0ubuntu2_amd64.deb**

Installing a Package

Installing a package creates the necessary directory structure for the package and installs the required files. The following command will install a package called *shim_0.8-0ubuntu2_amd64.deb* on *ubuntu14*:

user1@ubuntu14:~$ **sudo dpkg -i /mnt/pool/main/s/shim/shim_0.8-0ubuntu2_amd64.deb**
(Reading database ... 169769 files and directories currently installed.)
Preparing to unpack .../shim_0.8-0ubuntu2_amd64.deb ...
Unpacking shim (0.8-0ubuntu2) over (0.8-0ubuntu2) ...
Setting up shim (0.8-0ubuntu2) ...

If this package requires the presence of any missing packages, you will see an error message related to failed dependencies. You must then install the missing packages first in order for this package to be loaded.

Reconfiguring an Installed Package

The package management system allows us to reconfigure an installed package using the *dpkg-reconfigure* command. This task resets the configuration to the original state of the time of package installation. The following example runs this command on the "shim" package that we have just installed:

user1@ubuntu14:~$ **sudo dpkg-reconfigure shim**

Verifying Package Integrity

Verifying an installed package compares the attributes of files in the package with the original file attributes saved and stored in the package database at the time the package was installed. The verification process uses the *dpkg* command with the -V option to compare the MD5 checksum value. The command returns to the prompt without displaying anything if the current and the stored checksum values are identical.

Let's run this check on the tar package:

user1@ubuntu14:~$ **dpkg -V tar**

There is no output and, hence, the package and its files are in their original state.

Removing vs. Purging a Package

Removing a package uninstalls the package but leaves the package's configuration files installed on the system.

To remove the package "shim," use the -r option:

user1@ubuntu14:~$ **sudo dpkg -r shim**
(Reading database ... 169768 files and directories currently installed.)
Removing shim (0.8-0ubuntu2) ...

If you want the configuration files associated with the package to be weeded out as well, you will need to specify the -P option with the command. The following re-runs the above command with -P:

```
user1@ubuntu14:~$  sudo dpkg -P shim
```

Either you attempt to remove a package or purge it, *dpkg* performs a dependency check to find whether another installed package requires the existence of this package. The removal attempt results in a failure if the command sees a dependency.

Managing Debian Packages with APT

The *Advanced Package Tool* (APT) is a package management toolset used on Debian, Ubuntu, and other similar Linux distributions. The principal software management command within APT is *apt-get*, which is a front-end to *dpkg*. The *apt-get* utility requires that your system have access to at least one software repository. Ubuntu repositories are accessible to everyone free of charge, and access to them is pre-configured on new OS installations in the */etc/apt/sources.list* file. The main benefit of using *apt-get* is its ability to resolve dependencies automatically by finding, downloading, and installing any required packages for a successful installation of the specified package.

apt-cache is another APT tool. The focus of this utility is to run queries and report information about the packages.

A newer tool within APT is referred to as *apt*. This command offers a set of functions that are also offered by *apt-get* and *apt-cache*. A later subsection elaborates the similarities and differences.

There is another popular package manipulation tool called *aptitude*. This is a menu-driven front-end text interface to the APT toolset that provides all functionalities that the entire APT toolset offer combined. This interactive program may also be invoked directly at the command line by specifying an intended action.

In the following subsections, we look at all the four tools: *apt-get*, *apt-cache*, *apt*, and *aptitude*.

Repository Configuration

The */etc/apt/sources.list* is the primary file that stores entries that point to configured software repositories for access and use by the APT commandset. By default, this file has a number of entries for pre-configured repositories, and more can be added to it or to a file under the */etc/apt/sources.list.d* directory. The APT toolset checks the *sources.list* file and then consults the files in the *sources.list.d* directory to spot a suitable source to obtain software packages from for installation. The following displays a snapshot of the default entries from the *sources.list* file. For brevity, we have instructed the *grep* command to exclude (-v) both commented (^#) and empty (^$) lines.

```
user1@ubuntu14:~$  cat /etc/apt/sources.list | grep -vE '^#|^$'
deb http://us.archive.ubuntu.com/ubuntu/ trusty main restricted
deb-src http://us.archive.ubuntu.com/ubuntu/ trusty main restricted
deb http://us.archive.ubuntu.com/ubuntu/ trusty-updates main restricted
deb-src http://us.archive.ubuntu.com/ubuntu/ trusty-updates main restricted
deb http://us.archive.ubuntu.com/ubuntu/ trusty universe
deb-src http://us.archive.ubuntu.com/ubuntu/ trusty universe
```

Each uncommented line in the file begins with the specification of a source type, such as deb or deb-src, followed by the web location, nickname for Ubuntu 14.04, and other relevant parameters.

The APT commandset references the package administration directory */var/lib/dpkg* to ascertain what packages and what version levels are already installed on the system before attempting an installation or upgrade. It then scans the repositories defined in the *sources.list* file or in one of the files under the *sources.list.d* directory to find an appropriate repository hosting the package, and continues with the installation.

The apt-get Command

The *apt-get* command may be used to perform a number of package administration tasks, and as we know, it invokes the *dpkg* utility in the background. Table 5-2 summarizes the common software handling tasks that *apt-get* can perform. For more operators and options, review the manual pages.

Subcommand	Description
autoremove	Removes unused installed packages automatically
clean	Clears downloaded packages from /var/cache/apt/archives directory
dist-upgrade	Same as "upgrade" plus it weeds out any extant packages for a potential conflict resolution with any new packages. Can be used to upgrade the OS version.
download	Downloads a package to the local directory
install	Installs or upgrades one or more packages. It downloads the specified packages under the /var/cache/apt/archives directory.
purge	Eradicates a package completely including its configuration files
remove	Erases a package but leaves its configuration files intact
update	Updates the package database with available package information
upgrade	Upgrades existing packages to their newest available versions

Table 5-2 Common apt-get Operations

Let's look at a few examples in the following subsections to understand the usage of the command. The examples are based on the assumption that the system has access to the Internet (obtaining IP assignments from a DHCP server running on your home router was automatically set up during the OS installation in Chapter 1), and the default definitions for the pre-configured repositories are present in the */etc/apt/sources.list* file.

Downloading a Package

Downloading a package only downloads the specified package to the directory you issue the command in. Here is how you would download a package called "zsh." You need to issue the command with *root* privileges.

```
user1@ubuntu14:~$ sudo apt-get download zsh
Get:1 http://us.archive.ubuntu.com/ubuntu/ trusty/main zsh amd64 5.0.2-3ubuntu6 [607 kB]
Fetched 607 kB in 0s (1,808 kB/s)
user1@ubuntu14:~$ ll zsh*
-rw-r--r-- 1 root root 606764 Oct 10  2013 zsh_5.0.2-3ubuntu6_amd64.deb
```

Installing a Package

This action is performed to install the specified package as well as any dependent packages on the system. Here is how you would install a package called "aptitude" directly from a repository:

```
user1@ubuntu14:~$ sudo apt-get install aptitude
```
Reading package lists... Done

Building dependency tree

Reading state information... Done

Suggested packages:

  aptitude-doc-en aptitude-doc tasksel debtags

The following NEW packages will be installed:

  aptitude

0 upgraded, 1 newly installed, 0 to remove and 168 not upgraded.

Need to get 0 B/1,371 kB of archives.

After this operation, 4,703 kB of additional disk space will be used.

Selecting previously unselected package aptitude.

(Reading database ... 169890 files and directories currently installed.)

Preparing to unpack .../aptitude_0.6.8.2-1ubuntu4_amd64.deb ...

Unpacking aptitude (0.6.8.2-1ubuntu4) ...

Processing triggers for man-db (2.6.7.1-1ubuntu1) ...

Setting up aptitude (0.6.8.2-1ubuntu4) ...

update-alternatives: using /usr/bin/aptitude-curses to provide /usr/bin/aptitude (aptitude) in auto mode

If you only want to see how the installation would progress, simply add the -s (simulate) switch to the above command to look like **sudo apt-get install -s aptitude**.

The install subcommand downloads the specified package to the */var/cache/apt/archives* directory.

Updating the Package Database

Updating the package database pulls the latest information for the installed packages from the repositories and applies it to the local package database on the system to update it. Simply run *apt-get* with the update subcommand as *root*: **sudo apt-get update**.

Upgrading Packages

Upgrading software packages on the system upgrades all installed packages, as well as their dependent packages, to their latest available version levels. However, you should update the package database prior to issuing **sudo apt-get upgrade**. Here is a sample output from the command:

```
user1@ubuntu14:~$ sudo apt-get upgrade
```
Reading package lists... Done

Building dependency tree

Reading state information... Done

Calculating upgrade... Done

The following packages have been kept back:

  linux-generic-lts-xenial linux-headers-generic-lts-xenial

The following packages will be upgraded:

  accountsservice apparmor apport apport-gtk apt apt-transport-https apt-utils

. . . .

164 upgraded, 0 newly installed, 0 to remove and 4 not upgraded.

Need to get 193 MB of archives.

After this operation, 17.7 MB of additional disk space will be used.

Do you want to continue? [Y/n]

Enter "Y" to proceed with the upgrade of the listed packages or "n" to cancel. You can add the -y option to the command to instruct it to continue without prompting for confirmation.

Removing a Package Without or With Configuration Files

Removing a package is simple. Use the remove subcommand with *apt-get* and specify the name of the package to be deleted. For instance, to weed a package called "wget" out of the system, issue the following:

user1@ubuntu14:~$ **sudo apt-get remove wget**
Reading package lists... Done
Building dependency tree
Reading state information... Done
The following packages will be REMOVED:
  hplip printer-driver-postscript-hp ssh-import-id ubuntu-standard wget
0 upgraded, 0 newly installed, 5 to remove and 4 not upgraded.
After this operation, 2,273 kB disk space will be freed.
Do you want to continue? [Y/n]

Enter "Y" to proceed with the erasure of the package or "n" to cancel the action. You may add the -y option to the command to instruct it to continue without prompting for confirmation. If you only want to know how the removal would progress, simply add the -s (simulate) switch to the above command to look like **sudo apt-get remove -s wget**.

The remove subcommand leaves the configuration files of the deleted package on the system. If you want to erase them along with the package removal, you would have to use the purge subcommand instead. In that case, the above command with the addition of confirmation switch will look like **sudo apt-get purge wget -y**.

Removing Transitory Packages

One or more packages may be installed automatically to satisfy dependency requirements during an installation process, and they are no longer needed after the desired package(s) has been successfully installed. These transitory packages may be deleted from the system later by issuing **sudo apt-get autoremove**. The -y switch can be appended to the command for auto confirmation.

Alternatively, you can add the --auto-remove option to the install or remove subcommand to take care of this deletion automatically at that time.

Cleaning the APT Cache

Once you are done with the package installation or upgrade, run **sudo apt-get clean** to clear out the packages that were downloaded as part of either process from the */var/cache/apt/archives* APT cache directory. This will free up some disk space.

The apt-cache Command

The *apt-cache* command is used to perform a variety of query operations against the APT cache and generate reports for our review. Table 5-3 describes a few common operations that the *apt-cache* command can perform. For a detailed look on this utility, consult its manual pages.

Subcommand	Description
depends	Displays dependent, suggested, recommended, and conflicting packages for a package
pkgnames	Lists all package names
rdepends	Shows inverse of depends. Output of this subcommand is similar to that of the showpkg's.
search	Searches for a string in package names and descriptions
show	Shows a package's record
showpkg	Shows package name, versions, and forward (normal) and reverse dependencies
stats	Displays statistical information about the APT cache
unmet	Shows unmet dependency information for all the packages in APT cache

Table 5-3 Common apt-cache Operations

The *apt-cache* command has some interesting options that can be used to deviate from its default behavior. For instance, the --installed option with the depends subcommand limits the search to installed packages only.

Let's look at a few examples in the following subsections to understand the usage of the *apt-cache* command.

Searching for a Package

This operation allows you to spot the specified string in package names and descriptions. The following example shows how to search for the string "gunzip". You do not need the superuser privileges in order to perform this task.

```
user1@ubuntu14:~$ apt-cache search gunzip
libperlio-gzip-perl - module providing a PerlIO layer to gzip/gunzip
libio-compress-perl - bundle of IO::Compress modules
libwww-mechanize-gzip-perl - Perl module to fetch webpages with gzip-compression
```

Listing all Packages

You can use the pkgnames subcommand with *apt-cache* to list all installed packages on the system. Here is the syntax:

```
user1@ubuntu14:~$ apt-cache pkgnames
```

A very long output will be generated.

Displaying Package Information

The show subcommand with *apt-cache* is used to display information about a package. Here is how we run this command to view information about the "aptitude" package:

```
user1@ubuntu14:~$ apt-cache show aptitude
```

Among other information, the output shows the package name, installed size, processor architecture it is designed for, version, packages it depends on, packages it conflicts with, source filename location and size, and short and long descriptions.

Listing Forward Dependencies

The depends subcommand with *apt-cache* is used to list forward dependencies, as well as the recommended and conflicting packages for the specified package. A forward dependent package is the package that is required in order for the specified package to be installed or work. Here is how we run this command to view dependency information for the package "zip":

```
user1@ubuntu14:~$ apt-cache depends zip
```

Listing Reverse Dependencies

The showpkg or the rdepends subcommand with *apt-cache* may be used to list the packages that depend on the specified package for their installation or functioning. The following shows the usage to view reverse dependencies for the package "zip":

```
user1@ubuntu14:~$ apt-cache showpkg zip
user1@ubuntu14:~$ apt-cache rdepends zip
```

The showpkg subcommand produces a little more information than does the rdepends subcommand.

Showing APT Cache Statistics

The stats subcommand with *apt-cache* shows statistical information about package metadata stored in the APT cache. Here is a sample use and output of this command:

```
user1@ubuntu14:~$ apt-cache stats
Total package names: 61863 (1,237 k)
Total package structures: 105308 (5,897 k)
  Normal packages: 73679
  Pure virtual packages: 1885
  Single virtual packages: 8159
  Mixed virtual packages: 1920
  Missing: 19665
Total distinct versions: 87036 (6,267 k)
Total distinct descriptions: 99386 (2,385 k)
Total dependencies: 682488 (19.1 M)
Total ver/file relations: 97037 (2,329 k)
Total Desc/File relations: 99386 (2,385 k)
Total Provides mappings: 25982 (520 k)
Total globbed strings: 167 (2,188 )
Total dependency version space: 3,491 k
Total slack space: 26.1 k
Total space accounted for: 34.2 M
```

The output shows a total for various package metadata element and an amount of disk space each element is consuming.

Viewing Unmet Dependencies

The unmet subcommand with *apt-cache* shows a list of unmet dependencies for all the packages with their information available in the APT cache. The command produces a long output. Here is how we issue it:

```
user1@ubuntu14:~$ apt-cache unmet
```

apt vs. apt-get and apt-cache

The *apt* command is another interface available in Debian and its spinoffs that may be used in place of *apt-get* and *apt-cache* to perform a subset of package handling functions. Table 5-4 provides a comparison between the *apt* subcommands and their equivalent *apt-get*/*apt-cache* subcommands.

Task	apt	apt-get	apt-cache
Install or upgrade a package	install	install	
Update the package database with updated package data	update	update	
Upgrade packages to their newest versions	upgrade	upgrade	
Same as "upgrade" plus remove any existing packages for a potential conflict resolution with any new packages. Can be used to upgrade the OS version.	full-upgrade	dist-upgrade	
Remove a package without deleting its configuration files	remove	remove	
List packages	list		pkgnames
Search for a string in package names and descriptions	search		search
Display information about a package	show		show

Table 5-4 Equivalent apt and apt-get/apt-cache Subcommands

Table 5-4 summarizes the *apt* vs. *apt-get* and *apt* vs. *apt-cache* operations, and the equivalent subcommands. A point to note here is that the outputs generated by *apt* vs. *apt-cache* subcommands may differ. Use an appropriate tool for what you want to achieve.

For example, if you want to install a package called "pkg", you can use either of the following two:

```
user1@ubuntu14:~$ sudo apt-get install pkg
user1@ubuntu14:~$ sudo apt install pkg
```

This syntax is applicable to all the subcommands that are described in the Table 5-4.

Understanding and Using aptitude

aptitude is a menu-driven front-end visual text interface to the APT package manipulation commandset. It supports all the operations—listing, querying, showing, installing, upgrading, removing, and purging packages—of the entire APT toolset plus much more. This interactive program may also be invoked directly from the command line by specifying an intended action.

Figure 5-1 shows the main interface that appears when the *aptitude* command is invoked without an action.

Figure 5-1 aptitude Program Text Interface

The main screen may be divided into three windows. The area across the top presents the program's menu items, which are accessed by pressing the Ctrl+t (C-t) key combination. The next line right beneath the menu depicts help on how to access the menu (C-t), navigate within aptitude (?), close a current window (q), update the list of available packages (u), and perform any pending installations, removals, and upgrades (g). The third line from the top displays the version of the program and the amount of disk space that can be freed up.

The middle window is where we can make a selection to perform an action on. There are six categories available: (1) Security Updates, (2) Upgradable Packages, (3) Installed Packages, (4) Not Installed Packages, (5) Virtual Packages, and (6) Tasks. Each of these categories also shows the number of packages/tasks available in that category at that time. The bottom window provides information in relation to a selection made in the middle window. By pressing Enter on a category in the middle window, we can expand a category for more granular selections or collapse an expanded view. After selecting a category, go to the main menu by pressing Ctrl+t and choose an action you want to carry out on the selected items. You can press ? at any time to view help on navigation and executing operations. You can press the forward slash (/) character while on a category to search for a pattern in package names. Once you find the package(s) you were looking for, go to the main menu and mark them for installation or erasure, and then go to Actions→Install/Remove packages to apply the action. You can press q to close the current window or to exit out of the program.

aptitude can be run directly from the command prompt as well without invoking its interface by specifying an action using a subcommand. The behavior of *aptitude* in that case will match that of the three APT commands' that were discussed earlier. Some of the popular subcommands available for use with *aptitude* are clean, download, full-upgrade, install, purge, reinstall, remove, safe-upgrade, search, show, and update. Additional subcommands peculiar to *aptitude* are also available, and they include forbid-version, forget-new, hold/unhold, markauto/unmarkauto, and why/why-not. Check the manual pages of *aptitude* for details.

Here is the command syntax for your review:

```
user1@ubuntu14:~$ sudo aptitude install <some_pkg>
user1@ubuntu14:~$ sudo aptitude purge <some_pkg>
```

RPM Package Overview

RHEL and its spinoffs are essentially a set of RPM packages grouped together to form an operating system. They are prepackaged for installation and assembled for various intended uses. They are built around the Linux kernel and include thousands of packages that are digitally signed, tested, and certified. There are several concepts associated with packages and package management that are touched upon in the following subsections.

Packages and Packaging

Packages are a group of files, metadata, and intelligence that make up a software application. They are available in two types: *binary* (or *installable*) and *source*. Binary packages are installation-ready and are bundled for distribution. They have .rpm extension and contain install scripts, pre- and post-installation scripts, executables, configuration files, library files, and manual pages and other documentation.

All metadata related to packages is stored at a central location and includes information such as package version, installation location, checksum values, and a list of included files with their attributes. This allows management tools to handle package administration tasks efficiently by referencing this metadata.

The package intelligence is used by package administration toolset for a successful completion of the package installation process. It may include information on pre-requisites, user account setup (if required), directories to create, and soft links to create. The intelligence also includes the reverse of this process for uninstallation.

Source packages come with the original unmodified version of the software that may be unpacked, modified as desired, and repackaged in the binary format for installation or distribution. They are identified with the .src extension.

Package Naming

Red Hat software packages follow a standard naming convention. Typically, there are five parts to a package name: (1) the package name, (2) the package version, (3) the package release (revision or build), (4) the Enterprise Linux the package is created for, and (5) the processor architecture the package is built for. An installable package name always has the .rpm extension; however, this extension is removed from the installed package name.

For example, if the name of an installable package is openssl-1.0.1e-60.el7.x86_64.rpm, its installed name would be openssl-1.0.1e-60.el7.x86_64. Here is a description of each part of the package name:

- ✓ **openssl** – package name
- ✓ **1.0.1e** – package version
- ✓ **60** – package release
- ✓ **el7** – stands for Enterprise Linux 7 (some packages have it, some do not)
- ✓ **x86_64** – processor architecture the package is created for. If we see "noarch" instead, the package will be platform-independent and can be installed on any hardware architecture. If we see "src," it will contain source code for the package.
- ✓ **.rpm** – the extension

Package Dependency

An installable package may require the presence of one or more additional packages in order to be installed successfully. Likewise, a software package component may require the functionality provided by one or more other packages to exist in order to operate as expected. This is referred to as *package dependency*, where one package depends on one or more other packages for installation or execution. Package dependency information is recorded in each package's metadata from where it is read by package handling utilities.

Package Database

Metadata for installed package files is stored in the */var/lib/rpm* directory. This directory location is referred to as the *package database*, and it is referenced by package manipulation utilities to obtain information about ownerships, permissions, timestamps, and file sizes. The package database also contains information on dependencies. All this data aids management commands in listing and querying packages, verifying dependencies and file attributes, upgrading and uninstalling existing packages, installing new packages, and carrying out other package handling tasks.

RPM Package Management Tools

The primary tool for package management on Red Hat Enterprise Linux and its derivatives—CentOS and Scientific Linux—is called *rpm* (*redhat package manager*). This tool offers a number of options for easy package handling; however, one major caveat with using this tool is that it does not automatically download and install dependent packages if required. To overcome this gap, a more innovative tool called *yum* (*yellowdog update modified*) is employed, which offers an easier method for package handling and is able to find, get, and install dependencies automatically.

Managing RPM Packages with rpm

The *rpm* command performs a number of package management tasks: querying, installing, upgrading, freshening, verifying, removing, and extracting packages. One caveat with this command is that it does not automatically satisfy package dependencies, which can be frustrating during installation and upgrade.

The rpm Command

Before getting into the details, let's look at some common *rpm* command options described in Table 5-5. Both short and long option formats are provided. You may use whichever of the two you feel comfortable with.

Query Options	Description
-q (--query)	Queries and displays packages
-qa (--query --all)	Lists all installed packages
-qc (--query --configfiles)	Lists configuration files
-qd (--query --docfiles)	Lists documentation files
-qf (--query --file)	Displays what package a file comes from
-qi (--query --info)	Shows installed package information including version, size, installation status and date, signature, and description
-ql (--query --list)	Lists all files in a package
-qip (--query --info --package)	Shows installable package information including version, size, installation status and date, signature, and description

Query Options	Description
-q --whatprovides	Lists packages that provide the specified package or file
-qR (--query --requires)	Lists files and packages a package depends on (requires)
Install Options	**Description**
-F (--freshen)	Upgrades an installed package
-i (--install)	Installs a package
-U (--upgrade)	Upgrades an installed package or installs it if it is not already installed
Other Options	**Description**
-e (--erase)	Removes a package
-v (--verbose) or -vv	Displays detailed information
-V (--verify)	Verifies the integrity of a package or package files

Table 5-5 rpm Command Options

Let's perform a few package management tasks on *centos73* for practice. Attach the CentOS 7.3 image to the VM in the Oracle VirtualBox console, and then make it available on the system using the *mount* command. You need to switch into the *root* user account first with the *su* command in order to mount the image. Enter the password when prompted:

```
[user1@centos73 ~]$ su -
Password:
Last login: Mon Jan 30 22:24:52 EST 2017 on pts/0
```

Now mount the image on */mnt* directory in read-only mode:

```
[root@centos73 ~]# mount -r /dev/cdrom /mnt
```

And validate the mount with the *df* command:

```
[root@centos73 ~]# df -h | grep mnt
/dev/sr0      4.1G      4.1G      0      100%      /mnt
```

We should now be able to access the packages via */mnt* directory.

Querying Packages

Querying packages searches for the information in the package database or at the specified location and displays it on the screen. The following are some examples.

To query all installed packages:

```
[root@centos73 ~]# rpm -qa                   (or rpm --query --all)
libgphoto2-2.5.2-3.el7.x86_64
attr-2.4.46-12.el7.x86_64
ibus-table-1.5.0-5.el7.noarch
libXres-1.0.7-2.1.el7.x86_64
. . . . . . . .
```

To query the installation status of a package:

```
[root@centos73 ~]# rpm -q perl            (or rpm --query perl)
perl-5.16.3-291.el7.x86_64
```

To list all files in a package:

```
[root@centos73 ~]# rpm -ql iproute        (or rpm --query --list iproute)
```

To list only the documentation files in a package:

```
[root@centos73 ~]# rpm -qd audit          (or rpm --query --docfiles audit)
```

To list only the configuration files in a package:

```
[root@centos73 ~]# rpm -qc coreutils      (or rpm --query --configfiles coreutils)
```

To identify which package owns a file:

```
[root@centos73 ~]# rpm -qf /etc/passwd    (or rpm --query --file /etc/passwd)
setup-2.8.71-7.el7.noarch
```

To display information about an installed package including version, release, installation status and date, size, signatures, description, and so on:

```
[root@centos73 ~]# rpm -qi setup          (or rpm --query --info setup)
Name         : setup
Version      : 2.8.71
Release      : 7.el7
Architecture : noarch
Install Date : Wed 21 Dec 2016 09:05:08 AM EST
Group        : System Environment/Base
Size         : 696715
License      : Public Domain
Signature    : RSA/SHA256, Sun 20 Nov 2016 03:43:54 PM EST, Key ID 24c6a8a7f4a80eb5
Source RPM   : setup-2.8.71-7.el7.src.rpm
Build Date   : Sat 05 Nov 2016 01:19:36 PM EDT
Build Host   : worker1.bsys.centos.org
Relocations  : (not relocatable)
Packager     : CentOS BuildSystem <http://bugs.centos.org>
Vendor       : CentOS
URL          : https://fedorahosted.org/setup/
Summary      : A set of system configuration and setup files
Description  : The setup package contains a set of important system configuration and
setup files, such as passwd, group, and profile.
```

To list all file and package dependencies for a package:

```
[root@centos73 ~]# rpm -qR sox            (or rpm --query --requires sox)
```

To query what the installable package is for, run either of the following:

```
[root@centos73 ~]# rpm -qip /mnt/Packages/zsh*
[root@centos73 ~]# rpm --query --info --package /mnt/Packages/zsh*
```

Installing a Package

Installing a package creates the necessary directory structure for the package, installs the required files, and runs any post-installation steps. The following command installs a package called zsh-5.0.2-25.el7.x86_64.rpm on the system (you may use --install --verbose --hash instead of -ivh):

```
[root@centos73 ~]# rpm -ivh /mnt/Packages/zsh-5.0.2-25.el7.x86_64.rpm
warning: /mnt/Packages/zsh-5.0.2-25.el7.x86_64.rpm: Header V3 RSA/SHA256 Signature, key ID
f4a80eb5: NOKEY
Preparing...                   ################################# [100%]
Updating / installing...
  1:zsh-5.0.2-25.el7            ################################# [100%]
```

If this package requires the presence of any missing packages, you will see an error message related to failed dependencies. You must first install the missing packages in order for this package to be loaded successfully.

Upgrading a Package

Upgrading a package will upgrade an installed version of the package. In the absence of an existing version, the upgrade simply installs the package.

To upgrade the "sushi" package, sushi-3.12.0-3.el7.x86_64.rpm, use the -U (or --upgrade) option:

```
[root@centos73 ~]# rpm -Uvh /mnt/Packages/sushi-3.12.0-3.el7.x86_64.rpm
```

The command makes a backup of all the affected configuration files during the upgrade process and adds the extension *.rpmsave* to them.

Freshening a Package

Freshening a package requires that an older version of the package must already exist on the system.

To freshen the "sushi" package, sushi-3.12.0-3.el7.x86_64.rpm, use the -F (or --freshen) option:

```
[root@centos73 ~]# rpm -Fvh /mnt/Packages/sushi-3.12.0-3.el7.x86_64.rpm
```

To freshen all installed packages from the ISO image, execute the following:

```
[root@centos73 ~]# rpm -Fvh /mnt/Packages/*.rpm
```

The above will do nothing, as the packages that currently exist on the system were installed from this ISO image during the installation; however, the command will work if the ISO image contains a newer version of the OS.

Verifying Package Integrity

Verifying the integrity of an installed package compares the attributes of files in the package with the original file attributes saved and stored in the package database at the time of package installation. The verification process uses the *rpm* command with the -V option to compare the

MD5 checksum value. The command returns to the prompt without displaying anything if the current and the stored checksum values are identical. We may use the -v or -vv option with the command for verbose output if needed.

Let's run this check on the "sushi" package:

```
[root@centos73 ~]# rpm -V sushi
```

The command returned nothing, which implies that the file attributes are intact. Now let's change the permissions on one of the files in the "sushi" package, */usr/bin/sushi*, to 777 from the current value 755, and then re-run the verification:

```
[root@centos73 ~]# ll /usr/bin/sushi
-rwxr-xr-x. 1 root root 442 Nov 20 2015 /usr/bin/sushi
[root@centos73 ~]# chmod -v 777 /usr/bin/shshi
mode of '/usr/bin/sushi' changed from 0755 (rwxr-xr-x) to 0777 (rwxrwxrwx)
[root@centos73 ~]# rpm -V sushi
.M.......   /usr/bin/sushi
```

The output indicates a change in the permission mode on the file in the "sushi" package. We can run the verification check directly on the file as well, by adding the -f option to the command and passing the filename as an argument:

```
[root@centos73 ~]# rpm -Vf /usr/bin/sushi
.M.......   /usr/bin/sushi
```

Now, let's revert the permissions and re-run the verification:

```
[root@centos73 ~]# chmod -v 755 /usr/bin/shshi
mode of '/usr/bin/sushi' changed from 0777 (rwxrwxrwx) to 0755 (rwxr-xr-x)
[root@centos73 ~]# rpm -V sushi
```

The command will produce no output, indicating no changes in the file, or the package for that matter.

Removing a Package

Removing a package uninstalls the package and all the associated files, and the directory structure.

To remove the package sushi, use the -e (or --erase) option and also specify -v (--verbose) for verbosity:

```
[root@centos73 ~]# rpm -ev sushi
Preparing packages...
sushi-3.12.0-3.el7.x86_64
```

This command performs a dependency inspection to check whether other an installed package requires the existence of the package being weeded out, and fails the removal if it detects a dependency.

Extracting Files from an Installable Package

Files in an installable RPM package can be extracted using the *rpm2cpio* command for reasons such as examining the contents of the package, replacing a corrupted or lost command, or replacing a critical configuration file of an installed package to its original state.

Assuming you have lost the */etc/ntp.conf* configuration file and you want to retrieve it from its installable package and put it back. You first need to determine what package this file comes from:

```
[root@centos73 ~]# rpm -qf /etc/ntp.conf
ntp-4.2.6p5-25.el7..centos.x86_64
```

Now use the *rpm2cpio* command to extract (-i) all files from the "ntp" package and create (-d) the necessary directory structure during the retrieval. Before doing that, create a temporary directory to extract the contents in.

```
[root@centos73 ~]# mkdir /tmp/ntp ; cd /tmp/ntp
[root@centos73 ~]# rpm2cpio /mnt/Packages/ntp-4.2.6p5-18.el7.x86_64.rpm | cpio -id
2813 blocks
```

The semicolon (;) character used in the example is a special character that serves the purpose of separating two or more independent commands on the same command line.

Run the *find* command to locate the *ntp.conf* file:

```
[root@centos73 ~]# find . -name ntp.conf
./etc/ntp.conf
```

The above output shows that the file we were looking for is in the */tmp/ntp/etc* directory. You can copy it to the */etc* directory now, and we're back in business.

Managing RPM Packages with yum

The *yum* command (*yellowdog updater, modified*) is the front-end to the *rpm* command and is the preferred tool for package management on RHEL and its derivatives. This utility requires that your system have access to a local or web-based software repository with an appropriate definition file in the */etc/yum.repos.d/* directory. The primary benefit of using the *yum* command is that it automatically resolves dependencies by downloading and installing any additional required packages for a successful installation of the specified package. With multiple repositories configured, *yum* extracts the package being installed from wherever it finds it. The *yum* command is versatile and provides multiple ways for doing certain tasks. Check out the manual pages on how you can use this command with that flexibility.

Yum Configuration File

The key configuration data for *yum* is located in the */etc/yum.conf* file. The "main" section of the file sets directives with a global effect on yum operations. You may define discrete sections for each custom repository that you plan to set up on the system. However, a better approach is to store the repository data in the */etc/yum.repos.d/* directory, which is the standard location created for this purpose. The default contents of the *yum.conf* file are listed below:

```
[root@centos73 ~]# cat /etc/yum.conf
[main]
cachedir=/var/cache/yum/$basearch/$releasever
keepcache=0
debuglevel=2
logfile=/var/log/yum.log
exactarch=1
obsoletes=1
gpgcheck=1
plugins=1
installonly_limit=5
```

Table 5-6 explains the above directives.

Directive	Description
cachedir	Defines the location to store *yum* downloads. Default is */var/cache/yum/$basearch/$releasever*.
keepcache	Specifies whether to store the package and header cache following a successful installation. Default is 0 (disabled).
debuglevel	Sets the level between 1 (minimum) and 10 (maximum) at which the debug is to be recorded in the logfile. Default is 2. A value of 0 disables this feature.
logfile	States the name and location of the log file for *yum* activities. Default is */var/log/yum.log*.
exactarch	Tells the command to update only those packages that match the CPU architecture of the installed packages. Default is 1 (enabled).
obsoletes	Checks and replaces any obsolete packages during updates. Default is 1 (enabled).
gpgcheck	Sets GPG signature check for package authenticity. Default is 1 (enabled).
plugins	Defines whether to include plug-ins with the packages to be downloaded. Default is 1 (enabled).
installonly_limit	Specifies the maximum number of versions of a single package to coexist on the system at a time. Default is 5.

Table 5-6 Directives in /etc/yum.conf

The values of any of these directives may be modified as required.

Yum Repository

A *yum repository* (or simply a *repo*) is a digital library for storing software packages. A repository is accessed for package retrieval, query, update, and installation. There are a number of repositories available on the Internet that are maintained by software publishers, such as CentOS and Red Hat, for free or at cost. By default, CentOS installation sets access to a number of pre-configured repositories via definition files located under the */etc/yum.repos.d* directory, as listed below:

```
[root@centos73 ~]# ll /etc/yum.repos.d
-rw-r--r--. 1 root root 1664 Nov 29 13:12 CentOS-Base.repo
-rw-r--r--. 1 root root 1309 Nov 29 13:12 CentOS-CR.repo
-rw-r--r--. 1 root root  649 Nov 29 13:12 CentOS-Debuginfo.repo
-rw-r--r--. 1 root root  314 Nov 29 13:12 CentOS-fasttrack.repo
-rw-r--r--. 1 root root  630 Nov 29 13:12 CentOS-Media.repo
-rw-r--r--. 1 root root 1331 Nov 29 13:12 CentOS-Sources.repo
-rw-r--r--. 1 root root 2893 Nov 29 13:12 CentOS-Vault.repo
```

Furthermore, you can build your own repositories for internal IT use by configuring custom repos for stocking different types of software. This is a good practice for an organization with a large number of Linux systems, as it takes care of dependencies automatically and aids in maintaining software consistency across the board. If you have developed a new package or built one, you can add it to one of those repositories as well. It is important to obtain packages from authentic and reliable sources, such as CentOS and Red Hat, to prevent potential damage to your system and to circumvent possible software corruption.

A sample repository file is shown below with some key directives:

```
[centos7.3_repo]
name=centos7.3 repo
baseurl=file:///mnt
enabled=1
gpgcheck=0
```

The above example shows five entries in the sample repo file. It defines a unique ID within the square brackets, a brief description of the repo with the name directive, the location of the repodata directory with the baseurl directive, whether or not this repository is active, and if packages are to be GPG-checked for authenticity. Each repository file must have an ID and a baseurl directive defined at a minimum; other directives are set as required. The baseurl directive for a local directory path is defined as file:///local_path (three forward slash characters, two represent the URL convention and one for the absolute path to the destination directory) and that for an FTP path as ftp://hostname/network_path and an HTTP path as http://hostname/network_path. The network path should include a resolvable hostname or an IP address.

The yum Command

The *yum* command may be used to perform a number of package administration tasks, and as we know, it invokes the *rpm* utility in the background. Table 5-7 summarizes the key software handling tasks that *yum* can perform. For more operators and options, check out the manual pages.

Subcommand	Description
clean	Removes cached data
deplist	Lists dependencies for a packages
info	Displays package details including version, release, size, installation status, short and long descriptions, etc.
install	Installs a new package or updates an existing one
list	Lists installed and available packages
provides (or whatprovides)	Searches for packages that contain the specified file or feature

Subcommand	Description
remove / erase	Removes a package and its dependencies
reinstall	Reinstalls the exact version of an installed package
repolist	Shows a list of accessible and enabled repositories with a count of packages available from each
search	Searches for a string in package descriptions
update	Updates one, more than one, or all installed packages. Takes care of the dependencies as well.
upgrade	Same as update, but it removes obsoleted packages

Table 5-7 yum Subcommands

Let's look at a few examples in the following subsections to understand the usage of the *yum* command. The examples are based on the assumption that the system has access to the Internet (obtaining IP assignments from a DHCP server running on your home router was selected during the OS installation in Chapter 1), and the default definitions for pre-configured repositories are present in the */etc/yum.repos.d* directory as discussed earlier.

Viewing Enabled Repositories

Let's peruse which of the pre-configured repositories are active and accessible to us on our *centos73* system. We use the repolist subcommand with yum for this purpose. We can add the -v option for detailed information if needed.

```
[root@centos73 ~]# yum repolist
Loaded plugins: fastestmirror, langpacks
Loading mirror speeds from cached hostfile
 * base: centos.mirror.iweb.ca
 * extras: mirror.netaddicted.ca
 * updates: centos.mirror.netelligent.ca
repo id              repo name                status
base/7/x86_64        CentOS-7 – Base          9,363
extras/7/x86_64      CentOS-7 – Extras          263
updates/7/x86_64     CentOS-7 – Updates         799
repolist: 10,425
```

The output indicates a total of 10,425 packages accessible to us from three repositories.

Listing Packages

Listing packages allows us to view packages installed on the system and packages available for installation from available repositories. The following are some examples.

To list all installed packages along with their names, versions, and the repository names that were used to install them:

```
[root@centos73 ~]# yum list installed
Installed Packages
GConf2.x86_64              3.2.6-8.el7       @anaconda
GeoIP.x86_64               1.5.0-11.el7      @anaconda
. . . . . . . .
```

The repository name "anaconda" refers to the installation program.

To list all packages available for installation along with their names, versions, and the repository names they are available from:

```
[root@centos73 ~]# yum list available
Available Packages
389-ds-base.x86_64          1.3.5.10-15.el7_3        updates
Cython.x86_64               0.19-3.el7               base
. . . . . . . .
```

Try the following to list both installed and available packages. This command produces the sum of the above two.

```
[root@centos73 ~]# yum list
```

To list all available packages from all enabled repositories that should be able to update:

```
[root@centos73 ~]# yum list updates
```

To list whether a package "bc" (for instance) is installed or available for installation:

```
[root@centos73 ~]# yum list bc
```

To list all installed packages with their names containing the string "gnome" at the beginning:

```
[root@centos73 ~]# yum list installed gnome*
```

Listing Package Dependencies and Providers

A successful installation of a single package may require one or more dependent packages to be pre-installed. Listing what is required as a dependency and what package is needed to resolve that dependency will help us prepare for any unexpected consequences ahead of time.

The following shows how to use the deplist subcommand with *yum* on the installed "bc" package to list the dependencies this package has and the names of the provider packages that were pre-installed to resolve those dependencies:

```
[root@centos73 ~]# yum deplist bc
. . . . . . . .
package: bc.x86_64 1.06.95-13.el7
  dependency: /bin/sh
   provider: bash.x86_64 4.2.46-21.el7_3
  dependency: /sbin/install-info
   provider: info.x86_64 5.1-4.el7
  dependency: libc.so.6(GLIBC_2.14)(64bit)
   provider: glibc.x86_64 2.17-157.el7_3.1
. . . . . . . .
```

As you can see, a single package requires the presence of multiple other packages in order to be installed successfully or work as expected.

Installing and Updating a Package

Installing a package creates the necessary directory tree for the package and the dependent packages, installs the required files, and runs any post-installation steps. If the package being loaded is already present, the command updates it to the latest available version. By default, *yum* prompts for a yes or no confirmation unless the -y option at the command line is specified. It also allows us to download the package in the */var/cache/yum/$basearch/$releasever/packages* directory if we select "d" when prompted.

The following attempts to install a package called "zsh", but proceeds with an update to the newest available version if it detects the presence of an older version:

```
[root@centos73 ~]# yum -y install zsh
. . . . . . . .
Resolving Dependencies
--> Running transaction check
---> Package zsh.x86_64 0:5.0.2-25.el7 will be updated
---> Package zsh.x86_64 0:5.0.2-25.el7_3.1 will be an update
--> Finished Dependency Resolution
Dependencies Resolved
```

Package	Arch	Version	Repository	Size

```
Updating:
 zsh      x86_64     5.0.2-25.el7_3.1     updates     2.4 M
Transaction Summary
```

```
Upgrade  1 Package
Total download size: 2.4 M
Downloading packages:
. . . . . . . .
  Updating   : zsh-5.0.2-25.el7_3.1.x86_64       1/2
  Cleanup    : zsh-5.0.2-25.el7.x86_64           2/2
  Verifying  : zsh-5.0.2-25.el7_3.1.x86_64       1/2
  Verifying  : zsh-5.0.2-25.el7.x86_64           2/2
Updated:
  zsh.x86_64 0:5.0.2-25.el7_3.1
Complete!
```

To update an installed package ("autofs" for instance) to the latest available version, issue the following command. Note that *yum* will fail if the specified package is not already installed.

```
[root@centos73 ~]# yum update autofs
No packages marked for update
```

To update all installed packages to the latest version:

```
[root@centos73 ~]# yum update
. . . . . . . .
Transaction Summary
================================================================================
Install    1 Package
Upgrade  130 Packages
Total download size: 273 M
Is this ok [y/d/N]:
```

Reinstalling a Package

Reinstalling a package overwrites the files of an existing package and runs any post-installation steps. If the package being reinstalled is not already there on the system, the command will error out. A reinstallation may be required to reinstate a package's executables and other files to their original state as a result of corruption.

The following example will reinstall the "zsh" package to its original state:

```
[root@centos73 ~]# yum reinstall zsh -y
```

Displaying Package Information

Displaying a package information shows its name, architecture it is built for, version, release, size, whether it is installed or available for installation, repo name it is installed/available from, short and long descriptions, license, and so on. This information can be viewed by supplying the info subcommand to *yum*. For instance, to display information for the "zsh" package:

```
[root@centos73 ~]# yum info zsh
. . . . . . . .
Name        : zsh
Arch        : x86_64
Version     : 5.0.2
Release     : 25.el7_3.1
Size        : 5.6 M
Repo        : installed
From repo   : updates
Summary     : Powerful interactive shell
URL         : http://zsh.sourceforge.net/
License     : MIT
Description : The zsh shell is a command interpreter usable as an interactive
            : login shell and as a shell script command processor.  Zsh
            : resembles the ksh shell (the Korn shell), but includes many
            : enhancements.  Zsh supports command line editing, built-in
            : spelling correction, programmable command completion, shell
            : functions (with autoloading), a history mechanism, and more.
```

You may add the -v option to the command for more package details.

Determining What Provides

Determining package contents include search operations on installed or available packages. For instance, we can determine what package a specific file belongs to or what package comprises a certain string. The following examples show how to carry out these tasks.

To search for packages that contain a specific file such as *etc/passwd*, use the provides or the whatprovides subcommand with *yum*:

```
[root@centos73 ~]# yum provides /etc/passwd
. . . . . . . .
setup-2.8.71-7.el7.noarch : A set of system configuration and setup files
Repo      : base
Matched from:
Filename   : /etc/passwd

setup-2.8.71-7.el7.noarch : A set of system configuration and setup files
Repo      : @anaconda
Matched from:
Filename   : /etc/passwd
```

The output shows two instances of the file. The first one indicates that the */etc/passwd* file is part of a package called "setup", which is available from a repository called "base" and the second instance shows that the "setup" package was installed by the anaconda program during installation.

With the provides subcommand, we can also use a wildcard character for filename matching. For example, the following command will list all packages that contain filenames beginning with "system-config-printer" followed by any number of characters in the */usr/bin* directory:

```
[root@centos73 ~]# yum whatprovides /usr/bin/system-config-printer*
```

To search for all packages that match the specified string in their name, description, or synopsis:

```
[root@centos73 ~]# yum search system-config-printer
```

Removing a Package

Removing a package uninstalls the package and all associated files and directory structure. It also erases any dependent packages as part of the deletion process. The command prompts for confirmation to proceed unless we specify the -y option with the yum command.

To erase the "zsh" package from the system and any packages that depend on it, use either the remove or the erase subcommand with *yum*:

```
[root@centos73 ~]# yum -y remove zsh
Resolving Dependencies
--> Running transaction check
---> Package zsh.x86_64 0:5.0.2-25.el7_3.1 will be erased
--> Finished Dependency Resolution
Dependencies Resolved
================================================================================
```

Package	Arch	Version	Repository	Size
Removing:				
zsh	x86_64	5.0.2-25.el7_3.1	@updates	5.6 M
Transaction Summary				

Remove 1 Package
Installed size: 5.6 M
Downloading packages:

. . . .

| Erasing | : zsh-5.0.2-25.el7_3.1.x86_64 | 1/1 |
| Verifying | : zsh-5.0.2-25.el7_3.1.x86_64 | 1/1 |

Removed:
  zsh.x86_64 0:5.0.2-25.el7_3.1
Complete!

Downloading a Package

Though *yum install* and *yum update* provide you with an option to download a package, you can use another tool called *yumdownloader* to download individual packages directly from a repository. You may do this to install the package on a non-networked system or examine its contents before making a decision whether or not to proceed with its installation.

To download a single rpm package, specify the name of the package with the command. The -v option is used for verbose output, the --resolve option ensures that dependencies are also downloaded, and the --destdir option instructs the command to download in the specified directory location. In the absence of --destdir, the package is downloaded in the directory you issue the command from. In the following example, a package called "dhclient" is downloaded in the */var/local* directory along with any dependencies:

```
[root@centos73 ~]# yumdownloader --resolve --destdir /var/local dhclient
. . . . . . . .
--> Running transaction check
---> Package dhclient.x86_64 12:4.2.5-47.el7.centos will be reinstalled
--> Finished Dependency Resolution
dhclient-4.2.5-47.el7.centos.x86_64.rpm          | 280 kB  00:01
```

The package is downloaded successfully in the */var/local* directory. Run **ll /var/local** for verification.

Chapter Summary

This chapter discussed shared libraries and software management to a reasonable extent. We looked at the concept of Linux library files, and learned the purpose and use of shared libraries. We added and updated the library path and the cache for programs to locate the library files.

The subsequent topics were related to packages and package handling regarding Debian and Red Hat, which also applied to their spinoffs. We learned about packages, packaging, naming, dependency, and package database. We performed ample package management tasks on our lab systems using both toolsets, which included the configuration and use of repositories. This practice was helpful in comprehending the toolset usage.

Chapter Review at a Glance

The following presents a one-sentence review of each key topic discussed in this chapter:

- Shared (dynamic) libraries are external software code that are typically stored in files located under /usr/lib (or /lib) or /usr/lib64 (/lib64) directories, which are referenced by many commands, programs, and applications for their successful installation or execution.

- Static libraries are software code that is an integral part of a program, command, or application.

- There are two major software packaging formats—Debian-based with .deb extension and RHEL-based with .rpm extension—used in Linux.

- A binary .deb or .rpm package file is installation-ready and it stores binary executable files, installation program, configuration files, documentation files, library files, folder structure, and file and package metadata (package name, version, release, architecture, description, dependency information, etc.).

- Debian and its derivatives offer a software package management toolset—dpkg, apt, apt-get, apt-cache, and aptitude—that allows for a number of package handling operations, such as downloading, querying, installing, updating, upgrading, searching, listing, displaying information, reconfiguring, verifying, removing, and purging software packages.

- RHEL and its offshoots offer a software package management commandset—rpm, yum, and yumdownloader—that allows for a number of package manipulation tasks, such as downloading, querying, installing, reinstalling, updating, upgrading, searching, listing, displaying information, verifying, and removing software packages.

- When executed, these tools reference or update the package database.

- The concept of software repository is common on both Linux streams, allowing system administrators to use available repositories or configure their own for enterprise use.

- Commands we learned in this chapter are: ldd, ldconfig, dpkg, dpkg-reconfigure, apt-get, apt-cache, apt, aptitude, rpm, rpmcpio, yum, and yumdownloader.

- Files and directories we discussed in this chapter are: /usr/lib/ (/lib/), /usr/lib64/ (/lib64/), /etc/ld.so.conf, /etc/ld.so.conf.d/*.conf, /etc/ld.so.cache, /var/lib/dpkg/, /etc/dpkg/dpkg.cfg,, /var/log/dpkg.log, /etc/apt/sources.list, /var/lib/rpm/, /etc/yum.conf, and /etc/yum.repos.d/.

Booting Linux and Initializing the System

➢ Comprehend Linux boot process—firmware, GRUB, kernel, and initialization phases
➢ Overview of Upstart initialization scheme
➢ Understand GRUB Legacy and GRUB2, their configuration files, and how to interact with them to boot into different runlevels and targets
➢ Modify autoboot timeout value, install a corrupted bootloader, and regenerate configuration file
➢ Overview of command line kernel options and how to pass and view them
➢ Know SysVinit initialization scheme in detail, including runlevels, associated files, directories, and sequencing
➢ View and switch runlevels, and modify the default runlevel
➢ Manage SysVinit services—list, enable, disable, start, restart, and check status
➢ Comprehend systemd concepts and understand units and targets
➢ Understand the usage of the systemd command and administer units and targets
➢ Inspect boot messages and runtime alerts

101.2 Boot the system [this entire objective is described in this chapter]

9. Provide common commands to the bootloader and options to the kernel at boot time
10. Demonstrate knowledge of the boot sequence from BIOS to boot completion

11. Understanding of SysVinit and systemd
12. Awareness of Upstart
13. Check boot events in the log files

The following is a partial list of the used files, terms and utilities: dmesg, BIOS, bootloader, kernel, initramfs, init, SysVinit, and systemd

101.3 Change runlevels / boot targets and shutdown or reboot system [this entire objective is described in this chapter]

14. Set the default runlevel or boot target
15. Change between runlevels / boot targets including single user mode
16. Shutdown and reboot from the command line
17. Alert users before switching runlevels / boot targets or other major system events
18. Properly terminate processes

The following is a partial list of the used files, terms and utilities: /etc/inittab, shutdown, init, /etc/init.d, telinit, system, systemctl, /etc/systemd/, /usr/lib/system/, and wall

102.2 Install a boot manager [this entire objective is described in this chapter]

23. Providing alternative boot locations and backup boot options
24. Install and configure a bootloader such as GRUB Legacy
25. Perform basic configuration changes for GRUB 2
26. Interact with the bootloader

The following is a partial list of the used files, terms and utilities: menu.lst, grub.cfg and grub.conf; grub-install, grub-mkconfig, and MBR

L inux goes through multiple phases during the boot process. It starts selective

services during its transition from one phase into another and provides the administrator an opportunity to interact with a preboot program to boot the system into a non-default runlevel/target or pass an option to the kernel. It launches a number of services during its transition to the default or specified runlevel/target.

systemd is the new default system initialization scheme in newer distribution versions of Debian and RHEL, as well as their offshoots, replacing both SysVinit and Upstart. systemd has brought many enhancements, capabilities, and tools to the operating system. It allows the system to boot into one of several pre-defined targets. All legacy power management commands and runlevels are still available and can be used if needed.

The Linux Boot Process in a Nutshell

Linux goes through a *boot* process when the system is powered up or restarted. The boot process lasts until all enabled services are started and a login prompt appears on the screen, which allows users to log in to the system and do their work. The boot process is automatic; however, you might need to interact with it to take a non-default action, such as booting a non-default kernel, booting into a non-default runlevel or target, repairing the system, recovering from an unbootable state, and so on. The boot process on an x86 computer may be split into four major phases: (1) the firmware phase, (2) the bootloader phase, (3) the kernel phase, and (4) the initialization phase. The system accomplishes these phases one after the other while performing and attempting to complete the tasks identified in each phase. The following subsections briefly explain each phase, and the subsequent sections elaborate more on the last three phases.

The Firmware Phase (BIOS and UEFI)

The firmware is the BIOS or the UEFI code that is stored in flash memory on the x86 system board. The first thing it does is run the *Power-On-Self-Test* (POST) to detect, test, and initialize the system hardware components. While doing so, it installs appropriate drivers for the video hardware and displays system messages on the screen. The firmware scans the available storage devices in an effort to locate a boot device, starting with a 512-byte image containing 446 bytes of the bootloader program, 64 bytes for the partition table, and the last two bytes with the boot signature. This 512-byte tiny area is referred to as the *Master Boot Record* (MBR) and it is located on the first sector of the boot disk. As soon as it discovers a usable boot device, it loads the bootloader into memory and passes control over to it.

The BIOS is a small memory chip in the computer that stores system date and time, list and sequence of boot devices, I/O configuration, etc. This configuration is customizable. Depending on the computer hardware, you need to press a key to enter the BIOS setup or display a menu to choose a source to boot the system. The computer goes through the hardware initialization phase that involves detecting and diagnosing peripheral devices. It runs the POST on the devices as it finds them, installs drivers for the graphics card and the attached monitor, and begins exhibiting system messages on the video hardware. It discovers a usable boot device, loads the bootloader program into memory, and passes control over to it. Boot devices on most computers support booting from optical and USB flash devices, hard drives, network, and other media.

The UEFI is a new 32/64-bit architecture-independent standard that computer manufacturers have widely adopted in their latest hardware offerings replacing BIOS. This mechanism delivers enhanced boot and runtime services, and superior features such as speed over the legacy 16-bit

---

BIOS. It has its own device drivers, is able to mount and read Linux extended file systems, includes UEFI-compliant application tools, and supports one or more bootloader programs. It comes with a boot manager that allows you to choose an alternative boot source. Most computer manufacturers have customized the features for their hardware platform. You may find varying menu interfaces among other differences.

The Bootloader Phase

Once the firmware phase is over and a boot device is detected, the system loads a piece of software located in the boot sector called the *bootloader*. The primary job of the bootloader program is to spot the Linux kernel code, decompress it, load it into memory, and transfer control over to it to further the boot process.

There have been plenty of bootloader programs used in Linux over the years of which GRUB, *GRand Unified Bootloader*, is the most recent. There are two versions of it. The older version was used on older Linux distribution versions and is now referred to as *GRUB Legacy*. The other one is shipped with newer Linux versions as the default bootloader program and is called *GRUB2*, an enhanced, modular, and more capable version of GRUB Legacy. GRUB2 also supports UEFI firmware and GPT drives, in addition to the legacy BIOS firmware and MBR drives.

The Kernel Phase

The *kernel* is the central program of the operating system, providing access to hardware and system services. After getting control from the bootloader, the kernel extracts the initrd file system image found in the */boot* file system into memory, decompresses it, and mounts it as read-only to serve as a temporary . The kernel loads necessary modules from the initrd image to allow access to the physical disks and the partitions and file systems therein. It also loads any required drivers to support the boot process. Later, it unmounts the initrd image and mounts the actual physical root file system in read/write mode. At this point, the necessary foundation has been built for the boot process to carry on and start loading the enabled services.

The Initialization Phase (SysVinit, Upstart, and systemd)

This is the last phase in the boot process. In Debian 8, RHEL 7, and their offshoots, systemd has supplanted both SysVinit and Upstart as the default system initialization scheme. systemd starts all enabled userspace system and network services, and brings the system up to the preset boot target. The system boot process is considered complete when all enabled services are operational for the boot target and users are able to log in to the system.

Linux systems with older SysVinit or Upstart initialization scheme starts the */sbin/init* program after the kernel phase is over. This program continues to run on the system until the system is shut down. On newer Linux versions running systemd, */sbin/init* is merely a symbolic link to */lib/systemd/systemd* file, which is the systemd init process.

The init Program

The *init* program (short for *initialization*) is the first process that spawns in the userland at system boot. It is a daemon process that serves as the root process for all subsequent processes that start on the system thereafter; therefore, it is assigned a process identifier (PID) 1. The init process debuted as a single main shell script in BSD UNIX that would call additional shell scripts one after the other in a pre-determined sequence to initialize the system. If a script had to wait for something during the execution, init had no other choice but to pause further execution until what was required either became available to the script or the script timed out. The init process then continued to the next script in the sequence. This unexpected wait resulted in delays in the overall boot process. To support the system initialization, there was one configuration file with names of enabled services and one optional script for handling miscellaneous tasks. During the initialization, the system had to start all enabled services.

init was enhanced in UNIX System V (SysVinit) with the introduction of numbered runlevels. This enhanced approach modularized the entire initialization process by permitting the system to boot and run into one of several pre-configured operating states, such as system maintenance and multi-user states, with or without graphical support. Each operating state defined a set of services and numbered them serially to get to that state of system operation. Though the services were numbered, it was the system administrator's responsibility to ensure that each script was sequenced in an appropriate order of dependency to lessen the chances of service failures and delays. This dependency adjustment was a manual process. Additionally, there was still the issue of slower processing of shell scripts. In SysVinit, the *inittab* file was referenced to determine the default runlevel to boot the system to. Based on this default runlevel, the *rc* script (part of the init program) called numbered start/stop scripts corresponding to the default runlevel and executed them. On a running system, these same scripts were used to transition from one operating state to another by only stopping or starting the services associated with the desired target runlevel. Debian, Ubuntu, Red Hat, and other Linux distributions had had this boot model for many years before they switched over to a more competent system boot model called Upstart.

The Upstart Program

Upstart was introduced as a substitute for the SysVinit model. It offered three major benefits over its predecessor: (1) asynchronous service startup; (2) automatic restart of crashed services; and (3) event-based service start and stop triggered by a process, a change in hardware, or by the start or stop of another service. This enhanced boot model was first presented in Ubuntu 6.10 in 2006 and it later became the default initialization scheme in Debian, Ubuntu, RHEL, and others. Upstart, like its precursor, also referenced the *inittab* file, but only to ascertain the default runlevel to boot to. Upstart used a set of configuration files located in the */etc/init* directory and processed scripts from the */etc/rc.d* directory for bringing the system up to the default runlevel and for state transitioning during system runtime. It used the *initctl* command for service control including starting, stopping, listing, and perusing status of jobs, restarting the init process, and so on. Due to some shortcomings in the Upstart design, newer Linux distribution versions have switched or are switching to *systemd*. A later section in this chapter elaborates on systemd.

Let's drill down on what we can accomplish and how in the last three phases of the boot process: (1) the bootloader phase (GRUB Legacy and GRUB2), (2) the Kernel phase, and (3) the initialization phase (SysVinit and systemd).

The Bootloader Phase—GRUB Legacy

GRUB Legacy supports boot disks with MBR on BIOS-based systems. It recognizes the boot codes for multiple operating systems, such as *BSD, Linux, DOS, and Microsoft Windows, that share a common boot disk and allows booting them. It identifies a variety of file system types, provides a simple user interface to interact with, a bunch of helpful commands, and so on.

As GRUB Legacy and SysVinit are not available on our *centos73* and *ubuntu14* systems, we have stood up another VM and installed an older version of CentOS, version 5.11, in it. This new system has the hostname *centos511* and it also obtains IP assignments from DHCP.

Before you move on, download the ISO image of 1of2 DVD for CentOS 5.11 from *www.centos.org/download* (under Older Versions, then click Tree→isos→x86_64). Once downloaded, create a VM in Oracle VM VirtualBox, and install the OS in it. Use DHCP to obtain IP assignments for the network interface. Instructions to install this old version vary from CentOS 7.3 that we had installed in Chapter 1.

All references to GRUB Legacy configuration files and commands made in this section are based on this new host.

Understanding GRUB Legacy Configuration File

It is important to comprehend the contents of the GRUB Legacy configuration file *grub.conf*, used in old versions of Debian and RHEL, and their spinoffs. This file is located in the */boot/grub* directory with symbolic links from */etc/grub.conf* and */boot/grub/menu.lst* files, as shown below:

```
[root@centos511 ~]# ll /etc/grub.conf /boot/grub/menu.lst
lrwxrwxrwx. 1 root root 11 Feb 10 10:53 /boot/grub/menu.lst -> ./grub.conf
lrwxrwxrwx. 1 root root 22 Feb 10 10:53 /etc/grub.conf -> ../boot/grub/grub.conf
```

Here are the uncommented default lines from *grub.conf* as recorded on *centos511*. We have enumerated the lines for easy explanation.

```
[root@centos511 ~]# grep -v ^# /boot/grub/grub.conf | nl
     1  default=0
     2  timeout=5
     3  splashimage=(hd0,0)/grub/splash.xpm.gz
     4  hiddenmenu
     5  title CentOS (2.6.18-398.el5)
     6      root (hd0,0)
     7      kernel /vmlinuz-2.6.18-398.el5 ro root=/dev/VolGroup00/LogVol00 rhgb quiet
     8      initrd /initramfs-2.6.18-398.el5.img
```

Each of the rows is explicated below:

- ✓ Line #1: Sets the default kernel entry, as defined with the corresponding "title" on line #5, to boot. If the value is set to 1, it would point to the next kernel entry associated with "title", and so on for subsequent values.
- ✓ Line #2: Gives you 5 seconds to interrupt the autoboot process to interact with GRUB at system boot time.
- ✓ Line #3: Sets the location of the graphical GRUB screen to be displayed. The value includes the location of the file */grub/splash.xpm.gz* under the first partition (0 represents */boot*) on the first boot disk (hd0).
- ✓ Line #4: Instructs the system to hide the GRUB menu until a key is pressed to interrupt the autoboot process.
- ✓ Line #5: Specifies the name or short description of the kernel. All titles are displayed in the GRUB menu and you can use the up/down arrow keys to select the desired entry to boot.
- ✓ Line #6: Sub-entry that points to the boot disk device as defined in the */boot/grub/device.map* file:

```
[root@centos511 ~]# cat /boot/grub/device.map
(hd0)    /dev/sda
```

✓ Line #7: Sub-entry that provides the kernel directive the arguments to be used during the boot process. It includes the kernel file name (*vmlinuz-2.6.18-398.el5*) and its location with respect to */boot*. It instructs the boot process to load the kernel read-only (ro) from the root logical volume (*/dev/VolGroup00/LogVol00*). The last two parameters instruct the boot process to boot the kernel in *Red Hat Graphical Boot* (rhgb) mode and hide (quiet) all non-critical boot messages. Note that the sequence of the boot parameters as defined with the kernel directive may vary between systems and versions.

✓ Line #8: Sub-entry that initializes the RAM disk (initrd or initramfs) so the kernel starts up and mounts an initial root file system from the */boot/initramfs-2.6.18-398.el5.img* file. This file contains loadable kernel modules that are not part of the default Linux kernel including the ones necessary for mounting file systems. These modules are loaded in memory to support kernel initialization and loading process.

You may find modified values of these directives or additional directives in this file on other Linux versions.

If you intend to make any modifications to this file, you will need to reboot the system with the *reboot* command after making the changes in order for them to take effect and for you to validate their effectiveness. There is no need to run any GRUB-related commands following the file edit.

Interacting with GRUB Legacy

After GRUB Legacy has been loaded into memory at boot time and takes control over, it searches for boot entries in the *grub.conf* file and presents them as a list of available choices. The system allows you to disrupt the autoboot process by pressing any key (the Shift key on Ubuntu) within five seconds (timeout=5 in *grub.conf*) and interact with GRUB Legacy for other options. Alternatively, if you wish to boot the system using the default boot device with all other default settings in place, do not press any key and let the system go through the autoboot process. This is the message that you will see on the screen in that case:

    Booting CentOS (2.6.18-398.el5) in 5 seconds...

If, however, you choose to interrupt the autoboot process, you will get to the GRUB Legacy menu where you can perform a number of tasks, such as searching for other boot devices, booting from a different boot disk or kernel, viewing or altering boot configuration, and booting into a non-default runlevel. These tasks are usually carried out for testing or debugging. Figure 6-1 (next page) displays the main GRUB Legacy menu as it appears on *centos511*.

There is only one kernel currently installed on the system and it is displayed on the GRUB Legacy main screen in Figure 6-1. Also, there are three commands—e, a, and c—available to enter the edit mode, modify the kernel string, and access the grub> command prompt, respectively. At this moment, if you still want to continue with the system boot, simply press the Enter key and the highlighted entry will be booted.

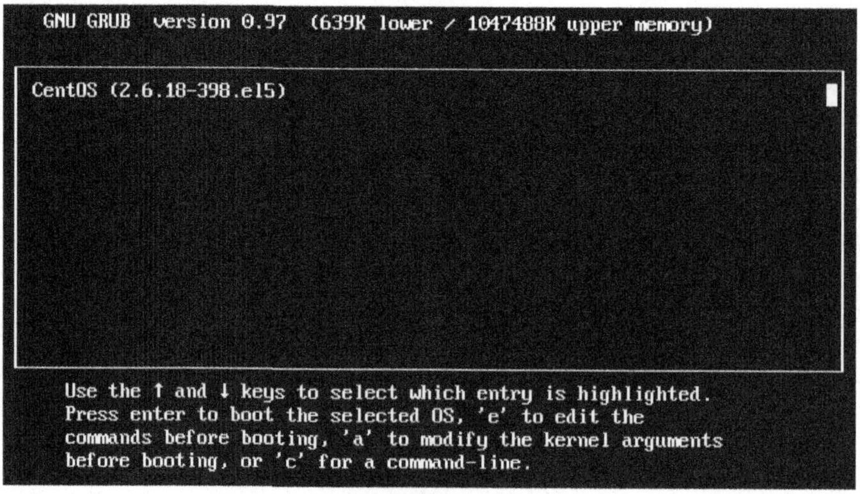

Figure 6-1 GRUB Legacy Main Menu

Figure 6-2 shows a picture of the boot directives that are displayed when the command *e* is entered.

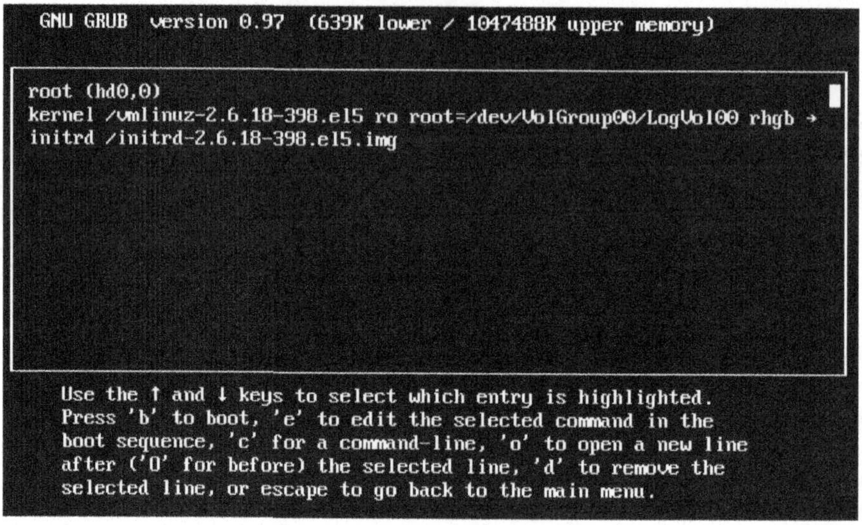

Figure 6-2 GRUB Legacy Edit Menu

As indicated in the bottom section of Figure 6-2, the up and down arrow keys are used to select an entry in the box, "b" to boot the system, "e" to edit the highlighted entry, "c" to access the grub> command prompt, "o" or "O" to open a new line before or after the highlighted entry, "d" to delete the highlighted entry, and ESC to return to the main menu. You may try some of these commands to familiarize yourself of their behavior, but avoid making any changes. When you are done, press the ESC key to go back to the main menu. Note that any changes you made while interacting with GRUB Legacy are temporary and will affect the system only for the current boot.

The next command "a" in the main menu allows you to modify the kernel string for booting the system into an alternative runlevel or for testing or troubleshooting. By default, it displays just the last portion of the boot string (see the kernel directive in the *grub.conf* file), as shown in Figure 6-3.

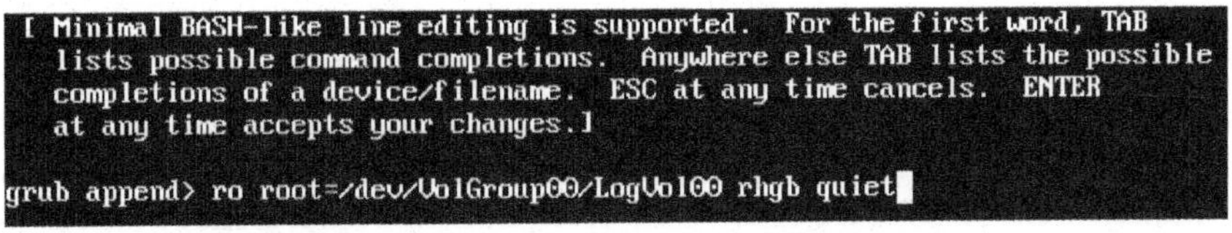

```
[ Minimal BASH-like line editing is supported.  For the first word, TAB
  lists possible command completions.  Anywhere else TAB lists the possible
  completions of a device/filename.  ESC at any time cancels.  ENTER
  at any time accepts your changes.]

grub append> ro root=/dev/VolGroup00/LogVol00 rhgb quiet
```

Figure 6-3 GRUB Legacy Kernel String

You can use the left and right arrow keys to scroll and edit any fragment of the string before pressing Enter to boot the system. For instance, if you want to boot into the single-user mode for maintenance, simply append an "s", "S", or "single" to the kernel string and press Enter. Replace it with "2" or "3" to boot the system into multi-user mode with graphical capabilities turned off.

The third and the last command "c" in the main menu takes you to the grub> command prompt where you can press TAB to list available commands to carry out diagnostic, recovery, and other functions.

Changing the Autoboot Timeout Value

The value of the timeout directive can be altered to adjust the autoboot delay as desired at system boot. This change is straightforward. Simply open the */boot/grub/grub.conf* file in the vi editor and change this directive's value to 10, for instance, as follows:

```
timeout=10
```

Save the file and quit vi. Reboot the system and observe the countdown timer before the list of bootable kernels is displayed. It would be something similar to the following:

Booting CentOS (2.6.18-398.el5) in **10** seconds...

Installing a Corrupted Bootloader

GRUB bootloader may get corrupted due to an inadvertent overwrite of some unwanted characters, losing its ability to boot Linux. For an event like that, GRUB Legacy offers the *grub-install* command that can be used to install GRUB on the boot disk. One key option with the command is --root-directory with which you can specify a directory location to store the new GRUB images produced, otherwise it will write directly to the MBR of the specified boot disk.

The use of this command is straightforward. Simply specify the boot device name with the command to reinstall the bootloader on. The following example shows how to execute this task on */dev/sda* on *centos511*:

[root@centos511 ~]# **grub-install /dev/sda**
Installation finished. No error reported.
This is the contents of the device map /boot/grub/device.map.
Check if this is correct or not. If any of the lines is incorrect, fix it and re-run the script `grub-install'.
this device map was generated by anaconda
(hd0)   /dev/sda

The installation is successful as depicted. The output also indicates the contents of the */boot/grub/device.map* file, which is used to store the default boot disk device name.

The Bootloader Phase—GRUB2

GRUB2 is available on the latest versions of RHEL and Debian and their clones as the default bootloader program with integrated support for both BIOS and UEFI firmware for MBR and GPT disks. The management of GRUB2 is different from that of GRUB Legacy's. It uses a different set of files to store configuration data and a different method to make configuration changes. This section covers the details.

Understanding GRUB2 Configuration Files

Unlike GRUB Legacy, the GRUB2 configuration file is */boot/grub2/grub.cfg* (or */boot/grub/grub.cfg* on Ubuntu) and it is referenced at boot time. This file is generated automatically when a new kernel is installed, updated, or upgraded, and, therefore, it is not advisable to modify it directly, as your changes will be overwritten. The source file that is used to regenerate *grub.cfg* is called *grub* and it is located under the */etc/default* directory. This file defines the directives that govern how GRUB2 should behave at boot time. Any changes made to the *grub* file will only take effect after the *grub2-mkconfig* (or *grub-mkconfig* on Ubuntu) utility has been executed.

Let's analyze the two files to understand their syntax and contents.

The /etc/default/grub File

The */etc/default/grub* file defines the directives that control the behavior of GRUB2 at boot time. Any changes in this file must be followed by the execution of the *grub2-mkconfig* (or *grub-mkconfig*) command in order to be reflected in the */boot/grub2/grub.cfg* (or */boot/grub/grub.cfg* on Ubuntu) configuration file.

Here is an enumerated list of the default settings from the *grub* file followed by an explanation in Table 6-1:

```
[root@centos73 ~]# nl /etc/default/grub
     1  GRUB_TIMEOUT=5
     2  GRUB_DISTRIBUTOR="$(sed 's, release .*$,,g' /etc/system-release)"
     3  GRUB_DEFAULT=saved
     4  GRUB_DISABLE_SUBMENU=true
     5  GRUB_TERMINAL_OUTPUT="console"
     6  GRUB_CMDLINE_LINUX="crashkernel=auto rd.lvm.lv=cl/root rd.lvm.lv=cl/swap rhgb quiet"
     7  GRUB_DISABLE_RECOVERY="true"
```

Directive	Description
GRUB_TIMEOUT	Defines the wait time, in seconds, before booting off the default kernel. Default value is 5.
GRUB_DISTRIBUTOR	Sets the name of the Linux distribution
GRUB_DEFAULT	Boots the selected option from the previous system boot
GRUB_DISABLE_SUBMENU	Enables/disables the appearance of GRUB2 submenu
GRUB_TERMINAL_OUTPUT	Sets the default terminal
GRUB_CMDLINE_LINUX	Specifies the command line options to pass to the kernel at boot time
GRUB_DISABLE_RECOVERY	Lists/hides system recovery entries in the GRUB2 menu

Table 6-1 GRUB2 Default Settings

Generally, you do not need to make any changes to this file, as the default settings are usually good for normal system operation.

The grub.cfg File

The *grub.cfg* is the main GRUB2 configuration file that supplies boot-time configuration information. This file can be regenerated manually with the *grub2-mkconfig* (or *grub-mkconfig*) utility, or it is automatically regenerated when a new kernel is installed, updated, or upgraded. In either case, this file will lose any previous manual changes made to it.

Here is how you would run this utility after making a change such as adjusting the GRUB_TIMEOUT value to 10 in the */etc/default/grub* file to reproduce *grub.cfg*:

```
[root@centos73 ~]# vi /etc/default/grub
GRUB_TIMEOUT=10
[root@centos511 ~]# grub2-mkconfig -o /boot/grub2/grub.cfg
Generating grub configuration file ...
Found linux image: /boot/vmlinuz-3.10.0-514.el7.x86_64
Found initrd image: /boot/initramfs-3.10.0-514.el7.x86_64.img
Found linux image: /boot/vmlinuz-0-rescue-19fc7726b26e46c7b95fd5656f943c63
Found initrd image: /boot/initramfs-0-rescue-19fc7726b26e46c7b95fd5656f943c63.img
done
```

Reboot the system with the *reboot* command and confirm the timeout value. On Ubuntu, run **grub-mkconfig** or **update-grub** instead.

grub2-mkconfig (or *grub-mkconfig*) also uses the settings defined in helper scripts located in the */etc/grub.d/* directory during the regeneration process. There are plenty of files located here, only a few are shown below:

```
[root@centos511 ~]# ll /etc/grub.d
-rwxr-xr-x. 1  root root  8702  Mar 20 10:34  00_header
-rwxr-xr-x. 1  root root 10781  Nov 22 10:51  10_linux
-rwxr-xr-x. 1  root root 11110  Nov 22 10:51  30_os-prober
-rwxr-xr-x. 1  root root   214  Nov 22 10:51  40_custom
-rwxr-xr-x. 1  root root   216  Nov 22 10:51  41_custom
```

The first script, *00_header*, sets the GRUB2 environment, the *10_linux* script searches for all installed kernels on the same disk partition, *30_os-prober* searches for the presence of other operating systems, and *40_custom* and *41_custom* are for us to add any customization. An example would be to add custom entries to the boot menu.

The *grub.cfg* file contains *menuentry* blocks for each installed kernel. Each block begins with a title and includes the names of the kernel and RAM disk image files, their location with respect to */boot*, and several options and modules to be loaded. These menu entry titles are displayed at the time of system boot, and you can choose one of them to boot. A sample menuentry block is shown below for the kernel 3.10.0-514.el7.x86_64 installed on *centos73*:

```
menuentry 'CentOS Linux  (3.10.0-514.el7.x86_64  7 (Core)' --class centos --class gnu-linux --class gnu
--class os --unrestricted $menuentry_id_option 'gnulinux-3.10.0-514.el7.x86_64-advanced-ae73-4f74-
b8bf-4a931f02bf91' {
```

```
        load_video
        set gfxpayload=keep
        insmod gzio
        insmod part_msdos
        insmod xfs
        set root='hd0,msdos1'
. . . . . . . .
        linux16 /vmlinuz-3.10.0-514.el7.x86_64 root=/dev/mapper/cl-root  ro  crashkernel=auto
rd.lvm.lv=cl/root  rd.lvm.lv=cl/swap  rhgb quiet  LANG=en_US.UTF-8
        initrd16 /initramfs-3.10.0-514.el7.x86_64.img
    }
```

If a new kernel is added to the system, it will automatically become the default boot kernel and it will be shown atop the list in GRUB2 menu at startup. The older entries will remain intact and can be chosen to boot in the GRUB2 menu if required.

Interacting with GRUB2

The GRUB2 main menu shows a list of bootable kernel entries as does GRUB Legacy, allowing us to move from one selection to another using the up or down arrow key. It lets us edit a selected kernel entry by pressing an "e" or go to the grub> command prompt by pressing a "c".

In the edit mode, GRUB2 loads the selected entry from the *grub.cfg* file (compare GRUB Legacy's *grub.conf* file) in an editor, enabling you to make a desired modification before booting the system. For instance, you can boot the system into a less capable operating mode by adding an "s", "S", "single", "2", "3", or "emergency" to the end of the line that begins with the keyword "linux16", as shown in Figure 6-4. Press Ctrl+x when done to boot. Remember that this is a one-time temporary change and it won't touch the *grub.cfg* file.

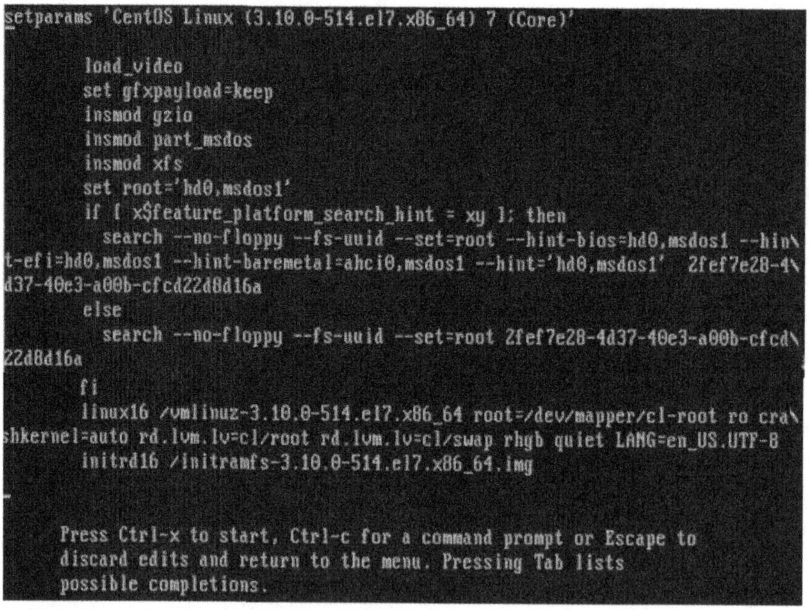

Figure 6-4 GRUB2 Kernel Edit

If you do not wish to boot the system at this time, you can press ESC to discard the changes and return to the main menu.

The grub> command prompt appears when you press Ctrl+c while in the edit window or "c" from the main menu. The command mode provides you with the opportunity to carry out debugging, recovery, and many other tasks. You can view available commands by pressing the TAB key. See Figure 6-5.

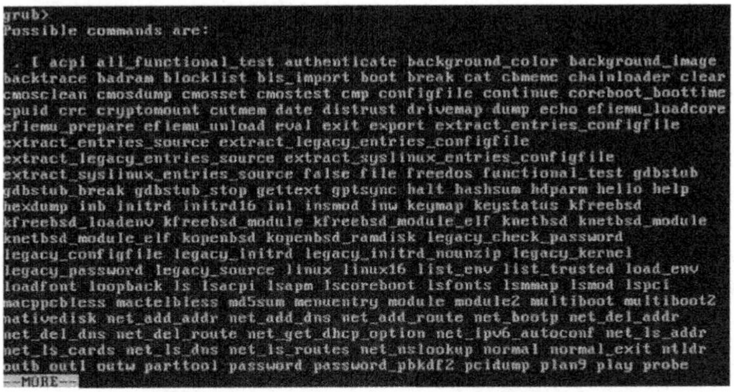

Figure 6-5 GRUB2 Commands

Compare the commands provided by GRUB Legacy with what GRUB2 offers. There is a big difference in the number of available commands.

The Kernel Phase

GRUB initializes the kernel and loads it into memory. Several messages appear on the console during the kernel initialization depending on the hardware and system configuration. These messages are logged to the */var/log/dmesg* file and may be examined later with a *less* on the file or the *dmesg* (diagnostic messages) command. The messages include information about the kernel version, memory, CPU, console, SELinux status, disks, root logical volume, network interfaces, swap logical volume, as well as any unusual events that occur in the system and may prove helpful in troubleshooting.

A few entries from the beginning of the *dmesg* file on *centos73* are shown below:

[user1@centos73 ~]$ **less /var/log/dmesg**
[0.000000] Initializing cgroup subsys cpuset
[0.000000] Initializing cgroup subsys cpu
[0.000000] Initializing cgroup subsys cpuacct
[0.000000] Linux version 3.10.0-514.el7.x86_64 (builder@kbuilder.dev.centos.org) (gcc version 4.8.5 20150623 (Red Hat 4.8.5-11) (GCC)) #1 SMP Tue Nov 22 16:42:41 UTC 2016
[0.000000] Command line: BOOT_IMAGE=/vmlinuz-3.10.0-514.el7.x86_64 root=/dev/mapper/cl-root ro crashkernel=auto rd.lvm.lv=cl/root rd.lvm.lv=cl/swap rhgb quiet
[0.000000] e820: BIOS-provided physical RAM map:
[0.000000] BIOS-e820: [mem 0x0000000000000000-0x000000000009fbff] usable
[0.000000] BIOS-e820: [mem 0x000000000009fc00-0x000000000009ffff] reserved

The *dmesg* command reads this information directly from the kernel buffer where it is recorded before it is written to the */var/log/dmesg* file.

Understanding Command Line Kernel Options

Command line kernel options, a.k.a. *boot-time kernel parameters*, are the options that are passed to the kernel at boot-time to override its default conduct during the boot process (booting into a non-default mode, using a different kernel, etc.) or to tune its runtime behavior. For testing and debugging purposes, you can pass an option via the GRUB interface to affect a single session only. Once the option is verified to work as expected, add it persistently to the system.

The entire kernel string, along with all the command line options that were used in the last system boot, is stored in the */proc/cmdline* file and can be viewed with any text file display tool. The following shows the contents as recorded on *centos73*:

[user1@centos73 ~]$ **cat /proc/cmdline**
BOOT_IMAGE=/vmlinuz-3.10.0-514.el7.x86_64 root=/dev/mapper/cl-root ro **crashkernel=auto rd.lvm.lv=cl/root rd.lvm.lv=cl/swap rhgb quiet**

The bolded text depicts the command line options that were used in the previous system boot.

In order to apply a command line option persistently to the default kernel, we edit the */etc/default/grub* file and append it to the value of the GRUB_CMDLINE_LINUX directive. For instance, to add an option, such as "kernstack" with a value of "1", modify the current directive in the file to look like:

GRUB_CMDLINE_LINUX="crashkernel=auto rd.lvm.lv=cl/root rd.lvm.lv=cl/swap rhgb quiet **kernstack=1"**

Next, issue the *grub2-mkconfig* (or *grub-mkconfig*) command to regenerate the *grub.cfg* file:

[user1@centos73 ~]$ **grub2-mkconfig -o /boot/grub2/grub.cfg**

Then reboot the system. After the system has been up, *cat /proc/cmdline* for confirmation:

[user1@centos73 ~]$ **cat /proc/cmdline**
BOOT_IMAGE=/vmlinuz-3.10.0-514.el7.x86_64 root=/dev/mapper/cl-root ro crashkernel=auto rd.lvm.lv=cl/root rd.lvm.lv=cl/swap rhgb quiet **kernstack=1**

The output confirms the addition of the option.

The System Initialization Phase—SysVinit

Once the kernel phase has concluded successfully, the system initialization phase begins during which several configuration files are referenced and numerous scripts are executed to start a number of services in preparation for system access and use. These scripts are grouped in multiple numbered control levels. The system executes the scripts defined in one control level before it goes to the subsequent level until it has started all the services that are marked to run at the default control level. The following subsections discuss control levels and how to manipulate them.

Runlevels

System *run control* (rc) levels are pre-defined sets of tasks that determine the operating state (or runlevel) of the system. Every Linux system supports eight standard runlevels, however, the way they implement them may vary from one distribution to another. The standard runlevels range from 0 to 6 and s or S. Four of them (0, 1, s or S, and 6) are reserved for system halt, maintenance, and reboot purposes, and the other four (2, 3, 4, and 5) are used for normal system operation. The default rc level is 5 if X Window and desktop software are installed. Table 6-2 describes the eight runlevels.

Runlevel	Description
0	Linux is down
1	Single-user state used by administrators to perform critical system administration tasks that cannot be done otherwise. All local file systems are mounted.
s or S	Single-user state used by administrators to perform critical system administration tasks that cannot be done otherwise. Provide limited capabilities than does runlevel 1.
2	Multi-user state with most services running
3	Multi-user state with all services running
4	Not implemented. Reserved for future use
5	Multi-user state with all services plus a graphical environment running. This is the default runlevel.
6	Linux reboots

Table 6-2 SysVinit Runlevels

Ubuntu provides an identical functionality at all runlevels from 2 to 5.

There is a special boot mode available called *emergency*. This mode is typically used to fix issues with an unbootable system. It executes most kernel phase programs and presents a command prompt without entering the initialization phase.

The kernel calls the */sbin/init* command and transfers the control over to it to initiate the system initialization process known as the *first process*. *init* consults the */etc/inittab* file to determine the default runlevel for the system to boot to. It reads plenty of other configuration files and calls a number of scripts in its effort to bring the system up to the default runlevel.

The /etc/inittab File

The *inittab* file establishes the default runlevel for the system. It also defines actions to be taken in other specific situations. There are four fields—id, runlevel, action, and process—per line entry separated by the colon (:) character. The following shows a few sample lines from the file on *centos511*:

```
id:5:initdefault:
si::sysinit:/etc/rc.d/rc.sysinit
l0:0:wait:/etc/rc.d/rc 0
ca::ctrlaltdel:/sbin/shutdown -t3 -r now
1:2345:respawn:/sbin/mingetty tty1
x:5:respawn:/etc/X11/prefdm -nodaemon
```

Table 6-3 expounds on the four fields:

Field	Description
Id	Defines a unique identification string containing one to four characters
Runlevel	Identifies one or more runlevels for which the action applies. An empty field is valid for all runlevels.
Action	Determines an action to be taken: **Initdefault:** determines the default runlevel for the system. The *init* command reads this line and boots the system to the specified runlevel. **Sysinit:** executes the specified process before *init* tries to access the system console. **Wait:** when an entry with this action is executed, other entries at the same runlevel will wait for its completion before their turn comes. **Ctrlaltdel:** runs the associated process when *init* receives the SIGINT signal such as the CTRL+ALT+DEL key sequence. The default action is to shut down the system and reboot it to the default runlevel. This action may be disabled by commenting this line entry out. **Respawn:** restarts the specified process if it dies. No action is taken if the process is already running.
Process	Defines the full pathname of the process or command that is to be executed along with any arguments

Table 6-3 The /etc/inittab File

If you modify anything in the *inittab* file, you will need to force the *init* process to re-read the updated information from it by running either of the following as *root*:

```
[root@centos511 ~]# init q
[root@centos511 ~]# telinit q
[root@centos511 ~]# kill -HUP 1
```

Sequencer, Configuration, and Initialization Directories

Part of the initialization process, *init* calls the */etc/rc.d/rc* (*/etc/init.d/rc* on Ubuntu) script to execute all startup scripts needed to bring the system up to the default runlevel. This script locates the service files in the sequencer directories */etc/rc.d/rc#.d* (*/etc/rc#.d* on Ubuntu), obtains configuration data from the files located in the */etc/sysconfig* (*/etc/default* on Ubuntu) directory, and starts them up from the initialization directory */etc/rc.d/init.d* (*/etc/init.d* on Ubuntu). It finally runs the */etc/rc.d/rc.local* (*/etc/init.d/rc.local* on Ubuntu) script to complete the initialization process. Run the *ll* command on these directories to get yourself familiarized with their content.

There are seven sequencer directories—*rc0.d, rc1.d, rc2.d, rc3.d, rc4.d, rc5.d,* and *rc6.d*—corresponding to the seven runlevels (except for "s" or "S"), and they contain two types of scripts:

start and *kill*. The names of the start scripts begin with an uppercase "S" and an uppercase "K" for the kill scripts. These scripts are symbolically linked to the actual start/kill scripts stored in the */etc/rc.d/init.d* (*/etc/init.d* on Ubuntu) directory. Each start/kill script contains start, stop, restart, reload, force-reload, and status functions, corresponding to service start, stop, stop and start, configuration file re-read, force configuration file re-read, and status check.

 Some Linux versions and distributions support additional functions.

During system initialization, the "S" scripts are executed one after the other in an ascending numerical sequence. Similarly, when the system goes down, the "K" scripts are executed in a descending numerical order.

Examining Current and Previous System Runlevels

Linux allows us to peruse the current and previous runlevels of the system using two different commands. First, we can use the *who* command with the -r switch:

```
[user1@centos511 ~]$ who -r
        run-level 5  2017-02-10 09:21              last=S
```

The output indicates that the system is currently running at runlevel 5 and its last runlevel was S. The output also displays the time when the runlevel change occurred.

The other option is the *runlevel* command, which displays the previous and current runlevels without any further details:

```
[user1@centos511 ~]$ /sbin/runlevel
N 5
```

Switching Runlevels and Modifying the Default Runlevel

We can switch from one runlevel to another using several different commands. Linux provides the *init* (or *telinit*) and *shutdown* commands to transition to any runlevel, as well as the *halt*, *poweroff*, and *reboot* commands for switching into one of the four reserved runlevels: 0, 1, s, and 6.

For a permanent change, however, modify the runlevel associated with the initdefault action in the */etc/inittab* file. You will need to reboot the system for the new value to take effect. As a precaution, do not enter 0 or 6 as the default runlevel in */etc/inittab*.

Using the init or telinit Command

On a running system, you can use the *init* or the *telinit* command to switch from the current runlevel to any of the eight available runlevels. The *telinit* command is symlinked to *init* (run **ll /sbin/telinit** to verify), so it does not really matter which of the two you run, as both will have an identical effect. After the switch is complete, you can use the *runlevel* command for confirmation.

By default, the *init* command goes ahead and starts stopping services and processes as soon as it is issued. It does not broadcast a notification to the users to alert them of system runlevel change or shutdown. Prior to issuing the *init* command, it is a good idea to compose a simple message as the *root* user and transmit it using the *wall* command as a warning to appear on the terminal screens of all logged-in users. The following shows an example. The message may or may not be quoted.

[root@centos511 ~]# **wall Hi users, please log off as the system is being taken down for maintenance at 8pm. Thank you for your cooperation.**
Broadcast message from root@centos73 (pts/1) (Mon Feb 13 22:20:42 2017):
Hi users, please log off as the system is being taken down for maintenance. Thank you for your cooperation.

At the specified maintenance time, you can go ahead and issue the *init* command as planned.

Let's see a few examples of switching runlevels with *init*.

Assuming the system is currently running at runlevel 5 and you want to switch to runlevel 3, issue either of the following and watch the messages that appear on the console screen:

```
[root@centos511 ~]# init 3
[root@centos511 ~]# telinit 3
```

This command gracefully stops all services that should not be running in level 3. It does not affect any other running processes and services.

Similarly, by initiating **init 1** from runlevel 3, most system services can be stopped for the system to transition into the single-user state.

Try the following additional examples and watch the console screen.

To switch from runlevel 1 to 5, run **init 5**.

To stop all services gracefully followed by a system shut down and reboot to the default runlevel, issue **init 6**.

To stop all services gracefully and bring the system down to the halt state, execute **init 0**.

Using the shutdown Command

The *shutdown* command is preferred over *init* and *telinit* for halting and rebooting the system, or switching it to the single-user mode. It stops all services and processes in a sequential and consistent fashion, as does *init* and *telinit*; however, it has a few distinctions. It broadcasts a message to all logged-in users, blocks new user login attempts, and waits for one minute, by default, for users to save their work and log off, after which time it begins stopping services and processes, and proceeds as per the options specified at the command line.

The following examples show some common options and arguments that may be supplied with *shutdown* as required:

[root@centos511 ~]# **shutdown -r 30**	broadcasts a message, waits for 30 seconds, blocks user login attempts, stops all services gracefully, shuts the system down, and reboots it to the default runlevel. Add the & sign to gain access to the command prompt by running the command in the background. A value of "0" or "now" replacing "30" will begin the shutdown process immediately.
[root@centos511 ~]# **shutdown -r 1:00**	broadcasts a message, stops all services gracefully starting at 1am, blocks user login attempts, shuts the system down, and reboots it to the default runlevel.

`[root@centos511 ~]# ` **`shutdown -h 20`**	broadcasts a message, waits for 20 minutes, and then brings the system down gracefully to the halt or power off state. Swap -h with -H to halt the system or with -P to power it off.
`[root@centos511 ~]# ` **`shutdown now -k`**	broadcasts a message, but does not actually bring the system down.
`[root@centos511 ~]# ` **`shutdown -t 75 0`**	broadcasts a message, blocks user login attempts, waits for 75 seconds after sending a warning message, and then start terminating services.
`[root@centos511 ~]# ` **`shutdown -c`**	(or `Ctrl+c`) Cancels a scheduled shutdown action.

The *shutdown* command calls the *init* command behind the scenes to perform runlevel changes. The shutdown begin time may be specified in the hh:mm format or as a number of minutes from the current time.

Using the halt, poweroff, and reboot Commands

The *halt, reboot,* and *poweroff* commands without any options perform the same action that the *shutdown* command would perform with "-h now", "-r now", and "-P now", respectively. You may specify the -f (force) switch with any of these commands to terminate the services and processes right away by calling the *kill* command with signal 9. This might, however, introduce the risk of damaging application files and file system structures; therefore, it is not recommended to use this option from any multi-user runlevel. Two of the three commands—*halt* and *reboot*—may be executed with the -p option to power off the system as well.

Managing SysVinit Services

There are plenty of system and network services available on Linux, which we can set to start automatically at each system reboot. These services can also be configured to remain disabled at system boot. Moreover, an automatic start and stop can be defined at individual runlevels. For example, you may want a specific service to start only if the system enters runlevel 5, but remain inactive at lower runlevels; view the operational status of a service; force a service to reload its configuration; and so on. A service can also be restarted manually.

The SysVinit scheme provides the *chkconfig* and *service* commands to manage services at the command prompt. The *chkconfig* command gives you the ability to display service startup settings and set a service to start or stop at appropriate runlevels. The *service* command allows you to start, stop, check the operational status of, and restart a service. This command also enables you to force the service to reload its configuration if there has been any change made to it.

Besides the two commands, a menu-driven program is also available for service management, and it is explained later in this section.

Exercise 6-1: List, Enable, and Disable Services

In this exercise, you will list the start/stop settings for a service called *ntpd*. You will enable this service for runlevel 3 only and validate the change. You will inspect the settings for all other services available on the system. Finally, you will enable this service to autostart at all multi-user runlevels, prevent it from autostarting at all runlevels, and validate the new settings.

1. Issue the *chkconfig* command and list the current start/stop settings for the *ntpd* service:

   [root@centos511 ~]# **chkconfig --list ntpd**
   ntpd   0:off 1:off 2:off 3:off 4:off 5:off 6:off

   The output indicates that *ntpd* is disabled for all runlevels.

2. Run *chkconfig* and turn *ntpd* on for runlevel 3:

   [root@centos511 ~]# **chkconfig --level 3 ntpd on**

3. Execute *chkconfig* and confirm the new setting:

   [root@centos511 ~]# **chkconfig --list ntpd**

4. Issue *chkconfig* again and list settings for all the services available on the system:

   [root@centos511 ~]# **chkconfig --list**
   NetworkManager   0:off 1:off 2:off 3:off 4:off 5:off 6:off
   acpid   0:off 1:off 2:on   3:on   4:on   5:on   6:off
   anacron   0:off 1:off 2:on   3:on   4:on   5:on   6:off
   atd   0:off 1:off 2:off 3:on   4:on   5:on   6:off
   . . . .

5. Run *chkconfig* to enable *ntpd* to start at all multi-user runlevels:

   [root@centos511 ~]# **chkconfig ntpd on**

6. Execute *chkconfig* to disable *ntpd* from autostarting at all multi-user runlevels:

   [root@centos511 ~]# **chkconfig ntpd off**

7. Confirm the new settings:

   [root@centos511 ~]# **chkconfig --list ntpd**
   ntpd   0:off 1:off 2:off 3:off 4:off 5:off 6:off

Exercise 6-2: Start, Restart, and Check Status of Services

In this exercise, you will check whether the *ntpd* service is running. You will start it and re-examine its running status. You will restart the service and peruse the running status for all the services available on the system.

1. Issue the *service* command to inspect the operating status of *ntpd*:

   [root@centos511 ~]# **service ntpd status**
   ntpd is stopped

2. Use the *service* command and start the *ntpd* service:

```
[root@centos511 ~]# service ntpd start
Starting ntpd:                              [ OK ]
```

3. Execute the *service* command to check whether the *ntpd* service was started:

```
[root@centos511 ~]# service ntpd status
ntpd (pid 4677) is running...
```

4. Issue the *service* command and restart *ntpd*:

```
[root@centos511 ~]# service ntpd restart
Shutting down ntpd:                         [ OK ]
Starting ntpd:                              [ OK ]
```

5. Run the *service* command to examine the operational status for all the services on the system:

```
[root@centos511 ~]# service --status-all
acpid (pid 2024) is running...
anacron is stopped
atd (pid  2262) is running...
. . . . . . . .
```

Configuring Service Start and Stop via Text Interface

The SysVinit system initialization scheme provides an alternative way of configuring service start and stop using a simple text interface called *ntsysv*. This program may be run with or without supplying one or more runlevels as an argument. Here are a few examples that will help you understand its usage.

To enable or disable services at the current system runlevel, run *ntsysv* without any arguments. It will bring up a text window similar to the one shown in Figure 6-6. You will see a list of all available services on the system. Select the ones you want enabled or disabled by pressing the Spacebar key. When you are done with the configuration use the TAB key to go to the OK button and press Enter.

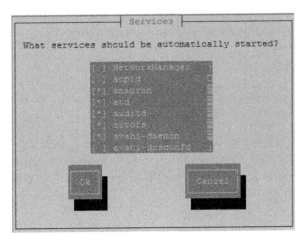

Figure 6-6 Service Start/Stop Management with ntsysv

To enable or disable several services at runlevels 2 and 3, for example, run this program as follows:

[root@centos511 ~]# **ntsysv --level 23**

By specifying runlevels at the command prompt this way, your start/stop selections will be effective only at those specific runlevels.

The System Initialization Phase—systemd

systemd (short for *system daemon*) is a system and service initialization and management mechanism that has superseded SysVinit and Upstart in terms of rapidity and capability. It has fast-tracked system initialization and state transitioning by introducing parallel processing of startup scripts, improved handling of service dependencies, and on-demand activation of services. systemd is the default system initialization mechanism used in most major mainstream Linux distributions, replacing both SysVinit and Upstart, and providing backward compatibility with SysVinit scripts. systemd is the first process with PID 1 that starts at boot and it is the last process that terminates at shutdown.

In order to benefit from parallelism, systemd initiates distinct services concurrently, taking advantage of multiple CPU cores and other computing resources. To achieve this, it creates sockets for all enabled services that support socket-based activation instantaneously at the very beginning of the initialization process, and passes them to daemon processes as they attempt to start in parallel. This approach lets systemd handle inter-service order dependencies and allows services to start without any delays. With systemd, dependent daemons need not be running, they only need the correct socket to be available. systemd creates all sockets first, all the daemons next, and any client requests to daemons not yet running are cached in the socket buffer and filled when the daemons come online. During the operational state, systemd maintains the sockets and uses them to reconnect other daemons and services that were interacting with an old daemon before it was terminated or restarted. Likewise, services that use activation based on D-Bus are started when a client application attempts to communicate with them the first time. Additional methods used by systemd for activation are device-based and path-based, with the former starting services when a specific hardware type such as USB is plugged in, and the latter starting services when a particular file or directory alters its state.

Socket is a communication method that allows a single process running on a system to talk to another process on the same or remote system.

D-Bus is another communication method that allows multiple services running in parallel on a system to talk to one another on the same or remote system.

With the on-demand activation, systemd defers the startup of services, such as Bluetooth and printing, until they are actually needed during the boot process or during runtime. Together, parallelization and on-demand activation save time and computing resources, and contribute to expediting the boot process considerably.

Units

Units are systemd objects used for organizing boot and maintenance tasks, such as hardware initialization, socket creation, file system mounts, and service startups. Unit configuration is stored in their respective configuration files, which are auto-generated from other configurations, created dynamically from the system state, produced at runtime, or user-developed. A unit can be in one of these operational states at a time: active, inactive, in the process of being activated or deactivated, or failed. A unit can be enabled or disabled. An enabled unit can be started to an active state; a disabled unit cannot be started.

A unit has a name and a type, and they are encoded in files with names in the form unitname.type. Some examples are tmp.mount, sshd.service, syslog.socket, and umount.target. There are two types of unit configuration files: (1) system unit files that are distributed with installed packages and located in the */usr/lib/systemd/system* (*/lib/systemd/system* on Ubuntu) directory, and (2) user unit files generated by users and stored in the */etc/systemd/user* directory (run **ll** on both directories to list their contents). The unit configuration files are a direct replacement for the initialization scripts found in the */etc/rc.d/init.d* (or */etc/init.d* on Ubuntu) directory.

Unit files contain common and specific configuration elements. Common elements fall under the [Unit] and [Install] sections, and comprise description, documentation location, dependency information, conflict information, and other options that are independent of the type of unit. The unit specific configuration data is located under the unit type section: [Service] for the service unit type, [Socket] for the socket unit type, and so forth. A sample unit file for *sshd.service* is shown below from the */usr/lib/systemd/system* directory on *centos73*:

```
[Unit]
Description=OpenSSH server daemon
Documentation=man:sshd(8) man:sshd_config(5)
After=network.target sshd-keygen.service
Wants=sshd-keygen.service

[Service]
Type=forking
PIDFile=/var/run/sshd.pid
EnvironmentFile=/etc/sysconfig/sshd
ExecStart=/usr/sbin/sshd $OPTIONS
ExecReload=/bin/kill -HUP $MAINPID
KillMode=process
Restart=on-failure
RestartSec=42s

[Install]
WantedBy=multi-user.target
```

Units can have dependency relationship among themselves based on a sequence (ordering) or a requirement. A sequence outlines one or more actions that need to be taken before or after the activation of a unit (options Before and After), and a requirement specifies what must already be running (option Requires) or not running (option Conflicts) in order for the successful launch of a unit. For instance, the *graphical.target* unit file (located in the */usr/lib/systemd/system* directory on *centos73*) shows that the system must already be operating in a multi-user mode and must not be

---

running in rescue mode in order for it to boot successfully into the graphical mode. Another option, Wants, may be used instead of Requires in the Unit or Install section so the unit is not forced to fail activation if a required unit fails to start.

There are a few other types of dependencies that you may see in unit configuration files. systemd generally sets and maintains inter-service dependencies automatically; however, this can be implemented manually as well.

Targets

Targets are simply logical collections of units. They are a special systemd unit type with the *.target* file extension. Some targets are equivalent to SysVinit runlevels; however, they are named rather than numbered. Targets are used to execute a series of units. This is typically true for booting the system to a specific operational level (similar to a numbered runlevel) with all the required services up and running at that level. Some targets inherit services from other targets and add their own to them. systemd includes several pre-defined targets that are described in Table 6-4, along with a comparable SysVinit runlevel.

Target	SysVinit Runlevel	Description
halt	0	Shuts down and halts the system
poweroff or runlevel0	0	Shuts down and powers off the system
shutdown	0	Shuts down the system
rescue or runlevel1	1, s, or single	Single-user target for administrative and recovery functions. All local file systems are mounted. Some essential services are started, but networking remains disabled.
multi-user or runlevel2|3|4	3	Multi-user target with full network support, but without GUI
graphical or runlevel5	5	Multi-user target with full network support and GUI
reboot or runlevel6	6	Shuts down and reboots the system
default	Typically set to 3 or 5	Default system boot target symlinked to either multi-user.target or graphical.target
emergency	N/A	Runs an emergency shell for critical system recovery
hibernate	N/A	Puts the system into hibernation by saving its running state on the hard disk and powering it off. When powered up, the system restores from its saved state rather than booting up.
suspend	N/A	Same as hibernation except that the system running state is saved in memory and power is not turned off
hybrid-sleep	N/A	Puts the system into hibernation and suspends its operation

Table 6-4 systemd Targets

Table 6-4 indicates one-to-one correspondence between most systemd targets and SysVinit runlevels. The default target is graphical.target, which is executed to boot the system with full networking and graphical support.

The systemctl Command

systemd comes with a set of management tools for querying and controlling its operations. The primary tool for interaction in this command suite is *systemctl*, which supports a number of administrative functions. This command also includes the combined functionality provided by the *chkconfig* and *service* commands.

The *systemctl* command is versatile and supports a variety of subcommands and flags. Table 6-5 lists and describes some common operations.

Subcommand	Description
enable / disable	Activates (deactivates) a unit for autostart at system boot
get-default (set-default)	Shows (sets) the default boot target
is-active	Checks whether a unit is running
is-enabled	Displays whether a unit is set to autostart at system boot
is-failed	Peruses whether a unit is in the failed state
isolate	Changes the running state of a system (similar to changing runlevels in SysVinit)
kill	Terminates all processes associated with a specific unit.
list-dependencies	Lists dependencies for a unit
list-unit-files	Lists installed unit files
list-units	Lists known units. This is the default subcommand when systemctl is executed without any arguments.
reload	Forces a running unit to re-read its configuration file
restart	Stops a running unit and restarts it
show	Shows unit properties
start / stop	Starts (stops) a unit
status	Presents the unit status information

Table 6-5 systemctl Subcommands

We will use a majority of these subcommands with *systemctl* going forward. Refer to the manual pages of this command for more details.

Managing Units

The *systemctl* command is used to view and manage all types of units. The following examples demonstrate some common operations related to inspecting units. These examples are run on our *centos73* system.

To list all known units and their status:

```
[root@centos73 ~]# systemctl
UNIT                           LOAD    ACTIVE SUB        DESCRIPTION
proc-sys-fs-binfmt_misc.automount  loaded active waiting   Arbitrary Executable File Formats
sys-devices-pci0000:00-0000:00:01.1-ata2-host1-target1:0:0-1:0:0:0-block-sr0.device loaded ac
sys-devices-pci0000:00-0000:00:03.0-net-enp0s3.device loaded active plugged   82540EM Gigabit
sys-devices-pci0000:00-0000:00:05.0-sound-card0.device loaded active plugged   82801AA AC'97
sys-devices-pci0000:00-0000:00:0d.0-ata3-host2-target2:0:0-2:0:0:0-block-sda-sda1.device load
```

The UNIT column in the above output shows the name of the unit and its location in the tree, LOAD reflects whether the unit configuration file was loaded properly, ACTIVE shows the high-level activation state, SUB depicts the low-level unit activation state, and DESCRIPTION illustrates the unit's content and functionality. By default, the *systemctl* command lists only the active units. You can use the --all option to see the inactive units also. If you want to list a specific type of unit, use the -t switch and specify a unit type. For instance, the following shows the list of all active and inactive units of type socket:

```
[root@centos73 ~]# systemctl -t socket --all
```

To list all units of type socket:

```
[root@centos73 ~]# systemctl list-sockets
LISTEN                      UNIT                        ACTIVATES
/dev/log                    systemd-journald.socket     systemd-journald.service
/run/dmeventd-client        dm-event.socket             dm-event.service
/run/dmeventd-server        dm-event.socket             dm-event.service
/run/lvm/lvmetad.socket     lvm2-lvmetad.socket         lvm2-lvmetad.service
/run/lvm/lvmpolld.socket    lvm2-lvmpolld.socket        lvm2-lvmpolld.service
/run/systemd/initctl/fifo   systemd-initctl.socket      systemd-initctl.service
```

To list all socket units and their status:

```
[root@centos73 ~]# systemctl --type=socket
```

To list all unit files installed on the system and their state:

```
[root@centos73 ~]# systemctl list-unit-files
UNIT FILE                           STATE
proc-sys-fs-binfmt_misc.automount   static
dev-hugepages.mount                 static
dev-mqueue.mount                    static
proc-fs-nfsd.mount                  static
```

To list all units that failed to start at the last system boot:

```
[root@centos73 ~]# systemctl --failed
  UNIT              LOAD    ACTIVE SUB     DESCRIPTION
● kdump.service     loaded  failed failed Crash recovery kernel arming
● postfix.service   loaded  failed failed Postfix Mail Transport Agent
```

Managing Service Units

The following examples demonstrate the use of the *systemctl* command on a service unit called *atd*.

To check the operational status of the *atd* service:

```
[root@centos73 ~]# systemctl status atd
atd.service – Job spooling tools
Loaded: loaded (/usr/lib/systemd/system/atd.service; enabled; vendor preset: enabled)
Active: active (running) since Mon 2017-02-13 09:53:49 EST; 3h 33min ago
Main PID: 1046 (atd)
CGroup: /system.slice/atd.service
        └─1046 /usr/sbin/atd -f
Feb 13 09:53:49 centos73 systemd[1]: Started Job spooling tools.
```

To disable the *atd* service from autostarting at the next system reboot:

```
[root@centos73 ~]# systemctl disable atd
Removed symlink /etc/systemd/system/multi-user.target.wants/atd.service.
```

To enable the *atd* service to autostart at the next system reboot:

```
[root@centos73 ~]# systemctl enable atd
Created symlink from /etc/systemd/system/multi-user.target.wants/atd.service to
/usr/lib/systemd/system/atd.service.
```

To peruse whether the *atd* service is set to autostart at the next system reboot:

```
[root@centos73 ~]# systemctl is-enabled atd
enabled
```

To check whether the *atd* service is running:

```
[root@centos73 ~]# systemctl is-active atd
active
```

To stop and start the *atd* service:

```
[root@centos73 ~]# systemctl stop atd
[root@centos73 ~]# systemctl start atd
```

To list all dependencies for the *atd* service:

```
[root@centos73 ~]# systemctl list-dependencies atd
atd.service
● ├─system.slice
● └─basic.target
●   ├─alsa-restore.service
●   ├─alsa-state.service
```

To show details for the *atd* service:

```
[root@centos73 ~]# systemctl show atd
Type=simple
Restart=no
NotifyAccess=none
RestartUSec=100ms
TimeoutStartUSec=1min 30s
TimeoutStopUSec=1min 30s
WatchdogUSec=0
WatchdogTimestamp=Mon 2017-02-13 13:30:31 EST
```

Managing Target Units

The *systemctl* command is used to manage the target units as well. It can be used to switch from one running target into another at the command line. Examples of some common target operations are provided below. You may use the *wall* command prior to initiating a target switch to announce your intention of doing so. See a usage example of the *wall* command earlier in this chapter.

To view a list of all loaded and active targets:

```
[root@centos73 ~]# systemctl -t target
UNIT                         LOAD    ACTIVE SUB     DESCRIPTION
basic.target                 loaded  active active  Basic System
cryptsetup.target            loaded  active active  Encrypted Volumes
getty.target                 loaded  active active  Login Prompts
graphical.target             loaded  active active  Graphical Interface
local-fs-pre.target          loaded  active active  Local File Systems (Pre)
local-fs.target              loaded  active active  Local File Systems
multi-user.target            loaded  active active  Multi-User System
network-online.target        loaded  active active  Network is Online
network.target               loaded  active active  Network
nfs-client.target            loaded  active active  NFS client services
nss-user-lookup.target       loaded  active active  User and Group Name Lookups
paths.target                 loaded  active active  Paths
remote-fs-pre.target         loaded  active active  Remote File Systems (Pre)
remote-fs.target             loaded  active active  Remote File Systems
```

For each target unit, the above output shows the target unit's full name, load state, high-level and low-level activation states, and a short description. Add the --all option to the above command to see all active and inactive loaded targets.

To look at the current default boot target:

```
[root@centos73 ~]# systemctl get-default
graphical.target
```

To change the current default boot target to multi-user.target:

```
[root@centos73 ~]# systemctl set-default multi-user
Removed symlink /etc/systemd/system/default.target.
Created symlink from /etc/systemd/system/default.target to /usr/lib/systemd/system/multi-user.target.
```

To switch to the multi-user target:

```
[root@centos73 ~]# systemctl isolate multi-user
```

You may run either the **runlevel** or the **who -r** command to verify the target switching.

To return to the graphical target:

```
[root@centos73 ~]# systemctl isolate graphical
```

To shut down the system to the halt or poweroff state, run **systemctl halt** or **systemctl poweroff**.

To shut down the system and then reboot it:

[root@centos73 ~]# **systemctl reboot**

To switch into the legacy runlevel 3 target:

[root@centos73 ~]# **systemctl isolate runlevel3**

Viewing System Boot Messages

The Linux system generates a ton of messages during the boot process. These messages are displayed on the system console and are also recorded in various log files at the same time for a later review if required. These messages show kernel information, hardware information and issues, services startup status and issues, and so on. The messages being displayed during the boot process may be concealed from viewing and replaced with a progress status bar by pressing the F2 key.

The three key files that record boot messages are *dmesg*, *boot.log*, and *messages* (*syslog* on Ubuntu) and all of them are located in the */var/log* directory. The *dmesg* file records kernel and hardware messages before the system logging service called *syslogd* (or *rsyslogd* on newer versions) is initiated, which is responsible for capturing messages and logging to *boot.log* and *messages* or *syslog* files.

The /var/log/dmesg File

This file is a store for recording kernel initialization and diagnostic messages. The messages may include information about the kernel version, memory, CPU, console, SELinux status, disks, root logical volume, swap logical volume, network interfaces, as well as any unusual events that occur in the system during boot-time or runtime and may prove helpful in troubleshooting.

A few initial entries from the *dmesg* file on *centos73* are shown below:

```
[user1@centos573 ~]$ head -15 /var/log/dmesg
[    0.000000] Initializing cgroup subsys cpuset
[    0.000000] Initializing cgroup subsys cpu
[    0.000000] Initializing cgroup subsys cpuacct
[    0.000000] Linux version 3.10.0-514.el7.x86_64 (builder@kbuilder.dev.centos.org) (gcc versi
on 4.8.5 20150623 (Red Hat 4.8.5-11) (GCC) ) #1 SMP Tue Nov 22 16:42:41 UTC 2016
[    0.000000] Command line: BOOT_IMAGE=/vmlinuz-3.10.0-514.el7.x86_64 root=/dev/mapper/cl-root
 ro crashkernel=auto rd.lvm.lv=cl/root rd.lvm.lv=cl/swap rhgb quiet kernstack=1
[    0.000000] e820: BIOS-provided physical RAM map:
[    0.000000] BIOS-e820: [mem 0x0000000000000000-0x000000000009fbff] usable
[    0.000000] BIOS-e820: [mem 0x000000000009fc00-0x000000000009ffff] reserved
[    0.000000] BIOS-e820: [mem 0x00000000000f0000-0x00000000000fffff] reserved
[    0.000000] BIOS-e820: [mem 0x0000000000100000-0x000000003ffeffff] usable
[    0.000000] BIOS-e820: [mem 0x000000003fff0000-0x000000003fffffff] ACPI data
```

Alternatively, you may run the *dmesg* command, which reads directly from the kernel ring buffer where the boot-time kernel information and runtime diagnostic messages are captured before they are written to the *dmesg* file.

The /var/log/boot.log File

Logs generated during system startup show the service startup sequence with a status stating whether the service was started successfully. This information may help in post-boot troubleshooting. Boot status messages are recorded in the *boot.log* file in */var/log*. Here is an excerpt from this file from *centos73*:

```
[user1@centos73 ~]$ head /var/log/boot.log
[  OK  ] Started Show Plymouth Boot Screen.
[  OK  ] Reached target Paths.
[  OK  ] Reached target Basic System.
[  OK  ] Found device /dev/mapper/cl-root.
         Starting File System Check on /dev/mapper/cl-root...
[  OK  ] Started File System Check on /dev/mapper/cl-root.
[  OK  ] Started dracut initqueue hook.
[  OK  ] Reached target Remote File Systems (Pre).
[  OK  ] Reached target Remote File Systems.
         Mounting /sysroot...
```

The /var/log/messages or /var/log/syslog File

The *messages* (or *syslog* on Ubuntu) file is the default location for logging system-wide activities including both boot-time and runtime messages. This file saves the information in plain text and may be viewed with any file display utility such as *cat, more, less, head,* or *tail*. This file may be observed in real time using the *tail* command with the -f (follow) option. It captures the date and time of the activity, hostname of the system, name and PID of the service, and a short description of the activity being logged. This file also records system shutdown messages and errors.

The following displays some sample entries from */var/log/syslog* as recorded on *ubuntu14*:

```
user1@ubuntu14:~$ head /var/log/syslog
Feb 14 06:12:05 ubuntu14 rsyslogd: [origin software="rsyslogd" swVersion="7.4.4" x-pid="490" x-info="http://www.rsyslog.com"] rsyslogd was HUPed
Feb 14 06:12:07 ubuntu14 anacron[1063]: Job `cron.daily' terminated
Feb 14 06:12:07 ubuntu14 anacron[1063]: Normal exit (1 job run)
Feb 14 06:17:01 ubuntu14 CRON[1793]: (root) CMD (   cd / && run-parts --report /etc/cron.hourly)
Feb 14 06:25:01 ubuntu14 CRON[1796]: (root) CMD (test -x /usr/sbin/anacron || ( cd / && run-parts --report /etc/cron.daily ))
Feb 14 07:17:01 ubuntu14 CRON[1798]: (root) CMD (   cd / && run-parts --report /etc/cron.hourly)
Feb 14 07:30:01 ubuntu14 CRON[1801]: (root) CMD (start -q anacron || :)
Feb 14 07:30:01 ubuntu14 anacron[1804]: Anacron 2.3 started on 2017-02-14
Feb 14 07:30:01 ubuntu14 anacron[1804]: Normal exit (0 jobs run)
Feb 14 08:17:01 ubuntu14 CRON[1808]: (root) CMD (   cd / && run-parts --report /etc/cron.hourly)
```

Chapter Summary

This chapter discussed the Linux boot process in depth, highlighting the complex process. We reviewed BIOS/firmware and looked at preboot administration tasks, and kernel and system startup phases. Preboot administration included interacting with GRUB Legacy and GRUB2, booting into specific runlevels/targets, and an analysis of the bootloader configuration file. We also explored the kernel initialization, boot-time options to the kernel, and system startup, which provided a detailed look at both SysVinit and systemd including their key components, directories, configuration files, and so on. We examined how to enable services and configure them to autostart. We used various tools to view and manage SysVinit runlevels and systemd units and targets.

Chapter Review at a Glance

The following presents a one-sentence review of each key topic discussed in this chapter:

- Linux boot process vary depending on the distribution and the system initialization method used; however, all Linux systems go through four major boot phases—the firmware phase, bootloader phase, kernel phase, and system initialization phase—before they are fully ready for their intended use.

- The firmware phase loads and executes the BIOS or the UEFI code to identify, examine, and initialize the system hardware components, installs the required drivers for video hardware to display messages on, scans and discovers the boot device, loads the bootloader program from the boot device's MBR/boot partition into memory, and passes control over to it to further the boot process.

- The bootloader code—GRUB Legacy or GRUB2—is stored in the boot sector of the boot device (MBR) or the boot partition (UEFI), and it locates the Linux kernel code, decompresses it, loads it into memory, and transfers control over to it to continue the boot process.

- System administrators can interact with GRUB to perform one-time, pre-boot administration tasks such as booting the system into a non-default runlevel/target, booting with an alternative kernel, supply a boot-time (commandline) kernel parameter, and so on.

- GRUB configuration files may be modified and regenerated to make permanent changes such as the autoboot timeout value and the addition of a boot-time kernel parameter.

- The kernel extracts a read-only copy of the root file system, decompresses it, mounts it temporarily to load necessary modules to support the boot process, and finally replaces it with the actual read-write root file system.

- The fourth and the final phase of the boot process is the system initialization phase, which takes the bulk of the boot process time.

- Depending on the Linux distribution and version in use, the system may be running SysVinit-, Upstart-, or the newest systemd-based system initialization scheme.

- SysVinit has been the most common and the longest-serving initialization scheme in Linux.

- The init program—also called the first-boot process with PID 1—is the first userland process that is started on the system in the SysVinit method; subsequent processes directly or indirectly spawn from it.

- SysVinit has multiple runlevels that correspond to system's various operating and power states, which may be changed using a host of commands that Linux provides.

- SysVinit services can be started, stopped, restarted, and reloaded, and can be set to autostart at system reboots.

- The Upstart program is more capable than SysVinit in the sense that it supports asynchronous service startup, auto-restart of failed services, and event-based service start and stop.

- The systemd is the system and service initialization and management mechanism that has replaced both SysVinit and Upstart in newest mainstream Linux distribution versions in terms of capabilities—parallelism, automatic service dependency handling, and on-demand activation of services—and speed.

- systemd targets are equivalent in concept to the runlevels in SysVinit.

- All boot, system operational, and other messages are logged to their respective log files.

- Commands we learned in this chapter are: grub-install, grub-mkconfig, grub2-mkconfig, update-grub, dmesg, init, telinit, who, runlevel, wall, shutdown, halt, poweroff, reboot, chkconfig, service, ntsysv, and systemctl.

- Files and directories we discussed in this chapter are: /etc/grub.conf, /boot/grub/grub.conf, /boot/grub/menu.lst, /boot/grub/device.map, /boot/grub2/grub.cfg, /boot/grub/grub.cfg, /etc/default/grub, /etc/grub.d/, /var/log/dmesg, /proc/cmdline, /etc/inittab, /etc/rc.d/rc, /etc/init.d/rc, /etc/rc.d/rc#.d/, /etc/rc#.d/, /etc/sysconfig/, /etc/default/, /etc/rc.d/init.d/, /etc/init.d/, /etc/rc.d/rc.local, /etc/init.d/rc.local, /etc/init.d, /etc/systemd/, /usr/lib/systemd/system/, /lib/systemd/system/, /var/log/boot.log, /var/log/messages, and /var/log/syslog.

## Chapter 7

Understanding and Configuring Hardware and Kernel Modules

This chapter describes the following major topics:

- ➤ Know PC hardware components including various communication channels
- ➤ Know devices and device files for PCI Express, mass storage, and USB
- ➤ Overview of processors and processor cores
- ➤ Compare hotplug and coldplug devices
- ➤ Dynamic hardware device handling
- ➤ Comprehend virtual file systems—Sysfs, Devices, and Procfs
- ➤ Understand D-Bus and how it works
- ➤ Interact with PC BIOS and view/modify common settings
- ➤ Identify current system kernel version and understand kernel modules
- ➤ Manage modules—query, load, and unload

This chapter covers the following objectives for LX0-103/101-400 Exam:

101.1 Determine and configure hardware settings [this entire objective is described in this chapter]

1. Enable and disable integrated peripherals
2. Configure systems with or without external peripherals such as keyboards
3. Differentiate between the various types of mass storage devices
4. Know the differences between coldplug and hotplug devices
5. Determine hardware resources for devices
6. Tools and utilities to list various hardware information (e.g. lsusb, lspci, etc.)
7. Tools and utilities to manipulate USB devices
8. Conceptual understanding of sysfs, udev, dbus

The following is a partial list of the used files, terms and utilities: /sys, /proc, /dev, modprobe, lsmod, lspci, and lsusb

Basic knowledge of key computer hardware components, such as communication channels, PCI devices, processors and cores, mass storage devices, and USB and other removable devices, is vital for system administrators. Moreover, the concept of hotplug and coldplug devices and how Linux manages the devices dynamically is important.

Linux maintains running system information in hundreds of files and directories organized hierarchically and located in memory-based file systems. These file systems are created at boot time, updated dynamically to reflect runtime changes, and destroyed at system shutdown. The stored information is referenced by a number of programs and commands for displaying, reporting, analysis, and troubleshooting. D-Bus and network sockets are communication mechanisms to facilitate processes to talk to one another on the same or different systems.

BIOS and UEFI are pre-boot menu-driven PC firmware interfaces designed to view and alter hardware settings, boot priorities, system date and time, and so on.

The Linux kernel is the colonel of the Linux system, controlling and regulating all system hardware and software. It comprises of hundreds of static and dynamic modules with each module bringing a unique functionality to the kernel. Modules may be listed, their information may be viewed, and they may be loaded or unloaded as required.

Computer Hardware

A computer is a set of physical components that work in unison to satisfy human computing needs. It comprises of several components, some of which must be present in order for the computer to be able to provide a minimum level of service, while more capabilities may be added with the inclusion of extra components to the base computer system. The physical components include, at a minimum, a microprocessor for running the code, memory for storing the code while it is running, a disk for offline data storage, a monitor for interfacing with the computer, and a keyboard for supplying input. Supplementary capability may be added by attaching a mouse for graphical input, network adapter for external network connectivity, storage adapter for storage networking, printer for printing documents, and so on. This section briefly examines common hardware components that are used in personal, laptop, and server computers (collectively referred to as computers in this chapter).

Communication Channels

In computers, communication takes place via three key channels: (1) *Interrupt Request* (IRQ), (2) *Input/Output port address* (I/O port address), and (3) *Direct Memory Address* (DMA). Most Linux systems automatically allocate and manage these communication channels dynamically without requiring manual intervention for configuration.

Interrupt Request (IRQ)

An interrupt request is a signal that devices on old computers sent to the processor to request processing time. The requesting device may be any internal or external device visible to the operating system. Each of these devices may require a dedicated IRQ number, which the PnP feature takes care of. USB and other similar devices share IRQs. The system maintains IRQ usage information in the */proc/interrupts* file for each processor and for each device. Here are a few lines from this file:

```
[user1@centos73 ~]$ cat /proc/interrupts
            CPU0        CPU1
   0:        121          0    IO-APIC-edge      timer
   1:         10          0    IO-APIC-edge      i8042
   8:          0          0    IO-APIC-edge      rtc0
   9:          0          0    IO-APIC-fasteoi   acpi
  12:        155          0    IO-APIC-edge      i8042
  14:          0          0    IO-APIC-edge      ata_piix
  15:        144       1493    IO-APIC-edge      ata_piix
  19:         41       2828    IO-APIC-fasteoi   enp0s3
  21:       6703       2178    IO-APIC-fasteoi   0000:00:0d.0, snd_intel8x0
  22:          0          0    IO-APIC-fasteoi   ohci_hcd:usb1
 NMI:          0          0    Non-maskable interrupts
 LOC:      50948      47956    Local timer interrupts
```

The output indicates four columns for each IRQ entry. The first column lists the IRQ number or name, followed by the number of that interrupt handled by a processor core, the type of interrupt, and a list of drivers, if any, receiving that interrupt.

I/O Port Address

An I/O port address is a storage location in memory that was used by devices on old computers to talk to the processor. Linux retains I/O port address information in the */proc/ioports* file, as shown below:

```
[user1@centos73 ~]$ head /proc/ioports
0000-0cf7 : PCI Bus 0000:00
  0000-001f : dma1
  0020-0021 : pic1
  0040-0043 : timer0
  0050-0053 : timer1
  0060-0060 : keyboard
  0064-0064 : keyboard
  0070-0071 : rtc_cmos
    0070-0071 : rtc0
  0080-008f : dma page reg
```

The output indicates I/O port addresses in hexadecimal in the first column along with the device names they are associated with in the second column.

Direct Memory Access (DMA)

A DMA channel is a communication technique that was used by devices on old computers to exchange data directly with main memory without involving system processors. This technique frees the system processors for other operations, resulting in improved system performance. Examples of such devices include sound and storage cards. To view a list of in-use DMAs, *cat* the */proc/dma* file:

```
[user1@centos73 ~]$ cat /proc/dma
4: cascade
```

PCI Express Devices

PCI Express (abbreviated as PCIe) is a successor to the older PCI (*Peripheral Component Interconnect*) and PCI-X bus technologies. PCIe includes a slot and an interface adapter that goes into the slot. It supports both 32-bit and 64-bit data paths for data exchange between the system processors and I/O adapters. In comparison with 32-bit versions, the 64-bit adapters are more common in newer computers, and they are much faster.

We can use the *lspci* command to display information about the PCI buses available on the system and devices connected to them. This command references the files stored in the */proc/bus/pci* directory and the */usr/share/hwdata/pci.ids* file to display the data. Without any options, it shows a basic view; however, you can specify the -v, -vv, or -vvv option for more details including the PCI bus speed, device IRQ settings, and device vendor identification. The output varies on the type of hardware you run this command on. For instance, the following is from *centos73*:

```
[user1@centos73 ~]$ lspci
00:00.0 Host bridge: Intel Corporation 440FX - 82441FX PMC [Natoma] (rev 02)
00:01.0 ISA bridge: Intel Corporation 82371SB PIIX3 ISA [Natoma/Triton II]
00:01.1 IDE interface: Intel Corporation 82371AB/EB/MB PIIX4 IDE (rev 01)
00:02.0 VGA compatible controller: InnoTek Systemberatung GmbH VirtualBox Graphics Adapter
00:03.0 Ethernet controller: Intel Corporation 82540EM Gigabit Ethernet Controller (rev 02)
00:04.0 System peripheral: InnoTek Systemberatung GmbH VirtualBox Guest Service
00:05.0 Multimedia audio controller: Intel Corporation 82801AA AC'97 Audio Controller (rev 01)
00:06.0 USB controller: Apple Inc. KeyLargo/Intrepid USB
00:07.0 Bridge: Intel Corporation 82371AB/EB/MB PIIX4 ACPI (rev 08)
00:0d.0 SATA controller: Intel Corporation 82801HM/HEM (ICH8M/ICH8M-E) SATA Controller [AHCI mo
de] (rev 02)
```

The output shows the slot number, class, vendor, and device description along with other optional data such as revision for each PCI device Linux sees. For instance, the last line in the above output has slot "00:0d.0" with 00 bus number, 0d device number, and 0 function number; class "SATA controller"; vendor "Intel Corporation"; device "82801/HM/HEM (ICH8M/ICH8M-E) SATA Controller [AHCI mode]"; and revision "02".

There are some common options available for use with the *lspci* command. Table 7-1 describes them.

Option	Action
-d	Shows information by vendor, device, or class
-D	Shows the PCI domain number also. It is usually 0000 on small computers.
-k	Shows the kernel driver in use for each device and the kernel module capable of handling it
-m	Shows information in more legible format
-n	Shows vendor and device codes in numerical format. Use -nn to view in both numerical and name format.
-s	Shows information for a specific slot containing PCI domain, bus, device, and function for each PCI device
-t	Shows information in tree-like structure

Table 7-1 lspci Command Options

Let's use some of these options in our examples below and observe the output.

To view the output that is more legible:

[user1@centos73 ~]$ **lspci -m**
00:00.0 "Host bridge" "Intel Corporation" "440FX - 82441FX PMC [Natoma]" -r02 "" ""
00:01.0 "ISA bridge" "Intel Corporation" "82371SB PIIX3 ISA [Natoma/Triton II]" "" ""

To view the output with vendor and device codes in numerical format:

[user1@centos73 ~]$ **lspci -n**
00:00.0 0600: 8086:1237 (rev 02)
00:01.0 0601: 8086:7000

To view more verbose information for devices in slot 01:

[user1@centos73 ~]$ **lspci -tvs 01**
-[0000:00]-+-01.0 Intel Corporation 82371SB PIIX3 ISA [Natoma/Triton II]
           \-01.1 Intel Corporation 82371AB/EB/MB PIIX4 IDE

To obtain vendor ID for a specific device such as Audio, use the -nn option:

[user1@centos73 ~]$ **lspci -nn | grep Audio**
00:05.0 Multimedia audio controller [0401]: Intel Corporation 82801AA AC'97 Audio Controller
[8086:2415] (rev 01)

To view information for a specific vendor device, Multimedia Audio Controller for instance, use the -d option (use vendor ID 8086:2415 from the previous output):

[user1@centos73 ~]$ **lspci -d 8086:2415 -v**
00:05.0 Multimedia audio controller: Intel Corporation 82801AA AC'97 Audio Controller (rev 01)
        Subsystem: Dell Device 0177
        Flags: bus master, medium devsel, latency 64, IRQ 21
        I/O ports at d100 [size=256]
        I/O ports at d200 [size=64]
        Kernel driver in use: snd_intel8x0
        Kernel modules: snd_intel8x0

Processors and Cores

Linux runs on a wide variety of computer hardware architectures with processors from Intel, AMD, IBM, and other manufacturers. Modern computers support processors that are single hardware components with several logical processors called *cores* on them. Each core acts as an independent processor and, together, they support aggressive parallel processing, boosting the overall performance of the system and applications. All mainstream Linux operating systems today support multi-core processors in both virtualized and non-virtualized environments.

Linux tracks and maintains processor information at two virtual locations: (1) the */proc/cpuinfo* file, and (2) under */sys* (a discussion on */sys* is provided later in this chapter). It records the number, type, and speed of processors, the count of sockets, cores per each socket, cache information, whether they support virtualization, and other details. We can use the *lscpu* command to view processor information. The following displays the processor data from *centos73*. Note that I have added one more processor to this system from VirtualBox console (with the VM powered off, go to its settings and then the Processor tab under System).

```
[user1@centos73 ~]$ lscpu
Architecture:              x86_64
CPU op-mode(s):            32-bit, 64-bit
Byte Order:                Little Endian
CPU(s):                    2
On-line CPU(s) list:       0,1
Thread(s) per core:        1
Core(s) per socket:        2
Socket(s):                 1
NUMA node(s):              1
Vendor ID:                 GenuineIntel
CPU family:                6
Model:                     58
Model name:                Intel(R) Core(TM) i7-3610QM CPU @ 2.30GHz
Stepping:                  9
CPU MHz:                   2294.794
BogoMIPS:                  4589.58
Hypervisor vendor:         KVM
Virtualization type:       full
L1d cache:                 32K
L1i cache:                 32K
L2 cache:                  256K
L3 cache:                  6144K
NUMA node0 CPU(s):         0,1
```

The output indicates two processors (0 and 1) that Linux sees, and both are online. There is one socket and both cores are located on that socket. You can calculate the total number of cores on the system by multiplying the core count (Cores per socket) with the number of sockets (Sockets). On *centos73*, it comes to 2. The command does not differentiate between "CPUs" and "Cores per socket" on a single processor system. We have an 8-core processor on the host of which 2 cores are allocated to *centos73*. The output and processor/core calculation may vary on other hardware platforms using different virtualization software.

Alternatively, running a file viewing utility such as the *cat* command on the */proc/cpuinfo* file will also show processor information:

```
[user1@centos73 ~]$ cat /proc/cpuinfo
Processor         : 0
vendor_id         : GenuineIntel
cpu family        : 6
model             : 58
model name        : Intel(R) Core(TM) i7-3610QM CPU @ 2.30GHz
stepping          : 9
microcode         : 0x19
cpu MHz           : 2294.794
cache size        : 6144 KB
```

physical id	: 0
siblings	: 2
core id	: 0
cpu cores	: 2
apicid	: 0
initial apicid	: 0
fpu	: yes
fpu_exception	: yes
cpuid level	: 13
wp	: yes
flags	: fpu vme de pse tsc msr pae mce cx8 apic sep mtrr pge mca cmov pat pse36 clflush

mmx fxsr sse sse2 syscall nx rdtscp lm constant_tsc rep_good nopl xtopology nonstop_tsc pni pclmulqdq monitor ssse3 cx16 sse4_1 sse4_2 x2apic popcnt aes xsave avx rdrand hypervisor lahf_lm

bogomips	: 4589.58
clflush size	: 64
cache_alignment	: 64
address sizes	: 36 bits physical, 48 bits virtual
power management:	

processor	: 1
. . . .	
physical id	: 0
siblings	: 2
core id	: 1
cpu cores	: 2
. . . .	

The file output indicates that the "physical id" of both processor 0 and 1 is the same, which indicates that both "cpu cores" are on the same physical component.

Mass Storage Devices

Personal computers use mass storage devices, such as Hard Disk Drives (HDD), Solid-State Drives (SDD), removable USB flash drives, and optical disc drives. These devices are attached to the system using a range of interfaces; however, bulk of them now support standard interfaces. Linux automatically detects the type and geometry of mass storage devices attached to the system at boot and dynamically during runtime. It allows us to partition them, except for the optical drives, using a variety of available disk partitioning tools.

Let's take a look at the four mass storage device types mentioned above.

Hard Disk Drives (HDD)

A hard disk drive is a mass storage device that has been in use for decades for storing large amounts of data, and it is more prevalent than any other types of mass storage device out there. Hard drives can be partitioned for various uses or their spaces can be pooled to construct volumes to address exceptionally large storage needs. They are physically connected to the computers using various attachment interfaces such as SATA, SAS, USB, and FireWire.

SATA (*Serial Advanced Technology Attachment*) is a popular mass storage attachment interface. It is the successor to the older PATA (*Parallel Advanced Technology Attachment*) standard, which

---

was slower, generally less efficient, and used primarily for internal disk attachments. A variant of SATA called *eSATA* is also available for connecting external mass storage devices to the system.

SAS (*Serial Attached SCSI*) is a replacement for the legacy SCSI (*Small Computer System Interface*) standard that had been in use for two decades. SAS uses the same commandset that the legacy SCSI standard used; however, SAS is faster and more flexible, scalable, and efficient than its predecessor.

USB (*Universal Serial Bus*) has become an industry standard for attaching external devices such as a hard drive to the computer. USB has supplanted the use of serial ports, parallel ports, game ports, and PS/2 mouse and keyboard ports on computers. It was designed with the principal objective to provide a universal interface to attach different kinds of devices—mass storage, keyboard, mouse, printer, network, camera, and media player—to the system. The USB interface also provides power to the connected devices. At the time of this writing, it supports multimedia and mobile devices, and it is used as a charging station as well. The latest USB standard is USB 3.1 with the support for data transfer speeds of up to 10Gbps, and it is backward compatible with older USB standards 3.0 and 2.0.

FireWire, originally designed and developed by Apple, is now recognized as IEEE 1394 interface standard for connecting external mass storage and multimedia devices to the computer. Similar to USB, FireWire also supports hot-plugging and plug-and-play features; however, the use of FireWire devices is less common.

We allocated an 8GB disk to *centos73* and *ubuntu14* at the time of their installation. We also have the ISO images for CentOS 7.3 and Ubuntu 14.04 attached to the virtual machines. We can use the *fdisk* command with the -l switch or the *lsblk* command to view the list of mass storage devices visible to the systems. Let's run the two commands on *centos73*:

```
[root@centos73 ~]# fdisk -l
Disk /dev/sda: 8589 MB, 8589934592 bytes, 16777216 sectors
Units = sectors of 1 * 512 = 512 bytes
Sector size (logical/physical): 512 bytes / 512 bytes
I/O size (minimum/optimal): 512 bytes / 512 bytes
Disk label type: dos
Disk identifier: 0x000ddf8a


Device  Boot    Start      End      Blocks   Id  System
/dev/sda1   *     2048   2099199   1048576   83  Linux
/dev/sda2       2099200  16777215  7339008   8e  Linux LVM


Disk /dev/mapper/cl-root: 6652 MB, 6652166144 bytes, 12992512 sectors
Units = sectors of 1 * 512 = 512 bytes
Sector size (logical/physical): 512 bytes / 512 bytes
I/O size (minimum/optimal): 512 bytes / 512 bytes


Disk /dev/mapper/cl-swap: 859 MB, 859832320 bytes, 1679360 sectors
Units = sectors of 1 * 512 = 512 bytes
Sector size (logical/physical): 512 bytes / 512 bytes
I/O size (minimum/optimal): 512 bytes / 512 bytes
```

The output shows (a) the disk name "/dev/sda" as identified by the operating system; (b) its size in megabytes, bytes, and sectors; (c) its geometry in the first block, followed by the partition information in the second block; and (d) logical volume names, sizes, and geometry in the third and fourth blocks.

And the *lsblk* command reports as follows:

```
[root@centos73 ~]# lsblk
NAME          MAJ:MIN  RM   SIZE  RO  TYPE        MOUNTPOINT
sda           8:0      0    8G    0   disk
├─sda1        8:1      0    1G    0   part        /boot
└─sda2        8:2      0    7G    0   part
  ├─cl-root   253:0    0    6.2G  0   lvm         /
  └─cl-swap   253:1    0    820M  0   lvm         [SWAP]
sr0           11:0     1    4.1G  0   rom         /mnt
```

The output shows the device (sda for hard disk and sr0 for optical disk), partition (sda1 and sda2), and logical volume (cl-root and cl-swap) names in the first column, their sizes in the fourth column; their types in the sixth column, and their mount points in the last column.

Older common mass storage device standards in use were ATA (AT Attachment, later called PATA and then SATA) and IDE (*Integrated Drive Electronics*). A variant of ATA referred to as ATAPI (*ATA Packet Interface*) was used for optical and other detachable devices.

Solid-State Drives

A Solid-State Drive (SSD) is an all electronic mass storage data device. Unlike the customary electromechanical hard disk drives, an SSD is manufactured with no moving parts, making it more reliable and compact, as well as lighter, faster, and lower-powered. However, these benefits come at a cost. SSDs are more expensive than their counterparts are. SSDs are now being used in desktop and laptop computers, and their deployment is fast growing. They may use the same interface as the traditional hard drives or the *Non-Volatile Memory Express* (NVMe) interface developed specifically for connecting SSDs via PCI Express (PCIe) bus. Linux partitioning tools do not differentiate between an HDD and an SSD; they view and treat them alike.

Removable USB Flash Drives

Flash drives are hot-pluggable, detachable, and reusable USB storage devices that are widely used for data mobility. They are reliable and fast with up to 256GB of data holding capacity as of this writing. Flash drives are also recognized by other names such as Thumb drives, USB drives, and Pen drives.

Optical Disc Drives

Optical disc drives are mass storage media (CD-ROM, DVD-ROM, and Blu-Ray devices) that use laser light to read and write data. A standard CD-ROM disc can hold up to 847MB of data. A single-layer DVD disc can hold up to 4.7GB of data and 8.7GB on dual-layered. A single-layer Blu-ray disc has the storage capacity of up to 25GB, with 50GB on dual-layered, 100GB on tri-layered, and 128GB on quad-layered. On newer computers, optical drives are attached using the same interfaces (SATA, SAS, USB, and FireWire) as the HDDs and SSDs. The read-only devices can be burnt only once but read as many times as you want; however, their writable versions can be written and overwritten more than once.

Universal Serial Bus (USB)

USB technology allows plenty of peripheral devices to be connected to a single USB port concurrently. Its design goal was to develop a standard universal interface to allow devices with varying and proprietary attachment requirements to be able to connect to the computer. The first release of the USB specification was called USB 1.0 and supported 12Mbps speed, followed by USB 2.0 at 480Mbps, USB 3.0 at 5Gbps, and the latest 3.1 support 10Gbps speed.

There is a wide array of devices available today that are designed to follow the USB specifications. These devices include mass storage drives, as well as input, networking, imaging, and multimedia devices. The system recognizes and creates device files dynamically as soon as it discovers a new USB device plugged in.

Linux provides the *lsusb* command to view USB information including the busses in the system and the devices connected to them. The examples provided below should be run on Linux systems with multiple USB devices attached for a better comprehension. The following output of *lsusb* is from *centos73*:

```
[root@centos73 ~]# lsusb
Bus 001 Device 001: ID 1d6b:0001 Linux Foundation 1.1 root hub
```

The output indicates that there is only one bus available on the system with only one device connected to it. It shows the bus number (001) to which the USB device "Linux Foundation 1.1 root hub" with manufacturer ID 1d6b and device ID 0001 is attached. If you wish to view the above information in detail, add the -v option with the command.

To view the above information in tree-like format, use the -t option with the command:

```
[root@centos73 ~]# lsusb -t
/:  Bus 01.Port 1: Dev 1, Class=root_hub, Driver=ohci-pci/12p, 12M
```

There are a few more switches with the *lsusb* command that are important to comprehend. These switches are: -d to show the information for a specific vendor and product ID, and -s to display information for a specific bus or bus number.

Let's look at the examples below to understand the use of the two options.

The above output indicates that there is only one USB bus with vendor ID 1d6b and product ID 0001 available on the system. To view more information about all the devices available on the system for this specific vendor, enter the vendor ID followed by the colon (:) character with the -d option:

```
[root@centos73 ~]# lsusb -d 1d6b:
```

From a multitude of product IDs specific to this one vendor, choose the one that you wish to see more information about, and enter it after the colon (:) character, as follows:

```
[root@centos73 ~]# lsusb -d 1d6b:0001
```

Similarly, to view information about all devices attached to a specific bus (001 for example), enter the bus number followed by the colon (:) character with the -s option:

```
[root@centos73 ~]# lsusb -s 001:
```

From a multitude of devices attached to this one bus, choose the one that you wish to see more information about, and enter it after the colon (:) character, as follows:

```
[root@centos73 ~]# lsusb -s 001:001
```

The device files for USB devices are located under the */dev/bus/usb* directory. Run the *ll* command on this directory to view the list. You can then run **lsusb -D /dev/bus/usb/001/001**, for instance, to view information about a specific device. The output will match to that of **lsusb -v**.

Hotplug and Coldplug Devices

The *hotplug* feature in Linux allows us to connect a removable device to a running system. Upon establishing a connection, the system recognizes the device and dynamically creates a device file for it under the */dev* directory and builds appropriate structures for it under */sys* (a discussion on */sys* is provided later in this chapter), allowing us to begin using the new device immediately. This feature is particularly useful with USB, FireWire, optical, Wi-Fi, Bluetooth, and pointing devices.

Cold plugging, on the contrary, is simply the opposite of hot plugging. It requires that the system must be powered off in order for a device to be connected to the system. Upon booting, the system discovers the new hardware, creates device files for it, builds device structures under */sys*, and makes it available for use by programs.

Probing and Managing Hardware Devices Dynamically with udev

udev is the dynamic device probing and management service in Linux for hotpluggable devices. It is used for automatic addition, modification, and deletion of hardware device files based on pre-configured rules. The support for udev is integrated in systemd in newer mainstream Linux distribution versions.

The udev configuration file is */etc/udev/udev.conf* where settings, such as the locations for device files and custom udev rules, along with an appropriate log level (error, informational, or debug) are defined. The defaults for these settings are */dev*, */etc/udev/rules.d*, and err, respectively. The pre-configured udev rules are stored in the */usr/lib/udev/rules.d* directory (or */lib/udev/rules.d* on Ubuntu). These rules may include device file names and their ownerships, owning groups, symlink names, and file permissions. They also include the commands intended to be executed.

The udev service has a single management command, *udevadm*. This command has several subcommands such as *control* to handle the behavior of the service daemon, *info* to query the udev database for device information, *monitor* to display kernel and udev events, *test* to simulate a udev execution for a device, and *trigger* to request kernel device events for cold-plugged devices. Each of these subcommands support multiple switches. Refer to the command's manual pages for details.

Here are a few examples to show you the command usage.

To display all devices currently configured in the udev database, run *udevadm* with the -e (export-db) option:

```
[user1@centos73 ~]$ udevadm info -e
P: /devices/LNXSYSTM:00
E: DEVPATH=/devices/LNXSYSTM:00
E: MODALIAS=acpi:LNXSYSTM:
E: SUBSYSTEM=acpi

P: /devices/LNXSYSTM:00/LNXCPU:00
E: DEVPATH=/devices/LNXSYSTM:00/LNXCPU:00
E: MODALIAS=acpi:LNXCPU:
E: SUBSYSTEM=acpi
. . . . . . . .
```

To query an individual device such as */sys/class/block/sda*, use -a (--attribute-walk) and -p (--path) options together:

```
[user1@centos73 ~]$ udevadm info -ap /sys/class/block/sda
  looking at device '/devices/pci0000:00/0000:00:0d.0/ata3/host2/target2:0:0/2:0:0:0/block/sda':
    KERNEL=="sda"
    SUBSYSTEM=="block"
    DRIVER==""
    ATTR{ro}=="0"
    ATTR{size}=="16777216"
    ATTR{stat}=="   4999   18  320404  11727  2798  223   29420  3031   0  5709  14753"
    ATTR{range}=="16"
    ATTR{discard_alignment}=="0"
. . . . . . . .
```

To view more information for a specific device *sda*, use the -q query) and -n (name) options:

```
[user1@centos73 ~]$ udevadm info -q all -n sda
P: /devices/pci0000:00/0000:00:0d.0/ata3/host2/target2:0:0/2:0:0:0/block/sda
N: sda
S: disk/by-id/ata-VBOX_HARDDISK_VBb45c2098-4658b5b4
S: disk/by-path/pci-0000:00:0d.0-ata-1.0
E: DEVLINKS=/dev/disk/by-id/ata-VBOX_HARDDISK_VBb45c2098-4658b5b4 /dev/disk/by-path/pci-
0000:00:0d.0-ata-1.0
E: DEVNAME=/dev/sda
E: DEVPATH=/devices/pci0000:00/0000:00:0d.0/ata3/host2/target2:0:0/2:0:0:0/block/sda
E: DEVTYPE=disk
. . . . . . . .
```

System Runtime Information

Linux stores runtime system information in three virtual (or memory-based) file systems called *Sysfs*, *Devices*, and *Procfs*. These file systems are created in memory at system boot and destroyed at system shut down. The Linux kernel automatically maintains a copy of runtime information in various virtual files under these file systems and, updates it dynamically to reflect additions, modifications, and deletions that may occur while the system is operational.

You can view the three file systems using the *df* command with the -a (all) option and then *egrep* for their types and send the output to the *head* command:

```
[user1@centos73 ~]$ df -ah | grep -E 'sysfs|dev|proc' | head -3
sysfs            0   0     0   -  /sys
proc             0   0     0   -  /proc
devtmpfs      481M   0  481M  0% /dev
```

The output indicates that the three virtual file systems are currently mounted on the system and they are accessible.

The Sysfs File System Mounted on /sys

The Sysfs (*system file system*) file system is accessible via the */sys* directory, and it is used to store kernel subsystem, hardware, and device driver information, which is referenced by user processes and commands. The following shows a listing of */sys*:

```
[user1@centos73 ~]$ ll /sys
drwxr-xr-x.   2 root  root  0 Feb 15 22:07  block
drwxr-xr-x.  27 root  root  0 Feb 15 22:07  bus
drwxr-xr-x.  47 root  root  0 Feb 15 22:07  class
drwxr-xr-x.   4 root  root  0 Feb 15 22:07  dev
drwxr-xr-x.  12 root  root  0 Feb 15 22:07  devices
drwxr-xr-x.   5 root  root  0 Feb 15 22:07  firmware
drwxr-xr-x.   6 root  root  0 Feb 15 22:07  fs
drwxr-xr-x.   2 root  root  0 Feb 15 22:07  hypervisor
drwxr-xr-x.   9 root  root  0 Feb 15 22:07  kernel
drwxr-xr-x. 161 root  root  0 Feb 15 22:07  module
drwxr-xr-x.   2 root  root  0 Feb 15 22:07  power
```

The output shows several sub-directories that store runtime information specific to mass storage devices, partitions, file systems, firmware, kernel, kernel modules, processors, memory, ports, controller cards, pseudo terminals, etc. You can *cd* into the */sys/block/sda* directory and find plenty of files and sub-directories holding detailed information on sda disk. Try navigating other sub-directories under */sys* to get yourself familiarized with the structure.

The Devices File System Mounted on /dev

The Devices (*dev file system*) file system is accessible via the */dev* directory, and it is used to store device nodes for physical hardware and virtual devices. The Linux kernel communicates with these devices through corresponding device nodes located under this file system. These device nodes are created and erased dynamically by the udev service as necessary based on defined rules.

There are two types of device files—*character* (or *raw*) and *block*—which the kernel uses to access the devices. Run the *ll* command on */dev* and grep for ^crw and ^brw to view the two types of files:

```
[user1@centos73 ~]$ ll /dev | grep ^crw | head -4
crw-------. 1  root  root  10, 235 Feb 15 22:07 autofs
crw-------. 1  root  root  10, 234 Feb 15 22:07 btrfs-control
crw-------. 1  root  root   5,   1 Feb 15 22:07 console
crw-------. 1  root  root  10,  61 Feb 15 22:07 cpu_dma_latency
```

```
[user1@centos73 ~]$ ll /dev | grep ^brw | tail -4
brw-rw----. 1  root disk     8,  0 Feb 15 22:07 sda
brw-rw----. 1  root disk     8,  1 Feb 15 22:07 sda1
brw-rw----. 1  root disk     8,  2 Feb 15 22:07 sda2
brw-rw----. 1  root cdrom   11,  0 Feb 15 22:07 sr0
```

Character devices are accessed serially with streams of bits transferred during kernel and device communication. Examples of such devices are serial printers, mice, keyboards, console screens, and terminals.

Block devices are accessed in a parallel fashion with data exchanged in blocks (parallel) during kernel and device communication. Block devices allow data access in a random fashion. Examples of block devices are mass storage devices and parallel printers.

The Procfs File System Mounted on /proc

The Procfs (*process file system*) file system is accessible via the */proc* directory, and it is used to maintain information about the current state of the running kernel including the details on CPU, memory, disks, partitioning, file systems, networking, running processes, IRQs, DMAs, and I/O port addresses. This virtual file system contains a hierarchy of sub-directories with thousands of zero-length files pointing to kernel-maintained relevant data in the memory. This virtual directory structure simply provides an easy interface to interact with the information. The Procfs file system is dynamically managed by the system. A directory listing of */proc* is provided below:

```
[user1@centos73 ~]$ ll /proc | head
dr-xr-xr-x. 9  root   root    0 Feb 15 22:07 1
dr-xr-xr-x. 9  root   root    0 Feb 15 22:07 10
dr-xr-xr-x. 9  root   root    0 Feb 15 22:07 100
dr-xr-xr-x. 9  root   root    0 Feb 15 22:07 102
dr-xr-xr-x. 9  root   root    0 Feb 15 22:07 1024
dr-xr-xr-x. 9  root   root    0 Feb 15 22:07 1025

. . . . . . . .
```

As mentioned, this file system contains thousands of files and sub-directories. Some sub-directory names are numerical and they store information for specific processes matching their Process IDs. Within each sub-directory, there are files and further sub-directories, which record information such as memory segment peculiar to that process. Other files and sub-directories point to configuration data for system components. If you wish to view configuration information for an item such as the CPU or memory, you can use the *cat* command. For instance, the following can be used to view what is stored in the *cmdline* and *version* files:

```
[user1@centos73 ~]$ cat /proc/cmdline
BOOT_IMAGE=/vmlinuz-3.10.0-514.el7.x86_64 root=/dev/mapper/cl-root ro crashkernel=auto
rd.lvm.lv=cl/root rd.lvm.lv=cl/swap rhgb quiet kernstack=1
[user1@centos73 ~]$ cat /proc/version
Linux version 3.10.0-514.el7.x86_64 (builder@kbuilder.dev.centos.org) (gcc version 4.8.5 20150623 (Red
Hat 4.8.5-11) (GCC) ) #1 SMP Tue Nov 22 16:42:41 UTC 2016
```

The data located under */proc* is referenced by a number of user and system utilities, including *top*, *ps*, *pstree*, *free*, *uname*, and *vmstat*.

D-Bus

D-Bus (*Desktop Bus*) is an interprocess communication mechanism that allows processes running on a system to talk to one another or processes running on multiple systems to talk to one another. In contrast to D-Bus, *socket* is another interprocess communication method that allows a single process running on a system to talk to another process on the same or remote system. These processes may include user processes, application processes, service processes, or a combination. Both communication methods are used for various purposes including sending a signal to a running application to perform some action. For instance, when an ISO image is attached to a Linux guest, a notification is generated for the udev service, which, based on a pre-defined rule, automatically mounts the image on a mount point.

Hardware Settings in the BIOS

It was discussed in Chapter 6 "Booting Linux and Initializing the System," that BIOS is the first code that is executed when the system is powered up or rebooted, and it is followed by the bootloader code, GRUB Legacy or GRUB2, which is stored in the first sector of the boot medium. Before the system loads the bootloader, we have the opportunity to enter the BIOS menu and view hardware settings or configure them to match our needs. These settings include adjusting system date and time; enabling or disabling integrated peripherals and CPU virtualization; configuring to boot without external peripherals, such as the keyboard; altering boot priorities; controlling access to the BIOS menu by setting an administrative password; and so on. Linux is only able to access or use a peripheral that is set to enabled in the BIOS.

Shortly after powering up the system, a manufacturer logo or a message appears for a brief period, inviting us to press a key to interact with the BIOS. Depending on the hardware manufacturer, this key may be ESC, Del, F1, F2, F8, F10, or F12. Let's look at various BIOS screens and see what they show and allow us to adjust. This presentation varies from one BIOS manufacturer to another, and you may have to use a slightly different set of keys for navigation within the BIOS.

The following figure presents the first screen after entering the BIOS.

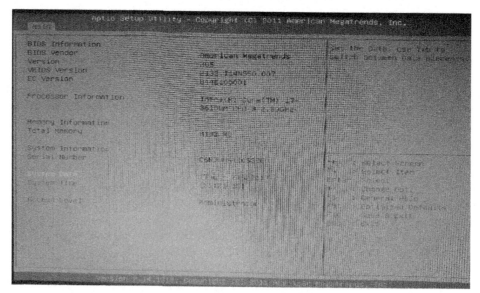

Figure 7-1 BIOS Setup – Main Category

At the top of the screen is a menu bar showing five categories: (1) Main, (2) Advanced, (3) Boot, (4) Security, and (5) Save & Exit. Each category is a representative of several items of which some are for display only and others are modifiable. Any item with an arrowhead next to it is expandable for further viewing or alteration. The context sensitive help appears in the top right-hand pane and it changes as we switch selections. The bottom right-hand pane shows help with navigation. It displays what keys to use to move from one category to another and from one item to another, change the value of a selected item, go back to the previous screen or exit the BIOS without saving changes, save the changes and exit the BIOS, obtain help, and load optimized defaults.

The Main category illustrated in Figure 7-1, shows the vendor and version of the BIOS; type, model, and speed of the processor; amount of memory; serial number of the system; date and time of the system; and access level. The only two changeable items here are the date and time.

The Advanced category, Figure 7-2, shows a number of items with many of them adjustable. You can expand the items with a triangle next to them to view or change their values. On computers, especially the server computers, you should be able to find an option such as "Halt On", "Halt On Errors", or "Keyboard Present" somewhere under this category that would, if configured appropriately, allow your computer to boot normally with no keyboard attached.

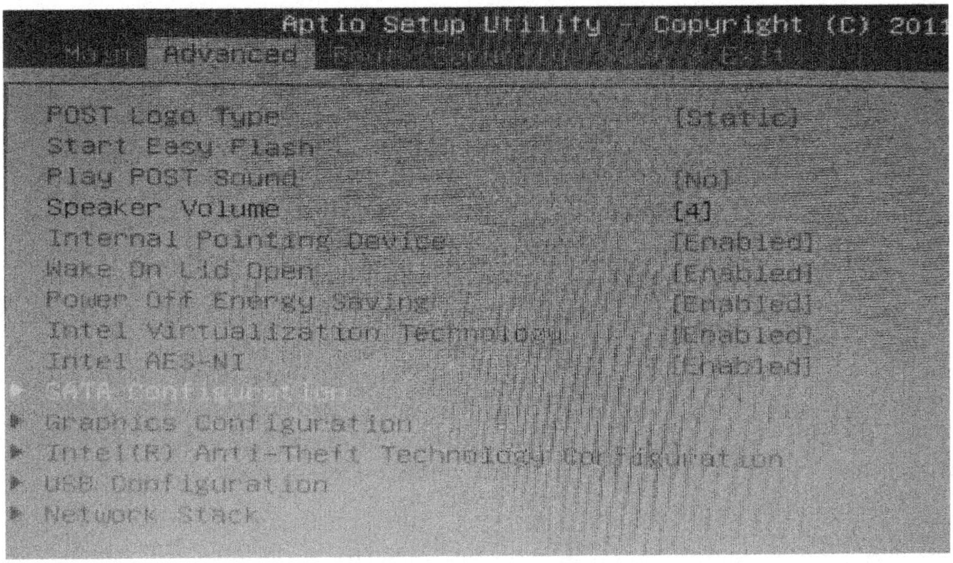

Figure 7-2 BIOS Setup – Advanced Category

The third category provides boot settings, as shown in Figure 7-3. Here you can enable the network booting, set boot priorities, add or delete boot options, and so on.

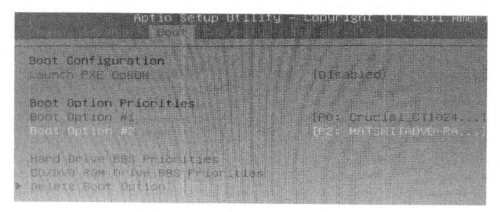

Figure 7-3 BIOS Setup – Boot Category

The Security category allows you to set administrator, user, and master passwords. You can also lock or unlock LAN, Wi-Fi, audio, hard disk, USB, and other interfaces.

The last category of menu items lets you save or discard changes and exit the BIOS, reset all values to the factory defaults, or boot with a non-default boot device.

While in the BIOS, you should make appropriate changes as required, and then save and exit. Linux will detect the changes and adjust itself accordingly and automatically.

Understanding and Managing Kernel Modules

The kernel is the core of the Linux system. It manages hardware, enforces security, regulates access on the system, as well as handles processes, services, and applications. It is a collection of software components called *modules* that work together as a single entity to provide a stable and controlled platform to programs, services, and applications to run smoothly and efficiently. Modules are *device drivers* that are used for controlling hardware devices—the processor, memory, controller cards, and peripheral equipment—as well as for interacting with software components—disk partitioning, file systems, and networking. Some of these modules are static to the kernel and are integral to system functionality, while others are loaded dynamically as needed, making it faster and more efficient in terms of overall performance, and less vulnerable to crashes.

Debian and RHEL Linux distributions and their spinoffs are available with the kernels that are designed to support diverse processor architectures, such as 64-bit Intel/AMD/PowerPC in single, multicore, and multiprocessor configurations. On the x86 system, **uname -m** shows the hardware architecture of the system.

Determining Kernel Version

We built three Linux systems (two in chapter 1 and one in chapter 6) to support the material presented in this book. These systems are *centos73* running CentOS version 7.3, *ubuntu14* running Ubuntu version 14.04.5, and *centos511* running CentOS version 5.11. To ascertain the version of the kernel running on these systems, we use the *uname* command with the -r switch:

```
[user1@centos73 ~]$ uname -r
3.10.0-514.el7.x86_64
user1@ubuntu14:~$ uname -r
4.4.0-31-generic
```

```
[user1@centos511 ~]$ uname -r
2.6.18-398.el5
```

The above output reveals that our three systems are running kernel versions 3.10.0, 4.4.0, and 2.6.18, respectively. Newer versions of Debian and Ubuntu are shipped with more recent kernel versions than 4.4.0. An anatomy of the kernel version on *centos73* is illustrated in Figure 7-4 and explained below.

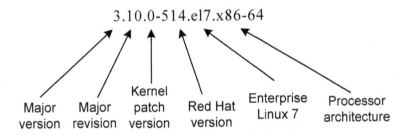

Figure 7-4 Anatomy of a Kernel Version

From left to right:

- ✓ (3) indicates the major version of the Linux kernel. The major number changes when significant alterations, enhancements, and updates to the previous major version are made.
- ✓ (10) determines the major revision of the third major version.
- ✓ (0) implies that this is the zeroth patched version of the tenth major revision of the third major version of the kernel.
- ✓ (514) identifies the Red Hat's customization of 3.10.0.
- ✓ (el7) represents the Enterprise Linux version this kernel is for.
- ✓ (x86_64) ascertains the architecture this kernel is built for.

A further analysis designates that 3.10.0 holds the general Linux kernel version information and the subsequent numbers and letters represent Red Hat specific information.

Managing Kernel Modules

Managing kernel modules involves performing several tasks such as listing, displaying details of, loading (adding), and unloading (removing) modules. Linux provides the *lsmod*, *modinfo*, and *modprobe* commands for their administration. Additional tools such as *insmod* and *rmmod* are also available; however, their substitute *modprobe* should be used instead. Let's look at each of these tools and see how we can use them.

Listing Loaded Modules

The *lsmod* command allows us to view modules that are currently loaded in the kernel. This command references the */proc/modules* file, and displays the information formatted. We can, alternatively, view the content of this file directly by using any text file display command. Both methods show module names, memory they are consuming, the number of processes using this and any dependent modules, and a list of dependent module names if applicable. Here is a partial output from the command and the file:

```
[user1@centos73 ~]$ lsmod
Module              Size    Used by
xt_CHECKSUM         12549   1
ipt_MASQUERADE      12678   3
. . . . . . . .
[user1@centos73 ~]$ cat /proc/modules
xt_CHECKSUM 12549 1 - Live 0xffffffffa052d000
ipt_MASQUERADE 12678 3 - Live 0xffffffffa0523000
. . . . . . . .
```

Displaying Module Information

We use the *modinfo* command to display details for a module that is loaded in the kernel. For instance, the following shows information about a disk mirroring module called "dm_mirror". We first run *lsmod* to check the load status of the module, and then run *modinfo*.

```
[user1@centos73 ~]$ lsmod | grep ^dm_mirror
dm_mirror              22135   0
[user1@centos73 ~]$ modinfo dm_mirror
filename:      /lib/modules/3.10.0-514.el7.x86_64/kernel/drivers/md/dm-mirror.ko
license:       GPL
author:        Joe Thornber
description:   device-mapper mirror target
rhelversion:   7.3
srcversion:    A1EDCA0CB7DD26013BEFC3F
depends:       dm-region-hash,dm-mod,dm-log
intree:        Y
vermagic:      3.10.0-514.el7.x86_64 SMP mod_unload modversions
signer:        CentOS Linux kernel signing key
sig_key:       D4:88:63:A7:C1:6F:CC:27:41:23:E6:29:8F:74:F0:57:AF:19:FC:54
sig_hashalgo: sha256
parm:          raid1_resync_throttle:A percentage of time allocated for raid resynchronization (uint)
```

The output disclosed the full path to the module file (filename), license type (license), author name (author), short description (description), Red Hat Enterprise Linux version (rhelversion), dependent module names (depends), and other information.

Loading and Unloading Modules

Use the *modprobe* command to add (insert or load) and remove (unload) a module dynamically to/from the Linux kernel. This command ensures that any unused dependent modules are also taken care of accordingly. The following example removes (-r) the *dm_mirror* module from the kernel along with all depended modules that are in its exclusive use. This command fails if any of the dependent modules or dm_mirror itself are in use. The -v option is used for verbose output.

```
[root@centos73 ~]# modprobe -vr dm_mirror
rmmod dm_mirror
rmmod dm_region_hash
rmmod dm_log
```

The modprobe command has replaced both insmod for module insertion and rmmod for module removal commands in newer Linux versions.

To confirm, use the *lsmod* command:

```
[root@centos73 ~]# lsmod | grep ^dm_mirror
```

The output should return nothing to indicate the removal of the module from the kernel.

We use the same command to insert (-i) the module along with all dependencies back to the running kernel. Here is how we do this:

```
[root@centos73 ~]# modprobe -vi dm_mirror
insmod /lib/modules/3.10.0-514.el7.x86_64/kernel/drivers/md/dm-log.ko
insmod /lib/modules/3.10.0-514.el7.x86_64/kernel/drivers/md/dm-region-hash.ko
insmod /lib/modules/3.10.0-514.el7.x86_64/kernel/drivers/md/dm-mirror.ko
[root@centos73 ~]# lsmod | grep ^dm_mirror
dm_mirror         22135 0
```

We can simulate the insertion and removal by specifying the -n (or --show or --dry-run) switch to the *modprobe* command. With this switch added, the command only reports what will actually happen if it is executed without this switch rather than performing either action. For instance, let's repeat the unload example with the -n option added:

```
[root@centos73 ~]# modprobe -vrn dm_mirror
```

We can verify with the *lsmod* command that the module is still in the loaded state.

Chapter Summary

In this chapter, we learned about common PC hardware components such as PCI devices; processors and cores; mechanical, static, and optical disk devices; and USB and FireWire ports. We looked deeply at the kernel, which is the "colonel" of the Linux system, in that it controls and regulates all system hardware and software. We described various channels that the kernel uses to communicate with PC components. We examined key differences between hot- and cold-pluggable devices and the dynamic search and handling of hardware devices.

We scrutinized virtual file systems that are used to store and maintain running system information. We viewed and analyzed the contents of a few files located in these file systems. We interacted with the BIOS and analyzed static and configurable items.

Finally, we explored a kernel version and examined kernel modules. We performed various module handling tasks, such as listing, viewing, loading, and unloading them, to develop a basic understanding of their management.

Chapter Review at a Glance

The following presents a one-sentence review of each key topic discussed in this chapter:

- A computer is a set of hardware components that is used by software programs and applications via an operating system, such as Linux.

- IRQs, I/O port addresses, and DMA are key communication channels used on old personal computers for devices to request processor attention, talk to the processor using specific memory addresses, and access memory without the involvement of the processor.

- PCIe technology is used in computers to connect peripheral devices to the computer.

- Processors are the CPU chips used in computers to execute user instructions.

- Cores are logical processors that share a processor chip; the use of multi-core processors are common on both physical and virtual computers.

- Mass storage devices are the physical or virtual storage devices, such as hard disk drives, solid-state drives, USB flash drives, and optical disc drives, that are used to store large amounts of data permanently.

- USB technology is widespread, supporting a number of peripheral devices, such as storage devices (hard disk drives, solid-state drives, optical drives, flash drives, FireWire drives), input devices (mice, keyboards, readers), network devices (WiFi, Bluetooth, Ethernet), and so on.

- Hotplug devices are auto-detected via the dynamic device probing and management service called udev without the need of a system reboot and while the system is operational; coldplug devices require a system shutdown in order to be installed, detected, and recognized by the system.

- Linux stores system runtime information—kernel subsystems, hardware, device drivers, device nodes, processes, and so on—in various memory-based file systems, such as Sysfs mounted on /sys, Devfs mounted on /dev, and Procfs mount on /proc, and updates the information dynamically as soon as there is change.

- Memory-based file systems are virtual file systems that are created automatically at system boot and destroyed automatically at system shutdown.

- D-bus is used by Linux to support communication between multiple processes running on the same or different systems; socket is used by Linux to support communication between two processes running on the same or different systems.

- BIOS stores basic hardware and system settings that can be altered to adjust the system hardware clock, enable or disable integrated peripheral devices, configure the system to boot without the presence of a keyboard, change boot priorities, and so on.

- Modules are the device drivers that form the core of the Linux system called kernel, which manages the system hardware, enforces security, and regulates access to system resources, services, and applications.

- Kernel modules may be individually loaded or unloaded as required.

- Commands we learned in this chapter are: lspci, lscpu, fdisk, lsblk, lsusb, udevadm, uname, lsmod, modinfo, and modprobe.

- Files and directories we discussed in this chapter are: /proc/interrupts, /proc/ioports, /proc/dma, /proc/bus/pci/, /usr/share/hwdata/pci.ids, /proc/cpuinfo, /etc/udev/udev.conf, /etc/udev/rules.d/, /usr/lib/udev/rules.d/, /sys/, /dev/, /proc/, and /proc/modules.

Chapter 8

Administering Partitions, File Systems, and Swap

This chapter describes the following major topics:

➢ MBR, GPT, and partitions—an overview
➢ Create, list, and erase partitions on MBR and GPT disks using fdisk, parted, and gdisk
➢ Understand Logical Volume Manager (LVM) concepts, objects, structure, and commands
➢ Describe common file system types—extended, XFS, optical, VFAT, Reiser, and Btrfs—and their use
➢ Expound on file system administration and monitoring tools and use them to mount and unmount file systems, determine their UUID, label them, automount them, monitor their usage, calculate their disk usage, and create them
➢ Mount and access removable media
➢ Dump disk image and back up partition table
➢ Examine, repair, and debug extended and XFS file system issues
➢ Dump XFS file system structural information to a file
➢ Overview of user and group quotas and how to activate quota support, and initialize, set, administer, and report quota usage
➢ Comprehend the purpose and use of swap space and how to build and activate it

102.1 Design hard disk layout [this entire objective is described in this chapter]

19. Allocate filesystems and swap space to separate partitions or disks
20. Tailor the design to the intended use of the system
21. Ensure the /boot partition conforms to the hardware architecture requirements for booting
22. Knowledge of basic features of LVM

The following is a partial list of the used files, terms and utilities: /(root) filesystem, /var filesystem, /home filesystem, /boot filesystem, swap space, mount points, and partitions

103.3 Perform basic file management [most of this objective is described in chapter 2, a part in chapter 4, the tar/cpio commands in chapter 1, and the dd command in this chapter]

46. Usage of dd

The following is a partial list of the used files, terms and utilities: dd

103.5 Create, monitor and kill processes [most of this objective is described in chapter 4, the uptime command in chapter 1, and the free command in this chapter]

The following is a partial list of the used files, terms and utilities: free

104.1 Create partitions and filesystems [this entire objective is described in this chapter]

64. Manage MBR partition tables
65. Use various mkfs commands to create various filesystems such as ext2/ext3/ext4, XFS, and VFAT
66. Awareness of ReiserFS and Btrfs
67. Basic knowledge of gdisk and parted with GPT

The following is a partial list of the used files, terms and utilities: fdisk, gdisk, parted, mkfs, and mkswap

104.2 Maintain the integrity of filesystems [this entire objective is described in this chapter]

68. Verify the integrity of filesystems
69. Monitor free space and inodes
70. Repair simple filesystem problems

The following is a partial list of the used files, terms and utilities: du, df, fsck, e2fsck, mke2fs, debugfs, dumpe2fs, tune2fs, and xfs tools (such as xfs_metadump and xfs_info)

104.3 Control mounting and unmounting of filesystems [this entire objective is described in this chapter]

71. Manually mount and unmount filesystems
72. Configure filesystem mounting on bootup
73. Configure user mountable removable filesystems

The following is a partial list of the used files, terms and utilities: /etc/fstab, /media, mount, and umount

104.4 Manage disk quotas [this entire objective is described in this chapter]

74. Set up a disk quota for a filesystem
75. Edit, check and generate user quota reports

The following is a partial list of the used files, terms and utilities: quota, edquota, repquota, and quotaon

Data is stored on disks that are divided into partitions. A partition can exist on a portion of a disk, on an entire disk, or it may span multiple disks. Each partition is accessed and managed independent of other partitions and may contain a file system or swap space. Partitioning information is stored at special disk locations that the system references at boot time. Linux offers a number of tools and a toolset for partition management. Partitions created with any of these can co-exist on a single disk.

Logical Volume Manager is a toolset that sets up an abstraction layer between the operating system and the disk hardware. It uses virtual objects for storage pooling and allocation, and offers a whole slew of management commands, each of which is developed to carry out a certain action.

Linux supports a variety of file system types with a range of pros and cons over one another. A file system is a logical container employed for file storage. It must be connected to the root of the directory hierarchy in order to be accessible. This may be accomplished automatically at system boot or manually when required. A file system can be mounted or unmounted using its unique identifier, label, or device file. There are several commands for file system creation and administration; some of them are file system type specific while others are not. Tools are available to monitor file system space utilization, examine and fix potential corruption in file system structures, debug a file system, and dump its structural information to a file.

A file system's byte-for-byte dump can be created for duplication or backup purposes. Similarly, the partition information stored at the beginning of a boot disk can be backed up and used to overwrite the original information in case of its corruption.

Quotas may be applied on users and user groups to limit their file system space use. There are several tools available for quota management and handling.

Swapping is a common feature used on Linux systems. In fact, a Linux installation cannot proceed without first defining a swap space. Swapping provides a mechanism to move out and in pages of data between the physical memory and the swap. A swap space acts as an extension to the physical memory.

MBR, GPT, and Partitions

A disk in Linux can be carved up into several partitions. This partition information is stored on the disk in a small region, which is read by Linux at boot time. This region is referred to as the *Master Boot Record* (MBR) on the BIOS-based systems, and *GUID Partition Table* (GPT) on the UEFI-based systems. At system boot, the BIOS/UEFI scans all storage devices, detects the presence of MBR/GPT areas, identifies the boot disks, loads the bootloader program in memory, executes the boot code to read the partition table and identify the */boot* partition, and continues with the boot process by loading the kernel in memory and passing control over to it. Though MBR and GPT are designed for different PC firmware types, their job is the same: to store disk partition information and the boot code.

Master Boot Record (MBR)

The MBR is resident on the first sector of the boot disk. It is a tiny 512-byte area of which 446 bytes are occupied by the bootloader program, 64 bytes by the partition table, and the remaining 2 bytes by the boot signature. MBR has limitations that led to the design, development, and use of GPT.

MBR allows the creation of three types of partition—primary, extended, and logical—on a single disk. Of these, only primary and logical can be used for data storage; the extended is a mere enclosure for holding the logical partitions and it is not meant for data storage. MBR supports the existence of up to 4 primary partitions numbered 1 through 4 at a time. In case additional partitions are required, one of the primary partitions must be deleted and replaced with an extended partition to be able to add logical partitions (up to 12) within that extended partition. Numbering for logical partitions begin at 5. MBR supports a maximum of 15 usable partitions (3 primary and 12 logical) on a single disk.

The other limitation of MBR is its lack of accessing disk space beyond 2TB. This is due to its 32-bit nature and the disk sector size of 512 byte that it uses. The MBR is non-redundant; the record it contains is not replicated, resulting in an unbootable system in the event of its corruption.

GUID Partition Table (GPT)

With the increasing use of disks larger than 2TB, a new 64-bit partitioning standard called *Globally Unique IDentifiers* (GUID) *Partition Table* (GPT) was developed and integrated in to the UEFI firmware. This new standard introduced plenty of enhancements, including the ability to construct up to 128 primary partitions (no concept of extended or logical partitions), utilize disks larger than 2TB, use 4KB sector size, and store a copy of the partition information before the end of the disk for redundancy. Moreover, this standard allows a BIOS-based system to boot from a GPT disk using the bootloader program stored in a protective MBR at the first disk sector. In addition, the UEFI firmware also supports the secure boot feature, which only allows signed binaries to boot.

Disk Partitions

The space on a hard disk is used to carve up one or more partitions. Care should be taken when adding a new partition to elude data corruption with the overlapping of an extant partition and wasting storage by leaving unused space between adjacent partitions. On our *centos73* and *ubuntu14* systems, the disk we allocated at the time of installation is recognized as *sda*, stands for SAS/SCSI/SATA disk **a** with the first partition identified as *sda1*, second partition *sda2*, third partition *sda3*, and so on. Any subsequent disks added to the system will be recognized as *sdb*, *sdc*, *sdd*, and so on, and will use 1, 2, 3, etc. for partition numbering.

Linux provides the *lsblk* command to list disk and partitioning information. Here is the output of this command from *centos73*:

```
[root@centos73 ~]# lsblk
NAME              MAJ:MIN     RM     SIZE    RO     TYPE   MOUNTPOINT
sda               8:0         0        8G    0      disk
├─sda1            8:1         0        1G    0      part   /boot
└─sda2            8:2         0        7G    0      part
  ├─cl-root       253:0       0      6.2G    0      lvm    /
  └─cl-swap       253:1       0      820M    0      lvm    [SWAP]
sr0               11:0        1      4.1G    0      rom    /mnt
```

The output indicates the presence of one disk *sda* on *centos73*. This disk is 8GB in size and it contains two partitions: *sda1* and *sda2*. The first partition holds */boot* and the second one is an LVM volume with *root* and *swap* logical volumes residing in it. Both *sda1* and *sda2* partitions occupy the entire disk capacity. The *sr0* represents the ISO image mounted as an optical medium.

We can also use additional tools such as *fdisk* and *parted* with the -l option to expose this information in more detail. Here is what *fdisk* displays on *centos73*:

```
[root@centos73 ~]# fdisk -l
Disk /dev/sda: 8589 MB, 8589934592 bytes, 16777216 sectors
Units = sectors of 1 * 512 = 512 bytes
Sector size (logical/physical): 512 bytes / 512 bytes
I/O size (minimum/optimal): 512 bytes / 512 bytes
Disk label type: dos
Disk identifier: 0x000ddf8a
```

Device	Boot	Start	End	Blocks	Id	System
/dev/sda1	*	2048	2099199	1048576	83	Linux
/dev/sda2		2099200	16777215	7339008	8e	Linux LVM

```
Disk /dev/mapper/cl-root: 6652 MB, 6652166144 bytes, 12992512 sectors
Units = sectors of 1 * 512 = 512 bytes
Sector size (logical/physical): 512 bytes / 512 bytes
I/O size (minimum/optimal): 512 bytes / 512 bytes


Disk /dev/mapper/cl-swap: 859 MB, 859832320 bytes, 1679360 sectors
Units = sectors of 1 * 512 = 512 bytes
Sector size (logical/physical): 512 bytes / 512 bytes
I/O size (minimum/optimal): 512 bytes / 512 bytes
```

The output indicates the size of *sda* in MBs, bytes, and sectors, followed by the type of label the disk has along with other information. It shows *sda1* as the bootable partition marked with an asterisk (*). The output also indicates the starting and ending sector number, size in 1KB blocks, and a type for each partition. Types 83 and 8e identify the two partitions as a regular Linux partition and an LVM partition, respectively. We can see a list of supported partition types using the l option within *fdisk*. The last two blocks of information are specific to the LVM logical volumes that exist within the *sda2* partition.

On older systems, the boot partition must reside within the first 1,024 cylinders of the boot disk, otherwise it wouldn't allow Linux to boot. On newer firmware, this limit does not apply.

Disk Management Tools

Linux offers several tools for partitioning and managing disk storage. These tools include *fdisk*, *gdisk* (*GPT fdisk*), and *parted*. *fdisk* is limited to manipulating MBR partitioning only, *gdisk* supports GPT and also understands MBR, while *parted* understands and supports both MBR and GPT. In addition, *Logical Volume Manager* (LVM) toolset is also available, which offers more granular and flexible disk management capabilities. Partitions created with a combination of most of these tools can co-exist on the same disk. In this chapter, we use the three commands to manipulate partitions and provide an overview of LVM.

Before we move on, we suggest adding three 200MB disks to *centos73* to perform exercises in the following sections. We will use one disk per administration tool. Here is what the *lsblk* command would show with three new disks added:

```
[root@centos73 ~]# lsblk | grep sd
NAME        MAJ:MIN     RM      SIZE    RO      TYPE    MOUNTPOINT
sda         8:0         0       8G      0       disk
├─sda1      8:1         0       1G      0       part    /boot
└─sda2      8:2         0       7G      0       part
sdb         8:16        0       200M    0       disk
sdc         8:32        0       200M    0       disk
sdd         8:48        0       200M    0       disk
```

The new disks added to the system are *sdb*, *sdc*, and *sdd*, and they all are 200MB in size.

Managing MBR Partitioning with fdisk

fdisk has been a popular tool for disk partitioning on Linux systems; however, its limitations has restricted its use on systems with storage devices larger than 2TB. This text-mode, menu-driven program allows us to display, add, modify, verify, and delete MBR partitions.

The main interface of *fdisk* can be invoked by specifying a disk device name such as */dev/sdb* with the command. Type *m* at the prompt that appears to view available subcommands.

```
[root@centos73 ~]# fdisk /dev/sdb
. . . . . . . .
Command (m for help): m
Command action
   a   toggle a bootable flag
   b   edit bsd disklabel
   c   toggle the dos compatibility flag
   d   delete a partition
   g   create a new empty GPT partition table
   G   create an IRIX (SGI) partition table
   l   list known partition types
   m   print this menu
   n   add a new partition
   o   create a new empty DOS partition table
   p   print the partition table
   q   quit without saving changes
   s   create a new empty Sun disklabel
   t   change a partition's system id
   u   change display/entry units
   v   verify the partition table
   w   write table to disk and exit
   x   extra functionality (experts only)
```

There are plenty of subcommands available. The ones that are deemed important for the purpose of this discussion have been bolded. These include *d* to delete a partition, *l* to list supported partition types, *n* to create a partition, *p* to print the partition table, *q* to discard the changes and quit the tool, *t* to change a partition id, *v* to verify the changes, and *w* to write the partition table information and quit *fdisk*.

Let us perform some exercises to understand the procedure on how to create and erase partitions with *fdisk*.

Exercise 8-1: Create a Partition

In this exercise, you will create a 50MB primary partition on */dev/sdb*, and confirm the creation.

1. Execute the *fdisk* command on */dev/sdb*:

    [root@centos73 ~]# **fdisk /dev/sdb**

2. Choose *n* to add a new partition and then press Enter for primary partition:

    Command (m for help): **n**
    Partition type:
      p   primary (0 primary, 0 extended, 4 free)
      e   extended
    Select (default p):

3. Press Enter to select the default partition number:

    Partition number (1-4, default 1):

4. Enter the sector number where you wish the partition to begin; the default is 2048. Select the default by pressing the Enter key:

    First sector (2048-409599, default 2048):

5. Specify +50M as the partition size in megabytes and press Enter. You can also enter the size in sectors, KBs, or GBs. The default is to use all available disk space.

    Using default value 2048
    Last sector, +sectors or +size{K,M,G} (2048-409599, default 409599): **+50M**
    Partition 1 of type Linux and of size 50 MiB is set

6. Execute *p* to print the partition table:

    Command (m for help): **p**
    . . . .

Device Boot	Start	End	Blocks	Id	System
/dev/sdb1	2048	104447	51200	83	Linux

7. Write this information to the disk with the *w* subcommand and exit out:

    Command (m for help): **w**
    The partition table has been altered!
    Calling ioctl() to re-read partition table.
    Syncing disks.

8. Confirm the partition information using *lsblk* or *fdisk*:

```
[root@centos73 ~]# lsblk | grep sdb
sdb              8:16   0  200M  0 disk
└─sdb1 8:17   0   50M  0 part
[root@centos73 ~]# fdisk /dev/sdb -l
/dev/sdb1      2048    104447    51200  83  Linux
```

Required partition has been created successfully.

Exercise 8-2: Delete a Partition

In this exercise, you will delete the */dev/sdb1* that was created in the previous exercise, and confirm the erasure.

1. Invoke the *fdisk* command on */dev/sdb*:

    ```
    [root@centos73 ~]# fdisk /dev/sdb
    ```

2. Execute *d1* at the prompt to delete partition 1:

    ```
    Command (m for help): d1
    Selected partition 1
    Partition 1 is deleted
    ```

3. Write this information to the disk using *w* and exit out of *fdisk*:

    ```
    Command (m for help): w
    ```

4. Confirm the partition deletion with *lsblk* or *fdisk*.

Managing MBR and GPT Partitioning with parted

parted is another popular tool that is used to carve up disks on Linux systems. This program may be run interactively by invoking its text-based interface or directly from the command prompt. It allows us to name, view, add, check, modify, copy, resize, and delete partitions. *parted* understands and supports both MBR and GPT schemes. It can be used to create up to 128 partitions on a single GPT disk.

The main interface of *parted* can be invoked by specifying a disk device name such as */dev/sdc* with the command. Type *help* at the prompt that appears to view available subcommands.

```
[root@centos73 ~]# parted /dev/sdc
GNU Parted 3.1
Using /dev/sdc
Welcome to GNU Parted! Type 'help' to view a list of commands.
(parted) help
  align-check TYPE N                check partition N for TYPE(min|opt) alignment
```

help [COMMAND]	print general help, or help on COMMAND
mklabel,mktable LABEL-TYPE	**create a new disklabel (partition table)**
mkpart PART-TYPE [FS-TYPE] START END	**make a partition**
name NUMBER NAME	name partition NUMBER as NAME
print [devices|free|list,all|NUMBER]	**display the partition table, available devices, free space, all found partitions, or a particular partition**
quit	**exit program**
rescue START END	rescue a lost partition near START and END
rm NUMBER	**delete partition NUMBER**
select DEVICE	choose the device to edit
disk_set FLAG STATE	change the FLAG on selected device
disk_toggle [FLAG]	toggle the state of FLAG on selected device
set NUMBER FLAG STATE	change the FLAG on partition NUMBER
toggle [NUMBER [FLAG]]	toggle the state of FLAG on partition NUMBER
unit UNIT	set the default unit to UNIT
version	display the version number and copyright information of GNU Parted

There are several subcommands available. The ones that are deemed important for the purpose of this discussion have been bolded. These include *mklabel* to label the partition table, *mkpart* to make a partition, *name* to name a partition, *print* to print the partition table, *quit* to discard the changes and quit *parted*, and *rm* to remove a partition.

At the *parted* prompt, we can invoke help for a specific subcommand. For example, to obtain help on *mklabel*, issue the following:

> (parted) **help mklabel**
>   mklabel,mktable LABEL-TYPE   create a new disklabel (partition table)
>   LABEL-TYPE is one of: aix, amiga, bsd, dvh, gpt, mac, msdos, pc98, sun, loop

Using this tool interactively is similar to using the *fdisk* command except that you need to use appropriate subcommands. For the basic partition creation and deletion exercises presented below, the following two exercises will show the use of this tool by directly invoking it from the command prompt.

Exercise 8-3: Create a Partition

In this exercise, you will assign partition type "msdos" to */dev/sdc* for using this disk as an MBR disk. You will create and confirm a 100MB primary partition on the disk.

1. Execute *parted* on */dev/sdc* to view the current partition information:

    ```
    [root@centos73 ~]# parted /dev/sdc print
    Error: /dev/sdc: unrecognised disk label
    Model: ATA VBOX HARDDISK (scsi)
    Disk /dev/sdc: 210MB
    Sector size (logical/physical): 512B/512B
    Partition Table: unknown
    Disk Flags:
    ```

There is an error on the first line of the output, indicating an unrecognized label. This disk needs to be labeled before it can be partitioned, as it is a new disk.

2. Assign disk label "msdos" to the disk with *mklabel*:

    [root@centos73 ~]# **parted /dev/sdc mklabel msdos**

 To use the GPT partition table type, run "mklabel gpt" instead.

3. Create a 100MB primary partition starting at 1MB using *mkpart*:

    [root@centos73 ~]# **parted /dev/sdc mkpart primary 1 101m**

4. Verify the new partition with *print*, or use the *lsblk* command:

    [root@centos73 ~]# **parted /dev/sdc print**
    Model: ATA VBOX HARDDISK (scsi)
    Disk /dev/sdc: 210MB
    Sector size (logical/physical): 512B/512B
    Partition Table: msdos
    Disk Flags:

    Number Start   End   Size   Type   File system Flags
    1   1049kB   101MB   99.6MB   primary
    [root@centos73 ~]# **lsblk /dev/sdc**

Required partition has been created successfully.

Exercise 8-4: Delete a Partition

In this exercise, you will delete the *sdc1* partition that was created in the previous exercise, and confirm the deletion.

1. Execute *parted* on */dev/sdc* with the *rm* subcommand to remove partition number 1:

    [root@centos73 ~]# **parted /dev/sdc rm 1**

2. Confirm the partition deletion with *lsblk* or **parted /dev/sdc print**.

Managing GPT Partitioning with gdisk

The *gdisk* utility is used to partition a disk in GPT format. This text-based, menu-driven program allows us to view, add, verify, modify, and delete partitions among other operations. *gdisk* can be used to create up to 128 partitions on a single disk on systems with UEFI firmware.

The main interface of *gdisk* can be invoked by specifying a disk device name such as */dev/sdd* with the command. Type *help* or *?* (question mark) at the prompt that appears to view available subcommands.

```
[root@centos73 ~]# gdisk /dev/sdd
GPT fdisk (gdisk) version 0.8.6
Partition table scan:
 MBR: not present
 BSD: not present
 APM: not present
 GPT: not present
Creating new GPT entries.

Command (? for help): help
b    back up GPT data to a file
c    change a partition's name
d    delete a partition
i    show detailed information on a partition
l    list known partition types
n    add a new partition
o    create a new empty GUID partition table (GPT)
p    print the partition table
q    quit without saving changes
r    recovery and transformation options (experts only)
s    sort partitions
t    change a partition's type code
v    verify disk
w    write table to disk and exit
x    extra functionality (experts only)
?    print this menu
```

The output indicates that there is no partition table currently assigned to the disk. It also shows a list of available subcommands that have close resemblance to those of the *fdisk* command's. The subcommands include *c* to change a partition name, *d* to delete a partition, *i* to display partition information, *l* to list supported partition types, *n* to create a partition, *o* to label the disk with an empty GPT, *p* to print the partition table, *q* to quit without saving the changes, *t* to change a partition id, *v* to verify the changes, and *w* to write the partition table information and exit.

The functionality of *gdisk* is similar to that of *fdisk*'s. Let's perform basic partition creation and deletion operations in the following exercises to understand the usage of the command.

Exercise 8-5: Create a Partition

In this exercise, you will assign partition type GPT to */dev/sdd*. You will create a 150MB partition and confirm its creation.

1. Invoke the *gdisk* interface by executing this command on */dev/sdd*:

    ```
    [root@centos73 ~]# gdisk /dev/sdd
    ```

2. Apply GPT as the partition table type to the disk and enter y for confirmation to proceed:

    ```
    Command (? for help): o
    This option deletes all partitions and creates a new protective MBR.
    ```

Proceed? (Y/N): **y**

3. Run the *p* subcommand to view the disk label:

Command (? for help): **p**
Disk /dev/sdd: 409600 sectors, 200.0 MiB
Logical sector size: 512 bytes
Disk identifier (GUID): **D3B16A7B-CBE6-4071-BA58-A4306BFA9F09**
Partition table holds up to 128 entries
First usable sector is 34, last usable sector is 409566
Partitions will be aligned on 2048-sector boundaries
Total free space is 409533 sectors (200.0 MiB)
Number Start (sector) End (sector) Size   Code Name

The output indicates the GUID and states that the partition table can hold up to 128 entries.

4. Create a 150MB partition. Press Enter to accept "1" as the partition number and "2048" as the starting sector number for the partition. Input +150M for the partition size and press Enter to accept the default hex code of 8300 for the type of partition (Linux filesystem).

Command (? For help): **n**
Partition number (1-128, default 1):
First sector (34-409566, default = 2048) or {+-}size{KMGTP}:
Last sector (2048-409566, default = 409566) or {+-}size{KMGTP}: **+150M**
Current type is 'Linux filesystem'
Hex code or GUID (L to show codes, Enter = 8300):
Changed type of partition to 'Linux filesystem'

5. Verify the new partition with *p*:

Command (? for help): **p**
. . . .
Number Start (sector)   End (sector)   Size   Code   Name
   1   2048   309247   150.0 MiB   8300   Linux filesystem

6. Run the *w* subcommand to write the partition information to the disk and exit out of the tool. Enter y when prompted for confirmation to proceed.

Command (? for help): **w**
Final checks complete. About to write GPT data. THIS WILL OVERWRITE EXISTING PARTITIONS!!
Do you want to proceed? (Y/N): **y**
OK; writing new GUID partition table (GPT) to /dev/sdd.
The operation has completed successfully.

7. Confirm the partition creation with either **lsblk** or **gdisk -l /dev/sdd**.

Required partition has been created successfully.

Exercise 8-6: Delete a Partition

In this exercise, you will delete the *sdd1* partition that was created in the previous exercise, and confirm the deletion.

1. Execute **gdisk /dev/sdd**.
2. Enter d1 at the prompt to delete partition number 1:

   Command (? for help): **d1**

3. Write the updated partition information to the disk and quit. Enter y for confirmation when prompted.

   Command (? for help): **w**

4. Confirm the partition deletion using **lsblk** or **gdisk -l /dev/sdd**.

Overview of Logical Volume Manager (LVM)

The Logical Volume Manager (LVM) solution is widely used for managing disk storage in Linux. LVM provides an abstraction layer between the physical storage and the file system, enabling the file system to be resized, span across multiple physical disks, use arbitrary disk space, etc. LVM allows us to accumulate spaces taken from one or several partitions or disks (called *physical volumes*) to form a logical container (called a *volume group*), which is then divided into logical partitions (called *logical volumes*). The other key benefits of LVM use include online resizing of volume groups and logical volumes, online data migration between logical volumes and between physical volumes, user-defined naming for volume groups and logical volumes, mirroring and striping across multiple physical disks, and snapshotting of logical volumes. Figure 8-1 depicts the LVM components.

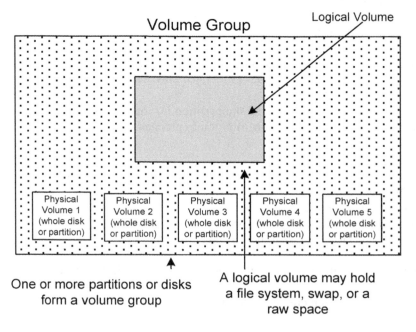

Figure 8-1 LVM Structure

Physical Volume

A physical volume (PV) is created when a partition or an entire disk is initialized and brought under LVM control. This process constructs LVM data structures on the device, including a label on the second sector and metadata shortly thereafter. The label includes a UUID, size, and pointers to the locations of data and metadata areas. Given the criticality of metadata, LVM stores a copy of it at the end of the physical volume as well. The rest of the space is available for use.

We can use the *pvs* command to scan and list available physical volumes on the system:

```
[root@centos73 ~]# pvs
  PV         VG    Fmt    Attr    PSize   PFree
  /dev/sda2  cl    lvm2   a--     7.00g   0
```

The output depicts the presence of one PV—*/dev/sda2*—that was created during *centos73* installation and was used to create the volume group called *cl*. The size of the PV is 7GB.

Volume Group

A volume group (VG) is created when at least one physical volume is added to it. The space from all physical volumes in a volume group is aggregated to form one large pool of storage, which is then used to build logical volumes. The physical volumes added to a volume group may be of varying sizes. LVM writes volume group metadata on each physical volume that is added to it. The volume group metadata contains its name, a unique identifier, the date and time of creation, how it was created, a list of included physical volumes and their attributes, a list of logical volumes, etc., and a copy of it is maintained at two locations on each physical volume within the volume group. A volume group can have any name assigned to it at the time of its creation. For example, it may be called *vg01*, *vgora*, or *vgweb* so as to identify the type of information it is constructed to store.

We can use the *vgs* command to scan and list available volume groups on the system:

```
[root@centos73 ~]# vgs
  VG      #PV    #LV    #SN    Attr     VSize    VFree
  cl      1      2      0      wz--n-   7.00g    0
```

The output indicates the presence of one VG called *cl* that was created during *centos73* installation from the */dev/sda2* physical volume. The size of the VG is currently equal to the size of the PV it contains.

Logical Volume

A volume group consists of a pool of storage taken from one or more physical volumes. This volume group space is used to create one or more logical volumes (LVs). A logical volume can be created or weeded out online, expanded or shrunk online, and can use space taken from one or several physical volumes inside the volume group.

The default naming convention for logical volumes is *lvol0, lvol1, lvol2*, and so on; however, we may assign any name that we wish. For example, a logical volume may be called *system*, *undo*, or *oraarch* so as to establish the type of information that it is constructed to store.

We can use the *lvs* command to scan and list available logical volumes on the system:

```
[root@centos73 ~]# lvs
  LV        VG    Attr        LSize   . . . . . . . .
  root      cl    -wi-ao----  6.20g
  swap      cl    -wi-ao----  820.00m
```

The output shows two logical volumes—root and swap—that were created during *centos73* installation in volume group *cl*. The sizes of the LVs are 6.2GB and 820MB, respectively.

LVM Operations and Commands

The LVM toolset offers a whole range of administrative commands to carry out various disk and volume management operations. These operations and their respective commands include creating and removing physical volumes (*pvcreate* and *pvremove*), creating and removing volume groups (*vgcreate* and *vgremove*), creating and removing logical volumes (*lvcreate* and *lvremove*), extending and reducing volume groups (*vgextend* and *vgreduce*), extending and reducing logical volumes (*lvextend* and *lvreduce*), and displaying physical volumes, volume groups, and logical volumes (*pvdisplay*, *vgdisplay*, and *lvdisplay*). All these tools accept the -v switch to show details during the performance of their operations. Refer to the manual pages of the commands for usage and details.

Understanding File Systems and File System Types

A *file system* is a logical container that is used to store files and directories. Each file system is created in a discrete partition or logical volume. A typical production Linux system usually has numerous file systems. During OS installation, if we select default disk layout, only two file systems are created—/ and /boot—though we can design a custom disk layout and construct separate containers to store dissimilar information. Typical additional file systems created during an installation are /home, /opt, /tmp, /usr, and /var. The two mandatory file systems—/ and /boot—are required for installation and booting.

Storing disparate data in distinct file systems versus storing all data in a single file system offers the following advantages. We can:

- ✓ Make any file system accessible (mount) or inaccessible (unmount) to users independent of other file systems. This hides or reveals information contained in that file system.
- ✓ Perform file system repair activities on individual file systems.
- ✓ Optimize or tune each file system independently.
- ✓ Grow or shrink a file system independent of other file systems.

Moreover, some native Linux backup tools such as *xfsdump* work only at the file system level.

Linux supports several types of file systems. These file systems may be categorized in three basic groups: *disk-based*, *network-based*, and *memory-based*. Disk-based file systems are typically created on physical drives using SCSI, iSCSI, SAS, SATA, USB, Fibre Channel, and other technologies. Network-based file systems are basically disk-based file systems shared over the network for remote access. Memory-based file systems are virtual; they are created automatically at system startup and destroyed when the system goes down. The first two types of file systems store information persistently, while any data saved in virtual file systems does not survive across system reboots. The following explains common disk-based file system types—Extended, XFS, and

ISO9660—that are supported in most Linux distributions and versions. Other less common types such as VFAT, ReiserFS/Reiser4, and Btrfs are also touched upon.

Extended File Systems

Extended file systems have been around in Linux for years. The first generation is obsolete and is no longer supported. The second, third, and fourth generations are currently available and supported. The fourth generation is the latest in the series and is superior with respect to features and enhancements to its predecessors.

The structure of an extended file system is built on a partition or logical volume at the time of file system creation. This structure is divided into two sets. The first set holds the file system's metadata and it is very tiny. The second set stores the actual data and it occupies almost the entire partition or the logical volume space.

The metadata includes the superblock, which keeps vital file system structural information, such as the type, size, and status of the file system and the number of data blocks it contains. Since the superblock holds such critical information, it is automatically replicated and maintained at various known locations throughout the file system. The superblock at the beginning of the file system is referred to as the *primary superblock*, and all of its copies as *backup superblocks*. If, for any reason, the primary superblock is corrupted or lost, it renders the file system inaccessible. One of the backup superblocks is then used to supplant the corrupted or lost primary superblock to bring the file system back to its normal state. The metadata also contains the inode table, which maintains a list of *index node* (inode) numbers. Each file is assigned an inode number at the time of its creation, and the inode number holds the file's attributes such as its type, permissions, ownership, owning group, size, and last access/modification time. The inode also holds and keeps track of the pointers to the actual data blocks where the file contents are located.

The ext3 and ext4 file systems support a journaling mechanism that provides them with the ability to recover swiftly after a system crash. Both ext3 and ext4 file systems keep track of their recent metadata changes in a *journal* (or log). Each metadata update is written in its entirety to the journal after completion. The system peruses the journal of each extended file system following the reboot after a crash to determine if there are any errors, and it recovers the file system rapidly using the latest metadata information stored in its journal. The ext2 file system does not support journaling; however, the support for journaling may be added to it if required.

In contrast to ext3 that supports file systems of sizes up to 16TiB and files of sizes up to 2TiB, ext4 supports very large file systems of sizes up to 1EiB (ExbiByte) and files of sizes up to 16TiB (TebiByte). Additionally, ext4 uses a series of contiguous physical blocks on the hard disk called *extents*, resulting in improved read and write performance with reduced fragmentation. ext4 supports extended user attributes, acl mount options (to support file permission allocation to specific users and groups), and metadata and quota journaling as well.

XFS File System

The *X File System* (XFS) is a high-performance 64-bit extent-based journaling file system type. XFS allows the creation of file systems and files of sizes up to 8EiB. It does not run file system checks at system boot; rather, it relies on us to use the *xfs_repair* utility manually to fix any issues if found. XFS sets the extended user attributes and acl mount options by default on new file systems. It enables defragmentation on mounted and active file systems to keep as much data in contiguous blocks as possible for faster access. The only major caveat with using XFS is its inability to shrink.

Like ext3 and ext4, xfs also uses journaling for metadata operations, guaranteeing the consistency of the file system against abnormal or forced unmounting. The journal information is read and any pending metadata transactions are replayed when the xfs file system is remounted.

XFS uses sophisticated techniques in its architecture for speedy IO performance. It can be snapshot in a mounted and active state. The snapshot thus produced can then be used for backup or other purposes.

ISO9660 File System

This file system type conforms to the ISO 9660 standard, hence the name. It is used for removable optical disc media such as CD/DVD drives for transporting software and patches, and operating system images in ISO format, between computers. The ISO9660 format originated from the *High-Sierra file system* (HSFS) format, and it has now been enhanced to include innovative features.

VFAT File System

VFAT (*Virtual File Allocation Table*) is an extension to the legacy FAT file system type, also called *FAT16*, that was introduced in early versions of MS-DOS. The support for FAT16 was later added to Microsoft Windows, Mac OS, and some UNIX versions, enabling them to read and write files written in that format. FAT16 had limitations; it was designed to use no more than 8.3 characters in filenames, limiting filenames to a maximum of eight characters plus three characters as an extension after the period. Moreover, it only allowed filenames to begin with a letter or number and to not contain spaces. FAT16 treated lowercase and uppercase letters alike.

VFAT was introduced with Microsoft Windows 95 and it has since been available. It supports 255 characters in filenames including spaces and periods; however, it still does not differentiate between lowercase and uppercase letters. VFAT support was added to Linux several years ago. A VFAT file system may be created on hard drives, but it is primarily used on removable media, such as floppy and USB flash drives, for exchanging data between Linux and Windows.

ReiserFS/Reiser4 File Systems

ReiserFS, occasionally referred to as *Reiser3*, was originally designed as a journaling filesystem with an exceptional capability of handling large amounts of small files to conserve disk space at the time. ReiserFS is now obsolete and it has been succeeded by *Reiser4*. Reiser4 also supports journaling and it allows expanding file systems online among other features. The support for Reiser4 is yet to be added to the mainline Linux distributions.

Btrfs File System

B-tree file system (Btrfs) is a copy-on-write file system that supports a file system size of up to 16EiB. It is capable of addressing and managing more files, larger files, and larger volumes than ext4. It supports snapshotting, compression, various RAID levels (Redundant Array of Independent Disks—a disk arrangement technique that allows for enhanced performance and fault tolerance), online defragmentation, online growth and shrinking, and online device addition and removal capabilities.

Managing File Systems

After reviewing various file system types, let's look at how to use some of them for data storage and access. This section covers the Extended, XFS, VFAT, and ISO9660 types only; others are beyond the scope of this book.

Managing file systems involves such operations as creating, mounting, labeling, viewing, growing, shrinking, unmounting, and removing them. These management tasks are common to both extended and xfs types. Most of these functions are also applicable to VFAT and a few to optical file systems, and will be covered in this chapter as well.

File System Administration Commands

In order to create and manage file systems, Linux offers a number of commands. Some of these commands are limited to their operations on the Extended, XFS, or VFAT file system type, while others are applicable to all file system types. Table 8-1 describes the commands that are important for our use and the exam.

Command	Description
Extended File System	
dumpe2fs	Displays file system metadata including superblock information
debugfs	Interactive debugging tool used to examine and change file system state, etc.
e2fsck	Peruses for file system inconsistencies, and repairs them if required. Can also be invoked as fsck.ext2, fsck.ext3, fsck.ext4, fsck -t ext2, fsck -t ext3, fsck -t ext4.
e2label	Modifies the label of a file system
mke2fs	Creates a file system. Can also be invoked as mkfs.ext2, mkfs.ext3, mkfs.ext4, mkfs -t ext2, mkfs -t ext3, and mkfs -t ext4. May be used with the -n option to determine the locations of the primary and backup superblocks.
tune2fs	Displays file system metadata including superblock information. Tunes file system attributes such as adding a journal to ext2, displaying and setting the maximum number of mounts before a check is enforced, adding a label, and so on.
XFS	
mkfs.xfs	Creates a file system. Can also be invoked as mkfs -t xfs.
xfs_admin	Tunes file system attributes
xfs_db	Debugs a file system
xfs_info	Displays information about a file system.
xfs_metadump	Copies a file system's metadata to a file for debugging
xfs_repair	Repairs file system inconsistencies
VFAT	
mkfs.vfat	Creates a file system. Equivalent to mkfs.fat
fsck.vfat	Examines a file system for inconsistencies, and repairs them if required. Can also be invoked as fsck -t vfat or fsck.fat.
Commands Common to All File Systems	
blkid	(block identifier). Displays UUID, label, and type of disk-based file systems
df	(disk free) Displays file system utilization
du	Calculates disk usage of directories and file systems
mount	Mounts a file system for user access. Displays currently mounted file systems. Use -t with a file system type to limit the view to that type.
umount	Unmounts a file system

Table 8-1 File System Management Commands

Most of these commands will be used in this chapter and subsequent chapters.

Mounting and Unmounting a File System

In order for user access to files and application programs in a file system, the file system has to be connected to the Linux directory at a desired attachment point, which is referred to as the *mount point*. A mount point is in essence any directory, preferably an empty directory, that is created solely for this purpose.

We can see many file systems already mounted on our system, such as the root file system mounted on / and the boot file system mounted on */boot* mount point. Both / and */boot* are essentially empty directories that are reserved by the system for the two file system mounts. We can use the *mount* command or the *df* command to view mounted file systems. The following shows only the / and */boot* file systems from *centos73*:

```
[user1@centos73 ~]$ mount -t xfs
/dev/mapper/cl-root on / type xfs (rw,relatime,seclabel,attr2,inode64,noquota)
/dev/sda1 on /boot type xfs (rw,relatime,seclabel,attr2,inode64,noquota)
[user1@centos73 ~]$ df -ht xfs
Filesystem            Size   Used   Avail   Use%   Mounted on
/dev/mapper/cl-root   6.2G   4.2G   2.1G    67%    /
/dev/sda1             1014M  172M   843M    17%    /boot
```

The "-t xfs" option limited the output of the commands to show only the xfs file system type and the -h option with the *df* command instructed the command to display the numbers in human-readable format (KB, MB, GB, and so on).

The default file system types assigned to / and */boot* on *ubuntu14* are ext2 and ext4, respectively. We can verify that by running **mount -t ext2** and **mount -t ext4** on that system.

The *mount* command is also used for mounting a file system to a mount point, and this action must be performed with root privileges. The command requires the absolute pathnames of the file system block device and the mount point name. It also accepts the UUID or label of the file system in place of a block device name. Options are available with this command to mount all or a specific type of file system. The *mount* command is also used to mount other types of file systems such as those located in removable media.

A mount point should be empty when an attempt is made to mount a file system on it, otherwise the contents of the mount point will hide. As well, the mount point must not be in use or the mount attempt will fail.

The *mount* command supports numerous options that may be used as required to override its default behavior. We can also specify more than one options by using a comma as a separator in between. Table 8-2 describes some of the options. Note that the options associated with "defaults" take effect if no other options are specified with the command.

Option	Description
async (sync)	Allows file system I/O to occur asynchronously (synchronously). This option does not have an effect on xfs file systems.
atime (noatime)	Updates (does not update) the inode access time for each access

Option	Description
auto (noauto)	Mounts (does not mount) a file system automatically at boot time or when the -a option is specified. The command references the */etc/filesystems* file for the order in which the file systems are to be probed for a type.
defaults	Accepts all default values (async, auto, dev, exec, nouser, rw, and suid)
dev (nodev)	Allows (disallows) the creation and use of device special files in the file system
exec (noexec)	Permits (does not permit) the execution of a binary that is located in the file system being mounted
remount	Remounts an already mounted file system with different options
ro (rw)	Mounts a file system read-only (read/write)
suid (nosuid)	Enables (disables) the execution of setuid and setgid programs that are located in the file system
users (nouser)	Allows (disallows) regular users to be able to mount or unmount a file system

Table 8-2 mount Command Options

The opposite of the *mount* command is *umount*, which is used to detach a file system from the directory hierarchy and make it inaccessible to users and applications. This command expects the absolute pathname to the block device containing the file system or its mount point name in order to detach it. Options are available with the *umount* command to unmount all or a specific type of file system.

Determining the UUID of a File System

Every extended and xfs file system has a 128-bit (32 hexadecimal characters) UUID (*Universally Unique IDentifier*) assigned to it at the time of its creation. In contrast, UUIDs assigned to vfat file systems are 32-bit (8 hexadecimal characters) in length. Assigning a UUID makes the file system unique among many other file systems that potentially exist on the system. The primary benefit of using a UUID is the fact that it always stays persistent across system reboots.

The */boot* file system on *centos73* is located in the */dev/sda1* partition and it is of type XFS. We can use the *xfs_admin* command with the -u option or the *blkid* command to determine its UUID:

```
[root@centos73 ~]# xfs_admin -u /dev/sda1
UUID = 2fef7e28-4d37-40e3-a00b-cfcd22d8d16a
[root@centos73 ~]# blkid /dev/sda1
/dev/sda1: UUID="2fef7e28-4d37-40e3-a00b-cfcd22d8d16a" TYPE="xfs"
```

The UUID reported by the two utilities is 2fef7e28-4d37-40e3-a00b-cfcd22d8d16a.

To determine the UUID of an extended file system, such as */dev/sda1* on *ubuntu14*, we can use the *blkid* command or either of the *tune2fs* or *dumpe2fs* commands; the latter two commands require root privileges.

```
user1@ubuntu14:~$ blkid /dev/sda1
/dev/sda1: UUID="650d5c17-363d-413e-a11e-d75220ca99ba" TYPE="ext2"
user1@ubuntu14:~$ sudo tune2fs -l /dev/sda1 | grep UUID
Filesystem UUID:        650d5c17-363d-413e-a11e-d75220ca99ba
```

```
user1@ubuntu14:~$ sudo dumpe2fs /dev/sda1
Filesystem UUID:        650d5c17-363d-413e-a11e-d75220ca99ba
```

The UUID reported by the three utilities is 650d5c17-363d-413e-a11e-d75220ca99ba.

Labeling a File System

A unique label may be used instead of a UUID to keep the file system association with its device file persistent across system reboots. A label is limited to a maximum of 12 characters on the xfs file system and 16 characters on the Extended file system. By default, no labels are assigned to a file system at the time of its creation.

The */boot* file system on *centos73* is located in the */dev/sda1* partition and it is of type XFS. We can use the *xfs_admin* command with the -l option or the *blkid* command to determine its label:

```
[root@centos73 ~]# xfs_admin -l /dev/sda1
label = ""
[root@centos73 ~]# blkid /dev/sda1
/dev/sda1: UUID="2fef7e28-4d37-40e3-a00b-cfcd22d8d16a" TYPE="xfs"
```

The output indicates that there is no label assigned to the file system.

To determine the label of an extended file system, such as */dev/sda1* on *ubuntu14*, we can use the *blkid* command or either of the *tune2fs* or *dumpe2fs* commands; the latter two commands require root privileges and they use the term "volume name" instead of "label" in the output:

```
user1@ubuntu14:~$ blkid /dev/sda1
/dev/sda1: UUID="650d5c17-363d-413e-a11e-d75220ca99ba" TYPE="ext2"
user1@ubuntu14:~$ sudo tune2fs -l /dev/sda1 | grep volume
Filesystem volume name:   <none>
user1@ubuntu14:~$ sudo dumpe2fs /dev/sda1 | grep volume
Filesystem volume name:   <none>
```

The output reports no existing labels on the file system.

A label is not needed on a file system if we intend to use its UUID, however, we can still apply one with the *xfs_admin* and *e2label* commands on respective file system types. Labeling an XFS file system requires that the target file system must be unmounted; this does not apply to Extended file systems.

The following example demonstrates the steps to unmount */boot*, set the label "bootfs" on */dev/sda1*, and remount it:

```
[root@centos73 ~]# umount /boot
[root@centos73 ~]# xfs_admin -L bootfs /dev/sda1
writing all SBs
new label = "bootfs"
[root@centos73 ~]# mount /boot
```

We can confirm the new label by executing either **xfs_admin -l /dev/sda1** or **blkid /dev/sda1**.

Now we can replace the string "UUID=2fef7e28-4d37-40e3-a00b-cfcd22d8d16a" for /boot in the /etc/fstab file with "LABEL=bootfs", and unmount and remount /boot as demonstrated above for confirmation. A discussion on the /etc/fstab file is provided in the next subsection.

The following example demonstrates how to apply a label called "bootvol" to /dev/sda1 on ubuntu14:

```
user1@ubuntu14:~$ sudo e2label /dev/sda1 bootvol
```

There is no need to remount the affected file system. Execute **e2label /dev/sda1, tune2fs -l /dev/sda1 | grep volume, dumpe2fs /dev/sda1 | grep volume**, or **blkid /dev/sda1** to confirm the new label on the file system.

We can swap the string "UUID=650d5c17-363d-413e-a11e-d75220ca99ba" for /boot in the /etc/fstab file with "LABEL=bootvol".

Automatically Mounting a File System at Reboots

File systems defined in the /etc/fstab file are mounted automatically at reboots. This file must contain proper and complete information for each listed file system. An incomplete or inaccurate entry might leave the system in an undesirable or unbootable state. Another benefit of adding entries to this file is that we only need to specify one of the four attributes—block device name, UUID, label, or mount point—of the file system that we wish to mount manually with the *mount* command. The *mount* command obtains the rest of the information from this file. Similarly, we only need to specify one of these attributes with the *umount* command to detach it from the directory hierarchy.

The default *fstab* file contains entries for file systems that are created at the time of installation. On *centos73*, for instance, this file currently has the following three entries:

```
[root@centos73 ~]# cat /etc/fstab
```

/dev/mapper/cl-root	/	xfs	defaults	0 0
UUID=2fef7e28-4d37-40e3-a00b-cfcd22d8d16a	/boot	xfs	defaults	0 0
/dev/mapper/cl-swap	swap	swap	defaults	0 0

ubuntu14 also has three entries in its *fstab* file:

```
user1@ubuntu14:~$ cat /etc/fstab
```

/dev/mapper/ubuntu--vg-root	/	ext4	errors=remount-ro	0 1
UUID=650d5c17-363d-413e-a11e-d75220ca99ba	/boot	ext2	defaults	0 2
/dev/mapper/ubuntu--vg-swap_1	none	swap	sw	0 0

The format of this file is such that each row is broken out into six columns to identify the required attributes for each file system to be successfully mounted. Here is what the columns contain:

- ✓ Column 1: defines a partition or logical volume name where the file system is resident, or its associated UUID or label.
- ✓ Column 2: identifies the mount point for the file system. For swap partitions, it is either "none" or "swap".

✓ Column 3: specifies the type of file system such as ext2, ext3, ext4, xfs, vfat, or iso9660. For swap, the type "swap" is used. You may use "auto" instead to leave it up to the *mount* command to determine the type of the file system.

✓ Column 4: identifies one or more comma-separated options to be used when mounting the file system. See Table 8-2 for a description of some of the options that you may use or consult the manual pages of the *mount* command or the *fstab* file for additional options and details.

✓ Column 5: is used by the *dump* utility to ascertain the file systems that need to be dumped. A value of 1 enables this check, and 0 or no value disables it.

✓ Column 6 (the last column): indicates the sequence number in which to run the *fsck* (file system check) utility on the file system at system reboots. By default, 0 is used for memory-based, remote, and removable file systems, 1 for /, and 2 for /boot and other physical file systems. 0 can also be used for any file system which we do not want to be examined.

This file is edited manually, so care must be observed to circumvent syntax and typo errors.

Monitoring File System Usage

On a live system, we often need to check file system usage to know if a mounted file system requires an expansion for growth or a clean up to generate free space. This involves examining the used and available spaces for a file system. We use the *df* (*disk free*) command for this purpose. It reports usage details for mounted file systems. By default, this command reports the numbers in KBs unless we use the -m or -h option to view the sizes in MBs or human-readable format.

Let's run this command on *centos73* with the -h option:

```
[root@centos73 ~]# df -h
Filesystem            Size   Used   Avail  Use%  Mounted on
/dev/mapper/cl-root   6.2G   4.2G   2.1G   67%   /
devtmpfs              481M   0      481M   0%    /dev
tmpfs                 497M   0      497M   0%    /dev/shm
tmpfs                 497M   6.9M   490M   2%    /run
tmpfs                 497M   0      497M   0%    /sys/fs/cgroup
tmpfs                 100M   0      100M   0%    /run/user/1000
/dev/sda1             1014M  172M   843M   17%   /boot
```

The output shows the file system name or type in the first column, followed by the total, used, and available spaces in the next three columns, and then the usage percentage and mount point in the last two columns.

There are a few other useful options available with the *df* command that we may use to produce the desired output. These options include:

-T to add a file system type to the output (example: **df -hT**)
-x to exclude the specified file system type from the output (example: **df -hx tmpfs**)
-t to limit the output to a specific file system type (example: **df -t xfs**)
-i to show inode information (example: **df -hi**)

You may use -h with any of these examples to print information in human-readable format.

Try running the *df* command with the different switches on *ubuntu14* and observe the output.

Calculating Disk Usage

In contrast to the *df* command that shows usage information for an entire file system, the *du* command reports the amount of space a file or directory occupies. By default, it shows the output in KBs; however, we can use the -m or -h option to view the output in MBs or human-readable format. In addition, we can view a usage summary with the -s option and a grand total with -c.

Let's run this command on the */usr/bin* directory on *centos73* to view the usage summary:

```
[root@centos73 ~]# du -hs /usr/bin
131M   /usr/bin
```

To add a "total" row to the output and with numbers displayed in KBs:

```
[root@centos73 ~]# du -sc /usr/bin
133892   /usr/bin
133892   total
```

Try this command with different options on the */usr/sbin/lvm* file and observe the results.

Exercise 8-7: Create and Mount an Extended File System

Redo Exercise 8-1 before attempting this exercise. In this exercise, you will format the *sdb1* partition created in Exercise 8-1 with the ext2 file system type. You will create */mntext* mount point and manually mount it. You will run appropriate commands to confirm its mount status, size, and type. You will upgrade the file system to ext3 and confirm with appropriate commands. You will append an entry to the *fstab* file for *sdb1* using its UUID. You will unmount the file system manually and remount it via the *fstab* file.

1. Format the partition with ext2 file system type using the *mke2fs* (or *mkfs.ext2* or *mkfs -t ext2*) command:

```
[root@centos73 ~]# mke2fs -t ext2 /dev/sdb1
mke2fs 1.42.9 (28-Dec-2013)
Filesystem label=
OS type: Linux
Block size=1024 (log=0)
Fragment size=1024 (log=0)
Stride=0 blocks, Stripe width=0 blocks
12824 inodes, 51200 blocks
2560 blocks (5.00%) reserved for the super user
First data block=1
Maximum filesystem blocks=52428800
7 block groups
8192 blocks per group, 8192 fragments per group
1832 inodes per group
Superblock backups stored on blocks:
      8193, 24577, 40961

. . . . . . . .
```

2. Create /mntext mount point with **mkdir -v /mntext**.
3. Mount /dev/sdb1 on /mntext with **mount /dev/sdb1 /mntext**.
4. Confirm the mount status and size with the *df* command, and type with the *mount* command:

    [root@centos73 ~]# **df -h | grep mntext**
    /dev/sdb1   49M   810KM 46M   2%   /mntext
    [root@centos73 ~]# **mount | grep mntext**
    /dev/sdb1 on /mntext type **ext2** (rw,relatime,seclabel)

5. Upgrade the file system to ext3 by adding journal using **tune2fs -j /dev/sdb1**.
6. Unmount and remount the file system, and confirm the file system type and new size with the *df* command:

    [root@centos73 ~]# **umount /mntext ; mount /dev/sdb1 /mntext**
    [root@centos73 ~]# **df -Th | grep mntext**

7. Determine the UUID for /dev/sdb1 using the *tune2fs* (or *blkid* or *dumpe2fs*) command:

    [root@centos73 ~]# **tune2fs -l /dev/sdb1 | grep UUID**
    Filesystem UUID: fed15b88-ae2c-4e5a-a369-0cb86573852b

8. Open the /etc/fstab file and append an entry for it:

    [root@centos73 ~]# **vi /etc/fstab**
    . . . .
    UUID=fed15b88-ae2c-4e5a-a369-0cb86573852b   /mntext   ext3   defaults 1 2

9. Unmount the file system and remount it with the entry in the *fstab* file:

    [root@centos73 ~]# **umount /mntext**
    [root@centos73 ~]# **mount -a**

10. Check the mount status as demonstrated in step 4.

Exercise 8-8: Create and Mount an XFS File System

Redo Exercise 8-3 before attempting this exercise. In this exercise, you will initialize the *sdc1* partition created in Exercise 8-3 with the xfs file system type. You will create /mntxfs mount point and manually mount the file system on to it. You will run appropriate commands to confirm its mount status, size, and type. You will apply the label "testxfs" to the file system and append an entry to the *fstab* file for it using the label. You will unmount the file system manually and remount it via the *fstab* file.

1. Initialize the /dev/sdc1 partition with the xfs file system type using the *mkfs* (or *mkfs.xfs*) command:

```
[root@centos73 ~]# mkfs -t xfs /dev/sdc1
meta-data=/dev/sdc1         isize=512          agcount=4, agsize=6080 blks
         =                  sectsz=512         attr=2, projid32bit=1
         =                  crc=1              finobt=0, sparse=0
data     =                  bsize=4096         blocks=24320, imaxpct=25
         =                  sunit=0            swidth=0 blks
naming   =version 2         bsize=4096         ascii-ci=0 ftype=1
log      =internal log      bsize=4096         blocks=855, version=2
         =                  sectsz=512         sunit=0 blks, lazy-count=1
realtime =none              extsz=4096         blocks=0, rtextents=0
```

2. Create */mntxfs* mount point with **mkdir /mntxfs**.
3. Mount */dev/sdc1* on */mntxfs* with **mount /dev/sdc1 /mntxfs**.
4. Confirm the mount status and size with the *df* command, and type with the *mount* command:

```
[root@centos73 ~]# df -h | grep mntxfs
/dev/sdc1          92M      5.0M     87M     6%        /mntxfs
[root@centos73 ~]# mount | grep mntxfs
```

5. Unmount the file system and apply label "testxfs":

```
[root@centos73 ~]# umount /mntxfs
[root@centos73 ~]# xfs_admin -L testxfs /dev/sdc1
```

6. Open the */etc/fstab* file and append an entry for this File systems:

```
[root@centos73 ~]# vi /etc/fstab
. . . . . . . .
LABEL=testxfs   /mntxfs            xfs        defaults   0   0
```

7. Execute **mount -a** to remount the file system with the entry in the *fstab* file.
8. Check the mount status and type as demonstrated in step 4.
9. Display file system information by running **xfs_info /mntxfs.**

Exercise 8-9: Create and Mount a VFAT File System

Redo Exercise 8-5 before attempting this exercise. In this exercise, you will initialize the *sdd1* partition created in Exercise 8-5 with the vfat file system type. You will create */mntvfat* mount point and manually mount this file system on to it. You will run appropriate commands to confirm its mount status, size, and type. You will append an entry to the *fstab* file for this file system. You will unmount the file system manually and remount it via the *fstab* file.

1. Initialize */dev/sdd1* partition with the vfat file system type using the *mkfs.vfat* (or *mkfs -t vfat*) command:

```
[root@centos73 ~]# mkfs.vfat /dev/sdd1
```

2. Create */mntvfat* mount point:

    [root@centos73 ~]# **mkdir /mntvfat -v**

3. Mount */dev/sdd1* on */mntvfat* using the *mount* command:

    [root@centos73 ~]# **mount /dev/sdd1 /mntvfat**

4. Confirm the mount status and size with the *df* command, and type with the *mount* command:

    ```
    [root@centos73 ~]# df -h | grep mntvfat
    /dev/sdd1          150M   0M      150M    0%        /mntvfat
    [root@centos73 ~]# mount | grep mntvfat
    ```

5. Open the */etc/fstab* file and append an entry for this File systems:

    ```
    [root@centos73 ~]# vi /etc/fstab
    . . . . . . . .
    /dev/sdd1          /mntvfat         vfat      defaults 1  2
    ```

6. Execute **mount -a** to remount the file system with the entry in the *fstab* file.
7. Check the mount status and type as demonstrated in step 4.

Accessing File Systems in Removable Media

You may need to access removable devices, such as an optical or a USB device, for installing some software located on them or transferring files. On a physical system, you insert the media into their respective ports and Linux automatically detects their presence. In a virtualized environment, however, you will need to attach the inserted media to your VM via the virtualization management program interface. You can mount them, inspect their sizes, view their contents, create file system structures (usb only) in them, transfer files (usb only), and so on. When you are done and you no longer need them, simply unmount them just like any other file system.

The following examples demonstrate how to work with these media on *centos73*. We have already attached the CentOS 7.3 ISO image to the system, plugged in a formatted USB flash drive, and attached it to the VM.

Linux has recognized the optical medium and we can access it via the */dev/sr0* or */dev/cdrom* device file. The USB medium is treated just like any other hard disk on the system. Let's run the *lsblk* command on *centos73* and see what it reports:

```
[root@centos73 ~]# lsblk
NAME           MAJ:MIN RM   SIZE RO TYPE MOUNTPOINT
sda              8:0    0     8G  0 disk
├─sda1           8:1    0     1G  0 part /boot
└─sda2           8:2    0     7G  0 part
  ├─cl-root    253:0    0   6.2G  0 lvm  /
  └─cl-swap    253:1    0   820M  0 lvm  [SWAP]
sdb              8:16   0   200M  0 disk
└─sdb1           8:17   0    50M  0 part /mntext
sdc              8:32   0   200M  0 disk
└─sdc1           8:33   0    95M  0 part /mntxfs
sdd              8:48   0   200M  0 disk
└─sdd1           8:49   0   150M  0 part
sde              8:64   1  14.6G  0 disk
└─sde1           8:65   1  14.6G  0 part
sr0             11:0    1   4.1G  0 rom
```

Other than the *sda* to *sdd* disks that we worked with before, we see two additional devices: *sde* with a partition *sde1* (USB) and *sr0* (DVD). Let's work with the media and perform some operations.

To mount the optical medium formatted with iso9660 file system type on */cdrom0* in read-only mode:

```
[root@centos73 ~]# mkdir /cdrom0
[root@centos73 ~]# mount -o ro /dev/cdrom /cdrom0
```

To mount the FAT32 file system in */dev/sde1* on the USB drive on */usb0* mount point:

```
[root@centos73 ~]# mkdir /usb0
[root@centos73 ~]# mount /dev/sde1 /usb0
```

Let's run the *df* and *mount* commands to verify the mount status, sizes, and type:

```
[root@centos73 ~]# df -h | egrep 'cdrom|usb'
/dev/sde1     15G    32K    15G     1%    /usb0
/dev/sr0     4.1G   4.1G      0   100%    /cdrom0
[root@centos73 ~]# mount | egrep 'cdrom|usb'
/dev/sde1 on /usb0 type vfat
(rw,relatime,fmask=0022,dmask=0022,codepage=437,iocharset=ascii,shortname=mixed,errors=remount-ro)
/dev/sr0 on /cdrom0 type iso9660 (ro,relatime)
```

The above outputs indicate the total storage capacity for the two devices, their usage, mount points, and types ("iso9660" for the optical file system and "vfat" for the one in the USB stick).

You can run **ls -l /cdrom0** and **ls -l /usb0** to view what the two media contain.

To unmount them both, issue the *umount* command and supply either their mount points or device files as an argument:

```
[root@centos73 ~]# umount /cdrom0 (or umount /dev/cdrom or umount /dev/sr0)
[root@centos73 ~]# umount /usb0 (or umount /dev/sde1)
```

With the information available for the two media, you should be able to add line entries for them to the *fstab* file for automatic mounting.

Disk Dumping and Backing up MBR

Disk dumping is the process of imaging an entire disk (a hard disk, optical disk, or a USB disk) or a disk partition to another disk or disk partition of the same or larger size. The resultant image is a clone of the source and may be used as a backup or on another computer if required.

Linux offers a command called *dd* (*disk dump*) for this purpose. This command performs a block-for-block duplication of the source disk or partition regardless of the type of data it contains or whether it is empty. The *dd* command can also be used to back up the MBR (*Master Boot Record*) of a boot disk or to create an image of a file or directory.

An elementary use of *dd* is shown below. It shows that a file */var/lib/rpm/Packages* of size ~71MB is duplicated in the */tmp* directory by the name *targetfile*. The source file is specified with the "if" (input file) parameter and the target is supplied with the "of" (output file) parameter.

```
[user1@centos73 ~]$ dd if=/var/lib/rpm/Packages of=/tmp/targetfile
139400+0 records in
139400+0 records out
71372800 bytes (71 MB) copied, 0.425475 s, 168 MB/s
```

The output indicates that the file was copied in 0.425475 seconds at the data transfer rate of 168 MB/second. It also shows the number of blocks read and written.

dd writes data in 512-byte (1/2K or 2x512=1K) blocks by default as evident from the above output, where 139400 blocks were copied. If you take this number (139400) and divide it by 2, you get an approximate size in kilobytes of the data copied, which in this example is about 71MB. Don't worry about the exact numbers. Some tools show sizes slightly differently from the others. For instance, the **ls -lh /var/lib/rpm/Packages** will show a different size.

This small block size may not be efficient in large duplications. To speed up the operation, you can use the ibs (input block size) and obs (output block size) options explicitly, or the bs (block size) option as a common denominator for both.

By default, the installations we did in Chapter 1 "Installing Linux and Using Basic Commands," created */dev/sda1* partitions of sizes 1GB and 243MB on our *centos73* and *ubuntu14* systems, respectively. Let's see how we can employ *dd* to back up this partition on *centos73* as *bootvol.bkp* (assign a 1.1GB virtual disk to this VM in Oracle VirtualBox console, create *sde1* on the entire disk, initialize the partition with *mkfs.xfs*, and mount it on */mntxfs1*). We will use a block size of 10MB for this operation to support large read and write operations.

```
[root@centos73 ~]# dd if=/dev/sda1 of=/mntxfs1/bootvol.bkp bs=10M
102+0 records in
102+0 records out
1073741824 bytes (1.1 GB) copied, 3.68623 s, 402 MB/s
```

The output shows that close to 1.1GB (102 x 10MB) of data was copied. Use the *ls* command to view the image file size:

```
[root@centos73 ~]# ls -lh /mntxfs1/bootvol.bkp
-rw-r--r--. 1 root root 1.0G Dec 22 13:12 /mntxfs1/bootvol.bkp
```

The command reports 1.0GB.

Likewise, the MBR of the boot disk can be backed up. Here is an example on how to back up the
first 512-byte boot block to a file called *mbr.bkp* under /root on *centos73*:

```
[root@centos73 ~]# dd if=/dev/sda of=/root/mbr.bkp count=1
1+0 records in
1+0 records out
512 bytes (512 B) copied, 0.000823808 s, 622 kB/s
```

To restore any of the three backups/images you've created, simply replace "if" with "of" and vice
versa. For instance, to restore the MBR, use **dd of=/dev/sda if=/root/mbr.bkp**.

Inspecting and Repairing File Systems

The structure of an extended file system could be damaged when an abnormal system shutdown or
crash occurs, potentially leaving the mounted and active file systems in an inconsistent state as the
system did not have enough time to unmount the file systems normally. To maintain file system
integrity, the operating system automatically runs a check at system boot time on file systems that it
finds in an abnormal state and attempts to repair and remount them. We can divide our learning on
this topic into extended and xfs file system types, as there are technical differences between the two
that affect how they are inspected and repaired.

Analyzing and Repairing Extended File Systems

At the time of this writing, Linux supports three generations of the extended file system type: ext2,
ext3, and ext4. By default, ext2 is without a journal. To maintain integrity, Linux uses the utility
called *e2fsck* (of *fsck*) for check and repair purposes. This utility is hardlinked to *fsck.ext2*, *fsck.ext3*,
and *fsck.ext4* commands that may be issued instead on the specific file system type. The *ll* output
below from *centos73* shows the inode number for *e2fsck* in the first column and the *find* command
lists all the hardlinked files with that inode number. They all have an identical inode number
508880.

```
[root@centos73 ~]# ll -i /usr/sbin/e2fsck
508880 -rwxr-xr-x. 4 root root 256384 Nov 5 14:59 /usr/sbin/e2fsck
[root@centos73 ~]# find /usr/sbin -inum 508880 -exec ls -li {} \;
508880 -rwxr-xr-x. 4 root root 256384 Nov 5 14:59 /usr/sbin/fsck.ext3
508880 -rwxr-xr-x. 4 root root 256384 Nov 5 14:59 /usr/sbin/fsck.ext4
508880 -rwxr-xr-x. 4 root root 256384 Nov 5 14:59 /usr/sbin/e2fsck
508880 -rwxr-xr-x. 4 root root 256384 Nov 5 14:59 /usr/sbin/fsck.ext2
```

The behavior of *e2fsck* is based on whether the file system has a journal. This utility is invoked
automatically with the -A option during the reboot after a system crash. It runs a full examination
on entire ext2 file systems as they are without a journal, reports inconsistencies, and attempts to
repair them automatically. It prompts for user intervention if it cannot resolve a discrepancy.
Conversely, if it determines that the file system has a journal (as in the case of ext3 and ext4), it
simply replays the journal and brings the file system back to its previous consistent state within no

---

time. This utility inspects all extended file systems with a passno (the sixth field) setting in the *fstab* file. If the passno field is empty or 0, the corresponding file system is left uninspected. By default, the root file system has passno set to 1 and other extended file systems have this value set to 2 or higher on older Linux distribution versions including our *ubuntu14* and *centos511*. This means that the root file system is examined first, and then those with 2 will have this inspection run in parallel. Memory-based file systems do not need an examination, and hence a 0 value.

The *e2fsck* command can also be executed manually on an unmounted (or read-only) file system from the command line using the file system's device file name, UUID, or type. During the check, it expects a "yes" or "no" response while in its attempt to correct discovered discrepancies, unless the -p (preen) option is specified, which gives the command a go ahead to fix problems automatically. We can also use the -f (force) option to run the analysis even if the file system is in clean and stable state.

Let's unmount the file system */dev/sdb1* that we created in Exercise 8-7 and execute the command on it in a variety of ways. We will use the -f option, as this file system has no current issues to view the full output of the inspection.

```
[root@centos73 ~]# umount /dev/sdb1
[root@centos73 ~]# e2fsck -f /dev/sdb1
[root@centos73 ~]# fsck.ext3 /dev/sdb1 -f
[root@centos73 ~]# fsck -t ext3 /dev/sdb1 -f
[root@centos73 ~]# e2fsck -f UUID=0dbc8566-1cc3-4b46-8dfa-1a0edf407454
e2fsck 1.42.9 (28-Dec-2013)
Pass 1: Checking inodes, blocks, and sizes
Pass 2: Checking directory structure
Pass 3: Checking directory connectivity
Pass 4: Checking reference counts
Pass 5: Checking group summary information
/dev/sdb1: 11/12824 files (9.1% non-contiguous), 6550/51200 blocks
[root@centos73 ~]# mount /dev/sdb1
```

The output shows that the command performed five passes on the file system during the process and it encountered no issues. We remounted the file system at the end.

> If we attempt to run e2fsck or fsck or any of their variations on a mounted file system, we will get an error message similar to "/dev/XXXX is mounted. e2fsck: Cannot continue, aborting."

During the scrutiny, if the command learns of a corruption in the primary superblock, it exits out to the command prompt, as it requires us to take a corrective measure. Linux does not allow a file system to be mounted if its primary superblock is lost or corrupted. In this situation, we identify the backup superblock locations with the *dumpe2fs* command for that file system, and then re-invoke *e2fsck* by specifying one of these locations to overwrite the primary superblock. We should be able to mount the file system back after the primary superblock has been fixed.

Exercise 8-10: Restore a Corrupted Primary Superblock

In this exercise, you will unmount the */mntext* file system that was created in Exercise 8-7. You will determine backup superblock locations and use one of them to overwrite the primary superblock assuming that it is corrupt. You will mount the file system back.

1. Unmount the */mntext* file system with **umount /mntext**.
2. Obtain the list of superblock locations using the *dumpe2fs* command:

    [root@centos73 ~]# **dumpe2fs /dev/sdb1 | grep superblock**
    Primary superblock at 1, Group descriptors at 2-2
    Backup superblock at 8193, Group descriptors at 8194-8194
    Backup superblock at 24577, Group descriptors at 24578-24578
    Backup superblock at 40961, Group descriptors at 40962-40962

    The output shows three backup locations at block numbers 8193, 24577, and 40961.

3. Run any of the following and specify the location of the first backup superblock (8193) to restore the primary. Use -y for confirmation to proceed with the overwrite.

    [root@centos73 ~]# **e2fsck -b 8193 /dev/sdb1 -y**
    [root@centos73 ~]# **fsck -b 8193 /dev/sdb1 -y**
    [root@centos73 ~]# **fsck -b 8193 /dev/sdb1 -y -t ext3**
    [root@centos73 ~]# **fsck.ext3 /dev/sdb1 -y -b 8193**

    . . . .
    Fix? yes
    /dev/sdb1: ***** FILE SYSTEM WAS MODIFIED *****
    /dev/sdb1: 11/12824 files (9.1% non-contiguous), 6550/51200 blocks

4. Mount the file system back with **mount /dev/sdb1**. The command will get the mount point information from *fstab*.

Debugging an Extended File System

We may examine an extended file system, change its state, undelete files, produce superblock statistics, navigate within the file system, and run plenty of basic Linux file manipulation commands using the interactive debugger program called *debugfs*. This tool offers many capabilities that both *tune2fs* and *dumpe2fs* include in them. These capabilities are incorporated in the command through numerous subcommands, which we can view by issuing *help* at its prompt.

To use this tool, execute *debugfs* on */dev/sdb1* as follows to open the file system in read-only mode. The output below shows a subset of the available subcommands.

    [root@centos73 ~]# **debugfs /dev/sdb1**
    debugfs: **help**
    show_super_stats, stats   Show superblock statistics
    change_working_directory, cd   Change working directory
    list_directory, ls   List directory
    show_inode_info, stat   Show inode information
    link, ln   Create directory link
    unlink   Delete a directory link

mkdir	Create a directory
rmdir	Remove a directory
rm	Remove a file (unlink and kill_file, if appropriate)
print_working_directory, pwd	Print current working directory
expand_dir, expand	Expand directory
mknod	Create a special file
list_deleted_inodes, lsdel	List deleted inodes
undelete, undel	Undelete file
write	Copy a file from your native filesystem
dump_inode, dump	Dump an inode out to a file
cat	Dump an inode out to stdout
lcd	Change the current directory on your native filesystem
rdump	Recursively dump a directory to the native filesystem
dirsearch	Search a directory for a particular filename
symlink	Create a symbolic link
quit, q	Leave the subsystem

debugfs supports a number of navigation and file manipulation subcommands including *cd*, *ls*, *ln*, *mkdir*, *rmdir*, *rm*, *pwd*, *undel*, and *cat* that have been covered in previous chapters. See the command's manual pages for details and usage. Try a few operations such as *stats*, *mkdir*, *rm*, and *undel* to get yourself familiarized with the usage of the tool. Type *q* and press Enter to quit and return to the command prompt.

You should start *debugfs* with the -w (writable) switch if you wish to make any changes to the file system.

Examining and Repairing an XFS File System

An xfs file system may be checked and repaired if a corruption in its metadata is suspected. The *xfs_repair* utility is available for this purpose. This tool requires that the file system be unmounted and in a clean state. When invoked, it replays the journal while performing all operations automatically without prompting for user input. The *xfs_repair* program goes through seven phases during its execution lifecycle on a file system. It peruses the elements such as inodes, directories, pathnames, link counts, and superblocks. The following is an example of running this tool on the */mntxfs* file system that resides in */dev/sdc1* partition we created in Exercise 8-8. Remember, we have to unmount the file system before running this command on it.

```
[root@centos73 ~]# umount /mntxfs
[root@centos73 ~]# xfs_repair /dev/sdc1
Phase 1 - find and verify superblock...
Phase 2 - using internal log
        - zero log...
        - scan filesystem freespace and inode maps...
        - found root inode chunk
Phase 3 - for each AG...
        - scan and clear agi unlinked lists...
        - process known inodes and perform inode discovery...
        - agno = 0
        - agno = 1
        - agno = 2
```

```
        - agno = 3
        - process newly discovered inodes...
Phase 4 - check for duplicate blocks...
        - setting up duplicate extent list...
        - check for inodes claiming duplicate blocks...
        - agno = 0
        - agno = 1
        - agno = 2
        - agno = 3
Phase 5 - rebuild AG headers and trees...
        - reset superblock...
Phase 6 - check inode connectivity...
        - resetting contents of realtime bitmap and summary inodes
        - traversing filesystem ...
        - traversal finished ...
        - moving disconnected inodes to lost+found ...
Phase 7 - verify and correct link counts...
done
[root@centos73 ~]# mount /mntxfs
```

The output indicates the seven phases of the check. We can add the -v flag for additional information in the output.

The *xfs_repair* command does not run at system boot even if an xfs file system was not cleanly unmounted. In the event of an abnormal unmount, this command simply replays the log at mount time, ensuring a consistent file system.

With this utility, we don't need to worry about locating copies of the superblock to repair the primary in case of its corruption. This tool takes care of that automatically by finding a backup and overwriting the primary with it.

Dumping XFS File System Metadata to a File

We have looked at the use of the *xfs_repair* utility for file systems with inconsistencies. In rare cases, it is possible that this utility is unable to fix an issue with the file system, leaving it inaccessible to users. Imagine a file system containing critical data and it must be repaired in order to be mounted! Linux provides the *xfs_metadump* utility to dump the metadata of a damaged xfs file system to a file for sending out to our company's technical support provider for analysis and debugging. This tool must only be run on a read-only or unmounted file system.

Here is how we unmount the xfs file system */dev/sdc1* (source), and run *xfs_metadump* on it to redirect the dump to a file called */tmp/xfsmntdump* (target):

```
[root@centos73 ~]# umount /dev/sdc1
[root@centos73 ~]# xfs_metadump /dev/sdc1 /tmp/xfsmntdump
```

We can inspect the file type produced with the *file* command:

```
[root@centos73 ~]# file /tmp/xfsmntdump
/tmp/xfsmntdump: XFS filesystem metadump image
```

This file may contain several megabytes of dump in it. Check the size with the *ls* command. If the file size is too large, you may compress it before forwarding it to the technical support group.

Understanding, Configuring, Managing, and Reporting Quota

By default, users can create as many files as they want in a file system provided there is enough room and inodes available. This opens up the door for them to consume a large chunk of file system space for personal files, which may include unnecessary data. With quota management, you can limit the file system space usage based on individual users or groups in order to prevent them from filling up the file system. Quota information for extended file systems is stored in *aquota.user* and *aquota.group* files for users and groups, and that for xfs within the file system metadata or in these files.

There is a variety of tools available for quota management for both extended and xfs file system types, and they are described in Table 8-3.

Command	Description
edquota	Edits/sets/copies user and group quota settings
quota	Displays quota settings and usage status
quotacheck	Examines quota usage and creates or repairs aquota.user and aquota.group files if they are lost or corrupted
quotaoff	Disables quota on a file system
quotaon	Enables quota on a file system
repquota	Reports quota usage
setquota	Sets disk quota at the command line

Table 8-3 Quota Management Commands

Quota can be set either by inodes (number of files a user can create) or disk size (amount of storage a user is entitled to use). The discussion in this section is restricted to quota application and management on extended file systems only; however, the concepts, commands, and procedures are also applicable to xfs file systems. You may practice the procedures presented on the xfs file system */dev/sdc1* mounted on */mntxfs* that we created earlier in Exercise 8-8.

Soft and Hard Quota Limits

When working with quotas, the concepts of *soft* and *hard* limits are essential.

A soft limit acts as a lower-level threshold, and it defines the maximum amount of disk space that a user or a group of users can use at will in a file system without being warned. If this threshold is met, the user or group is still permitted to use the file system space until the point they hit the absolute maximum upper-level threshold, called the hard limit, beyond which they cannot use any additional file system space.

If a grace period is also enforced, the user or group members must move or remove their files within that time frame to bring their usage down to below the soft limit or they will be rejected from further using the file system. Note that the grace period is only set for soft limits.

Activating Quota Support

Before we are able to set any quotas for users and groups on a file system, we need to ensure that the file system is mounted with quota support enabled. Let's work on the */dev/sdb1* ext3 file system that we created in Exercise 8-7. This file system is mounted on */mntext*. We can use the *mount* command to check whether quota support is enabled:

```
[root@centos73 ~]# mount | grep sdb1
/dev/sdb1 on /mntext type ext3 (rw,relatime,seclabel,data=ordered)
```

The output does not show an indication of quota support added to it. In order to be able to work with quotas on this file system, we need to remount it with usrquota and grpquota options to enable quota support for both users and groups:

```
[root@centos73 ~]# mount -o remount,usrquota,grpquota /mntext
[root@centos73 ~]# mount | grep sdb1
/dev/sdb1 on /mntext type ext3 (rw,relatime,seclabel,quota,usrquota,grpquota,data=ordered)
```

The output confirms the activation of quota.

Initializing Quota Databases

Next, execute the *quotacheck* command on the file system in verbose mode (-v) to perform a quota scan for all users (-u) and groups (-g). This command will create (-c) *aquota.user* and *aquota.group* databases in that file system to store quota information.

```
[root@centos73 ~]# quotacheck -cguv /mntext
quotacheck: Scanning /dev/sdb1 [/mntext] quotacheck done
quotacheck: Checked 3 directories and 0 files
```

Check for the creation of *aquota.user* and *aquota.group* files under */mntext*:

```
[root@centos73 ~]# ll /mntext/aquota*
-rw------- 1 root  root  6144 Mar 2  14:55 /mntext/aquota.group
-rw------- 1 root  root  6144 Mar 2  14:55 /mntext/aquota.user
```

Enabling and Disabling Quota Enforcement

Now, we need to enable quota enforcement on */mntext* using the *quotaon* command. Use -v for verbose output.

```
[root@centos73 ~]# quotaon -v /mntext
/dev/sdb1 [/mntext]: group quotas turned on
/dev/sdb1 [/mntext]: user quotas turned on
```

The *quotaon* command also has the -a (all) option that we can use to enable quota enforcement on all the file systems that are listed in the */etc/fstab* file and the -p (print state) option to tell us whether the quota is on.

The reverse of the above is the *quotaoff* command, which is used to turn quota enforcement off. Both *quotaon* and *quotaoff* commands support -a (all), -p (print state), -u (user), -g (group), -v (verbose) options.

Setting and Viewing User and Group Quotas

At this point, we are ready to set quotas for users and groups on the */mntext* file system. We use the *edquota* command to accomplish this goal. This command opens the *aquota.user* or *aquota.group* file in the *vi* editor, and allows us to manually modify the values according to our needs. The following example opens the user quota file for *user1*:

```
[root@centos73 ~]# edquota user1
Disk quotas for user user1 (uid 1000):
  Filesystem        blocks    soft     hard    inodes   soft    hard
  /dev/sdb1           0        0        0        0       0       0
```

The output shows two sets of three settings beside the file system name. The first set is to configure soft and hard limits at the block level, and the second set applies the limits at the inode level. We can specify number of 1K blocks, such as 10240000 for 10MB for the first set or 2000 for the second. Let's look at a couple of examples to cognize the usage. Currently, all values are set to 0, which means the user currently has no restrictions on the file system space usage.

Let's set the block soft and hard limits to 5MB and 8MB, respectively, and leave the inode settings intact:

```
  /dev/sdb1           0       5120     8192      0       0       0
```

Alternatively, you can use the *setquota* command to modify the limits directly from the command prompt. This command automatically writes to the *aquota.user* file.

```
[root@centos73 ~]# setquota -u user1 5M 8M 0 0 /mntext
```

To confirm the new setting, use the *quota* command with the -v option:

```
[root@centos73 ~]# quota -v user1
Disk quotas for user user1 (uid 1000):
  Filesystem      blocks   soft    hard   grace   files   quota   limit   grace
  /dev/sdb1          0     5120    8192            0       0       0
```

The output shows a few additional columns that are currently set to zero.

To test the limits, set full permissions on */mntext* with the *chmod* command as the *root* user and then log off and log back in as *user1*. Now, try to make a file larger than 8MB under */mntext* and see what happens. You may instead try copying a large amount of data over in an attempt to cross the boundary. For example, copy the contents of */usr/sbin*:

```
[root@centos73 ~]# chmod 777 /mntext
[user1@centos73 ~]$ cp /usr/sbin/* /mntext
. . . . . . . .
sdb1: warning, user block quota exceeded.
```

```
cp: cannot open '/usr/sbin/build-locale-archive' for reading: Permission denied
sdb1: write failed, user block limit reached.
. . . . . . . .
```

As soon as it hit the 8MB threshold, it stopped copying and produced quota warning messages. You may run **df -h** to view /mntext utilization.

Let's try this exercise for group *dba* (run **groupadd dba** as the *root* user to create this group) by modifying the *aquota.group* file with *edquota*. The following sets a soft limit of 10MB and a hard limit of 20MB for *dba* group members:

```
[root@centos73 ~]# edquota -g dba
/dev/sdb1   0      10240  20480  0      0      0
```

With the *setquota* command, it would be **setquota -g dba 10M 20M 0 0 /mntext**. You can verify the group quota settings by running **quota -vg dba**.

Modifying Grace Period for Soft Limits

We modified the block level soft and hard limits for a user and group, and we can use the same procedure to apply limits based on inodes. In the event a user or group exceeds their configured soft threshold, they will be allowed to use the file system space for a grace period of time, giving them an opportunity to move or remove their files to bring their usage down below the soft limit in order to be able to continue using the file system. If the grace period is surpassed and the usage is still over the limit, the user or group will not be permitted to use the file system space anymore.

The default grace period for both users and groups is 7 days, which can be verified by running **edquota -t** and **edquota -tg**, respectively. This limit can be modified and set to desired values in units of days, hours, minutes, or seconds. Let's see how this can be done.

To modify the grace period on both block and inode usage to 4 days for all users, use the -t option with the *edquota* command:

```
[root@centos73 ~]# edquota -t
/dev/sdb1          4days  4days
```

To modify the grace period to 12 hours on block usage for only *user1*, use the -T option with the *edquota* command:

```
[root@centos73 ~]# edquota -T user1
/dev/sdb1          12hours        unset
```

To modify the grace period to 6 hours on block usage for only group *dba*, specify either the group name or its GID with the command:

```
[root@centos73 ~]# edquota -Tg dba
/dev/sdb1          6hours  unset
```

We can perform the above three operations with the *setquota* command as well, but it only accepts the time in seconds. Here are the equivalent commands:

```
[root@centos73 ~]# setquota -ut 345600 345600 /mntext
[root@centos73 ~]# setquota -u user1 -T 43200 unset /mntext
[root@centos73 ~]# setquota -gT dba 21600 unset /mntext
```

Duplicating User and Group Quota Settings

In a large environment, you may simply want to duplicate quota settings for an existing user or group and apply them to another user or group account to save time. We can use the *edquota* or the *setquota* command for this purpose as well but with the -p (prototype) option. Here is how:

To copy quota settings for *user1* to *user15* (run **useradd user15** to create this account prior to running the following command), run any of the following:

```
[root@centos73 ~]# edquota -p user1 user15
[root@centos73 ~]# setquota -p user1 user15 /mntext
```

Verify the settings for *user15* by running **edquota user15**.

The same procedure applies to group accounts, except that we add the -g option and specify source and target group names. For example, **edquota -gp dba dba1** or **setquota -gp dba dba1 /mntext** (run **groupadd dba1** if this group does not already exist prior to running either of these commands).

Activating Quota Automatically at System Reboots

To auto-activate disk quota settings on a file system each time the system is rebooted, we define the usrquota and grpquota options in the */etc/fstab* file for it. As we had already added an entry for the ext3 file system /dev/sdb1 to the *fstab* file in Exercise 8-7, we need to reopen this file and modify the corresponding entry to look like the following:

UUID=fed15b88-ae2c-4e5a-a369-0cb86573852b   /mntext   ext3   defaults,**usrquota,grpquota**   1   2

Adding these options will ensure that the system will execute *quotacheck* and *quotaon* commands on the file system on subsequent reboots.

Reporting Quota Usage

After quota has been set for users and groups, we can monitor the usage and generate reports as appropriate. Linux provides us with the *repquota* command to accomplish this task. This tool reports the usage for users and groups on quota-enabled file systems. Options such as -a (all) to display a usage report for all quota-enabled file systems, -u and -g to limit the output to users and groups, and -v for verbosity are common with this reporting utility. Here are a few examples.

To report quota usage for all users with files in quota-enabled file systems:

```
[root@centos73 ~]# repquota -a
*** Report for user quotas on device /dev/sdb1
Block grace time: 4days; Inode grace time: 4days
```

| User | | Block limits | | | | File limits | | | |
		used	soft	hard	grace	used	soft	hard	grace
root	--	3155	0	0		640	0	0	
user1	+-	31765	5120	8192	3days	696	0	0	

The + (plus) sign is an indication of over usage.

To report quota usage for all groups with files in quota-enabled file systems, use **repquota -ag**.

We may specify a file system name with the command to limit the exam to that particular File systems:

```
[root@centos73 ~]# repquota -u /mntext        (or repquota /dev/sdb1)
[root@centos73 ~]# repquota -g /mntext        (or repquota -g /dev/sdb1)
```

Try the -v option with all of the above to see additional information in the report.

Understanding and Managing Swap

Physical memory (or main memory) in the system is a finite temporary storage resource employed for loading kernel and running user programs and applications. *Swap space* is an independent region on the physical disk used for holding idle data momentarily until it is needed (Linux also supports the use of *swap file* created in a file system, but its use is not encouraged due to performance issues.) The system splits the physical memory into small logical chunks called *pages* and maps their physical locations to virtual locations on the swap to facilitate access by system processors. This physical-to-virtual mapping of pages is stored in a data structure called *page table*, and is maintained by the kernel.

When a program or process is spawned, it requires space in the physical memory to run and be processed. Although numerous programs can run concurrently, the physical memory cannot hold all of them at once. The kernel monitors the memory usage. As long as the free memory remains below a high threshold, nothing happens. However, when the free memory falls below that threshold, the system starts moving selected idle pages of data from physical memory to the swap space in an effort to make room to accommodate other programs. This piece in the process is referred to as *page out*. Since the system CPU performs the process execution in a round-robin fashion, when the system needs this paged-out data for execution, the CPU looks for that data in the physical memory and a *page fault* occurs, resulting in returning the pages to the physical memory from the swap. This data return to the physical memory is referred to as *page in*, and the entire process of paging data out and in is known as *demand paging*.

Determining Current Swap Usage

The size of a swap area should not be less than the amount of physical memory; however, depending on application requirements, it may be twice the size or larger. It is also not uncommon to see systems with less swap than the actual amount of physical memory. This is especially witnessed on systems with a huge physical memory size.

Linux offers a few tools for us to view memory and swap space utilization. These tools include the *free* and *vmstat* commands. We use the *free* command to view how much physical memory is installed (total), used (used), available (free), used by shared library routines (shared), holding data before it is written to disk (buffers), and used to store frequently accessed data (cached) on the system. The -h flag may be specified with the command to list the values in human-readable format, otherwise -k for KB, -m for MB, -g for GB, and so on are also supported. Add -t with the command to display a line with the "total" at the bottom of the output. Here is a sample output from *centos73*:

```
[root@centos73 ~]# free -ht
                  total           used    free    shared  buffers  cached
Mem:              992M            835M    157M    2.7M    75M      292M
-/+ buffers/cache:                468M    524M
Swap:             819M            0M      819M
Total:            1.8G            835M    976M
```

The output indicates that the system has 992MB of total memory of which 835MB is in use and 157MB is free. It shows, on the second line, that the figures 468MB (835-75-292) and 524MB (992-468) are the used and free memory amounts excluding and including buffers and cache numbers, respectively. It reports swap space utilization on the third line, showing that it is not in use. The last line prints the combined usage summary of the main memory and swap.

Try **free -hts 2** and **free -htc 2** to refresh the output every two seconds (-s) and to display the output twice (-c).

The *free* command reads the information from the */proc/meminfo* file to produce the report. The values are shown in KBs by default, and they'll be slightly off from what we have just seen with *free*. Here are the relevant fields from this file:

```
[root@centos73 ~]# cat /proc/meminfo | grep -E 'Mem|Swap|Inactive'
MemTotal:        1016344 kB
MemFree:         221164 kB
MemAvailable:    344268 kB
SwapCached:           0 kB
SwapTotal:       839676 kB
SwapFree:        839676 kB
Inactive:        428340 kB
```

There is about 1GB (MemTotal) of total memory on this system. For better performance, the kernel uses as much memory as it can for caching data. As reads and writes occur constantly, the kernel struggles to keep the data in cache as pertinent as possible. The caching information is reported as the sum of the number of buffers and cached pages. The portion of the cache memory used by a certain process is released when the process is terminated, and is allocated to a new process as needed. The above output indicates that about 468MB (Inactive) of the total memory is available for use by new processes. The output also displays the total configured swap (SwapTotal) and how much of it is currently available (SwapFree).

The *vmstat* (*virtual memory statistics*) command is another tool that we may use to view virtual memory statistics. Without any options, this command reports the numbers in KBs; however, we can use "-S m" or "-S g" to view output in MBs or GBs.

```
[root@centos73 ~]# vmstat
procs -------------memory------------- --swap-- -----io---- ---system-- --------cpu----------
 r  b   swpd   free    buff   cache    si  so   bi  bo    in   cs   us sy id  wa st
 1  0    0    190204  76800  299008    0   0    3   2     11   14    0 0 100   0  0
```

The columns under memory and swap depict similar numbers that we saw earlier. Try running *vmstat* with the -s switch to view the output in a different format.

Swap Space Administration Commands

In order to create and manage swap spaces on the system, we have the *mkswap*, *swapon*, and *swapoff* commands available. We use *mkswap* to initialize a partition for use as a swap space. Once the swap area is ready, we can activate or deactivate it from the command line with the help of the other two commands, or set it up for automatic activation by placing an entry in the *fstab* file. The *fstab* file accepts the swap area's device file, UUID, or label.

Exercise 8-11: Create a Swap Partition and Activate Swap

In this exercise, you will create an 80MB primary partition on */dev/sdc* using *parted* for use as a swap partition. You will create swap structures in *sdc2* and enable the area. You will add an entry to the */etc/fstab* file for auto-activation. Finally, you will use appropriate commands to view statistics.

1. Create an 80MB primary partition starting at 102MB using *parted*:

   `[root@centos73 ~]#` **parted /dev/sdc mkpart pri 102 182m**

2. Create swap structures in *sdc2* using *mkswap*:

   `[root@centos73 ~]#` **mkswap /dev/sdc2**
   mkswap: /dev/sdc2: warning: wiping old signature.
   Setting up swapspace version 1, size = 78844 KiB
   no label, UUID=7610af04-fea0-4ac6-b1a0-44ce8aec31d6

3. Enable paging in the partition using **swapon -v /dev/sdc2**.
4. Confirm swap space activation in the new area by running **swapon -s**.
5. Edit the *fstab* file and add an entry for the new swap area:

   UUID=7610af04-fea0-4ac6-b1a0-44ce8aec31d6   swap   swap   defaults 0 0

6. Issue **free -ht** to view the reflection of the swap space numbers on the Swap and Total lines.

You can reboot the system at this point and re-run step 6 after the system has been booted up to ensure that the new space is automatically activated.

Exercise 8-12: Deactivate and Remove Swap Space

In this exercise, you will deactivate the swap region manually and remove its entry from the *fstab* file. You will eliminate the *sdc2* partition and confirm the erasure.

1. Deactivate swap in *sdc2* using **swapoff -v /dev/sdc2**.
2. Use **free -ht** to validate the removal.
3. Edit the *fstab* file and remove the corresponding entry.
4. Remove the partition using **parted /dev/sdc rm 2**.
5. Confirm the partition erasure using **parted /dev/sdc print**. You should not see *sdc2* partition anymore.

Chapter Summary

This chapter discussed concepts and theory surrounding MBR and GPT partitioning schemes, LVM, file systems, user quotas, and swap.

The chapter started with an overview of MBR and GPT partitioning schemes, and partition creation and administration tools. We used different utilities and created and deleted partitions. We examined the benefits of using the LVM disk partitioning solution and learned of its foundation objects and management commands.

We reviewed file system concepts and looked at a variety of supported file system types. We covered file system administration and monitoring utilities. We studied the concepts around mounting and unmounting file systems. We examined the UUID associated with file systems and applied labels to file systems. We analyzed the file system table and added entries for auto-activating file systems at reboots. We looked at tools for reporting file system usage and calculating disk usage. We learned about file system image duplication and MBR backups. We used utilities for debugging, determining, and fixing issues related to unhealthy file systems. We performed a number of exercises on file system creation, administration, and repair to reinforce the concepts and theory learned.

On some Linux systems, implementation of quota on file system space usage for certain users and groups is imminent. We studied types of quota, and how to set and view it. We learned how to initialize quota database; enforce, modify, and auto-activate quota; duplicate quota settings and apply them to other users and groups; and report its usage.

We touched upon the concepts of swapping and paging, and looked at how they worked. We performed exercises on creating, activating, viewing, deactivating, and removing swap spaces, as well as configuring them for auto-activation at system reboots.

Chapter Review at a Glance

The following presents a one-sentence review of each key topic discussed in this chapter:

- Storage drives are partitioned to create multiple containers, which are then initialized to store files or use as a swap space.

- MBR is a tiny region on a 32-bit BIOS-based system disk that is used to store disk partition information and a bootloader program; GPT is a small administrative partition on a 64-bit UEFI-based system disk that stores disk partition information and, optionally, a bootloader program.

- MBR is non-redundant, allows the creation of up to 15 usable partitions (3 primary and 12 logical) on a single disk, and cannot access disk space beyond 2TB; GPT stores a copy of the metadata on the disk, allows the creation of up to 128 primary partitions on a single disk, and supports disks of sizes larger than 2TB.

- Linux offers plenty of native partition management tools, of which some support MBR disks only while others understand and support both MBR and GPT.

- LVM is a widely-used, flexible alternative for disk management that provides a virtual layer over the underlying physical disks for convenient and granular partition management.

- LVM initializes a partition or an entire disk and calls it a physical volume, which is then used in a volume group to create one or more logical volumes.

- LVM logical volumes are synonym to standard disk partitions that are created with non-LVM tools, however, the logical volumes can span multiple underlying physical disks, and be resized, snapshot, migrated, mirrored, or striped.

- A file system is a logical structure that is created in a partition or logical volume by initializing it for storing files and directories.

- A minimum of two partitions—the root (/) and /boot file systems—are created on all Linux installations, along with a third partition that is used as a swap space; any number of additional partitions or logical volumes may be created on the system during or after the operating system installation as required.

- Several file systems can be created to hold dissimilar data and each one of them can be accessed, repaired, optimized, tuned, extended, reduced, and backed up independent of the rest.

- Disk-based file systems store information persistently and are created on physical (or virtual) media—hard disks, solid-state disks, or USB disks; network-based file systems are essentially disk-based file systems or directories that are shared for network access using protocols, such as NFS or CIFS; and memory-based file systems store an in-memory copy of the running system and they are automatically created, maintained, and destroyed by the kernel.

- Linux supports a variety of disk-based file system types, such as ext2, ext3, ext4, xfs, iso9660, vfat, ReiserFS/Reiser4, and Btrfs, with either ext4 or xfs being the default on most newer distribution versions; each file system type has its own advantages.

- File system metadata stores superblock and inode table information.

- The superblock stores crucial file system structural information, such as the type, size, and status of the file system and the number of data blocks it contains.

- An inode number holds a file's attributes, such as its type, permissions, ownership, owning group, size, last access/modification time, and keeps track of the pointers to the actual data blocks where the file contents are stored.

- A file system must be attached (mounted) to the directory structure in order to be accessed and used.

- The UUID of a file system is automatically assigned at the time of its creation to make it unique among all other file systems that may exist on the system; a file system label would serve the same purpose as the UUID; however, it has to be manually assigned to a file system.

- A file system must be defined using its UUID, label, or device file in the file system table in order to be automatically mounted at system restarts.

- File system space usage must be properly monitored and enough extra space must be maintained in a file system to prevent it from filling up, which may result in an application or system crash.

- The image of a disk partition or an entire disk can be dumped to an alternative location of the same or larger size for backup or importing on another Linux system; the MBR can also be backed up the same way.

- A file system may be corrupted or may develop inconsistencies in the event of an abnormal system reboot or force file system unmount, leaving it in an unclean and unmountable state, which then requires a thorough examination and repair to restore it to its previous clean and healthy state.

- XFS file system metadata may be dumped to a file and sent to technical support personnel to obtain help in repairing a corruption that cannot be fixed with native check and repair tools.

- Quota establishment is a method for controlling file system space usage by setting limits on individual user and group accounts.

- Soft and hard limits can be applied when setting quota to establish minimum and maximum thresholds on file system space usage.

- Quota support must be activated and quota databases must be initialized before applying quota settings on the system for the first time.

- Swap space complements the main Linux system memory and it is used to hold idle data temporarily.

- Demand paging is the process of swapping pages of idle blocks of data in and out of the main system memory.

- Commands we learned in this chapter are: lsblk, fdisk, parted, gdisk, pvs, pvdisplay, pvcreate, pvremove, vgs, vgdisplay, vgcreate, vgremove, vgextend, vgreduce, lvs, lvdisplay, lvcreate, lvremove, lvextend, lvreduce, lvrename, dumpe2fs, debugfs, fsck, e2fsck, fsck.ext2, fsck.ext3, fsck.ext4, e2label, mkfs, mke2fs, mkfs.ext2, mkfs.ext3, mkfs.ext4, tune2fs, mkfs.xfs, xfs_admin, xfs_db, xfs_info, xfs_metadump, xfs_repair, mkfs.vfat, fsck.vfat, blkid, df, du, mount, umount, edquota, quota, quotacheck, quotaoff, quotaon, repquota, setquota, free, vmstat, mkswap, swapon, and swapoff.

- Files and directories we discussed in this chapter are: /etc/fstab, /media/, aquota.user, aquota.group, and /proc/meminfo.

PART
TWO

LX0-104/102-400

Chapter 9

Writing Shell Scripts and Managing a SQL Database

This chapter describes the following major topics:

- ➤ Overview of shell scripts
- ➤ Write scripts to display basic system information
- ➤ Execution and setuid-rights on shell scripts
- ➤ Write scripts using variable and command substitutions
- ➤ Write scripts employing shell, special, and positional parameters
- ➤ Know and use functions
- ➤ Write interactive scripts
- ➤ Employ number sequencing and replace current shell process
- ➤ Grasp exit codes and test conditions
- ➤ Comprehend and use logical constructs: if-then-fi, if-then-else-fi, and if-then-elif-fi
- ➤ Understand and use looping constructs: for-do-done and while-do-done
- ➤ Control loop behavior
- ➤ Introduction to databases, database management systems, SQL, and MySQL/MariaDB
- ➤ Install and configure MariaDB and interact with its shell
- ➤ Create, manage, and drop database and tables
- ➤ Insert, query, update, and delete records

105.1 Customize and use the shell environment [a part of this objective is described in this chapter; most of it in chapter 10; and env, export, set, unset, alias, and lists commands/topics are explained in chapter 4]

2. Write Bash functions for frequently used sequences of commands

The following is a partial list of the used files, terms and utilities: source, function

105.2 Customize or write simple scripts [most of this objective is described in this chapter and the rest in chapter 15]

5. Use standard sh syntax (loops, tests)
6. Use command substitution
7. Test return values for success or failure or other information provided by a command
9. Correctly select the script interpreter through the shebang (#!) line
10. Manage the location, ownership, execution and suid-rights of scripts

The following is a partial list of the used files, terms and utilities: for, while, test, if, read, seq, and exec

105.3 SQL data management [this entire objective is described in this chapter]

11. Use of basic SQL commands
12. Perform basic data manipulation

The following is a partial list of the used files, terms and utilities: insert, update, select, delete, from, where, group by, order by, and join

$\mathbb{S}$ hell scripts are essentially a group of Linux commands along with control structures and optional comments stored in a text file. Their primary purpose of creation is the automation of long and repetitive tasks. Scripts may include any simple to complex command and can be executed directly at the command prompt. They do not need to be compiled because they are interpreted by the shell line by line. This chapter presents example scripts and analyzes them to solidify the learning. These scripts begin with simple programs and advance to those that are more complicated. As with any other programming language, the scripting skill develops over time as more and more scripts are read, written, and examined.

SQL is a common database query language employed to interact with a database management system such as MariaDB. It is used to create and administer databases, perform queries against them in a variety of ways, and handle data stored in them.

Shell Scripts

Shell scripts (a.k.a. *shell programs* or simply *scripts*) are text files that contain Linux commands and control structures for the automation of lengthy, complex, or repetitive tasks, such as managing packages and users, administering partitions and file systems, monitoring file system utilization, trimming log files, archiving and compressing files, removing unnecessary files, starting and stopping database services and applications, and producing reports. Commands in the script are interpreted and run by the shell one at a time in the order in which they are listed in the script. Each line is executed as if it is typed and run at the command prompt. Control structures are utilized for creating and managing logical and looping constructs. Comments are also usually included to add general information about the script such as the author name, creation date, previous modification dates, purpose of the script, and its usage. If the script encounters an error during execution, an error message is displayed on the screen.

Scripts presented in this chapter are written in the bash shell and may be used in other shells with slight modifications.

You can use any available text editor to write the scripts; however, it is suggested to use the *vi* editor so that you get an opportunity to practice this popular editing tool as you learn scripting. To quickly identify where things are in our scripts, we use the *nl* command to enumerate the lines. We store our shell scripts in the */usr/local/bin* directory and add it to the PATH variable. All scripts presented in this chapter are created and executed on *centos73* as *user1*.

Displaying System Information—Script01

Let's create our first script called *sys_info.sh* in the */usr/local/bin* directory and examine it line by line. Before we do that, we need to establish full access on this directory by running **chmod 777 /usr/local/bin** as the *root* user. After this step has been executed successfully, *cd* into this directory and start by typing what you see below. Do not enter the line numbers, as they are used for explanation and reference.

```
[user1@centos73 bin]$ nl sys_info.sh
1   #!/bin/bash
2   # This script is called sys_info.sh and it was written by Asghar Ghori on December 11, 2014.
3   # This script should be located in the /usr/local/bin directory.
4   # The script was written to show basic Linux and system information.
5   echo "Display Basic System Information"
```

```
6    echo "==========================="
7    echo
8    echo "The hostname of this system is:"
9    /usr/bin/hostname
10   echo
11   echo "The following users are currently logged on to this system:"
12   /usr/bin/who
```

 Within vi, press the ESC key and then type :set nu to view line numbers associated with each line entry.

In this script, comments and commands are used as follows:

The first line indicates the shell that will run the commands in the script. This line must start with the "#!" character combination (called *shebang*) followed by the full pathname to the shell file.

The next three lines contain comments: the script name, author name, creation time, default location for storage, and purpose. The number (#) sign implies that anything to the right of it is informational and will be ignored during script execution. Note that the first line also uses the number character (#), but it is followed by the exclamation mark (!); this combination has a special meaning to the shell.

The fifth line has the first command of the script. The *echo* command prints on the screen whatever follows it. In our case, we will see "Display Basic System Information" printed.

The sixth line will highlight the text "Display Basic System Information" by underlining it.

The seventh line has the *echo* command followed by nothing. This will insert an empty line in the output.

The eighth line will print "The hostname of this system is:".

The ninth line will execute the *hostname* command to display the basic system information.

The tenth line will insert an empty line.

The eleventh line will print "The following users are currently logged on to this system:" on the screen.

The twelfth line will execute the *who* command to list the logged-in users.

Here is the *sys_info.sh* file created in the */usr/local/bin* directory:

```
-rw-rw-r--. 1 user1 user1 512 Mar 07 14:38 /usr/local/bin/sys_info.sh
```

Executing a Script

The script created above does not have the execute permission bit since the default umask value for a regular user is set to 0002, which allows read/write access to the owner and group members, and read-only access to the rest. We will need to run the *chmod* command on the file and add the execute bit for everyone:

```
[user1@centos73 bin]$ chmod +x sys_info.sh
```

Any user on the system can now run this script using either its relative or full pathname:

```
[user1@centos73 bin]$ sys_info.sh
[user1@centos73 bin]$ ./sys_info.sh
[user1@centos73 bin]$ /usr/local/bin/sys_info.sh
```

By default, the *usr/local/bin* directory is included in the PATH of all users. However, if it is not, we will need to define it in the *etc/profile* file so that whoever logs on to the system gets this path set automatically. Alternatively, individual users may add the path to their *~/.bash_profile* file. The following shows how to add the new pathname to the existing PATH setting at the command prompt:

```
[user1@centos73 bin]$ export PATH=$PATH:/usr/local/bin
```

If you store the script at a directory location that is not in your PATH or if your script does not have the execute permission, you can use the built-in bash shell command called source (abbreviated as period .) to run the script. For instance, if the sys_info.sh script is located in /tmp, you can either run it as "./sys_info.sh" or "source sys_info.sh" while you are in /tmp. If the script does not have the execute permission, you can run it as "source sys_info.sh" or as "bash sys_info.sh".

Let's run *sys_info.sh* and see what the output will look like:

```
[user1@centos73 bin]$ sys_info.sh
Display Basic System Information
===============================

The hostname of this system is:
centos73

The following users are currently logged on to this system:
user1         tty1      2017-03-07 15:06
```

The output reflects the execution of commands as scripted.

A Word on SUID-Rights on Shell Scripts

As described in Chapter 2 "Working with Files and File Permissions", the setuid (suid) bit is enabled on binary executables to allow non-owners to execute them with owner privileges. This typically applies to commands, such as */usr/bin/su* (or */bin/su*), that are owned by the *root* user to give normal users the ability to execute them successfully.

The setuid bit is not intended for executable shell scripts due to serious security issues that its use may inflict or cause to inflict on the system. The default behavior of the operating system is to ignore this bit if it is set on a shell script at the time of its execution. The suggested alternative is to use the *sudo* command.

Here is how the system overlooks this bit when a setuid-enabled shell script is executed. A shell script typically starts with the "#!" character combination (a.k.a. *shebang*) followed by the absolute pathname of the shell, such as */bin/sh* for the Bash shell or */bin/ksh* for the Korn shell, that is to be used to run the script. Let's say we have a shell script called *start.sh* located in the */usr/local/bin* directory, containing #!/bin/sh on the first line and some code on subsequent lines. When we

---

execute this script, the system will run it as "**/bin/sh /usr/local/bin/start.sh**", ignoring the setuid bit that is enabled on the script. This is because the setuid capability is only usable when it is applied on the command or program itself and not on the supplied argument. In our case here, */bin/sh* is the command and */usr/local/bin/start.sh* is the argument supplied to it. Therefore, the system disregards the presence of the setuid bit.

Using Variable Substitution—Script02

The following script called *pre_env.sh* will display the values of SHELL and LOGNAME environment variables. Recall from Chapter 4 "Dealing with the Bash Shell and Processes" that these are pre-defined environment variables that are set when a user logs in to the system.

```
[user1@centos73 bin]$ nl pre_env.sh
1    #!/bin/bash
2    echo "The location of my shell command is:"
3    echo $SHELL
4    echo "I am logged in as $LOGNAME".
```

Add the execute bit to this script, and run to view the result:

```
[user1@centos73 bin]$ pre_env.sh
The location of my shell command is:
/bin/bash
I am logged in as user1.
```

Using Command Substitution—Script03

During the execution of a script, we can use the command substitution feature of the bash shell and store the output generated by the command into a variable. For example, the following script called *cmd_out.sh* will run the *hostname* and *uname* commands and store their output in variables. This script shows two different ways to use command substitution. Make sure to use the backticks to enclose the *uname* command.

```
[user1@centos73 bin]$ nl cmd_out.sh
1    #!/bin/bash
2    SYSNAME=$(hostname)
3    KERNVER=`uname -r`
4    echo "The hostname of this system is $SYSNAME".
5    echo "This system is running kernel version: $KERNVER".
```

Add the execute bit and run the script:

```
[user1@centos73 bin]$ cmd_out.sh
The hostname of this system is centos73.
This system is running kernel version: 3.10.0-514.el7.x86_64.
```

Understanding Shell Parameters

A *shell parameter* (or simply a *parameter*) is an entity that holds a value such as a name, special character, or number. The parameter that holds a name is referred to as a variable; a special character is referred to as a *special parameter*; and one or more digits, except for 0 is referred to as a *positional parameter* (a.k.a. a *command line argument*). We discussed variables in Chapter 4 "Dealing with the Bash Shell and Processes". A special parameter represents the command or script itself ($0), count of supplied arguments ($* or $@), all arguments ($#), and PID of the process ($$). A positional parameter ($1, $2, $3 . . .) is an argument supplied to a program at the time of its invocation, and its position is determined by the shell based on its location with reference to the calling program. Figure 9-1 gives a pictorial view of the special and positional parameters.

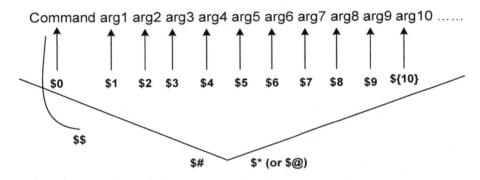

Figure 9-1 Special and Positional Parameters

Figure 9-1 also shows that positional parameters beyond the number 9 are to be enclosed in curly brackets. Just like the variable and command substitutions, the shell uses the dollar ($) sign for special and positional parameter expansion as well.

Using Special and Positional Parameters—Script04

The script *sp_po.sh* below will show furnished command line arguments, their total count, the value of the first argument, and the process ID of the script:

```
[user1@centos73 bin]$ nl sp_po.sh
1    #!/bin/bash
2    echo "There are $# arguments specified at the command line".
3    echo "The arguments supplied are: $*"
4    echo "The first argument is: $1"
5    echo "The Process ID of the script is: $$"
```

The result will be as follows when this script is executed with four arguments. Do not forget to add the execute bit.

```
[user1@centos73 bin]$ sp_po.sh baku timbuktu xingyang quito
There are 4 arguments specified at the command line.
The arguments supplied are: baku timbuktu xingyang quito
The first argument is: baku
The Process ID of the script is: 15913
```

Understanding Functions

A *function* is a bash shell feature that allows us to group sets of tasks and be able to run them individually if required. A function has a name followed by () and then a command or sequence of commands that may be specified on the same line as the function or separately on individual lines and must be enclosed within curly brackets. A function definition may be prepended with the keyword "function"; however, it is not required and not recommended to be used. The following shows two syntaxes. Notice how the semicolon (;) character is employed to segregate commands in the first composition and it is not needed in the second one.

```
funcname () { command1; command2; }

function funcname ()
{
command1
command2
}
```

Let's define a simple function called testfunc at the command prompt:

```
[user1@centos73 bin]$ testfunc () { echo "There are $# args"; echo "They are: $@"; }
```

Now execute this function with a few arguments such as Toronto, Ottawa, and Detroit:

```
[user1@centos73 bin]$ testfunc Toronto Ottawa Detroit
There are 3 args
They are: Toronto Ottawa Detroit
```

The output shows that the shell expanded both special parameters and processed the function.

Using Function—Script05

A function can be defined within a shell script as well. The script will treat it and run it just like any other command. Script *scr_func.sh* will define two functions: use_func and ano_func to echo simple statements and print the PID of the script:

```
[user1@centos73 bin]$ nl scr_func.sh
1    #!/bin/bash
2    function use_func ()
3    {
4    echo "I am learning Linux."
5    echo "I am preparing for my certification exam."
6    }
7    ano_func ()  { echo "The script name is: $0"; }
8    use_func
9    ano_func
```

Add the execute bit to the script and run it:

```
[user1@centos73 bin]$ scr_func.sh
I am learning Linux.
I am preparing for my certification exam.
The script name is: scr_func.sh
```

Writing Interactive Scripts—Script06

Interactive scripts prompt for input and continue their execution based on the input received. They store the input in a variable. The *read* command is used for receiving the input and saving it in a variable (FILE in the following example). This command may be preceded by a message telling the user what is expected as an input.

The *inter_read.sh* script below will list files and prompt to enter the file name to be removed. The PWD environment variable is used in the script to display our location in the directory tree.

```
[user1@centos73 bin]$ nl inter_read.sh
1    #! /bin/bash
2    echo "Here is a list of all files in the $PWD directory:"
3    /bin/ls -l
4    echo "Enter the name of file to be removed: "
5    read FILE
6    echo "Type 'y' to remove, 'n' if you do not want to:"
7    /bin/rm -i $FILE
```

Here is what the *inter_read.sh* script will do. Do not forget to add the execute bit.

```
[user1@centos73 bin]$ inter_read.sh
```
Here is a list of all files in the /usr/local/bin directory:

. . . .

Enter the name of file to be removed:

scr_func.sh

Type 'y' to remove, 'n' if you do not want to:

/bin/rm: remove regular empty file 'scr_func.sh? **n**

There may be plenty of files in the directory. We entered "scr_func.sh" when prompted and then "n" to instruct the command not to delete it.

Generating Number Sequences

The *seq* (sequence) command produces a sequence of numbers and displays them as a list on the screen. It produces a sequence starting at 1 (the default start value) up to the supplied number (the end value).

The following shows an example with number 4 as the end value:

```
[user1@centos73 bin]$ seq 4
1
2
3
4
```

We can also provide a start value to the command to commence from there. As an example, **seq 5 15** will print all numbers from 5 to 15. By default, this command uses an incremental value (or step value) of 1, which exists between the start and end values. We can add a custom step value squeezed in between to have the command get a different sequence. For instance, **seq 4 3 18** will show 4, 7, 10, 13, and 16 in the output.

Two options -s (separator) and -w (width) may be used if desired to view the output differently. For example, **seq -s : 4 3 18** will print 4:7:10:13:16 on a single line with the colon (:) character as the separator between the printed values and will equalize width in the output by padding with leading zeros if the -w switch is also added (**seq -ws : 4 3 18**).

Replacing Current Shell Process with exec

The *exec* command is another built-in shell command that you can use to run another command without invoking a new process for it. In other words, *exec* transfers the PID of the current shell to the specified command. This process is irreversible, meaning that once the new command assumes the PID, you cannot go back to the originating shell. For instance, if you are logged in and your shell PID is 12923, and you run **exec sh**, *sh* will take over your shell's PID (12923) without spawning a new process for itself. Assuming you are running the bash shell, run the *ps* command and jot down the PID of the bash shell process:

```
[user1@centos73 bin]$ ps
25542        pts/0     00:00:00        bash
```

The PID is 25542. Now run **exec sh** at the command prompt to invoke the Bourne shell, and re-run *ps*:

```
[user1@centos73 bin]$ ps
25542        pts/0     00:00:00        sh
```

Notice that the new process "sh" has replaced the original process "bash" and has assumed its PID.

The *exec* command may be used in situations where you do not want to allow users to be able to log in to the system, rather, simply run an assigned program and log off upon program termination. As an example, try running **exec top** at the command prompt and then press q to quit *top*. Your terminal session should terminate.

Logical Statements or Conditionals

So far, we have talked about simple scripts that run the code line by line. The shell lets us employ logical constructs to control the flow of scripts. It does this by allowing us to use test conditions, which decides what to do next based on the true or false status of the condition.

The shell offers two logical constructs: the *if-then-fi* construct and the *case* construct. The if-then-fi construct has a few variations and those will be covered as well. A discussion on the case construct is beyond the scope of this book and the exams.

Before starting to look at the example scripts and see how logical constructs are used, let's discuss exit codes and various test conditions. We will use them later in our example scripts.

Exit Codes

Exit codes, or *exit value*, refer to the value returned by a command or script when it concludes execution. This value is based on the outcome of the program. If the program runs successfully, we typically get a zero exit code; otherwise, we get a non-zero value. This code or value is also referred to as a *return code,* and it is stored in a special shell parameter called *?* (question mark). Let's look at the following two examples to cognize their usage:

```
[user1@centos73 bin]$ ls
scr_func.sh
[user1@centos73 bin]$ echo $?
0
[user1@centos73 bin]$ man
What manual page do you want?
[user1@centos73 bin]$ echo $?
1
```

In the first example, the *ls* command ran successfully and it produced the desired result, hence a zero exit code was returned and stored in the ?. In the second example, the *man* command did not run successfully because of a missing argument, therefore a non-zero exit code was returned and stored in the ?. In either case, we echoed the ? value.

We can define exit codes within a script at distinct locations in order to help debug the script by knowing exactly where the script terminated.

Test Conditions

Test conditions are used in logical constructs to decide what to do next. They can be set on integer values, string values, or files using the *test* command or by enclosing them within square brackets []. Table 9-1 describes various test condition operators.

Operation on Numeric Value	Description
integer1 -eq (-ne) integer2	Integer1 is equal (not equal) to integer2
integer1 -lt (-gt) integer2	Integer1 is less (greater) than integer2
integer1 -le (-ge) integer2	Integer1 is less (greater) than or equal to integer2
Operation on String Value	**Description**
string1=(!=)string2	Tests whether the two strings are identical (not identical)
-l string or -z string	Tests whether the string length is zero
string or -n string	Tests whether the string length is non-zero
Operation on File	**Description**
-b (-c) file	Tests whether the file is a block (character) device file
-d (-f) file	Tests whether the file is a directory (normal file)
-e (-s) file	Tests whether the file exists (non-empty)
-L file	Tests whether the file is a symlink
-r (-w) (-x) file	Tests whether the file is readable (writable) (executable)
-u (-g) (-k) file	Tests whether the file has the setuid (setgid) (sticky) bit
file1 -nt (-ot) file2	Tests whether file1 is newer (older) than file2
Logical Operators	**Description**
!	The logical NOT operator
-a or && (two ampersand characters)	The logical AND operator. Both operands must be true for the condition to be true. Syntax: [-b file1 && -r file1]
-o or || (two pipe characters)	The logical OR operator. Either of the two or both operands must be true for the condition to be true. Syntax: [(x == 1 -o y == 2)]

Table 9-1 Test Conditions

Having described the exit codes and test conditions, let's look at a few example scripts and observe their effects.

The if-then-fi Statement—Script07

The if-then-fi statement evaluates the condition for true or false. It executes the specified action if the condition is true; otherwise, it exits the construct. The if-then-fi statement begins with an "if" and ends with a "fi", as depicted in Figure 9-2:

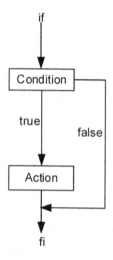

Figure 9-2 The if-then-fi Construct

The syntax of this statement can be written as follows:

```
if   Condition
        then
                Action
fi
```

We saw earlier how to check the number of arguments supplied at the command line. The following example script called *if_then_fi.sh* determines the number of arguments and prints an error message if there are none provided:

```
[user1@centos73 bin]$ nl if_then_fi.sh
1    #!/bin/bash
2    if       [ $# -ne 2 ]
3    then
4            echo "Error: Invalid number of arguments supplied."
5            echo "Usage: $0 source_file destination_file."
6            exit 2
7    fi
8    echo "Script terminated."
```

This script will display the following messages on the screen if it is executed without exactly two arguments specified at the command line:

Error: Invalid number of arguments supplied.
Usage: if_then_fi.sh source_file destination_file

A value of 2 will appear upon examining the return code with **echo $?**. This value reflects the exit code that we defined in the script on line number 6.

Conversely, the return code will be 0 and the message will be "Script terminated" if we supply two arguments.

The if-then-else-fi Statement—Script08

The if-then-fi statement has a limitation and it can execute an action only if the specified condition is true. It quits the statement if the condition is untrue. The if-then-else-fi statement, in contrast, is more advanced in the sense that it can execute an action if the condition is true and another action if the condition is false. The general syntax of this structure is:

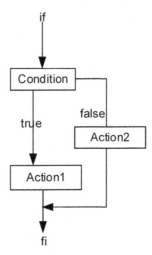

Figure 9-3 The if-then-else-fi Construct

The syntax of this statement can be written as follows:

```
if   Condition
then
     Action1
else
     Action2
fi
```

Action1 or Action2 is performed for a true or false evaluation of the condition. The following script called *if_then_else_fi.sh* will accept an integer value as an argument and tell if the value is positive or negative.

```
[user1@centos73 bin]$ nl if_then_else_fi.sh
1    #!/bin/bash
2    if        [ $1 -gt 0 ]
3    then
4            echo  "$1 is a positive integer value".
5    else
6            echo  "$1 is a negative integer value".
7    fi
```

Apply the execute bit and then run it one time with a positive integer value and the next time with a negative value:

```
[user1@centos73 bin]$ if_then_else_fi.sh 10
10 is a positive integer value.
[user1@centos73 bin]$ if_then_else_fi.sh -10
-10 is a negative integer value.
```

The if-then-elif-fi Statement—Script09

The if-then-elif-fi is a more sophisticated construct than the other two if-then-fi statements. We can define multiple conditions and associate an action with each one of them. During the evaluation of this construct, the action corresponding to the true condition is performed. The general syntax of this structure is shown in Figure 9-4:

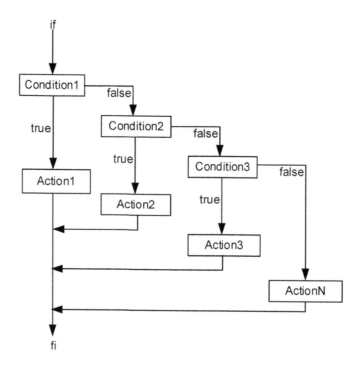

Figure 9-4 The if-then-elif-fi Construct

The syntax of this statement can be written as follows:

```
if      Condition1
then
        Action1
elif    Condition2
then
        Action2
............
............
else
        ActionN
fi
```

The following script called *lpi.sh* will display the name of the exam LX0-103 or LX0-104 for the entered exam code lx103 or lx104. If a random or no argument is provided, it will print "Usage: Acceptable values are lx103 and lx104".

```
[user1@centos73 bin]$ nl lpi.sh
1    #!/bin/bash
2    if       [ "$1" = lx103 ]
3    then
4            echo "LX0-103"
6    elif     [ "$1" = lx104 ]
7    then
8            echo "LX0-104"
9    else
10           echo "Usage: Acceptable values are lx103 and lx104".
11   fi
```

After adding the execute bit, run this script three times: the first time with argument lx103, the second time with lx104, and the third time with something arbitrary or nothing:

```
[user1@centos73 bin]$ lpi.sh lx103
LX0-103
[user1@centos73 bin]$ lpi.sh lx104
LX0-104
[user1@centos73 bin]$ lpi.sh
Usage: Acceptable values are lx103 and lx104.
```

Looping Statements

As a Linux user and administrator, you often want to perform certain task on a number of given elements or repeatedly until the specified condition becomes true or false. For instance, if plenty of disks need to be initialized for use in LVM, you can either run the *pvcreate* command on each disk one at a time or employ a loop to do it for you. Likewise, based on a condition, you may want a program to continue to run until the condition becomes either true or false.

There are three constructs—*for-do-done*, *while-do-done*, and *until-do-done*—that you can use to implement looping. The for loop is also referred to as the *foreach* loop.

The for-do-done construct iterates on a list of given values until the list is exhausted. The while-do-done statement runs repeatedly until the specified condition becomes false. The until-do-done structure does just the opposite of while-do-done; it performs an operation repeatedly until the specified condition becomes true.

Test Conditions

The *let* command is used in looping constructs to evaluate the condition at each iteration. It compares the value stored in a variable against a pre-defined value. Each time the loop does an iteration, the variable value is altered. You can enclose the test condition for arithmetic evaluation within double parentheses (( )) or double quotation marks instead of using the *let* command explicitly.

Table 9-2 lists operators that can be used in test conditions.

Operator	Description
!	Negation
+ / − / * / /	Addition / subtraction / multiplication / division
%	Remainder
< / <=	Less than / less than or equal to
> / >=	Greater than / greater than or equal to
=	Assignment
== / !=	Comparison for equality / non-equality

Table 9-2 let Operators

Having described various test condition operators, let's look at a few example scripts and observe their implications.

The for-do-done Loop—Script10

The for-do-done loop is executed on an array of elements until all the elements in the array are consumed. Each element is assigned to a variable one after the other for processing. The syntax of this looping construct is displayed in Figure 9-5:

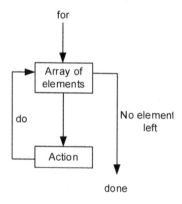

Figure 9-5 The for-do-done Construct

The syntax of this construct can be written as follows:

```
for VAR in list
do
     Action
done
```

The *for_do_done.sh* script below initializes a variable COUNT to 0. The for loop will read each letter sequentially from the range placed within curly brackets (no spaces before the letter A and after the letter Z), assign it to another variable LETTER, and display the value on the screen. The COUNT variable is incremented by 1 at each iteration of the loop.

```
[user1@centos73 bin]$ nl for_do_done.sh
1    #!/bin/bash
2    COUNT=0
3    for LETTER in {A..Z}
4    do
5            COUNT=$((COUNT + 1))
6            echo "Letter $COUNT is [$LETTER]"
7    done
```

The output of the script when run after adding the execute permission bit will be:

```
[user1@centos73 bin]$ for_do_done.sh
Letter 1 is [A]
Letter 2 is [B]
Letter 3 is [C]
. . . . . . . .
Letter 24 is [X]
Letter 25 is [Y]
Letter 26 is [Z]
```

The while-do-done Loop—Script11

The while-do-done loop checks for a condition and goes on executing a block of commands until the specified condition becomes false. The general syntax of this construct is:

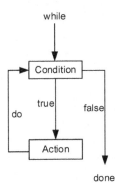

Figure 9-6 The while-do-done Construct

The syntax of this construct can be written as follows:

```
while        Condition
do
             Action
done
```

The condition specified is usually an arithmetic expression containing the *test* or the *let* command in either an implicit or an explicit mode, but they are normally used implicitly.

Let's look at a simple *while_do_done.sh* program that initializes a variable COUNT to 0. The while loop will count up to and including 20 and display the value on the screen. It will increment the COUNT variable by 2 at each iteration.

```
[user1@centos73 bin]$ nl while_do_done.sh
1    #!/bin/bash
2    COUNT=0
3    while [ $COUNT -le 20 ]
4    do
5            echo "Counter is $COUNT"
6            COUNT=$((COUNT + 2))
7    done
```

Try running this program after making it executable and observe the output. Modify the script and exchange "while" with "until" and "-le" with "-ge" and re-run to see what it produces.

You may use "while true" or "while :" instead of "while [$COUNT . . ." on line 3 to run the loop endlessly. The opposite behavior can be witnessed by substituting "while" with "until" and amending line 6 accordingly.

Controlling Loop Behavior

In shell scripts with looping constructs, we often see the commands *break* and *continue* employed. These commands are used to control the behavior of loops. The *break* command discontinues the execution of a loop immediately and transfers the control to the command following the done keyword. The *continue* command skips execution of the remaining part of the loop and transfers the control back to the beginning of the loop for next iteration. These commands may be used in the construct where necessary.

Another command that is also common in shell scripts is the *sleep* command. This command suspends the execution of the script for a period specified in seconds (the default is one second). It may be used within the looping and logical statements as well as anywhere else within the script for this purpose.

Modify the *while_do_done.sh* script and insert a line after line 6 with command "break" and run the script. You will notice that the loop terminates as soon as it encounters the *break* command right after its first iteration.

Next, try this script again by replacing "break" with "sleep 3", which will instruct the loop to wait for three seconds after each repetition.

Understanding Databases, DBMS, and SQL

A *database* is a structured collection of data, comprising facts and figures of something, and can be processed to generate meaningful results. An example of "something" is a database that stores data about airlines, hotels, car rentals, and vacation packages. People access this database via a website to search and make bookings and reservations using a number of different combinations and options that are configured in the database. Moreover, the database also provides people with the ability to limit their searches to a specific service or expand to include two or more.

Databases are widely used in both public and private sectors for storage and retrieval of data to meet general and specific business requirements.

A database with a large amount of stored data accessed by a number of users concurrently using a variety of combinations and options requires a *database management system* (DBMS) that is able to store, manage, and manipulate that data. A DBMS is a software application, such as MariaDB, MySQL, Oracle, IBM DB2, HP HANA, Sybase, Ingress, Informix, PostgreSQL, and Microsoft SQL Server. Such management systems allow the definition, creation, configuration, administration, performance management, backup, and recovery of a database; storage, modification, and weeding out of data in the database; and querying and retrieving of that data to produce desired reports for users or to feed to a requesting application. Furthermore, a DBMS also allows the administrator to place security controls on users in terms of what they can do.

Databases can be accessed by directly logging in to them. This type of access is typically granted to database architects and administrators with design, build, and management responsibilities. Databases are accessed by end users or applications through other applications for data query and retrieval. This type of access does not require direct logging into the database.

What is a Relational Database?

A *relational database* is a type of database that is structured based on the relational model suggested by Edgar. F. Codd in 1970. It is a set of *tables* comprising *rows* (a.k.a. *tuples* or *records*) and *columns* (a.k.a. *fields* or *attributes*) for data storage and organization. Each row represents a single record, which comprises of column values. A column is made up of the same type of values such as character or integer. See Figure 9-7 for the three table components: row, column, and value.

Sno	First	Last	Born	Died	Age
1	Albert	Einstein	1879	1955	76
2	Isaac	Newton	1643	1727	84
3	Marie	Curie	1867	1934	67
4	Galileo	Galilei	1564	1642	78
5	Thomas	Edison	1847	1931	84
6	Alexander	Bell	1847	1922	75
7	Benjamin	Franklin	1706	1790	84
8	Louis	Pasteur	1822	1895	73

Figure 9-7 Components of a Database Table

In order to protect against entering duplicate records in a table, a column with unique values for each record is identified, and defined as a *primary key*. In Figure 9-7, column "Sno" can be chosen as a primary key, as it contains a distinctive value for each record.

 A table is like a simple spreadsheet.

For flexible data storage, organization, and retrieval, a DBMS allows the creation and use of multiple tables in a database to store distinct records about something, and then linking the tables together using a unique key. For instance, we can have a database with two tables, one consisting of the records shown in Figure 9-7, and the other with data about their inventions and a "Sno". We can then define the "Sno" column as a *foreign key* to establish a relationship between the two tables. A user querying record "1" will get information from both tables. This is an example of a one-to-one table relationship. All DBMS support one-to-many and many-to-many relationships.

Understanding SQL

SQL (*Structured Query Language*) is the standard programming language employed for DBMS management, as well as for querying and manipulating data they store. It comes with all the necessary tools that allow for database creation and administration, data handling and manipulation, and data searching, retrieval, and reporting. All open source and proprietary DBMS software mentioned earlier support this language with or without exclusive additions.

Managing and Querying a Database

There are a number of RDBMS available, some in the open source space and others in the proprietary world. For demonstrations in this chapter, we use MariaDB, an enhanced binary fork of the famous MySQL database.

MariaDB is not installed on the system by default. We need to use **yum install mariadb-server** on *centos73* or **apt-get install mariadb-server** on *ubuntu14* to install the software. Prior to initiating the installation, we need to ensure that the systems have access to a repository hosting the software.

After the installation has been completed, we configure the MariaDB service and perform simple management and query tasks, such as listing, creating, and dropping databases; creating, describing, listing, renaming, and dropping tables; and inserting, updating, querying, and deleting records in tables.

All exercises in this section are done on *centos73*.

Exercise 9-1: Install and Configure MariaDB

In this exercise, you will install the MariaDB server software, including any dependent packages. You will perform an initial configuration, and enable and start the service for use.

1. Install the MariaDB server software:

    [root@centos73 ~]# **yum -y install mariadb-server**

2. Set MariaDB service to autostart at system reboots:

    [root@centos73 ~]# **systemctl enable mariadb** (or **chkconfig mariadb on**)

3. Secure access to MariaDB installation using the *mysql_secure_installation* script and enter information as described in square brackets:

[root@centos73 ~]# **mysql_secure_installation**
. . . .
Enter current password for root (enter for none): **[Press the Enter key here]**
OK, successfully used password, moving on...
Setting the root password ensures that nobody can log into the MariaDB root user without the proper authorisation.
Set root password? [Y/n]   **[Press Enter to set the root database user password. This account is not the same as the system root account]**

New password: **[Enter a password for the database user *root*]**
Re-enter new password: **[Re-enter the password for the database user *root*]**
Password updated successfully!
Reloading privilege tables..
... Success!
By default, a MariaDB installation has an anonymous user, allowing anyone to log into MariaDB without having to have a user account created for them. This is intended only for testing, and to make the installation go a bit smoother. You should remove them before moving into a production environment.
Remove anonymous users? [Y/n]   **[Press Enter to remove all anonymous users]**
... Success!
Normally, root should only be allowed to connect from 'localhost'. This ensures that someone cannot guess at the root password from the network.
Disallow root login remotely? [Y/n] **n**   **[Do not disallow remote root user login]**
... skipping.
By default, MariaDB comes with a database named 'test' that anyone can access. This is also intended only for testing, and should be removed before moving into a production environment.
Remove test database and access to it? [Y/n]   **[Press Enter to remove the test database]**
 - Dropping test database...
... Success!
 - Removing privileges on test database...
... Success!
Reloading the privilege tables will ensure that all changes made so far will take effect immediately.
Reload privilege tables now? [Y/n] **[Press Enter for the changes to take effect right away]**
... Success!
Cleaning up...
All done! If you've completed all of the above steps, your MariaDB installation should now be secure.
Thanks for using MariaDB!

4. Start the MariaDB service and examine its operational status:

[root@centos73 ~]# **systemctl start mariadb** (or **service mariadb start**)
[root@centos73 ~]# **systemctl status mariadb** (or **service mariadb status**)
mariadb.service – MariaDB database server
   Loaded: loaded (/usr/lib/systemd/system/mariadb.service; enabled; vendor preset: disabled)
   Active: active (running) since Mon 2017-03-13 09:33:23 EDT; 36min ago

Process: 14451 ExecStartPost=/usr/libexec/mariadb-wait-ready $MAINPID (code=exited, status=0/SUCCESS)

Process: 14370 ExecStartPre=/usr/libexec/mariadb-prepare-db-dir %n (code=exited, status=0/SUCCESS)

Main PID: 14450 (mysqld_safe)

. . . .

This completes the installation and initial configuration of MariaDB service.

Starting the MariaDB Shell and Checking Connection Status

Once you have the MariaDB server software installed and *root* user password setup, you can invoke its shell interface with the *mysql* command. Enter the *root* user (-u) password (-p) when prompted.

[root@centos73 ~]# **mysql -u root -p**
Enter password:
Welcome to the MariaDB monitor. Commands end with ; or \g.
Your MariaDB connection id is 26
Server version: 5.5.35-MariaDB MariaDB Server
Copyright © 2000, 2013, Oracle, Monty Program Ab and others.
Type 'help;' or '\h' for help. Type '\c' to clear the current input statement.
MariaDB [(none)]>

The MariaDB shell prompt appears, indicating that you have successfully logged in to it. The prompt indicates that there is no current connection to a database. There are several subcommands available here that you can view by entering *help*. All subcommands have a short description indicating what they are for. We will use the *status*, *use*, and *exit* subcommands in this chapter.

The *status* subcommand shows the connection status:

MariaDB [(none)]> **status**
----
mysql Ver 15.1 Distrib 5.5.52-MariaDB, for Linux (x86_64) using readline 5.1
Connection id: 10
Current database:
Current user: root@localhost
SSL: Not in use
Current pager: stdout
Using outfile: "
Using delimiter: ;
Server: MariaDB
Server version: 5.5.52-MariaDB MariaDB Server
Protocol version: 10
Connection: Localhost via UNIX socket
. . . .
Uptime: 1 hour 8 min 50 sec
Threads: 1 Questions: 22 Slow queries: 0 Opens: 0 Flush tables: 2 Open tables: 26 Queries per second avg: 0.005

The output provides general information about the connection, including an ID assigned to this session, the database it is connected to, the user name who invoked this session, and so on.

The mysql Command for Database and Table Operations

The prime command for managing and querying MariaDB is *mysql*. This command offers a variety of subcommands of which some are described in Table 9-3.

Subcommand	Description
Database and Table Operations	
create	Creates a database or table
drop	Drops a database or table
show	Lists databases or tables
Table Operations	
delete	Removes a record from a table
describe (or desc)	Shows the table structure
group by	Groups values from a column to find their sum, average, count, or minimum or maximum value
insert	Inserts data into a table
join	Queries two or more tables on a common key
order by	Sorts the output; may be used with ASC or DESC to sort in ascending or descending order.
rename	Renames a table
select	Retrieves data from a table
update	Updates a record in a table

Table 9-3 Database Administration Commands

Table 9-3 separates subcommands specific to both databases and tables, and tables only. Typical operations performed on both databases and tables include creating, listing (or showing), and dropping them. Likewise, typical operations for table-only administration include the rename and join functions, as well as inserting, updating, querying, and deleting records in tables.

Each subcommand executed at the MariaDB prompt expects a semicolon (;) at the end.

The usage of these subcommands is demonstrated in the following exercises.

Exercise 9-2: Create a Database and Table, and Insert Records

In this exercise, you will create a database called *lpicdb*. You will create a table called *lx103* in the *lpicdb* database using the column names and data as provided in Table 9-4 below.

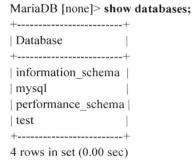

Sno	FirstName	LastName	City	Country	Age
1	Albert	Einstein	Ulm	Germany	76
2	Isaac	Newton	Woolsthorpe	UK	84
3	Marie	Curie	Warsaw	Poland	67
4	Galileo	Galilei	Pisa	Italy	78
5	Thomas	Edison	Milan	USA	84
6	Alexander	Bell	Edinburg	UK	75
7	Louis	Pasteur	Dole	France	73
8	Nicolaus	Copernicus	Toruri	Poland	70
9	James	Maxwell	Edinburg	UK	48
10	Pierre	Curie	Paris	France	47

Table 9-4 Data for use with Exercises

1. List what databases are currently available on the system using the *show* subcommand:

    ```
    MariaDB [none]> show databases;
    +------------------------+
    | Database               |
    +------------------------+
    | information_schema |
    | mysql                  |
    | performance_schema |
    | test                   |
    +------------------------+
    4 rows in set (0.00 sec)
    ```

    It shows the presence of four default databases.

2. Create a database called *lpicdb* using the *create* subcommand:

    ```
    MariaDB [none]> create database lpicdb;
    Query OK, 1 row affected (0.00 sec)
    ```

3. Verify the database creation using the *show* subcommand:

    ```
    MariaDB [none]> show databases;
    . . . . . . . .
    | lpicdb   |
    . . . . . . . .
    ```

    The output shows the new database on the list.

4. Select the new database for further actions using the *use* subcommand:

    ```
    MariaDB [(none)]> use lpicdb;
    Database changed
    MariaDB [lpicdb]>
    ```

Observe that the prompt has changed to reflect the selected database.

5. Create table called *lx103* in the new database using the *create* subcommand. For text columns, limit the number of characters to 20, and use integer type for Sno and Age columns.

```
MariaDB [lpicdb]> create table lx103 (Sno int,FirstName varchar(20),LastName
varchar(20),City varchar(20),Country varchar(20),Age int);
Query OK, 0 rows affected (0.07 sec)
```

6. Display the structure of the table with the *describe* (or *desc*) subcommand:

```
MariaDB [lpicdb]> desc lx103;
+---------------+-------------+------+-----+---------+-------+
| Field         | Type        | Null | Key | Default | Extra |
+---------------+-------------+------+-----+---------+-------+
| Sno           | int(11)     | YES  |     | NULL    |       |
| FirstName     | varchar(20) | YES  |     | NULL    |       |
| LastName      | varchar(20) | YES  |     | NULL    |       |
| City          | varchar(20) | YES  |     | NULL    |       |
| Country       | varchar(20) | YES  |     | NULL    |       |
| Age           | int(11)     | YES  |     | NULL    |       |
+---------------+-------------+------+-----+---------+-------+
6 rows in set (0.00 sec)
```

The output shows six columns. The first column indicates the field name, the second column specifies the type of data that can be stored in the field along with a character limit, the third column tells whether it is allowed to store a null value, the fourth column denotes whether the field is a table key, the fifth column shows the default value to be used for the field if an empty record is added, and the last column displays any special properties associated with the field.

7. Insert the records into the table using the *insert* subcommand, ensuring that values are enclosed within quotes:

```
MariaDB [lpicdb]> insert into lx103 values('1','Albert','Einstein','Ulm','Germany','76');
MariaDB [lpicdb]> insert into lx103 values('2','Isaac','Newton','Woolsthorpe','UK','84');
MariaDB [lpicdb]> insert into lx103 values('3','Marie','Curie','Warsaw','Poland','67');
MariaDB [lpicdb]> insert into lx103 values('4','Galileo','Galilei','Pisa','Italy','78');
MariaDB [lpicdb]> insert into lx103 values('5','Thomas','Edison','Milan','USA','84');
MariaDB [lpicdb]> insert into lx103 values('6','Alexander','Bell','Edinburg','UK','75');
MariaDB [lpicdb]> insert into lx103 values('7','Louis','Pasteur','Dole','France','73');
MariaDB [lpicdb]> insert into lx103 values('8','Nicolaus','Copernicus','Toruri','Poland','70');
MariaDB [lpicdb]> insert into lx103 values('9','James','Maxwell','Edinburg','UK','48');
MariaDB [lpicdb]> insert into lx103 values('10','Pierre','Curie','Paris','France','47');
```

8. Query the records to confirm the addition using the *select* subcommand:

```
MariaDB [lpicdb]> select * from lx103;
+------+---------------+------------+---------------+-----------+------+
| Sno  | FirstName     | LastName   | City          | Country   | Age  |
+------+---------------+------------+---------------+-----------+------+
|   1  | Albert        | Einstein   | Ulm           | Germany   |  76  |
|   2  | Isaac         | Newton     | Woolsthorpe   | UK        |  84  |
|   3  | Marie         | Curie      | Warsaw        | Poland    |  67  |
|   4  | Galileo       | Galilei    | Pisa          | Italy     |  78  |
|   5  | Thomas        | Edison     | Milan         | USA       |  84  |
|   6  | Alexander     | Bell       | Edinburg      | UK        |  75  |
|   7  | Louis         | Pasteur    | Dole          | France    |  73  |
|   8  | Nicolaus      | Copernicus | Toruri        | Poland    |  70  |
|   9  | James         | Maxwell    | Edinburg      | UK        |  48  |
|  10  | Pierre        | Curie      | Paris         | France    |  47  |
+------+---------------+------------+---------------+-----------+------+
```

10 rows in set (0.00 sec)

This completes the addition and verification of all 10 records to the *lx103* table in the *lpicdb* database.

Exercise 9-3: Perform Basic SQL Queries

In this exercise, you will perform a number of queries against the database *lpicdb*. Note that column names are case-insensitive.

1. Query *lx103* and show only a count of the records it contains:

   MariaDB [lpicdb]> **select count(*) from lx103;**

2. Query *lx103* for records of scientists who died at the age of 84:

   MariaDB [lpicdb]> **select * from lx103 where Age=84;**

3. Query *lx103* for records of scientists who lived for 70 or more years:

   MariaDB [lpicdb]> **select * from lx103 where age > 70;**

4. Query *lx103* for records of scientists with last name "Curie":

   MariaDB [lpicdb]> **select * from lx103 where lastname='Curie';**

5. Query *lx103* for records of scientists who died between the ages of 70 and 85:

   MariaDB [lpicdb]> **select * from lx103 where age between 70 and 85;**

6. Query *lx103* for records of scientists who were born in Poland and Germany:

   MariaDB [lpicdb]> **select * from lx103 where Country='Poland' or Country='Germany';**

7. Query *lx103* for countries where the scientists in the database were born:

     MariaDB [lpicdb]> **select Country from lx103;**

8. Query *lx103* for records of scientists who died in their 70s. The percentage (%) sign is used as a wildcard character.

     MariaDB [lpicdb]> **select * from lx103 where age like '7%';**

9. Query *lx103* for records of scientists who lived for more than 60 years and sort the records by the Age column in ascending order:

     MariaDB [lpicdb]> **select * from lx103 where age > 60 order by age;**

10. Query *lx103* for cities and countries where the scientists in the database were born and sort the records in reverse order by city name:

     MariaDB [lpicdb]> **select City,Country from lx103 order by city desc;**

11. Show the combined age of all the scientists with last name Curie under a new column Total_Age:

     MariaDB [lpicdb]> **select lastname, sum(age) as Total_Age from lx103 where lastname='Curie' group by lastname;**

12. Show how many scientists were born in UK under a new column Total_Country:

     MariaDB [lpicdb]> **select country, count(*) as Total_Country from lx103 where country='UK' group by country;**

Exercise 9-4: Perform Queries on Two Tables Using Join

For this exercise, create a table called *lx104* and add columns Sno, BornYear, and DiedYear as shown in Table 9-5. Consult Exercise 9-2 on how to do it.

Sno	BornYear	DiedYear
1	1879	1955
2	1643	1727
3	1867	1934
4	1564	1642
5	1847	1931
6	1847	1922
7	1822	1895
8	1473	1543
9	1831	1879
10	1859	1906

Table 9-5 Data for lx104

In this exercise, you will run queries against *lx103* and *lx104* tables on a common field (Sno) using the join clause. Both tables contain different information about the same set of scientists; however, they have a matching Sno.

1.   Run the following to obtain scientists' first and last names and the years they were born and died, and use Sno as the matching key. Sort the data by BornYear.

   MariaDB [lpicdb]> **select firstname, lastname, bornyear, diedyear from lx103, lx104 where lx103.sno = lx104.sno order by bornyear;**

2.   Modify the above to sort in reverse order by Age:

   MariaDB [lpicdb]> **select firstname, lastname, bornyear, diedyear,age from lx103, lx104 where lx103.sno = lx104.sno order by age desc;**

3.   A modified version of the above is:

   MariaDB [lpicdb]> **select firstname, lastname, bornyear, diedyear,age from lx103 join lx104 on lx103.sno = lx104.sno order by age desc;**

Exercise 9-5: Update Records

In this exercise, you will update records in tables *lx103* and *lx104*.

1.   Replace the fields Albert Einstein with Benjamin Franklin in *lx103* using the *update* subcommand:

   MariaDB [lpicdb]> **update lx103 set firstname='Benjamin',lastname='Franklin' where sno='1';**

2.   Substitute the fields 1822 and 1895 for Sno 9 in *lx104* with 1800 and 1890 using the *update* subcommand:

   MariaDB [lpicdb]> **update lx104 set bornyear='1800',diedyear='1890' where sno='9';**

3.   Confirm the above changes:

   MariaDB [lpicdb]> **select * from lx104 where sno='9';**

Exercise 9-6: Delete Records

In this exercise, you will delete records from tables *lx103*.

1.   Delete record numbers 1 and 7 from *lx103* using the *delete* subcommand:

   MariaDB [lpicdb]> **delete from lx103 where Sno='1' or Sno='7';**

2.   Confirm the deletion:

   MariaDB [lpicdb]> **select * from lx103;**

Exercise 9-7: Drop Tables and Database

In this exercise, you will drop both tables and then the entire database.

1. Drop *lx103* and *lx104* along with content using the *drop* subcommand and verify with *show*:

   MariaDB [(lpicdb)]> **drop table lx103,lx104;**

2. Confirm the removal:

   MariaDB [(lpicdb)]> **show tables;**

3. Drop the *lpicdb* database:

   MariaDB [(none)]> **drop database lpicdb;**

4. Confirm the removal:

   MariaDB [(none)]> **show databases;**

5. Type *quit* and press Enter to exit out of the MariaDB shell.

Chapter Summary

In this chapter, we learned the basics of bash shell scripting and database creation and query. This chapter began with an overview of scripting and then demonstrated how to write and analyze test scripts using a number of shell's built-in features. We wrote and inspected simple code and gradually advanced to more complicated scripts, including writing and examining interactive scripts and scripts employing logical and looping constructs.

We also learned about databases, database management systems, and the SQL language. SQL is a common database query language employed to interact with a database management system. We installed and configured a database software for practice, connected to it, created and dropped a database, created and dropped tables, accomplished a variety of queries against the database, and updated and erased records we stowed in the tables. The performance of these hands-on tasks strengthened our learning.

Chapter Review at a Glance

The following presents a one-sentence review of each key topic discussed in this chapter:

- Shell scripts are programs that contain commands, comments, and control structures—conditionals and loops—, and are written to automate lengthy and repetitive tasks, such as creating multiple user accounts at once, installing and managing software packages, constructing and administering partitions and file systems, trimming logs and deleting unnecessary files, compressing and archiving files, generating custom reports, monitoring system resource utilization, and starting, stopping, and status checking services, databases, and applications.

- The shebang at the beginning of a shell script identifies the shell to be used to execute the script.

- Shell scripts should not be assigned setuid rights to avoid potential damages that this privileged access might bring to the system; use sudo instead.

- There are three shell parameters discussed in this chapter and are referred to as a variable that is used to hold a name, such as $VAR="Beautiful Day"; a special parameter that stores a special character, such as $* and $$; and a positional parameter that is used to hold a numeric value, except for 0, such as $1 and $20.

- A function is a shell feature that may be used in shell scripts to define sets of tasks within separate containers that may be run individually.

- An interactive shell script prompts the user for an input and continues its execution based on the user response entered.

- A number sequence can be generated using different start, end, and step values, with or without some basic formatting done to the output.

- A running process can be replaced with a new process without changing the PID of the running process or invoking a new shell.

- There are two types of conditionals used in this chapter: if-then-fi (and its variants) and case.

- There are three types of looping constructs used in this chapter: for-do-done, while-do-done, and until-do-done.

- Exit codes determine the exit point of a shell script or success or failure of a command.

- Test conditions are used in conditionals and loops to make decisions on what action to take next.

- The behavior of a loop may be controlled by breaking out of a loop or returning to the beginning of a loop

- A command's execution can be suspended for a specified period.

- A database is a structured collection of data, which can be processed to generate meaningful results.

- A database management system (DBMS) is used to manage, manipulate, and query data stored in a database via the standard programming language called SQL.

- A DBMS uses tables of rows (tuples or records) and columns (fields or attributes) to store and organize data in a database.

- Commands we learned in this chapter are: source, read, exit, seq, function, exec, echo, if, for, while, test, break, continue, sleep, mysql_secure_installation, mysql, insert, update, select, delete, from, where, group by, order by, and join.

- Files and directories we discussed in this chapter are: /usr/local/bin/.

Managing Users and Groups

➢ Analyze user authentication files—passwd, shadow, group, and gshadow
➢ Enable and disable shadow password mechanism
➢ Know default attributes used at user creation time
➢ Create, modify, and delete user accounts with default and custom values, and no-login shell
➢ Set password aging on user accounts
➢ List who is logged-in and view successful and failed user login attempts and reboot history
➢ Use su and sudo commands
➢ Display and apply user limits on system resources
➢ Create, modify, and delete group accounts
➢ Search and get entries from user authentication files
➢ Comprehend system-wide (global) and per-user shell startup files

This chapter covers the following objectives for LX0-104/102-400 Exam:

105.1 Customize and use the shell environment [a part of this objective is described in chapter 9; most of it in this chapter; and env, export, set, unset, alias, and lists commands/topics are explained in chapter 4]

1. Set environment variables (e.g. PATH) at login or when spawning a new shell
3. Maintain skeleton directories for new user accounts
4. Set command search path with the proper directory

The following is a partial list of the used files, terms and utilities: /etc/bash.bashrc, /etc/profile, ~/.bash_profile, ~/.bash_login, ~/.profile, ~/.bashrc, and ~/.bash_logout

107.1 Manage user and group accounts and related system files [this entire objective is described in this chapter]

23. Add, modify and remove users and groups
24. Manage user/group info in password/group databases
25. Create and manage special purpose and limited accounts

The following is a partial list of the used files, terms and utilities: /etc/passwd, /etc/shadow, /etc/group, /etc/skel, chage, getent, groupadd, groupdel, groupmod, passwd, useradd, userdel, usermod

110.1 Perform security administration tasks [most of this objective is described in this chapter, and the rest is split between chapters 11 and 15]

64. Set or change user passwords and password aging information
66. Set up limits on user logins, processes and memory usage
67. Determine which users have logged in to the system or are currently logged in
68. Basic sudo configuration and usage

The following is a partial list of the used files, terms and utilities: passwd, chage, sudo, /etc/sudoers, su, usermod, ulimit, who, w, and last

110.2 Setup host security [this objective is split equally among this chapter and chapters 11 and 14; the /etc/inittab and /etc/init.d/* are explained in chapter 6]

69. Awareness of shadow passwords and how they work

The following is a partial list of the used files, terms and utilities: /etc/nologin, /etc/passwd, and /etc/shadow

An authorized user gains access to a Linux system using their unique login name, which must exist on the system. A user is a member of one or more groups at a time. Members of a group have identical group-level permissions on files and directories. Other users and members of other groups may also be given access to those files and directories. User and group information is recorded in authentication files. Default values used at the time of user creation are stored in definition files.

Password aging may be applied on user accounts for increased access control. A user may be assigned a no-login shell in order to restrict their ability to log on to the system. A list of the currently logged-in users and a history of users' previous login attempts can be viewed for reporting or auditing.

A user may switch into other user accounts, including the root user, provided they have the knowledge of the target user's password. A regular user on the system may be allowed access to privileged commands.

Limits may be placed on certain system resources to restrict their usage. Information stored in authentication files may be obtained for a specific user or group. At user login, plenty of system and user startup scripts are executed.

Understanding User Authentication Files

Linux supports three fundamental user account types: *root, normal,* and *service.* The *root* user is the superuser or the administrator with full access to all services and administrative functions on the system. This user account is created by default during installation. The normal users have user-level privileges. They cannot perform any administrative functions but can run applications and programs that they are authorized to execute. The service accounts are responsible for taking care of their respective installed services. These accounts include apache, ftp, mail, ntp, postfix, and qemu.

User account information for local users is stored in four files that are located in the */etc* directory. These files are *passwd, shadow, group,* and *gshadow,* and they are updated when a user or group account is created, modified, or erased. The same files are referenced to examine and validate credentials for a user at the time of their login attempt into the system, and therefore, they are referred to as *user authentication* files. These files are so critical to the operation of the system that, by default, the system maintains a backup of each of them as *passwd-, shadow-, group-,* and *gshadow-* in the */etc* directory.

The passwd File

The */etc/passwd* file is a plain text file and contains vital user login data. Each line in the file represents one user account, and there are seven colon-separated (:) fields per line. A sample line entry from the file is displayed in Figure 10-1.

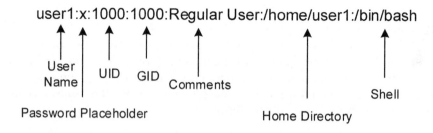

user1:x:1000:1000:Regular User:/home/user1:/bin/bash

User Name | Password Placeholder | UID | GID | Comments | Home Directory | Shell

Figure 10-1 The /etc/passwd File

Here is what is stored in each field:

✓ The first field contains the login name that is used to log in to the system. Usernames up to 255 characters, including the underscore and hyphen characters, are supported; however, usernames should not use any special characters or uppercase letters.

✓ The second field can contain an "x" (points to the /etc/shadow file for the actual password), an asterisk * character to pinpoint a disabled account, or an encrypted password containing a combination of random letters, numbers, and special characters in the absence of *shadow* file.

✓ The third field comprises a unique number between 0 and approximately 2 billion. This number is known as the *User ID* (UID). User ID 0 is reserved for the *root* account; UIDs between 1 and 999 are reserved for system accounts; and UIDs 1000 and beyond are used for normal user and application accounts. By default, newer versions of major Linux distributions assign UIDs to new users starting at 1000.

✓ The fourth field holds a number referred to as the *Group ID* (GID). This number corresponds with a group entry in the /etc/group file. By default, Linux creates a group for every new user matching their username and the same GID as their UID. The GID defined in this field represents a user's primary group.

✓ The fifth field optionally stores general comments about the user that may include the user's name, contact information, and location to help identify the person for whom, or the application for which, the account was set up.

✓ The sixth field defines the absolute path to the user home directory. A *home* directory is the location where a user is placed after logging in to the system, and it is used for personal storage. The default location for user home directories is /home.

✓ The last field consists of the absolute path of the shell file that the user uses as their primary shell after logging in. The default shell assigned to users is the bash shell.

An excerpt from the *passwd* file is shown below:

```
[root@centos73 ~]# cat /etc/passwd
root:x:0:0:root:/root:/bin/bash
bin:x:1:1:bin:/bin:/sbin/nologin
daemon:x:2:2:daemon:/sbin:/sbin/nologin
. . . . . . . .
user1:x:1000:1000:user1:/home/user1:/bin/bash
```

 Permissions on the /etc/passwd file should be 644, and the file must be owned by *root*.

The shadow File

The implementation of the shadow password mechanism provides a more secure password security for local users. With this mechanism in place, not only are the user passwords encrypted and stored in a more secure */etc/shadow* file, but certain limits on user passwords in terms of expiration, warning period, etc., can also be applied on a per-user basis. These limits and other settings are defined in the */etc/login.defs* file, which the shadow password mechanism enforces on user accounts. This is referred to as *password aging*. Unlike the *passwd* file, which is world-readable, the *shadow* file has no non-*root* access. This is done to safeguard the file's content.

With the shadow password mechanism active, a user is initially checked in to the *passwd* file for existence and then in the *shadow* file for authenticity.

The *shadow* file contains user authentication and aging information in plain text. Each row in the file corresponds to one entry in the *passwd* file. There are nine colon-separated (:) fields per line. A sample entry from this file is exhibited in Figure 10-2.

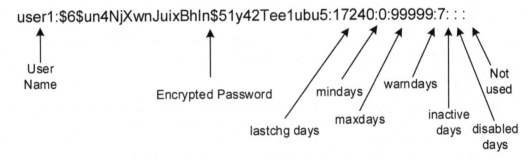

Figure 10-2 The /etc/shadow File

Here is what is stored in each field:

- ✓ The first field contains the login name as it appears in the *passwd* file.
- ✓ The second field consists of an encrypted password. An exclamation mark (!) at the beginning of this field implies that the user account is locked.
- ✓ The third field sets the number of days since the UNIX epoch (January 01, 1970) when the password was last modified. An empty field represents the passiveness of password aging features, and a 0 in this field forces the user to change their password upon next login.
- ✓ The fourth field expresses the minimum number of days that must elapse before the user can change their password. A 0 or null value in this field disables this feature.
- ✓ The fifth field defines the maximum number of days of password validity before the user starts getting warning messages to change it. A null value in this field disables this feature as well as the maximum password age, warning alerts, and user inactivity period.
- ✓ The sixth field consists of the number of days for which the user gets warnings for changing their password. A 0 or null value in this field disables this feature.
- ✓ The seventh field contains the maximum allowable number of days of user inactivity. A null value in this field disables this feature.
- ✓ The eighth field expresses the number of days since the UNIX epoch after which the account expires.
- ✓ The last field is reserved for future use.

UNIX epoch, also referred to as UNIX time, is a reference point from which UNIX/Linux system time is measured. All time calculations on the system are based on this epoch. UNIX epoch is set to midnight on Thursday January 01, 1970 UTC.

An excerpt from the *shadow* file is shown below:

[root@centos73 ~]# **cat /etc/shadow**
root:6FMJOkYh4j/sYOKkx$JAnW/tsfJJBiHK4qhukwpD/Zz0XvhsRt.NZ5nwAmkYpVgCEyswKI9tF
M9SMKERsx8cpZLJM5dE9AtZAUl6m9w1::0:99999:7:::
bin:*:17110:0:99999:7:::
daemon:*:17110:0:99999:7:::

. . . .
user1:6MLh61oeJ$T5aPryISioEomPgfvY/gm.fb5RCxQ3gu95Z7YGvATwzbuylWWQA1zYYA/bSKIb
ZYHF2RnBMsWEkv6HgkIFNor1:17240:0:99999:7:::

Permissions on the *shadow* file should be 000 (*centos73*) or 640 (*ubuntu14*), the file must be owned by *root* with owning group *root* (*centos73*) or *shadow* (*ubuntu14*).

The group File

The */etc/group* file is a plain text file and contains the group information. Each row in the file stores one group entry. Every user on the system must be a member of at least one group, which is referred to as the user's *primary* group. By default, the primary group name matches the user name it is associated with. Additional groups may be set up and users with common file access requirements can be added to them. There are four colon-separated (:) fields per line in the file. A sample entry from the file is exhibited in Figure 10-3.

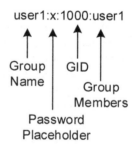

Figure 10-3 The /etc/group File

Here is what is stored in each field:

- ✓ The first field holds a unique group name, which must begin with a letter. By default, each user gets a unique group matching their name. Additional groups may be created as per need and users assigned to them. Group names up to 255 characters are supported.
- ✓ The second field is not typically used and is left blank. It may, however, contain an encrypted group-level password (copied and pasted from the *shadow* file or an x that points to the *gshadow* file for password). We may set a password on a group if we want non-members to

be able to change their group identity to this group temporarily using the *newgrp* command. The non-members must enter the correct password in order to do so.

✓ The third field defines the group identifier (GID), which is also placed in the GID field of the *passwd* file. By default, groups are created with GIDs starting at 1000 with the same name as the user name that is assigned to them. The system allows several users to belong to a single group; it also allows a single user to be a member of plenty of groups at the same time.

✓ The last field identifies the membership for the group. Note that a user's primary group is defined in the *passwd* file, and not in the *group* file.

An excerpt from the *group* file is shown below:

```
[root@centos73 ~]# cat /etc/group
root:x:0:
bin:x:1:
daemon:x:2:
. . . . . . . .
user1:x:1000:user1
```

 Permissions on the *group* file should be 644, and the file must be owned by *root*.

The gshadow File

The shadow password implementation also provides an added layer of protection at the group level. With this mechanism active, the group passwords are encrypted and stored in a more secure */etc/gshadow* file. Unlike the *group* file, which is world-readable, the *gshadow* file has no non-*root* access. This is done to safeguard the file's content.

The *gshadow* file stores encrypted group passwords. Each row in the file corresponds to one entry in the *group* file. There are four colon-separated (:) fields per line entry. A sample entry from this file is exhibited in Figure 10-4.

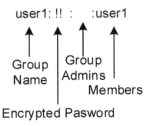

Figure 10-4 The /etc/gshadow File

Here is what is stored in each field:

✓ The first field consists of the group name as it appears in the *group* file.
✓ The second field can contain an encrypted password. A single exclamation point (!) in this field disallows users from gaining access to this group with the *newgrp* command; a pair of exclamation marks (!!) places the same restriction as the single exclamation point, plus it also

indicates that a group password was never set; and a null value restricts the group members to change into this group with *newgrp*.

✓ The third field lists usernames of group administrators that are authorized to add or remove members to and from this group.

✓ The last field holds the usernames that belong to the group.

An excerpt from the *gshadow* file is shown below:

```
[root@centos73 ~]# cat /etc/gshadow
root:::
bin:::
daemon:::
. . . . . . . .
user1:!!:::user1
```

Permissions on the *gshadow* file should be 000 (*centos73*) or 640 (*ubuntu14*), the file must be owned by *root* with owning group *root* (*centos73*) or *shadow* (*ubuntu14*).

Activating and Deactivating Shadow Password Mechanism

The shadow password mechanism that enables the use of *shadow* and *gshadow* files for storing user and group passwords and password aging information may be deactivated if desired. However, this is an undesirable and un-recommended action unless there is a specific need to do so. Linux offers four tools: two (*pwconv* and *grpconv*) to activate the mechanism, and the other two (*pwunconv* and *grpunconv*) to deactivate it. These are described in Table 10-1.

Command	Description
pwconv	Creates and updates the shadow file and moves user passwords over from the passwd file
pwunconv	Moves user passwords back to the passwd file and removes the shadow file
grpconv	Creates and updates the gshadow file and moves group passwords over from the group file
grpunconv	Moves group passwords back to the group file and removes the gshadow file

Table 10-1 Shadow Mechanism Control Commands

The *pwconv* command references the */etc/login.defs* file for some password aging attributes while being executed. The use of these commands is straightforward. You simply run the desired command without any options for an action.

Managing User Accounts and Password Aging

Managing user accounts involves creating accounts with the *useradd* command, assigning them passwords using the *passwd* command, modifying their attributes with the *usermod* command, and deleting them using the *userdel* command. Managing password aging involves setting and modifying aging attributes on user accounts, and Linux provides us with the *chage* and *passwd* commands for the performance of these tasks. The following sub-sections elaborate on these commands and demonstrate their use.

The useradd, usermod, and userdel Commands

This set of commands is used to add, modify, and delete a user account from the system. The *useradd* command adds entries to the four user authentication files for each account added to the system. It creates a home directory for the user and copies the default user startup files from the *skeleton* directory */etc/skel* into the user's home directory. This command supports several options; Table 10-2, however, lists some common options in both short and long versions, with an explanation.

Option	Description
-c (--comment)	Describes useful information about the user
-d (--home-dir)	Defines the absolute path to the user home directory
-D (--defaults)	Displays or modifies default user settings
-e (--expiredate)	Specifies a date YYYY-MM-DD after which a user account is automatically disabled
-f (--inactive)	Denotes maximum days of inactivity before a user account is declared invalid
-g (--gid)	Specifies a primary GID. Without this option, a group account matching the user name is created with the GID matching the UID.
-G (--groups)	Specifies the membership for up to 20 comma-separated supplementary groups
-k (--skel)	Specifies the location for the skeleton directory (default is /etc/skel), which stores default user startup files. Three hidden bash shell files—.bash_profile, .bashrc, and .bash_logout—are available in this directory by default. We can customize these files or add our own under /etc/skel for user accounts created thereafter.
-m (--create-home)	Creates a home directory if it does not already exist
-o (--non-unique)	Creates a user account sharing the UID of an existing user
-s (--shell)	Defines the absolute path to the shell file
-u (--user-group)	Indicates a unique UID. Without this option, the next available UID from the /etc/passwd file is used.
login	Specifies a login name to be assigned to the user account

Table 10-2 useradd Command Options

We can modify the attributes of a user account with the *usermod* command. The syntax of this command is similar to that of the *useradd* command's, with most options identical. Table 10-3 describes the options that are specific to *usermod* only, and shows them in both short and long versions.

Option	Description
-a (--append)	Adds a user to a supplementary group(s)
-l (--login)	Specifies a new login name
-L (--lock) / -U (--unlock)	Locks/unlocks a user account

Option	Description
-m (--move-home)	Creates a new home directory and moves the content from the old location to here

Table 10-3 usermod Command Options

The *userdel* command is simple. It removes entries for the specified user from the authentication files, and deletes the user's home directory if the -r option is also specified. The -f flag may be used to force the removal even if the user is still logged in.

The useradd and login.defs Files

The *useradd* command picks up the default values from the */etc/default/useradd* and */etc/login.defs* files for any options that are not specified at the command line. Moreover, the *login.defs* file is also consulted by the *usermod*, *userdel*, *chage*, and *passwd* commands as needed. We can view the *useradd* file content with a command such as *cat* or *less*, or display the settings by running **useradd -D**.

The other file *login.defs* comprises of additional directives that set several defaults. User and group management commands consult this file to obtain information that is not specified at the command line. Some common directives and their default values are shown below:

```
MAIL_DIR              /var/spool/mail
PASS_MAX_DAYS         99999
PASS_MIN_DAYS         0
PASS_MIN_LEN          5
PASS_WARN_AGE         7
UID_MIN               1000
UID_MAX               60000
GID_MIN               1000
GID_MAX               60000
CREATE_HOME           yes
UMASK                 077
USERGROUPS_ENAB       yes
ENCRYPT_METHOD        SHA512
```

These directives define the mail directory location for the user (MAIL_DIR), password aging attributes (PASS_MAX_DAYS, PASS_MIN_DAYS, PASS_MIN_LEN, and PASS_WARN_AGE), range of UIDs and GIDs to be allocated to new user and group accounts (UID_MIN, UID_MAX, GID_MIN and GID_MAX), approval for home directory creation (CREATE_HOME), default umask (UMASK), confirmation for user's group erasure if it contains no more members (USERGROUPS_ENAB), and the algorithm to be used for user password encryption (ENCRYPT_METHOD).

Exercise 10-1: Create a User Account with Default Attributes

In this exercise, you will create a user account *user2* with all preset default values. You will assign the user a password and show the line entries from all four authentication files for this user.

1. Create *user2* with all the default values:

    ```
    [root@centos73 ~]# useradd user2
    ```

2. Assign a password to this user and enter it twice when prompted:

    ```
    [root@centos73 ~]# passwd user2
    ```

3. *grep* for *user2* on the *passwd*, *shadow*, *group*, and *gshadow* files to examine what the *useradd* command has added:

    ```
    [root@centos73 ~]# cd /etc; grep user2 passwd shadow group gshadow
    passwd:user2:x:1001:1002::/home/user2:/bin/bash
    shadow:user2:$6$k/f7iJvT$95exj7aYt01lA.7uNFKKFx1z80OmILBx9S2cDcHEK4kyGwZBy.E9oB
    DsW4YQua47fSG2gZ.9p8.kFNIrYb.n61:17240:0:99999:7:::
    group:user2:x:1002:
    gshadow:user2:!::
    ```

As we can see, the command used the next available UID (1001) and GID (1001), and the default settings for the home directory (*/home/user2*), shell file (*/bin/bash*), and password aging (0:99999:7:::).

4. Test this new account by running **su - user2** and supplying the password. Run the **id** command after logging in to view the user and group information. Ignore the context information, as it is related to a topic that is beyond the scope.

    ```
    [user2@centos73 ~]$ id
    uid=1001(user2) gid=1002(user2) groups=1002(user2)
    context=unconfined_u:unconfined_r:unconfined_t:s0-s0:c0.c1023
    ```

Exercise 10-2: Create a User Account with Custom Values

In this exercise, you will create an account *user3* with UID 1010, home directory */home/user3c*, shell */bin/csh*, membership in group *user2* with GID 1002, and default startup files copied into this user's home directory. You will assign this user a password and show the line entries from all four authentication files.

1. Create *user3* with UID 1010 (-u), home directory */home/user3c* (-m and -d), shell */bin/csh* (-s) membership in group 1002 (-g), and default startup files copied into this user's home directory (-k):

    ```
    [root@centos73 ~]# useradd -u 1010 -m -d /home/user3c -g 1002 -k /etc/skel -s
    /bin/csh user3
    ```

2. Assign user123 as password (passwords assigned this way is not recommended; however, it is okay in a lab environment):

    ```
    [root@centos73 ~]# echo user123 | passwd --stdin user3
    ```

3. *grep* for *user3* on the *passwd, shadow, group,* and *gshadow* files to see what was added for this user:

[root@centos73 ~]# **cd /etc ; grep user3 passwd shadow group gshadow**
passwd:user3:x:1010:1002::/home/user3c:/bin/csh
shadow:user3:6hRFFsMzP$uNFGn7OipZ2CehftpHWrKC8IErqdSc2H/18Oc2EkgbBWelTmdRZm
WZAnq4DAJsQbonfcy.SEjGhN4Z0VgO2rc.:17240:0:99999:7:::

Notice that nothing was added to the *group* and *gshadow* files. This is because we used an existing group with the command.

4. Test this new account by running **su - user3** and supplying the password. Run the **id** command after logging in to view the user and group information. Ignore the context information, as it is related to a topic that is beyond the scope.

[user3@centos73 ~]$ **id**
uid=1010(user3) gid=1002(user2) groups=1002(user2)
context=unconfined_u:unconfined_r:unconfined_t:s0-s0:c0.c1023

The passwd Command for Password Aging

The common use of the *passwd* command is to set or modify a user's password; however, we can also use this command to lock and unlock a user account and modify their password aging attributes. Table 10-4 lists some key options in both short and long versions, and describes them.

Option	Description
-d (--delete)	Erases a user password without expiring the user account
-e (--expire)	Forces a user to change their password upon next logon
-i (--inactive)	Defines the number of days of inactivity after password expiry and before the account is locked. With -1, this feature can be disabled.
-k (--keep)	Re-activates an expired user account without changing the password
-l (--lock) / -u (--unlock)	Locks/unlocks a user account
-n (--minimum)	Specifies the number of days that must elapse before the password can be changed. A value of 0 allows the user to change their password at any time.
-w (--warning)	Defines the number of days a user gets warning messages to change password before the password expiry
-x (maximum)	Denotes the maximum days of validity of the password before a user starts getting warning messages to change password. With -1, this feature can be disabled.

Table 10-4 passwd Command Options

We will use some of the *passwd* command options in this chapter.

The chage Command for Password Aging

The *chage* command is used to set and alter password aging parameters on a user account. It supports a number of options in both short and long versions. Table 10-5 describes most of them.

Option	Description
-d (--lastday)	Specifies a date in the YYYY-MM-DD format, or number of days since the UNIX epoch when the password was last modified. With -d 0, the user is forced to change the password at next login.
-E (--expiredate)	Sets a date in the YYYY-MM-DD format, or number of days since the UNIX epoch on which the user account is deactivated. With -1, this feature can be disabled.
-l (--inactive)	See the description for -i in Table 10-4
-l	Lists password aging attributes for a user
-m (--mindays)	See the description for -n in Table 10-4
-M (--maxdays)	See the description for -x in Table 10-4
-W (--warndays)	See the description for -w in Table 10-4

Table 10-5 chage Command Options

We will use most of the *chage* command options later in this chapter.

Exercise 10-3: Set up Password Aging on User Accounts

In this exercise, you will configure password aging for *user2* using the *passwd* command. You will modify the values for mindays, maxdays, and warndays. You will run the *chage* command to display the aging settings on this account.

Next, you will configure aging for *user3* using the *chage* command. You will modify mindays, maxdays, warndays, and account expiry. You will run the *chage* command to display the updated settings.

1. Configure password aging for *user2* with mindays set to 7, maxdays to 28, and warndays to 5 using the *passwd* command:

    ```
    [root@centos73 ~]# passwd -n 7 -x 28 -w 5 user2
    ```

2. Confirm the new settings by issuing **chage -l user2**.
3. Configure password aging for *user3* with mindays set to 10, maxdays to 30, warndays to 7, and account expiry set to December 31, 2018:

    ```
    [root@centos73 ~]# chage -m 10 -M 30 -W 7 -E 2018-12-31 user3
    ```

4. Display the new settings for confirmation by executing **chage -l user3**.

The No-Login User Account

The *nologin* shell, located in the */usr/sbin* (or */sbin*) directory, is a special purpose program that can be employed for user accounts that do not require login access to the system. Typical examples of these accounts are service accounts such as *ftp*, *apache*, and *sshd*. With this shell assigned, the user is politely refused with the message, "This account is currently not available." displayed on the screen. If a custom message is needed, we can create a file called *nologin.txt* in the */etc* directory and add the desired text to it. The content of this file is printed on the screen upon user access denial, instead of the default message.

An alternative to the nologin shell is the use of the *false* (or *true*) command in the shell field of the *passwd* file. These commands are located in the */usr/bin* (or */bin*) directory, and their purpose is to instruct the login program to do nothing and return to the calling program. The use of the nologin shell is the preferred method for preventing user logins.

There is also a way to disallow all users from logging in to the system. With this approach, there is no need to change user login shells. We simply create a file called *nologin* (or *nologin.txt* on some Linux distributions) under the */etc* directory and add whatever text we desire. The presence of this file will prevent all users, except for the *root* user, from logging in to the system. They will see the contents of this file on their terminal screens.

Exercise 10-4: Create a User Account with No-Login Access

In this exercise, you will create an account *user4* with all the default values but without login access. You will assign this user the nologin shell. You will display the line entry for this user from the *passwd* file and test the account.

1. Create *user4* with the shell file */sbin/nologin*:

   [root@centos73 ~]# **useradd -s /sbin/nologin user4**

2. Assign password user123:

   [root@centos73 ~]# **echo user123 | passwd --stdin user4**

3. *grep* for *user4* on the *passwd* file and verify the shell field containing the nologin shell:

   [root@centos73 ~]# **grep user4 /etc/passwd**
   passwd:user4:x:1011:1011::/home/user4:/sbin/nologin

4. Test access by attempting to log in as *user4*:

   [root@centos73 ~]# **su - user4**
   This account is currently not available.

Exercise 10-5: Modify a User Account

In this exercise, you will modify certain attributes for *user2* and *user3*, and then delete *user4*. You will change the login name for *user2* to *user2new*, UID to 2000, home directory to */home/user2new*, and login shell to */bin/false*. You will *grep* the *passwd* file for *user2new* to validate the updates. You will set a new expiry on this user to February 28, 2018 and validate it.

1. Modify the login name for *user2* to *user2new* (-l), UID to 2000 (-u), home directory to */home/user2new* (-m and -d), and login shell to */bin/false* (-s):

   [root@centos73 ~]# **usermod -u 2000 -m -d /home/user2new -s /bin/false -l user2new user2**

2. Confirm the changes:

   [root@centos73 ~]# **grep user2new /etc/passwd**

3. Set February 28, 2018 as the new expiry date for *user2new*:

    [root@centos73 ~]# **usermod -e 2018-02-28 user2new**

4. Confirm the new expiry for *user2new* by running **chage -l user2new**.

Exercise 10-6: Modify Password Aging and Delete a User Account

In this exercise, you will modify *user3* to force this user to change password at next login, be unable to change password within five days following the last password change, and disable account expiry. You will validate the change with *chage*.

Next, you will lock *user4*, delete it, and confirm the removal.

1. Modify *user3* to expire this user's password and prompt to change it at next login (-d), be unable to change password within five days following the last password change (-m), and disable account expiry (-E -1):

    [root@centos73 ~]# **chage -d 0 -m 5 -E -1 user3**

2. Confirm the aging updates for *user3* by issuing **chage -l user3**.
3. Lock *user4* using either **usermod -L user4** or **passwd -l user4**.
4. Remove *user4* along with their home and mail spool directories (-r):

    [root@centos73 ~]# **userdel -r user4**

5. Confirm the deletion with **grep user4 /etc/passwd**.

Listing Currently Logged-In Users

Users log on to the system for work and then they exit out upon completion of their work. In many cases, users leave their login sessions open for extended periods of time for no apparent reason. The recommended practice from a hardening standpoint is to log on, perform work, and log off. We may use the *who* command to list who is currently logged in:

```
[root@centos73 ~]# who
root       :0       2017-03-16  08:02  (:0)
user1      pts/0    2017-03-16  08:03  (:1)
user1      :1       2017-03-16  08:03  (:1)
```

The first column displays the username, the second column shows the terminal session name, the next two columns indicate the date and time the user logged in, and the last column shows whether the terminal session is graphical (:0, :1) or remote (an IP address is shown for a remote connection).

On a system with plenty of users on with multiple sessions open, we can use the *who* command with the "am i" arguments to view the information just for the user who is running this command:

```
[root@centos73 ~]# who am i
user1      pts/0    2017-03-16  08:03  (:1)
```

The *w* (*what*) command displays information similar to the *who* command, but in more detail. It also tells the length of time the user has been idle for, along with the CPU utilization and current activity. On the first line, it shows the current system time, the length of time the system has been up for, number of users currently logged in (each session is considered a separate user), and the current average load on the system over the past 1, 5, and 15 minutes.

```
[root@centos73 ~]# w
08:05:13 up 9:28, 3 users, load average: 0.12, 0.20, 0.12
USER  TTY   FROM          LOGIN@  IDLE  JCPU  PCPU  WHAT
root   :0    :0            08:02   ?xdm?  1:02  0.28s  gdm-session-worker [pam/gdm
user1  pts/0 :1            08:03   1.00s  0.05s  0.02s  w
user1  :1    :1            08:03   1.00s  0.05s  0.02s  gdm-session-worker [pam/gdm
```

Viewing History of Successful User Login Attempts

Sometimes you need to know which users have logged on to the system or how many times and when the system was rebooted. The *last* command reports the history of successful user login attempts and system reboots. It reports all login and logout activities, including the login time, session duration, and session source the attempt was made from.

Let's run this command to view a report:

```
[root@centos73 ~]# last
user1          pts/1           :1                     Thu Mar 16 08:03  still logged in
user1          pts/0           :1                     Thu Mar 16 08:03  still logged in
user1          :0              :0                     Thu Mar 16 08:02  still logged in
reboot         system boot     3.10.0-514.el7.x  Wed Mar 15 22:36 - 08:16     (09:39)
. . . . . . . .
```

If you wish to list the system reboot details only:

```
[root@centos73 ~]# last reboot
reboot         system boot     3.10.0-514.el7.x  Wed Mar 15 22:36 - 08:20     (09:44)
reboot         system boot     3.10.0-514.el7.x  Wed Mar 15 12:02 - 08:20     (20:18)
reboot         system boot     3.10.0-514.el7.x  Wed Mar 15 07:26 - 08:20     (1+00:54)
```

The output shows, among other details, the kernel version booted in the third column and the duration the system has/had been up for in the last column.

Viewing History of Failed User Login Attempts

The *lastb* command reports the history of unsuccessful user login attempts, including the login name, program used, session source the attempt was made from, timestamp, and duration.

Here is a sample report from *centos73*. Only the *root* user has the ability to run this command.

```
[root@centos73 ~]# lastb
user1    ssh:notty   :1    Thu Mar 16 08:29 - 08:29  (00:00)
```

Switching (or Substituting) Users

Even though we can log in to the system directly as *root*, it is not a recommended practice. The recommended practice is to sign in with our own normal user account and then switch into the *root* account if necessary. This is safer and ensures system security and protection. In addition to becoming *root*, we can substitute with another user account as well. In either case, we need to know the password for the target user account in order for a successful substitution. The *su* command available in Linux provides us this ability. The following presents a few examples to comprehend the usage.

To switch from *user1* into *root* without executing startup scripts for the target user (startup scripts are explained later in this chapter). Enter the *root* user password when prompted.

```
[user1@centos73 ~]$ su
Password:
```

To repeat the above while ensuring that startup scripts for the target user are also executed to provide an environment similar to a real login, use the hyphen character (or -l) with the command:

```
[user1@centos73 ~]$ su -
```

To switch into a different user account, such as *user3*, specify the name of the target user with the command. Enter the password when prompted.

```
[user1@centos73 ~]$ su - user3
```

To issue a command as a different user without switching into that user, we can use the -c option. For example, the *firewall-cmd* command with the --list-services option requires superuser privileges. *user1* can use *su* as follows and execute this privileged command to obtain desired results:

```
[user1@centos73 ~]$ su -c 'firewall-cmd --list-services'
Password:
dhcpv6-client ssh
```

The *root* user can switch into any other user account without being prompted for that user's password.

Doing as Superuser

On production Linux servers, we take necessary steps to ensure that users have the ability to carry out their assigned job without hassle. In most cases, this requires privileged access to certain tools and functions, which the *root* user is normally allowed to run.

Linux provides normal users the ability to run a set of privileged commands or to access non-owning files without the knowledge of *root* password. These users can precede one of those commands with a utility called *sudo* (*superuser do*) at the time of executing that command. The users are prompted to enter their own password, and if correct, the command is executed successfully for them. The *sudo* utility is designed to provide protected access to administrative functions as defined in the */etc/sudoers* file. It can also be used to allow a user or a group of users to run scripts and applications owned by a different user.

Any normal user that requires privileged access to commands or non-owning files is defined in the *sudoers* file. This file may be opened and edited with a command called *visudo*.

The syntax for user and group entries in the file is similar to the following example entries for user *user1* and group *dba*:

    user1   ALL=(ALL)   ALL
    %dba   ALL=(ALL)   ALL

These entries may be added to the beginning of the file, and they are intended to provide full access to every administrative function to both *user1* and members of the *dba* group (group is prefixed by the percentage (%) sign)). In other words, *user1* and *dba* group members will have full *root* user authority on the system with these settings in place.

Now, when *user1* or a *dba* group member attempts to access a privileged function, they will be required to enter their own password. For instance:

    [user1@centos73 ~]$ sudo cat /etc/sudoers
    Password:

If we want the user and group members not to be prompted for a password, we can modify their entries in the *sudoers* file to look like:

    user1   ALL=(ALL)   NOPASSWD: ALL
    %dba   ALL=(ALL)   NOPASSWD: ALL

Rather than allowing them full access to the system, we can restrict their access to the functions that they need access to. For example, to limit their access to a single command */usr/bin/cat*, modify the directives as follows:

    user1   ALL=/usr/bin/cat
    %dba   ALL=/usr/bin/cat

These users should now be able to use the *cat* command to view the content of the */etc/sudoers* file. Try **cat /etc/sudoers** as *user1* and then again as **sudo cat /etc/sudoers**. You will see the difference.

Configuring sudo to work the way it has just been explained may result in a cluttered *sudoers* file with too many entries. A preferred method is to use pre-defined aliases—User_Alias, Cmnd_Alias, and Host_Alias—to configure groups of users, commands, and hosts. For instance, we can define a Cmnd_Alias called PKGCMD containing *yum* and *rpm* commands, and a User_Alias called PKGADM for *user1* to *user3*. These users may or may not belong to the same Linux group. We then give PKGADM access to PKGCMD. This way we set one rule that allows a group of users access to a group of commands. We can add or remove commands and users anytime as needed. Here is how this configuration will look like:

    Cmnd_Alias   PKGCMD = /usr/bin/yum, /usr/bin/rpm
    User_Alias   PKGADM = user1, user2, user3
    PKGADM   ALL = PKGCMD

Append the above to the bottom of the *sudoers* file as user *root* and then try running the *yum* or *rpm* command preceded by *sudo* as one of the users listed. You will be able to perform software management tasks just like the *root* user.

The *sudo* command logs successful authentication and command data to the */var/log/secure* file under the name of the actual user executing the command (and not *root*).

Displaying and Setting User Limits

Users may experience degraded performance of their applications on a heavily used system. Linux allows us to place limits on certain user-accessible system resources, such as processes, memory, and files, to help guarantee continuous execution of their key processes. By default, the limits are wide open or unlimited in many cases, which give users running less critical processes the same allowance on resource utilization. The *ulimit* command is available in Linux to help us control this distribution.

ulimit is used to display and set user resource controls. When executed with -a, it reports the current user limits. An excerpt of essential resources is provided below for *user1* on *centos73*. This output is sorted on the last column.

```
[user1@centos73 ~]$ ulimit -a
file size           (blocks, -f)      unlimited
max memory size  (kbytes, -m)      unlimited
cpu time           (seconds, -t)     unlimited
virtual memory     (kbytes, -v)      unlimited
file locks           (-x)            unlimited
scheduling priority  (-e)            0
open files           (-n)            1024
max user processes   (-u)            3847
```

As you can see in the output, there are no size, time, and amount restrictions for *user1* on the first five resources. Every process they run will automatically get the default priority of 0 (just like any other process on the system). The user can open up to a maximum of 1,024 files with the ability to run a maximum of 3,847 processes. The options that you see in parentheses in the above output can be used with the *ulimit* command to alter that particular value.

Limits are categorized as either soft or hard. With *ulimit*, you can change soft limits up to the maximum set by hard limits. Hard limits can be configured only by *root*.

The following example of the *ulimit* command can be used to change the maximum file size to a different value such as 1MB that *user1* can create:

```
[user1@centos73 ~]$ ulimit -f 1024
```

Verify the new value by reissuing **ulimit -a**.

Now try to create or copy a file larger than 1MB in size as *user1*. The system will inhibit you from doing that.

At this point if you log off and log back in as *user1*, you will notice that the value is reset to the original value. In order to ensure that the new value remains available across future logins, you need to edit the *.bash_profile* file located in *user1*'s home directory and add the above command to it. A discussion on this file is provided later in this chapter.

Managing Group Accounts

Managing group accounts involves creating accounts with the *groupadd* command, modifying their attributes using the *groupmod* command, and deleting them using the *groupdel* command. The following two sub-sections describe the basic use of these commands.

The groupadd, groupmod, and groupdel Commands

This set of commands is used to add, alter, and remove a group account from the system. The *groupadd* command adds entries to the *group* and *gshadow* files for each group added to the system. It supports several options of which a few are common. Table 10-6 lists them in both short and long versions, and explains them.

Option	Description
-g (--gid)	Specifies the GID to be used for the group
-o (--non-unique)	Allows sharing a GID between two or more groups
-r	Creates a system group account with a GID below 1000
groupname	Specifies a group name

Table 10-6 groupadd Command Options

The *groupadd* command picks up the default values from the *login.defs* file.

We can modify the attributes of a group account with the *groupmod* command. The syntax of this command is very similar to that of the *groupadd* command's, with most options identical. One different option with the *groupmod* command is -n, which allows us to rename an existing group.

The *groupdel* command is straightforward. It removes entries for the specified group from both *group* and *gshadow* files.

Exercise 10-7: Create, Modify, and Delete Group Accounts

In this exercise, you will create a group called *linuxadm* with GID 5000 and another group called *sales* sharing the GID. You will change the group name from *sales* to *mgmt* and then change the GID for *linuxadm* to 6000. You will add *user1* to *linuxadm* and verify this action with the *id* and *groups* commands. Finally, you will remove the *mgmt* group.

1. Create group *linuxadm* with GID 5000:

   [root@centos73 ~]# **groupadd -g 5000 linuxadm**

2. Create group *sales* sharing (-o) the GID of *linuxadm*:

   [root@centos73 ~]# **groupadd -og 5000 sales**

3. Alter the name of group *sales* to *mgmt*:

   [root@centos73 ~]# **groupmod -n mgmt sales**

4. Change the GID of *linuxadm* to 6000:

    [root@centos73 ~]# **groupmod -g 6000 linuxadm**

5. Add (-a) *user1* to *linuxadm* while retaining (-G) the user's existing memberships:

    [root@centos73 ~]# **usermod -aG linuxadm user1**

6. Verify group memberships for *user1*:

    [root@centos73 ~]# **id user1**
    uid=1000(user1) gid=1000(user1) groups=1000(user1),6000(linuxadm)
    [root@centos73 ~]# **groups user1**
    user1 : user1 linuxadm

7. Delete the *mgmt* group:

    [root@centos73 ~]# **groupdel mgmt**

Getting Entries from Local Authentication Files

The *getent* (*get entries*) command is a simple tool that we can use to lookup matching entries in administrative databases—passwd, shadow, group, gshadow, hosts, services, etc.—that are defined in the */etc/nsswitch.conf* file. This command reads the specified database and displays the line entry that corresponds to the supplied key. For instance, if you want to check whether *user1* exists in the *passwd* and *shadow* databases, run the *getent* command as follows:

    [root@centos73 ~]# **getent passwd user1**
    user1:x:1000:1000:user1:/home/user1:/bin/bash
    [root@centos73 ~]# **getent shadow user1**
    user1:6MLh61oeJ$T5aPryISioEomPgfvY/gm.fb5RCxQ3gu95Z7YGvATwzbuylWWQA1zYYA/bSKIb
    ZYHF2RnBMsWEkv6HgkIFNor1:17240:0:99999:7:::

And for group *user1*, for instance, specify the appropriate database name:

    [root@centos73 ~]# **getent group user1**
    user1:x:1000:user1
    [root@centos73 ~]# **getent gshadow user1**
    user1:!!::user1

If a key is not supplied, the command simply prints the entire database content on the screen.

Notice that the function of this command is equivalent to that of *grep*'s. You can use **grep user1 /etc/passwd** instead of **getent passwd user1** for instance. This rule can be applied on other databases as well.

Shell Startup Files

In Chapter 4 "Dealing with the Bash Shell and Processes," we used local and environment variables, and modified the default command prompt to add useful information to it. In other words, we modified the default shell environment to suit our needs. The changes we made were lost when we logged off. What if we wanted to make those changes permanent so that each time we logged in they were available for us?

Modifications to the default shell environment are typically stored in *startup* (or *initialization*) files. These files are sourced by the shell following user authentication at the time of logging in and before the initial command prompt appears. In addition, aliases, functions, and scripts can be added to these files as well. There are two types of startup files: *system-wide* (a.k.a. *global*) and *per-user*.

System-wide Shell Startup Files

System-wide shell startup files set the general environment for all users at the time of their login to the system. These files are located in the */etc* directory and are maintained by the system administrator. System-wide files can be modified to include general environment settings and customizations that are needed by every user or most users on the system.

Table 10-7 lists and describes system-wide startup files for bash shell users.

File	Comments
/etc/profile	Sets common environment variables such as PATH, USER, LOGNAME, MAIL, HOSTNAME, HISTSIZE, and HISTCONTROL for all users, establishes umask for user accounts with a login shell, processes the shell scripts located in the /etc/profile.d directory, and so on.
/etc/bashrc (centos73) /etc/bash.bashrc (ubuntu14)	Defines functions and aliases, sets umask for user accounts with a non-login shell, establishes the command prompt, etc. Contents of the two files have distribution-specific differences.

Table 10-7 System-wide Startup Files

Excerpts from the *profile* and *bashrc* files are presented below:

```
[root@centos73 ~]# cat /etc/profile
........
if [ -x /usr/bin/id ]; then
    if [ -z "$EUID" ]; then
        # ksh workaround
        EUID=`id -u`
        UID=`id -ru`
    fi
    USER="`id -un`"
    LOGNAME=$USER
    MAIL="/var/spool/mail/$USER"
fi
........
```

```
[root@centos73 ~]# cat /etc/bashrc
. . . . . . . .
if [ "$PS1" ]; then
 if [ -z "$PROMPT_COMMAND" ]; then
  case $TERM in
  xterm*|vte*)
   if [ -e /etc/sysconfig/bash-prompt-xterm ]; then
      PROMPT_COMMAND=/etc/sysconfig/bash-prompt-xterm
   elif [ "${VTE_VERSION:-0}" -ge 3405 ]; then
      PROMPT_COMMAND="__vte_prompt_command"
   else
      PROMPT_COMMAND='printf "\033]0;%s@%s:%s\007" "${USER}" "${HOSTNAME%%.*}"
"${PWD/#$HOME/~}"'
. . . . . . . .
```

Per-user Shell Startup Files

Per-user shell startup files override or modify system default definitions set by the system-wide startup files. These files may be customized by individual users to suit their needs. By default, two such files (in addition to the *.bash_logout* file) located in the skeleton directory */etc/skel* are copied into user home directories at the time of their creation.

We may create additional files in our home directories to set more environment variables or shell properties if required.

Table 10-8 lists and describes common per-user startup files for bash shell users.

File	Comments
.bash_profile (centos73)	Sets environment variables and sources the .bashrc file to set functions and aliases
.profile (ubuntu14)	Sets environment variables and sources the .bashrc file to set functions and aliases. This file is used in the absence of both .bash_profile and .bash_login.
.bashrc (both)	Defines functions and aliases. This file sources global definitions from the /etc/bashrc (or /etc/bash.bashrc) file.
.bash_logout (both)	Executed when the user logs off

Table 10-8 Per-user Startup Files

Excerpts from the *.bash_profile* and *.bashrc* files for the *root* account are displayed below:

```
[root@centos73 ~]# cat ~/.bashrc
# .bashrc
# User specific aliases and functions
alias rm='rm -i'
alias cp='cp -i'
alias mv='mv -i'
# Source global definitions
if [ -f /etc/bashrc ]; then
    . /etc/bashrc
fi
```

```
[root@centos73 ~]# cat ~/.bash_profile
# .bash_profile
# Get the aliases and functions
if [ -f ~/.bashrc ]; then
        . ~/.bashrc
fi
# User specific environment and startup programs
PATH=$PATH:$HOME/bin
export PATH
```

The order in which the system-wide and per-user startup files are executed is important to grasp. The system runs the */etc/profile* file first, followed by *.bash_profile* (or *.bash_login* in the absence of *.bash_profile*), *.profile* (if neither *.bash_profile* nor *.bash_login* exists), *.bashrc*, and finally the */etc/bashrc* file.

The per-user file *.bash_logout* is executed when the user leaves the shell or logs off.

Chapter Summary

In this chapter, we built a solid comprehension of user authentication files. We analyzed their contents and syntax in detail. We looked at files that store default values used at the time of user creation. We discussed password shadowing and password aging. We performed exercises to create user accounts with default and custom attributes and with no-login access. Through additional exercises, we placed aging restrictions on user accounts, and modified and deleted them. We learned how to list currently logged-in users and view users' previous login attempts history. We developed the knowledge of using the tools to switch into other user accounts and to issue privileged commands as a normal user. We learned about placing user limits on the usage of certain system resources. We created, altered, and erased group accounts. We used a whole slew of commands for the performance of user and group management tasks.

In addition, we also learned about reading specific entries from authentication files and examined system-wide and per-user startup files.

Chapter Review at a Glance

The following presents a one-sentence review of each key topic discussed in this chapter:

- There are three types of user accounts: root (with full administrative rights on the system), normal (with limited user-level rights), and service (with rights on the applications or services they are associated with).

- Four primary files—/etc/passwd, /etc/shadow, /etc/group, and /etc/gshadow—that store user authentication, password aging, and group information, with their backup files: passwd-, shadow-, group-, and gshadow- also located in the /etc/ directory.

- Any user with UID 0 will have full administrative rights on the system, just like the root user that also has the UID 0; UIDs from 1 to 999 are reserved for service accounts, and UIDs 1000 and beyond are for normal user accounts.

- A user's primary group is defined in the /etc/passwd file.

- User passwords and password aging information are stored in the /etc/shadow file on systems using the password shadowing mechanism.

- All four files must be owned by the root user with 644 permissions on the passwd and group files, and 000 (or 640) on shadow and gshadow files.

- UNIX time (UNIX epoch) begins at midnight January 1, 1970 UTC, and all time and timestamp calculations on Linux are based on this time.

- Linux uses the concept of User Primary Group (UPG) by which each user account that is created on the system has a corresponding group account matching the username.

- Shadow password mechanism can be deactivated, in which case the encrypted passwords will move from the /etc/shadow file to the /etc/passwd file; by default, it is activated.

- A list of currently logged-in users can be generated to view basic information on their activities.

- Linux keeps track of successful and failed user login attempts history as well as a history of all system reboots, which can be viewed using appropriate commands.

- A user may switch into another user's account provided the user's password is known; the root user does not need to know the password of the user being switched into.

- Sudo mechanism is the default native mechanism in Linux, which gives normal users the ability to execute one or more privileged commands.

- Certain limits on user accounts may be placed to control their ability to use system resources—processes, memory, and files—to help guarantee unhindered execution of the processes that really need more resources.

- User and group information may be pulled from the authentication files using a simple lookup tool.

- Initialization (or shell startup) files—both system-wide and per-user—are executed or parsed after a user successfully enters their credentials upon login.

- Commands we learned in this chapter are: pwconv, pwunconv, grpconv, grpunconv, useradd, usermod, userdel, passwd, chage, who, w, last, lastb, su, sudo, visudo, ulimit, groupadd, groupmod, groupdel, and getent.

- Files and directories we discussed in this chapter are: /etc/passwd, /etc/shadow, /etc/group, /etc/gshadow, /etc/login.defs, /etc/skel/, /sbin/nologin (or /usr/sbin/nologin), /etc/nologin.txt, /etc/nologin, /bin/false (or /usr/bin/false), /etc/sudoers, /var/log/secure, /etc/nsswitch.conf, /etc/profile, /etc/profile.d/, /etc/bash.bashrc, /etc/bashrc, ~/.bash_profile, ~/.bash_login, ~/.profile, ~/.bashrc, and ~/.bash_logout.

Chapter 11

Understanding Networking and Administering Network Interfaces

This chapter describes the following major topics:

- ➢ Introduction to the OSI reference model and the TCP/IP protocol suite
- ➢ Understand the terms: encapsulation, de-encapsulation, and peer-to-peer
- ➢ Fundamentals of networking—hardware address, ARP, hostname, IPv4, network classes, subnetting, subnet mask, CIDR notation, protocol, TCP/UDP, well-known ports, ICMP, and IPv6
- ➢ Compare the differences between IPv4 and IPv6
- ➢ Understand network interfaces, configuration files, hosts table, and management commands
- ➢ Configure and activate network interfaces
- ➢ Overview of routing and routing table
- ➢ Add static and default routes manually and persistently
- ➢ Discuss and use various network interface testing and debugging tools—ping, netstat, netcat, traceroute, tracepath, nmap, and arp
- ➢ Review general Internet services and configuration files
- ➢ Enable and activate Internet services

This chapter covers the following objectives for LX0-104/102-400 Exam:

109.1 Fundamentals of internet protocols [this entire objective is described in this chapter]

48. Demonstrate an understanding of network masks and CIDR notation
49. Knowledge of the differences between private and public "dotted quad" IP addresses

50. Knowledge about common TCP and UDP ports and services (20, 21, 22, 23, 25, 53, 80, 110, 123, 139, 143, 161, 162, 389, 443, 465, 514, 636, 993, 995)
51. Knowledge about the differences and major features of UDP, TCP and ICMP
52. Knowledge of the major differences between IPv4 and IPv6
53. Knowledge of the basic features of IPv6

The following is a partial list of the used files, terms and utilities: /etc/services, IPv4, IPv6, subnetting, TCP, UDP, and ICMP

109.2 Basic network configuration [this entire objective is described in this chapter, with the exception of the /etc/nsswitch.conf file that is explained in chapter 12]

54. Manually and automatically configure network interfaces
55. Basic TCP/IP host configuration
56. Setting a default route

The following is a partial list of the used files, terms and utilities: /etc/hostname, /etc/hosts, ifconfig, ifup, ifdown, ip, route, and ping

109.3 Basic network troubleshooting [this entire objective is described in this chapter, with the exception of the host and dig commands that are explained in chapter 12]

57. Manually and automatically configure network interfaces and routing tables to include adding, starting, stopping, restarting, deleting or reconfiguring network interfaces
58. Change, view, or configure the routing table and correct an improperly set default route manually
59. Debug problems associated with the network configuration

The following is a partial list of the used files, terms and utilities: ifconfig, ip, ifup, ifdown, route, hostname, netstat, ping, ping6, traceroute, traceroute6, tracepath, tracepath6, netcat

110.1 Perform security administration tasks [most of this objective is described in chapter 10, and the rest is split between this chapter and chapter 15]

65. Being able to use nmap and netstat to discover open ports on a system

The following is a partial list of the used files, terms and utilities: nmap and netstat

110.2 Setup host security [this objective is split equally among chapters 10 and 14, and this chapter; the /etc/inittab and /etc/init.d/* are explained in chapter 6]

70. Turn off network services not in use

The following is a partial list of the used files, terms and utilities: /etc/xinetd.d/*, /etc/xinetd.conf, /etc/inetd.d/*, /etc/inetd.conf

A computer network is formed when two or more physical or virtual computers are connected together for resource and information sharing. There are numerous concepts and terms that need to be grasped in order to be able to work effectively and efficiently with network interface configuration and troubleshooting, routing, and other network services. This chapter provides a wealth of that information.

The OSI reference model is a seven layer networking model that provides the foundation for network communication. Each layer in the model exchanges information with its neighboring layer, except for the first and the last layer. The TCP/IP protocol suite has four layers (or five layers) that match with the OSI model's layers with some layers have one-to-one correspondence, while others combine the functionality of multiple layers into one.

Additional terms and concepts related to networking include hardware and IP addresses, hostnames, network classes, subnetting and subnet masks, and protocols and ports. A good comprehension of these concepts is invaluable.

For a system to be able to talk to other systems on the network, one of its network interfaces must be configured appropriately with a unique IP address, hostname, and other essential network parameters. The network assignments may be assigned statistically or obtained automatically from a DHCP server. Few files are involved in the configuration, which may be modified by hand or using commands. Testing follows the configuration to confirm the system's ability to communicate with other systems on the network.

Routing selects network paths for the transmission of traffic between two computing devices that may be located far apart on distinct networks. Proper routes must be configured on Linux in order for it to be able to direct the traffic accurately. Routes may be added manually with commands or permanently by editing files or using commands.

Linux delivers a range of network interface testing and troubleshooting commands for tasks, such as connectivity verification, interface examination, connection debugging, traffic flow tracing, and network scanning.

There are plenty of network services that run or may be run on the Linux system. Some start on their own while the startup of others is controlled through the Internet services daemon program. Non-essential services are typically completely turned off as a result of system hardening.

Networking Fundamentals

The primary purpose of computer networks is to allow users to share data and resources. A simple network is formed when two computers are interconnected. Using a networking device called *switch*, this network can be expanded to include additional computers, as well as printers, scanners, storage, and other devices (collectively referred to as *nodes* or *entities*). A computer on the network can be configured to act as a file server, storage server, or as a gateway to the Internet for the rest of the networked computers. Nodes may be interconnected using electrical or fiber cables, or some sort of wireless medium. A complex network may have thousands of nodes linked via a variety of data transmission media.

There are many elementary concepts and terms that you need to grasp before being able to configure network interfaces and client/server setups. As well, there are many configuration files and commands related to various network services that you need to thoroughly understand. Some of the concepts, terms, configuration files, and commands are explained in this chapter and in later chapters.

Introduction to OSI Reference Model

The *Open Systems Interconnection* (OSI) is a reference networking model developed to provide guidelines to networking product manufacturers. These guidelines have enabled them to develop products capable of communicating and working with one another's software and hardware products in a heterogeneous computing environment. The OSI reference model is defined and divided for ease in seven layers, as depicted in Figure 11-1, with each layer performing a unique function independent of other layers.

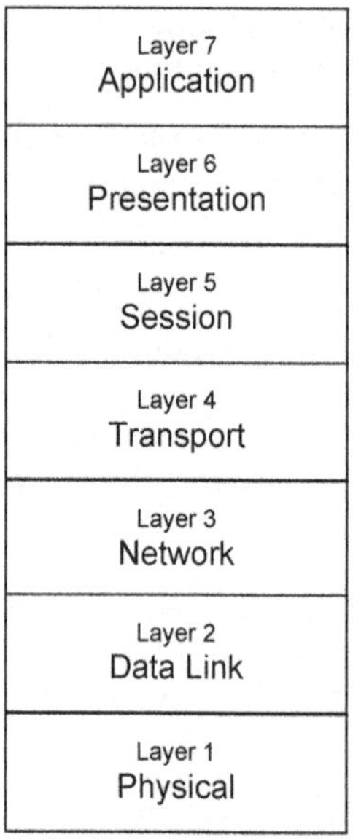

```
┌─────────────────────┐
│       Layer 7       │
│     Application     │
├─────────────────────┤
│       Layer 6       │
│     Presentation    │
├─────────────────────┤
│       Layer 5       │
│       Session       │
├─────────────────────┤
│       Layer 4       │
│      Transport      │
├─────────────────────┤
│       Layer 3       │
│       Network       │
├─────────────────────┤
│       Layer 2       │
│      Data Link      │
├─────────────────────┤
│       Layer 1       │
│       Physical      │
└─────────────────────┘
```

Figure 11-1 The OSI Reference Model

Each layer in the model interacts directly with two layers, one above it and one below it, except for the top and the bottom layers. The functionality provided by the seven layers is typically separated into three categories: (1) application (such as ftp or ssh), (2) set of transport/network protocols (such as TCP and IP), and (3) related software and hardware (such as cables).

The function of the seven layers can be segregated into two groups. One group, containing the upper three layers (5 to 7), relates to user applications such as formatting of data. The other group, containing the lower four layers (1 to 4), add transport information such as the address of the destination node.

Each layer of the OSI reference model is briefly touched upon in the following subsections.

Layer 7: The Application Layer

The *application* layer is where a user or program requests initiation of some kind of service on a remote node. Utilities and programs that work at this layer include *ftp*, *ssh*, *telnet*, SMTP, HTTP, DHCP, and X Window. On the remote node, server daemons for these services (*ftpd*, *sshd*, *telnetd*, and so on) respond by providing access to the requested service. In other words, client and server programs for these services work at this layer.

Layer 6: The Presentation Layer

The *presentation* layer converts the incoming data from the application layer into a format understandable by the remote node where this message is destined. This layer manages the presentation of the data to be independent of the node hardware architecture.

Layer 5: The Session Layer

The *session* layer sets up, synchronizes, sequences, and terminates a communication session established between a client program on the source node and the corresponding server program on the destination node. This layer deals with session and connection coordination between the source and destination nodes.

Layer 4: The Transport Layer

The *transport* layer manages end-to-end data transfer reliability. It makes sure that data from source to destination arrives error-free; otherwise, it retransmits it. The protocols that work at this layer are *Transmission Control Protocol* (TCP) and *User Datagram Protocol* (UDP).

Layer 3: The Network Layer

The network layer routes and forwards data packets to the right destination using the right network path. This layer manages data addressing and delivery functions. Protocols that work at this level are *Internet Protocol* (IP), *Address Resolution Protocol* (ARP), *Internet Control Message Protocol* (ICMP), *Point to Point Protocol* (PPP), etc.

A *router* is a common device that works at the network layer, routing data packets from one network to another. The source and destination networks may be located thousands of miles apart. A router is widely employed on corporate networks as well as the Internet.

Layer 2: The Data Link Layer

The *data link* layer manages the delivery of data packets beyond the physical network. This layer implements packet framing and provides error detection functionality. Protocols available at this layer include *Ethernet*, *token ring*, and *Fibre Distributed Data Interchange* (FDDI).

A *switch* is a common device that works at this layer. It inspects the MAC address contained within each incoming packet and determines the output port to forward the packet to. Once it has that information handy, it switches the packet to the port and the packet ultimately reaches the destination node.

Layer 1: The Physical Layer

The *physical* layer transmits data packets through the network. It describes network hardware characteristics including electrical, mechanical, optical, and functional specifications to ensure compatibility between communicating nodes. Protocols available at this layer include XBase-T. Network devices *repeaters* and *hubs* work at this layer. Cables, connectors, and LAN interfaces also fall under this layer.

Summary of OSI Layers

A summary of the functions provided by the OSI layers is presented in Table 11-1 for a quick reference.

OSI Layer	Description
Application (7)	Requests initiation of service on a remote node
Presentation (6)	Manages presentation of data to be independent of hardware architecture
Session (5)	Establishes, synchronizes, sequences, and terminates communication session setup between the source and destination
Transport (4)	Controls end-to-end data transfer reliability
Network (3)	Manages data addressing and delivery functions
Data Link (2)	Performs packet framing and provides error detection functionality
Physical (1)	Describes network hardware characteristics including electrical, mechanical, optical, and functional specifications

Table 11-1 OSI Layer Summary

Encapsulation and De-encapsulation

Data transmission between nodes takes place in the form of packets. When a message is created at the application layer, subsequent layers add header information to the message as it passes down through to the physical layer. Headers contain layer-specific information. When the message along with header information reaches the physical layer, it is referred to as a *packet*. The process of forming a packet through the seven layers of the OSI model is called *encapsulation*.

The packet is transmitted as a stream of 1s and 0s through the medium to the destination node where the physical layer receives the data stream and a reverse process begins. Headers are detached at each subsequent layer as the message passes up through to the application layer. This reverse process is referred to as *de-encapsulation*. Figure 11-2 illustrates the encapsulation and de-encapsulation processes.

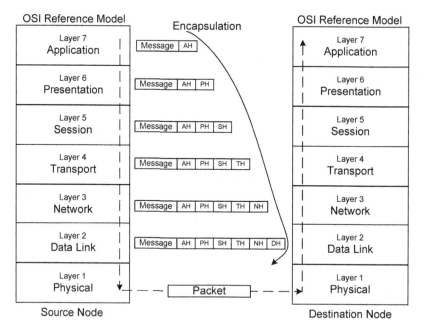

Figure 11-2 Encapsulation and De-encapsulation

Peer-to-Peer Model

Each layer on the source acts as a peer layer to its corresponding layer on the destination node, making the OSI model *peer-to-peer*. Header information attached at the application layer can only be read, understood, and removed by the application layer on the receiving side. Similarly, header attached at the session layer can only be read, understood, and removed by the session layer on the receiving end, and so on for the other layers.

Introduction to TCP/IP

The *Transmission Control Protocol / Internet Protocol* (TCP/IP) is a suite of protocols that is used as the global standard for information exchange on networks and the Internet. Although there are scores of protocols within the TCP/IP suite, the name is derived from the two key protocols: Transmission Control Protocol (TCP) and Internet Protocol (IP).

TCP/IP uses the client/server model of communication in which a client program on a node requests a service and the server program on the destination node responds. TCP/IP communication is primarily point-to-point, meaning that each communication session is between two network entities.

TCP/IP Layers

TCP/IP is layered similar to the OSI model. It is, in fact, based on the OSI reference model. Some vendors have defined the TCP/IP suite in four layers, while others in five. Figure 11-3 shows the suite in four layers and compares it with the OSI reference model discussed earlier.

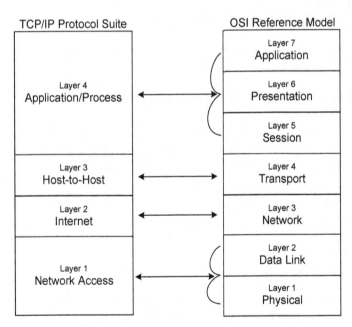

Figure 11-3 The TCP/IP Protocol Suite

The figure illustrates the TCP/IP protocol stack (left) and compares it with the OSI reference model (right). Each layer in the TCP/IP model provides an equivalent function of one or more of the corresponding layers in the OSI model. For instance, the TCP/IP application layer is equivalent to the top three OSI layers—application, presentation, and session—and the network access layer

---

Chapter 11: Understanding Networking and Administering Network Interfaces   **319**

merges the functionality of the bottom two OSI layers—data link and physical. For a description of each layer and how it interacts with its neighbors, refer to the previous section.

Hardware Address

A *hardware* address is a unique 48-bit address that is used to identify the correct destination entity for data packets transmitted from a source entity. The data packets include hardware addresses for both the source and the destination. A network protocol called ARP maps a hardware address to the destination entity's IP address. A hardware add

ress is also referred to as *Ethernet, physical, MAC,* or *station* address.

We can use the *ifconfig* or the *ip* command to list the network interfaces along with their hardware addresses. Here is how to accomplish this on *centos73* using three different methods:

```
[user1@centos73 ~]$ ifconfig | grep Ethernet
     ether 08:00:27:ae:f3:5b  txqueuelen  1000  (Ethernet)
[user1@centos73 ~]$ ip addr
2: enp0s3: <BROADCAST,MULTICAST,UP,LOWER_UP> mtu 1500 qdisc pfifo_fast state UP qlen
1000
   link/ether 08:00:27:ae:f3:5b brd ff:ff:ff:ff:ff:ff
[user1@centos73 ~]$ ip link
2: enp0s3: <BROADCAST,MULTICAST,UP,LOWER_UP> mtu 1500 qdisc pfifo_fast state UP mode
DEFAULT qlen 1000
   link/ether 08:00:27:ae:f3:5b brd ff:ff:ff:ff:ff:ff
```

The bolded text represent the hardware address for the primary network interface *enp0s3* on the system. Rest of the output is removed for brevity.

Address Resolution Protocol (ARP)

As you know, IP and hardware addresses work hand in hand with each other and a combination of both is critical to identifying the correct destination system. A protocol called *address resolution protocol* (ARP) is employed to enable IP and hardware addresses to work together. ARP determines the hardware address of the destination entity with a known IP address.

ARP broadcasts messages over the network requesting each alive node to reply with its hardware and IP addresses. The addresses received are cached locally in a special memory area called *ARP cache,* and can be viewed with the *arp* command as follows:

```
[user1@centos73 ~]$ arp -a
gateway (10.0.2.2) at 52:54:00:12:35:02 [ether] on enp0s3
```

The *arp* command reports duplicate IP addresses if there are any on the network. Examine the output for any conflicts. Use the -v option for additional details.

Hostname

A *hostname* is a unique alphanumeric label (the hyphen, underscore, and period characters are also allowed) that is assigned to a node to identify it on the network. It can consists of up to 64 characters by default. It is normally allotted based on the purpose and principal use. The hostname for a Linux system is stored in the */etc/hostname* or the */etc/sysconfig/network* file depending on the distribution and version of the Linux OS.

The hostname can be viewed with the *hostname* or the *uname* command, or by displaying the contents of the */etc/hostname* (or the */etc/sysconfig/network*) file. On versions with systemd system initialization, you can use the *hostnamectl* command as well for this purpose.

```
[user1@centos73 ~]$ hostname
[user1@centos73 ~]$ uname -n
[user1@centos73 ~]$ cat /etc/hostname
centos73
[user1@centos73 ~]$ hostnamectl
   Static hostname: centos73
. . . . . . . .
```

IPv4 Address

IPv4 stands for *Internet Protocol version 4* and it represents a unique 32-bit software address that every single entity on the network must have in order to communicate with other entities. It was the first version of IP that was released for public use. IPv4 addresses are also referred to as *dotted-quad* addresses, and they can be assigned on a temporary or permanent basis. Temporary addresses are referred to as *dynamic* addresses and are typically leased from a DHCP server for a period of time. Permanent addresses, on the other hand, are called *static* addresses and they are manually set.

We can use the *ifconfig* or the *ip* command to list the network interfaces along with their IP addresses. Here is how to accomplish this on *centos73*:

```
[user1@centos73 ~]$ ifconfig
enp0s3: flags=4163<UP,BROADCAST,RUNNING,MULTICAST>  mtu 1500
        inet 10.0.2.15  netmask 255.255.255.0  broadcast 10.0.2.255
[user1@centos73 ~]$ ip addr
2: enp0s3: <BROADCAST,MULTICAST,UP,LOWER_UP> mtu 1500 qdisc pfifo_fast state UP qlen 1000
        inet 10.0.2.15/24 brd 10.0.2.255 scope global dynamic enp0s3
```

The bolded text represents the IPv4 address for the primary network interface *enp0s3* on the system. Rest of the output is removed for brevity.

Network Classes

An IPv4 address is comprised of four period-separated octets (4 x 8 = 32 bit address) that are divided into a *network* portion (or network ID/bits) comprising of the *most significant bits* (MSBs) and a *node* portion (or node/host ID/bits) containing the *least significant bits* (LSBs). The network portion identifies the correct destination network, and the node portion represents the correct destination node on that network. Public network addresses are classified into three categories: class A, class B, and class C. Private network addresses are classified into two categories: class D and class E. Class D addresses are multicast and they are employed in special use cases only. Class E addresses are experimental and are reserved for future use.

Class A

Class A addresses are used for large networks with up to 16 million nodes. This class uses the first octet as the network portion and the rest of the octets as the node portion. The total number of usable network and node addresses can be up to 126 and 16,777,214, respectively. The network address range for class A networks is between 0 and 127. See an example below of a random class A IP address, which also shows two reserved addresses:

10.121.51.209	(class A IP address)
10.121.51.**0**	(network address)
10.121.51.**255**	(broadcast address)

0 and 255 (highlighted) are network and broadcast addresses and are always reserved.

Class B

Class B addresses are used for mid-sized networks with up to 65 thousand nodes. This class employs the first two octets as the network portion and the other two as the node portion. The total number of usable network and node addresses can be up to 16,384 and 65,534, respectively. The network address range for class B networks is between 128 and 191. See an example below of a random class B IP address, which also shows two reserved addresses:

161.121.51.209	(class B IP address)
161.121.51.**0**	(network address)
161.121.51.**255**	(broadcast address)

0 and 255 (highlighted) are network and broadcast addresses and are always reserved.

Class C

Class C addresses are employed for small networks with up to 254 nodes. This class uses the first three octets as the network portion and the last octet as the node portion. The total number of usable network and node addresses can be up to 2,097,152 and 254, respectively. The network address range for class C networks is between 192 and 223. See an example below of an arbitrary class C IP address, which also shows two reserved addresses:

215.121.51.209	(class C IP address)
215.121.51.**0**	(network address)
215.121.51.**255**	(broadcast address)

0 and 255 (highlighted) are network and broadcast addresses and are always reserved.

Class D

Class D addresses the range from 224 to 239.

Class E

Class E addresses the range from 240 to 255.

Subnetting

Subnetting is a technique by which a large network address space is divided into several smaller and more manageable logical sub-networks, referred to as *subnets*. Subnetting results in reduced network traffic, improved network performance, and de-centralized and easier administration, among other benefits. Subnetting does not touch the network bits; it uses the node bits only.

The following should be kept in mind when dealing with subnetting:

✓ Subnetting does not increase the number of IP addresses in a network. In fact, it reduces the number of usable addresses.
✓ All nodes in a given subnet have the same subnet mask.
✓ Each subnet acts as an isolated network and requires a router to talk to other subnets.
✓ The first and the last IP address in a subnet are reserved. The first address points to the subnet itself and the last address is the broadcast address.

Subnet Mask

A *subnet mask* or *netmask* is the network portion plus the subnet bits. It separates the network bits from the node bits. It is used by routers to pinpoint the start and end of the network/subnet portion and the start and end of the node portion for a given IP address.

The subnet mask, like an IP address, can be represented in either decimal or binary notation. The 1s in the subnet mask isolate the subnet bits from the node bits that contain 0s. The default subnet masks for class A, B, and C networks are 255.0.0.0, 255.255.0.0, and 255.255.255.0, respectively.

To determine the subnet address for an arbitrary IP address, such as 192.168.12.72 with netmask 255.255.255.224, write the IP address in binary format and then write the subnet mask in binary format with all network and subnet bits set to 1 and all node bits set to 0. Then perform a logical AND operation. For each matching 1 you get a 1, otherwise you get a 0. The following highlights the ANDed bits:

```
11000000.10101000.00001100.01001000    (IP address 192.168.12.72)
11111111.11111111.11111111.11100000    (subnet mask 255.255.255.224)
================================
11000000.10101000.00001100.01000000    (subnet IP 192.168.12.64 in binary format)
    192  .  168  .  12  .  64          (subnet IP in decimal format)
```

This calculation enables you to ascertain the subnet address from a given IP and subnet mask.

Classless Inter-Domain Routing (CIDR) Notation

Classless Inter-Domain Routing (CIDR) is a technique designed to control the quick depletion of IPv4 addresses and the rapid surge in the number of routing tables required to route IPv4 traffic on the network and the Internet. This technique was introduced as a substitute for the *classful* scheme, which was not scalable and had other limitations. Using CIDR, IPv4 addresses can be allocated in custom blocks suitable for networks of all sizes, resulting in smaller and less cluttered routing tables. CIDR was originally designed to address IPv4 needs; however, it has been extended to support IPv6 as well.

An IPv4 address written in CIDR notation has a leading forward slash (/) character followed by the number of routing bits. A sample class C IP address of 192.168.0.20 with the default class C subnet mask of 255.255.255.0 will be written as 192.168.0.20/24. This notation presents a compact method of denoting an IP address along with its subnet mask.

Protocol

A *protocol* is a set of rules governing the exchange of data between two networked entities. These rules include how data is formatted, coded, and controlled. The rules also provide error handling, speed matching, and data packet sequencing. In other words, a protocol is a common language that all nodes on the network speak and understand. Some common protocols are TCP, UDP, IP, and ICMP. Protocols are defined in the */etc/protocols* file. An excerpt from this file on *centos73* is provided below:

```
[user1@centos73 ~]$ cat /etc/protocols
ip          0    IP        # internet protocol, pseudo protocol number
hopopt      0    HOPOPT    # hop-by-hop options for ipv6
icmp        1    ICMP      # internet control message protocol
igmp        2    IGMP      # internet group management protocol
ggp         3    GGP       # gateway-gateway protocol
ipv4        4    IPv4      # IPv4 encapsulation
st          5    ST        # ST datagram mode
tcp         6    TCP       # transmission control protocol
```

TCP and UDP Protocols

TCP and UDP protocols are responsible for transporting data packets between network entities. TCP is reliable, connection-oriented, and point-to-point. It inspects for errors and sequencing upon a packet's arrival on the destination node, and returns an acknowledgement to the source node, establishing a point-to-point connection with the peer TCP layer on the source node. If the packet is received with an error or if it is lost in transit, the destination node requests a resend of the packet. This ensures guaranteed data delivery and makes TCP reliable. Due to its reliability and connection-oriented nature, TCP is widely implemented in network applications.

UDP, in contrast, is unreliable, connectionless, and multi-point. If a packet is lost or contains errors upon arrival at the destination, the source node is unaware of it. The destination node does not send an acknowledgment back to the source node. A common use of this protocol is in broadcast-only applications where reliability is not sought.

Well-Known Ports

Both TCP and UDP use ports for data transmission between a client and its server program. Ports are either well-known or private. A well-known port is reserved for an application's exclusive use, and it is standardized across all network operating systems. Well-known ports are defined in the */etc/services* file, excerpts of which are shown below from *centos73*:

```
# service-name     port/protocol     [aliases ...]     [# comment]
ftp-data           20/tcp
ftp-data           20/udp
ftp                21/tcp
ftp                21/udp            fsp fspd
ssh                22/tcp                               # The Secure Shell (SSH) Protocol
ssh                22/udp                               # The Secure Shell (SSH) Protocol
telnet             23/tcp
telnet             23/udp
```

The first column in the above output lists the official name of a network service, followed by the port number and transport layer protocol the service uses, optional aliases, and comments in successive columns.

Some common services and the ports they listen on are: ftp 20 and 21, ssh 22, telnet 23, SMTP mail 25, DNS 53, HTTP 80, POP3 110, Network Time Protocol (NTP) 123, NetBIOS session service 139, IMAPv2 143, SNMP 161, SNMP trap 162, LDAP 389, secure HTTP (HTTPs) 443, secure SMTP (SMTPs) 465, syslog 514, secure LDAP (LDAPs) 636, secure IMAP (IMAPs) 993, and secure POP (POP3s) 995.

A private port, on the other hand, is an arbitrary number generated when a client application attempts to establish a communication session with its server process. This port number no longer exists after the session has ended.

ICMP Protocol

The *Internet Control Message Protocol* (ICMP) is one of the key protocols in the TCP/IP suite. This protocol is primarily used for testing and diagnosing network connections. Commands such as *ping* uses this protocol to send a stream of messages to network devices to examine their health and report statistical and diagnostic messages. The report includes the number of packets transmitted, received, and lost; a round-trip time for individual packets with an overall average; a percentage of packets lost during the communication; and so on. Other commands, such as *traceroute* and *tracepath*, also employ this protocol for route determination and debugging between network entities.

The IPv6 version of ICMP is referred to as ICMPv6 and it is used by tools such as *ping6*, *traceroute6*, and *tracepath6*.

IPv6

With an explosive growth of the Internet, the presence of an extremely large number of network nodes requiring an IP, and an ever-increasing demand for additional addresses, the conventional IPv4 address space, which provides approximately 4.3 billion addresses, has been exhausted. To meet the future demand, a new version of IP is now available and its use is on the rise. This new version is referred to as *IPv6* (IP version 6) or *IPng* (IP next generation). By default, IPv6 is enabled in most newer versions of popular Linux distributions for all network interfaces.

IPv6 is a 128-bit software address, providing access to approximately 340 undecillion (340 followed by 36 zeros) addresses. This is an extremely large space, and it is expected to fulfill IP requirements for several decades to come.

IPv6 uses a messaging protocol called *neighbor discovery protocol* (NDP) to probe the network to discover neighboring IPv6 devices, determine their reachability, and map their associations. This protocol also includes enhanced functionalities (provided by ICMP and ARP on IPv4 networks) for troubleshooting issues pertaining to connectivity, duplicate address detection, and routing.

Unlike IPv4 addresses, which are denoted by four period-separated octets, IPv6 addresses contain eight colon-separated groups of four hexadecimal numbers. A sample v6 IP could be 1204:bab1:21d1:bb43:23a1:9bde:87df:bac9. It looks a bit daunting at first sight; however, methods to simplify their representation do exist.

Also, the *ip addr* command output from *centos73* shows the IPv6 address for *enp0s3* interface in CIDR notation:

```
[user1@centos73 ~]$  ip addr | grep inet6
    inet6 fe80::a00:27ff:feae:f35b/64 scope link
```

Major Differences between IPv4 and IPv6

There are a number of differences between IPv4 and IPv6 protocols. Some of the major ones are described in Table 11-2.

IPv4	IPv6
Uses 4 8-bit, period-separated decimal number format for address representation. Example: 192.168.0.100	Uses 8 16-bit, colon-separated hexadecimal number format for address representation. Example: fe80::a00:27ff:feae:f35b
Number of address bits: 32	Number of address bits: 128
Maximum number of addresses: ~4.3 billion.	Maximum number of addresses: virtually unlimited
Common testing and troubleshooting tools: ping, traceroute, tracepath, etc.	Common testing and troubleshooting tools: ping6, traceroute6, tracepath6, etc.
Support for IP autoconfiguration: no	Support for IP autoconfiguration: yes
Packet size: 576 bytes	Packet size: 1280 bytes

Table 11-2 IPv4 vs IPv6

These and other differences not listed here are due to enhancements and new features added to IPv6.

Network Interfaces

Network Interface Cards (NICs) are hardware adapters that provide one or more Ethernet ports for network connectivity. NICs may also be referred to as *network adapters* and individual ports as *network interfaces*. NICs may be built-in to the system board or are add-on adapters. They are available in one, two, or four port configurations on a single adapter. Individual interfaces can be configured with IPv4 or IPv6 (or both) assignments by editing files or using commands. Additional tasks, such as activating and deactivating them manually and auto-activating them at system reboots, can also be performed with these methods. We will discuss interface configuration and their administration in this chapter. In newer mainline Linux distribution versions, there is a distinction between a device and a connection. A device is a network interface, while a connection is the configuration used for the device (collection of settings). A device can have multiple connection configurations; however, only one of them is active at a time.

Understanding Interface Configuration Files

Each network interface has a configuration file to store IP assignments and other relevant parameters for the interface. The system reads this file and applies the settings at the time the interface is activated. Configuration files for all interfaces on RHEL and its clones are stored in a central location under the *config/sysconfig/network-scripts* directory. The interface file names begin with *ifcfg-* and they are appended with the name of the interface by which the system recognizes them. Some instances of interface file names are *ifcfg-eth0*, *ifcfg-enp0s3*, *ifcfg-br0*, and *ifcfg-em1*. Debian and its clones store network configuration for all interfaces in a single file called *interfaces* that is located in the */etc/network* directory.

On *centos73*, *ubuntu14*, and *centos511*, the installation program automatically assigned *enp0s3*, *eth0*, and *eth0*, respectively, to their primary network interfaces. Let's look at the current *enp0s3* interface configuration file, as it contains more directives than *eth0* on *centos511*. The following command excludes IPv6 settings in the output:

```
[user1@centos73 ~]$ cat /etc/sysconfig/network-scripts/ifcfg-enp0s3 | grep -vi ipv6
TYPE="Ethernet"
BOOTPROTO="dhcp"
DEFROUTE="yes"
PEERDNS="yes"
PEERROUTES="yes"
NAME="enp0s3"
UUID="4eae1c93-c572-44ca-a447-798954808d11"
DEVICE="enp0s3"
ONBOOT="yes"
NM_CONTROLLED=no
```

These and some additional directives are described in Table 11-3 in alphabetical order.

Directive	Description
BOOTPROTO	Defines the boot protocol to be used. Values include "dhcp" to obtain IP from a DHCP server and "none" or "static" to use a static IP as set with the IPADDR directive.
DEFROUTE	Whether to use this interface as the default route
DEVICE	Specifies the device name for the network interface
GATEWAY	Specifies a gateway address for the interface if the BOOTPROTO directive is set to "none" or "static"
HWADDR	Describes the hardware address for the interface
IPADDR	Specifies a static IP for the interface if the BOOTPROTO directive is set to "none" or "static"
NAME	Any description given to this connection
NETMASK	Sets a netmask address for the interface if the BOOTPROTO directive is set to "none" or "static"
NM_CONTROLLED	Whether the NetworkManager service is allowed to modify the configuration in this file. It should be turned off on computers that use static IP addresses.
ONBOOT	Whether to auto-activate this interface at system boot
PEERDNS	Whether to modify the DNS client resolver file /etc/resolv.conf. Default is "yes" if BOOTPROTO=dhcp is set.
UUID	The UUID associated with this interface
TYPE	Specifies the type of this interface

Table 11-3 Network Interface Configuration File (CentOS)

Let's take a look at the current *eth0* interface configuration file on *ubuntu14*:

```
[user1@ubuntu14 ~]$ cat /etc/network/interfaces
auto lo
iface lo inet loopback
auto eth0
iface eth0 inet dhcp
```

These and additional directives are described in Table 11-4 in alphabetical order.

Directive	Description
address	Specifies a static IP for the interface if the inet directive is set to "static"
auto	Auto-activates the specified interface at system boot
gateway	Specifies a gateway address for the interface if the inet directive is set to "static"
hwaddress	Describes the hardware address for the interface
iface	Specifies the device name for the network interface
inet	Defines the boot protocol to be used. Values include "dhcp" to obtain IP from a DHCP server and "static" to use a static IP.
nameserver	Uses the specified IP as the DNS server
netmask	Sets a netmask address for the interface if the inet directive is set to "static"

Table 11-4 Network Interface Configuration File (Ubuntu)

There are numerous other directives including those for IPv6 that may be defined in interface configuration files on both CentOS and Ubuntu. View manual pages for details.

Interface Administration Tools

There are two commands—*ifconfig* and *ip*—available for network interface configuration and administration. Of them, *ifconfig* is now obsolete in the latest mainline Linux distribution versions and users are encouraged to use the *ip* command instead, which is more versatile and flexible. The *ip* command is also a substitute for the *netstat* and *route* commands that we will learn later in this chapter. Furthermore, we may configure network interfaces manually by directly editing their configuration files with appropriate IP assignments.

Additional tools have been introduced in newer distribution versions. A discussion of those is beyond the scope of this book.

Once the desired network configuration is in place for an interface, we can either restart the network service to deactivate and reactivate all configured network interfaces on the system (this action is not desirable on live production systems) or use the *ifup* command to bring a specific interface up with new IP assignments. The reverse for the *ifup* command is *ifdown*, which is used to deactivate a specific interface.

The next three exercises, 11-1 to 11-3, will show different procedures to configure new network interfaces on *centos73*, *ubuntu14*, and *centos511*.

Exercise 11-1: Configure and Activate a New Network Interface Non-Persistently and Persistently on centos73

In this exercise, you will add a new bridged network adapter to *centos73* VM in Oracle VirtualBox console and point it to a working wireless network adapter on your computer. Your *centos73* system should recognize this interface as *enp0s8* (or something similar). You will configure this new interface with static IP assignment (192.168.0.100/24 and gateway 192.168.0.1) non-persistently at the command prompt and then persistently by creating an appropriate file for it and adding entries to it. You will set auto-activation for this interface. You will deactivate and reactivate this interface manually at the command prompt and re-validate the settings after a reboot.

1. Shut down *centos73* and power the VM off. Open the Oracle VirtualBox console and select *centos73*. Click Settings→Network→Adapter 2. Check mark "Enable Network Adapter". From the drop-down lists for "Attached to" and "Name", choose "Bridged Adapter" and an appropriate wireless network adapter. On our VBox console, it looks like the following:

Click OK to complete the new interface addition and then power up the system.

2. Log on to *centos73* as *root* and run the *ip* command to confirm the addition of the new interface:

[root@centos73 ~]# **ip addr**
3: **enp0s8**: <BROADCAST,MULTICAST> mtu 1500 qdisc noop state DOWN qlen 1000
   link/ether 08:00:27:3f:2c:c3 brd ff:ff:ff:ff:ff:ff

The output indicates the presence of the new interface by the name *enp0s8*, and it is currently down with no IP assignment.

3. Apply IP 192.168.0.100/24 to the new interface manually with the following and verify with the **ip a** or **ifconfig enp0s8** command:

[root@centos73 ~]# **ip a add 192.168.0.100/24 broadcast 192.168.0.255 dev enp0s8**

Alternatively, you can run **ifconfig enp0s8 192.168.0.100/24 broadcast 192.168.0.255** to achieve the same.

At this point, if you reboot the system, this IP will be lost. You need to configure the setting persistently.

4. Open */etc/sysconfig/network-scripts/ifcfg-enp0s8* file in the vi editor and add the following:

```
DEVICE=enp0s8
BOOTPROTO=static
ONBOOT=yes
IPADDR=192.168.0.100
NETMASK=255.255.255.0
GATEWAY=192.168.0.1
```

Save the file and exit out of the editor.

5. Deactivate and reactivate this interface manually using the *ifdown* and *ifup* commands:

   [root@centos73 ~]# **ifdown enp0s8 ; ifup enp0s8**

   Issue the **ip a** or **ifconfig enp0s8** command to confirm the setting.

6. Reboot the system using the **reboot** command and validate the assignment with either **ip a** or **ifconfig enp0s8** after the system has been up.

Run PuTTY, the ssh client program downloaded in Chapter 1 to your MS Windows desktop, and enter the new IP in the space provided to access *centos73*. See Chapter 1 "Installing Linux and Using Basic Commands" for more details.

Exercise 11-2: Configure and Activate a New Network Interface Non-Persistently and Persistently on ubuntu14

In this exercise, you will add a new bridged network adapter to *ubuntu14* VM in Oracle VirtualBox console and point it to a working wireless network adapter on your computer. Your *ubuntu14* system should recognize this interface as *eth1*. You will manually remove the IP that is automatically assigned to it. You will configure this new interface with static IP assignments (192.168.0.101/24 and gateway 192.168.0.1) non-persistently at the command prompt and then persistently by adding appropriate entries to the interface configuration file. You will set auto-activation for this interface. You will deactivate and reactivate this interface manually at the command prompt and re-validate the settings after a reboot.

1. Follow step 1 from Exercise 11-1 to assign a new interface to *ubuntu14*.
2. Log on to *ubuntu14* as *user1* and run the **ip a** or **ifconfig** command to confirm the addition of the new interface (*eth1*) with some arbitrary IP address allotted to it by DHCP.
3. Remove the DHCP-allotted IP (assuming it is 192.168.0.19/24) using either of the following:

   [user1@ubuntu14 ~]$ **sudo ip a del 192.168.0.19/24 dev eth1**
   [user1@ubuntu14 ~]$ **sudo ifconfig eth1 0.0.0.0**

4. Apply IP 192.168.0.101/24 to *eth1* with either of the following and verify with the **ip a** or **ifconfig eth1** command:

   [user1@ubuntu14 ~]$ **sudo ip a add 192.168.0.101/24 broadcast 192.168.0.255 dev eth1**

Alternatively, you can run **sudo ifconfig eth1 192.168.0.101/24 broadcast 192.168.0.255** to achieve the same.

At this point, if you reboot the system, this IP will be lost. You need to configure the setting persistently.

5. Open */etc/network/interfaces* file in the vi editor and append the following to the bottom of the file:

    auto eth1
    iface eth1 inet static
    address 192.168.0.101
    netmask 255.255.255.0
    gateway 192.168.0.1

Save the file and exit out of the editor.

6. Deactivate and reactivate this interface manually using the *ifdown* and *ifup* commands:

    [user1@ubuntu14 ~]$ **sudo ifdown eth1 ; sudo ifup eth1**

Issue the **ip a** or **ifconfig eth1** command to confirm the setting.

7. Reboot the system using the **reboot** command and validate the assignment with either **ip a** or **ifconfig eth1** after the system has been up.

Run PuTTY, the ssh client program downloaded in Chapter 1 to your MS Windows desktop, and enter the new IP in the space provided to access *ubuntu14*. See Chapter 1 "Installing Linux and Using Basic Commands" for more details.

Exercise 11-3: Configure and Activate a New Network Interface Persistently on centos511

Your *centos511* system will recognize the new network interface as *eth1*, allot a DHCP-supplied IP to it, and create *ifcfg-eth1* file under */etc/sysconfig/network-scripts/* directory. You will modify this new interface file to use the static IP 192.168.0.102/24 with gateway 192.168.0.1 and auto-activation turned on. You will deactivate the interface to remove the DHCP-allotted IP and reactivate it to apply the new IP assignments stored in the file.

1. Follow step 1 from Exercise 11-1 to assign a new interface to *centos511*.
2. Log on to *centos511* as *root* and run the **ip a** or **ifconfig** command to confirm the addition of the new interface (*eth1*) with some arbitrary IP address allotted to it by DHCP.
3. Open */etc/sysconfig/network-scripts/ifcfg-eth1* file in the vi editor and replace the current information with the following:

    DEVICE=eth1
    BOOTPROTO=static
    ONBOOT=yes
    IPADDR=192.168.0.102
    NETMASK=255.255.255.0
    GATEWAY=192.168.0.1

Save the file and exit out of the editor.

4. Deactivate and reactivate this interface using the *ifdown* and *ifup* commands:

[root@centos511 ~]# **ifdown eth1 ; ifup eth1**

Issue the **ip a** or **ifconfig eth1** command to confirm the new setting.

5. Reboot the system using the **reboot** command and validate the assignment with either **ip a** or **ifconfig eth1** after the system has been up.

Run PuTTY, the ssh client program downloaded in Chapter 1 to your MS Windows desktop, and enter the new IP in the space provided to access *centos511*. See Chapter 1 "Installing Linux and Using Basic Commands" for more details.

Understanding and Updating the Hosts Table

Each IP configured on an interface has a hostname assigned to it. In an environment with multiple networked systems, it is prudent to have some kind of a hostname to IP address resolution method in place to avoid typing a destination system IP repeatedly when trying to access it. DNS is one such method. It is designed for large networks such as corporate networks and the Internet. For small, internal networks, the use of a local host table (the */etc/hosts* file) is more common. This table is used to maintain hostname to IP mapping for all systems on the local network, allowing us to access any system by simply employing its hostname. From the standpoint of this book, we have three systems in place, each with one DHCP-supplied IP address and one static IP address. As DHCP addresses are not persistent and should not be used on servers, we will use the static IPs instead and create their mappings with existing hostnames in the *hosts* table. Here is what we will need to add to the existing */etc/hosts* files on all three systems:

```
192.168.0.100       centos73
192.168.0.101       ubuntu14
192.168.0.102       centos511
```

Each row in the file has an IP address in the first column followed by the *official* (or *canonical*) hostname in the second column, and one or more optional aliases thereafter. The official hostname and one or more aliases give users the flexibility of accessing a system using any of these names.

As indicated earlier, the *hosts* file is used on small networks only and therefore must be updated on each individual system to reflect any changes.

Routing

Routing is the process of choosing paths on the network along which to send traffic to a destination node. This process is implemented with the deployment of specialized and sophisticated hardware devices called *routers*. Routers are widely used on the Internet and in corporate networks for traffic routing. A Linux system may also be configured as a router; however, that capability will not be as sophisticated.

When systems on two distinct networks communicate with each other, proper routes must be in place for them to be able to talk. For instance, if system A on network A sends a data packet to system B on network B, one or more routing devices are involved in routing the packet to system B. The packet passes from one router to another until it reaches the router that is able to deliver the packet directly to system B. Each router along the path is referred to as a *hop*. If system A has no explicit route defined to reach system B, the packet is forwarded to the *default route* (or the *default gateway*), which attempts to search for an appropriate route to the destination system. If found, it delivers the packet to it, otherwise it errors out.

Routing Table

A *routing table* preserves information about available routes and their status. It may be built and updated dynamically or manually by adding or removing routes. The *ip*, *route*, or the *netstat* command can be used to view entries in the routing table. Here is how to use the *ip* command on *centos511*:

```
[root@centos511 ~]# ip route
default via 192.168.0.1 dev eth1
169.254.0.0/16 dev eth1 scope link
192.168.0.0/24 dev eth0 proto kernel scope link src 192.168.0.100
192.168.0.0/24 dev eth1 proto kernel scope link src 192.168.0.101
```

The output begins with the address and netmask of the destination network. The keyword "default" identifies the IP address of the default gateway for transmitting data to other networks in the absence of a proper route. The "dev" keyword signifies the name of the interface that is used to transmit traffic. "proto" identifies the routing protocol as either "kernel" (installed by the kernel during auto-configuration) or "static" (installed by the user). The "scope" keyword determines the scope of the destination to be global, nowhere, host, or link. "src" shows the source address associated with the interface, and "metric" (not shown) displays the number of hops to the destination system. Systems on the local network are one hop, and each subsequent router thereafter is an additional hop.

Now, let's look at what it shows with the *route* command on *centos511*, which is equivalent to using **ip route** on older Linux systems. Here is a sample output:

```
[root@centos511 ~]# route
Kernel IP routing table
```

Destination	Gateway	Genmask	Flags	Metric	Ref	Use	Iface
192.168.0.0	*	255.255.255.0	U	0	0	0	eth0
192.168.0.0	*	255.255.255.0	U	0	0	0	eth1
169.254.0.0	*	255.255.0.0	U	0	0	0	eth0
default	192.168.0.1	0.0.0.0	UG	0	0	0	eth1

The first, second, third, fifth, and eighth columns display the same information as does *ip route*. "Flags" shows the status or type of route being used (U identifies the route as up, H denotes the destination as a host, and G represents a gateway route). The "Ref" for references is not used in Linux. The "Use" column indicates the count of lookups for the route.

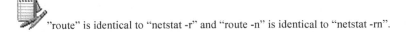

"route" is identical to "netstat -r" and "route -n" is identical to "netstat -rn".

Try running this command by adding the -n option to view the output in numerical format where applicable.

Managing Routes

Managing routes involves adding static routes to a specific host or network via an interface, modifying or deleting current routes, and setting the default route. The *ip* or the *route* command can be used for management. Route entries added with these commands do not survive system reboots, therefore, you need to add them to the interface-specific *route-** file (such as *route-eth1*) in the */etc/sysconfig/network-scripts* directory for persistence. The global default gateway for use by all configured interfaces on the system is set in the */etc/sysconfig/network* file with the GATEWAY directive. On system with a single network interface, it can alternatively be defined in the interface-specific ifcfg-* file (such as *ifcfg-eth1*) with the same directive. The next two exercises will demonstrate how to add static and default routes manually and persistently on *centos511*.

 The route command is obsolete on latest mainline Linux distribution versions. Users are, therefore, encouraged to use the ip command instead.

 Both static and default routes are defined in the /etc/network/interfaces file on Ubuntu with the gateway directive.

Exercise 11-4: Add a Static Route Non-Persistently and Persistently

In this exercise, you will add a static route non-persistently to network 192.168.3.0/24 via *eth1* with gateway 192.168.0.1 using both *ip* and *route* commands. You will permanently re-add this route by creating a file under the */etc/sysconfig/network-scripts* directory and adding appropriate entries to it. You will reboot the system to confirm the activation of the new route. Finally, you will delete the route manually at the command line.

1. Add a static route to 192.168.3.0/24 via *eth1* with gateway 192.168.0.1 using either of the following:

    ```
    [root@centos511 ~]# ip route add 192.168.3.0/24 via 192.168.0.1 dev eth1
    [root@centos511 ~]# route add -net 192.168.3.0/24 gw 192.168.0.1 dev eth1
    ```

2. Show the routing table to validate the addition of the new route. Use **ip route** or **route**.
3. Reboot the system and run **ip route** or **route** again to confirm an automatic deletion of the route as the entries are non-persistent. You can also run **ifdown eth1** and then **ifup eth1** instead of rebooting the system.
4. To ensure the route is persistent across restarts, create a file *route-eth1* under */etc/sysconfig/network-scripts/* and insert the following entries:

    ```
    ADDRESS0=192.168.3.0
    NETMASK0=255.255.255.0
    GATEWAY0=192.168.0.1
    ```

    Or, you can place the entry in the following format:

    ```
    192.168.3.0/24 via 192.168.0.1 dev eth1
    ```

5. Restart the *eth1* interface for the route to take effect:

    [root@centos511 ~]# **ifdown eth1 ; ifup eth1**

6. Run the **ip route** or the **route** command to validate the new route.
7. Delete this route by removing its entry from the routing table using either of the following:

    [root@centos511 ~]# **ip route del 192.168.3.0/24**
    [root@centos511 ~]# **route del -net 192.168.3.0/24**

8. Confirm the removal with **ip route** or **route**.

You should not see the route in the output. You can remove the *route-eth1* file if this route is no longer needed.

Once a route is in place and you need to modify it, the *route* command does not provide any options for alteration. You will need to weed out the route entry and re-add it with correct specifications. The *ip* command, however, does offer the "change" option for this purpose. You simply replace the "add" option with the "change" option and enter correct assignments with the command.

Exercise 11-5: Delete and Add the Default Route Non-Persistently and Persistently

The default route via 192.168.0.1 using *eth0* is already configured on *centos511*. In this exercise, you will remove this route and set it again over *eth1* instead using both *ip* and *route* commands. You will permanently add this route to the */etc/sysconfig/network* file and reboot the system to confirm its activation.

1. Show the current default route using **ip route** or **route**.
2. Delete this route using either of the following:

    [root@centos511 ~]# **ip route del default**
    [root@centos511 ~]# **route del default**

3. Confirm the deletion with **ip route** or **route**.
4. Re-add the default route via *eth1* using either of the following:

    [root@centos511 ~]# **ip route add default via 192.168.0.1 dev eth1**
    [root@centos511 ~]# **route add default gw 192.168.0.1 dev eth1**

5. Confirm the addition with **ip route** or **route**.
6. Open the */etc/sysconfig/network* file and set GATEWAY and GATEWAYDEV directives as follows:

    GATEWAY=192.168.0.1
    GATEWAYDEV=eth1

7. Reboot the system and run **ip route** or **route** to confirm the persistence and activation of the default route on *eth1*.

Testing and Debugging Network Interfaces

Now that we know how to configure network interfaces and routes manually and automatically, let's look at the tools available for testing and debugging network interface connections, and how to use them.

Network problems generally involve physical connectivity or configuration issues. Physical connectivity issues may include a network card that is not seated properly in the slot, a cable is plugged into a wrong network port, a broken cable, bad or loose connectors, router or switch port disabled or malfunctioning, and so on. Configuration issues may involve missing interface support in kernel, duplicate IP addresses on the network, incorrect IP assignments, improper routing table entries, IP assignments lost after a system reboot, and so on.

The following subsections present various tools for help in testing connectivity, and debugging and resolving issues pertaining to network connectivity. These tools include *ping* (*ping6*), *netstat*, *netcat*, *traceroute* (*traceroute6*), *tracepath* (*tracepath6*), *nmap*, *ip*, *ifconfig*, *route*, and *arp*. The *ping6*, *traceroute6*, and *tracepath6* commands are specific to IPv6. For problems related to incorrect configuration, examine the settings in interface and route configuration files stored under */etc/sysconfig/network-scripts/* (or in the */etc/network/interfaces* file on Ubuntu) and in */etc/hosts*, */etc/hostname*, and */etc/sysconfig/network* files.

Testing Network Connectivity with ping

After the new connection has been established on *centos511* on *eth1* with IP 192.168.0.102, we need to test whether this address is pingable and accessible from other systems. To this end, log on to *centos73* and run the *ping* command. The *ping* command is used to peruse the network connectivity at the IP level when the physical connectivity is established and proper IP assignments are in place. This command sends out a series of 64-byte *Internet Control Message Protocol* (ICMP) test packets to the destination IP and waits for a response. With the -c option, we can specify the number of packets that we want to transmit.

The following will send two packets from *centos73* to 192.168.0.102:

```
[user1@centos73 ~]$ ping -c2 192.168.0.102
PING 192.168.0.10 (192.168.0.10) 56(84) bytes of data.
64 bytes from 192.168.0.102: icmp_seq=1 ttl=64 time=0.565 ms
64 bytes from 192.168.0.102: icmp_seq=2 ttl=64 time=0.208 ms

--- 192.168.0.10 ping statistics ---
2 packets transmitted, 2 received, 0% packet loss, time 1000ms
rtt min/avg/max/mdev = 0.208/0.386/0.565/0.179 ms
```

Under "ping statistics," it shows the number of packets transmitted, received, and lost. The packet loss should be 0% and the round trip time should not be too high for a healthy connection. In general, we can use this command to test connectivity with the system's own IP, the loopback IP (127.0.0.1), a static route, the default gateway, and other addresses on the local or remote network.

If *ping* fails in any of the situations, we need to check if the network adapter is seated properly, its driver is installed, network cable is secured appropriately, IP and netmask values are set correctly, and the default or static route is accurate.

Inspecting Network Interfaces with netstat

netstat (*network statistics*) shows active network connections and their statistics, as well as routing tables along with miscellaneous network information such as open ports and sockets. This tool has several useful switches available for generating desired reports, and it plays an essential role in testing and debugging network interfaces. It displays incoming and outgoing packet data per configured interface with the -i (interface) option. The use of this option is beneficial to inspect statistics for a suspected interface. You can add the -t or -u option to restrict the output to TCP-only or UDP-only traffic. If you are interested in viewing the kernel routing table, this command provides the -r option, which is equivalent to using the *route* and *ip route* commands. With both -rn options, the routing table report is in the numerical format. The -a (all) option with *netstat* instructs the command to display the status of both open and non-open sockets. With -l (listening) or without any options, this command limits the output to open sockets only. The -s (statistics) option is another valuable switch; *netstat* depicts abridged statistics on the usage of each protocol—IP, ICMP, TCP, and UDP—on the system. The -v option is also available for use with the command to add more detail to reports.

The netstat command is obsolete in latest mainline Linux distribution versions and users are encouraged to use its replacements: the ss command or "ip -s link".

From network connectivity troubleshooting and interface misbehavior debugging perspectives, use *netstat* to validate routes and IP addresses, identify the direction of packet flow, determine ports applications are listening on, list sources for established connections, and so on.

Try **netstat -rn, netstat -l, netstat -a, netstat -t**, and **netstat -s**, and observe the output. You don't need to spend time on analyzing the reports.

Exploring and Debugging Network Connections with netcat

netcat (a.k.a. *nc* or *ncat*) is a handy tool for exploring and monitoring network connections and troubleshooting issues with the connections by reading and writing data across network connections over the TCP or UDP protocol. This tool has the ability to listen on a port for incoming connection requests, establish a network connection on a host, send packets, and perform port scanning. It supports both IPv4 and IPv6 networks.

Some common options are:

-l to run in listen (server) mode
-p to specify a source port number
-r to use an auto-generated random port number
-s to stipulate the IP of the interface to be used for sending out packets
-v for verbosity
-u to operate in UDP mode instead of the default TCP
-z to perform port scanning to ascertain what ports are open and what services are using them

Let's look at the following examples to understand some of its usages.

To scan *ubuntu14* (from *centos511*) to identify the ports (one or a range) it is listening on. This is used to determine what network services are active on the system. Here is how you would run the scanner on port range 1 to 100:

```
[user1@centos511 ~]$ nc -z 192.168.0.101 1-100
Connection to 192.168.0.101 22 port [tcp/ssh] succeeded!
```

The output indicates that the only network port currently open on *ubuntu14* between 1 and 100 is port 22, which is associated with the secure shell service.

To run *netcat* in client/server mode, open another terminal window on *centos511* and run the command to listen on port 5000:

```
[user1@centos511 ~]$ tty
/dev/pts/1
[user1@centos511 ~]$ nc -l 5000
```

Issue the following on the other terminal window to establish a client/server connection on port 5000:

```
[user1@centos511 ~]$ tty
/dev/pts/0
[user1@centos511 ~]$ nc localhost 5000
```

Type anything on either terminal and the text will replicate on the other terminal. Enter Ctrl+c to terminate the session when done. You can run the client session from a remote system as well to test a port. Check the manual pages of the command for more information and usage examples.

If this tool is not already installed on the system, use **yum install nc** or **apt-get install netcat** as appropriate to load it.

Tracing Flow of Network Traffic with traceroute and tracepath

traceroute and *tracepath* commands are employed for tracing the flow of traffic to a destination system on the local or remote network using either IPv4 or IPv6 protocol. These commands may be helpful in isolating and troubleshooting connectivity issues when *ping* has failed. Both tools work in a similar fashion except that *traceroute* requires the *root* user privileges to function correctly. The commands require the destination system's hostname or IP address to be specified.

To trace the route from *centos511* to *ubuntu14* using the default interface chosen from the routing table, use either of the following:

```
[user1@centos73 ~]$ traceroute 192.168.0.102
traceroute to 192.168.0.102 (192.168.0.102), 30 hops max, 40 byte packets
 1  (192.168.0.102) 0.033 ms  0.058 ms  0.015 ms
[user1@centos73 ~]$ tracepath 192.168.0.102
 1:  192.168.0.102 (192.168.0.102)         0.047ms pmtu 16436
 1:  192.168.0.102 (192.168.0.102)         0.054ms reached
     Resume: pmtu 16436 hops 1 back 1
```

The first column shows the time-to-live (TTL) of the probe followed by the hop name or its IP and the times in milliseconds for miscellaneous calculations.

The *traceroute* command has some useful options available for use with it. These options include -i to specify an alternative interface on the system to transmit the probe packets through, -m to change the maximum number of hops from the default of 30, and -I, -T, or -U to use ICMP, TCP, or UDP protocols for probes. Check the manual pages of this and the *tracepath* command for more information.

Scanning Networks with nmap

nmap (*network mapper*) is a powerful network probing and security auditing tool that may be used to scan and inventory hosts on the network for the type and version of operating system they are running, services along with ports and protocols they are using, firewall in use, host up time, and so on.

The primary use of this tool, however, has been to scan ports on remote hosts and report on their state as being open, closed, filtered, unfiltered, open/filtered, or closed/filtered. The open and closed states indicate whether or not a service is listening on a port, the filtered and unfiltered states report the inability of *nmap* to determine whether a responsive or an unresponsive port is open or closed, and the last two states show the weakness of the command to determine which of the two states describe a port.

With this tool, you can specify a range of ports to scan, hosts or networks to probe, detect open ports to discover service and version information, and so on.

The following shows an example using some common options. This example will run *nmap* on *centos511* against *ubuntu14* with the -A option for OS and version discovery as well as traceroute information, -sV for services and ports they are listening on, and -v for verbosity. You can run this command as a normal user; however, it is able to retrieve more information with *root* privileges.

```
[root@centos511 ~]# nmap -AvsV 192.168.0.102
. . . . . . . .
Discovered open port 22/tcp on 192.168.0.102
Discovered open port 111/tcp on 192.168.0.102
Discovered open port 627/tcp on 192.168.0.102
The SYN Stealth Scan took 0.04s to scan 1680 total ports.
Initiating service scan against 3 services on 192.168.0.102 at 17:33
The service scan took 11.00s to scan 3 services on 1 host.
Initiating RPCGrind Scan against 192.168.0.102 at 17:33
The RPCGrind Scan took 0.00s to scan 2 ports on 192.168.0.102.
For OSScan assuming port 22 is open, 1 is closed, and neither are firewalled
Host 192.168.0.102 appears to be up ... good.
Interesting ports on 192.168.0.102:
Not shown: 1677 closed ports
PORT   STATE SERVICE VERSION
22/tcp  open  ssh    OpenSSH 4.3 (protocol 2.0)
111/tcp open  rpc
. . . . . . . .
Nmap finished: 1 IP address (1 host up) scanned in 20.485 seconds
        Raw packets sent: 1728 (77.604KB) | Rcvd: 3462 (147.480KB)
```

Try running *nmap* against *scanme.nmap.org* and see what it reports.

This command has many other options available for host discovery, port scanning, service/version detection, OS recognition, timing and performance, and so on. Review the manual pages of this command for options, examples, and detailed explanation. If this tool is not already installed on the system, use **yum install nmap** or **apt-get install nmap** as appropriate to load it.

Manipulating the ARP Cache with arp

A hardware address is used to spot the correct destination node for data packets transmitted from the source node. The data packets include hardware addresses for both entities. The ARP protocol obtains hardware and IP addresses from network nodes and caches it locally. We can use the *arp* command to view, add, or erase entries manually.

The arp command is obsolete in latest mainline Linux distribution versions; users are encouraged to use "ip neighbor" as its replacement.

Here is how we run this command to view cached entries:

```
[user1@centos511 ~]$ arp -v
Address              HWtype HWaddress           Flags   Mask    Iface
192.168.0.1          ether  18:D6:C7:6C:D3:71   C               eth1
192.168.0.11         ether  DC:85:DE:02:71:EF   C               eth1
Entries: 2     Skipped: 0     Found: 2
```

The output indicates the IP and hardware address mappings for the discovered nodes, and names of the network interfaces they are associated with. It also provides a summary at the bottom.

Now, let's add a new entry (-s) for *ubuntu14* to the cache. The hardware address is 08:00:27:4d:a9:85 as determined with the *ip addr* or *ifconfig* command for *eth1* on *ubuntu14*. Run the following as *root* and verify:

```
[root@centos511 ~]# arp -s 192.168.0.101 08:00:27:4d:a9:85
[root@centos511 ~]# arp
Address              HWtype HWaddress           Flags   Mask    Iface
192.168.0.101        ether  08:00:27:4D:A9:85   CM              eth1
192.168.0.1          ether  18:D6:C7:6C:D3:71   C               eth1
192.168.0.11         ether  DC:85:DE:02:71:EF   C               eth1
```

The new entry is included in the output. The *arp* command provides the -d option to delete an entry from the cache. For instance, **arp -d 192.168.0.101** will clear this entry from the cache. Check the manual pages of the command for more information.

The Internet Services

When services are accessed and used over the network, two software pieces called *client* and *server* are involved. The client program requests for a service running on a remote system. The server program on the remote system responds to and serves the client request, establishing a client/server communication channel. A single system can act as both a server and a client at the same time, providing services to other systems and using their services as a client.

Server programs are started in one of two ways: (1) via the startup scripts located in sequencer directories, or (2) via the master server program daemon called *xinetd* (the *extended internet daemon*) or *inetd* (*internet daemon*), which is also referred to as the *super-server*.

xinetd is a more secure and modern open-source substitutes for the old inetd, which is no longer available in popular Linux distributions.

xinetd is available on older Linux versions with SysVinit method of system initialization by default. Systems running systemd have a superior and more secure mechanism for service management and, therefore, xinetd is not installed on these systems by default. It is, however, available for installation and use.

A detailed discussion on the startup scripts and sequencer directories is provided in Chapter 8 "Administering Partitions, File Systems, and Swap."

Common Internet Services

Linux supports numerous Internet services to give users the ability to perform various tasks over the network. These services include *rexec* for remote command executions, *finger* for user information lookups, *rcp* and *ftp* for remote file transfers, and *rlogin* and *telnet* for remote logins. Additional popular services such as *named* (BIND or DNS), *rsync*, and *sendmail* are also available for use in hostname resolutions, network file synching, and sending and receiving email messages. Many of these services work under the hood of *xinetd*, while the rest have their own startup mechanisms.

/etc/xinetd.conf and /etc/xinetd.d

The *xinetd* super-server daemon is launched by one of the startup scripts when the system boots to run level 3. This daemon reads its configuration file */etc/xinetd.conf* and sits in the memory, listening on ports listed in the */etc/services* file for services defined and enabled in the */etc/xinetd.d* directory, and waiting for respective client connection requests to come in. Upon arrival of a service request on a port, the super-server launches the server program corresponding to that port. It establishes a connection between the client and server processes, gets itself out of that communication, and restarts listening on that port on behalf of that service. Every service uses a unique port number as defined in the *services* file.

The equivalent for the /etc/xinetd.conf file is /etc/inetd.conf and that for /etc/xinetd.d is /etc/inetd.d for inetd.

Here is an excerpt from the *xinetd.conf* file that shows a few basic directives:

```
defaults
{
# The next two items are intended to be a quick access place to temporarily enable or disable services.
#     enabled     =
#     disabled    =
}
includedir /etc/xinetd.d
```

The defaults section, the only section in the file by default, defines some common settings that apply to all the services listed in the *xinetd.d* directory. Of particular interest is the includedir directive at the bottom of the file. This directive indicates the storage location for service configuration files. The default location is */etc/xinetd.d*.

The following output shows the directory contents of *xinetd.d*:

```
[root@centos511 ~]# ls /etc/xinetd.d
chargen-dgram      daytime-stream   echo-stream     klogin        rsync
chargen-stream     discard-dgram    eklogin         krb5-telnet   tcpmux-server
cups-lpd           discard-stream   ekrb5-telnet    kshell        time-dgram
daytime-dgram      echo-dgram       gssftp          rmcp          time-stream
```

All services are set to the default value of yes for the disable directive, which implies that no service is currently marked for use. This statement can be validated by grepping for string "disable" as follows:

```
[root@centos511 ~]# grep disable /etc/xinetd.d/*
chargen-dgram:      disable   = yes
chargen-stream:     disable   = yes
cups-lpd:           disable   = yes
daytime-dgram:      disable   = yes
daytime-stream:     disable   = yes
. . . . . . . .
```

Enabling and Activating an xinetd-Controlled Service

As depicted in the *grep* output of the *xinetd.d* configuration files in the previous subsection, all services are disabled by default. We can enable (or disable) a service using the *chkconfig* command. This utility modifies the disable directive's value directly in the service's configuration file. For instance, issue the following to enable the klogin service:

```
[root@centos511 ~]# chkconfig klogin on
```

You can verify the switching by executing **grep disable /etc/xinetd.d/klogin**. You should see "disable = no" in the output.

Moreover, if you want to activate this service right now without a system reboot, use the *service* command to force the super-server to re-read all service configuration files:

```
[root@centos511 ~]# service xinetd reload
```

The klogin service is now enabled and activated, and the super-server is listening for client requests for this service.

The reverse of this activation and allowance is performed with **chkconfig klogin off** and **service xinetd reload**.

One of the best practices from a Linux server hardening standpoint is to enable only those services that are in use on the system, and leave all others disabled.

Chapter Summary

This chapter discussed the rudiments of networking. It started with an introduction to the OSI reference networking model. It outlined the seven layers, described the process of encapsulation and de-encapsulation, and examined the peer-to-peer nature of the OSI model.

Next, we looked at the TCP/IP protocol suite and saw how the layers in this suite correspond with the layers in the OSI model. A discussion on this topic was followed by a study of several networking concepts and terms that included hardware and IP addresses, hostname, network classes, subnetting and subnet mask, CIDR notation, protocols and ports, and so on. A basic understanding of these terms was essential.

We configured a new network interface and applied IP assignments to it, one time from a DHCP server and the second time manually. We analyzed the file involved in the configuration. We activated and deactivated the interface by hand and defined the IP and hostname mapping for the interface in the hosts database. We performed a ping test for functional validation.

The subsequent topic expounded on the concept and implementation of routing. Routing is vital, as it lays the foundation for transferring IP traffic among networks over public and private networks. We looked at the function of the routing table and saw how to view entries in the table. We added static and default routes using commands and by editing interface-specific route configuration files.

Linux includes an assortment of tools for testing and debugging network connectivity and network interfaces. A good working knowledge of these tools is crucial.

The chapter concluded with a short discussion on the Internet services and their global and per-service configuration files. We examined various services controlled by the super-server process and how we could enable or disable them.

Chapter Review at a Glance

The following presents a one-sentence review of each key topic discussed in this chapter:

- Computer networks are built to share resources and data, using devices, such as switches, over wired or wireless links.

- The OSI reference model is a seven-layer—application, presentation, session, transport, network, data link, and physical—networking model that provides a set of guidelines for manufacturers to follow to develop their networking products with the ability to work in a multi-vendor computing environment.

- Each layer in the OSI reference model defines a specific function, along with protocols and hardware that support that function.

- Encapsulation is the process of forming a network packet through the OSI layers for transmission to other network entities; de-encapsulation is the reverse of encapsulation.

- TCP/IP is a four- (or five-) layer—application, host-to-host, internet, and network access layers—protocol stack that corresponds to the seven layers of the OSI model.

- TCP and IP are the two primary protocols in the TCP/IP protocol suite to transport data packets between source and destination entities.

- Each network device has a unique 48-bit hardware address, which is also called a MAC address, Ethernet address, station address, or physical address.

- The ARP protocol identifies the hardware address of a network entity with a known IP address.

- A hostname is an alphanumeric name of a network entity that uniquely identifies it on the network.

- IPv4 is a unique 32-bit software address that identifies a node on the network; IPv6 is a unique 128-bit software address that is designed to fulfill the future requirement.

- IPv4 has four network classes from class A to class E, with the first three classes used in public networks and the latter two in scientific and other special purpose cases.

- Subnetting allows the division of a large network address space into multiple, smaller sub-networks for performance and de-centralized management.

- A subnet mask is the boundary that segregates one subnet from the other.

- CIDR notation is implemented to control the quick depletion of IPv4 addresses and the rapid surge in the number of routing tables that are needed to route traffic on the network.

- A protocol, such as TCP, IP, UDP, and ICMP, is a "common language" that network entities use to communicate and understand one another.

- Ports—well-known or private—are used to allow a client program to communicate with its corresponding server program.

- NICs are hardware (or virtualized) components that allow a network entity to communicate with other devices on the network.

- Routing is the process of choosing network paths on which to send data packets; routers implement this process.

- The default route (or default gateway) is used to route network traffic in the absence of static routes.

- A routing table stores and maintains information about available routes and their status.

- Network connectivity and interface configuration issues can be ascertained and resolved using available testing and debugging tools.

- Every network service or application has two primary components—a server program that offers a service and a client program that accesses it.

- A network service, such as DNS, FTP, or sshd, can be started automatically (or manually) using an explicit startup script or via the super-server Internet daemon program.

- Commands we learned in this chapter are: ifconfig, ip, arp, hostname, uname, ifup, ifdown, route, ping (ping6), netstat, netcat (nc or ncat), traceroute (traceroute6), tracepath (tracepath6), and nmap.

- Files and directories we discussed in this chapter are: /etc/hostname, /etc/protocols, /etc/services, /etc/sysconfig/network-scripts/ifcfg-*, /etc/network/interfaces, /etc/hosts, /etc/sysconfig/network, /etc/xinetd.conf (/etc/inetd.conf), and /etc/xinetd.d/ (/etc/inetd.d/).

## Chapter 12

Understanding Internationalization, and Configuring Localization, NTP, and DNS

This chapter describes the following major topics:

- ➤ Introduction to internationalization and localization
- ➤ Review character set and character encoding
- ➤ Display and alter system-wide and per-user locale
- ➤ Convert text input into a different character encoding
- ➤ Exhibit and set system-wide and per-user timezone values
- ➤ Introduction to the Network Time Protocol service
- ➤ Overview of time sources, NTP roles, and stratum levels
- ➤ Understand NTP packages and tools, and analyze the configuration file
- ➤ Configure and test NTP client
- ➤ Query NTP servers and update system clock spontaneously
- ➤ Show and set Linux system and hardware clocks
- ➤ Comprehend domain name system and the terms name resolution, name space, and domains
- ➤ Understand DNS roles and describe DNS client configuration files and lookup tools
- ➤ Set up DNS client and test with dig, host, nslookup, and getent

This chapter covers the following objectives for LX0-104/102-400 Exam:

107.3 Localisation and internationalization [this entire objective is described in this chapter]

29. Configure locale settings and environment variables
30. Configure timezone settings and environment variables

The following is a partial list of the used files, terms and utilities: /etc/timezone, /etc/localtime, /usr/share/zoneinfo, environment variables (LC_*, LC_ALL, LANG, TZ), /usr/bin/locale, tzselect, tzconfig, date, iconv, UTF-8, ISO-8859, ASCII, and unicode

108.1 Maintain system time [this entire objective is described in this chapter]

31. Set the system date and time
32. Set the hardware clock to the correct time in UTC
33. Configure the correct timezone
34. Basic NTP configuration
35. Knowledge of using the pool.ntp.org service
36. Awareness of the ntpq command

The following is a partial list of the used files, terms and utilities: /usr/share/zoneinfo, /etc/timezone, /etc/localtime, /etc/ntp.conf, date, hwclock, ntpd, ntpdate, and pool.ntp.org

109.2 Basic network configuration [this entire objective is described in chapter 11, with the exception of the /etc/nsswitch.conf file that is explained in this chapter]

The following is a partial list of the used files, terms and utilities: /etc/nsswitch.conf

109.3 Basic network troubleshooting [this entire objective is described in chapter 11, with the exception of the host and dig commands that are explained in this chapter]

59. Debug problems associated with the network configuration

The following is a partial list of the used files, terms and utilities: host, dig

109.4 Configure client side DNS [this entire objective is described in this chapter]

60. Query remote DNS servers
61. Configure local name resolution and use remote DNS servers
62. Modify the order in which name resolution is done
The following is a partial list of the used files, terms and utilities: /etc/hosts, /etc/resolv.conf, /etc/nsswitch.conf, host, dig, and getent

L**inux** community is diversified in terms of the languages they speak and the cultural rulesets they use, and it is disseminated globally. Linux has been adapted over time to accommodate varying needs and requirements of this large and dispersed community of users and developers. Linux may be configured to use a specific language, a particular ruleset (date and time formats, number and currency formats, measurement units, etc.), and a precise time zone to provide regional working conditions. These settings may be set for all users on the system or individual users.

The Network Time Protocol service maintains the clock on the system and keeps it synchronized with a more accurate and reliable source of time. Providing accurate and uniform time for systems on the network allows time-sensitive applications to perform correctly and precisely. It also aids the logging service to capture and record messages and alerts perfectly. A Linux system (virtual or physical) obtains time from the computer's hardware clock. They both can be adjusted if either of the two is out of sync.

Domain Name System is the standard network service used for hostname lookups on the Internet as well as on local and corporate networks. DNS clients use this service to communicate with remote systems. There are several lookup programs that use DNS to obtain information.

Internationalization and Localization

As we know, Linux has its source code available at no cost to the worldwide community of developers and users for use, modification, repackaging, and redistribution. At the same time, it is one of the most widely deployed and used operating system in homes and data centers. This developer and user community is scattered geographically, speak or understand a variety of languages containing different *character sets* (abbreviated as *charsets*), and use diverse currencies, date/time formats, measurement units, paper sizes, number formats, etc. In order to accommodate their needs and requirements, Linux has been adapted to support various languages, cultural rules, and time zones. This adaptation is referred to as *Internationalization* and it is commonly abbreviated as the numeronym *i18n* (the first and the last letter of the word with a count of the rest of the letters in between) due to the word's length. The support for internationalization is particularly important for European and East Asian communities that use a multitude of character sets in their languages.

Localization, on the other hand, is the ability of Linux to adapt itself to a specific language, cultural requirement (collectively known as *locale*), and time zone. Currently, Linux offers locale and time zone support for a number of different languages, cultures, and time zones. We choose the ones appropriate for our need during Linux installation. The term localization is abbreviated as *L10n*— the first and the last letter of the word with a count of the remaining letters in between.

Character Set and Character Encoding

A number of differences must be handled between locales during text conversion, translation, and screen presentation. An industry-standard character encoding system called the *Unicode Standard* was designed to handle the variances and provide a consistent mapping for every character to a unique number regardless of the language, program, or platform the character belongs to or is associated with. This resulted in an exclusive, integrated, and universal representation of each character as well as overcoming the issues of conflicts and concurrences that existed in various legacy encoding schemes. The Unicode Standard contains code mappings, character database, and all relevant definitions and details, and it is updated regularly. Most vendors have adopted this global standard in their software products and operating systems including Linux. One major benefit of using Unicode is the ability to create and use multilingual, multinational, and multiregional websites, software products, and operating systems.

The support for Unicode character set is implemented in software and operating systems through various *character encoding* schemes, most popular of which are *UTF-8* and *UTF-16* (8-bit and 16-bit *Unicode Transformation Format*). Other regional encoding mechanisms, such as Shift-JIS used in Japan, Big5 used in China, and variants of ISO 8859 used in Europe, the Middle East, and North Africa also use Unicode.

UTF-8 is the default character encoding scheme employed in popular Linux distributions for text transformation based on the Unicode standard. It is capable of encoding all Unicode characters, and provides backward compatibility with the ASCII character set that comprises of 128 characters and uses eight bits for each character representation. For non-ASCII characters, UTF-8 uses 16, 24, or 32 bits for encoding. UTF-8 is the preferred encoding mechanism employed for websites and email programs.

Displaying Locale Information

The global locale setting is selected at the time of Linux installation, and it is stored in the LANG environment variable. This value may be viewed with the *echo* command as follows:

```
[user1@centos511 ~]$ echo $LANG
en_US.UTF-8
```

The output indicates that the system is set to use the US English as the native language with UTF-8 character encoding. The value stored in the LANG variable plays an important role in testing or debugging a script or program during development or execution. This variable may be modified by individual programmers or administrators as appropriate. The new global value is reflected in the locale-specific environment variables, also called *locale categories*, as well.

Another command called *locale* located in the */usr/bin* directory can be used to view the current value of LANG as well as associated variables that govern the user environment:

```
[user1@centos511 ~]$ locale
LANG=en_US.UTF-8
LC_CTYPE="en_US.UTF-8"
LC_NUMERIC="en_US.UTF-8"
LC_TIME="en_US.UTF-8"
LC_COLLATE="en_US.UTF-8"
LC_MONETARY="en_US.UTF-8"
LC_MESSAGES="en_US.UTF-8"
LC_PAPER="en_US.UTF-8"
LC_NAME="en_US.UTF-8"
LC_ADDRESS="en_US.UTF-8"
LC_TELEPHONE="en_US.UTF-8"
LC_MEASUREMENT="en_US.UTF-8"
LC_IDENTIFICATION="en_US.UTF-8"
LC_ALL=
```

The *locale* command displays the current LANG variable and sub-ordinate categories prefixed with LC_. Table 12-1 describes the LC_* environment variables from the previous output.

LC_ Variable	Description
LC_CTYPE	Defines the character type and case conversion
LC_NUMERIC	Sets non-monetary numbering formats, including the thousands separator
LC_TIME	Governs date and time formats, such as YYYY-MM-DD, MM-DD-YYYY, 12-hour clock, and 24-hour clock
LC_COLLATE	Identifies collation rules for sorting and regular expressions
LC_MONETARY	Defines currency formats, including the currency sign and its position, and the thousands separator
LC_MESSAGES	Sets the language to use to write messages and their responses
LC_PAPER	Governs the paper size to use, such as A4 and letter
LC_NAME	Defines how to address a person, such as Mr. and Mrs.
LC_ADDRESS	Defines the format for location addressing
LC_TELEPHONE	Sets the formatting used in telephone numbers such as (123) 456 7890 and 123-456-7890
LC_MEASUREMENT	Governs measurement units such as those for the Metric and US systems
LC_IDENTIFICATION	Describes the metadata for the default locale
LC_ALL	Global locale variable. If set, it will override the values of LANG as well as all LC_* environment variables. This is primarily used in testing or diagnostics. By default, the value is empty.

Table 12-1 LC Variables

The *locale* command has the -a and -m switches that may be used to display the list of all available locales and character mappings. Try the command with these options and observe the output. Add the -v option with -a to view more detailed output. Before you are able to modify the locale or mapping to a new value, you need to ensure that it is listed in the output of the above commands.

There are two other interesting options available with the *locale* command that you may use for enhanced readability. These options are -c and -k, and they instruct the command to show the values of all available keywords within a category and add a keyword name with each value, respectively. Here is what the command will produce when executed with no option, and with -k, -c, and -ck options:

```
[user1@centos511 ~]$ locale LC_MEASUREMENT
2
UTF-8
[user1@centos511 ~]$ locale LC_MEASUREMENT -k
measurement=2
measurement-codeset="UTF-8"
[user1@centos511 ~]$ locale LC_MEASUREMENT -c
LC_MEASUREMENT
2
UTF-8
```

```
[user1@centos511 ~]$ locale LC_MEASUREMENT -kc
LC_MEASUREMENT
measurement=2
measurement-codeset="UTF-8"
```

The first output displays the values for the specified category (LC_MEASUREMENT), the second one associates a keyword name for each value, the third output excludes the keyword names but adds the category name at the beginning, and the fourth result is a combination of the last two.

Modifying System-Wide Locale

By default, the LANG variable is set to en_US.UTF-8 on our three systems and stored in various files depending on the distribution and version. Here are the file names and their locations along with default contents:

```
[user1@centos73 ~]$ cat /etc/locale.conf
LANG="en_US.UTF-8"
[user1@centos511 ~]$ cat /etc/sysconfig/i18n
LANG="en_US.UTF-8"
SYSFONT="latarcyrheb-sun16"
[user1@ubuntu14 ~]$ cat /etc/default/locale
LANG=en_US.UTF-8
```

We may change this setting to a different value such as en_CA for all users on the system. Simply edit this file and replace the value. You will need to log off and log back in to experience the effects.

On Debian and clones, you can also run the *update-locale* command to change this setting directly in the */etc/default/locale* file without making a manual modification. This is how you would do it to alter the value to C.UTF-8:

```
[user1@ubuntu14 ~]$ sudo update-locale LANG=C.UTF-8 LANGUAGE
```

On systemd-based systems, you can use the *localectl* command with status, list-locales, and set-locale options to examine the current locale and keyboard mapping, list available locales, and modify the locale setting, in addition to the *locale* command. Here are examples on how to use this command with the three options:

```
[user1@centos73 ~]$ localectl status
    System Locale: LANG=en_US.UTF-8
        VC Keymap: us
       X11 Layout: us
[user1@centos73 ~]$ localectl list-locales
[root@centos73 ~]# localectl set-locale LANG=en_CA.UTF-8
```

The list-locales option is equivalent to running *locale -a*. The output is useful in determining the current locale prior to setting it to a new value with the set-locale option, which directs the command to make a direct change in the */etc/locale.conf* file.

Modifying Per-User Locale

Individual users can modify their *.bash_profile* or *.bashrc* file, whichever is applicable, in their home directories and define the LANG variable with a value of their preference. In addition, they can also set an individual variable (category) explicitly. For instance, they can add **export LC_TELEPHONE=en_GB.UTF-8** to their profile or run it at the command prompt to use the British telephone number format.

Converting Text from One Character Encoding to Another

It is possible to convert text entered in one encoding into another. Linux provides the *iconv* command for the purpose. Some key options available with this tool are -l to display the list of all known charset encodings, -f to specify the source encoding, and -t to stipulate the desired one. Here is what you would see when you run this command with the -l option:

```
[user1@centos511 ~]$ iconv -l
```
The following list contain all the coded character sets known. This does not necessarily mean that all combinations of these names can be used for the FROM and TO command line parameters. One coded character set can be listed with several different names (aliases).

437, 500, 500V1, 850, 851, 852, 855, 856, 857, 860, 861, 862, 863, 864, 865, 866, 866NAV, 869, 874, 904, 1026, 1046, 1047, 8859_1, 8859_2, 8859_3, 8859_4, 8859_5, 8859_6, 8859_7, 8859_8, 8859_9, 10646-1:1993, 10646-1:1993/UCS4, ANSI_X3.4-1968, ANSI_X3.4-1986, ANSI_X3.4, ANSI_X3.110-1983, ANSI_X3.110, ARABIC, ARABIC7, ARMSCII-8, ASCII, ASMO-708, ASMO_449, BALTIC, BIG-5, BIG-FIVE, BIG5-HKSCS, BIG5, BIG5HKSCS, BIGFIVE, BS_4730, CA, CN-BIG5, CN-GB, ...

The output shows all encodings available on the system. Now, for instance, if you wish to convert the string 421$#@ stored in a file called *testencode* into Japanese EBCDIC encoding, run the following at the command prompt:

```
[user1@centos511 ~]$ iconv ~/testencode -t EBCDIC-JP-E
```

You may redirect the output of the above command to a file by specifying a name preceded by the > sign or the -o option. For instance:

```
[user1@centos511 ~]$ iconv ~/testencode -t EBCDIC-JP-E -o iconv.out
```

You can view the content of the output file using *cat*, *less*, *more*, *view*, etc.

Displaying Time Zone Information

As Linux is used around the world, the requirement to support local time zones is obvious. As part of internationalization, support for various time zones is added to the operating system in order to allow users to make time adjustments based on their geography.

The default time zone in Linux is selected and configured at the time of installation and it is typically based on the geographic location the system is intended to operate at or for. The system maintains a number of files under */usr/share/zoneinfo/* to store time zone information for various cities, countries, and regions. For instance, the file *America/Toronto* in this directory contains the time zone information that applies to the city of Toronto in Canada and the sub-directory *Pacific* stores time zone files for countries and islands in the Pacific Rim.

The current time zone may be determined by issuing the *date* and *hwclock* handy tools. They show the date and time on the system as well. Here are sample outputs from the two commands:

Wed Apr 19 21:02:53 **EDT** 2017
Wed 19 Apr 2017 09:12:42 PM **EDT** -0.985325 seconds

On Linux systems, there is a file called *localtime* under */etc/* that is either a symlink to the actual time zone file under */usr/share/zoneinfo/* or a copy of it. This file is referenced by the *date*, *hwclock*, and other commands to determine the current time zone on the system. The contents of this file are illegible though. On *centos511* and *ubuntu14*, the */etc/sysconfig/clock* and */etc/timezone* files, respectively, store the current time zone value in readable format. These files are automatically updated when the time zone value is altered.

Setting System-Wide Time Zone

There are different tools available in Linux for modifying the time zone on the system depending on the distribution and version. These tools include the *timeconfig* (*centos511*) and *dpkg-reconfigure* (*ubuntu14*) text-interfaced programs and the *timedatectl* command line program on *centos73*. The following show the interfaces for the first two, the third command is discussed later in this subsection.

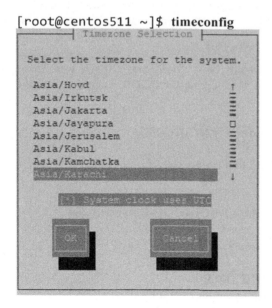

```
[root@ubuntu14 ~]$ sudo dpkg-reconfigure tzdata
```

```
 Package configuration

 lqqqqqqqqqqqqqqqqqqqqqqqqqu Configuring tzdata tqqqqqqqqqqqqqqqqqqqqqqqqqqk
 x Please select the geographic area in which you live. Subsequent        x
 x configuration questions will narrow this down by presenting a list of  x
 x cities, representing the time zones in which they are located.         x
 x                                                                        x
 x Geographic area:                                                       x
 x                                                                        x
 x                         Africa                                         x
 x                         America                 a                      x
 x                         Antarctica                                     x
 x                         Australia               a                      x
 x                         Arctic Ocean            a                      x
 x                         Asia                    a                      x
 x                         Atlantic Ocean                                 x
 x                                                                        x
 x                                                                        x
 x                                                                        x
 x            <Ok>                             <Cancel>                    x
 x                                                                        x
```

You have to scroll up or down the list to choose the desired continent and city. Press the TAB key to go to the OK button and press Enter to make the selection and exit out of the programs. Both tools also update their respective */etc/sysconfig/clock* and */etc/timezone* files.

There is another command called tzconfig on Debian and derivatives; however, it has been deprecated and users need to use "dpkg-reconfigure tzdata" as a replacement.

On systems running systemd, a different command called *timedatectl* is available for time zone management. This tool allows us to view available time zones (list-timezones option) and modify the time zone (set-timezone option). Here is how we would list time zones with this command:

```
[root@centos73 ~]# timedatectl list-timezones
```

You can *grep* for a time zone name to save time in browsing through the entire list to find a desired value. Use "**timedatectl list-timezones | grep Moncton**", for example, to see whether an entry exists for that city. If a match is found and you want to change the current time zone to it, issue the command as follows:

```
[root@centos73 ~]# timedatectl set-timezone America/Moncton
```

This command will create/update the symlink */etc/localtime* to point to */usr/share/zoneinfo/America/Moncton* file:

lrwxrwxrwx. 1 root root 37 Apr 20 15:01 /etc/localtime -> ../usr/share/zoneinfo/America/Moncton

You can validate the change by executing the *timedatectl*, *date*, or *hwclock* command.

Without invoking any of the tools discussed above, you can simply remove the /etc/localtime file and create a soft link pointing to the actual time zone file under /usr/share/zoneinfo/ that you want to set the time zone as. Alternatively, you can copy the desired time zone file from /usr/share/zoneinfo/ and overwrite /etc/localtime.

Setting Per-User Time Zone

Linux provides the *tzselect* command to identify a time zone value that can be used in an individual user's ~/.*bash_profile* or ~/.*profile* file with the TZ environment variable. This practice is only required if we want to set a different time zone for an individual user. This command prompts to enter a continent or ocean, country, and an optional city or time zone and then displays a suitable value to be used with TZ.

On systems running systemd, you can also use the "timedatectl list-timezones", as described in the previous subsection, to spot a particular time zone value for use with TZ.

Let's examine the current setting of TZ for *user1* with the *echo* command on *centos511*, and see what it is currently set to:

```
[user1@centos511 ~]$ echo $TZ
```

The output produced nothing, which implies that TZ is not currently set for this user.

Now, let's run *tzselect* as *user1* and determine what value we should use with TZ for the country Panama in the continent Americas. The output is truncated where necessary. We choose options 2 and 35, and then 1 for confirmation.

```
[user1@centos511 ~]$ tzselect
Please identify a location so that time zone rules can be set correctly.
Please select a continent or ocean.
 1) Africa
 2) Americas
. . . . . . . .
#? 2
Please select a country.
. . . . . . . .
 8) Bolivia          35) Panama
. . . . . . . .
#? 35
The following information has been given:
     Panama
Therefore TZ='America/Panama' will be used.
Local time is now:     Thu Apr 20 10:26:07 EST 2017.
Universal Time is now:  Thu Apr 20 15:26:07 UTC 2017.
Is the above information OK?
 1) Yes
 2) No
#? 1
You can make this change permanent for yourself by appending the line
     TZ='America/Panama'; export TZ
to the file '.profile' in your home directory; then log out and log in again.
. . . . . . . .
```

Based on the bolded comments at the bottom of the output, you need to edit your *.bash_profile* or *.profile*, whichever is applicable, in your home directory and define TZ in it as indicated. You will need to log off and log back in for the new value to take effect. Run **echo $TZ** for confirmation after logging back in.

The Network Time Protocol

Network Time Protocol (NTP) is a networking protocol for synchronizing the system clock with remote timeservers for accuracy and reliability. This protocol has been in use with tens of millions of computing devices employing it to obtain time from tens of thousands of NTP servers deployed across the globe. When using this protocol, time accuracies are typically within a millisecond. Having precise time on networked systems allows time-sensitive applications, such as logging and monitoring software, backup and scheduling tools, financial and billing systems, authentication and email applications, and file and storage sharing protocols, to function with precision.

NTP sends a stream of messages to configured NTP servers and binds itself to the one with least amount of delay in its responses, most accurate, and may or may not be the closest distance-wise. The client system maintains a drift in time in a file and references this file for gradual drop in inaccuracy.

The NTP server program is called *ntpd* and it uses the UDP protocol over well-known port 123. If enabled, this daemon program starts at system boot and continuously operates to keep the system clock in sync with a more accurate source of time. This daemon can be started manually with **systemctl start ntpd** on systems running systemd and with **service ntpd start** on SysVinit systems (replace start with stop, restart, reload, and status as appropriate).

In order to understand NTP, a discussion of its components and roles is imperative. A subsequent look at the required software, configuration file, and client configuration and testing follows.

Time Sources

A *time source* is any device that acts as a provider of time to other devices. The most precise sources of time are the atomic clocks. They use *Universal Time, Coordinated* (UTC) for time accuracy. They produce radio signals that radio clocks use for time propagation to computer servers and other devices that require accuracy in time. When choosing a time source for a network, preference should be given to the one that takes the least amount of time to respond. This server may or may not be physically closest.

The common sources of time employed on computer networks are the local system clock, an Internet-based public timeserver, and a radio clock.

The local system clock can be used as a provider of time. This requires the maintenance of correct time on the server either manually or automatically via *cron*. Keep in mind, however, that this server has no way of synchronizing itself with a more reliable and precise external time source. Therefore, using the local system clock as a timeserver is the least recommended option.

Several public timeservers (visit *www.ntp.org* for a list) are available over the Internet for the provision of time on the network. These timeservers are typically operated by government agencies, research organizations, large software vendors, and universities around the world. One of the systems on the local network is identified and configured to obtain time from one or more of the public timeservers. This option is preferred over the use of the local system clock. The official *ntp.org* site also provides a common pool called *pool.ntp.org* for vendors and organizations to register their own NTP servers voluntarily for general public use. Examples include *centos.pool.ntp.org* and *ubuntu.pool.ntp.org* for Linux distribution-specific NTP pools and *ca.pool.ntp.org* and *oceania.pool.ntp.org* for country and continent/region-specific NTP pools. Under these sub-pools, the owners maintain multiple NTP servers with enumerated hostnames such as *0.centos.pool.ntp.org*, *1.centos.pool.ntp.org*, *2.centos.pool.ntp.org*, and so on. In many Linux distributions, these public pooled NTP servers are pre-defined in their NTP configuration file.

A radio clock is regarded as the perfect provider of time, as it receives time updates straight from an atomic clock. *Global Positioning System* (GPS), WWVB, and DCF77 are some popular radio clock methods. A direct use of signals from these sources requires connectivity of some hardware to the computer identified to act as an organizational or site-wide timeserver.

NTP Roles

From an NTP standpoint, a system can be configured to operate as a primary server, secondary server, peer, or client.

A *primary* server gets time from one of the time sources mentioned above, and provides time to secondary servers or clients, or both.

A *secondary* server receives time from a primary server and can be configured to provide time to a set of clients to offload the primary or for redundancy. The presence of a secondary server on the network is optional, though highly recommended.

A *peer* reciprocates time with an NTP server. All peers work at the same stratum level and all of them are considered equally reliable. Both primary and secondary servers can be peers of each other.

A *client* receives time from a primary or a secondary server and adjusts its clock accordingly.

NTP servers, peers, and clients can also be configured to operate in a broadcast mode (the polling mode is the default). In broadcast mode, a server broadcasts time over the network and a client binds with it. Both server and client must be configured in this mode in order for this setup to work.

Stratum Levels

As we know, there are different types of time sources available for us to synchronize the system clock with. These time sources are categorized hierarchically into several levels referred to as *stratum levels* based on their distance from the reference clocks (atomic, radio, and GPS). The reference clocks operate at stratum level 0 and are the most accurate provider of time with little to no delay. Besides stratum 0, there are fifteen additional levels that range from 1 to 15. Of these, servers operating at stratum 1 are considered perfect, as they get time updates directly from a stratum 0 device. See Figure 12-1 for a sample hierarchy.

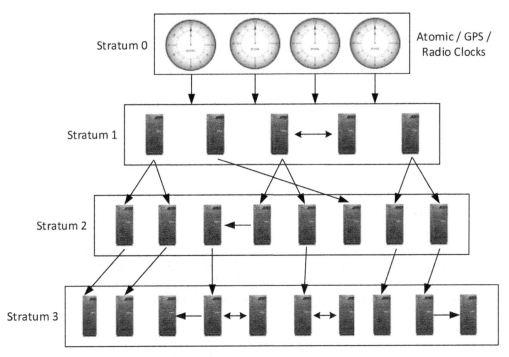

Figure 12-1 NTP Stratum Levels

A stratum 0 device cannot be used on the network directly. It is attached to a computer, which is then configured to operate at stratum 1. Servers functioning at stratum 1 are called *timeservers* (or *primary timeservers*) and they can be set up to deliver time to stratum 2 servers. Similarly, a stratum 3 server can be configured to synchronize its time with a stratum 2 server and deliver time to the next lower level server, and so on. Servers sharing the same stratum can be configured as peers to exchange time updates with each other.

> If a secondary server is also configured to get time from a stratum 1 server directly, it will act as a peer to the primary server.

There are a number of public NTP servers available for free to synchronize the system time with. They normally operate at higher stratum levels such as 2 and 3.

NTP Packages and Utilities

In order for us to be able to configure and use NTP, we have to ensure that software packages—ntp and ntpdate—are installed on the system. You can use the *rpm* or the *dpkg* command, as appropriate, to examine their installation state:

```
[user1@centos73 ~]$ rpm -qa | grep ^ntp
ntp-4.2.6p5-25.el7.centos.x86_64
ntpdate-4.2.6p5-25.el7.centos.x86_64
[user1@ubuntu14 ~]$ dpkg -l | grep ntp
ii  ntp  1:4.2.6.p5+dfsg-3ubuntu2.14.04.10  amd64  Network Time Protocol daemon and utility programs
ii  ntpdate  1:4.2.6.p5+dfsg-3ubuntu2.14.04.10  amd64  client for setting system time from NTP servers
```

The ntp package brings the core NTP server and client functionalities to the system including the */etc/ntp.conf* configuration file, the *ntpd* daemon process that must run on every participating NTP system, and the *ntpq* and *ntpstat* commands for querying and status checking.

If the packages are not already installed, run **yum install ntp ntpdate** or **apt-get install ntp ntpdate** as appropriate to load them.

The ntpdate package installs the *ntpdate* command line tool that gives us the ability to bring the system time immediately at par with the time on an NTP server. This command only works when the NTP service is down on the system.

NTP Configuration File

The key configuration file for NTP is *ntp.conf* located in the */etc* directory. This file is referenced by the NTP daemon at startup to determine the synchronization sources, operating modes, log file name and location, and other details. This file can be modified by hand to set directives based on the role the system is going to play. Some common directives used in this file along with real or mock values are provided below with an explanation in Table 12-2:

```
driftfile          /var/lib/ntp/drift
logfile            /var/log/ntp.log
server             0.centos.pool.ntp.org  iburst
server             1.centos.pool.ntp.org  iburst
server             2.centos.pool.ntp.org  iburst
server             3.centos.pool.ntp.org  iburst
server             127.127.1.0                       # local clock
peer
broadcast          192.168.1.255  autokey            # broadcast server
broadcastclient                                      # broadcast client
```

Table 12-2 describes these directives.

Directive	Description
driftfile	Indicates the location of the driftfile (default is /var/lib/ntp/drift). This file is used by the ntpd daemon for maintaining local system clock accuracy.
logfile	Sets the location of the log file
server	Defines the hostname or IP address of the timeserver. There are four default public timeserver entries: 0, 1, 2, and 3 on our CentOS and Ubuntu systems in centos.pool.ntp.org and ubuntu.pool.ntp.org vendor-specific sub-pools. The server directive with IP 127.127.1.0 specifies the use of the local system clock as the provider of time.
peer	Identifies the hostname or IP address of the peer
broadcast	Specifies the hostname or IP address of the broadcasting timeserver. This option is preferred in an environment with a large number of NTP clients.
broadcastclient	The presence of this directive sets the system as a broadcast client of a broadcast NTP server

Table 12-2 Description of ntp.conf Directives

There are plenty of additional directives and options that may be defined in this file. Use **man 5 ntp.conf** for details.

Exercise 12-1: Configure NTP Client

By default, the NTP software comes pre-configured for use as an NTP client with four public timeserver entries defined in the configuration file. In this exercise, you will simply activate the NTP service without making any changes to the default configuration and validate the binding and operation. The procedure in this exercise stipulates the commands to be executed on our three lab systems. Use the commands that apply to your OS distribution and version. If no hostname follows a command, it applies to all three systems. Make sure that you run the commands directly as the *root* user or with sudo access.

1. Ensure that pre-configured public timeserver entries are present in the */etc/ntp.conf* file by issuing **grep ^server /etc/ntp.conf**.
2. Enable the *ntpd* daemon to autostart at reboots using **systemctl enable ntpd** (*centos73*), **chkconfig ntpd on** (*centos511*), or **sudo update-rc.d ntp enable** (*ubuntu14*).
3. Start the NTP service using **systemctl start ntpd** (*centos73*), **service ntpd start** (*centos511*), or **sudo service ntp start** (*ubuntu14*).
4. Examine the NTP service status using **systemctl status ntpd** (*centos73*), **service ntpd status** (*centos511*), or **sudo service ntp status** (*ubuntu14*).
5. Inspect whether the system has established binding to an NTP server using **ntpq -p**:

remote	refid	st	t	when	poll	reach	delay	offset	jitter
+mail.stygium.ne	209.51.161.238	2	u	50	64	377	14.221	-29.571	8.492
+bitdonut.co	128.105.39.11	3	u	51	64	377	16.036	-20.181	15.913
ellen.linuxgene	142.3.100.2	2	u	2	64	1	16.452	0.881	4.770
*ntp3.torix.ca	.PPS.	1	u	47	64	377	18.853	-26.535	10.077

The output indicates that the *ntpd* daemon has established binding with an NTP server *ntp3.torix.ca*, which is indicated by the asterisk (*) character beside it. Details for the columns are available in the next subsection.

6. Check the binding summary with **ntpstat** (*centos73* and *centos511*) or **sudo ntptime** (*ubuntu14*):

```
[root@centos73 ~]# ntpstat
synchronised to NTP server (67.215.197.149) at stratum 3
   time correct to within 61 ms
   polling server every 128 s
```

The output will vary on the three systems.

Querying NTP Servers

We used the *ntpq* tool in the previous exercise to query the status of server association. This command sends out requests to and receives responses from NTP servers, and reports the output on the screen. This utility may also be run interactively.

Run this tool with the -p (print) option to list NTP servers known to the system along with details:

---

remote	refid	st	t	when	poll	reach	delay	offset	jitter
+ntp-1.asininete	128.252.19.1	2	u	681	1024	377	49.962	0.396	1.125
c1110364-13198.	206.108.0.133	2	u	603	1024	377	17.652	-7419.5	5606.63
ns2.dargalsolut	.INIT.	16	u	-	1024	0	0.000	0.000	0.000
*ks4001083.ip-19	192.93.2.20	2	u	774	1024	377	27.667	2.601	1.366
192.168.0.255	.BCST.	16	u	-	64	0	0.000	0.000	0.000

The report shows IP addresses or hostnames of the NTP servers that were contacted. The plus (+) sign besides an entry symbolizes that the NTP server was considered for sync and the asterisk (*) symbol indicates the current selection. You might also see a number (#) or a dash (–) character or nothing at all. These would mean that the NTP server was selected for binding, but the distance exceeded the maximum; not considered for binding; and rejected due to a high stratum level or failed sanity checks.

Other interesting columns in the report indicate a stratum level (16 designates an invalid stratum) (st), the last time (in seconds) a response was received from the server (when), polling interval (default is 64 seconds) (poll), number of successful attempts (000: no recent probes were answered; 377: all recent probes were answered) to reach the server (reach), length of time (in milliseconds) for a returned response (delay), and the current time difference (in milliseconds) between the server and the local clock (offset).

Updating System Clock Instantly

At times, it is necessary to synchronize the local system clock with an NTP server instantaneously. The ntpdate software package provides the *ntpdate* utility to fulfill this purpose. It is employed to accomplish a one-time sync only. This command requires that the NTP service must not be running on the local system. It accepts the hostname or IP address of an NTP server as an argument to synchronize time with.

Assuming the NTP service is stopped with **systemctl stop ntpd** (*centos73*), **service ntpd stop** (*centos511*), or **sudo service ntp stop** (*ubuntu14*), run **ntpdate 2.centos.pool.ntp.org** on any of the systems. The output will be something similar to the following:

    25 Apr 10:02:36 ntpdate[6817]: step time server 206.108.0.133 offset 0.008547 sec

Restart the service after executing *ntpdate* so that the local clock continues to receive time updates.

The *ntpdate* command is deprecated in the latest mainline Linux distribution versions in favor of **ntpd -q** (query). With this option, the *ntpd* command queries a timeserver, adjusts the clock, and then quits. Try running it as highlighted and observe the output. Other options such as -g and -x are also available. Consult the manual pages for details.

Displaying and Setting System Date and Time

System date and time can be manually adjusted with native Linux tools if the system has no access to an external NTP server. The *timedatectl* command is available on *centos73* and *ubuntu14*, which can be used to display and set the system date and time. We used this tool earlier in this chapter to display the current system date, time, and time zone, and to modify the time zone. This command outputs this information when executed without an option. It shows the local time, Universal time (formerly called GMT—*Greenwich Mean Time*), RTC (*real-time clock*, a battery-backed hardware clock located on the system board), and time zone. It also shows information related to the NTP and DST (*daylight saving time*). Let's look at how to modify the date and time with this command on *centos73*.

To modify the current date to August 12, 2017:

    [root@centos73 ~]# **timedatectl set-time 2017-08-12**

To change the time to 11:00 a.m.:

    [root@centos73 ~]# **timedatectl set-time 11:00**

To display the date and time after the above changes:

    [root@centos73 ~]# **timedatectl**
        Local time: Fri 2017-08-11 10:01:28 EDT
    Universal time: Fri 2017-08-11 14:01:28 UTC
          RTC time: Fri 2017-08-11 14:01:28
          Timezone: America/Toronto (EDT, -0400)
    . . . .

Alternatively, we can use the *date* command to view or modify the system date and time. This command can be used on older as well as the newest Linux distributions.

To view current date and time:

    [root@centos73 ~]# **date**

To change the system date and time to April 25, 2017 10:43 a.m.:

    [root@centos73 ~]# **date --set "2017-04-25 10:43:00"**
    Tue Apr 25 10:43:00 EDT 2017

Querying and Setting the Hardware Clock

We have seen how to view and set the system time locally and remotely. Our computer systems have a battery-operated clock referred to as the *real-time clock* (RTC) or the *hardware clock* that feeds time to the operating system(s) running on the computer. Typically, the operating system time is in harmony with this hardware clock; however, we can manually synchronize either clock with the other using the *hwclock* command. This command can be used to display date and time as well.

    [root@centos73 ~]# **hwclock**
    Sat 22 Apr 2017 10:56:29 AM EDT -0.491962 seconds

To alter the system date and time to Saturday December 30, 2017 UTC at 8:00 a.m., run the command as follows:

    [root@centos73 ~]# **hwclock --set --date "Sat Dec 30 08:00:00 UTC 2017"**

Verify the adjustment with the **hwclock** or **timedatectl | grep RTC** as appropriate.

DNS and Name Resolution

Domain Name System (DNS) is an inverted tree-like structure employed on the Internet and private networks (including home and corporate networks) as the de facto standard for resolving hostnames to their numerical IP addresses. DNS is platform-independent with support integrated in every operating system. DNS is also referred to as BIND, *Berkeley Internet Name Domain*, which is an implementation of DNS, and it has been the most popular DNS application in use. *Name resolution* is the technique that uses DNS/BIND for hostname lookups.

In order to understand DNS, a brief discussion of its components and roles is imperative. A subsequent look at the client-side configuration files and commands follows, along with examples on how to use the tools for name resolution.

DNS Name Space and Domains

The DNS *name space* is a hierarchical organization of all the domains on the Internet. The root of the name space is represented by a period. The hierarchy right below the root denotes the *top-level domains* (TLDs) with names such as .com, .net, .edu, .org, .gov, .ca, and .de. A DNS *domain* is a collection of one or more systems. Sub-domains fall under their parent domains and are separated by a period. For example, centos.org is a second-level sub-domain that falls under .org and wiki.centos.org is a third-level sub-domain that falls under centos.org.

Figure 12-2 exhibits a sample hierarchy of the name space, showing the top three domain levels.

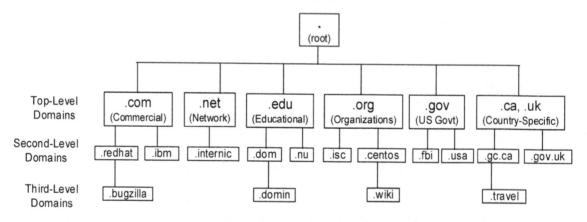

Figure 12-2 DNS Hierarchy

At the deepest level of the hierarchy are the *leaves* (systems, nodes, or any device with an IP address) of the name space. For example, a network switch *net01* in *.travel.gc.ca* sub-domain will be known as *net01.travel.gc.ca*. If a period is added to the end of this name to look like *net01.travel.gc.ca.*, it will be referred to as the *Fully Qualified Domain Name* (FQDN) for *net01*.

DNS Roles

From a DNS perspective, a system can be configured to operate as a primary server, secondary server, or client. A DNS server is also referred to as a *nameserver*.

A *primary* (a.k.a. *master*) *server* is responsible for its domain (or sub-domain). It maintains a master database of all the hostnames and their associated IP addresses that are included in that domain. Any changes in the database is done on this server. Each domain must have one primary server with one or more optional *secondary* (a.k.a. *slave*) servers for load balancing and redundancy. A secondary server also stores an updated copy of the master database and it continues to provide name resolution service in the event the primary server becomes unavailable.

A *DNS client* queries nameservers for name resolution. Every system with access to the Internet or other external network will have the DNS client functionality configured and operational. Setting up DNS client on Linux involves only two text files. These files are discussed in the next two subsections.

Understanding Resolver Configuration File

The *resolv.conf* file under */etc/* is the DNS resolver configuration file where information to support hostname lookups is defined. This file may be edited manually with a text editor. It is referenced by resolver utilities to obtain necessary information to construct and transmit queries. There are three key directives set in this file—domain, nameserver, and search—and they are described in Table 12-3.

Directive	Description
domain	Identifies the default domain name to be searched for queries
nameserver	Declares up to three DNS server IP addresses to be queried one at a time in the order in which they are listed. Nameserver entries may be defined as separate line items with the directive or on a single line.
search	Specifies up to six domain names, of which the first must be the local domain. No need to define the "domain" directive if this directive is used.

Table 12-3 The Resolver Configuration File

A sample entry showing the syntax is provided below for reference:

```
domain      example.com
search      example.net  example.org  example.edu  example.gov
nameserver  191.11.11.23  8.8.8.8  8.8.4.4
```

A variation of the above is:

```
domain      example.com
search      example.net  example.org  example.edu  example.gov
nameserver  191.11.11.23
nameserver  8.8.8.8
nameserver  8.8.4.4
```

Currently, we only have the "nameserver 192.168.0.1" entry defined in our */etc/resolv.conf* file on *centos73* and *centos511*, and in the */etc/network/interfaces* file on *ubuntu14*.

Viewing and Adjusting Name Resolution Sources and Order

The *nsswitch.conf* file under */etc/* directs the lookup utilities to the correct source to get hostname information from. In the presence of multiple sources, this file also identifies the order in which to consult them and an action to be taken next. There are four keywords—success, notfound, unavail, and tryagain—that oversee this behavior, and are described along with default actions in Table 12-4.

Keyword	Meaning	Default Action
success	Information found in source and provided to the requester	return (do not try the next source)
notfound	Information not found in source	continue (try the next source)
unavail	Source down or not responding; service disabled or not configured	continue (try the next source)
tryagain	Source busy, retry later	continue (try the next source)

Table 12-4 Name Service Source and Order Determination

The following example entry shows the syntax of the relevant entry from the *nsswitch.conf* file. It shows two sources for name resolution: files (*/etc/hosts*) and DNS (the */etc/resolv.conf* file).

    hosts: files dns

Based on the default behavior, the search will terminate if the requested information is found in the *hosts* table. However, we can alter this behavior and instruct the lookup programs to return if the requested information is not found there. The modified entry will look like:

    hosts: files [notfound=return] dns

This altered entry will ignore the DNS.

 See Chapter 11 "Understanding Networking and Administering Network Interfaces" for details on /etc/hosts file.

Once the */etc/resolv.conf* and */etc/nsswitch.conf* files are configured appropriately, we can use the client tools for lookups. Common query tools include *dig, host, nslookup,* and *getent,* and are elaborated in the following subsections.

Performing Name Resolution with dig

dig (*domain information groper*) is a DNS lookup utility. It queries the nameserver specified at the command line or consults the *resolv.conf* file to determine the nameservers to be queried. This tool may be used to troubleshoot DNS issues due to its flexibility and verbosity. The following shows a few usage examples.

To get the IP for *ubuntu.com* using the nameserver listed in the *resolv.conf* file:

```
[user1@centos73 ~]$ dig ubuntu.com

. . . . . . . .
;; ANSWER SECTION:
ubuntu.com.            505    IN    A    91.189.94.40
. . . . . . . .
;; Query time: 25 msec
;; SERVER: 192.168.0.1#53(192.168.0.1)
;; WHEN: Wed Apr 26 10:28:42 EDT 2017
;; MSG SIZE  rcvd: 205
```

The output shows the total time (25 milliseconds) it took to get the result, the IP address (91.189.94.40) of ubuntu.com, the nameserver IP (192.168.0.1) used for the query, the DNS port number (53), and other information.

To perform a reverse lookup on the IP, use the -x option with the command:

```
[user1@centos73 ~]$  dig -x 91.189.94.40

. . . . . . . .
;; ANSWER SECTION:
40.94.189.91.in-addr.arpa. 3600 IN     PTR     ovinnik.canonical.com.

. . . . . . . .
```

Reference the command's manual pages for details.

Performing Name Resolution with host

host is an elementary DNS lookup utility that works on the same principles as the *dig* command in terms of nameserver determination. This tool produces lesser data in the output by default; however, you can add the -a or -v option for verbosity. Here are a few examples on its usage.

To perform a lookup on *redhat.com*:

```
[user1@centos73 ~]$  host redhat.com
redhat.com has address 209.132.183.105
redhat.com mail is handled by 5 mx1.redhat.com.
redhat.com mail is handled by 10 mx2.redhat.com.
```

To perform a reverse lookup on the IP of *redhat.com*:

```
[user1@centos73 ~]$  host 209.132.183.105
105.183.132.209.in-addr.arpa domain name pointer redirect.redhat.com.
```

Refer to the command's manual pages for details.

Performing Name Resolution with nslookup

nslookup queries the nameservers listed in the *resolv.conf* file or specified at the command line. The following shows a few usage examples.

To get the IP for *redhat.com* using nameserver 8.8.8.8 instead of the nameserver defined in */etc/resolv.conf*:

```
[user1@centos73 ~]$ nslookup redhat.com 8.8.8.8
Server:       8.8.8.8
Address:      8.8.8.8#53
Non-authoritative answer:
Name:         redhat.com
Address:      209.132.183.105
```

To perform a reverse lookup on the IP address of *redhat.com* using the default nameserver:

```
[user1@centos73 ~]$ nslookup 209.132.183.105
Server:        192.168.0.1
Address:       192.168.0.1#53
Non-authoritative answer:
105.183.132.209.in-addr.arpa   name = redirect.redhat.com.
. . . . . . . .
```

Consult the command's manual pages on how to use it in interactive mode.

Performing Name Resolution with getent

The *getent* (*get entries*) command is a rudimentary tool that can be employed to fetch matching entries from the databases defined in the */etc/nsswitch.conf* file. This command reads the corresponding database and displays the line entry matching the specified key. For instance, if you want to check whether a match for *centos.org* exists in the *hosts* table or in DNS, run this command as follows:

```
[user1@centos73 ~]$ getent hosts centos.org
85.12.30.226   centos.org
```

Check the command's manual pages for additional usages.

Chapter Summary

There were three major topics covered in this chapter: (1) internationalization and localization, (2) NTP, and (3) DNS.

One topic of discussion was internationalization, which reflects the diversity of Linux and its users, the purpose behind its presence in Linux, and how it was different from localization. We learned how to view locale and time zone settings and how to modify them to match system-wide and individual preferences.

Next, we discussed the Network Time Protocol service and described various sources for obtaining time, different roles that systems could play, and elaborated on the strata paradigm. We looked at packages and utilities available for performing NTP management tasks, and continued with an analysis of the NTP configuration file. We performed an exercise to strengthen the concepts and theory learned. Finally, we saw how to query NTP servers, update the system clock instantly, and set the system and hardware clocks.

We concluded the chapter with a deliberation of DNS and name resolution. We discussed the concepts and roles, and analyzed the resolver configuration file and the source/order determination file. We examined and used various client tools for hostname lookup.

Chapter Review at a Glance

The following presents a one-sentence review of each key topic discussed in this chapter:

- Internationalization (abbr. i18n) is the support included in Linux to adapt itself to any of the variety of supported regional environments (languages, cultural rulesets, and time zones).

- Localization (abbr. L10n) is the ability of Linux to adapt itself to a specific regional environment.

- Text in one character encoding can be converted into a different character encoding.

- NTP is a networking protocol to synchronize the system clock with a more reliable source of time.

- Depending on the requirement, a Linux system can be configured as a provider or receiver of time on the network.

- NTP strata categorize sources of time based on their proximity with a reference clock.

- The DNS service is used on large networks and the Internet to resolve hostnames to their IP addresses, and vice versa.

- A Linux system can be configured as a provider or user of the name resolution service.

- There are several name resolution tools available in Linux that may be used to perform client queries.

- Commands we learned in this chapter are: locale, update-locale, localectl, iconv, timeconfig, timedatectl, tzselect, tzconfig, ntpq, ntpstat, ntptime, ntpd, ntpdate, date, hwclock, dig, host, nslookup, and getent.

- Files and directories we discussed in this chapter are: /etc/locale.conf, /etc/sysconfig/i18n, /etc/default/locale, /usr/share/zoneinfo, /etc/localtime, /etc/sysconfig/clock, /etc/timezone, /etc/ntp.conf, /var/lib/ntp/drift, /var/log/ntp.log, /etc/resolv.conf, and /etc/nsswitch.conf.

Chapter 13

Managing User Interfaces, Desktops, and Printers

This chapter describes the following major topics:

➢ Overview of X Window System and X server
➢ View monitor settings
➢ Analyze X configuration file and configure and start X server
➢ Manage X font server start and stop
➢ Grasp display manager, desktop environment manager, and window manager terms
➢ Make basic changes and customization—change default display manager, modify greetings, turn display manager on or off, and customize LightDM interface
➢ Run X client applications over the network
➢ Review and comprehend available accessibility options—keyboard navigation, onscreen keyboard, screen readers, speech synthesizers, screen magnifiers, mouse cursors and gestures, and visual and audible alerts
➢ Modify accessibility options in desktop managers
➢ Understand CUPS concepts and its directory tree
➢ Know printer configuration types
➢ Determine available printer drivers and devices
➢ Configure local, remote, and network printers
➢ Use CUPS tools to administer printers—enable and disable a printer, accept or reject incoming print requests, check printer status, and remove a printer
➢ Employ available tools to work with print requests: submit, list, and remove print requests
➢ Review and debug common printing issues

106.1 Install and configure X11 [this entire objective is described in this chapter]

13. Verify that the video card and monitor are supported by an X server
14. Awareness of the X font server
15. Basic understanding and knowledge of the X Window configuration file

The following is a partial list of the used files, terms and utilities:
/etc/X11/xorg/xorg.conf, xhost, DISPLAY, xwininfo, xdpyinfo, and X

106.2 Setup a display manager [this entire objective is described in this chapter]

16. Basic configuration of LightDM
17. Turn the display manager on or off
18. Change the display manager greeting
19. Awareness of XDM, KDM and GDM

The following is a partial list of the used files, terms and utilities: lightdm and /etc/lightdm

106.3 Accessibility [this entire objective is described in this chapter]

20. Basic knowledge of keyboard accessibility settings (AccessX)
21. Basic knowledge of visual settings and themes
22. Basic knowledge of assistive technology (ATs)

The following is a partial list of the used files, terms and utilities: Sticky/repeat keys, mouse keys, high contrast/large print desktop themes, screen reader, braille display, screen magnifier, on-screen keyboard, gestures (used at login, for example gdm), orca, GOK, emacspeak

108.4 Manage printers and printing [this entire objective is described in this chapter]

44. Basic CUPS configuration (for local and remote printers)
45. Manage user print queues
46. Troubleshoot general printing problems
47. Add and remove jobs from configured printer queues

The following is a partial list of the used files, terms and utilities: CUPS configuration files, tools and utilities; /etc/cups, and lpd legacy interface (lpr, lprm, lpq)

X Window System provides the foundation for running graphical applications, which includes system administration tools, user applications, as well as Linux graphical display, desktop, and window manager programs. This is convenient for users with limited command line knowledge to interact with the operating system. The X Window System also offers a variety of accessibility options for users with vision, hearing, mobility, and speech impairments to help them interact with the operating system without difficulty and use applications with ease.

The Linux CUPS printing system is a set of utilities, configuration files, and other hooks for configuring and managing printers and print queues, and submitting and administering user print requests. Issues pertaining to printing may arise and efforts to troubleshoot and fix them need to be taken, which require a solid familiarity of how CUPS work and a firm knowledge of appropriate tools.

X Server

Most modern Linux distributions use an open source implementation of the X Window System provided by *X.Org Foundation*, an open source organization with focus on managing and overseeing the development of X and technologies surrounding it. X (short for *X Window System* and originally derived from the XFree86 Project) is based on the client/server architecture whereby a software daemon runs on a system and serves graphical client requests initiated on the local or a remote system. The X server (also called a *display server*) manages the graphics and associated video hardware, and the X client is any graphical application such as *xclock*, *xterm*, or *gedit* that communicates with the X server. The X server process is multi-threaded, meaning that it can serve multiple X client application requests concurrently. All Linux graphical user and configuration tools are X clients of the X server.

The configuration for the X server and graphical desktops is performed during Linux installation if we choose to include the X Window System support. The video hardware is detected and automatically configured for optimum performance and results.

In order for the X server and graphical desktops to run properly and efficiently, we need to ensure that the system has enough memory and supported video hardware—the video card, monitor, and mouse—installed. By default, X.Org supports a variety of multivendor video hardware devices. If a device we intend to use on our system is not recognized by our Linux system, we can obtain an appropriate software package containing the driver module from a trustworthy source or may use a built-in generic driver such as the generic VGA for the video card, if available.

Viewing X Configuration

In almost all cases, the video and input device configuration done during installation is sufficient; however, you may modify the settings for certain precise needs. There are plenty of X software packages installed on the system during installation, of which xorg-x11-server-Xorg provides the X server daemon process called *Xorg*. This daemon delivers the support on which a selected graphical display/desktop manager program runs. The other packages xorg-x11-server-utils and xorg-x11-utils include a number of client utilities, including the commands such as *xrandr*, *xwininfo*, and *xdpyinfo*.

The *xrandr* command can be used to view display monitor settings such as the screen size, orientation, and reflection. Here is an example from *centos73*. Make sure to run this command in a graphical terminal window.

```
[user1@centos73 ~]$ xrandr
```
Screen 0: minimum 640 x 480, current 1024 x 768, maximum 1024 x 768
default connected primary 1024x768+0+0 0mm x 0mm
   1024x768   61.00*
   800x600   61.00
   640x480   60.00

The *xwininfo* command prints geometrical information about the X terminal window in which it is executed. When executed without an option, it shows the window id (0x1a00007 in the below output) and terminal's location and appearance data. Here is a sample output of this command from *centos73*. You will need to click the mouse in the window when prompted.

```
[root@centos73 ~]# xwininfo
```
xwininfo: Please select the window about which you would like information by clicking the mouse in that window.
xwininfo: Window id: 0x1a00007 "root@centos73:~"
  Absolute upper-left X: 0
  Absolute upper-left Y: 67
  Relative upper-left X: 0
  Relative upper-left Y: 39
  Width: 1024
  Height: 667
  Depth: 32
. . . .
  Corners: +0+67 -0+67 -0-34 +0-34
  -geometry 112x35+0+28

There are several options available with this command to obtain desired information. These options include: -stats (the default option to show window location and appearance); -all (display all possible data); -id and -name (show information by the specified id or name); and -root (print root window information). Check the manual pages of this command for details.

The *xdpyinfo* command is used to display detailed information about the X server and its capabilities. The output produced when this command is executed without any options may spread over hundreds or thousands of lines. Most of the data shown is technical in nature. Here is an excerpt of the output from *centos73*. This command needs to be run in an X terminal window.

```
[root@centos73 ~]# xdpyinfo
```
name of display: :0
version number: 11.0
vendor string: The X.Org Foundation
vendor release number: 11702000
X.Org version: 1.17.2
maximum request size: 16777212 bytes
. . . .
default screen number: 0
number of screens: 1
screen #0:
  dimensions: 1024x768 pixels (271x203 millimeters)

resolution: 96x96 dots per inch
depths (7):   24, 1, 4, 8, 15, 16, 32
root window id: 0x25d
depth of root window: 24 planes
number of colormaps: minimum 1, maximum 1
default colormap: 0x20
default number of colormap cells: 256
preallocated pixels: black 0, white 16777215
options: backing-store WHEN MAPPED, save-unders NO
largest cursor: 1024x768
. . . .

Understanding X Configuration File and Rebuilding X Server

The other command line tool that can be used to print X server configuration and rebuild the X server is the *Xorg* command. This command can be run with the -configure option to obtain current configuration settings. The output is redirected to a file called *xorg.conf.new* in the *root* user's home directory. This file can then be modified if desired to alter current settings, renamed to *xorg.conf*, and placed in the */etc/X11* (or */etc/X11/xorg*) directory from where the X server will pick up the updates.

Modifying configuration in this file and applying it is not recommended in most circumstances, as the configuration auto-detected and applied at the OS installation time is usually accurate and best for the type of hardware in place.

Before you run *Xorg* command, stop the X service on the system:

```
[root@centos73 ~]# init 3
[root@centos73 ~]# Xorg -configure
```

Here are significant contents of this file. You will notice that the configuration is segregated in several sections. Each section is enclosed within the keywords "Section" and "EndSection", and controls or points to a specific characteristic of the X server.

```
Section "ServerLayout"
    Identifier    "X.org Configured"
    Screen    0  "Screen0" 0 0
    InputDevice    "Mouse0" "CorePointer"
    InputDevice    "Keyboard0" "CoreKeyboard"
EndSection
Section "Files"
    ModulePath   "/usr/lib64/xorg/modules"
    FontPath    "catalogue:/etc/X11/fontpath.d"
    FontPath    "built-ins"
EndSection
Section "Module"
    Load "glx"
```

```
EndSection
Section "InputDevice"
     Identifier  "Keyboard0"
     Driver      "kbd"
EndSection
Section "InputDevice"
     Identifier  "Mouse0"
     Driver      "mouse"
     Option      "Protocol" "auto"
     Option      "Device" "/dev/input/mice"
     Option      "ZAxisMapping" "4 5 6 7"
EndSection
Section "Monitor"
     Identifier  "Monitor0"
     VendorName  "Monitor Vendor"
     ModelName   "Monitor Model"
EndSection
Section "Device"
     Identifier  "Card0"
     Driver      "vesa"
     BusID       "PCI:0:2:0"
EndSection
Section "Screen"
     Identifier  "Screen0"
     Device      "Card0"
     Monitor     "Monitor0"

. . . . . . . .
```

The output shows eight sections, which may be reordered if desired. This information will vary from system to system and from one Linux distribution to another. The section contents are briefly described below:

- ✓ The ServerLayout section signifies the screen and input devices to be used.
- ✓ The Files section specifies the directory locations where modules and fonts are found.
- ✓ The Module section identifies the modules to be loaded to support X server functionality.
- ✓ The InputDevice sections show information about the keyboard and mouse, and what device drives to be used for them.
- ✓ The Monitor section highlights information about the monitor being used, along with vendor and model names.
- ✓ The Device section displays the video card and the driver in use. It also shows the location of the video card on the computer.
- ✓ The Screen section shows the device and monitor being used.

If you wish to apply the new configuration at this point, copy this file to the X configuration directory with **cp ~/xorg.conf.new /etc/X11/xorg.conf** (or *letc/X11/xorg/xorg.conf* on some distributions) and then execute the **startx** command or **init 5** to bring up the X server based on the new configuration. By default, X uses the *xorg.conf* file for configuration settings.

The startx and xinit Commands

The *startx* command, located in the */usr/bin* directory, is a shell script that can be used to start the X server manually if it is not already running. This script is the front-end to the *xinit* command, which starts the X server by calling the *X* (symbolically linked to *Xorg*) command. During the X startup process, configuration files, such as */etc/X11/xorg.conf*, are referenced. The *startx* (or *xinit*) also brings up any pre-defined graphical display and desktop programs such as GNOME or KDE during the startup process.

Overview of the X Font Server

X requires fonts to display the text properly. Older Linux distribution versions provided fonts to local and network X applications through a central service via the *X font server* (xfs), which was based on the core X font subsystem. This practice has largely been replaced by Fontconfig, a subsystem of commands, configuration files, and other necessary support for customizing and managing access to fonts. Fontconfig provides simple font management and direct access to fonts. A further coverage of Fontconfig is beyond the scope of this book.

The X font server name, the port it listened on, and (optionally) the font location was supplied in the Files section of the *xorg.conf* file via the FontPath directive (FontPath "www.example.com:8919"). The X server was dependent on the availability of the X font server in order to start up successfully and operate properly.

The X font server operations such as start, stop, restart, status check, and enable/disable for autostart were managed just like any other Linux service with the *service* and *chkconfig* commands.

Working In a Graphical Environment

Linux allows users to work in both text and graphical environments. Text interface might be cumbersome for many; however, numerous administrators and programmers prefer to work in a text-mode setting without needing the graphics capabilities of the operating system at all. Nevertheless, graphical environment provides easier and convenient interaction with the operating system by hiding the challenges that users might otherwise have to experience working in text-mode.

X begins at the end of the Linux boot process if the system is configured to boot to SysVinit run level 5 or the systemd graphical target. X sets up the foundation for users to log in and run tools, programs, and applications in a graphical setting. There are three programs that are critical to the overall functionality of the graphical environment. These programs are called the *display manager* (a.k.a. *login manager*), *desktop manager*, and *window manager*, and they are invoked following the completion of the groundwork set up by X for them. All major Linux distributions come standard with or support at least one set of these programs to furnish users with end-to-end graphical experience on top of X.

Display/Login Manager

A display/login manager—such as *GNOME display manager* (GDM), *Light display manager* (LightDM), *X display manager* (XDM), and *K display manager* (KDM)—is responsible for the presentation of a login screen (may also be referred to as a *greeter*). This allows users to enter credentials to log on to the system, and the preparation for the desktop environment for the user after the credentials has been verified. Figures 13-1 and 13-2 show images of two common display managers GDM and LightDM taken from *centos511* and *ubuntu14*, respectively.

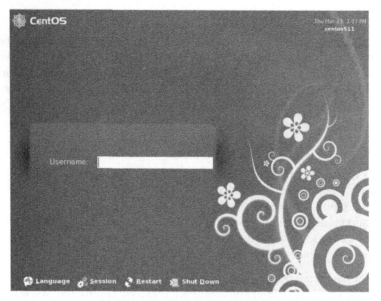

Figure 13-1 GNOME Display/Login Manager

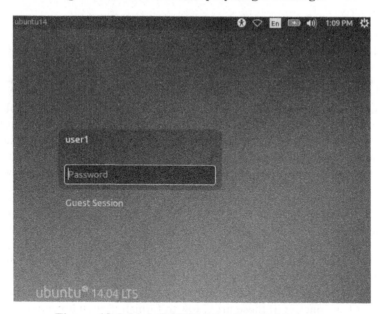

Figure 13-2 LightDM Display/Login Manager

The greeter screens present a login prompt, show hostname and system time, allow us to shut down or reboot the system, and a few other manager-specific controls.

GDM is the default display manager program used on CentOS whereas LightDM is the default on Ubuntu. Both provide advanced and convenient features, outclassing XDM. XDM is the default display manager in the absence of GDM, LightDM, and other sophisticated display managers. Introduced some three decades ago, XDM is very rudimentary in nature and it was loaded as part of the X11 software installation. KDM has been retired in favor of another advanced display manager called SDDM (*simple desktop display manager*); however, it is still available on older Linux versions.

Desktop Environment Manager

Once the credentials are validated, the display/login manager establishes a *desktop environment* (DE) using a desktop management program such as Unity, GNOME, or *K desktop environment* (KDE) for users to work in. A desktop environment provides users with an easy and point-and-click interface to interact with the operating system and applications viz., a file manager and control panel to perform functions, such as setting wallpapers and screen savers, managing desktop icons and widgets, accessing configuration tools, programs, removable media, and web, and so on. Figures 13-3 and 13-4 show images of two common desktop environment management programs: GNOME and Unity, taken from *centos511* and *ubuntu14*, respectively.

Figure 13-3 GNOME Desktop Environment Manager

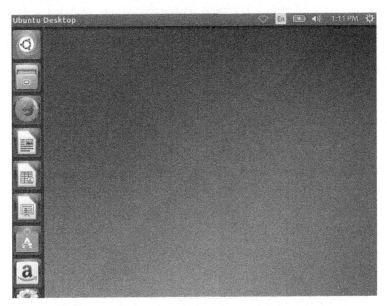

Figure 13-4 Unity Desktop Environment Manager

Generally, the look and feel, and features included in a desktop environment are similar to one another. If you are familiar with Microsoft Windows desktop interface, you should not have any difficulty using any of these interfaces. The default screens include some icons on the desktop and the rest of the programs can be opened by clicking the drop-down menu items across the top (GNOME) or clicking one of the icons to the left of the main screen (Unity). Both environments allow you to open several virtual desktops. The desktop and the menus are customizable and allow you to create icons for additional applications. Plenty of tools are included by default.

Window Manager

A DE works closely with a *window manager* program to control the presentation, location, and adornment of the various windows that the system and users would open on the desktop. There is a whole of slew of window management programs available in Linux, some of which are Metacity, Kwin, and TWM (*tab window manager*).

Changing Default Display Manager

In most cases, we do not want to change the default display manager for our desktop environments; however, the system allows us to use a different login manager if desired. To accomplish this, we simply need to create/modify the */etc/sysconfig/desktop* file on *centos511* and set the DISPLAYMANAGER directive value to GDM, XDM, KDE, or any other supported program provided it is already installed on the system. On *ubuntu14*, we modify the */etc/X11/default-display-manager* file and add the pathname of the program such as */usr/bin/xdm*, */usr/sbin/gdm*, or */usr/bin/kdm* that we wish to use.

 Use **yum install xdm gdm kdm** on *centos511* and **sudo apt-get install xdm gdm kdm** on *ubuntu14* if these display manager programs are not already on the system.

In the absence of these files, CentOS defaults to GDM and Ubuntu defaults to LightDM.

Now execute **init 3** and then **init 5**, or reboot the system to test the settings.

Modifying GDM and XDM Greetings

All display managers allow us to customize their faces to how we want to see them. For instance, we can modify the default greeting, background colors, text fonts, and border width; choose whether or not to show the list of user accounts; enable autologon for a specific user; and so on. These settings are primarily stored in the */etc/X11/xdm/Xresources* file for XDM and GDM, */etc/gdm/custom.conf* file for GDM, *kdmrc* file for KDM (*kdmrc* file may be located in the */etc/kde4/kdm*, */usr/share/kde4/config/kdm*, or */etc/X11/kdm* directory). Some of the configuration might be located in other files under the */etc/X11*, */etc/gdm*, and */etc/kde4* directories.

In this subsection, we will only set a greeting message to appear on the display manager. The rest of the configuration is beyond the scope of this book; however, you can explore the files further and make customization if interested.

To add a custom greeting for GDM on *centos511*, you need to ensure that DISPLAYMANAGER=GDM is set in the */etc/sysconfig/desktop* file before proceeding. Next, edit the *custom.conf* file in */etc/gdm* and add the following lines to it:

```
[greeter]
Defaultwelcome=false
Welcome="Hello, this is our GDM test server centos511."
```

Save the file and exit out of the editor. To test the setting, either reboot the system or issue **init 3** and then **init 5** after a few seconds. You should see the greeting on the login screen.

For XDM, set DISPLAYMANAGER=XDM in */etc/sysconfig/desktop*, and add or modify the following line in the */etc/X11/xdm/Xresources* file:

```
xlogin*greeting: Hello, this is our XDM test server centos511.
```

Save the file, exit out of the editor, and test by rebooting the system or issuing the **init 3** and **init 5** commands.

On *ubuntu14*, the changes for GDM and XDM in the *custom.conf* and *Xresources* files are identical; however, you need to ensure that the pathname to the corresponding display manager is appropriately defined in the */etc/X11/default-display-manager* file as explained earlier.

Switching Display Manager On or Off

We might want to turn the display manager off for security or other reasons. The system will display the console login prompt instead, and everything else will work just as fine except with the unavailability of the graphical environment. CentOS and Ubuntu have slightly different ways to achieve this. Here is how we do it on our *centos511* and *ubuntu14* systems.

On *centos511*, we edit the */etc/inittab* file and change the default run level from 5 to 3, as highlighted in bold below:

```
x:3:respawn:/etc/X11/prefdm -nodaemon
```

And on *ubuntu14*, we prepend the display manager pathname with a # sign in the */etc/X11/default-display-login* file to look like:

```
#/usr/sbin/lightdm
```

Both changes will require a system reboot to implement the new setting. We should not see the display manager screen following the startup.

Reverse the changes to turn the display manager back on.

Customizing LightDM Interface

LightDM, compared to GDM, is lighter and faster. As shown in the default interface in Figure 13-2, it lists normal user accounts from the *passwd* file for login selection, indicates a no-password guest user account with restricted access, and shows no welcome message on the screen. We can transpose the defaults to change the look of the screen and for tighter security. For example, we can define the option greeter-hide-users=true to hide user list, allow-guest=false to disable guest logins, autologin-user=user1 to allow a specific user to log in to the system automatically after waiting for 5 seconds (autologin-user-timeout=5).

LightDM has several configuration files that influence its behavior. They store many defaults and are located in files under the */usr/share/lightdm/lightdm.conf.d* directory. These files should not be

---

altered manually; rather, any required modification should be recorded in a file by the name *lightdm.conf* in the */etc/lightdm* directory. This file does not exist by default on Ubuntu 14.04.

Let's create *lightdm.conf* and disable guest logins and hide user list. You must add the identifier "SeatDefaults" and enclose it within square brackets before listing the two options in the file.

```
[user1@ubuntu14 ~]$ sudo vi /etc/lightdm/lightdm.conf
[SeatDefaults]
allow-guest=false
greeter-hide-users=true
```

Save the file and quit *vi*. Reboot the system and observe the changes on the screen. The screen should now look similar to the one shown in Figure 13-5.

Figure 13-5 LightDM Interface without Guest and User List

Edit the file again and place options autologin-user=user1 and autologin-user-timeout=5 to the end of the file, and reboot the system. You will notice that the display manager will wait for 5 seconds and then log *user1* in automatically.

Remote X Sessions

As we know X is a client/server application and it is capable of running in the networked environment in addition to running locally on the same Linux computer. This allows us to initiate graphical user and administrative tools on a remote Linux system without the need to log on to the console of that system and invoke them. In order to set this access up, we need to enable remote X access on the local system with the *xhost* command and set the DISPLAY variable on the remote system to show the graphics there.

Exercise 13-1: Run X Application Remotely

In this exercise, you will enable remote X access on *centos511* (local system) as *user1*, log on to *ubuntu14* (remote system) as *user1*, check or set the environment variable DISPLAY to point to the local system and run the *xlock* application to appear on the remote system. You will configure this access over the secure shell protocol (ssh). After the completion of the test, disable remote X access on the local system. The assumptions for this exercise are that (1) a desktop environment is running on both systems and (2) the IP for *centos511* is 192.168.0.102 and that for *ubuntu14* is 192.168.0.101.

1. Ensure that the secure shell service (*sshd*) is running on *centos511*:

```
[user1@centos73 ~]$ ps -ef | grep sshd | grep -v grep
root    2327   1 0  10:14  ?     00:00:00  /usr/sbin/sshd
```

2. Enable (the + sign) remote X access using the *xhost* command on *centos511*. To limit this access to only *ubuntu14*, use **xhost +192.168.0.102** instead (use **xhost +ubuntu14** if hostname resolution is configured).

    ```
    [user1@centos73 ~]$ xhost +
    access control disabled, clients can connect from any host
    ```

3. Log on to the graphical console of *ubuntu14*, open a terminal session, and run the following to establish an X session to *centos511*. If this is the first time you are logging in remotely to *centos511* from *ubuntu14* as *user1*, you will need to enter "yes" when prompted to provide your confirmation to proceed with the connectivity. You will not be prompted again on subsequent connection attempts. Enter *user1* password as set on *centos511* to log on.

    ```
    [user1@ubuntu14 ~]$ ssh -X 192.168.0.102
    The authenticity of host '192.168.0.102 (192.168.0.102)' can't be established.
    RSA key fingerprint is 6d:41:14:56:25:f7:8c:1c:b2:c0:e5:5a:df:ba:3f:37.
    Are you sure you want to continue connecting (yes/no)? yes
    Warning: Permanently added '192.168.0.102' (RSA) to the list of known hosts.
    user1@192.168.0.102's password:
    Last login: Sun Mar 26 10:14:36 2017
    [user1@centos511 ~]$
    ```

4. Check the DISPLAY variable value. It might be the hostname or IP address of *centos511* appended with :0 or :0.0, or something similar to what is shown below on my system. In most cases, a correct DISPLAY variable value is automatically established.

    ```
    [user1@centos511 ~]$ echo $DISPLAY
    localhost:10.0
    ```

5. Run *xlock* at the command prompt to test remote X functionality. The clock should appear on *ubuntu14*.

6. Close *xclock* and terminate the remote X session by issuing the **exit** command at the command prompt.

7. Return to *centos511* and run the *xhost* command as follows to disable (the - sign) remote X access. To disable this access for only *ubuntu14*, use **xhost -192.168.0.101** instead (use **xhost -ubuntu14** if hostname resolution is configured).

```
[user1@centos511 ~]$ xhost -
access control enabled, only auhorized clients can connect
```

This completes the exercise to configure and use remote X access.

Accessibility Options

Most major Linux distributions provide numerous desktop accessibility tools and features for users with a hearing, speech, vision (partially sighted or completely blind), or mobility impairment to assist them in their interaction with the operating system and applications. Additional tools may be downloaded and installed as desired. These tools, along with any required hardware devices, may collectively be referred to as *Assistive Technologies* (ATs) that most modern Linux graphical environments support, such as GDM, KDE, and Unity. Assistive technologies encompass tools and applications for keyboard navigation, onscreen virtual keyboards, screen readers and speech synthesizers, screen magnifiers and resolution adjustments, mouse cursors and gestures, and visual and audible alerts. The following subsections discuss them in brief.

Keyboard Navigation

There are several keyboard accessibility features available within the desktop environments that allow us to adjust the settings for keyboard usage for physically impaired users. Here is a short description for each feature:

Bounce Keys

The bounce keys (a.k.a. delay keys) feature adds a little delay between each acceptance of a single key that is depressed more than once inadvertently.

Mouse Keys

Mouse keys assist users who have trouble using a mouse to use the keypad instead for cursor movements and clicks.

Repeat Keys

This feature enables the system to ignore keys depressed quickly one after the other and a key depressed for a longer period of time.

Slow Keys

This feature helps users who have trouble pressing keys by accident. It adds a delay between the time a key is pushed and the time its action is accepted.

Sticky Keys

Sticky keys help users with trouble pressing multiple keys simultaneously (Ctrl+Alt, Alt-F1, or Ctrl+c for example). With this feature turned on, users can carry out operations with a single finger by locking one key (called a *modifier* key such as Shift, Ctrl, and Alt) and then pressing the other.

Toggle Keys

With this feature on, a sound alert is generated when keys such as `NumLock` and `CapsLock` are pushed. This feature is especially useful for the blind.

Onscreen Keyboard

The onscreen keyboard application such as the *GNOME Onscreen Keyboard* (GOK) help users who cannot type but can use a pointing device, such as a mouse or touchpad, to point and click on the desired keys on an onscreen virtual keyboard. As an alternative to GOK, you may install and use another onscreen keyboard software called IOK.

Screen Readers and Speech Synthesizers

Screen readers for text-to-audio conversions are valuable for blind users. The conversions are forwarded to a speech synthesizer program for reading out the text loud. Common screen reader applications include Emacspeak, eSpeak, Speakup, and Orca, and they all support external Braille terminals as well. Common speech synthesizer applications include Festival and ViaVoice. You may download and install the desired application combo on the target system using an appropriate software installation command.

Screen Magnifiers and Resolution Adjustments

Screen magnifiers are useful for an enlarged view of a portion of the screen for partially sighted people. Several applications are available in this area including KMag and Xzoom. Use an appropriate command to install the one of your liking.

The use of high contrast themes for better screen resolution (colors, background, etc.) and enlarged text for easy reading provide invaluable assistance to partially sighted users. Such users can enhance the screen contrast level and use `CtrlAlt+` or `CtrlAlt-` to adjust the onscreen font size for better visibility and legibility.

Mouse Cursors and Gestures

Mouse cursors are available in assorted shapes and sizes to aid users with difficulty in sighting or following them. For users with physical difficulties, mouse gestures may be configured to enable them to log in to the system without having to type in their credentials.

Visual and Audible Alerts

Visual alerts may be configured for users with hearing disorders to enable them to see onscreen warnings and notifications. Similarly, sound controls may be set for users with vision problems so that they can hear audible warnings and notifications as they pop up.

Accessibility Configuration in GDM and Unity

GNOME and Unity desktop managers have many of the accessibility options built-in to them. Figure 13-6 shows them when we select Applications from the main menu in GDM on *centos73* and click System Tools → Settings and then Universal Access. It would be System Settings from menu items in Unity. Older versions of CentOS, version 5.11 for instance running on *centos511*, provide accessibility settings under System → Preferences.

 The terms Settings, All Settings, and System Settings are synonymous to Control Panel in MS Windows.

The look and placement of features and options vary between the two desktop environments and amongst versions of the same desktop program. Some of the features may simply be turned on or off by sliding the on/off switch, while others present granular control options in popped up windows.

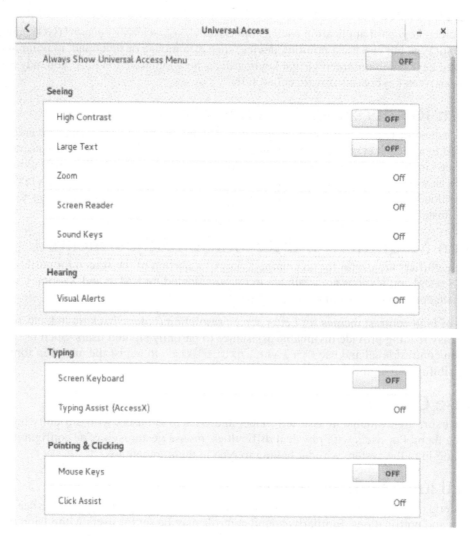

Figure 13-6 Accessibility Settings in GDM & Unity

One example of granular controls is of Typing Assist (AccessX) under Typing in Figure 13-6 above (GDM). It opens up a window, Figure 13-7, when we click on it to let us customize it as desired.

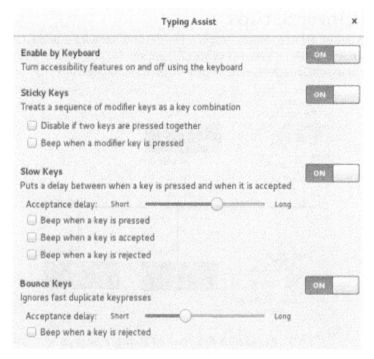

Figure 13-7 Accessibility Settings in GDM & Unity | Typing Assist (AccessX)

In addition to accessing the accessibility options by clicking on the Universal Access icon, there are Keyboard, Mouse & Touchpad, and Sound control icons on the main Settings page as well that you may check out for a few other settings related to these resources.

Understanding the Linux Printing System

The standard printing service available on most Linux distributions is referred to as CUPS (originally an abbreviation of *Common UNIX Printing System*). CUPS is the UNIX/Linux implementation of the *Internet Printing Protocol* (IPP), and has succeeded the UNIX LP *line printer daemon* (lpd) print service due to its modular design, ease of use, wide acceptance, and functionality. Linux distributions offer a helper program called cups-lpd for converting UNIX-style LPD print jobs into IPP for compatibility with CUPS. IPP runs on top of HTTP protocol to provide network access to printers. CUPS also supports the *PostScript Printer Definition* (PPD) files.

CUPS is based on the client/server architecture where a print client sends a file to a print server for printing. The print client is typically the *lp* or the *lpr* command that submits a file to the print server. The print server is the print scheduler daemon called *cupsd*, which is started when the system enters runlevel 2 or multi-user target and stopped when the system changes runlevel to 1 or shuts down. The scheduler daemon listens on port 631 and supports both TCP and UDP protocols for network printing. The print job submitted by the print client goes through a filter or translator program such as Ghostscript for transformation into a format that the printer understands. The print job is then queued into a spooler location from where it is picked up by the scheduler process and forwarded to the destination printer for printing.

CUPS offers both browser-based and GUI-based configuration tools, in addition to a set of commands, for printer management.

Types of Printer Setups

There are three types of printer setups—*local*, *remote*, and *network*—and CUPS support all of them. Figure 13-8 illustrates our three systems *centos73*, *ubuntu14*, and *centos511*, and one printer (*prn2*) connected to the network. There is another printer (*prn1*) attached directly to *centos73*.

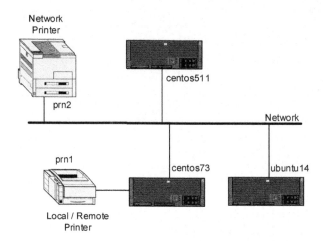

Figure 13-8 Types of Printer Setups

Local Printer

A printer attached physically to a system's USB, parallel, or serial port, and accessed by users of that system only is called a *local printer*. CUPS also supports printing to a PDF file. In Figure 13-8, *prn1* is a local printer for users on *centos73*.

Remote Printer

A local printer acts as a remote printer for users on remote systems. In Figure 13-8, *prn1* acts as a *remote printer* for users on *ubuntu14* and *centos511* systems.

Network Printer

A *network printer* is physically connected to a network or Wi-Fi and has its own hostname and IP address. CUPS supports network printer discovery as well as several protocols for network printing. In Figure 13-8, *prn2* is a network printer accessible to users on all three systems.

CUPS Directory Hierarchy

The CUPS directory hierarchy comprises of different types of files to support the printing system end-to-end. These files are primarily stored in five directory locations—*/etc/cups*, */usr/bin*, */usr/sbin*, */var/spool/cups*, and */var/log/cups*. Table 13-1 describes some key CUPS configuration files and directories.

File / Sub-directory	Purpose
/etc/cups/	Parent directory for storing all printer-related configuration as well as filter, transformer, interface, and model programs.
/etc/cups/client.conf	Defines the default CUPS server
/etc/cups/cupsd.conf	Default CUPS configuration file. Also contains who can access or browse a shared printer and from where

File / Sub-directory	Purpose
/etc/cups/printers.conf	Stores printer configuration including information about the default printer
/usr/bin/	Contains user print request submission and management commands such as lp, lpr, lpq, lprm, lpstat, and cancel
/usr/sbin/	Contains privileged printer and print queue administration commands such as lpadmin, cupsenable, cupsdisable, cupsaccept (or accept), and cupsreject (or reject)
/var/spool/cups/	Parent directory for storing printer status and print requests
/var/spool/cups/tmp/	Temporary holding area for print requests before they are sent for printing
/var/log/cups/	Contains CUPS log files

Table 13-1 CUPS Directory Hierarchy

In addition, the CUPS printing system uses the */run/cups* (or */var/run/cups* on older versions) directory to hold runtime information for the service.

Configuring and Managing Printers and Print Queues

The printing system may be configured and managed via commands, the browser-based tool, or a graphical tool available on most mainline Linux distributions. Printer configuration includes tasks such as adding a local, remote, or network printer, while printer and print queue administration includes operations such as setting the default print destination, enabling and disabling a printer, making a print queue accept or reject print requests, perusing the printer and print queue status, and removing a printer. The following subsections elaborate on how to manage the CUPS service start and stop, and perform the operations using the command line tools described in Table 13-1.

Managing the CUPS Service

The *cupsd* daemon can be started, restarted, and stopped manually just like any other service on the Linux system. It can also be configured to start automatically at specific runlevels or targets. Let's look at some basic operations.

To start *cupsd* using the *service* command on *centos511* and the *systemctl* command on *centos73*:

```
[root@centos511 ~]# service cups start
[root@centos73 ~]# systemctl start cups
```

Switch "start" with restart or stop as desired to perform that operation. Also try running **service cups status** or **systemctl status cups** to check the operational status of the service.

To enable *cupsd* to start at subsequent system reboots, use the *chkconfig* command on *centos511* or the *systemctl* command on *centos73*:

```
[root@centos511 ~]# chkconfig cups on
[root@centos73 ~]# systemctl enable cups
```

CUPS Management Tools

Linux offers a suite of command line tools for printer management. These tools are located in the */usr/sbin* directory and require *root* privileges for execution. These administrative tools include *lpinfo*, *lpadmin*, *cupsenable*, *cupsdisable*, *cupsaccept* (or *accept*), and *cupsreject* (or *reject*), and they are used to list available printer drivers and devices, administer printers, enable printers, disable printers, accept print requests in print queues, and reject print requests from being accepted into print queues, respectively.

Listing Available Drivers and Devices with lpinfo

The *lpinfo* command is helpful in identifying an available driver (-m) and device (-v) for use with a new printer configuration. For example, if you wish to know whether the driver for Samsung ML-7300N printer is installed, you can run the *lpinfo* command as follows:

```
[root@centos73 ~]# lpinfo -m | grep 'Samsung ML-7300N'
gutenprint.5.2://samsung-ml-7300n/expert Samsung ML-7300N - CUPS+Gutenprint v5.2.9
gutenprint.5.2://samsung-ml-7300n/simple Samsung ML-7300N - CUPS+Gutenprint v5.2.9 Simplified
```

The output confirms the presence of the desired driver.

 Gutenprint and Foomatic (not shown) are extensive sets of free printer drivers for CUPS and LPD services.

Next, we need to know what devices are available on the system that we may be able to use for this printer. We run the *lpinfo* command but this time with the -v option:

```
[root@centos73 ~]# lpinfo -v
```

The output will show a list of supported network protocols as well as other available devices.

Administering Printers with lpadmin

lpadmin is the prime printer command line administration tool and it can be used to add, modify, or remove a printer, and to set a default print destination. This command has several options:

-p to assign a name to a printer
-m to specify a model
-v to specify a port or URL
-D to add a general description
-E to enable a printer to begin accepting user print requests
-d to set a printer as the system-wide default destination for user print requests
-x to remove a printer.

Checking the Status of Printers and Print Queues with lpstat

The *lpstat* command shows the status of printers and queued print requests. This tool has plenty of options that you might find useful to use during print system management. Some basic options are described in Table 13-2.

Option	Description
-a	Displays the accept/reject status
-d	Indicates the default destination printer
-o	Lists queued requests only
-p	Shows the enable/disable status
-r	Identifies *cupsd* status
-s	Displays the summary information
-t	Provides detailed information about all configured printers and queued requests
-u	Lists queued jobs by submitting user names
-v	Presents the devices configured printers are attached to

Table 13-2 lpstat Options

The -t option is equivalent to using -a, -d, -o, -p, -r, and -v combined.

Exercise 13-2: Add a Local Printer

In this exercise, you will use the *lpadmin* command to add an HP LaserJet P3005 printer as a local printer (or print queue) *prn1* (-p) on *centos73* on USB port (-v) */dev/usb0*. You will use the description "Test LaserJet Printer" (-D) and printer model (-m) gutenprint.5.2://hp-lj_p3005/simple. You will specify -E to enable the printer to accept print requests. You will set the new printer as the default queue and display detailed status.

1. Add the printer as per the details provided in the exercise description:

    [root@centos73 ~]# **lpadmin -p prn1 -m gutenprint.5.2://hp-lj_p3005/simple -v usb:/dev/usb0 -D "Test LaserJet Printer" -E**

2. Set *prn1* as the default print queue:

    [root@centos73 ~]# **lpadmin -d prn1**

3. Check the status:

    [root@centos73 ~]# **lpstat -t**
    scheduler is running
    system default destination: prn1
    device for prn1: usb:/dev/usb0
    prn1 accepting requests since Thu 30 Mar 2017 06:47:19 AM EDT
    printer prn1 is idle. enabled since Thu 30 Mar 2017 06:47:19 AM EDT

The status shows that the scheduler *cupsd* is running with *prn1* as the default print destination. It shows that the printer is accepting requests and it is enabled. You should now be able to send a test print request to this printer using its name.

Exercise 13-3: Add Access to a Remote Printer

In this exercise, you will add access to *prn1* from another system *centos511* (client). You will run the *lpadmin* command on *centos511* and assign the print queue a name such as *prn1* (same as on the print server) and the ipp location with port 631 as the device file (-v). You will make an assumption that IP 192.168.0.100 is configured on the print server.

1. Add support for the remote printer on *centos511*:

    [root@centos511 ~]# **lpadmin -p prn1 -D "Test LaserJet Printer on centos73" -v http://192.168.0.100:631/printers/prn1 -E**

2. Set *prn1* as the default printer:

    [root@centos7511 ~]# **lpadmin -d prn1**

3. Check the status:

    [root@centos511 ~]# **lpstat -t**
    scheduler is running
    system default destination: prn1
    device for prn1: http://192.168.0.100:631/printers/prn1
    prn1 accepting requests since Thu 30 Mar 2017 06:58:38 AM EDT
    printer prn1 is idle. enabled since Thu 30 Mar 2017 06:58:38 AM EDT

You should be able to send a print request from *centos511* to the remote printer using its name.

Exercise 13-4: Add Access to a Network Printer

In this exercise, you will configure network print access to *prn2* (IP 192.168.0.110, model HP LaserJet 1609DN) from client *ubuntu14* and assign name *prn2*:

1. Add access to the network printer on *ubuntu14*:

    [user1@ubuntu14 ~]$ **sudo lpadmin -p prn2 -v socket://192.168.0.110 -E -m drv:///hpcups.drv/hp-laserjet_professional_p1609dn.ppd**

2. Check the status of the print system:

    [user1@ubuntu14 ~]$ **lpstat -t**

Execute **sudo lpadmin -d prn2** if you wish to set this print queue as the default destination. Use other options with *lpstat* to view the status of individual items. Refer to Table 13-2.

Enabling and Disabling a Printer

A printer is automatically enabled and started to accept print requests from users right after it is created. However, you can enable it if it is not. The *cupsenable* command is used for this purpose. The opposite of enabling is the disable function, which you can perform with the *cupsdisable* command. When you disable a printer, you may add a reason using the -r option so that users who try to submit new requests for printing will see the reason for the printer's unavailability on their terminals. Here is how you would disable and enable the printer *prn1*:

To disable *prn1*:

```
[root@centos73 ~]# cupsdisable prn1
```

To disable *prn1* with a reason:

```
[root@centos73 ~]# cupsdisable -r "prn1 is unavailable for 1 hour" prn1
```

To re-enable *prn1*:

```
[root@centos73 ~]# cupsenable prn1
```

Check the printer status anytime with **lpstat -t** for confirmation.

Accepting and Rejecting Print Requests

A printer (or a print queue in this context) must be accepting requests in its queue before it can actually print them. The *cupsaccept* (or *accept*) command allows user print requests to be queued for printing and the *cupsreject* (or *reject*) command does the opposite of it. When you set your print queue in rejection mode, you may add a reason using the -r option so that users who try to submit new requests for printing will see the reason for print queue's unavailability on their terminals. Here is how you would use these commands for print queue *prn2* on *ubuntu14*:

To reject user print requests with or without a reason:

```
[user1@ubuntu14 ~]$ cupsreject -r "prn2 is down for toner replacement" prn2
[user1@ubuntu14 ~]$ cupsreject prn2
```

To restart accepting user requests:

```
[user1@ubuntu14 ~]$ cupsaccept prn2
```

Examine the printer status anytime with **lpstat -t** for confirmation.

Exercise 13-5: Remove a Printer

In this exercise, you will use a sequence of steps to remove the active printer *prn1* from *centos511*. You will use an appropriate reason to reject new print requests from accumulating in the print queue. You will inspect the status once the procedure is complete.

1. Reject user print requests on *prn1*:

    ```
    [root@centos511 ~]# reject -r "prn1 has been removed permanently" prn1
    ```

2. Disable the printer:

    ```
    [root@centos511 ~]# cupsdisable prn1
    ```

3. Remove the printer:

    ```
    [root@centos511 ~]# lpadmin -x prn1
    ```

4. Confirm the removal:

```
[root@centos511 ~]# lpstat -t
```

Submitting and Managing Print Requests

Once printers and print queues have been configured and ready for use, users can submit print jobs to the default (or any desired) print queue and manage them with simple commands. Print queue management involves listing, modifying, moving, and removing print requests. The following subsections describe how to perform these tasks.

Print Request Management Tools

Linux provides a set of commands for print job submission and queue management. These commands are *lp* (or *lpr*) for request submissions, *lprm* for request removals, and *lpq* for queue status viewing. These commands are located in the */usr/bin* directory.

Submitting Print Requests

As you know, the primary command line tool for print request submission is the *lp* command. Some common options that this command supports are:

-d to specify a destination other than the default or if there is no default destination set
-h to send a print request to a specified host
-m to notify the user by email of job completion
-n to specify the number of copies to print
-t to print a custom title on the first page (the default is to print the submitting user's name)

Alternatively, if you prefer to use the *lpr* command, replace the option -d with -P, -h with -H, -n with -#, and -t with -T; the use of -m is identical. *lpr* is one of the legacy tools that has been inherited from the old UNIX LP print service. Let us look at some examples on the usage of these commands.

To print the */etc/group* file on the default printer *prn1*:

```
[root@centos73 ~]# lp /etc/group
request id is prn1-1 (1 file(s))
[root@centos73 ~]# lpr /etc/group
request id is prn1-2 (1 file(s))
```

The output indicates that prn1-1 and prn1-2 are the two print requests submitted to this print queue.

To print two copies of the */etc/passwd* file on a non-default printer *prn1* (assuming *prn1* is not the default printer) with the title "This is a test print", and inform by email of job completion:

```
[root@centos73 ~]# lp -dprn1 -t "This is a test print" -n2 -m /etc/passwd
request id is prn1-3 (1 file(s))
[root@centos73 ~]# lpr -#2 -m -Pprn1 -T "This is a test print" /etc/passwd
request id is prn1-4 (1 file(s))
```

Listing Queued Print Requests

Now that you have submitted four print jobs to *prn1*, let's examine their status with the *lpstat* and *lpq* commands. These commands list all print requests submitted to all print queues by default:

```
[root@centos73 ~]# lpstat -o
prn1-1     root    2048    Fri 31 Mar 2017 09:00:12 AM EDT
prn1-2     root    2048    Fri 31 Mar 2017 09:00:17 AM EDT
prn1-3     root    3072    Fri 31 Mar 2017 09:00:35 AM EDT
prn1-4     root    3072    Fri 31 Mar 2017 09:01:11 AM EDT
[root@centos73 ~]# lpq
prn1 is ready and printing
Rank        Owner   Job     File(s)                 Total Size
active      root    1       group                   2048 bytes
1st         root    2       group                   2048 bytes
2nd         root    3       This is a test print    3072 bytes
3rd         root    4       This is a test print    3072 bytes
```

As shown in the first output, *lpstat* lists the job ID, submitting user name, file size, and submission timestamp for each print request in the *prn1* queue. You may add the -u option to the command and specify the name of a user to view jobs submitted by that particular user and the -p option with a queue name (e.g. -p prn1) to see jobs held in that individual queue.

The *lpq* command, on the other hand, shows similar information. It tells us the job priority, submitting user name, job ID, title, and file size. This command also supports viewing jobs by a specific user (-U) or print queue (-P).

Removing Queued Print Requests

There are currently four print jobs in the *prn1* queue. You can remove them one at a time or all at once using the *lprm* command. A regular user can remove their own requests while the *root* user can erase anyone's. This command requires a job ID number to be deleted as reported by *lpq* in the third column of its output. Here is how you run it to remove job ID 1:

```
[root@centos73 ~]# lprm 1
```

To remove all print requests for a specific user or held in a specific queue, use the command with the -U or the -P option and supply a user or queue name.

Troubleshooting General Printing Problems

The printing subsystem generally works without issues as long as a proper maintenance schedule is followed for printing devices, and print cartridges are replaced on time. However, apart from hardware malfunctioning, there could be reasons related to printer configuration or network misbehavior that would result in no printing. Depending on whether a printer is local or not, troubleshooting could involve an examination of error messages being generated, a review of log files, a re-inspection of configuration files, and an execution of numerous commands. Once a root cause is identified, necessary steps are taken to fix the issue in order to bring the printing service back to normal.

In this brief section, we will present a few pointers to help you with troubleshooting general printing problems. This review is based on three presumptions: (1) printing devices are operational with no hardware problems, (2) the printing setup was in working condition, and (3) there are no network issues.

1. Check to ensure that the CUPS service *cupsd* is running. Use the *ps, lpstat, systemctl* (systemd), or *service* (SysVinit) command. Here are examples:

   ```
   [root@centos73 ~]# ps -ef | grep cupsd
   root    1087   1  0 Apr01 ?    00:00:00 /usr/sbin/cupsd -f

   [root@centos73 ~]# lpstat -t
   scheduler is running
   system default destination: prn1
   device for prn1: usb:/dev/usb0
   prn1 accepting requests since Thu 30 Mar 2017 08:48:45 AM EDT
   printer prn1 is idle.  enabled since Thu 30 Mar 2017 08:48:45 AM EDT

   [root@centos73 ~]# systemctl status cups
   cups.service - CUPS Printing Service
      Loaded: loaded (/usr/lib/systemd/system/cups.service; enabled; vendor preset: enabled)
      Active: active (running) since Sat 2017-04-01 19:37:46 EDT; 12h ago
    Main PID: 1087 (cupsd)

   [root@centos511 ~]# service cups status
   cupsd (pid 2329) is running...
   ```

The above outputs confirm the operational status of the scheduler service. If the service is not running, execute (systemd) **systemctl start cups** or (SysVinit) **service cups start** to bring them up.

2. The printer (or the print queue) might not be accepting new print requests. Check with **lpstat -a** or **lpstat -t**. This command will show whether the printer is rejecting requests. If yes, run the **cupsaccept** command to change the mode to accepting.
3. The printer (or the print queue) is accepting new print jobs, but the printer is not printing them. The printer might not be in enabled mode. Examine with **lpstat -p** or **lpstat -t**. This command will show whether the printer is disabled. If yes, run the **cupsenable** command to change the mode to enabling.
4. In case of a remote or network printer, try submitting a print request from a different system and see if that works.

In addition to inspecting the printing service and printer state, you also need to determine whether the command you are issuing is syntactically correct. The *lp* and *lpr* commands have subtle differences when it comes to command line options. For instance, *lp* accepts -d to specify a destination printer (or print queue) while *lpr* uses -P.

Chapter Summary

This chapter discussed X Window System, common GUI managers, accessibility options, and the CUPS printing system. We learned about the X server with a brief analysis of its configuration file, as well as the X startup programs and X font server.

Next, we learned about graphical display, desktop, and window managers, and reviewed some common programs in those spaces. We made a few configuration changes, such as setting the default display manager, modifying the greeters, turning display managers on and off, and customizing one of the display managers. The topic concluded with the setup and testing of an X application over the network.

Linux provides accessibility options as part of the X Window System and graphical manager programs for users with vision, speech, hearing, and mobility impairments. These options include assertive technologies and assistance with the keyboard and mouse. We examined various options available and looked at how to adjust them to align with individual user needs.

We developed a good understanding of the CUPS printing system, its directory structure, configuration file, daemon program, and so on. We reviewed local, remote, and network printer configuration types and defined them. We checked the start and stop status of the CUPS daemon program and configured it for auto startup.

We interacted with various administration tools for adding a printer, setting a default print destination, enabling and disabling a printer, allowing and disallowing users to submit print requests, checking printer status, and removing a printer. We used various tools to submit, list, and remove print requests.

Lastly, we touched upon troubleshooting common printing problems and how to fix them.

Chapter Review at a Glance

The following presents a one-sentence review of each key topic discussed in this chapter:

- X.Org's X Window system is an open source implementation on most modern Linux distributions.

- An X server is a multi-threaded service that is responsible for managing the graphics and associated video hardware, as well as X client requests; an X client is a program that works with an X server to run graphical applications, such as gedit and xterm.

- X font server is a central service that is used to provide fonts to X client applications in order to display the text properly.

- X font server has been largely replaced by Fontconfig subsystem that includes commands, configuration files, and other required support to display and manage fonts.

- The X service is automatically started when Linux enters runlevel 5 (SysVinit) or graphical target (systemd).

- Three programs are critical to the functionality of the graphical environment: display/login manager, which presents a login screen for users to enter their credentials (examples: GDM, LightDM, XDM, KDM, and SDDM); desktop manager, which is where the users work (examples: Unity, GNOME, and KDE); and window manager, which controls the presentation, location, and adornment of various windows (examples: Metacity, Kwin, and TWM).

- X client applications may be invoked on a remote X server.

- In addition to a wide variety of third-party hardware and software solutions available for accessible users, Linux provides several native desktop accessibility tools and features for impaired users to enable them to use the operating system and applications with ease.

- Assistive technologies include tools and applications for keyboard navigation, onscreen virtual keyboards, screen readers, speech synthesizers, screen magnifiers, screen resolution adjustments, mouse cursors, mouse gestures, and visual and audible alerts.

- CUPS, based on the IPP, is a standard feature-rich client/server printing service available in most Linux distributions and it is a replacement for the UNIX LPD print service.

- A printer may be configured as a local, remote, or network printer.

- Troubleshooting a printing problem requires several basic checks to be performed to pinpoint the issue.

- Commands we learned in this chapter are: xwininfo, xdpyinfo, Xorg, X, init, startx, xinit, xhost, xclock, ssh, lpinfo, lpadmin, lpstat, cupsenable, cupsdisable, cupsaccept, accept, cupsreject, reject, lp, lpr, lprm, and lpq.

- Files and directories we discussed in this chapter are: /etc/X11/xorg.conf, /etc/X11/xorg/xorg.conf, /etc/sysconfig/desktop, /etc/X11/default-display-manager, /etc/X11/xdm/Xresources, /etc/gdm/custom.conf, (/etc/kde4/kdm/, /etc/X11/kdm/, or /usr/share/kde4/config/kdm/), /etc/inittab, /etc/X11/default-display-login, /etc/lightdm/lightdm.conf, /usr/share/lightdm/lightdm.conf.d/, /etc/cups/, /var/spool/cups/, /var/log/cups/, /run/cups/, /var/run/cups/, /etc/cups/client.conf, /etc/cups/cupsd.conf, and /etc/cups/printers.conf.

## Chapter 14

Scheduling Tasks, Logging Messages, and Using TCP Wrappers

- ➢ Comprehend job scheduling
- ➢ Control who can schedule jobs
- ➢ Overview of the scheduler log file
- ➢ Use at for one-time scheduling—submit, view, list, and remove a job
- ➢ Understand crontable syntax and use it to schedule recurring jobs
- ➢ Overview of anacron
- ➢ Introduction to system logging and an analysis of its configuration file
- ➢ Log custom messages manually
- ➢ Log local messages to remote servers
- ➢ Receive remote messages and log them locally
- ➢ Rotate log files to manage file sizes and disk space usage
- ➢ Overview of syslog-ng
- ➢ Understand systemd journal and view its content
- ➢ Control network access to system and services via TCP Wrappers

This chapter covers the following objectives for LX0-104/102-400 Exam:

107.2 Automate system administration tasks by scheduling jobs [this entire objective is described in this chapter]

26. Manage cron and at jobs
27. Configure user access to cron and at services
28. Configure anacron

The following is a partial list of the used files, terms and utilities:
/etc/cron.{d,daily,hourly,monthly,weekly}, /etc/at.deny, /etc/at.allow, /etc/crontab, /etc/cron.allow, /etc/cron.deny, /var/spool/cron/*, crontab, at, atq, atrm, anacron, /etc/anacrontab

108.2 System logging [this entire objective is described in this chapter]

37. Configuration of the syslog daemon
38. Understanding of standard facilities, priorities and actions
39. Configuration of logrotate
40. Awareness of rsyslog and syslog-ng

The following is a partial list of the used files, terms and utilities: syslog.conf, syslogd, klogd, /var/log/, logger, logrotate, /etc/logrotate.conf, /etc/logrotate.d/, journalctl, /etc/systemd/journald.conf, /var/log/journal

110.2 Setup host security [this objective is split equally among chapter 10, this chapter, and chapter 11; the /etc/inittab and /etc/init.d/* are explained in chapter 6]

71. Understand the role of TCP wrappers

The following is a partial list of the used files, terms and utilities: /etc/hosts.allow and /etc/hosts.deny

Job scheduling allows a user to schedule a command for a one-time or recurring execution in the future. A job is submitted and managed by authorized users only. All executed jobs are logged. Anacron is a service that automatically runs jobs that were missed while the system was down.

Linux logs system activities in various log files for storage and analysis, and possible troubleshooting. Logs generated on one system may be forwarded to and stored on a remote system. This makes the remote system a central repository for all messages generated on that system. The remote system may be configured to receive forwarded messages from several clients.

Log files grow over time and need to be rotated periodically to prevent from filling the file system space. System log file records custom messages sent to it for recording. Syslog-ng is another powerful logging service available for use in Linux. systemd has introduced a new service for viewing and managing system logs in addition to the traditional syslog.

TCP Wrappers is a simple system and service access control mechanism. It may be configured to permit (or prevent) specific hosts, networks, and domains to access one or more network services running on the system.

Understanding Job Scheduling

Job scheduling is a feature that allows a user to submit a command for execution at a specified time in the future. The execution of the command could be one time or periodic based on a pre-determined time schedule. A one-time execution may be scheduled for an activity that needs to be performed at a time of low system usage. One example of such an activity would be the execution of a lengthy shell program. In contrast, a recurring activity could include creating a compressed archive, trimming log files, monitoring the system, running a custom script, or removing unwanted files from the system.

Job scheduling and execution is taken care of by two service daemons: *atd* and *crond*. While *atd* manages the jobs scheduled to run one time in the future, *crond* is responsible for running jobs repetitively at pre-specified times. At startup, this daemon reads the schedules in files located in the */var/spool/cron* (or */var/spool/cron/crontabs* for Ubuntu) and */etc/cron.d* directories, and loads them in the memory for on-time execution. It scans these files at short intervals and updates the in-memory schedules to reflect any modifications made. This daemon runs a job at its scheduled time only and does not entertain any missed jobs. In contrast, the *atd* daemon retries a missed job at the same time next day. For any additions or changes, neither daemon needs a restart.

Controlling Who Can Access

By default, all users are allowed to schedule jobs using the at and cron services. However, this access may be controlled and restricted to specific users only. This can be done by listing users in the allow or deny file located in the */etc* directory for either service. These files are named *at.allow* and *at.deny* for the at service and *cron.allow* and *cron.deny* for the cron service.

The syntax for the four files is identical. We only need to list usernames that are to be allowed or denied access to these scheduling tools. Each file takes one username per line. The *root* user is always permitted; it is affected neither by the existence or non-existence of these files nor by the inclusion or exclusion of its entry in these files.

Table 14-1 shows various combinations and their impact on user access.

---

at.allow / cron.allow	at.deny / cron.deny	Impact
Exists, and contains user entries	Existence does not matter	All users listed in allow files are permitted
Exists, but is empty	Existence does not matter	No users are permitted
Does not exist	Exists, and contains user entries	All users, other than those listed in deny files, are permitted
Does not exist	Exists, but is empty	All users are permitted
Does not exist	Does not exist	No users are permitted

Table 14-1 User Access Restrictions to Scheduling Tools

By default, the *deny* files exist on RHEL and its derivatives and are empty, and the *allow* files are non-existent. This opens up full access to using both tools for all users. On Ubuntu, none of the files are available by default, which closes the access for everyone except for the *root* user.

The following message appears if an unauthorized user attempts to execute *at*:

You do not have permission to use at.

And the following message appears for unauthorized access attempt to the cron service:

You (user1) are not allowed to use this program (crontab)
See crontab(1) for more information

To generate the denial messages, I placed entries for *user1* in the *deny* files.

Scheduler Log File

All activities for *atd* and *crond* services are logged to the */var/log/cron* file. Information such as the time of activity, hostname, owner, PID, and a message for each invocation is captured. The file also keeps track of other activities for *crond* such as the service start time and any delays. A few sample entries from the log file on *centos73* are shown below:

Apr 3 14:10:01 centos73 CROND[2874]: (root) CMD (/usr/lib64/sa/sa1 1 1)
Apr 3 14:20:02 centos73 CROND[3618]: (root) CMD (/usr/lib64/sa/sa1 1 1)
Apr 3 14:30:01 centos73 CROND[4197]: (root) CMD (/usr/lib64/sa/sa1 1 1)

Using at

The *at* command is used to schedule a one-time execution of a program in the future. All submitted jobs are spooled in the */var/spool/at* directory and executed by the *atd* daemon at the specified time. Each submitted job will have a file created containing the settings for establishing the user's shell environment to ensure a successful execution. This file also includes the name of the command or script to be run. There is no need to restart the *atd* daemon after a job submission.

There are multiple ways for expressing the time with the *at* command. Some examples are:

at 1:15am	(executes the task at the next 1:15am)
at noon	(executes the task at 12pm)
at 23:45	(executes the task at 11:45pm)

at midnight	(executes the task at 12am)
at 20:05 tomorrow	(executes the task at 8:05pm on the next day)
at now + 5 hours	(executes the task 5 hours from now. We can specify minutes, days, or weeks instead)
at 3:00 11/15/17	(executes the task at 3am on November 15, 2017)

 at assumes the current year if no year is mentioned and today's date if no date is mentioned.

You may supply a filename with the *at* command using the -f option. The command will execute that file at the specified time. For instance, the following will run *script1.sh* (create this file in *user1*'s home directory, add the *ls* command to it, and ensure that it is executable by the user) for *user1* from their home directory two hours from now:

[user1@centos73 ~]$ **at -f ~/script1.sh now + 2 hours**
job 1 at Mon Apr 3 16:42:00 2017

The at service is installed on RHEL and its clones by default; however, you may have to load it on Ubuntu. Use appropriate software management tools to confirm or install. See Chapter 5 "Managing Shared Libraries and Software Packages" for details.

Exercise 14-1: Submit, View, List, and Remove an at Job

In this exercise, you will submit an at job as the *root* user to run the *date* command at 11:30 p.m. on August 31, 2018, and have the output and any error messages generated redirected to the */tmp/date.out* file. You will list the submitted job, display contents for verification, and then remove the job.

1. Run the *at* command and specify the correct time and date for the job execution. Press Ctrl+d at the at> prompt when done.

    [root@centos73 ~]# **at 11:30pm 8/31/18**
    at> **date &> /tmp/date.out**
    at> **<EOT>**
    job 2 at Thu Aug 31 23:30:00 2018

    The system has assigned ID 2 to this job.

2. List the job file created in the */var/spool/at* directory:

    [root@centos73 ~]# **ll /var/spool/at**
    -rwx------. 1 user1 user1 2639 Apr 3 14:50 a00002018e8c12

3. Display the contents of this file with either of the following. Specify the job ID if using the *at* command.

    [root@centos73 ~]# **less /var/spool/at/a00005016d1f72**
    [root@centos73 ~]# **at -c 2**

4. List the spooled job with either of the following:

```
[root@centos73 ~]# at -l
[root@centos73 ~]# atq
```

5. Finally, remove the spooled job with the *at* or *atrm* command:

```
[root@centos73 ~]# at -d 2
[root@centos73 ~]# atrm 2
```

This should remove the job file from the */var/spool/at* directory as well. You can confirm the deletion with the *atq* command.

Using crontab

Using the *crontab* command is the other method for scheduling tasks for running in the future. Unlike *atd*, *crond* executes cron jobs on a regular basis if they comply with the format defined in the */etc/crontab* file. Crontables for users are located in the */var/spool/cron* (or */var/spool/cron/crontabs* for Ubuntu) directory. Each authorized user with a scheduled job has a file matching their login name in this directory.

For example, the crontab file for *user1* would be */var/spool/cron/user1*. The other location where system crontables are stored is the */etc/cron.d* directory; however, only the *root* user is allowed to create, modify, or delete them. The *crond* daemon scans entries in the files at the two locations to determine the execution plan. The daemon runs the commands or scripts at the specified time and adds a log entry to the */var/log/cron* file. There is no need to restart the daemon after submitting or modifying a cron job.

By default, cron and crontable files are installed on the system as part of the Linux installation. Use appropriate software management tools to confirm. See Chapter 5 "Managing Shared Libraries and Software Packages" for details.

The *crontab* command is used to edit (-e), list (-l), and remove (-r) crontables. The -u option is also available for users who wish to modify a different user's crontable, provided they are allowed to do so and that the user is listed in the *cron.allow* file. The *root* user can also use the -u option to alter other users' crontables, even if the users are not listed in the *allow* file. By default, crontab files are opened in the vi editor when the *crontab* command is issued to edit them.

Syntax of User Crontab Files

The */etc/crontab* file stipulates the syntax that each user cron job must comply with in order for *crond* to interpret and execute it successfully. Based on this structure, each line in a user crontable with an entry for a scheduled job is comprised of six fields. See Figure 14-1 for the syntax.

Compared to user crontables, the system crontab files have seven fields. The first five and the last fields are identical; however, the sixth field specifies the user name of who will be executing the specified command or script.

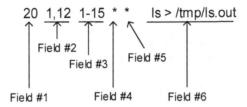

20 1,12 1-15 * *   ls > /tmp/ls.out

Field #2

Field #3   Field #5

Field #1   Field #4   Field #6

Figure 14-1 Syntax of Crontables

A description of each field is given in Table 14-2.

Field	Field Content	Description
1	Minute of hour	Valid values are 0 (the exact hour) to 59. This field can have one specific value (see #1), multiple comma-separated values (see #2), a range of values (see #3), a mix of #2 and #3 (1-5,6-19), or an * representing every minute of the hour (see #4 and #5).
2	Hour of day	Valid values are 0 (midnight) to 23. Same usage applies as in the minute of hour field.
3	Day of month	Valid values are 1 to 31. Same usage applies as in the minute of hour field.
4	Month of year	Valid values are 1 to 12 or jan to dec. Same usage applies as in the minute of hour field.
5	Day of week	Valid values are 0 to 6 or sun to sat, with 0 representing Sunday, 1 representing Monday, and so on. Same usage applies as in the minute of hour field.
6	Command or script to execute	Specifies the absolute pathname of the command or script to be executed, along with any arguments that it requires.

Table 14-2 Description of Crontable Syntax

Exercise 14-2: Add, List, and Remove a Cron Job

For this exercise, assume that no users other than *root* are currently allowed to schedule cron jobs on *centos73*.

In this exercise, you will submit a cron job for *user1* to run *script1.sh* (create this file, add "echo Hello, this is a test" to it, and ensure the script is executable by *user1*) located in this user's home directory. You will schedule this script to execute at the 5th minute past the hour from 1:00 a.m. to 5:00 a.m. on the 20th and the 25th of every month. You will have the output redirected to the */tmp/script1.out* file, list the cron entry, and then remove the crontable. You can open two terminals on the system, one with *user1* logged in and the other one with a *root* session.

1. As *user1*, open the crontable and append the following schedule to it. Save the file when done and exit out of the editor.

```
[user1@centos73 ~]$ crontab -e
5  1-5  20,25  *  *  /home/user1/script1.sh > /tmp/script1.out
```

2. As *root*, list the crontable for *user1* in the */var/spool/cron* directory:

    ```
    [root@centos73 ~]# ll /var/spool/cron/user1
    -rw-------. 1 user1 user1  70  Apr 3 20:01 user1
    ```

3. As *root*, edit the */etc/cron.allow* file and add *user1* to it:

    ```
    [root@centos73 ~]# vi /etc/cron.allow
    user1
    ```

4. As *user1*, list the contents of the crontable:

    ```
    [user1@centos73 ~]$ crontab -l
    5 1-5 20,25 * *  /home/user1/script1.sh > /tmp/script1.out
    ```

5. As *user1*, remove the crontable and confirm the erasure:

    ```
    [user1@centos73 ~]$ crontab -r
    [user1@centos73 ~]$ crontab -l
    no crontab for user1
    ```

What is anacron?

Anacron is a service that runs after every system reboot, checking for any *cron* and *at* jobs that were scheduled for execution during the time the system was down, and, therefore, they were missed. Anacron proves useful on laptop, desktop, and similar purpose systems with extended periods of frequent downtimes and are not intended for 24/7 operations. Anacron scans the */etc/cron.hourly/0anacron* file for three factors to learn whether to run missed jobs. The three factors it examines are: (1) the presence of the */var/spool/anacron/cron.daily* file, (2) the elapsed time of 24 hours since anacron was last run, and (3) if the system is plugged in to an AC source. If all three factors are affirmative, anacron goes ahead and automatically executes the scripts located in the */etc/cron.daily*, */etc/cron.hourly*, */etc/cron.weekly*, and */etc/cron.monthly* directories, based on the settings and conditions defined in anacron's own configuration file */etc/anacrontab*. The default non-commented contents of the */etc/anacrontab* file from *centos73* are displayed below:

```
[root@centos73 ~]# cat /etc/anacrontab
. . . . . . . .
SHELL=/bin/sh
PATH=/sbin:/bin:/usr/sbin:/usr/bin
MAILTO=root
RANDOM_DELAY=45
START_HOURS_RANGE=3-22
1          5     cron.daily     nice  run-parts  /etc/cron.daily
7          25    cron.weekly    nice  run-parts  /etc/cron.weekly
@monthly   45    cron.monthly   nice  run-parts  /etc/cron.monthly
```

This file has five variables defined: (1 and 2) the SHELL and PATH variables set the shell and path to be used for executing the scripts; (3) MAILTO defines the username or an email of the user who is to be sent any output and error messages; (4) RANDOM_DELAY expresses the maximum arbitrary delay in minutes added to the base delay of the jobs as defined in the second column of the last three lines; (5) and START_HOURS_RANGE states the hour range within which the missed jobs could begin.

The last three lines define the schedule and the scripts to be executed. The first column represents the period in days (or @daily, @weekly, @monthly, or @yearly), which anacron uses to inspect whether the specified job has been executed in this period; the next column specifies the delay in minutes after the system has been booted up for anacron to wait before executing the job; the third column contains a unique job identifier; and the fourth column represents the command to be used to execute the scripts located under the *etc/cron.daily*, */etc/cron.weekly*, and */etc/cron.monthly* directories. Here the *run-parts* command is invoked for execution at the default niceness.

For each job, anacron examines whether the job was already run in the specified period (column 1) and executes it after waiting for the number of minutes (column 2) plus the RANDOM_DELAY value if it wasn't. When all missed jobs are executed and there is none pending, anacron exits.

Anacron may be run manually at the command prompt. For example, to run all the jobs that are scheduled in the */etc/anacrontab* file but were missed, simply type the **anacron** command and press the Enter key.

Anacron stores job execution dates in files located in the */var/spool/anacron* directory for each defined schedule. There are several options available with the *anacron* command. Check the manual pages for further information.

System Logging

System logging (*syslog* for short) is an essential and one of the most rudimentary elements of the operating system. Its purpose is to capture messages generated by the kernel, daemons, commands, user activities, applications, and other events, and forward them to various log files, which store them for security auditing, service malfunctioning, system troubleshooting, or informational purposes.

The daemon that is responsible for system logging is called *rsyslogd*. This daemon is multi-threaded, with support for enhanced filtering, encryption protected message relaying, and a variety of configuration options. The *rsyslogd* daemon reads its configuration file */etc/rsyslog.conf* and the configuration files located in the */etc/rsyslog.d* directory at startup. The default depository for most system log files is the */var/log* directory. Other services such as audit, Apache, and GNOME desktop manager also have sub-directories under */var/log/* for storing their respective log files.

> On older Linux versions, a service called *klogd* is used for capturing kernel messages and events, and feeding them to another service called *syslogd*. The *klogd* service has its own PID file located in the */var/run* directory called *klogd.pid*. In newer versions, the *klogd* functionality is incorporated into *syslogd*, and the resulting service with other enhancements is now called *rsyslogd*.

The syslog service is modular, allowing the modules listed in its configuration file to be dynamically loaded in the kernel as and when needed. Each module brings a new functionality to the system upon loading.

The *rsyslogd* daemon can be stopped manually with **systemctl stop rsyslog** on systems running systemd and with **service rsyslog stop** on SysVinit systems. Replace stop with start, restart, reload, and status as appropriate.

A PID is assigned to the daemon at startup and a file by the name *syslogd.pid* (or *rsyslogd.pid*) is created under */run/* to save the PID. The reason this file is created and stores the PID is to inhibit the initiation of multiple instances of *rsyslogd*.

The Syslog Configuration File

The primary syslog configuration file is located in the */etc* directory and it is called *rsyslog.conf*. This file contains three sections: Modules, Global Directives, and Rules (on Ubuntu, this file contains the Modules and Global Directives sections; the Rules section is outlined in the */etc/rsyslog.d/50-default.conf* file). The Modules section provides the support for manual logging via the *logger* command and access to the systemd journal. The Global Directives section consists of the directives that influence the syslog service as a whole. The Rules section dictates what to capture and where to send it. A few sample line entries from the Rules section are shown below and explained subsequently:

```
*.info;mail.none;authpriv.none;cron.none        /var/log/messages
authpriv.*                                      /var/log/secure
mail.*                                          /var/log/maillog
cron.*                                          /var/log/cron
*.emerg                                         :omusrmsg:*
uucp,news.crit                                  /var/log/spooler
local7.*                                        /var/log/boot.log
```

As depicted, each line entry comprises of two fields. The left field is called *selector*, and the right field is referred to as *action*. The selector field is further divided into two period-separated sub-fields called *facility* (left) and *priority* (right), with the former representing one or more system process categories that generate messages and the latter identifying the severity associated with the messages. The semicolon (;) character is used as a distinction mark if multiple facility.priority groups are present. The action field determines the destination to send the messages to.

There are numerous supported facilities such as auth, authpriv, cron, daemon, kern, lpr, mail, news, syslog, user, uucp, and local0 through local7. The asterisk (*) character represents all of them.

Similarly, there are several supported priorities, and they include emerg, alert, crit, err, warn, notice, info, debug, and none. This sequence is in the descending criticality order. The asterisk (*) represents all of them. If a lower priority is selected, the daemon logs all messages of the service at that and higher levels.

The first line entry above instructs the daemon to catch and store informational messages from all services to the */var/log/messages* file (or the */var/log/syslog* file on Ubuntu) and ignore all messages generated by mail, authentication, and cron services. The second, third, and fourth line entries command the daemon to collect and log all messages produced by authentication, mail, and cron to the *secure, maillog,* and *cron* files, respectively. The fifth line orders the daemon to display emergency messages on the terminals of all logged-in users. The sixth line shows two comma-separated facilities that are set at a common priority. These facilities tell the daemon to gather critical messages from uucp and news facilities, and log them to the */var/log/spooler* file. The last line entry is for recording the boot-time service startup status to the */var/log/boot.log* file.

If you have made any modifications to the *rsyslog.conf* file (or the *50-default.conf* file on Ubuntu), run the *rsyslogd* command with the -N switch and specify a numeric verbosity level to inspect whether the file has any errors:

```
[root@centos73 ~]# rsyslogd -N 1
rsyslogd: version 7.4.7, config validation run (level 1), master config /etc/rsyslog.conf
rsyslogd: End of config validation run. Bye.
```

With no issues reported in the output, the syslog service can be restarted (or reloaded) in order for the changes to take effect.

Logging Custom Messages

Many times it is worthwhile to add a note to the system log file to mark the start or end of an activity, or something in-between, for a future reference. This is especially important when you run a script to carry out certain task and you want to record its status or add comments at various stages of its execution. This is also beneficial in debugging the startup of an application to know exactly where it is failing.

The Modules section in the *rsyslog.conf* file provides the support to record custom messages to the *messages* (or *syslog*) log file using the *logger* command. This command may be run by normal users or the *root* user. For instance, if you want to add the note "System Rebooted by $USER" as *user1* with the PID of the process also recorded (-i), use the following:

```
[user1@centos73 ~]$ logger -i System Rebooted by $USER
```

Now *tail* the *messages* or *syslog* file and you'll see this message recorded along with a timestamp, hostname, and PID:

```
Apr 5 23:12:14 centos73 user1[8516]: System Rebooted by user1
```

You may add the -p option and specify a priority level either as a numerical value or in the facility.priority format. The default priority at which the messages are recorded is user.notice. See the manual pages for the *logger* command for more details.

Logging System Messages Remotely

Capturing and logging local messages on the system is the default behavior of the syslog service. However, there may be circumstances that demand for consolidation of all local logs on to a central system, called *loghost*, for reasons such as auditing or ease of system management.

The syslog service supports network logging as well. You set up a loghost to receive remote messages for storage and configure clients to forward their messages to the loghost. You may use either the TCP or the UDP protocol for communication between a loghost and clients; the changes in the configuration between the two are minor.

The */etc/rsyslog.conf* file has a pair of twin directives in the Modules section, one pair is to use with the TCP protocol and the other one to use with the UDP protocol. The directives for TCP are:

```
$ModLoad imtcp
$InputTCPServerRun 514
```

And those for UDP are:

```
$ModLoad imudp
$InputUDPServerRun 514
```

The syslog service loads the kernel module (imtcp or imudp) specified with the $ModLoad directive to enable the support needed on the system to function as a loghost. The other directive $InputTCPServerRun (or $InputUDPServerRun) identifies the network port to be used for the service.

On the client side, this file requires a single line entry to enable the local syslog service to forward all alerts to the loghost. Here are sample entries for use with TCP and UDP:

```
*.*  @@192.168.0.101:514     [TCP]
*.*  @192.168.0.101:514      [UDP]
```

The *.* represents all facilities at all priorities. We prepend two @ signs for TCP and one @ sign for UDP to the IP address or hostname of the loghost server, followed by the network port number (514) after the colon (;) delimiter.

 On Ubuntu, the line entry on the client may be added to the /etc/rsyslog.d/50-default.conf file instead.

Exercise 14-3: Configure a System as a Loghost

This exercise should be done on *ubuntu14*.

In this exercise, you will configure *ubuntu14* as a loghost to serve the client *centos73* on the default port. You will use the TCP protocol.

1. Open the /etc/rsyslog.conf file in a text editor and uncomment the following two directives located in the Modules section:

    ```
    $ModLoad imtcp
    $InputTCPServerRun 514
    ```

2. Save the file and exit out of the editor. Restart the syslog service:

    ```
    [user1@ubuntu14 ~]$ sudo service rsyslog restart
    rsyslog stop/waiting
    rsyslog start/running, process 3307
    ```

This completes the setup for loghost and it is now ready to receive and record client messages.

Exercise 14-4: Configure a System as a Loghost Client

This exercise should be done on *centos73*.

In this exercise, you will configure *centos73* to forward all messages to the loghost that was configured in the previous exercise. After the setup, you will generate a custom message on the client and check for its appearance in the /var/log/syslog file on the loghost for validatation.

1. Open the /etc/rsyslog.conf file in a text editor and add the following line to the bottom of the file:

    ```
    *.*  @@192.168.0.101:514
    ```

2. Restart the syslog service:

    [root@centos73 ~]# **systemctl restart rsyslog**

3. Generate a custom log message:

    [root@centos73 ~]# **logger -i "This is a test message from centos73…"**

4. Log on to the loghost (*ubuntu14*) and tail the */var/log/syslog* file:

    [user1@ubuntu14 ~]$ **tail /var/log/syslog**
    . . . .
    Apr 6 8:19:25 centos73 root[3307]: This is a test message from centos73…

You should be able to see the alert in the *syslog* file on the loghost. This completes the setup of a loghost client and confirms the operation of the service as configured.

Rotating Log Files

We know that Linux records all system activities in log files that are stored in a central location under the */var/log* directory, as defined in the configuration file. A listing of this directory reveals the files along with sub-directories that may have multiple service-specific logs. Here is a sample listing from *centos73*:

```
-rw-r--r--.  1 root    root      13813 Apr  5 08:26 boot.log
-rw-------.  1 root    root      36794 Apr  5 09:10 cron
drwxr-xr-x. 2 lp       sys         267 Apr  2 03:27 cups
-rw-r--r--.  1 root    root      32042 Apr  5 08:26 dmesg
-rw-r--r--.  1 root    root     584292 Apr  5 09:08 lastlog
-rw-------.  1 root    root        784 Apr  5 08:26 maillog
drwxr-x---. 2 mysql    mysql        25 Mar 13 09:24 mariadb
-rw-------.  1 root    root     423300 Apr  5 09:10 messages
-rw-------.  1 root    root      12453 Apr  5 09:08 secure
-rw-r--r--.  1 root    root      66472 Apr  5 09:06 Xorg.0.log
-rw-------.  1 root    root       7980 Mar 28 09:36 yum.log
```

The output shows log files for various services. Depending on the usage and the number of messages generated and captured, log files may quickly fill up the */var* file system, resulting in unpredictable system behavior. Also, they may grow to an extent that would make it difficult to load, read, send, or analyze them. To avoid getting into any unwanted situation, we need to ensure that they be rotated on a regular basis and their archives be removed automatically. To that end, a script called *logrotate* under */etc/cron.daily/* invokes the *logrotate* command on a daily basis via Anacron to run a rotation as per the schedule defined in the */etc/logrotate.conf* file and the configuration files for various services located in the */etc/logrotate.d* directory. These configuration files may be modified to alter the schedule or include additional tasks such as removing, compressing, and emailing selected log files.

Here is an excerpt from the */etc/logrotate.conf* file on *centos73*:

```
[root@centos73 ~]# cat /etc/logrotate.conf
# rotate log files weekly
weekly
# keep 4 weeks worth of backlogs
rotate 4
# create new (empty) log files after rotating old ones
create
# use date as a suffix of the rotated file
dateext
# uncomment this if you want your log files compressed
#compress
# RPM packages drop log rotation information into this directory
include /etc/logrotate.d
# no packages own wtmp and btmp -- we'll rotate them here
/var/log/wtmp {
    monthly
    create 0664 root utmp
        minsize 1M
    rotate 1
}
/var/log/btmp {
    missingok
    monthly
    create 0600 root utmp
    rotate 1
}
```

The file content shows the default log rotation frequency (weekly). It indicates the period of time (4 weeks) to retain the rotated logs before deleting them. Each time a log file is rotated, a replacement file is created with the date as a suffix to its name, and the *rsyslogd* daemon is restarted. The script presents the option of compressing the rotated files using the *gzip* utility. During the script execution, the *logrotate* command checks for the presence of additional log configuration files in the */etc/logrotate.d* directory and includes them as necessary. For the *wtmp* and *btmp* files, discrete rules are in place elaborating the frequency, permissions, ownership, and the number of times to rotate them. The directives defined in the *logrotate.conf* file have a global effect on all log files.

What is syslog-ng?

syslog-ng is a flexible and powerful logging service that may be used to collect, classify, correlate, and forward system and kernel messages and events to log files on local or remote servers for storage and analysis. The primary configuration file for this service is located in the */etc/syslog-ng* directory and it is called *syslog-ng.conf*. The daemon for this service is referred to as *syslog-ng* with its PID stored in the */var/run/syslog-ng* file. In Linux distributions with *systemd*, you may be able to run *syslog-ng* alongside *systemd-journald*, or you may choose to disable *systemd-journald* and use *syslog-ng* instead.

By default, the software for syslog-ng is not included in mainstream Linux distributions; however, you can point your system to appropriate repositories and install it. See Chapter 5 "Managing Shared Libraries and Software Packages" for help on how to configure a repository and install rpm and deb software packages.

Understanding the systemd Journal

In addition to rsyslog, newer mainline Linux distributions with systemd system initialization scheme offers a new service for viewing and managing log files. This service is implemented via the *systemd-journald* daemon. The function of this service is to collect and manage log messages from both kernel and daemon processes, as well as from syslog. It stores the alerts in a non-legible format in files called *journals* in the */run/log/journal* directory. These files are structured and indexed for faster and easier searches, and may be viewed and managed using the *journalctl* command. As we know, */run* is a virtual file system that is created in memory at system boot and destroyed at system shut down. Therefore, the log data stored therein is non-persistent; however, we can enable persistent storage for the logs.

Linux allows the concurrent execution and use of both *rsyslogd* and *systemd-journald*. In fact, the data gathered by *systemd-journald* may be forwarded to *rsyslogd* for further processing and storage in text format.

The main configuration file for this service is */etc/systemd/journald.conf*, which contains numerous default settings that affect the overall functionality of the service. These settings may be modified as required.

Viewing the Journal

systemd offers the *journalctl* command to read the journals in a variety of different ways using various options. One common usage is to run the command without any options to see all messages generated since the last system reboot. The following shows a few initial entries from the journal:

```
[root@centos73 ~]# journalctl
-- Logs begin at Thu 2017-04-06 21:54:57 EDT, end at Fri 2017-04-07 09:30:01 EDT
Apr 06 21:54:57 centos73 systemd-journal[96]: Runtime journal is using 6.2M (max
Apr 06 21:54:57 centos73 kernel: Initializing cgroup subsys cpuset
Apr 06 21:54:57 centos73 kernel: Initializing cgroup subsys cpu
Apr 06 21:54:57 centos73 kernel: Initializing cgroup subsys cpuacct
Apr 06 21:54:57 centos73 kernel: Linux version 3.10.0-514.el7.x86_64 (builder@kb
Apr 06 21:54:57 centos73 kernel: Command line: BOOT_IMAGE=/vmlinuz-3.10.0-514.el
Apr 06 21:54:57 centos73 kernel: e820: BIOS-provided physical RAM map:
Apr 06 21:54:57 centos73 kernel: BIOS-e820: [mem 0x0000000000000000-0x0000000000
```

Notice that the format of the messages is similar to that of the messages logged to the */var/log/messages* (or */var/log/syslog* on Ubuntu) file. Each line begins with a timestamp followed by the system hostname, process name with or without a PID, and an actual message.

We may add "-o verbose" to the command to view the output in a structured form. Other useful options such as -k limits the output to kernel-generated messages only, -n with a numeric value restricts the output to that many line entries, and -f shows log entries in real-time (similar to how *tail -f* works). The *journalctl* command also allows us to view messages for a specific service. For instance, we can see all messages related to the *crond* service by issuing **journalctl /sbin/crond**.

TCP Wrappers

TCP Wrappers is a host-based service that allows us to control access into the system from remote hosts sending service requests via the super-server daemon called *xinetd* (or the older insecure

---

inetd) or directly to standalone network services that do not use *xinetd*. The access mechanism is controlled via the TCP Wrappers' daemon called *tcpd* at the host level (network and domain level controls are also a part of it) through configuration files *hosts.allow* and *hosts.deny*. Both files are located in the */etc* directory and their default versions enforce no restrictions.

Here is how the host-based access control mechanism works. When an *xinetd*-controlled client request comes in, *xinetd* scans the *hosts.allow* file via the *tcpd* daemon and allows the request served if it finds a match in the file. In case of a match failure, *tcpd* inspects the *hosts.deny* file and rejects the request if a corresponding entry exists there. If neither file has a matching entry, *xinetd* grants access to the request. TCP Wrappers entertains only the first match as it scans the files and ignores any subsequent matching entries that are defined in the files. Any edits on either file take effect immediately.

Format of Access Control Files

TCP Wrappers provides access control using two files in the */etc* directory: *hosts.allow* and *hosts.deny*. The format of both files is identical and is based on the "what:where" format as shown below:

<service daemon> : <clients>

The first column indicates the name of a service daemon such as *telnetd*, *sshd*, and *ftpd*, and the second column lists a hostname, network address, or domain name of the client requesting the service. Keywords ALL and EXCEPT may be used in either field to represent "open to all" or an "exception". Keywords LOCAL, KNOWN, or UNKNOWN may be used in the second field to match hostnames without a leading dot, that can be resolved, or that cannot be resolved.

Table 14-3 describes several sample combinations to comprehend the usage and syntax of the files.

Entry	hosts.allow	hosts.deny
ALL:ALL	Requests from all hosts, networks, and domains are allowed	Requests from all hosts, networks, or domains are denied
ALL:ubuntu14.example.com	Requests from the specified host is allowed	Requests from the specified host is denied
ALL:.example.com	Requests from the specified domain are allowed	Requests from the specified domain are denied
ALL:192.168.2.	Requests from the specified network are allowed	Requests from the specified network are denied
sshd:ALL	Requests to the service are allowed from everywhere	Requests to the service are denied from everywhere
sshd:LOCAL	Requests to the service are allowed from the local network	Requests to the service are denied from the local network
telnetd:192.168.2.	Requests to the service are allowed from the specified network.	Requests to the service are denied from the specified network.

Table 14-3 TCP Wrappers Access Control Files

A number of additional combinations can be created and added to the files as per the requirement. TCP Wrappers logs access control information to the */var/log/secure* file.

Chapter Summary

This chapter discussed three major topics. The first topic discussed submitting and managing tasks to run in the future one time or on a recurring basis. We looked at the daemons that control the task execution and the control files where we list users who can or cannot submit jobs. We looked at the log file that stores information about all executed jobs. We reviewed the syntax of the crontab file and a variety of calendar formats for use with both at and cron job submissions. We performed exercises to get a grasp on their usage.

Next, we studied the system logging service and briefly touched the syslog-ng and systemd journaling services. These three services are different logging mechanisms available in Linux for capturing and storing alerts from scores of subsystems and services. We examined a log configuration file and discussed log file rotation at length. We looked at setting up a central logging environment with one loghost and one client after briefly discussing the benefits associated with central logging. We tested the client/server setup by generating and capturing log messages.

The last topic discussed was TCP Wrappers, a host-based access control mechanism that is used to control which services on the system can be accessed and from which hosts, networks, or domains. The configuration is simple and it is manually defined in files.

Chapter Review at a Glance

The following presents a one-sentence review of each key topic discussed in this chapter:

- Authorized users can schedule a task, such as a shell program, command, large copy or archival job, log file trimming, system monitoring, or deletion of unwanted files, for one-time execution in the future or on a recurring basis.

- Separate services, atd and crond daemons, run on the system to take care of one-time and recurring executions.

- All activities of both services are logged for reporting or analysis.

- The anacron service is responsible for running the jobs that could not be executed due to system shutdown or reboot.

- System logging is an essential operating system service that is responsible for capturing automated or custom alerts and messages generated by system and user activities and storing them in log files for auditing, troubleshooting, referencing, or analysis.

- The default system logging service is network-ready and can be slightly modified to send or receive alerts to and from remote Linux systems for central storage.

- As log files grow fast, the default Linux configuration automatically rotates and compresses the log files based on a configurable schedule to avoid filling up the file system.

- Syslog-ng is an optional logging service that may be used to gather, classify, correlate, and forward kernel and system messages and alerts to log files for local or remote storage and inspection.

- Linux systems running systemd system and service management mechanism can use the systemd journald service for collecting, viewing, and managing messages and alerts from syslog as well as from system and kernel subsystems, and storing them in journals for fast and easy retrieval.

- TCP Wrappers is a host-based simple access-control mechanism that can be used to regulate remote client requests from accessing corresponding services on the system.

- Commands we learned in this chapter are: at, atq, atrm, crontab, anacron, rsyslogd, logger, logrotate, and journalctl.

- Files and directories we discussed in this chapter are: /var/spool/cron/, /var/spool/cron/crontabs/, /etc/cron.d/, /etc/at.allow, /etc/at.deny, /etc/cron.allow, /etc/cron.deny, /var/log/cron, /var/spool/at/, /etc/crontab, /etc/cron.hourly/, /var/spool/anacron/cron.daily, /etc/cron.daily/, /etc/cron.monthly, /etc/cron.weekly, /etc/anacrontab, /etc/rsyslog.conf, /var/log/, /run/syslogd.pid, /run/rsyslogd.pid, /etc/rsyslog.d/50-default.conf, /var/log/messages, /var/log/spooler, /var/log/boot.log, /etc/logrotate.conf, /etc/logrotate.d/, /etc/syslog-ng/syslog-ng.conf, /var/run/syslog-ng, /run/log/journal/, /etc/systemd/journald.conf, /var/log/journal, /var/log/syslog, /etc/hosts.allow, /etc/hosts.deny, and /var/log/secure.

Chapter 15

Sending and Receiving Email and Securing Access with Secure Shell and GnuPG

This chapter describes the following major topics:

- ➢ Introduction to SMTP and the email system
- ➢ Overview of key email terms and how the email system works
- ➢ Write, send, receive, and check user email
- ➢ Send alerts and notifications to the root user
- ➢ Forward incoming email to another user or email address
- ➢ Understand the OpenSSH service and basic encryption techniques
- ➢ Review OpenSSH versions, algorithms, server process, client tools, and authentication agent
- ➢ Analyze system-wide server and client configuration and key files
- ➢ Set up trusted logins without and with authentication agent
- ➢ Use OpenSSH client commands to remote log in and copy
- ➢ Comprehend port tunneling and configure it
- ➢ Introduction to GNU privacy guard and overview of its commands
- ➢ Generate and list private/public key pair
- ➢ Export, share, and import public key
- ➢ Encrypt and decrypt files with and without signing
- ➢ Produce annulment certificate
- ➢ Find files with special permissions turned on for auditing
- ➢ Use lsof and fuser to list open files and PIDs accessing a file

105.2 Customize or write simple scripts [most of this objective is described in chapter 9 and the rest in this chapter]

8. Perform conditional mailing to the superuser

108.3 Mail Transfer Agent (MTA) basics [this entire objective is described in this chapter]

41. Create e-mail aliases
42. Configure e-mail forwarding
43. Knowledge of commonly available MTA programs (postfix, sendmail, qmail, exim) (no configuration)

The following is a partial list of the used files, terms and utilities: ~/.forward, sendmail emulation layer commands, newaliases, mail, mailq, postfix, sendmail, exim, qmail

110.1 Perform security administration tasks [most of this objective is described in chapter 10, and the rest is split between chapter 11 and this chapter]

63. Audit a system to find files with the suid/sgid bit set

The following is a partial list of the used files, terms and utilities: find, fuser, lsof

110.3 Securing data with encryption [this entire objective is described in this chapter]

72. Perform basic OpenSSH 2 client configuration and usage
73. Understand the role of OpenSSH 2 server host keys
74. Perform basic GnuPG configuration, usage and revocation
75. Understand SSH port tunnels (including X11 tunnels)
The following is a partial list of the used files, terms and utilities: ssh, ssh-keygen, ssh-agent, ssh-add, ~/.ssh/id_rsa and id_rsa.pub, ~/.ssh/id_dsa and id_dsa.pub, /etc/ssh/ssh_host_rsa_key and ssh_host_rsa_key.pub, /etc/ssh/ssh_host_dsa_key and ssh_host_dsa_key.pub, ~/.ssh/authorized_keys, /etc/ssh_known_hosts, gpg, and ~/.gnupg/*

Email is one of the most common network services in use today, and it has become an essential part of our lives. Every major operating system supports it. There are a wealth of email programs available that allow us to configure a system as a server or client for composing, sending, listing, receiving, reading, and redirecting email messages.

Secure Shell is a network protocol that delivers a secure mechanism for data transmission between source and destination systems over insecure network paths. It provides a set of utilities that allows users to generate key pairs and use them to set up trusted logins between systems for themselves. Additional utilities in the set gives remote users the ability to log in and transfer files securely using advanced encryption and authentication mechanisms. These tools have predominantly supplanted their insecure counterparts in the corporate world.

The principal use of the GNU Privacy Guard is to encrypt and sign email messages for privacy and confidentiality, making the messages, including any attachments, exceptionally hard for unauthorized people to crack or tamper with. GNU Privacy Guard also supports file encryption.

Finding files with special permission bits turned on is useful for reporting and auditing. Processes open one or more files when they run; such processes may be identified, and, optionally, terminated.

SMTP and the Email System

Simple Mail Transport Protocol (SMTP) is a networking protocol that is used to transport email messages from one email server to another. It establishes a reliable connection between the source and the destination email server for message handover. This protocol runs on top of the IP protocol and uses well-known TCP port 25 for its operation. Using a combination of these protocols, a message is transported on the network or the Internet, passing through one or several routing devices to reach its ultimate destination.

An email message typically has four parts to it: (1) the sender's ID and domain name, (2) the receiver's email address, (3) a subject line, and (4) a message body. The SMTP protocol uses the first two items to determine the sender and receiver's domains based on which it decides whether the message is destined for the local network. If the message is intended for the local network, it delivers the message to the receiving user's mailbox. If not, it sends the message across the Internet to the correct target system.

Common Terms

An email system typically performs four key functions: *Mail User Agent* (MUA), *Mail Submission Agent* (MSA), *Mail Transport Agent* (MTA), and *Mail Delivery Agent* (MDA). Some programs are designed to perform one of these functions only; however, most programs have the ability to accomplish more than one function.

Mail User Agent (MUA)

A *Mail User Agent* is an email client program used to compose messages, and to submit them to an outgoing MTA via an MSA. On the receiving side, an MUA pulls the message into the inbox of the user and allows them to read. An MUA uses either the POP or IMAP protocol for mail retrieval. Some common MUAs are *mail*, *mailq*, *mailx*, and *mutt*.

Mail Submission Agent (MSA)

A *Mail Submission Agent* is responsible for accepting new mail messages from an MUA. Most MUAs and MTAs have this functionality built-in to their programs.

Mail Transport Agent (MTA)

A *Mail Transport Agent* is responsible for transporting a message from a sending mail server and another MTA is responsible for accepting the message at a receiving mail server, and they both use SMTP. There are plenty of MTA software available and they all have their own strengths and weaknesses. The most widely used MTAs are Postfix, sendmail, Qmail, and Exim.

Mail Delivery Agent (MDA)

A *Mail Delivery Agent* is responsible for delivering an incoming message to a local mail spool directory for storage from where an MUA pulls it for viewing. The MDA is either a separate program or its functionality is integrated within an MTA.

Post Office Protocol (POP) and Internet Message Access Protocol (IMAP)

The *Post Office Protocol* and the *Internet Message Access Protocol* are used by MUAs for retrieving user mail messages from a mail server to their local inboxes. The latest versions of the two protocols are POP3 and IMAP4, and they listen on TCP ports 110 and 143, respectively. Their secure cousins are POP3s and IMAPs, which provide secure authentication and data privacy. The secure versions use TCP ports 995 and 993 for operation.

Mail Queue

A *mail queue* (equivalent to an outbox) is a directory location where user-submitted email messages are stored temporarily before they are transported out by an MTA.

Mailbox

A *mailbox* (equivalent to an inbox) is a location for storing received user email messages. By default, a mailbox file is created under the */var/spool/mail* directory for each existing user account with a matching name.

How the Email System Works

A fully functional email system from a sender standpoint requires an email client (MUA) to compose an email message, a program (MSA) that takes this email message and submits it to a temporary location (mail queue) for further processing, and another program (MTA) for transporting that email message over the network or the Internet to the destination system (another MTA) using the SMTP protocol. On the receiving side, the MTA receives the message and invokes an MDA, which forwards the message to a temporary mail spool location and holds it there until an MUA retrieves and saves it in the mailbox of the user via either POP3 or IMAP protocol. See Figure 15-1 for a high-level process flow.

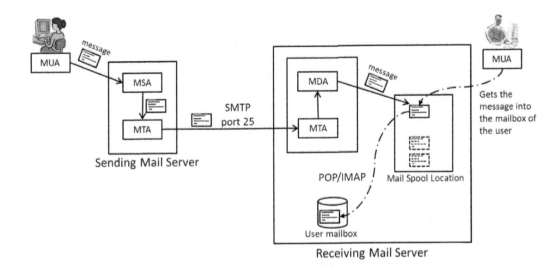

Figure 15-1 Email – From Sender to Receiver

We can analogize the entire process of the email system to the traditional postal system for delivery of a letter (email message). From a sender perspective, a person (MUA) writes a letter and puts it in an envelope with a receiver's name, destination address, and appropriate postage, and drops it at a mail facility. A postal worker (MSA) picks up the letter and takes it to a postal facility (mail queue) for culling, postmarking, scanning, barcoding, sorting, etc. After the processing is complete, the letter is transported (MTA) via a carrier (SMTP) to the delivery post office (another MTA) close to the destination address. A postal worker (MDA) gets the letter and delivers it to the mailbox (inbox) of the receiver (MUA) who uses their mailbox key (authentication) to gain access to the letter.

Composing, Sending, Receiving, and Checking Mail

Linux provides an elementary tool that we can use to compose, send, receive, and check email messages. This tool is called *mail* (or *mailx* in newer versions). Depending on how we stipulate a recipient's ID, we can send a message to a local user by simply specifying that user's name or to a remote user by entering their email address. Another useful tool is *mailq*, which shows us and allows us to control what is in the mail queue on the mail server.

Both *mail* and *mailq* commands need to be installed on the system if they do not already exist. The *mail* (or *mailx*) command is part of the mailx package on *centos73* and *centos511*, and the mailutils package on *ubuntu14*; *mailq* is part of both postfix and sendmail packages on either distribution. Use (CentOS) **yum -y install mailx postfix** or (Ubuntu) **apt-get -y install mailutils postfix** to install them. Consult Chapter 5 "Managing Shared Libraries and Software Packages" for additional help on performing installations on the two Linux distributions.

Moreover, an MTA must be configured and operational on the system in order to send and receive emails. Postfix is the default MTA on *centos73* and *ubuntu14*, and sendmail is the default MTA on *centos511*. They were installed as part of our Linux installations earlier or using the above commands and are good to go with the default configuration; however, you may need to start the service using **systemctl start postfix** or **service postfix start**, as elucidated in Chapter 6 "Booting Linux and Initializing the System." Make sure that an MTA is running before you proceed further.

In most, if not all, Linux distributions, notifications generated by various subsystems for task completions or failures are automatically dispatched to the *root* user, and we can list or view them by issuing the *mail* command as *root*. Moreover, users can manually send messages to one another on the same or remote systems using this command. Let's look at the following example in which a subject (-s option) "Task 24 completed." and a local recipient (*root*) are specified at the command line. Type in a message on the new line that is opened and press Enter when done typing to mark the completion of the message body. Press Ctrl+d to submit the message for delivery.

```
[user1@centos73 ~]$ mail -s "Task 24 completed." root
Testing email message composition....
EOT
```

This message may alternatively be *echo*'ed and piped to the *mail* command for non-interactive submission:

```
[user1@centos73 ~]$ echo "Task 24 completed." | mail root
```

We can use the **mailq** command (or its alternative **sendmail -bp**) at this time to list the contents of the mail queue. The commands, however, will report nothing if the queue is empty and the messages have already been sent out.

Now let's check whether the recipient, the *root* user, has received the two emails. Log in or switch account into *root* and run *mail* or *mailx*:

```
[root@centos73 ~]# mail
Heirloom Mail version 12.5 7/5/10.  Type ? for help.
"/var/spool/mail/root": 2 messages 2 new
>N  1 user1          Mon May  1 13:48  18/648  "Task 24 completed."
 N  2 user1          Mon May  1 13:49  17/601
& (Enter)
Message  1:
From user1@centos73.localdomain  Mon May  1 13:48:38 2017
Return-Path: <user1@centos73.localdomain>
X-Original-To: root
Delivered-To: root@centos73.localdomain
Date: Mon, 01 May 2017 13:48:37 -0400
To: root@centos73.localdomain
Subject: Task 24 completed.
. . . . . . . .
Testing email message composition....

& (Enter)
Message  2:
From user1@centos73.localdomain  Mon May  1 13:49:01 2017
Return-Path: <user1@centos73.localdomain>
X-Original-To: root
Delivered-To: root@centos73.localdomain
Date: Mon, 01 May 2017 13:49:01 -0400
To: root@centos73.localdomain
```

```
. . . . . . . .
Task 24 completed.

& d
& q
Held 1 message in /var/spool/mail/root
You have mail in /var/spool/mail/root
```

The output lists both messages in the user's inbox. Press Enter at the & (ampersand) prompt to view the first message, Enter again to view the next message, *d* to delete a message, or *q* to quit.

Linux also allows us to run a command and email its output. The following example shows how to email the *date* command output to *root*. This example will not include a subject line.

```
[user1@centos73 ~]$ date | mail root
```

Switch into *root* and run *mailx* to check the message.

For testing with an email address, supplant the recipient's name with a valid personal email address.

Forwarding email notifications to the *root* or other administrative user is typically done for automated tasks to apprise the receiver of any issues or errors encountered during the execution of a task, or its progress or completion status. The first two and the fourth command examples in this subsection are instances of such usages that may be added to automated programs or shell scripts.

Refer to the manual pages of the *mail* command for additional options and details.

Redirecting User Mail

Sometimes we want our incoming email to be forwarded to one or more local or Internet email addresses so we don't miss any updates. There are two popular methods for doing this. One is to create a hidden file called *.forward* in the user's home directory and simply add the destination email addresses. Two is to add a mapping of incoming and destination email addresses to the */etc/aliases* file and build a database out of it for reference by the MTA running on the system.

Redirecting User Mail Using the .forward File

This is a simple process and it works for individual user accounts only. Each user that requires redirection of their email will need to create this file in their home directory. As an example, let's configure the redirection for *user1*'s emails to *abc@yahoo.com* (replace with a valid email account for test purposes) by running the following as *user1*:

```
[user1@centos73 ~]$ echo abc@yahoo.com > ~/.forward
```

Now, all emails meant for *user1* on *centos73* will be relayed to the specified email address. Try sending a test message to *user1* with the *mail* utility and check the inbox.

Redirecting User Mail Using the aliases Database

In contrast to the *.forward* file solution that any normal user on the system can accomplish for their personal mail redirection, the *aliases* file method requires someone with the *root* user privileges to be able to modify the file and regenerate its database for reference by the mail server. The *aliases* file and its database *aliases.db* are located in the */etc* directory.

Let's look at the two sample entries (one of them is modified) from the *aliases* file to understand the syntax:

```
bin:        root
daemon:     root,abc@yahoo.com
```

The output shows examples of mail forwarding for users *bin* and *daemon* to *root*. Each user name has the colon (:) character appended to it followed by a local user name, an Internet email address, or a combination.

Let's use this technique to configure mail redirection for *user1*. Open the */etc/aliases* file in a text editor, go to the end of the file, and add the following entry (substitute abcd@yahoo.com with a valid email address):

```
user1:      abcd@yahoo.com
```

After completing the modification, transform the file contents into *aliases.db* by executing the *newaliases* command (or its equivalent **sendmail -I**) as *root*:

```
[root@centos73 ~]# newaliases
```

 The aliases procedure works for deleted and non-existing user accounts as well.

Lastly, restart the mail service for the updates to take effect. Use the *systemctl* or the *service* command as appropriate. Issue **cal | mail user1** as *root* and check the inbox of the recipient for an email containing the *cal* command output.

The OpenSSH Service

Secure Shell (SSH) delivers a secure mechanism for data transmission between source and destination systems over IP networks. It was designed to replace the old remote login programs that transmitted user passwords in clear text and data unencrypted. SSH employs digital signatures for user authentication with encryption to secure a communication channel, making it extremely hard for people to gain unauthorized access to passwords or the data in transit. It also monitors the data being transferred throughout a session to ensure integrity. SSH includes a set of utilities, providing remote users the ability to log in, transfer files, and execute commands securely. Due to strong security features, SSH utilities have supplanted their conventional, unsecured login and file copy counterpart programs.

OpenSSH is a free, open-source implementation of proprietary SSH, and it comes bundled with most Linux distributions. Once applied successfully on the system, the unsecure services—*telnet*, *rlogin*, and *rcp*—can be disabled after a careful examination to eliminate potential impact. The secure command that has substituted *telnet* and *rlogin* remote login services is called *ssh* and that for *rcp* is called *scp*.

OpenSSH also supports *port tunneling* (a.k.a. *port forwarding*), which allows data transmission via unencrypted protocols over ssh-encrypted channels. This feature is common for X11 forwarding, allowing the graphical portion of an application to take advantage of the secure connection.

Access to OpenSSH server may be configured via TCP Wrappers. Refer to Chapter 11 "Understanding Networking and Administering Network Interfaces" for details. Access may also be configured via its own configuration file (discussed later) or firewall.

Basic Encryption Techniques

Encryption is a way of scrambling information with the intent of hiding the real information from unauthorized access. OpenSSH can utilize various encryption techniques during an end-to-end communication session between two entities (client and server). Two common but basic techniques are *symmetric* and *asymmetric*. They are also referred to as *secret key encryption* and *public key encryption* techniques.

Symmetric uses a single key called a *secret* key that is generated as a result of a negotiation process between two entities at the time of their initial contact. Both sides use the same secret key during subsequent communication for data encryption and decryption.

Asymmetric, on the other hand, uses a combination of pre-generated *private* and *public* keys, which are randomly generated strings of alphanumeric characters attached to messages being exchanged. The client transmutes the information with a *public* key and the server decrypts it with the paired *private* key. The private key must be kept secure since it is private to a single sender; the public key is disseminated to clients. This technique is used for channel encryption as well as user authentication.

OpenSSH Versions and Algorithms

OpenSSH currently has two versions—v1 and v2—and they both are available in most Linux distributions. The newer version has many enhancements, improvements, and sophisticated configuration options. The default is v2 as defined with the Protocol directive in the */etc/ssh/sshd_config* file, with v1 as the fallback. v2 supports various algorithms for data encryption and user authentication (digital signatures) such as RSA and DSA. RSA is more common and it is widely employed partly because it supports both encryption and authentication. In contrast, DSA is restricted to authentication only. These algorithms are used to generate public and private key pairs for the asymmetric technique.

OpenSSH Server Daemon and Client Commands

The OpenSSH server software provides a service daemon process called *sshd*. By default, the server software is installed during OS installation with this program pre-configured to run, allowing users the ability to log in to the system using an ssh client program such as PuTTY or the *ssh* command right after the installation is complete. This daemon listens on well-known TCP port 22 as documented in the */etc/ssh/sshd_config* file with the Port directive.

The client software is also installed during OS installation, and it provides plenty of utilities such as those listed and described in Table 15-1.

Utility	Description
scp	Secure remote copy program. Replaced the non-secure rcp command.
ssh	Secure remote login program. Replaced the non-secure telnet and rlogin commands.
ssh-add	Adds private key identities to the authentication agent (ssh-agent)
ssh-agent	Authentication Agent. Holds and manages user private keys for automatic authentication.

Utility	Description
ssh-keygen	Generates and manages private and public key pairs

Table 15-1 OpenSSH Client Commands

The use of these commands is demonstrated in the following subsections.

System-Wide Server Configuration and HostKey Files

The OpenSSH server configuration file defines the global settings for the *sshd* daemon to control how it should operate. This file is located in the */etc/ssh* directory and it is called *sshd_config*. There are a number of directives preset in this file that affect all incoming client ssh communication requests and are well-tuned to work as-is for most environments. From the perspective of this book, three additional directives—AuthorizedKeysFile, HostKey, and X11Forwarding—are worth mentioning here.

The AuthorizedKeysFile directive specifies the name and location of the file containing a user's identification information to be used by the server to authenticate the user. The default is *~/.ssh/authorized_keys*.

A set of the HostKey directives defines the locations and names of the files to be used to determine the private host keys for *sshd*. The defaults are based on the type of algorithm used. For instance, the *ssh_host_key* file is the default for v1 and the *ssh_host_rsa_key* and *ssh_host_dsa_key* files are the defaults for v2. These files also have their corresponding public host key files with a *.pub* extension and they are stored in the same directory location as well. All keys stored in these files are generated at the time of OS installation. For any additional host keys we may use for a different algorithm, we use the *ssh-keygen* command to generate them.

The X11Forwarding directive allows or disallows remote access to graphical applications. The default may be set to either yes or no depending on the version and distribution.

As indicated earlier, the default settings work fine for most environments. However, any changes made in this file will take effective only when the *sshd* program is notified with the *service* or the *systemctl* command, whichever is applicable, to reload the configuration or restart *sshd*.

System-Wide Client Configuration and Per-User Key Files

The OpenSSH client configuration file defines the global settings for the *ssh* client utilities (*ssh*, *scp*, etc.) to control how they should behave. This file is located in the */etc/ssh* directory and it is called *ssh_config*. There are a number of directives preset in this file that affect all outgoing ssh communication requests and are well-tuned to work as-is for most environments. From the perspective of this book, two additional directives—ForwardX11 and IdentityFile—are worth mentioning here.

The ForwardX11 directive is used to enable or disable automatic redirection of X11 traffic over an SSH channel. By default, this directive is set to no. It works in conjunction with the X11Forwarding directive on the SSH server side. Both directives must be set to yes in order for the graphical redirection to work properly.

A set of the IdentityFile directives defines the locations and names of the files containing a user's authentication identity. The defaults are based on the type of algorithm used. For instance, the *~/.ssh/identity* file is the default for v1 and the *~/.ssh/id_rsa* and *~/.ssh/id_dsa* files are the defaults for v2. These files also have their corresponding public key files with a *.pub* extension and they are stored in the same directory location as well. The *~/.ssh* directory does not exist by default; it is created when a user executes the *ssh-keygen* command for the first time to generate keys or connects to an SSH server and accepts the server's host (public) key for the first time. In the second case, the client stores the server's host (public) key locally in a file called *known_hosts* (or */etc/ssh/ssh_known_hosts*) along with its hostname or IP address. On subsequent access attempts from the client, the client will use this information to verify the authenticity of the server.

Exercise 15-1: Configure Trusted Login on a Host

To avoid entering your password each time you log in to a specific system, you may set up a password-free and passphrase-free entry to it.

In this exercise, you will configure this setup for *user1* on *centos73* and *ubuntu14*. You will generate a DSA private/public key combination for this user on *centos73* and copy it over to *ubuntu14*. You will run the *ssh* command on *centos73* to log on to *ubuntu14* with no questions asked.

1. Log on to *centos73* as *user1*.
2. Generate DSA keys and save (-f) them under *~/.ssh/* in the *id_dsa* and *id_dsa.pub* files. Enter a null passphrase (-N) and suppress (-q) the output.

   [user1@centos73 ~]$ **ssh-keygen -f ~/.ssh/id_dsa -N "" -q**

3. Copy the public key file to *ubuntu14* under */home/user1/.ssh*. Accept the host key for *ubuntu14* when presented. Then enter the password for *user1* as set on *ubuntu14* to continue with the file copy. The file will be copied as *authorized_keys*.

   [user1@centos73 ~]$ **ssh-copy-id -i ~/.ssh/id_dsa.pub 192.168.0.101**
   The authenticity of host '192.168.0.101 (192.168.0.101)' can't be established.
   ECDSA key fingerprint is 35:17:a9:5a:98:a7:2c:8a:07:a4:e6:5a:7d:5a:3e:e0.
   Are you sure you want to continue connecting (yes/no)? **yes**
   . . . .
   user1@192.168.0.101's password:
   Number of key(s) added: 1
   Now try logging into the machine, with: "ssh '192.168.0.101'"
   and check to make sure that only the key(s) you wanted were added.

   At the same time, this command also creates or updates the *known_hosts* file on *centos73* and stores the host key for *ubuntu14* in it.

4. Run the *ssh* command as *user1* on *centos73* to connect to *ubuntu14* without being prompted:

   [user1@centos73 ~]$ **ssh 192.168.0.101**
   Welcome to Ubuntu 14.04.5 LTS (GNU/Linux 4.4.0-31-generic x86_64)
   . . . .
   user1@ubuntu14:~$

The setup and the testing is complete.

What is Authentication Agent?

Rather than employing no-password, no-passphrase ssh logins, we can use a more secure approach with the help of *ssh-agent* and *ssh-add* programs. The setup for this alternative entails a one-time generation of passphrase-protected keys and an addition of the decrypted private key to the authentication agent's cache. Once added, the agent will automatically authenticate the user for each invocation of an ssh utility (*ssh*, *scp*, etc.) using the user's stored decrypted key. This will save the user from entering the passphrase each time they use an ssh program for the duration of the session. This facility is particularly convenient for users who require a frequent use of the ssh tools. Note that a re-addition of the private key to the agent's cache is required each time you log off and log back in to take advantage of this facility.

Exercise 15-2: Configure Trusted Login with Authentication Agent

In this exercise, you will generate an RSA key pair for *user1* on *centos511* (create *user1* account on *centos511* if it does not already exist there) and copy their public key over to *ubuntu14*. You will start the authentication agent and add the user's private key to the agent's cache on *centos511*. You will verify the addition of the key to the cache and run a test *ssh* connection attempt to *ubuntu14*.

1. Log on to *centos511* as *user1*.
2. Generate RSA keys for *user1* (RSA is the default key type, so there is no need to specify the type). Press Enter to accept the default file name and location for the keys. Enter a passphrase when prompted.

   [user1@centos511 ~]$ ssh-keygen -q
   Enter file in which to save the key (/home/user1/.ssh/id_rsa):
   Enter passphrase (empty for no passphrase):
   Enter same passphrase again:

3. Copy the public key to *ubuntu14* at the default location. Accept the server's host key when presented. Enter the password for *user1* as set on *ubuntu14* to continue with the file copy. The file will be copied as *authorized_keys*.

   [user1@centos511 ~]$ ssh-copy-id -i ~/.ssh/id_rsa.pub 192.168.0.101
   . . . .
   Are you sure you want to continue connecting (yes/no)? **yes**
   . . . .

4. Start the authentication agent process:

   [user1@centos511 ~]$ eval $(ssh-agent)
   Agent pid 3157

5. Add the user's private key to the authentication agent's cache (no need to specify the file name or location for RSA). Enter the passphrase to decrypt the key and insert it in the cache. Verify the addition by listing (-l) the cache content.

```
[user1@centos73 ~]$ ssh-add
```
Enter passphrase for /home/user1/.ssh/id_rsa:
Identity added: /home/user1/.ssh/id_rsa (/home/user1/.ssh/id_rsa)
```
[user1@centos73 ~]$ ssh-add -l
```
2048 17:8c:ff:67:cf:b5:5e:31:4c:60:cc:2e:93:cc:85:98 /home/user1/.ssh/id_rsa (RSA)

6. Execute **ssh 192.168.0.101** as *user1* to initiate a remote session on *ubuntu14*. You should not be prompted for passphrase.

The setup is complete and it is good for the duration of the session. This setup will also work for other Linux systems (such as *centos73*) if the user's public key is copied to them.

Copying Files Remotely Using scp

The secure copy program, *scp*, is part of the SSH and it allows us to transfer files from one Linux system to another. This program can be run by a regular user as long as the user has the required read and write permissions on the source and destination, or by the *root* user. Here are a few examples to understand the program's syntax and usage. Enter a password/passphrase if prompted.

To copy the */etc/ntp.conf* file from *centos511* to *ubuntu14* in *user1*'s home directory:

> `[user1@centos73 ~]$ scp /etc/ntp.conf 192.168.0.101:/home/user1`

To copy the */etc/ntp.conf* file over from *ubuntu14* in the current directory:

> `[user1@centos73 ~]$ scp 192.168.0.101:/etc/ntp.conf .`

To copy the */etc/fstab* file to *ubuntu14* under */tmp* as *user2* (*user2* must exist on *ubuntu14*; enter their password when prompted):

> `[user1@centos73 ~]$ scp /etc/fstab user2@192.168.0.101:/tmp`

Check the manual pages of the command for more details and usage examples.

Understanding and Configuring SSH Port Tunneling

One of the features of OpenSSH is to allow unencrypted protocols to tunnel their data through ssh-encrypted network channels. This feature works for several unencrypted protocols such as SMTP, IMAP, POP3, HTTP, and VNC. It also works for X11 (X Window system), allowing the graphical portion of an application to take advantage of the secure network connection.

Let's consider an example of setting up X11 port tunneling over SSH on *centos511* (server) and access it on *ubuntu14* (client). In order for this setup to work, we need to ensure that the directives AllowTcpForwarding and X11Forwarding are set to "yes" in the OpenSSH server configuration file *sshd_config*. We will need to notify the OpenSSH service, if we have modified the file, by executing **service sshd reload** or **systemctl reload sshd** as appropriate. On the client side, the ForwardX11 directive in the *ssh_config* file also needs to be turned on. The next step is to log on to the client desktop, open a terminal session, and issue the *ssh* command to receive X11 traffic on an arbitrary local port 5015 from the server via its port 5020 (-L). The -f option will direct *ssh* to run in the background, and the -N option will prevent the execution of any commands on the server. The remote host to establish the tunnel with is specified at the end of the command line.

```
[user1@ubuntu14 ~]$ ssh -L 5015:192.168.0.102:5020 -fN 192.168.0.102
```

Enter the password/passphrase for *user1* on *centos511* when prompted. Execute a command such as **xclock** to run a graphical program. You will see an X clock appear on the client desktop. This program will use the ssh tunnel established with the *ssh* command above.

GNU Privacy Guard (GnuPG)

GNU Privacy Guard, abbreviated GnuPG or GPG, is an implementation of the proprietary *Pretty Good Privacy* (PGP) program and it is primarily used to encrypt email messages for privacy and sign them for confidentiality by utilizing a combination of public and secret (private) key cryptographic techniques. This makes email messages containing possible sensitive information extremely hard to be cracked or altered while in transit. In addition to emails, GnuPG may also be used for file encryption.

The gpg and gpg2 Commands

In order to work with GnuPG, you require the gnupg software or its newer version gnupg2 installed on the system. On most newer Linux distribution versions, either package is installed as part of the operating system installation, so you do not have to worry about installing it.

The gnupg2 (gnupg) package provides the *gpg2* (*gpg*) command for encryption, signing, and key management—generating, listing, verifying, exporting, and importing public/secret key pairs. This command may also be invoked by issuing *gpg* (in fact, *gpg* is a soft link to *gpg2*) on newer versions. The *gpg2* program is powerful and flexible with a number of options available to work with. Table 15-2 lists a few of them in alphabetical order and describes them. The options are provided in both long and short formats where applicable.

Option	Description
--armor (-a)	Generates the output in ASCII format
--clearsign	Signatures are in clear text. Creates a file with .asc extension.
--decrypt (-d)	Decrypts data
--encrypt (-e)	Encrypts data
--export/--import	Exports/imports a key
--gen-key	Generates a new key pair
--gen-revoke	Generates a revocation certificate
--keyserver	Specifies a key server name or IP in hkp:// or ldap:// format
--list-keys (-k)	Lists available keys
--output (-o)	Specifies a file name to redirect the output to
--recipient (-r)	Specifies the UID of the intended recipient
--recv-keys	ID of the keys to be pulled or used from a key server, which must be specified
--sign	Signatures are not in clear text. Creates a file with .gpg extension. May be combined with --encrypt to also encrypt the message.

Table 15-2 gpg2 Options

Refer to the manual pages of the command for additional options and details.

Generating and Listing Keys

GnuPG key pairs are generated using the --gen-key option with the command. You may direct the command to keep the output as quiet as possible by specifying the -q option. There will be a series of questions asked during the process. Let's generate a keypair for *user1* on *centos73*. Accept the default values at the first four prompts and enter "user1" and "user1@centos73.example.com" for the next two questions. Press the Enter key for no comments and accept the selections by pressing "o". All the selections made are highlighted in bold. Input a passphrase when prompted to generate the keys and complete the process.

```
[user1@centos73 ~]$ gpg2 -q --gen-key
. . . . . . . .
Please select what kind of key you want:
   (1) RSA and RSA (default)
   (2) DSA and Elgamal
   (3) DSA (sign only)
   (4) RSA (sign only)
Your selection? 1
RSA keys may be between 1024 and 4096 bits long.
What keysize do you want? (2048)
Requested keysize is 2048 bits
Please specify how long the key should be valid.
      0 = key does not expire
   <n>  = key expires in n days
   <n>w = key expires in n weeks
   <n>m = key expires in n months
   <n>y = key expires in n years
Key is valid for? (0)
Key does not expire at all
Is this correct? (y/N) y
GnuPG needs to construct a user ID to identify your key.
Real name: user1
Email address: user1@centos73.example.com
Comment:
You selected this USER-ID:
   "user1 <user1@centos73.example.com>"
Change (N)ame, (C)omment, (E)mail or (O)kay/(Q)uit? o
You need a Passphrase to protect your secret key.
. . . . . . . .
gpg: key 30283245 marked as ultimately trusted
public and secret key created and signed.
. . . . . . . .
pub   2048R/9EF4A26C 2017-05-03
      Key fingerprint = 63A8 DF9F D859 904D 8FAA  3A34 AA7C 5293 9EF4 A26C
uid    user1 <user1@centos73.example.com>
sub   2048R/89F54121 2017-05-03
```

The last four lines in the output indicate the public key (9EF4A26C) and the relevant fingerprints, user ID, and subkey. All this information is stored in a hidden directory called *.gnupg* in the home directory of the user who executed the command. This directory is created as part of the process if it does not already exist.

After the keys have been produced, you can list them for confirmation using the --list-keys option with the *gpg2* command:

```
[user1@centos73 ~]$ gpg2 --list-keys
/home/user1/.gnupg/pubring.gpg
-------------------------------
pub   2048R/9EF4A26C 2017-05-03
uid     user1 <user1@centos73.example.com>
sub   2048R/89F54121 2017-05-03
```

You may use the --list-public-keys and --list-secret-keys options with the command to restrict the listing to public-only or secret-only keys.

Exporting and Sharing Public Key

The public key we just generated for *user1* may be exported to a file for distribution to other systems. To this end, we use the --export option with the command and specify the UID (user1) and a target file name (such as *user1key.pub*) to store the exported public key information:

```
[user1@centos73 ~]$ gpg2 --export user1 > user1key.pub
```

The next step is to share the output file with intended recipients so that they import the key on their systems for decrypting your incoming emails, validating your signatures, and encrypting emails that they write to you. If you prefer to share the exported file as an email attachment, add the --armor option to the above command to look like **gpg2 --export --armor user1 > user1key.pub** before sending it out. This option directs the tool to export the information in ASCII format.

An alternative, and a more convenient method, is to share the public key via a keyserver so you do not have to send it to potential individual recipients by email. This way any person who needs to exchange confidential and private information with you can get the key from the keyserver. GnuPG provides a free central repository at *keys.gnupg.net* for public to store their keys. To use this service, simply execute **gpg2 --send-keys 9EF4A26C hkp://keys.gnupg.net** or **gpg2 --send-keys 9EF4A26C**. To verify the success of the key submission, open a browser window, point it to *keys.gnupg.net*, and enter 0x9EF4A26C to search for the key. The result should be similar to the following:

Search results for '0x9ef4a26c'

```
Type bits/keyID      cr. time    exp time   key expir
-----------------------------------------------------------------
pub   2048R/9EF4A26C 2017-05-03
            Fingerprint=63A8 DF9F D859 904D 8FAA  3A34 AA7C 5293 9EF4 A26C

uid user1 <user1@centos73.example.com>
sig   sig3  9EF4A26C 2017-05-03 _____ _____ [selfsig]

sub   2048R/89F54121 2017-05-03
sig sbind  9EF4A26C 2017-05-03 _____ _____ []
```

The output confirms the key upload to the keyserver.

Importing Public Key

Once the key has been received by email, the other party (recipient) can import it to add it to their keyring (keys maintained by GPG) using the --import option with the command. Here is how they would do it as *user1* on *ubuntu14* assuming that the file was already transferred to this server under the */home/user1* directory:

```
[user1@ubuntu14 ~]$ gpg2 --import user1key.pub
gpg: directory `/home/user1/.gnupg' created
gpg: new configuration file `/home/user1/.gnupg/gpg.conf' created
gpg: WARNING: options in `/home/user1/.gnupg/gpg.conf' are not yet active during this run
gpg: keyring `/home/user1/.gnupg/secring.gpg' created
gpg: keyring `/home/user1/.gnupg/pubring.gpg' created
gpg: /home/user1/.gnupg/trustdb.gpg: trustdb created
gpg: key 9EF4A26C: public key "user1 <user1@centos73.example.com>" imported
gpg: Total number processed: 1
gpg:               imported: 1  (RSA: 1)
```

They can run **gpg2 --list-keys** to view and confirm the import on *ubuntu14*.

To import the key from the keyserver *keys.gnupg.net* and add it to the keyring, use **gpg2 --recv-keys** command and specify the 8-digit hex key ID (such as 9EF4A26C). If the keyserver is a different server, add the --keyserver option and specify the correct URI with hkp:// or ldap://. Verify the import by issuing **gpg2 --list-keys**.

Encrypting and Decrypting Files With or Without Signing

GnuPG also allows us to encrypt files using the *gpg2* command. It provides us the option to also sign the file alongside encryption. The following example encrypts (--encrypt) the */etc/default/useradd* file on *ubuntu14* for *user1* (--recipient) and store the output (--output) in a file called *useradd.gpg* in plain text (--armor):

```
[user1@ubuntu14 ~]$ gpg2 --armor --recipient user1 --output useradd.gpg --encrypt
/etc/default/useradd
```

You can use the *cat* command to view the contents of *useradd.gpg* file as the output was stored in plain ASCII format. Note that you do not have to use the --armor option if you want the output stored in a non-readable format. Similarly, without the --output option, the output will be stored in a file called *useradd.asc* under */etc/default/* (will require *root* user privileges). Copy *useradd.gpg* to *centos73* using the *scp* command.

On *centos73*, decrypt the file with the *user1*'s passphrase that was entered above. Run **gpg2 --decrypt useradd.gpg** and you will see the original file contents on the screen. It you wish to restore the original, unencrypted version of the *useradd* file, run **gpg2 useradd.gpg** instead.

We can also sign a file alongside encryption using the --sign option with the *gpg2* command. Here is an example. Let's encrypt and sign */etc/fstab* file on *centos73*, copy it to *ubuntu14*, and decrypt it. To this end, run **gpg2 --armor --recipient user1 --output fstab.sig --sign --encrypt /etc/fstab** on *centos73*. Use the *scp* command to copy *fstab.sig* to *ubuntu14*. On *ubuntu14*, run **gpg2 --decrypt fstab.sig** or **gpg2 fstab.sig** to display the file contents on the screen or restore the original, unencrypted version of the *fstab* file. A message similar to "Good signature from XXXX" will confirm the authenticity of the file.

Generating Revocation Certificate

One optional but recommended step is to generate a revocation certificate so that you can use it to nullify your key pair in case you lose the secret key or it is compromised, superseded, or no longer required. The *gpg2* command offers the --gen-revoke option for this purpose. Run this command as follows for *user1*:

```
[user1@ubuntu14 ~]$ gpg2 --gen-revoke user1
```

Enter a reason for the creation, an optional description, and a passphrase to unlock the secret key for *user1*. The certificate is generated and will be displayed on the screen. Copy and paste it in a file and store the file in a separate, secure location for use with **gpg2 --edit-key user1** command in the future if needed to invalidate the key pair.

Miscellaneous Topics

Throughout Part Two of the book, we have explicated several security-related topics that are aligned with LX0-104/102-400 exam objectives 110.1, 110.2, and 110.3. These topics were covered where they seemed to be a better fit with the matter being discussed, such as in Chapters 10, 11, 14, and earlier in this chapter. However, there is one additional topic: finding files with special permission bits for auditing, and two commands: *fuser* and *lsof*, that are pending coverage. These topic and commands are expounded in the following subsections.

Finding Files with Special Permission Bits for Auditing

In Chapter 2 "Working with Files and File Permissions", we discussed three special permission bits: setuid (a.k.a. suid), setgid (a.k.a. sgid), and sticky. These permission bits may be set on binary executable files, executable files and shared directories, and public-writable directories, respectively.

The setuid bit may be defined on binary executable files to provide non-owners the ability to run them with the privileges of the owner. The setgid bit has the same effect as that of the setuid bit; however, it works at the group level. The setgid bit may also be set on shared directories for group collaboration. The sticky bit is set on public-writable directories for prohibiting file deletions by non-owners.

Chapter 2 also discussed how to use the *chmod* command to apply or unset the three permission bits using u+s or u-s for the setuid bit, g+s or g-s for the setgid bit, and o+t or o-t for the sticky bit. We may alternatively use the octal notation with digits "4", "2", and "1" prepended to the standard permissions for the three special bits, respectively.

The use of the special bits should be regulated and monitored to evade potential security issues to system operations and applications. The use of the first two bits—setuid and setgid—on user or application files, including the shell scripts, is highly discouraged. Standard Linux executable binary files, such as */usr/bin/su* (or */bin/su*) and */usr/bin/wall* (or */bin/wall*) with either of the bit set as the default, are an exception to this rule.

In order to determine which files and directories have the special bits set, we use the -perm option with the *find* command. The use of the *find* command is discussed at length in Chapter 2 and in various other chapters in Part One of the book. Let's look at the examples provided below and see how this command can be used to search for files and directories with special permissions enabled.

The following examples show two ways to specify permissions with the -perm option. One method is to use the hyphen (-) character and the other method is to use the forward slash (/) character with the permission mode. With a hyphen, the command searches for matches with all of the permission bits set. On the other hand, the forward slash directs the command to match any of the permission bits. Both methods accept octal and symbolic notations.

To search for all files with the setuid bit applied, use either of the following. The "000" represents any standard permission at the user, group, and other level.

```
[root@centos73 ~]# find / -perm -4000
[root@centos73 ~]# find / -perm /u+s
```

The setuid bit has no effect on directories.

To search for all files under /usr with the setgid bit defined:

```
[root@centos73 ~]# find /usr -perm /2000 -type f
[root@centos73 ~]# find /usr -type f -perm -g+s
```

To search for all group-shared directories under /run with the setgid bit set:

```
[root@centos73 ~]# find /run -perm -g+s -type d
[root@centos73 ~]# find /run -type d -perm /2000
```

To search for all directories with the sticky bit applied:

```
[root@centos73 ~]# find / -type d -perm -1000
[root@centos73 ~]# find / -type d -perm /o+t
```

The sticky bit has no effect on files.

Refer to the manual pages of the *find* command for additional details on the usage of the -perm option.

Identifying Files Used by Processes (Listing Open Files)

The *lsof* (*list open files*) command shows the running processes and the files they have opened. An open file may be a regular file, a directory file, a block or character device file, or a network socket (hostname or IP plus port or client program name). This tool is powerful and versatile, and it may be helpful in debugging and system hardening. This command may be run without any options to list all the files that are currently open on the system by active processes. Here is a sample output:

```
[root@centos73 ~]# lsof
COMMAND PID TID USER FD   TYPE DEVICE SIZE/OFF NODE     NAME
systemd  1       root cwd  DIR  253,0  4096     64       /
systemd  1       root rtd  DIR  253,0  4096     64       /
systemd  1       root txt  REG  253,0  1482128  13286014 /usr/lib/systemd/systemd
systemd  1       root mem  REG  253,0  20040    149232   /usr/lib64/libuuid.so.1.3.0
```

systemd	1	root	mem	REG	253,0	256960	458916	/usr/lib64/libblkid.so.1.1.0
systemd	1	root	mem	REG	253,0	90664	149207	/usr/lib64/libz.so.1.2.7
systemd	1	root	mem	REG	253,0	157424	149263	/usr/lib64/liblzma.so.5.2.2

. . . .

The above output shows a wealth of information about open files and the processes employing them. It includes the process name (COMMAND), process ID (PID), process owner (USER), file type (TYPE), major and minor numbers of the device the file is located on (DEVICE), file size or offset (SIZE/OFF), file's inode number (NODE), and name of the open file (NAME).

The output produced by the *lsof* command may contain thousands of lines of data, and it is too cumbersome to look for a specific piece of information. The *lsof* command provides several options that can limit the output and fine-tune the search. The following five options are particularly useful for narrowing the search:

-c: lists the files opened by a specific daemon (**lsof -c crond**)
+D: lists the files opened in the specified directory (**lsof +D /etc**)
-p: lists the open files associated with a particular PID (**lsof -p 2**)
-u: lists the open files associated with a particular logged-in user (**lsof -u user1**)
-t: lists the PIDs that are accessing a certain file (**lsof -t /etc/passwd**)

You can also supply a file name directly with the *lsof* command to view the processes that are using it (**lsof /etc/passwd**). Try all the bolded command examples and ponder over the outputs.

From a networking standpoint, the *lsof* command may be used as an alternative to the *netstat* command to list open ports and the services that are using them. The -i option is useful; it instructs the command to generate a mapping of services and associated port numbers. This option may be followed by "4" or "6" to restrict the output further to either the IPv4 or the IPv6 service. Here is a sample output when this command is issued with the -i option to find IPv4 services:

```
[root@centos73 ~]# lsof -i4
COMMAND    PID    USER   FD   TYPE DEVICE SIZE/OFF NODE NAME
systemd      1    root   44u  IPv4  15526      0t0  TCP *:sunrpc (LISTEN)
avahi-dae  710   avahi   12u  IPv4  17034      0t0  UDP *:mdns
avahi-dae  710   avahi   13u  IPv4  17035      0t0  UDP *:46047
chronyd    724  chrony    1u  IPv4  16161      0t0  UDP localhost:323
cupsd     1084    root   12u  IPv4  23447      0t0  TCP localhost:ipp (LISTEN)
sshd      1110    root    3u  IPv4  18171      0t0  TCP *:ssh (LISTEN)
mysqld    1581   mysql   14u  IPv4  22088      0t0  TCP *:mysql (LISTEN)
dnsmasq   2742  nobody    3u  IPv4  25651      0t0  UDP *:bootps
dnsmasq   2742  nobody    5u  IPv4  25659      0t0  UDP centos73:domain
dnsmasq   2742  nobody    6u  IPv4  25660      0t0  TCP centos73:domain (LISTEN)
sshd      2766    root    3u  IPv4  25718      0t0  TCP centos73:ssh->192.168.0.11:64361 (ESTABLISHED)
```

The first and last columns in the above output list services (COMMAND) that are running on the system and the associated socket information (NAME). The last entry shows an SSH client connection established via IP 192.168.0.11 and port 64361. With the -i option, the *lsof* command allows us to view what ports are open and which services are using them, and to decide whether we close unused ports for system hardening. In other words, we can leave a service associated with a port running or turn it off. By default, the *lsof* command attempts to resolve IP addresses that it encounters to their hostnames, which results in a slower command response. Similarly, the command tries to resolve port numbers with their service names as defined in the */etc/services* file, which also contributes in slowing down the process. To disable both the features, we can use the -n and the -P options, respectively. Try running **lsof -i4 -nP** and observe the command response and information displayed under the NAME column.

You may further limit the output down to the protocol name, port number, or connection status. For instance, to view a UDP-only service using port 67, modify the above command to look like **lsof -i4udp:67 -nP** and observe the output. Similarly, try **lsof -i 4 -nP -s tcp:listen** for all IPv4 TCP services that are listening. Both usages of the *lsof* command are helpful in determining the network services that are running on the system, the protocol they are using, their connection status, and whether they are IPv4 or IPv6.

For additional options and usage, consult the command's manual pages. You may also run **lsof -h** for a quick look at available options.

Identifying and Terminating PIDs Using a Specific File

Just like the *lsof* program that is used to identify files that are opened by processes, the *fuser* (*file user*) program is used to identify process IDs that have a particular file opened. The *fuser* command offers a subset of the *lsof* functionality. It may also be used to perform one task that *lsof* is not designed for, and that is to terminate or kill the PIDs using a particular file or file system.

Let's look at the following example in which *fuser* is run on a library file */usr/lib64/libuuid.so.1.3.0*:

```
[root@centos73 ~]# fuser /usr/lib64/libuuid.so.1.3.0
/usr/lib64/libuuid.so.1.3.0:  1m  524m  534m  1081m  1095m  1849m  2209m  2462m  2486m  2554m  2574m
```

The output shows a bunch of process IDs (1, 524, 534, 1081, and so on) that are accessing the specified library file. The trailing letter "m" identifies the access type as memory-mapped or shared library. Additional access-type identifiers include c, e, f, F, and r, and they represent:

c: the current working directory (CWD) for the process
e: executable being run
f: the file is opened in read-only mode
F: the file is opened in writable mode
r: the root directory

With the addition of the -v option, the output of the *fuser* command is verbose, as shown in the following example:

```
[root@centos73 ~]# fuser /usr/lib64/libuuid.so.1.3.0 -v
                    USER      PID ACCESS COMMAND
/usr/lib64/libuuid.so.1.3.0:
                    root         1 ....m systemd
                    root       524 ....m lvmetad
                    root       534 ....m systemd-udevd
                    root      1081 ....m rsyslogd
                    root      1095 ....m libvirtd
                    gdm       1849 ....m gnome-session
                    gdm       2209 ....m gnome-settings-
                    gdm       2462 ....m gnome-shell
                    gdm       2486 ....m pulseaudio
```

Try this command on other open files that were reported in the *lsof* command output in the previous subsection. Also try running **cd /boot** and then **fuser /boot -u**. The -u option will make the command report the process owner name as well. You may be able to terminate all the processes that are accessing a particular file, directory, or file system. For instance, after running **cd /boot** and **fuser /boot -u**, you can run **fuser -k /boot** to kill the process accessing */boot*.

For additional options and usage, consult the *fuser* command's manual pages. You may also run **lsof -h** for a quick look at available options.

Chapter Summary

In this chapter, we have had a thorough examination of the SMTP protocol and elaborated on common terms and protocols that are associated with the email system. At length, the discussion described how the email system works and analogized it to the traditional postal system. It demonstrated the composition, sending, receipt, and checking of email messages, as well as how to redirect incoming email to another user on the system or to an email address.

We discussed an open source version of the secure shell service—what it is, how it works, available versions, and algorithms it uses. We skimmed through various encryption techniques and authentication methods. We touched upon the daemon, configuration files, and commands. We performed setups to demonstrate different methods for authenticating trusted users. We used client tools to demonstrate remote login and file transfer capabilities. We examined the use of secure shell tunnels for insecure protocols to channel their data through.

The topic on the GnuPG was the last topic in the chapter and of the book. We looked at what GnuPG is and what it does. We demonstrated our understanding of the topic by performing several operations, such as generating and listing private/public key pair; exporting, sharing, and importing a public key; encrypting and decrypting files with or without adding digital signatures; and creating a dissolution certificate.

The chapter concluded with an explanation of several miscellaneous topics. These topics included searching for files and directories with special permission bits applied for auditing purposes; listing files, directories, and network sockets opened by PIDs; and determining PIDs using a specific file, and, optionally, killing the PIDs.

Chapter Review at a Glance

The following presents a one-sentence review of each key topic discussed in this chapter:

- SMTP is a well-known networking protocol that is used to carry email messages from one email server to another.

- An email message contains a sender's and a receiver's email address, along with a subject and a message body.

- An MUA is a program that is used to compose an email message and submit to an MSA.

- An MSA is a program that accepts an email message from an MUA and forwards it to an MTA.

- An MTA accepts a submitted email message and transports it to another MTA on the destination end.

- An MDA fetches a received email message and deposits it to a storage location for the receiver to pull it via an MUA.

- POP3 (POP3s) and IMAP4 (IMAPs) are client-side protocols that are used to retrieve email messages into a user's inbox.

- A mail queue is a temporary directory location to hold submitted email messages before they are sent out.

- A mailbox is a directory location where user email messages are stored.

- An incoming email message can be forwarded to a different user on the Linux system or to an email address.

- OpenSSH is an open source implementation of the secure shell service on Linux to provide a secure mechanism to transmit data between network entities.

- OpenSSH tools have successfully supplanted many older, insecure network services, such as rcp, rlogin, and telnet.

- OpenSSH also supports port tunneling (or port forwarding) to allow data transmission via unencrypted protocols, such as X11, over its secure channel.

- Encryption is a process of distorting information to conceal the actual data from unauthorized users.

- Symmetric and asymmetric are two common encryption techniques that are used for data encryption purposes.

- DSA is a common algorithm that supports user authentication over OpenSSH channels; RSA is another common algorithm that also encrypts data in addition to the user authentication function.

- OpenSSH client-side configuration can be done at the system-wide or per-user level.

- The authentication agent is a more secure method of implementing trusted user logins.

- GnuPG is a common program that is used to encrypt and sign email messages using a combination of public and secret keys.

- Linux provides a way to search for files in the system with special permission bits—setuid, setgid, and sticky—enabled for auditing.

- Files that are opened by a process for reading or writing can be identified and displayed.

- PIDs that have a particular file opened can be identified and, optionally, terminated.

- Commands we learned in this chapter are: mail, mailx, mailq, sendmail, newaliases, ssh, ssh-keygen, ssh-copy-id, ssh-agent, ssh-add, scp, xclock, gpg, gpg2, find, lsof, and fuser.

- Files and directories we discussed in this chapter are: ~/.forward, /etc/aliases, /etc/aliases.db, /etc/ssh/sshd_config, ~/.ssh/authorized_keys, /etc/ssh/ssh_host_key, /etc/ssh/ssh_host_rsa_key, ssh_host_rsa_key.pub, /etc/ssh/ssh_host_dsa_key, ssh_host_dsa_key.pub, /etc/ssh/ssh_config, ~/.ssh/identity, ~/.ssh/id_rsa, ~/.id_rsa.pub, ~/.ssh/id_dsa, ~/.ssh/id_dsa.pub, /etc/ssh_known_hosts, /etc/ssh/ssh_known_hosts, ~/.ssh/known_hosts, and ~/.gnupg/.

Appendix A: Sample LX0-103/ 101-400 Quiz

This appendix provides 414 sample questions for CompTIA Linux+ Powered by LPI/LPIC-1 exam LX0-103/101-400. Answers to these questions are available in Appendix B. I recommend that you first read and understand the material in Part ONE thoroughly and then take this quiz. You may find similar questions in Appendix C (Sample LX0-104/102-400 quiz), that's intentional. Do not consult the material or seek external help while taking this quiz. Mark the questions that you answer incorrectly. Revisit the relevant topics and try again.

Note that a success on this sample quiz does not guarantee passing the relevant CompTIA Linux+/LPIC-1 exam. In fact, you can create thousands of questions based on the exam objectives and the material presented in this book. However, a thorough study of the topics, a good practice of the commands, and a decent knowledge of various files, directories, and terms discussed in this book increase your chances of scoring higher on the exams.

1. The default umask for regular user with Bash shell is 0027. True or False?

2. What digit represents the setuid bit in the chmod command?
   A. 2   B. 3   C. 1   D. 4

3. Which file system is used to store kernel and GRUB files?
   A. /etc   B. /boot   C. /etc   D. /usr/boot

4. What would the following sed command do?

   sed -n '/root/p' /etc/group

   A. Display lines from the /etc/group file that contain the pattern root
   B. Display lines from the /etc/group file that do not contain the pattern root
   C. Hide lines from the /etc/group file that contain the pattern root
   D. Display lines in duplicate from the /etc/group file that contain the pattern "root"

5. A file compressed with bzip2 can be uncompressed using the gunzip command. True or False?

6. What is the use of the apropos command?
   A. To perform a keyword search in manual pages   B. To show the manual pages of a command
   C. To show the syntax of a configuration file   D. All of the above

7. What is the purpose of using the -a option with the ls command?
   A. To show the listing alphabetically sorted   B. To include socket files in the listing
   C. To include hidden files in the listing   D. To show the directory listing recursively

8. What type of help does section 5 of the manual pages contain?
   A. File types   B. Directory creation techniques
   C. Special commands   D. File formats

9. Both id and groups commands are useful for displaying a user identification. True or False?

10. Which THREE of the following commands can be used to create and manage disk partitions?
   A. The pvcreate command
   B. The gdisk command
   C. The parted command
   D. The fdisk command

11. What are the TWO common uses of the square brackets [] wildcard characters?
   A. To match a range of numeric characters
   B. To match a set of characters
   C. To match a range of characters
   D. To match a set of numeric characters

12. What would the command **echo "I am Linux certified"** print on the screen?
   A. I am Linux certified
   B. echo I am Linux certified
   C. "I am Linux certified"
   D. echo "I am Linux certified"

13. Which command can be used to determine the file type?
   A. The file command
   B. The type command
   C. The what command
   D. The filetype command

14. In vi, which of the following would you use to copy 2 lines and paste them below the current line?
   A. 2yyP (uppercase P)
   B. 2yyp (all lowercase)
   C. 2pyy (all lowercase)
   D. yy2P (uppercase P)

15. Type the name of the command that is used to print the first few lines of a file?

   _____

16. Which umask setting should be set to have new files and directories get permissions 660 and 770, respectively?
   A. 777   B. 077   C. 666   D. 007

17. Which of the following is a file search criteria with the find command?
   A. Searching by type
   B. Searching by inode number
   C. Searching by size
   D. Searching by modification time
   E. Searching by name
   F. All of the above

18. The output generated by the umask command shows the current user mask in four digits. What is the significance of the left-most digit?
   A. Enabled umask if the digit is 1
   B. Disabled umask if the digit is 0
   C. No significance
   D. Most significant bit

19. Default permissions are calculated by subtracting the umask value from the initial permissions. True or False?

20. Which of the following are true in regards to hotplugging and coldplugging? Select TWO.
   A. Coldplugging requires a system shutdown to connect a device
   B. Hotplugging requires a system shutdown to connect a device
   C. Coldplugging is an OS feature that recognizes a device and creates appropriate device files and structures for it without requiring a system poweroff
   D. Hotplugging is a feature that recognizes a device and creates appropriate device files and structures for it without requiring a system shutdown or reboot

21. Type the name of the command that is used to update the shared library cache.

   _____

22. Name the three permission classes.
   A. User, group, and public   B. Read, write, and execute
   C. +, -, and =   D. All of the above

23. Type the name of the GRUB Legacy configuration file that is referenced at system boot time.
   A. grub   B. grub.cfg   C. grublegacy.conf   D. grub.conf

24. Name THREE permission modes from the following:
   A. User, group, and public   B. Read, write, and execute
   C. +, -, and =   D. All of the above

25. Write the digit that represents the sticky bit in the chmod command.

   _____

26. The chgrp command may be used to modify both ownership and group membership simultaneously.
   True or False?

27. The chown command may be used to modify both ownership and group membership on a file. True or
   False?

28. What is the default sorting mode of the sort command?
   A. To sort numerically   B. To sort alphabetically
   C. To sort on the last column   D. To sort numerically on the first column

29. What is the equivalent symbolic value for permissions 751?
   A. rwxr-x---   B. rwxr-xr-x   C. rwxr----x   D. rwxr-x--x

30. A file must have the .sh extension in order to be executed. True or False?

31. Select TWO that are true for a hard link.
   A. Source and target have a common inode number
   B. Source and target must not be in different filesystems
   C. Source and target must be in different filesystems
   D. Source and target have different inode numbers

32. What happens to the remaining hard-linked files if one of the files is removed? Select TWO.
   A. Data they point to is lost   B. Data they point to remains intact
   C. Link count is changed   D. Link count remains unchanged

33. What is the use of the pwd command?
   A. To show the relative path of the previous working directory
   B. To show the absolute path of the current working directory
   C. To show the absolute path of the previous working directory
   D. To show the relative path of the current working directory

34. /boot is not a memory-based file system. True or False?

35. Name the two types of path representation:
A. There is only one type of path
B. Full and empty
C. Absolute and relative
D. None of the above

36. What are the indicators in the ll command output that identify a file as a soft link?
A. Line entry begins with an "l", has 777 permissions, and has an arrow pointing to the linked file
B. Line entry begins with an arrow, has 777 permissions, and has an "l" pointing to the linked file
C. Line entry begins with an "l", has 777 permissions, and has an arrow pointing to the source file
D. Line entry begins with an arrow, has 666 permissions, and has an "l" pointing to the source file

37. The rmdir command cannot be used to remove a directory hierarchy. True or False?

38. What permissions would the owner of a file get if the chmod command is executed with 555?
A. Read and execute   B. Read and write   C. Read only   D. Write and execute

39. What would the command **find / -name core -ok rm {} \; do?**
A. Search for files by the name "core" in the entire directory tree and prompt for removal confirmation as they are found
B. Search for all files by the name "core" in the root user's home directory and remove them
C. Display matching files from the root directory and remove them
D. Search for all files by the name "core" in the entire directory hierarchy and remove them as they are found

40. The who command may be used to view logged out users. True or False?

41. Which THREE of the following are valid statements about copying and linking files?
A. A copied file has no impact on the source file if it is removed or renamed
B. Editing a link file actually edits the file the link points to
C. A copied file can have different access permissions than the source file
D. Deleting a link deletes the source file

42. Write the name of the command that can be used to display the vi editor tutorial.

_____

43. Which of the following commands can be used to view processes running on the system?
A. print   B. process   C. top   D. list

44. The ll command produces nine columns in the output by default. True or False?

45. Name TWO usages of the pipe character.
A. To send output to two destinations
B. As an AND operator
C. As an OR operator
D. To send output of one command as input to another

46. What are the TWO commands to list the PID of a specific process?
A. pshow   B. pidof   C. pgrep   D. pid

47. Which built-in shell command can be used to move a running job to the background and continue its execution there?
   A. background   B. daemon   C. bg   D. All of these

48. What is the principal advantage of using the yum command over the rpm command?
   A. Both commands resolve dependencies automatically
   B. There are no major differences between the two commands
   C. The yum command automatically resolves dependencies
   D. The rpm command automatically resolves dependencies

49. What are the default and maximum nice values?
   A. -10 and 20   B. +5 and -18   C. 0 and 19   D. 10 and 10

50. What is the default priority assigned to a process when it is started?
   A. 80   B. +5   C. 0   D. 70

51. Which of the following is not a correct command?
   A. xz file1   B. bunzip2 file1.xz   C. xz -l file1.xz
   D. bzip2 file1   E. bunzip2 file1.bz2

52. Why would we use the renice command?
   A. To change the niceness of a defunct process   B. To start a process with a different nice value
   C. To remove dead processes   D. To change the priority of a running process

53. What are the TWO commands that can be used to terminate a process?
   A. kill   B. term   C. pkill   D. prockill

54. The default location to record system alerts is the system log file. True or False?

55. What is the -R option used for with the ls command?
   A. To show a directory listing numerically sorted   B. To show hidden files
   C. To show hidden files under a directory   D. To show a directory listing recursively

56. What is the difference between owner-level permissions "rws" and "rwS" on a setuid file?
   A. They indicate that the file has/does not have read and write permission bits set for the file owner
   B. They indicate that the file does not have/has an underlying owner-level execute permission bit set
   C. There is no difference between the two
   D. They indicate that the file has/does not have an underlying owner-level execute permission bit set on it

57. Linux commands may be divided into privileged and non-privileged commands. True or False?

58. Which command is used to create a directory?
   A. makedir   B. touch   C. mkdir   D. createdir

59. Which command besides the uptime command can be used to display system load averages and the length of time the system has been up for?
   A. who   B. w   C. load   D. whodo

60. Which of the following is not a process state?
    A. Running   B. Waiting   C. Sleeping   D. Stopped   E. Terminated   F. Zombie

61. Which THREE statements are true for the command **date2 && hostname**?
    A. The && characters are list operators
    B. The && characters are used to perform a logical AND operation on the given commands
    C. The hostname command will be executed and its result will be displayed
    D. There will be an error saying "date2 not found" when the above is executed

62. Signal 9 is used for a soft termination of a process. True or False?

63. What would the command **rpm -ql kernel** do?
    A. List all files in the specified package
    B. List only the configuration files in the specified package
    C. List only the documentation files in the specified package
    D. List all directory names in the specified package

64. Which of the following directives is used in the GRUB Legacy configuration file to control the length of time the GRUB menu should be displayed before the default kernel boots up?
    A. time   B. timeout   C. delay   D. defaulttime

65. Select THREE features of the Filesystem Hierarchy Standard.
    A. It describes the layout of directories
    B. It describes which Linux versions and distributions can use it
    C. It describes the type of information the directories should store
    D. It describes whether the directories can be shared

66. What is the purpose of the rpm2cpio command?
    A. To back up files in an rpm package
    B. To copy files from an rpm package and append them to another rpm package
    C. To extract files from an rpm package and remove them
    D. To extract files from an rpm package

67. The systemd command may be used to rebuild a new kernel. True or False?

68. What is the use of the -y option with the **yum install** and **yum remove** commands?
    A. No confirmation will be required   B. Confirmation prompt will appear
    C. To display the command's usage   D. The option is invalid

69. Which of the following is accomplished when the SIGHUP signal is passed to a service process?
    A. The service process is restarted without changing the PID
    B. The service process is restarted with a new PID assigned to it
    C. All client connections to the service process are terminated
    D. The service process is forced to re-read its configuration file

70. What information would be displayed when the command **rpm -qf /bin/bash** is executed? Select TWO.
    A. File's version   B. Name of the package the file belongs to
    C. File's inode number   D. File's dependencies

71. What is the difference between installing and upgrading a package?
   A. Installing installs a new package and removes the old one, and upgrading upgrades an existing package or installs it if it is not already installed
   B. Installing installs a new package and upgrading upgrades an existing package or installs it if it is not already installed
   C. Installing installs or upgrades a package and upgrading installs a package
   D. Both install a new package only

72. What must be the extension of a yum repository configuration file?
   A. .r   B. .yum   C. No extension is necessary   D. .repo

73. Soft-linked directories cannot cross file system boundaries but hard-linked directories can. True or False?

74. What would the command **yum list kernel** do?
   A. Show whether the kernel package is installed or available for installation
   B. Show whether the kernel package is installed
   C. Show whether the kernel package was removed
   D. Show whether the kernel package is available for installation

75. Which of the following is correct to create a 200MB primary partition on /dev/sdb disk?
   A. parted /dev/sdb mkpart pri 10 210m   B. parted /dev/sdb mklabel pri 10 210m
   C. parted /dev/sdb1 mkpart pri 10 210m   D. parted /dev/sdb mkpart 10 210m

76. What would the options ivh cause the rpm command to do?
   A. Install a package and show files as they are extracted from the package
   B. Install a package and capture the detailed output and progress in a log file
   C. Install a package and show installation details and progress
   D. Install a package and hide installation details and progress

77. Which command would show a specified command's absolute pathname in the directory structure as well as the location of its manual pages?
   A. what   B. showwhat   C. whereis   D. which

78. What would the command **who | tr -s ' '** do?
   A. Substitute all white spaces between columns of the who command output with a single white space
   B. Squeeze all TAB spaces between columns of the who command output to a single TAB space
   C. Replace each white space between columns of the who command output to one TAB space
   D. Replace all white spaces between columns of the who command output to a single TAB space

79. We can use the downloadyum command to download a package. True or False?

80. What would the command **yum list installed *gnome*** do?
   A. Display all installed packages that contain "gnome" in their names
   B. Display all available packages that contain "gnome" in their names
   C. Display all installed packages that do not contain "gnome" in their names
   D. Display all available packages that do not contain "gnome" in their names

81. Which THREE commands can be used to view the absolute pathname of a command in the directory structure?

   A. type   B. file   C. whereis   D. which

82. What would the command **rpm -qa** do?

   A. List all uninstalled packages   B. List both installed and available packages

   C. List all installed packages   D. List all available packages

83. What would the command **yum info kernel** do?

   A. Display package information

   B. List files that the package contains

   C. Show whether the package is deleted

   D. Show whether the package is available for installation

84. Most newer computers support both BIOS and UEFI. True or False?

85. Which of the following can be used to update the timestamp on file1?

   A. cat > file1   B. type file1   C. view file1   D. touch file1

86. What would happen if the timeout value is set to 0 in GRUB configuration file?

   A. The system will list available kernels for one second and then continue with the boot process

   B. The system will boot the default kernel immediately and will not let the user interact with GRUB

   C. The system will boot the second kernel that is listed in GRUB configuration

   D. The system will not boot

87. By default, GRUB is stored in the MBR on BIOS-based systems. True or False?

88. Which file stores the location information of the boot partition on BIOS-based systems?

   A. bios.cfg   B. grub.env   C. boot.cfg   D. grub.cfg

89. Which of the statements about the locate command are valid? Select THREE.

   A. It discovers all occurrences of the specified string as they appear in file pathnames

   B. It references the /var/lib/mlocate/mlocate.db file for discovery

   C. It is run automatically once a day

   D. A statistics of its database can be viewed with locate -S.

90. What would the command **fg %1** do?

   A. Bring background job 1 to the foreground   B. Send foreground job 1 to the background

   C. Display background job 1 status   D. Show information about job 1

91. What would the nice command display without any options or arguments?

   A. The current nice value   B. The previous nice value

   C. The default priority value   D. The priority value

92. What would /dev/sde3 represent?

   A. Third partition on the fifth SATA/SCSI disk   B. Fifth partition on the third SATA/SCSI disk

   C. Third partition on the first SATA/SCSI disk   D. Third partition on the fourth SATA/SCSI disk

93. Which TWO of the following are the variants of input redirection?
   A. >   B. <<   C. <<<   D. |

94. Every process that runs on the system has a unique identifier called PID. True or False?

95. Which THREE of the following can the debugfs command be used for on extended file systems?
   A. Change file system state   B. Produce superblock stats
   C. Delete files   D. Examine file system

96. Type the name of the filter that can be used to print distinctive or identical lines.
   _____

97. Which command is used to manage services on systems running systemd?
   A. chkconfig   B. systemctl   C. systemd   D. service

98. Name the TWO directory paths where systemd unit files are stored.
   A. /etc/system/systemd   B. /etc/systemd/system
   C. /usr/lib/system/systemd   D. /usr/lib/systemd/system

99. What is the name of the boot log file?
   A. alerts.log   B. bootinfo.log   C. boot.log   D. bootlog

100.   Which two virtual files store processor and memory information? Select TWO.
   A. /proc/cpuinfo   B. /dev/meminfo   C. /dev/cpuinfo   D. /proc/meminfo

101.   Select THREE features of LVM.
   A. Online resizing of logical volumes
   B. Online expansion and reduction of volume groups
   C. Online snapshotting
   D. Online migration from standard partitioning solution to LVM

102.   Which TWO of the following can be used to view an extended file system label/volume?
   A. dumpe2fs -l /dev/sdb1   B. lsblk /dev/sdb1
   C. blkid /dev/sdb1   D. tune2fs -l /dev/sdb1

103.   Which THREE commands can be used to find a package name that includes the specified file?
   A. rpm --query /etc/shadow   B. rpm -qf /etc/shadow
   C. yum whatprovides /etc/shadow   D. yum provides /etc/shadow

104.   Which of the following is invalid to force checking an ext3 file system /dev/sdc2?
   A. fsck -f /dev/sdc2   B. fsck -t ext3 /dev/sdc2 -f
   C. e2fsck -t ext3 /dev/sdc2   D. fsck.ext3 /dev/sdc2 -f
   E. None of the above

105.   What would the command **systemctl restart rsyslog** do?
   A. Stop the syslog service permanently   B. Restart the systemd service
   C. Restart the syslog service   D. Restart the systemctl service

106. In which target on the Linux system with systemd does the X window and the graphical desktop interface start?
A. Graphical   B. Multi-user   C. Network   D. Single-user

107. Which command can be used to determine the kernel release information?
A. probe   B. uname   C. kernel   D. w

108. The lsmod command is used to rebuild kernel modules. True or False?

109. Which command can be used to unload a module?
A. The modload command with -u switch   B. The modunload command
C. The modprobe command   D. The lsmod command

110. We cannot use the yum command to upgrade the Linux kernel. True or False?

111. Write the name of the new system initialization scheme introduced in latest versions of popular Linux distributions.

_____

112. XFS is the default file system type in RHEL7 and its clones. True or False?

113. What type of information does the blkid command display?
A. Attributes for block devices   B. Attributes for both block and character devices
C. Attributes for all devices on the system   D. Attributes for optical devices

114. What is the process of paging out and paging in known as?
A. Thrashing   B. Virtual memory   C. Substituting   D. Demand paging

115. What would the command **mkswap /dev/sdc2** do?
A. Create file system swap in /dev/sdc2
B. Create swap structures in /dev/sdc2
C. Create XFS structures in /dev/sdc2
D. Copy swap structures from /dev/sdc2 to the local directory

116. The parent process gets the nice value of its child process. True or False?

117. What would happen if we mount a file system on a directory that already contains files in it?
A. The directory contents will be visible
B. The directory contents will be deleted
C. The directory contents will hide
D. You must create a new directory to use as a mount point

118. A UUID is automatically assigned to a file system at the time of its creation. True or False?

119. A label is automatically assigned to a file system at the time of its creation. True or False?

120. Which of the following command must be run in order for the changes made to GRUB Legacy configuration file to take effect?
A. grub-mkconfig   B. mkconfig-grub   C. mkconfig   D. none

121. Select TWO of the following to apply sticky bit to a public-writable directory.
   A. chmod +t   B. chmod o+s   C. chmod 1777   D. chmod 2777

122. Type the name of the GRUB2 configuration file that is referenced at system boot time.

   _____

123. The difference between the primary and backup superblocks is that the primary superblock includes pointers to the data blocks where the actual file contents are stored whereas the backup superblocks don't. True or False?

124. Which TWO of the following can be used to delete only the bootloader portion on the boot disk /dev/sda?
   A. dd if=/dev/zero of=/dev/sda bs=512 count=1
   B. dd of=/dev/sda if=/dev/zero bs=446 count=1
   C. dd of=/dev/sda if=/dev/zero bs=512 count=1
   D. dd if=/dev/zero of=/dev/sda bs=446 count=1

125. What would the command **mkfs.ext4 /dev/vgtest/lvoltest** do?
   A. Make ext4 file system structures in the logical volume
   B. Remove ext4 file system structures from the logical volume
   C. Build swap structures of type ext4 in the logical volume
   D. Replace swap structures from the logical volume with ext4 file system structures

126. Select TWO from the following to list partition table information for disk /dev/sdd?
   A. fdisk -l /dev/sdd   B. parted -l /dev/sdd
   C. fdisk /dev/sdd print   D. parted /dev/sdd print

127. What is the difference between the update and upgrade options of the yum command?
   A. The update option updates installed packages; the upgrade option removes obsolete packages as well
   B. The upgrade option updates installed packages; the update option removes obsolete packages as well
   C. Both update and upgrade options are identical
   D. The update option installs new packages; the upgrade option replaces installed packages

128. The aptitude command in Debian and spinoffs can be run directly at the command prompt to perform an action without invoking the command's user interface. True or False?

129. Type the command that is used to view file system space utilization.

   _____

130. What would the command **ls /etc | less** do?
   A. Run both ls and less command on the /etc/ directory concurrently
   B. Send the input of the less command to the ls command for viewing one page at a time
   C. Send the output of the less command to the ls command for viewing one page at a time
   D. Send the output of the ls command to the less command for viewing one page at a time

131. What would the command **ps -U user5** do?
   A. Show all processes with owning user user5   B. Show all processes with owning group user5
   C. Show all processes not owned by user5   D. Both A and B are correct

132. Arrange the tasks in correct sequence for a file system: umount, mount, create, remove
    A. Unmount, create, remove, mount   B. Unmount, create, mount, remove
    C. Create, mount, remove, unmount   D. Create, mount, unmount, remove

133. The parted utility may be used to create LVM logical volumes. True or False?

134. What would the command **cpio -iv < /tmp/home.cpio** do?
    A. Restore all files from /tmp/home.cpio archive and display output in verbose mode
    B. List all files in the /tmp/home.cpio archive and display output in verbose mode
    C. Copy /home directory to a file called /tmp/home.cpio
    D. Restore selective files from /tmp/home.cpio archive and display output in verbose mode

135. Which command can be used to create a label for an XFS file system?
    A. xfs_admin   B. xfs_label   C. xfs_repair   D. xfs_metadata

136. What is the use of the xargs command?
    A. To use the input of one command as arguments to another command
    B. To use the output of one command as arguments to another command
    C. To use the arguments of one command as input to another command
    D. None of the above

137. What would the mount command do with the -a switch?
    A. Remove all file systems listed in the fstab file
    B. Unmount all file systems listed in the fstab file
    C. Mount all file systems listed in the fstab file
    D. Unmount all mounted file systems and remount them

138. What would the command **df -t xfs** do?
    A. Mount all file systems of type XFS from fstab file
    B. Unmount all mounted file systems of type XFS
    C. List mounted file systems of type XFS
    D. List unmounted file systems of type XFS

139. How can we send the SIGINT signal to interrupt a process?
    A. By pressing Ctrl+d   B. By pressing Ctrl+c
    C. By pressing Ctrl+a   D. By pressing Ctrl+z

140. Which TWO of the following statements are true for the mkfs.ext4 and mke2fs commands?
    A. Both can be used to create extended file systems
    B. The former is used to create an ext4 file system and the latter an xfs file system
    C. Neither can be used to create an ext3 file system
    D. Both can be used to create an ext4 file system

141. Which of the following commands can be used to determine the total and used physical memory and
    swap in the system?
    A. free   B. du   C. df   D. stats

142. Which THREE statements are true about /dev/?
A. It is automatically mounted at system startup
B. Its contents are destroyed at system shutdown
C. It is created on the boot disk during installation
D. It is a memory-based filesystem

143. What would you see in the output if you run **grep -w pr....e /etc/profile**?
A. Words matching exactly seven characters from the /etc/profile file
B. Matching words that begin with "pr" and end in "e" with exactly four characters in between from the /etc/profile file
C. Words matching exactly seven lowercase characters from the /etc/profile file
D. Words matching exactly seven uppercase characters from the /etc/profile file

144. Swap spaces listed in the /etc/fstab file are automatically activated at system reboots. True or False?

145. Select THREE valid statements about Sysfs.
A. Sysfs is created on the boot disk at the time of Linux instsallation
B. It stores kernel subsystem, hardware, and device driver information
C. User processes and commands reference information stored under /sys
D. Sysfs is a memory-based file system that is mounted on /sys directory

146. The xfs_repair command must be run on a mounted file system. True or False?

147. The swapon command is used to activate a swap space. Write the name of the command that is used to deactivate a swap space.

_____

148. Select the command to add physical volumes to an existing volume group.
A. vgdisplay   B. vgextend   C. pvextend   D. vgs

149. Select the command to show file system usage, type, and inode information.
A. free -Ti   B. du -Thi   C. tune2fs -iTh   D. df -Ti

150. Which THREE of the following are the basic redirection operators?
A. <   B. >   C. >>   D. <<

151. What is the primary difference between a here doc and a here string?
A. A here doc uses markers to mark the start and end of input; a here string does not
B. A here string uses markers to mark the start and end of input; a here doc does not
C. Both are identical
D. A here doc uses the $ sign to mark the start and end of input; a here string uses the > symbol instead

152. Where is the partition table information stored by default on BIOS-based systems?
A. In the partition table   B. In the BIOS
C. In the MBR   D. In the grub.cfg file

153. What is the maximum number of partitions that can be created on a GPT disk?
A. 64   B. 128   C. 32   D. 256

154. Can you link files or directories across file systems using symbolic links?
   A. Yes   B. No

155. Which command can be used to report quota usage?
   A. edquota   B. quotacheck   C. quotaon   D. repquota

156. Which file stores in-memory disk partition information?
   A. /proc/system_part   B. /sys/partitions   C. /proc/partitions/info   D. /proc/partitions

157. Depending on the Linux distribution and version, which THREE commands can be used to regenerate GRUB2 configuration file?
   A. grub2-mkconfig   B. grub-mkconfig   C. mkconfig   D. update-grub

158. What is the vgs command used for?
   A. To list LVM volume groups
   B. To list LVM volume groups along with logical and physical volumes
   C. To list LVM logical volumes
   D. To scan volume groups and update the configuration file

159. Which special character would you add to a command to run it in the background?
   A. ?   B. !   C. &   D. %

160. Select THREE of the following that can be used to identify a file system block device in the /etc/fstab file.
   A. Device file   B. Mount point   C. Label   D. UUID

161. When can a disk or partition be referred to as a physical volume?
   A. After it is initialized with pvcreate command   B. Before it is initialized with pvcreate command
   C. After it is added to a volume group   D. After it is used to hold a logical volume

162. Write the name of the command that is used to remove an LVM logical volume.
   _____

163. What are the TWO main uses of the built-in Bash shell command set?
   A. To enable or disable a shell feature
   B. To display local and environment variables and their values
   C. To set local and environment variables
   D. To enable or disable a service

164. It is necessary to create a file system in a logical volume before it can be used to store files in it. True or False?

165. What would the output of **join file1 file2** be?
   A. Display lines from the two files if their join fields are identical
   B. Modify the two files and display lines from the two files side by side
   C. Display lines from the two files side by side and ignore the join field
   D. Display the contents of the two files

166. What would the command **pvcreate /dev/sdd** do?
A. Remove LVM structures from the disk
B. Initialize the disk for use in gdisk
C. Add the disk to an LVM volume group
D. Initialize the disk for use in LVM

167. Which TWO of the following would extract the contents of a gzipped tar archive?
A. tar tzf filename.tar.gz
B. tar vzxf filename.tar.gz
C. gunzip filename.tar.gz ; tar xf filename.tar
D. tar vztf filename.tar.gz

168. A single disk can be used by both parted and LVM at the same time. True or False?

169. Which of the following can be used to redirect both standard error and standard output to a file and overwrite any previous content?
A. 2>1
B. 2<&1
C. 2>&1
D. 1>&2

170. Write the name of the command to create an LVM logical volume.

_____

171. Select THREE uses of the cat command.
A. It can be used to edit a text file
B. It can be used to display a text file
C. It can be used to create a text file
D. It can be used to concatenate two files

172. What TWO statements are correct about initramfs?
A. It is a read-only image of the root file system
B. It is a read-only image of the boot file system
C. The initramfs is updated with the update-init command
D. It is mounted at an early boot stage to support kernel loading and initialization

173. Why do we use the su command?
A. To log out of the system
B. To shut down the system
C. To switch user id
D. To display a list of logged in users

174. Which command can be used to view information about an XFS file system?
A. xfs_info
B. xfs_admin
C. xfs_metadump
D. xfs_repair

175. The mkfs command is used to create file systems. What is the default file system type used if it is not specified with the command?
A. ext2
B. xfs
C. vfat
D. ntfs

176. Which command would we use to view the details of a volume group and logical and physical volumes within it? Write the name of the command.

_____

177. Messages generated by the kernel are displayed on the screen during system boot. Which of the following boot-time parameter can be passed to the kernel to suppress them?
A. quiet
B. nomessage
C. suppress
D. console

178. Which command pair can be used to convert TABs to Spaces and vice versa?
A. cut and uniq
B. expand and unexpand
C. suppress and unsuppress
D. convert and unconvert

179. Which TWO commands can be used to display a user's current group memberships?
    A. groups   B. id   C. who   D. whoami

180. The lsusb command is used to display USB device information. What information can be viewed in the output? Select FOUR.
    A. USB busses and the devices attached to them
    B. Bus number associated with each identified USB bus
    C. Manufacturer ID of a USB device
    D. Health status of a USB device
    E. Device ID of a USB device

181. What would the command **systemctl isolate multi-user** do?
    A. Switch from multi-user mode back to the graphical mode on systems running systemd
    B. Switch to multi-user mode on systems running SysVinit
    C. Switch to multi-user mode on systems running Upstart
    D. Switch to multi-user mode on systems running systemd

182. The ldd command is used to perform the following.
    A. Configure dynamic dependencies   B. Display package dependencies
    C. Display dynamic dependencies   D. Display static library files

183. Which command displays disk and partition information?
    A. blkid   B. lsusb   C. cat /proc/cpuinfo   D. lsblk

184. The cp command is used to copy files and directories. True or False?

185. Regular expressions are also referred to as regex or regexp. True or False?

186. What does the PATH variable contain?
    A. Directories to cd into   B. Directory search order to locate a command for execution
    C. Disk pathnames   D. Directory search order for the find command

187. What is the difference between the --remove (-r) and --purge (-P) options of the dpkg command?
    A. The former removes a package along with configuration files, the latter only deletes a package
    B. The former only removes a package, the latter deletes a package as well as its configuration files
    C. The former removes a package along with its manual pages, the latter deletes a package but leaves its manual pages intact
    D. The former removes a package, the latter deletes a package along with its manual pages

188. Select THREE system initialization schemes.
    A. Upstart   B. Bootloader   C. SysVinit   D. BIOS   E. Kernel   F. systemd

189. Which TWO LVM commands can be used to grow the size of a logical volume without affecting the file system it contains?
    A. fsadmin   B. lvextend   C. lvresize   D. fsextend

190. What benefit does the scp command provide over the cp command?
    A. Security   B. Speed   C. More options   D. None of the above

191. A volume group can be created without any physical volume in it. True or False?

192. Which THREE of the following can bring a system running SysVinit down to single-user mode?
    A. shutdown   B. init 1   C. telinit 1   D. shutdown -r

193. The SysVinit initialization program is located in the /sbin directory. Type its name in the space provided below.

_____

194. Which of the following would extract all lines from file1 that do not contain the specified pattern?
    A. egrep -v pattern file1   B. grep -v pattern file1
    C. grep -n pattern file1   D. fgrep -v pattern file1

195. How would you rename "scripts1" directory to "scripts2" in the present working directory?
    A. ln scripts1 scripts2   B. ren scripts1 scripts2
    C. mv scripts1 scripts2   D. mv scripts2 scripts1

196. What does the command chown do?
    A. Changes user id
    B. Makes you the owner of all files in your home directory
    C. Changes the time stamp on a file or directory
    D. Changes the ownership of a file or directory

197. How would you capture the result of the who command in a variable called WHO? Select TWO.
    A. WHO=$(who)   B. who=$(WHO)   C. WHO=`who`   D. who>WHO

198. A disk or partition can be added to a volume group without being initialized. True or False?

199. Write the command that can be used to count the number of lines in the input supplied.

_____

200. What command would you use to influence the execution priority of a command?
    A. pri   B. priority   C. nice   D. chpri

201. What would the command **cd ..** do?
    A. Move one level down to a child directory   B. Move one level up to the parent directory
    C. Change into the root directory   D. Switch to a child directory

202. The which command is used to determine:
    A. The current version and release of a command
    B. Pseudo terminal your session is running from
    C. The absolute path of a command
    D. Compiler options used to create a command

203. Which of the following would display memory and swap usage in human-readable format, with a summary line at the bottom and output refreshing every fifth second?
    A. free -ets 5   B. free -hss 5   C. free -htT 5   D. free -hts 5

204. Type the name of the command that can be used with the -p option to create a directory hierarchy?

_____

205. The main function of the bootloader program is to:
A. Load the kernel into memory
B. List the /boot directory contents
C. Execute the POST
D. Rebuild the kernel

206. Which of the following can be used to log in to a default installation of a Linux system with graphical user environment running?
A. On the desktop console
B. Using the telnet command
C. Using the secure shell
D. All of the above

207. Which component of the Linux structure a user interacts with?
A. Directory structure
B. Kernel
C. Shell
D. None of the above

208. /boot is a recommended shareable file system. True or False?

209. What are valid statements in order to view modules currently loaded in the kernel? Select TWO.
A. Use cat /sys/modules
B. Use cat /proc/modules
C. Run the modprobe command
D. Run the lsmod command

210. Which of the following find command would perform a case-insensitive search for directory names that begin with xyz?
A. find /usr -name xyz*
B. find / -iname xyz*
C. find /etc -inum xyz*
D. find / -icase xyz*

211. What would the command **find /var -mtime -200** do?
A. Search for files in the /var directory that are modified within the past 200 days
B. Search for files in the /var directory that were modified at least 200 days ago
C. Search for files in the /var directory that were modified exactly 200 days ago
D. Search for files in the /var directory that were accessed within the last 200 days

212. Which TWO of the following can be used to display information about a Debian package?
A. apt-cache show
B. dpkg -s
C. apt-get show
D. dpkg -S

213. Type the name of the command that can be used to number lines in output.

_____

214. How many arguments are there in the **cal 10 2018** command?
A. 3
B. 2
C. 1
D. 0

215. Which THREE statemnets are true for the mv command.
A. It can be used to copy files
B. It can be used to move files
C. It can be used to rename files
D. It can be used to move directories

216. Where would **cd ~user2** takes the root user?
A. To user1's home directory
B. To user2's home directory
C. To user2 sub-directory under user1's home directory
D. To root user's home directory

217. What information do logname and whoami commands provide?
   A. Home directory path   B. Login information   C. UID   D. Username

218. What do the -i, -t, and -o switches do with the cpio command? Select ONE.
   A. The -t switch is used to list a cpio archive content
   B. The -o switch is used to create a cpio archive
   C. The -i switch is used to extract from a cpio archive
   D. These switches are used to restore, list, and create cpio archives

219. Which command only displays a user's group memberships?
   A. id   B. newgrp   C. groups   D. usermod

220. The lspci command is used to display hardware information specific to PCI buses and the devices connected to them. Select ONE of the following that is not included in the output.
   A. Device health status   B. Device description   C. PCI bus speed   D. Slot number

221. Which TWO commands can be used to display the previous runlevel of the system?
   A. runlevel   B. system   C. who -r   D. systemctl

222. Select FOUR of the following whose settings can be viewed or modified in BIOS?
   A. System date and time   B. CPU virtualization and integrated peripherals
   C. Network time   D. Booting without a keyboard   E. Boot priorities

223. Which command provides help on the syntax of the /etc/passwd file?
   A. man 5 passwd   B. man passwd   C. man -k passwd   D. help passwd

224. Which of the following shows the current system runlevel?
   A. whodo   B. who   C. uptime   D. who -r

225. Select TWO directory names from the following that may be shared over the network?
   A. /opt   B. /etc   C. /var/opt   D. /var/lock

226. Is the path /home/user1/dir1/scripts1 absolute or relative?
   A. Absolute   B. Relative

227. Which TWO of the following can be used to list reverse dependencies for a Debian package?
   A. apt-cache showpkg   B. apt-cache rdepends   C. apt-cache depends   D. apt-cache show

228. What information does the inode of a symbolic link contain?
   A. Nothing   B. The creation time of the linked file
   C. The name of the linked file   D. The path to the linked file

229. Which command can be used to copy an entire disk image to a USB drive or another disk?
   A. cpio   B. tar   C. diskcopy   D. dd

230. How would you change group ownership to testgrp recursively on a directory called /dir1? Select TWO.
   A. chown -R testgrp /dir1   B. chgrp testgrp /dir1
   C. chgrp -R testgrp /dir1   D. chown -vR :testgrp /dir1

231. Which of the following would list only the installed rpm packages? Select THREE.
    A. rpm --query --all   B. yum list   C. rpm -qa   D. yum list installed

232. Type the name of the command that you would use to create a zero-length file.
    _____

233. To view the last 20 lines of a file, which of the following would you run.
    A. tail filename   B. tail +20 filename   C. tail -20 filename   D. tail 20 filename

234. The grep command is used to display lines in a file that match a certain pattern. What modifications
    does the grep command make in the file?
    A. None   B. Removes the matched lines from the file
    C. Removes the file contents   D. Modifies the file

235. Which of the following would list active terminal screens created with the screen command?
    A. screen -l   B. screen -list   C. term -l   D. term -list

236. What is not a criteria for finding files using the find command?
    A. Modification time   B. hostname   C. Directory name   D. File name

237. Can you link two directories using the hard link method?
    A. Yes   B. No

238. Which option would you use with the ls command to view inode numbers of the files and directories?
    A. -I   B. -i   C. -inode   D. -Inode

239. In vi, which of the following would you use to copy 5 lines and paste them above the current line?
    A. 5yyP (uppercase P)   B. 5yyp (all lowercase)
    C. 5pyy (all lowercase)   D. yy5P (uppercase P)

240. What TWO modes are available to modify file permissions?
    A. chmod   B. symbolic   C. chown   D. octal

241. What are THREE common wildcard characters that are used in filename globbing?
    A. ?   B. *   C. \   D. []

242. To modify permissions on a file to get 751, which of the following would you run?
    A. chmod -751 filename   B. chmod rwxr-x--x filename
    C. chmod u+rwxrxx filename   D. chmod 751 filename

243. What option would you use with the umask command to display the umask value in symbolic
    notation?
    A. -O   B. -A   C. -S   D. -N

244. Which of the following syntax of the chown command is correct to change the ownership and owning
    group on file1 to user1 and group1, respectively?
    A. chown group1:user1 file1   B. chown user1:group1 file1
    C. chown -u user1 -g group1 file1   D. chown user1 group1 file1

245. To prevent users from removing other users' files in a public directory, what would you do?
   A. Set setuid bit on the directory
   B. Set setgid bit on the directory
   C. Set setpid bit on the directory
   D. Set sticky bit on the directory

246. Which option with the chown command enables you to change file ownership recursively?
   A. -R   B. -A   C. -r   D. -a

247. Given a file consisting of 10,509 lines, which command would you use to break the file into multiple, smaller files containing not more than 1000 lines in each of the output file?
   A. truncate   B. split   C. break   D. filter

248. What is the use of the xfs_metadump command?
   A. To dump XFS file system metadata
   B. To restore XFS file system metadata
   C. To unmount an XFS file system
   D. To overwrite XFS file system metadata

249. Which command in the vi editor removes a character preceding the current cursor position?
   A. R   B. x   C. X   D. r

250. What would the following sed command do?

   sed 's/profile/Profile/g' /etc/group

   A. Displays the contents of the /etc/group file with all the occurrences of the word "profile" substituted with "Profile"
   B. Displays the contents of the /etc/group file with all the occurrences of the word "Profile" substituted with "profile"
   C. Changes all the occurrences of the word "profile" with "Profile" and save it to the /etc/group file
   D. Changes all the occurrences of the word "Profile" with "profile" and save it to the /etc/group file

251. Which option is used with the sed command to perform multiple edits on the input?
   A. -E   B. -I   C. -s   D. -e

252. A major number represents a specific type of device driver in the kernel. True or False?

253. Which directory holds the system initialization files on SysVinit systems?
   A. /var/init.d   B. /etc/init.d   C. /etc/sysvinit.d   D. /etc/vinit.d

254. The -r option is used with the cp and rm commands to copy/remove an entire directory hierarchy recursively. True or False?

255. Which command can be used to (only) download a given rpm package?
   A. downloader   B. rpmdownloader   C. download   D. yumdownloader

256. What kind of information a minor number represents?
   A. It represents the type of device
   B. It lists a specific device within a category of devices
   C. It represents a specific device within a device category
   D. All of the above

257. The ps and the top command cannot be used to view processes running on the system. True or False?

258. What would the output of the command **type whatis** be?
A. The absolute path of the whatis command that will be used to run it if it is issued without using its full pathname
B. The relative path of the whatis command that will be used to run it if it is issued without using its full pathname
C. The absolute path of the type command that will be used to run the whatis command
D. The relative path of the type command that will be used to run the whatis command

259. Which of the following can be used to display the value contained in the variable EDITOR?
A. display $EDITOR   B. display EDITOR   C. echo EDITOR   D. echo $EDITOR

260. Which mount point is used on some Linux distributions for automatic mounting of removable media?
A. /opt   B. /media   C. /net   D. /mnt

261. Which of the following is not a pre-defined environment variable?
A. HOME   B. LOGNAME   C. NAME   D. TZ

262. Which command can be used to modify or copy user and group quota information?
A. edquota   B. quotacheck   C. quotaon   D. repquota

263. Which TWO of the following would redirect error messages to an alternate location?
A. 2>>   B. 2<<   C. 2<   D. 2>

264. Which command is used to unset an alias?
A. unsetalias   B. unalias   C. alias rm   D. unset alias

265. What is the use of the pipe character in Bash shell?
A. To take output of one command and pass it as input to the next command
B. To take input from one command and pass it as input to the next command
C. To take output from two files and pass it as input to the next command
D. All of the above

266. Which TWO of the following would continue to run even if the user who initiated them logs off?
A. nohup cp -rp dir1 dir2 &   B. nohup chown -R user1 dir1 &
C. cp -rp dir1 dir2 &   D. nohup scp -rp dir1 server2:/dir2

267. What does]] do in the vi editor?
A. Takes you to the start of the current line   B. Takes you to the first line of the file
C. Takes you to the end of the current line   D. Takes you to the last line of the file

268. What commands are available in the vi editor to enter the edit mode?
A. A, a, I, i, o, and O   B. A, E, and O   C. a, e, and o   D. append, insert and open

269. Which TWO built-in shell commands would run a program in the current shell?
A. program.sh   B. source   C. sh   D. . (dot)

270. Which character is used at the end of a command line to run that command in the background?
   A. @   B. %   C. $ D. &

271. Which of the following would you use to execute the top command at a niceness of +2? Select THREE.
   A. nice -2 top   B. nice +2 top   C. nice --adjustment 2 top   D. nice -n 2 top

272. Which command can be used to display the boot-time and diagnostic messages?
   A. dmesg   B. diag   C. lsmesg   D. dmessages

273. By default, CentOS and Ubuntu installation programs create three logical volumes—/, /boot, and swap. True or False?

274. What is the location of the rpm database?
   A. /var/lib/sw   B. /var/lib/software   C. /var/lib/rpm   D. /var/sw/rpm

275. Linux supports a number of disk-based file system types. Select FIVE from the following.
   A. Extended   B. XFS   C. NFS   D. VFAT   E. ISO9660   F. Btrfs

276. Select the command to recursively add read and write access permission bits for group members on all files under /tmp/dir1.
   A. chown -R g+rw /tmp/dir1   B. chmod -R g+rw /tmp/dir1
   C. chmod -R g=rw /tmp/dir1   D. chmod -R 666 /tmp/dir1

277. What would the command **cut -f1 -d: /etc/passwd | xargs** do?
   A. Print a list of all group names that exist on the system on one line
   B. Print a list of all usernames that will be created on the system
   C. Print a list of all usernames that exist on the system on one line
   D. Print a list of all usernames that exist on the system one per line

278. Which of the following will sort the ls -l command output by month and record the sorted output in /tmp/sort.out file?
   A. ls -l / | sort -k 6 -r /tmp/sort.out   B. ls -l / | sort -s 6 -s /tmp/sort.out
   C. ls -l / | sort 6M -o /tmp/sort.out   D. ls -l / | sort -k 6M -o /tmp/sort.out

279. What would the output of **paste -d: file1 file2** be?
   A. Display corresponding lines from the two files side by side with the colon (:) character used as a delimiter
   B. Modify the two files and then display corresponding lines side by side
   C. Display lines from the two files with the colon (:) character used as a delimiter
   D. Display the contents of the two files

280. What would the command **who | tr [a-z] [A-Z]** do?
   A. Display the entire output of the who command in uppercase letters
   B. Display the entire output of the who command in lowercase letters
   C. Display selective output of the who command in mixed case letters
   D. Display the entire output of the who command in mixed case letters

281. Which THREE are the components of LVM?
    A. Physical volume   B. Disk group   C. Volume group   D. Logical volume

282. Type the vi editor command that would delete three lines starting at the current line.
    _____

283. Which LVM object is used to hold one or more physical volumes?
    A. Logical volume   B. Volume group   C. Another physical volume   D. Physical extent

284. What does the mount command with -a option do?
    A. Mounts all network file systems listed in the /etc/fstab file
    B. Mounts all file systems that are currently not mounted, but are listed in the /etc/fstab file
    C. Mounts all optical file systems listed in the /etc/fstab file
    D. Mounts all virtual file systems listed in the /etc/fstab file

285. Which THREE of the following are valid subcommands that can be used with apt-get?
    A. remove   B. install   C. upgrade   D. delete

286. Which of the following is an incorrect command?
    A. gzip file1   B. gunzip file1.gz   C. gzip -l file1.gz   D. gunzip -l file1.gz

287. How many fields per line entry are there in the /etc/group, /etc/fstab, /etc/passwd, and /etc/shadow files?
    A. 9, 7, 6, and 4   B. 9, 6, 7, and 4   C. 4, 6, 7, and 9   D. 4, 7, 6, and 9

288. Which TWO of the following would create a logical volume, lvol1, of size 100MB in vg00 volume group?
    A. lvcreate -L 100 -n lvol1 vg00   B. lvcreate /dev/vg00/lvol1 -l 100
    C. lvcreate -l 100 vg00 lvol1   D. lvcreate -l 25 -n lvol1 vg00

289. What would the option -U cause the rpm command to do?
    A. Install or upgrade a package and show progress
    B. Install a package
    C. Upgrade an installed package and display an error if it is not already installed
    D. Upgrade an installed package or install it if it is not already installed

290. Which THREE commands are used for group account management?
    A. groupadd   B. groupmod   C. delgroup
    D. groupdel   E. modgroup   F. addgroup

291. What are TWO benefits of using the less command over the more command?
    A. more does not read an entire file before it starts to display its contents
    B. less does not read an entire file before it starts to display its contents
    C. more is faster than less
    D. less is faster than more

292. Which file systems, besides / and /boot, are recommended for creation during OS installation? Choose FOUR.
    A. /home   B. /var   C. /usr   D. /etc   E. /opt

293. What is the purpose of using the ? and * wildcard characters in regex?
   A. The ? is used to match one character and * is used to match two characters in the given input
   B. The ? is used to match two characters and * is used to match three characters in the given input
   C. The ? is used to match any number of characters and * is used to match one character in the given input
   D. The ? is used to match one character and * is used to match any number of characters in the given input

294. Which command is used to reduce a logical volume and a volume group? Choose TWO.
   A. vgshrink   B. vgreduce   C. lvreduce   D. lvshrink

295. What kind of file systems can the mkfs command create? Choose THREE.
   A. xfs   B. vfat   C. ext2   D. swapfs

296. Which of the following is correct to mount a file system?
   A. mount -t ext2 lvtest fs1   B. mount -t ext2 /fs1 /dev/vgtest/lvtest
   C. mount -t ext2 /dev/vgtest/lvtest /fs1 D. mount -t /fs1 ext2 /dev/vgtest/lvtest

297. Which file contains the file systems that are intended for automatic mounting at system reboots?
   A. /etc/sysconfig/fstab   B. /etc/fstab   C. /etc/sbtab   D. /etc/fs.conf

298. Which of the following will change the default boot target to multi-user on systems running systemd?
   A. chkconfig enable multi-user   B. systemctl set-default multi-user
   C. systemctl get-default multi-user   D. service enable multi-user

299. What is the significance of the semicolon (;) character in syntax **command1 ; command2**?
A. The shell waits for the completion of command2 before it executes command2
   B. The shell runs both command1 and command in parallel
   C. The shell runs command2 only if command1 is successful
   D. The shell waits for the completion of command1 before it executes command2

300. What does the mount command do when run without any options or arguments?
   A. Displays all currently mounted network file systems
   B. Displays all currently mounted special file systems
   C. Displays all currently mounted file systems
   D. Displays all currently mounted optical file systems

301. Which command is used to broadcast a message to all logged-in users?
   A. write   B. talk   C. wall   D. broadcast

302. With LVM, you can span a logical volume on multiple physical disks or partitions. True or False?

303. Which command is used to check and repair a damaged CDROM file system?
   A. fsck   B. fsck.cd   C. fscd   D. A CD file system does not require a repair

304. Which environment variable defines pathnames to non-standard directory locations that contain
   additional shared libraries?
   A. PATH   B. LD_LIBRARY   C. LD_LIB_PATH   D. LD_LIBRARY_PATH

305. Which of the following would display the utilization of all active swap spaces?
A. swapinfo   B. swapon   C. swap -a   D. swapon -a

306. The tr filter can be used to delete, squeeze, or translate input characters. True or False?

307. The dpkg command can be used to perform the following. Select FIVE.
A. To remove a package   B. To verify the integrity of a package
C. To search which package owns a file   D. To show contents of a package
E. To unconfigure a package   F. To purge a package

308. What is the typical default runlevel on systems running SysVinit initialization scheme in a graphical user environment?
A. 1   B. 2   C. 3   D. 5

309. Which of the following statements are true for a mount point? Select THREE.
A. It must be an empty directory
B. It may or may not be an empty directory
C. It can be used to mount a disk-based, memory-based, or removable file system
D. It is created with the mkdir command

310. What does the shutdown command do which the init command does not? Choose TWO.
A. Starts the shutdown process right away
B. Waits for one minute before commencing system shutdown
C. Broadcasts a message to all logged-in users
D. Both A and C

311. Which file on the SysVinit system determines the default boot level at system startup?
A. /etc/inittab.conf   B. /etc/init.conf   C. /etc/inittab   D. /sbin/init

312. Which log file stores the system boot messages?
A. /etc/boot.log   B. /var/log/boot.log   C. /etc/boot.conf.log   D. /var/adm/boot.log

313. What would executing **!100** at the Bash shell command prompt do?
A. Run the Bash shell built-in command called !100
B. Run the command that is located on the 100th line in the user's history file
C. Run the command ! with argument 100
D. It will display an error message on the screen

314. Which built-in Bash shell command would show us the absolute pathname of a command that is within a defined path?
A. type   B. whereis   C. which   D. locate

315. Which command can be used to merge short files created with the split command to regenerate the original file?
A. less   B. tail   C. head   D. cat

316. Which command can be used to view unnecessary characters in a file or supplied input?
A. print   B. fmt   C. cat   D. od

317. What would the command **ls -ld /var/log/???** display?
   A. List of directory names which contain exactly three alphanumeric characters
   B. List of directory names which contain three or more alphabetic characters
   C. List of directory names which contain three or less alphabetic characters
   D. List of directory names which contain exactly three alphabetic characters

318. Which of the following are vi editor modes? Choose THREE.
   A. Edit mode   B. Last line mode   C. Command mode   D. Save mode

319. What would the command **ls -ld /etc/systemd/system/[!m-z]** display?
   A. List of sub-directories under /etc/systemd/system whose names begin with letters m and z
   B. List of sub-directories under /etc/systemd/system whose names do not begin with letters m through z
   C. List of sub-directories under /etc/systemd/system whose names do not begin with m and z
   D. List of sub-directories under /etc/systemd/system whose names begin with letters m through z

320. The Bash shell allows us to run jobs in the background. Which command can we use to display what is running in the background?
   A. tasks   B. bg   C. fg   D. jobs

321. Which of the following would search files and directories under /usr with ownership not belonging to the root user? Select THREE.
   A. find /usr -not root   B. find /usr -not -user root
   C. find /usr -not -user root -print   D. find /usr ! -user root

322. Specific functions within a shared library may be referenced by multiple executables concurrently. True or False?

323. Which command can be used to display the value contained in a variable?
   A. display   B. var   C. show   D. echo

324. The -v is a common option that is used with many commands. What would it do when it is used with the grep, egrep, or the fgrep command?
   A. Shows details in the output   B. Hides details in the output
   C. Shows matching line entries in the output   D. Shows non-matching line entries in the output

325. What is the meaning of the character "+" if it appears in the ll command output right after the permissions column?
   A. Setuid bit is set   B. Setgid bit is set   C. Sticky bit is set   D. ACL is set

326. Which command would list processes running on the system?
   A. topps   B. ps   C. psstat   D. proc

327. Which signal is sent by default with the kill command to terminate a process gracefully?
   A. 15   B. 9   C. 2   D. 1

328. Which of the following can be used to send the output of a command to the terminal screen as well as to a file called file1?
   A. command 2>&1   B. command | file1 tee
   C. file1 | tee command   D. command | tee file1

329. Which command would display all available signals?
A. kill -s   B. kill -l   C. kill -a   D. kill

330. Which THREE commands (in order) may be used to display physical volume, logical volume, and volume group information?
A. lvdisplay, vgdisplay, pvdisplay   B. vgdisplay, lvdisplay, pvdisplay
C. pvdisplay, lvdisplay, vgdisplay   D. pvdisplay, vgdisplay, lvdisplay

331. Which is not a boot phase on a Linux system running systemd?
A. GRUB   B. init   C. BIOS   D. Kernel

332. What would **2>>file1** do?
A. Redirects output to file1   B. Redirects error messages and appends them to file1
C. Receives input from file1   D. Redirects input to file1

333. What would the command **chmod g-w file1** do?
A. Remove write permission bit from file1 for group
B. Remove write permission bit from file1 for public
C. Add write permission bit to file1 for group
D. Add write permission bit to file1 for public

334. Where would you start entering the text in vi when you press the A key while in the command mode?
A. Beginning of the current line   B. Middle of the current line
C. End of the current line   D. Opens up a new line and you insert text there

335. What would **:%s/old/new** do in vi?
A. Replaces the first occurrence of the pattern "new" with "old" on the same line
B. Replaces the first occurrence of the pattern "old" with "new" on the same line
C. Replaces all occurrences of the pattern "old" with "new" in the entire file
D. Replaces all occurrences of the pattern "new" with "old" in the entire file

336. What would **grep ^$ /etc/group** produce in the output?
A. Displays all lines from the /etc/group file that contain at least one character
B. Displays no lines from the /etc/group file
C. Displays all lines from the /etc/group file that begin with the character ^ and end with the character $
D. Displays all empty lines in the /etc/group file

337. The aptitude command in Debian and its spinoffs is a menu-driven program that may be used instead of the APT commands. True or False?

338. Which command would you use to navigate within the Linux directory tree?
A. pwd   B. cd   C. where   D. nav

339. What does the execute permission on a directory mean?
A. You can create files in the directory   B. You can execute a command located in the directory
C. You can execute the directory   D. You can cd into the directory

340. What is the recommended command to use to bring down a SysVinit system gracefully? Type only the name of the command.

_____

341. Which is the default home directory for the root user?
A. /var/root   B. /usr/root   C. /etc/root   D. /root   E. /tmp/root

342. Which TWO of the following are the default directory locations as defined in FHS to store library files?
A. /lib   B. /usr/lib   C. /lib64   D. /usr/lib64

343. What is the primary difference in the output of the **cat /etc/profile** and **cat < /etc/profile** commands?
A. The first command will display the file contents and the second will create the file
B. If executed together, these commands will concatenate their contents into a new file
C. No difference
D. The first command will create the file and the second will display the file contents

344. Which directory stores the manual pages on the Linux system?
A. /lib/share/man   B. /usr/share/man   C. /var/share/man   D. /etc/share/man

345. Which of the following would you run to disable file overwriting in output redirection?
A. set +o noclobber   B. set -a noclobber   C. set +a noclobber   D. set -o noclobber

346. Type the name of the command that is used to reinstall GRUB Legacy on the boot disk.

_____

347. Which TWO commands can be used to display environment variables and their values?
A. print   B. env   C. unset   D. export

348. Which of the following can be used to search for a string in Debian package names and descriptions? Select TWO.
A. dpkg search   B. apt search   C. apt-get search   D. apt-cache search

349. What would the entry **ca::ctrlaltdel:/sbin/shutdown -t3 -r now** in /etc/inittab file cause the system to do when Ctrl+Alt+Del key sequence is pressed on the system?
A. Wait for three seconds and then shut down and power off the system
B. Wait for three seconds and then shut down and reboot the system
C. Start the shutdown process immediately and power off the system
D. Start the shutdown process immediately and reboot the system

350. Which of the following shows the number of lines in file15?
A. wc -w file15   B. wc -a file15   C. wc -c file15   D. wc -l file15

351. Type the name (not the entire path) of the file on the system running SysVinit where the Ctrl+Alt+Del key sequence can be enabled or disabled.

_____

352. Which directory holds most of the log files?
A. /var/log   B. /var/adm/log   C. /var/adm   D. /var/adm/syslog

353. Which of the following is correct for command **sort -k 2 -n file1**?
A. It will sort file1
B. It will sort file1 alphabetically on the second column
C. It will sort file1 on the second column
D. It will sort file1 numerically on the second column

354. In addition to the shutdown, init, and telinit commands, which TWO additional commands on SysVinit systems can also be used to bring a system down without rebooting it?
A. stop
B. halt
C. reboot
D. poweroff

355. Which of the following is the software repository configuration file under the /etc/apt directory on Debian and derivatives?
A. repos.d
B. sources.d
C. sources.list
D. repos.list

356. Which command can be used to alter attributes (adding journal, changing file system check frequency, adding a label, etc.) of an extended file system?
A. fstune
B. mount
C. mkfs
D. tune2fs

357. Which TWO filesystem types allocate inodes as they are needed?
A. ext2
B. ext3
C. ext4
D. xfs

358. What is the alias command used for?
A. To create nick names for users
B. To create nick names for groups
C. To create shortcuts to commands and directories
D. To setup cron jobs

359. A DVD is mounted on /cdrom mount point. The root user attempts to unmount it but gets a device busy message. Select TWO possible reasons.
A. A file is open under /cdrom
B. There is nothing mounted on /cdrom
C. The root user does not have enough permission to carry out the task
D. A user is sitting in it

360. Which shell built-in command would set environment variables?
A. echo
B. set
C. env
D. export

361. Which TWO statements are true about /proc/?
A. It is a virtual file system
B. Runtime changes that the system store under /proc/ are instantly recognized by the kernel
C. It is a disk-based file system
D. Runtime changes that the system store under /proc/ are recognized by the kernel after the system reboot

362. What would the command **find /etc -maxdepth 3 | xargs /usr/bin/file** do?
A. Search for files under /etc and show their file type
B. Search for files to a maximum of three directory levels below /etc/ and determine their file type
C. Display file types of all files in under the /etc directory
D. Search for files to a maximum of four directory levels below / and determine their file type

363. Which of the following commands can be used to reconfigure an installed Debian package?
A. dpkg
B. dpkg-configure
C. dpkg-reconfigure
D. dpkg configure

364. What is the significance of the -d option with the cut command?
   A. It signifies the field to be used as a separator
   B. It signifies the delimiter character to be used as a field separator
   C. It signifies the delimiter character to be used as a command separator
   D. It signifies the delimiter character to be used to display output

365. Which command would display only the third column in the output of the ls -l command?
   A. ls -l | cut -f2 -d " "   B. ls -l | cut -f3 -d " "
   C. ls -l | cut -d "" -f3   D. ls -l | cut -d " " -f2

366. In vi, what is the significance of the digit that precedes the yy (yank) command?
   A. It indicates the number of lines to yank   B. It indicates the number of words to yank
   C. It indicates the number of characters to yank   D. It indicates the number of bytes to yank

367. Who can change a user password?
   A. Only the user him/herself   B. Only the root user
   C. Both the user and the root   D. Any user on the system

368. What is the default secondary command prompt in Linux?
   A. >   B. <   C. $ D. #

369. VAR=`hostname` and VAR=$(hostname) are examples of:
   A. Filename completion   B. Command completion
   C. Tilde substitution   D. Command substitution

370. Which TWO of the following can be used to unmount a CD file system (/dev/cdrom) that is mounted on /mnt?
   A. umount /mnt   B. unmount /mnt
   C. unmount /dev/cdrom   D. umount /dev/cdrom

371. What are the ways of saving and exiting in vi? Choose THREE.
   A. :w!   B. ZZ   C. :wq!   D. :q!   E. :x!

372. What is the name of the default file that is stored in the HISTFILE variable to store user command history?
   A. ~/bash_history   B. ~/.bash_history   C. /etc/bash_history   D. /etc/.bash_history

373. What is the location of the GRUB Legacy menu.lst file?
   A. /boot/grub2   B. /etc/grub   C. /var/grub   D. /boot/grub

374. Which TWO commands can be used to display password aging information?
   A. chpw   B. chage   C. passwd   D. lsage

375. Which steps should be performed to add custom library information to the cache?
   A. Update the /etc/ld.so.conf file and run the ldconfig command
   B. Update the /etc/ld.so.conf file and run the ldd command
   C. Update the /etc/ldd.conf file and run the lddconfig command
   D. Update the /etc/ld.so.conf file and that's it

376. Which of the following THREE can be used to shut down and reboot a system using SysVinit scheme?

A. telinit 6   B. init 6   C. shutdown   D. shutdown -r

377. Which of the following commands can be used to list the dependencies of a Debian package?

A. apt-cache dependencies   B. apt-get dependencies   C. apt-cache depends   D. apt-get depends

378. Parameters can be supplied to the kernel at system boot time. Which file under /proc/ can be viewed when the system is up to check what was supplied? Type the file name only.

_____

379. What is the difference between the update and upgrade subcommands of apt-get?

A. The former would update the installed packages database and the latter would upgrade installed packages
B. The former would update the installed packages and the latter would upgrade the package database with the latest information
C. There is no difference between the two
D. The former would update or install new packages and the latter would upgrade the installed packages database

380. Select THREE usages of the fmt command.

A. It can be used to print a file   B. It can be used to add indentation
C. It can be used to set column width   D. It can be used to add spacing between words
E. It can be used to modify text

381. What is the default priority of a child process?

A. It gets the average priority   B. It gets the highest priority
C. It inherits from its parent process   D. It gets the lowest priority

382. Which THREE of the following would initialize /dev/sdd1 as an ext3 file system?

A. mkfs.ext3 /dev/sdd1   B. mkfs -t ext3 /dev/sdd1
C. mke2fs -t ext3 /dev/sdd1   D. tune2fs -t ext3 /dev/sdd1

383. What is true about d-bus and socket. Select TWO.

A. D-bus is a communication method that allows multiple processes to talk to one another on the same or remote system
B. Socket is an inter-process communication method that allows multiple processes to talk to one another on the same or remote system
C. Socket is a communication method that allows a single process to talk to other process on the same or remote system
D. D-bus is an inter-process communication method that allows a single process to talk to other process on the same or remote system

384. What would the command **udevadm info -e** produce?

A. Display coldplug devices configured in the udev database
B. Display PCI devices currently configured in the udev database
C. Display devices previously configured in the udev database
D. Display all devices currently configured in the udev database

385. Select TWO of the following methods to zero out the contents of logfile.
    A. cat < /dev/trim > logfile   B. cat < /dev/null > logfile   C. > logfile   D. trim logfile

386. Which TWO of the following will end your terminal session?
    A. ctrl+d   B. out   C. exit   D. quit

387. Which THREE statements are true for the pr filter?
    A. It can be used to format text for printing
    B. It can be used to print a text file
    C. It can be used to add date and time of printing
    D. It can be used to add a footer before printing a file

388. Which THREE of the following are list operators?
    A. &   B. &&   C. | D. || E. ;   F. ;;

389. Which of the following is not an entry in the /etc/passwd file?
    A. UID   B. username   C. shell   D. pwd

390. Boot device order is stored in the BIOS. True or False?

391. Which THREE statements are true for udev?
    A. It is a dynamic device probing service
    B. It has pre-configured rules defined for various types of devices in the /etc/udev/udev.conf file
    C. The udevmgt command is its main management command
    D. The udevadm command is its main management command

392. Which command can be used to view USB device information including a specific vendor's information?
    A. lspci   B. lsusb   C. lsmod   D. lsinfo

393. Which command line option would prevent the find command from searching below the specified number of sub-directories?
    A. depth   B. mindepth   C. below   D. maxdepth

394. Which of the following can be used to search for a command whose directory path is not included in the PATH variable?
    A. find   B. type   C. which   D. whereis

395. Which of the following would define a local variable called VAR with a value "exam"?
    A. VAR=$exam   B. VAR=exam   C. $VAR=exam   D. VAR = exam

396. What would the command **who | tr -d root** do?
    A. Deletes the pattern "root" from the output of the who command and replaces it with "who"
    B. Replaces the pattern "root" in the output of the who command with "d"
    C. Deletes the pattern "root" from the output of the who command
    D. Replaces the pattern "root" in the output of the who command with "tr"

397. Type the name of the directory under /etc/, which stores yum repository definition files.

_____

398. What are the THREE methods to start the vi editor?
A. By running the vi command without a file name specified
B. By running the vi command with an existing file name specified
C. By running the vi command with a non-existing file name specified
D. By running the vi command with a directory name specified

399. Which file would you consult to check if a service failed to start during system boot?
A. /var/log/rc.log   B. /etc/boot.log   C. /var/log/boot.log   D. /etc/syslog.boot

400. **alias rm="rm -i"** is an example of:
A. Filename completion   B. Alias substitution
C. Tilde substitution   D. Command substitution

401. RPM packages may be verified for integrity after they have been installed by executing rpm --verify. Which of the following is compared for verification?
A. Files in the rpm package   B. Package size   C. Timestamp   D. MD5 checksum

402. Which of the following can be used to view the second and fourth columns from the /etc/group file?
A. cut -f 2,4 /etc/group   B. cut -f2,4 -d: /etc/group
C. cat /etc/group | cut -d: D. cat /etc/group | cut -f 2,4

403. Which file system (or directory) is used to hold variable files, such as log files, status files, and spool files?
A. /var   B. /usr   C. /etc   D. /root   E. /tmp

404. To ensure that a file system has user and group quota automatically enabled for it each time the system is rebooted, which TWO options would you place in the /etc/fstab file for the file system?
A. enquota   B. usrquota   C. grpquota   D. quotaon

405. Which of the following would display an enumerated list of empty lines from the /etc/profile file?
A. grep -v ^$ /etc/profile   B. grep -Ev ^$ /etc/profile
C. fgrep -v ^$ /etc/profile   D. grep -n ^$ /etc/profile

406. Which command is used to create and initialize aquota.user and aquota.group files to store user and group quota information?
A. setquota   B. quotacheck   C. quotaon   D. edquota

407. How would you remove a file by the name * located in the current directory?
A. By executing rm *   B. By executing rm *
C. By executing rm *\   D. By executing rm ?*

408. What is not true about the mlocate.db file?
A. It is located in the /etc/mlocate/ directory
B. Its configuration file is /etc/updatedb.conf
C. It may be updated manually with the updatedb command
D. It is updated periodically via cron

409. Which of the following fall under the category of mass storage devices?
A. Solid-state device   B. Hard disk drive   C. USB key
D. DVD drive   E. All of the above

410. Type the name of the command that can be used to terminate all processes that match a criteria.

_____

411. Which of the following can be used to calculate and display disk usage summary in human-readable format?
A. du -h /etc   B. df -hs /etc   C. du -sh /etc   D. df -sh /etc

412. Type the name of the file that stores the secondary group memberships for a user.

_____

413. The setuid bit is set on:
A. Executable files at group level   B. Executable files at owner level
C. Shell scripts   D. Executable files at public level

414. Which TWO runlevels should not be defined as the default boot runlevels on SysVinit systems?
A. 0   B. 3   C. 2   D. 6

Appendix B: Answers to Sample LX0-103/101-400 Quiz

1.	False	2.	D	3.	B	4.	D	5.	False
6.	A	7.	C	8.	D	9.	False	10.	BCD
11.	BC	12.	A	13.	B	14.	B	15.	head
16.	D	17.	F	18.	C	19.	True	20.	AD
21.	ldconfig	22.	A	23.	D	24.	B	25.	1
26.	False	27.	True	28.	B	29.	D	30.	False
31.	AB	32.	BC	33.	B	34.	True	35.	C
36.	C	37.	True	38.	D	39.	A	40.	False
41.	ABC	42.	vimtutor	43.	C	44.	True	45.	CD
46.	BC	47.	C	48.	C	49.	C	50.	A
51.	B	52.	D	53.	AC	54.	True	55.	D
56.	D	57.	True	58.	C	59.	B	60.	E
61.	ABD	62.	False	63.	A	64.	B	65.	ACD
66.	D	67.	False	68.	A	69.	D	70.	B
71.	B	72.	D	73.	False	74.	B	75.	A
76.	C	77.	C	78.	A	79.	False	80.	A
81.	ACD	82.	C	83.	A	84.	True	85.	D
86.	B	87.	True	88.	D	89.	BCD	90.	A
91.	A	92.	A	93.	BC	94.	True	95.	ABD
96.	uniq	97.	B	98.	BD	99.	C	100.	AD
101.	ABC	102.	CD	103.	BCD	104.	C	105.	C
106.	A	107.	B	108.	False	109.	C	110.	False
111.	systemd	112.	True	113.	A	114.	D	115.	B
116.	False	117.	C	118.	True	119.	False	120.	D
121.	AC	122.	grub.cfg	123.	False	124.	BD	125.	A
126.	AD	127.	A	128.	True	129.	df	130.	D

131.	A	132.	D	133.	False	134.	B	135.	A
136.	B	137.	C	138.	C	139.	B	140.	AD
141.	A	142.	ABD	143.	B	144.	True	145.	BCD
146.	False	147.	swapoff	148.	B	149.	D	150.	ABC
151.	A	152.	C	153.	B	154.	A	155.	D
156.	D	157.	ABD	158.	A	159.	C	160.	ACD
161.	A	162.	lvremove	163.	AB	164.	True	165.	A
166.	D	167.	BC	168.	True	169.	C	170.	lvcreate
171.	BCD	172.	AD	173.	C	174.	A	175.	A
176.	vgdisplay	177.	A	178.	B	179.	AB	180.	ABCE
181.	D	182.	C	183.	A	184.	True	185.	True
186.	B	187.	B	188.	ACF	189.	BC	190.	A
191.	False	192.	ABC	193.	init	194.	B	195.	C
196.	D	197.	AC	198.	False	199.	wc	200.	C
201.	B	202.	C	203.	D	204.	mkdir	205.	A
206.	AC	207.	C	208.	False	209.	BD	210.	B
211.	A	212.	AB	213.	nl	214.	B	215.	BCD
216.	B	217.	D	218.	D	219.	C	220.	A
221.	AC	222.	ABDE	223.	A	224.	D	225.	AC
226.	A	227.	AB	228.	D	229.	D	230.	CD
231.	ACD	232.	touch	233.	C	234.	A	235.	B
236.	B	237.	B	238.	B	239.	A	240.	BD
241.	ABD	242.	D	243.	C	244.	B	245.	D
246.	A	247.	B	248.	A	249.	C	250.	A
251.	D	252.	True	253.	B	254.	True	255.	D
256.	C	257.	False	258.	A	259.	D	260.	B
261.	C	262.	A	263.	AD	264.	B	265.	A
266.	AB	267.	D	268.	A	269.	BD	270.	D
271.	ACD	272.	A	273.	True	274.	C	275.	ABDEF
276.	B	277.	C	278.	D	279.	A	280.	A
281.	ACD	282.	3dd	283.	B	284.	B	285.	ABC

286.	D	287.	C	288.	AD	289.	D	290.	ABD
291.	BD	292.	ABCE	293.	D	294.	BC	295.	ABC
296.	C	297.	B	298.	B	299.	D	300.	C
301.	C	302.	True	303.	D	304.	D	305.	B
306.	True	307.	ABCDF	308.	D	309.	BCD	310.	BC
311.	C	312.	B	313.	B	314.	A	315.	D
316.	D	317.	A	318.	ABC	319.	B	320.	D
321.	BCD	322.	True	323.	D	324.	D	325.	D
326.	B	327.	A	328.	D	329.	B	330.	C
331.	B	332.	B	333.	A	334.	C	335.	B
336.	D	337.	True	338.	B	339.	D	340.	shutdown
341.	D	342.	BD	343.	C	344.	B	345.	A
346.	grub-install	347.	BD	348.	BD	349.	B	350.	D
351.	inittab	352.	A	353.	D	354.	BD	355.	C
356.	D	357.	CD	358.	C	359.	AD	360.	D
361.	AB	362.	B	363.	C	364.	B	365.	B
366.	A	367.	C	368.	A	369.	D	370.	AD
371.	BCE	372.	B	373.	D	374.	BC	375.	A
376.	ABD	377.	C	378.	cmdline	379.	A	380.	BCD
381.	C	382.	ABC	383.	BD	384.	D	385.	BC
386.	AC	387.	ACD	388.	BDE	389.	D	390.	True
391.	ABD	392.	B	393.	D	394.	A	395.	B
396.	C	397.	yum.repos.d	398.	ABC	399.	C	400.	B
401.	D	402.	B	403.	A	404.	BC	405.	D
406.	B	407.	A	408.	A	409.	E	410.	killall
411.	C	412.	/etc/group	413.	B	414.	AD		

Appendix C: Sample LX0-104/102-400 Quiz

This appendix provides 376 sample questions for CompTIA Linux+ Powered by LPI/LPIC-1 exam LX0-104/102-400. Answers to these questions are available in Appendix D. I recommend that you first read and understand the material in Part TWO thoroughly and then take this quiz. You may find similar questions in Appendix A (Sample LX0-103/101-400 quiz), that's intentional. Do not consult the material or seek external help while taking this quiz. Mark the questions that you answer incorrectly. Revisit the relevant topics and try again.

Note that a success on this sample quiz does not guarantee passing the relevant CompTIA Linux+/LPIC-1 exam. In fact, you can create thousands of questions based on the exam objectives and the material presented in this book. However, a thorough study of the topics, a good practice of the commands, and a decent knowledge of various files, directories, and terms discussed in this book increase your chances of scoring higher on the exams.

1. Which command can be used to add or remove a CUPS printer?
   A. lpadmin   B. lpstat   C. cups   D. cupscon

2. The size of an IPv6 packet is smaller than that of an IPv4. True or False?

3. What would **echo $?** do?
   A. Echo the character ?
   B. Display the message "command not found"
   C. Display total number of command line arguments specified at the last executed command
   D. Display the exit code of the last command executed

4. Type the name of the command that a user may run to determine the time zone that they can use in their shell startup file.

   _____

5. What is the default CUPS server configuration file?
   A. /etc/cups/printers.conf   B. /etc/cupsd.conf
   C. /etc/cups/cups.conf   D. /etc/cups/cupsd.conf

6. Which TWO of the following can be used to remove a submitted at job with ID# 4?
   A. at -d 4   B. at -l 4   C. atrm 4   D. atrm -q 4

7. What is the significance of using two @ signs in syslog client configuration file?
   A. They signify the use of the IP protocol   B. They signify the use of the TCP protocol
   C. They signify the use of the UDP protocol   D. They signify the use of the ICMP protocol

8. The setuid bit on an executable file gives regular users the ability to run that executable with the owner's privileges. True or False?

9. Depending on the Linux distribution and version, which TWO are valid configuration files to enable or disable a display manager?
   A. /etc/X11/default-display-manager
   B. /etc/inittab
   C. /etc/sysconfig/desktop
   D. /etc/X11/default-display-login

10. The following is an example of command substitution. Select TWO.
   A. echo "The hostname of the system is $(hostname)"
   B. echo "The hostname of the system is (hostname)"
   C. echo "The hostname of the system is $hostname"
   D. echo "The hostname of the system is `hostname`"

11. What does a system logging service do? Select THREE.
   A. Forwards alerts and messages to remote logging servers
   B. Deletes forwarded alerts and messages
   C. Logs alerts and messages to appropriate local destinations
   D. Captures alerts and messages

12. Which TWO of the following files does the groupdel command update?
   A. /etc/user   B. /etc/profile   C. /etc/group   D. /etc/gshadow

13. Which of the following would you use to enable file overwriting in output redirection?
   A. set +o noclobber   B. set -a noclobber   C. set +a noclobber   D. set -o noclobber

14. What would the command **seq 5 15** print on the screen?
   A. Prints numbers 5 and 15   B. Prints numbers 5 to 15
   C. Prints numbers 1 to 5 and 15   D. Prints numbers 1 to 15 with number 5 skipped

15. How would you generate a GnuPG revocation certificate for a user called user7?
   A. By running gpg2 --gen-revoke user7   B. By running gpg2 --gen-key user7
   C. By running gpg2 --gen-key --revoke user7   D. By running gpg2 --gen-key2 user7

16. Depending on the Linux distribution and version, which TWO files should be modified to enable or disable all network services that the xinetd or the inetd daemon control?
   A. /etc/inetd.conf   B. /etc/network.conf
   C. /etc/xinetd.conf   D. /etc/inetd.cf

17. What is the command to search for files with suid/sgid bits enabled?
   A. which   B. whereis   C. find   D. locate

18. Which of the TWO are correct syntaxes to change date and time on the system?
   A. hwclock set-time 11:44 2017-12-12   B. timedatectl -d "2017-12-12 11:44"
   C. timedatectl set-time 11:44 2017-12-12   D. date --set "2017-12-12 11:44"

19. What would the command **xhost +** do?
   A. Execute the xhost command on the local system
   B. Disable remote X access on the local system
   C. Enable remote X access on the local system
   D. Execute the xhost command on the local system for a regular user

20. Depending on the Linux distribution and version, which THREE commands can be used to display hostname of the system? Select THREE.
    A. hostname   B. uname   C. hostnamectl   D. host

21. Which TWO commands can be used to list submitted email messages in a mail queue before they are transmitted?
    A. mail   B. sendmail -bp   C. sendmail without any options   D. mailq

22. Which of the following SQL statements is correct to insert a record in table "ex102t"?
    A. insert into ex102t values('FirstName','LastName')
    B. select * from ex102t insert FirstName=Albert, LastName=Einstein;
    C. insert ex102t set FirstName=Albert, LastName=Einstein;
    D. insert into ex102t values('Albert','Einstein');

23. Which of the following can be defined in shell startup files? Select TWO.
    A. Email addresses   B. Variables   C. Functions   D. Address

24. Why do we use NTP?
    A. For administering file timestamps
    B. For local clock synchronization with a more reliable time source
    C. For sending packets to test remote connectivity
    D. All of the above with proper options and arguments

25. Which TWO files in the /etc/ directory control user access to the at service?
    A. at.deny   B. at.conf   C. at.ctrl   D. at.allow

26. Which file does TCP Wrappers log messages to?
    A. /var/log/wrappers B. /var/log/secure   C. /var/log/su   D. /var/log/tcp

27. Depending on the Linux distribution and version, which THREE commands can be used to activate or deactivate a network interface?
    A. ifconfig   B. ip   C. ifcli   D. nmcli

28. How would the condition **COUNT=$((COUNT + 1))** cause a for loop to behave when the initial value of the COUNT variable is set to 0?
    A. Add "1" to the counter at each loop iteration
    B. Subtract "0" from the counter at each loop iteration
    C. Subtract "1" from the counter at each loop iteration
    D. Add "0" to the counter at each loop iteration

29. Select a benefit of using the CIDR notation in IP addresses.
    A. More usable IP addresses   B. Less usable IP addresses
    C. Shorter IP addresses   D. Less entries in routing tables

30. What would the command **useradd -D** do?
    A. Display the range of values used at the time of user creation or modification
    B. Display the default values used at the time of user creation or modification
    C. Suggest values that cannot be used for new users
    D. Suggest values that must be used when creating user accounts

31. Which command is used to unset an alias?
   A. unsetalias   B. unalias   C. alias rm   D. unset alias

32. An alias hostname is just another name for a host. True or false?

33. Which THREE of the following are true for the nmap command?
   A. It can be used to discover open ports on remote systems
   B. It can detect the type and version of operating system running on remote systems
   C. It can detect the commands that users running on remote systems
   D. It can be used to map remote services according to port numbers defined in the /etc/services file
   E. It is a network probing tool

34. How many bits does an IPv6 address contain?
   A. 64   B. 96   C. 128   D. 160   E. 192

35. What would the command **find /usr -perm /2000 -type f** do?
   A. Search for files and directories under /usr with sgid bit enabled
   B. Search for files under /usr with sgid bit enabled
   C. Search for files under /usr with suid and sgid bits enabled
   D. Search for files under /usr with sgid bit enabled and 000 permissions

36. Which command can be used to print geometrical information of an X terminal window including the window id and terminal's location and appearance data?
   A. xterm   B. xwininfo   C. display   D. xdpyinfo

37. Which protocol is used by an MTA?
   A. SNMP   B. LDAP   C. DNS   D. SMTP

38. Which command executes another program without invoking a sub-shell for it?
   A. bash   B. source   C. exec   D. invoke

39. The adaptability of Linux to a wide variety of languages, cultural settings, and time zones is referred to as:
   A. Internationalization   B. Regionalization   C. Globalization   D. Localization

40. What needs to be done to update the aliases.db database after updating the /etc/aliases file?
   A. Restart Sendmail daemon   B. Run the newaliases command
   C. Run the aliases command   D. Reboot the system

41. Name the default configuration file for LightDM that is located in the /etc/lightdm directory and can be used to enable or disable guest logins and show or hide user list.
   _____

42. What are the benefits of using the OpenSSH utilities?
   A. Use encryption during data transfer   B. Use hidden keys during data transfer
   C. Log audit trail   D. Both A and B

43. Depending on the Linux distribution and version, static and default routes can be defined in network interface configuration files. True or False?

44. Which sequence of commands is appropriate to offline a printer for maintenance, and then back online?
A. cupsreject, cupsenable, cupsaccept, cupsdisable
B. cupsenable, cupsaccept, cupsdisable, cupsreject
C. cupsreject, cupsdisable, cupsenable, cupsaccept
D. cupsreject, cupsaccept, cupsdisable, cupsenable

45. How many address bits do IPv4 and IPv6 addresses contain?
A. 16/64   B. 64/256   C. 32/64   D. 32/128

46. Type the name of the configuration file for the anacron service.

_____

47. Which THREE tools can be used for DNS queries?
A. dig   B. nslookup   C. nsswitch   D. host

48. Which command is used to cancel a print request?
A. lpalt   B. lpcancel   C. cancel   D. lpadmin

49. Write an SQL query to display all records stored in a table called ex102t matching the name "Abraham".
A. select * from ex102t where name='Abraham'
B. select all from ex102t where name='Abraham';
C. select all in ex102t where name='Abraham';
D. select * from ex102t where name='Abraham';

50. Which THREE commands can be used to display network interface statistics and routing table?
A. netstat   B. ifconfig   C. ip   D. ss

51. Type the default netmask address for a class B network?

_____

52. Which file documents the well-known network port numbers, along with service names and protocols they are associated to use?
A. /usr/bin/protocols   B. /etc/protocols   C. /etc/services   D. Both B and C

53. Type the name of the file that must be edited to disallow a user from scheduling an at job.

_____

54. OpenSSH host key files are located in the /etc/ssh directory. True or False?

55. What would the command **useradd user500** do?
A. It will display an error message
B. It will create user500 using the default values
C. It will create user500 with all custom values
D. It will create user500 without using the default values

56. Which file is consulted in Ubuntu at system boot to activate network interfaces and apply IP addresses to the interfaces?
   A. /etc/network/interfaces
   C. /etc/sysconfig/interfaces
   B. /etc/network/networks
   D. /etc/sysconfig/network-scripts/ifcfg-eth0

57. Type the name of the primary syslog service configuration file.
   _____

58. Which file contains the IP address to hostname mapping?
   A. /etc/hosts
   B. /etc/sysconfig/hosts
   C. /etc/hostnames
   D. /etc/hosts.map

59. Which command is used to lookup matching entries in administrative databases such as /etc/passwd and /etc/group?
   A. grep
   B. getent
   C. getadm
   D. egrep

60. Which TWO of the following are the IPv4 versions of the tracepath6 and traceroute6 commands?
   A. traceroute4
   B. tracepath4
   C. traceroute
   D. tracepath

61. What would having the entry sshd:ALL in the /etc/hosts.deny file mean?
   A. Remote login access via the secure shell service is enabled
   B. Remote login access through all services on the system are enabled
   C. Remote login access through all services on the system are disabled
   D. Remote login access via the secure shell service is disabled

62. Which THREE commands can be used to display and modify network interface configuration?
   A. nmcli
   B. ifconfig
   C. nm
   D. ip

63. Which TWO commands can be used to check connectivity between two network nodes using the ICMP protocol?
   A. ping6
   B. netstat
   C. ping
   D. linkstatus

64. Which command can be used to convert text from one character encoding to another?
   A. iconv
   B. convert
   C. enconvert
   D. txtconvert

65. Which file is referenced by the date and hwclock command to determine the current time zone?
   A. /usr/share/zoneinfo
   B. /etc/localtime
   C. /etc/timezone
   D. /var/time

66. To configure trusted login for OpenSSH, which command would you use to generate a private/public keypair?
   A. ssh
   B. ssh-keygen
   C. ssh.key.gen
   D. ssh.keygen

67. Type the well-known port that the OpenSSH service uses?
   _____

68. Which of the TWO time sources can be used to sync time of your Linux system?
   A. An internet-based time server
   C. A watch
   B. A wall clock
   D. The local system clock

69. Which TWO shell built-in commands would run a program in the current shell?
   A. program.sh   B. source   C. . (dot)   D. sh

70. Which TWO commands can be used to discover open ports on a system?
   A. netstat   B. mapper   C. probe   D. nmap

71. Type the name of the file that stores a user's RSA identity for use with OpenSSH.

   _____

72. When two time servers work at the same stratum level, they are called peers. True or False?

73. Which of the following shows the correct syntax of entries in the /etc/hosts file?
   A. hostname alias1 alias2 IP   B. IP alias1 alias2 hostname
   C. IP hostname alias1 alias2   D. alias1 alias2 hostname IP

74. Depending on the Linux distribution and version, which TWO files are used to store a system's hostname?
   A. /etc/hosts.conf   B. /etc/sysconfig/network
   C. /etc/hostname   D. /etc/default/network

75. Which command can be used to check the status of NTP associations?
   A. ntpdd   B. xntpd   C. ntptrace   D. ntpq

76. Which TWO commands can be used to display environment variables and their values?
   A. print   B. env   C. unset   D. export

77. What would the command **ssh-add -l** do?
   A. Add user's public and private keys to authentication agent's cache
   B. Add a user's public key to authentication agent's cache
   C. Add a user's private key to authentication agent's cache
   D. List authentication agent's cache

78. Which TWO of the following show the correct syntax to remove a static route to a network non-persistently?
   A. ip route del 192.168.2.0/24   B. ifconfig route del 192.168.2.0/24
   C. ip route 192.168.2.0/24 del   D. route del -net 192.168.2.0/24

79. Which looping construct can be used to perform an action on listed items?
   A. while-do-done   B. until-do-done   C. if-then-fi   D. for-do-done

80. Normal users do not have access to list, create, or cd into the /var/spool/cron directory that stores crontab files. True or False?

81. Which is the de facto service used on the Internet for hostname resolution?
   A. DNS   B. NetworkManager   C. NIS   D. LDAP

82. Type the command to terminate all processes using a mounted file system.

   _____

83. On a small network with a few Linux systems, which hostname resolution method can be used?
   A. LDAP   B. DNS   C. NetworkManager   D. /etc/hosts

84. Any user on the system can modify the /etc/shadow and /etc/passwd files. True or False?

85. Which of the following is not included in the /etc/passwd file?
   A. GID   B. Home directory   C. Shell
   D. Comments   E. UID   F. User's secondary group

86. Type the name of the journald configuration file that is located in the /etc/systemd directory.

   _____

87. Select FOUR of the following that are valid for group accounts.
   A. A user can be a member of multiple groups at a time
   B. A user can have only one group as their primary group at a time
   C. Every group on the system must have a unique GID
   D. A user can switch into another group temporarily
   E. Two groups may share a GID

88. Which THREE of the following are included in the /etc/group file?
   A. GID   B. Group members   C. Shell   D. Group name

89. What would happen to an incoming email if the recipient user has a .forward file in their home directory
    containing email address user25@server25.example.com?
   A. The first 25 emails received will be redirected to user25
   B. Any email received by user25@server25.example.com will be forwarded to the recipient user
   C. Any email received by the recipient user will be forwarded to user25@server25.example.com
   D. Nothing will happen

90. What is the well-known port number used for the HTTP service?
   A. 8080   B. 80   C. 443   D. 880

91. Which of the following is not included in the /etc/shadow file?
   A. Username   B. GID   C. Encrypted password   D. Aging information

92. What is the name of the X11 configuration file?
   A. xorg.conf   B. x11.conf   C. xorgx11.conf   D. x11org.conf

93. What daemon must run on DNS clients to enable hostname resolution?
   A. named   B. name   C. dnsd   D. None

94. Select the name of the file that, if created in the /etc directory, would disallow normal users from being
    able to log on to the system.
   A. nologin   B. nousers   C. nouserlogins   D. nologins

95. Type the well-known port number for the LDAP service.

   _____

96. The primary use of the ICMP protocol is in testing and diagnosing network connections. True or False?

97. What would the command **lpadmin -d prn1** do?
   A. Print the /etc/hosts file on prn1 printer
   B. Set prn1 as the default printer and prints a test page
   C. Set prn1 as the default printer
   D. Print a test page on the default printer and deletes it

98. The new syslog service combines the functionalities of both syslogd and klogd services. True or False?

99. Identify TWO differences between TCP and UDP protocols.
   A. TCP does not guarantee packet delivery; UDP does
   B. TCP is reliable; UDP is not
   C. TCP is connectionless; UDP is connection-oriented
   D. TCP is point-to-point; UDP is not

100. What would the command **lp -d prn1 /etc/hosts** do?
   A. Prints the /etc/hosts file on prn1 printer
   B. Sets prn1 as the default printer
   C. Sets prn1 as the default printer and prints the /etc/hosts file
   D. Prints the /etc/hosts file on the default printer and deletes it

101. Define NTP stratum levels. Select TWO.
   A. They determine the reliability of time sources
   B. They determine the proximity of time sources
   C. They determine the accuracy of time sources
   D. They determine the availability of time sources

102. What would the command **ping -c3 192.168.0.2** do?
   A. Send packets of size 3KB to the IP
   B. Send three packets to the IP and continue if there is no response
   C. Send packets to the IP every third second
   D. Send three packets to the IP and quit

103. The ability of Linux to adapt itself to a specific language and cultural requirement is referred to as:
   A. Internationalization   B. Regionalization   C. Globalization   D. Localization

104. Which TWO of the following show the correct syntax for adding a static route non-persistently?
   A. ifconfig route add 192.168.4.0/24 via 192.168.0.1 dev eth1
   B. ip route add 192.168.4.0/24 via 192.168.0.1 dev eth1
   C. route add -net 192.168.4.0/24 gw 192.168.0.1 dev eth1
   D. ifconfig route add -net 192.168.4.0/24 gw 192.168.0.1 dev eth1

105. What is the function of the shift command?
   A. To switch the positions of two arguments
   B. To move all arguments to the left
   C. To move all arguments to the right
   D. To move only the last argument to the left

106. GDM is faster than LightDM. True or False?

107. OpenSSH enables:
   A. Authentication based on standard 128-bit encryption
   B. Authentication based on standard mode security extension
   C. Authentication based on hidden keys
   D. Authentication based on trusted mode security

108. Which of the following DNS query tools can also be used for DNS troubleshooting?
    A. dig   B. host   C. nslookup   D. nsswitch

109. Depending on the Linux distribution and version, which FOUR tools can be used to set or modify the time zone on the system?
    A. dpkg-reconfigure tzdata   B. timeconfig   C. timedatectl
    D. tzconfig   E. hostnamectl

110. Which pair of commands can be used to activate and deactivate shadow password mechanism for users?
    A. pwconv/pwunconv   B. shconv/shunconv
    C. passconv/passunconv   D. conv/unconv

111. Select THREE accessibility features that are available in GDM and Unity for users with disability.
    A. Contrast setting   B. Screen size setting
    C. Visual alert setting   D. AccessX

112. The ulimit command can be used to display and place user limits on computing resources, such as processors, memory, and files. True or False?

113. Which command can be used to determine the route a packet would take to reach the destination system?
    A. tracert   B. traceroute   C. route find   D. findroute

114. The OpenSSH toolset provides a non-secure network tunnel for accessing a Linux system. True or False?

115. Which command can be used to update system time instantly?
    A. xntpd   B. ntpdate   C. chdatentp   D. hostnamectl

116. The w command shows the following pieces of information in its output. Select THREE.
    A. System uptime information   B. List of logged-in users and what they're doing
    C. The logout time of a user   D. The length of time a user has been idle for

117. The equivalent for the mailq command is:
    A. mail   B. mailx   C. sendmail --mail   D. sendmail -bp

118. Write an SQL query to display all records stored in a table called ex102t and sort the output by city name.
    A. select * from ex102t order by city;   B. select all from ex102t order by city;
    C. select all in ex102t order by city;   D. select * from ex102t order by city

119. What is the purpose of subnetting?
    A. To create multiple smaller networks out of an IP
    B. To divide the network portion of an IP into multiple addresses
    C. To create larger networks
    D. To concatenate multiple IP addresses to form large networks

120. The X font server may be configured on older Linux versions to provide a central location to store and access fonts. True or False?

121. Which THREE of the following are list operators?
A.   B. &&   C. | D. || E. ;   F. ;;

122. The break command terminates the execution of a loop and returns the control to the command immediately after it. True or False?

123. What is the minimum number of nodes required to form a network?
A. 1   B. 2   C. 3   D. 0

124. How many layers are in there in the OSI reference networking model?
A. 8   B. 9   C. 7   D. 5

125. What is the term used for adding a header message at each layer of the OSI reference model?
A. De-encapsulation   B. Encapsulation   C. Packet-forming   D. Peer-to-peer

126. Which directory is used to store a user's authentication files by default?
A. /etc/ssh   B. ~/.ssh   C. ~/ssh   D. /etc/.ssh

127. Type the name of the command that is used to modify a group account.

_____

128. What signifies the end of an "if" statement in a shell script?
A. endif   B. if   C. }   D. fi

129. Select TWO from the following to print two copies of /tmp/file1 to prn1 printer and send an email when printing is complete.
A. lpr -dprn1 -#2 -m /tmp/file1   B. lpr -Pprn1 -#2 -m /tmp/file1
C. lp -dprn1 -nm2 /tmp/file1   D. lp -dprn1 -n2 -m /tmp/file1

130. Type the name of the command that is used to convert input text from one character encoding into another.

_____

131. A relational database has two or more tables linked by a common key. True or False?

132. What TWO components must be defined at a minimum for every cron job in a crontable?
A. Schedule   B. Group name   C. Username   D. Command

133. How would you capture the result of the who command in a variable called WHO?
A. WHO=$(who)   B. who=$(WHO)   C. WHO=who   D. who>WHO

134. Which of the following is the correct syntax in the /etc/aliases file to forward emails received by user30 to root and ab@ab.com?
A. root,ab@ab.com: user30   B. user30 root ab@ab.com
C. user30: root,ab@ab.com   D. user30,root,ab@ab.com

135. Which command can be used to make a printer to disallow new print requests from queuing?
 A. cupsstop   B. cupsdisallow   C. cupsdisable   D. cupsreject

136. Which of the following would print the contents of the /etc/profile file on printer prn3?
 A. lp -p prn3 /etc/profile   B. lp -dprn3 /etc/profile
 C. lp -a prn3 /etc/profile   D. lp -pprn3 /etc/profile

137. OSI layers provide a set of rules for data transmission. True or False?

138. The lpadmin command is used to display the health of configured printers. True or False?

139. Which file would you modify to add the following default gateway information persistently on RHEL and spinoffs?

   GATEWAY=<IP>
   GATEWAYDEV=eth2

 A. /etc/network.conf   B. /etc/sysconfig/network
 C. /etc/default/network   D. /etc/network/interfaces

140. At what layers the TCP and IP protocols are defined? Choose TWO.
 A. Data link layer   B. Application layer   C. Transport layer   D. Network layer

141. Which directory is the default location for storing log files?
 A. /tmp/log   B. /etc/log   C. /var/log   D. /usr/log

142. Locale settings may be configured at per-user and system-wide levels. True or False?

143. What is the default subnet mask for a class B IP address?
 A. 255.255.255.0   B. 255.255.0.0   C. 255.0.0.0   D. 0.0.0.255

144. Which is not another name for MAC address?
 A. IP address   B. Hardware address   C. Station address   D. Ethernet address

145. Where do the at and cron scheduling daemons store history of executed jobs?
 A. /etc/cron   B. /etc/log/cron   C. /var/log/cron/cron   D. /var/log/cron

146. What is the term "journal" refers to on systems running systemd?
 A. A journal is a file under /var/log/journal directory that stores alerts captured by the syslog service
 B. A journal is a file under /var/log/journal directory that stores alerts captured by the journald service
 C. A journal is a file under /run/log/journal directory that stores alerts captured by the syslog service
 D. A journal is a file under /run/log/journal directory that stores alerts captured by the journald service

147. Which TWO of the following can be used to set or change password aging attributes on a user account?
 A. chattr   B. passwd   C. set   D. chage

148. Which THREE of the following can be used to view routing table information?
 A. netstat -r   B. ip route   C. ifconfig -a   D. route

149. Which TWO of the following have syntax problems?
  A. mail -s "Hello, This is me." user20
  B. echo "Hello, This is me." | mail user20
  C. mail "Hello, This is me." user20
  D. echo user20 | mail "Hello, This is me."

150. Which file is referenced to determine sources to look up hostname information?
  A. /etc/network.conf
  B. /etc/nsswitch.conf
  C. /etc/resolv.conf
  D. /etc/sysconfig/network

151. Type the name of the legacy command that is still used to submit print requests.

  _____

152. What would the command **usermod -aG nixadm user10** do?
  A. Add user10 to group nixadm without affecting user10's current group memberships
  B. Replace user10's current group memberships with group nixadm
  C. Change user10's primary group to nixadm
  D. Replace user10's supplementary groups with group nixadm

153. What would the command **ssh-keygen -f ~/.ssh/id_rsa -N "" -q** do?
  A. Generate OpenSSH DSA keys with all the defaults
  B. Generate OpenSSH RSA keys quietly with a null passphrase and store them in ~/.ssh/id_rsa file
  C. Generate OpenSSH RSA keys with all the defaults
  D. Generate OpenSSH DSA keys quietly with a null passphrase and store them in ~/.ssh/id_rsa file

154. Type the name of the command to list available devices on the system that can be used to set up a printer.

  _____

155. Which FOUR of the following components can be parts of a shell script?
  A. Conditional statements
  B. Comments
  C. Loops
  D. Commands
  E. Location

156. Which TWO of the following can be used to set or change some password aging attributes for a user account?
  A. useradd
  B. usermod
  C. groupadd
  D. groupmod

157. The Neighbor Discovery Protocol (NDP) is used for the following TWO purposes.
  A. To probe an IPv4 network
  B. To discover IPv6 devices
  C. To probe an IPv6 network
  D. To discover IPv4 and IPv6 devices

158. Which command can be used to determine a time zone value that an individual user can set for themselves?
  A. tzconfig
  B. tzselect
  C. echo $TZ
  D. timedatectl

159. What does the echo command do without any arguments?
  A. Removes an empty line
  B. Adds a comments line
  C. Cleans comments
  D. Adds an empty line

160. Which THREE are valid keywords for the /etc/resolv.conf file?
   A. Nameserver   B. Domain   C. Search   D. Hostname

161. The until-do-done loop continues to run until the specified condition becomes false. True or False?

162. POP3 and IMAP4 use the following port numbers.
   A. 100/200   B. 995/993   C. 110/143   D. 25/28

163. What would the test condition [$1 -ge 0] do in an if-then-fi statement?
   A. Test whether an integer value supplied as the first argument is less than 0
   B. Test whether an integer value supplied as the first argument is greater than 0
   C. Test whether an integer value supplied as the first argument is less than or equal to 0
   D. Test whether an integer value supplied as the first argument is greater than or equal to 0

164. The tracepath and traceroute commands may be used to troubleshoot a network connection when a ping test has failed. True or False?

165. Which command can be used for both composing and reading email messages?
   A. mailq   B. mail   C. mailx   D. postfix

166. What are TWO good reasons to use exit codes in a shell script?
   A. To determine where exactly a script concluded execution
   B. To help debug a script
   C. To help determine how to write a new script
   D. To help understand how a script works

167. What is the name of the command that can be used to run the anacron service manually?
   A. cron   B. anac   C. anacron   D. anacrontab

168. Type another name used for the default gateway.
   _____

169. What is the unicode standard?
   A. It consists of various standards to support users
   B. It helps translate code mappings into character definitions
   C. It transforms character mappings and store them in a character database
   D. It comprises code mappings, character database, and relevant definitions and details

170. Which TWO files the useradd command consults to get default user attributes?
   A. /etc/default/useradd   B. /etc/default/logins
   C. /etc/sysconfig/useradd   D. /etc/login.defs

171. What is the impact of the setuid bit on directories?
   A. Directories cannot be shared with other users
   B. Directories will allow only setuid-enabled files to be stored in them
   C. No impact
   D. Directories can be shared among group members

172. What could the command **Xorg -configure** be used for? Select TWO.
  A. To configure remote X access
  B. To view current X configuration settings
  C. To invoke the X tool
  D. To modify X configuration settings

173. What is the advantage of using port tunneling (port forwarding)? Select TWO.
  A. It allows only encrypted protocols to use this feature
  B. It allows data transmission via unencrypted protocols over ssh-encrypted channels
  C. X11 can take advantage of this feature by allowing the graphical portion of an application to use the secure connection.
  D. This feature requires a lot of configuration and therefore it is barely used

174. What would the following function called funtest do?

  funtest () { echo "There are $# args"; echo "They are: $@"; }

  A. There is a syntax error in the function
  B. Display a list and count of arguments
  C. Display a count and list of arguments, and then delete them
  D. Display a count and list of arguments

175. Which TWO of the following can be used to restart the syslog service?
  A. systemctl restart rsyslog
  B. systemctl restart rsyslogd
  C. service rsyslog restart
  D. service rsyslogd restart

176. Depending on the Linux distribution and version, which TWO directories store files to enable or disable individual network service?
  A. /etc/inetd.conf.d
  B. /etc/networkd.d
  C. /etc/xinetd.d
  D. /etc/inetd.d

177. Write an SQL query to display all records stored in a table called ex102t with a common last name.
  A. select * from ex102t where lastname='LN" group by lastname;
  B. select * from ex102t where lastname='LN" sort by lastname;
  C. select * from ex102t where lastname='LN" order by lastname;
  D. select * from ex102t where lastname='LN" list by lastname;

178. Which command is used to write interactive scripts?
  A. interact
  B. tellme
  C. read
  D. write

179. What are THREE possible benefits of writing shell scripts?
  A. To automate lengthy tasks
  B. To simplify the performance of Linux administration tasks
  C. To automate repetitive tasks
  D. To complicate Linux administration tasks

180. A database is a non-structured collection of data. True or False?

181. The CUPS printing system uses files to store configuration information. What is the name of the directory where these files are stored?
  A. /usr/cups
  B. /etc/cups
  C. /usr/print
  D. /etc/print

182. What are THREE major components of a database table?
  A. Column
  B. Value
  C. Sort
  D. Row

183. A subnet mask is used to identify the start and end of the network and node portion of an IP address. True or False?

184. What are TWO fundamental types of logical constructs used in shell scripting?
A. for-do-done   B. case   C. if-then-elif-fi   D. if-then-fi

185. Which of the following would run an at job 6 hours from now?
A. at + 6 hours   B. at 6 pm   C. atd now + 6 hours   D. at now + 6 hours

186. Select FOUR Mail Transfer Agent (MTA) program names from the following.
A. Sendmail   B. Postfix   C. Evolution
D. Mutt   E. Exim   F. Qmail

187. Which of the THREE commands can be used to work with variables?
A. var   B. env   C. set   D. export

188. What is the difference between a primary key and a foreign key in database terminology?
A. A primary key is used within a table to uniquely identify a record; a foreign key is used to relate two or more tables
B. A primary key is used to relate two or more tables; a foreign key is used within a table to uniquely identify a record
C. There is no difference between the two
D. Both primary and foreign keys are used within a single table

189. How can we determine which processes are using a mounted file system or a network port?
A. With the help of the ps command   B. With the help of the top command
C. With the help of the lsof command   D. With the help of the fuser command

190. Why do we usually define multiple NTP servers on the NTP client for time maintenance? Select TWO.
A. To improve time precision   B. To improve efficiency
C. To increase availability   D. To expand network efficiency

191. Which command shows a list of users who are currently logged on to the system?
A. 'who am i'   B. who   C. login   D. whoami

192. What information does the lastb command display?
A. It reports the history of successful user login attempts
B. It reports the history of successful and unsuccessful user login attempts
C. It reports the history of superuser login attempts
D. It reports the history of unsuccessful user login attempts

193. What does the "x" in the second field of the /etc/passwd file imply?
A. It implies that the encrypted password is stored in the /etc/gshadow file
B. It implies that the encrypted password is stored in the /etc/shadow file
C. It implies that the shadow password mechanism is disabled
D. It implies that the encrypted password for this user is stored at the beginning of the /etc/shadow file

194. The journald service records alerts in a non-legible format. Which command do we use to read them?
   A. syslog   B. journalctl   C. journal   D. strings

195. Write the SQL command to create a database called exam102.
   A. create database exam102;   B. create exam102 database;
   C. create database exam102   D. create database db exam102;

196. What would the command **ssh-copy-id -i ~/.ssh/id_rsa.pub 192.168.0.20** do?
   A. Copy file ~/.ssh/id_rsa.pub to 192.168.0.20 using the sftp command under the same directory location
   B. Copy file ~/.ssh/id_rsa.pub to 192.168.0.20 using the ssh command under /etc
   C. Copy file ~/.ssh/id_rsa.pub to 192.168.0.20 using the ssh command under the same directory location
   D. Copy file ~/.ssh/id_rsa.pub to 192.168.0.20 using the rcp command under the same directory location

197. Select the FOUR local user authentication files that are affected when a user or group account is created, modified, or removed.
   A. passwd   B. fstab   C. gshadow   D. resolv.conf   E. group   F. shadow

198. Type the name of the sudo configuration file that is located in the /etc directory.
   _____

199. What are the TWO types of shell startup files?
   A. Per-user   B. Normal-user   C. Service-wide   D. System-wide

200. Write an SQL statement to update the field "FirstName" with value "Abraham" matching serial number "Sno" to "1" in table "ex102t".
   A. update ex102t set FirstName=Abraham where Sno=1;
   B. update ex102t update FirstName=Abraham where Sno=1;
   C. update ex102t set FirstName=Abraham where Sno=1
   D. select * from ex102t set FirstName=Abraham where Sno=1;

201. What would the command passwd -l user10 do?
   A. Change aging for user10   B. Unlock user10   C. Lock user10   D. Delete user10

202. Which THREE network classes are used on public networks?
   A. Class A   B. Class B   C. Class C   D. Class D   E. Class E

203. What is the first UID assigned to a regular user on newer Linux distributions?
   A. 500   B. 100   C. 900   D. 1000

204. What is the impact of the sticky bit on files?
   A. No impact
   B. Normal users will not be able to delete the files
   C. The root user will be able to delete or modify the files
   D. Files cannot be shared with other users

205. Which TWO of the following can be used to search for files with suid bit set?
   A. find / -perm /u+s -type f   B. find / -perm -4000
   C. find / -type f -perm /o+s   D. find / -perm /o+t

206. Every user in Linux gets a private group by default. True or False?

207. The selector field in the rsyslog.conf file is segregated into three sub-fields called facility, priority, and action. True or False?

208. Which TWO commands can be used to display queued print requests?
   A. lpq -o   B. lpq   C. lpadmin -o   D. lpstat -o

209. The last command is used to report successful user login attempts and system reboot history. True or False?

210. Depending on the Linux distribution and version, which THREE files store system-wide locale information?
   A. /etc/default/locale   B. /etc/sysconfig/L10n
   C. /etc/locale.conf   D. /etc/sysconfig/i18n

211. What would the userdel command do if it is run with the -r option?
   A. Delete a user along with their home directory
   B. Delete a user without touching their home directory
   C. Delete home directory of a user
   D. Delete a user along with their system-wide shell startup files

212. Which directory stores time zone information for various cities, countries, and regions?
   A. /etc/timezones   B. /usr/zonefiles
   C. /etc/zoneinfo   D. /usr/share/zoneinfo

213. Which command can be used to start the X server manually?
   A. start   B. startx   C. X   D. xstart

214. Type the name of the command that is used to enable or disable remote X access on the local system.
   _____

215. What is the first GID assigned to a group on newer Linux distributions?
   A. 500   B. 100   C. 1000   D. 900

216. ALL and LOCAL are valid keywords that can be used in TCP Wrappers configuration files hosts.deny and hosts.allow to represent every host and hosts on the local network, respectively. True or False?

217. What is the name of the default backup file for /etc/shadow?
   A. /etc/shadow.sh   B. /etc/shadow-   C. /etc/shadow.bak   D. /etc/shadow.old

218. Linux allows us to use the same number as both UID and GID. True or False?

219. What would the command **chage -E 2018-12-31 user20** do?
   A. Set December 31, 2018 as the account expiry date for user10
   B. Set December 31, 2018 as the account deletion date for user10
   C. Set December 31, 2018 as a reminder to recreate user10 account
   D. Run a shell script for user10 on December 31, 2018

220. Which TWO of the following show the correct syntax to remove an IP non-persistently from the system?
A. ip a del 192.168.2.20/24 dev eth1
B. ifconfig del 192.168.2.20/24 dev eth1
C. ip dev eth1 del 192.168.2.20/24
D. ifconfig eth1 del 192.168.2.20/24

221. What would the command **chage -l user5** do?
A. List user5 account information
B. Lock user5 account
C. Unlock user5 account
D. Display aging attributes for user5

222. Rotating log files on a regular basis is a valuable feature to ensure availability of enough free space. Which command does the system use for log file rotation and subsequent compression and mailing out?
A. rotate
B. rotatelog
C. logrotate
D. rotation

223. Which command can be used to print detailed information about X server and its capabilities?
A. xterm
B. xdpyinfo
C. display
D. xwininfo

224. Which TWO statements are correct for using the hyphen character with the su command?
A. The su command does not process the specified user's shell startup files
B. The su command processes the specified user's shell startup files
C. The su command processes the root user's shell startup files if no user account name is supplied
D. The use of the hyphen character is unnecessary

225. What is the well-known port number associated with the secure HTTP service?
A. 80
B. 143
C. 993
D. 443

226. Which TWO of the following are correct to list GnuPG keys?
A. gpg2 --list-keys
B. gpg2 --show-keys
C. gpg --list-keys
D. gpg --show-keys

227. What is the significance of the -o option with the groupadd and groupmod commands?
A. It allows the commands to allocate an in-use GID to other groups
B. It prevents the commands from allocating an in-use GID to other groups
C. It instructs the commands to create or modify a group account without allocating a GID
D. It disallows the commands from re-allocating an in-use GID to a new/different group

228. Type the name of the command that is used to change a user's primary group temporarily.
_____

229. What would the command **iconv /tmp/testcode -t EBCDIC-JP-E -o /tmp/testcode.out** do?
A. Translate the content of /tmp/testcode into Japanese and record output in /tmp/testcode.out
B. Translate the content of /tmp/testcode into Japanese language
C. Convert the content of /tmp/testcode into Japanese EBCDIC encoding and record output in /tmp/testcode.out
D. Convert the content of /tmp/testcode.out into Japanese EBCDIC encoding and record output in /tmp/testcode

230. The /etc/bashrc file contains shell scripts that are executed at user login. True or False?

231. What would the command **chage -d 0 user60** do?
A. Disable password aging for user60   B. Disable user60's ability to change password
C. Force user60 to change password right now   D. Force user60 to change password at next login

232. Which user does not need to be defined in *.allow or *.deny file to run the at and cron jobs?
A. The bin user   B. The root user   C. user1   D. All service user accounts

233. Depending on the Linux distribution and version, which TWO of the following could be the directory locations where user crontab files are stored?
A. /etc/spool/cron/crontabs   B. /etc/spool/cron
C. /var/spool/cron/crontabs   D. /var/spool/cron

234. By default the *.allow files for at and cron exist. True or False?

235. Which languages does the ISO-8859 standard support?
A. East Asian   B. European   C. African   D. South Asian

236. Which TWO of the following are true for a subnet mask?
A. It increases the number of usable IP addresses
B. Subnets require a router in between in order to communicate with one another
C. Each network node within a subnet will have a unique subnet address
D. Subnetting results in harder administration
E. Subnetting results in improved network performance

237. Which option with the crontab command would allow a user to modify their crontables?
A. -l   B. -a   C. -m   D. -e

238. Which file stores default password aging attributes?
A. /etc/login.defs   B. /etc/default/logins   C. /etc/sysconfig/logins   D. /etc/logins

239. Which class of IP addresses has the least number of node addresses?
A. Class A   B. Class B
C. Class C   D. All three classes have the same number of node addresses

240. Which command would display the status of all configured print queues?
A. lpadmin -d   B. lp -t   C. lpadmin -t   D. lpstat -t

241. What are the uses of the ifup and ifdown commands?
A. To activate and deactivate the NTP service   B. To activate and deactivate the HTTP service
C. To remove and redefine a network interface   D. To activate and deactivate a network interface

242. Individual users may set a different time zone for themselves using the TZ environment variable in a per-user shell startup file. True or False?

243. The passwd file stores secondary user group information. True or False?

244. **alias rm="rm -i"** is an example of:
A. Filename completion   B. Alias substitution
C. Tilde substitution   D. Command substitution

245. Which THREE of the following methods can be used to share GnuPG keys with intended recipients?
A. As an email attachment
B. Via a keyserver
C. By running gpg --send-keys user@email
D. Via a USB key

246. Which TWO commands can be used to display the hardware address of a network interface?
A. ping   B. netstat   C. ifconfig   D. ip

247. Select FOUR facilities that the syslog service recognizes.
A. cron   B. user   C. rsyslog   D. daemon   E. auth

248. Which file defines the protocols in the system?
A. /etc/protocols/protocols   B. /etc/protocols   C. /etc/services   D. /etc/tcp

249. What is the purpose of the ONBOOT directive in the interface configuration file in RHEL and derivatives?
A. Whether to activate an interface at system boot
B. Whether to perform a ping test at system boot
C. Whether to allow the system to boot up
D. Whether to activate network services at system boot

250. List THREE benefits of subnetting.
A. Better management
B. Smaller networks
C. More usable IP addresses
D. Less traffic

251. What would the command **passwd -n 7 -x 15 -w 3 user6** do?
A. Set warndays to 7, maxdays to 15, and mindays to 3 for user6
B. Set mindays to 7, warndays to 15, and maxdays to 3 for user6
C. Set maxdays to 7, mindays to 15, and warndays to 3 for user6
D. Set mindays to 7, maxdays to 15, and warndays to 3 for user6

252. Which TWO files in the /etc/ directory control user access to the cron service?
A. cron.allow   B. crontab   C. anacron   D. cron.deny

253. What is the function of the default gateway?
A. It is used only in the presence of static routes
B. It is used only in the absence of static routes
C. It is used when the system is unable to find an appropriate route to a destination
D. It is always used

254. What is the range of a class B network?
A. 128 to 191   B. 127 to 192   C. 193 to 223   D. 224 to 240

255. Which file or directory stores network interface configuration on Debian and derivatives?
A. /etc/network
B. /etc/network/interfaces
C. /etc/sysconfig/network-scripts
D. /var/network/interfaces

256. Which environment variable must be set appropriately to work with X applications?
A. XHOST   B. DISPLAY   C. X11   D. SHOW

257. CUPS printing system is a replacement for the LPD print service. True or False?

258. What is the default NTP polling interval, in seconds?
   A. 128   B. 32   C. 256   D. 64

259. Which of the following is correct to view a list of current NTP time sources?
   A. ntpq -p   B. ntpq -q   C. ntpstat -p   D. ntpstat -q

260. What port and protocol does NTP use?
   A. 321/UDP   B. 124/UDP   C. 123/UDP   D. 123/ICMP

261. Which of the following is not a syslog priority?
   A. emerg   B. warn   C. log   D. debug

262. What is the purpose of the NTP drift file /var/lib/ntp/drift?
   A. NTP uses it to keep track of remote clock accuracy
   B. NTP uses it to keep track of hardware clock accuracy
   C. NTP uses it to keep track of Windows clock accuracy
   D. NTP uses it to keep track of local clock accuracy

263. Depending on the Linux distribution and version, static and/or default routes can be defined
     persistently in THREE of the following files?
   A. The /etc/sysconfig/network file
   B. Interface-specific route configuration files under /etc/sysconfig/network-scripts directory
   C. The /etc/network/interfaces file
   D. The /etc/resolv.conf file
   E. The /etc/nsswitch.conf file

264. What is the name of the system-wide shell startup file that defines shell variables for all users?
   A. /etc/profile   B. ~/profile   C. /etc/.profile   D. /etc/profile.sh

265. Which environment variable overrides the values of all individual locale environment variables?
   A. LC_ALL   B. LC_*   C. LOCALE_ALL   D. LANG

266. What would the command **ntpdate 0.server.centos.ntp.org** do?
   A. It will start the local clock synchronization process with the specified NTP server
   B. It will instantly synchronize the local system clock with the specified NTP server
   C. It will instantly bind the local system clock with the specified NTP server
   D. It will instantly synchronize the specified server's time with the system's local clock

267. What THREE would the command **ip addr** show in the output?
   A. Display MAC address for all network interfaces
   B. Display DNS assignments for all network interfaces
   C. Display IPv6 assignments for all network interfaces
   D. Display IPv4 assignments for all network interfaces

268. Which TWO of the following can be used to list submitted at jobs?
   A. atq -e   B. at -l   C. atq   D. at -q

269. Write an SQL query to display all records stored in tables ex101t and ex102t with matching key Sno. Select TWO correct answers.
   A. select all in ex101t join ex102t on ex101t.sno = ex102t.sno;
   B. select * from ex101t,ex102t where ex101t.sno = ex102t.sno;
   C. select * in ex101t,ex102t on ex101t.sno = ex102t.sno;
   D. select * from ex101t join ex102t on ex101t.sno = ex102t.sno

270. What would the entry "hosts: files dns" mean in the /etc/nsswitch.conf file?
   A. To consult the /etc/hosts file and then DNS
   B. To consult the /etc/hosts file and then time out
   C. To consult the /etc/hosts file only
   D. To consult the DNS and then the /etc/hosts file

271. The journald service is available on systems that run either SysVinit or systemd. True or False?

272. What would the command **host 10.22.112.22** do? Select TWO.
   A. Query the specified IP for a DNS server
   B. Provide a hostname associated with the specified IP
   C. Query available name resolution sources for the specified IP
   D. There is a syntax problem

273. Is the DNS name space hierarchical, flat, or winding? Type your answer in the space provided.

   _____

274. Which directory contains the default user startup template files that are copied to the home directory of a user account at the time of creation?
   A. /etc/skeleton   B. /etc/default/user   C. /etc/default   D. /etc/skel

275. What is the well-known port number for the DNS service?
   A. 51   B. 52   C. 53   D. 54

276. Which THREE of the following are true for an MTA?
   A. It is responsible for downloading email messages to a recipient's inbox
   B. It is responsible for transporting email messages between mail servers
   C. It uses the POP and IMAP protocols over port 25
   D. It uses port 25
   E. It uses the SMTP protocol

277. Type the name of the file that defines the mapping between users and email addresses.

   _____

278. What is the secure equivalent that OpenSSH provides for the rcp command?
   A. scp   B. cp   C. ftp   D. No equivalent, use rcp

279. What is the significance of the character combination (#!) at the beginning of a shell script?
   A. It outlines the absolute path of the Bash shell file to be used to run the script
   B. It outlines the absolute path of the shell to be used to run the script
   C. It outlines the absolute path of the Korn shell to be used to run the script
   D. It outlines the absolute path of the C shell to be used to run the script.

280. Select TWO of the following that can be used to redirect incoming user email to one or more recipients.
A. By using the ~/.forward file   B. By using the /etc/aliases file
C. By using the /etc/forward file   D. By using the mail command

281. Which of the following correctly lists the features included in assistive technologies?
A. Text size adjustments   B. Audible and visual alerts   C. Onscreen virtual keyboards
D. Mouse gestures   E. Screen resolution adjustments   F. All of the above

282. Which of the following should be run after making changes to the rsyslog.conf file to check for any errors?
A. service rsyslog restart   B. rsyslogd   C. systemctl rsyslog restart   D. rsyslogd -N 1

283. Which TWO of the following commands can be used for tracing flow of network traffic?
A. route   B. tracepath   C. netstat   D. traceroute

284. Type the name of the OpenSSH client configuration file located in the /etc/ssh directory.

_____

285. Depending on the Linux distribution and version, which TWO are valid configuration files to store the default display manager?
A. /etc/default/display   B. /etc/X11/desktop
C. /etc/sysconfig/desktop   D. /etc/X11/default-display-manager

286. What would the command **groupadd -g 4000 dba** do? Select TWO.
A. Create a group called dba with GID 4000   B. Create a group called 4000 with GID dba
C. Update the /etc/group and /etc/gshadow files   D. Add a group called dba using the next available GID

287. How many characters does the ASCII character set comprises of?
A. 64   B. 128   C. 256   D. 512

288. Which directory stores the user SSH keys?
A. /tmp/ssh   B. /etc/ssh   C. ~/.ssh   D. /etc/.ssh

289. Which directory stores the interface configuration files in RHEL and derivatives?
A. /var/lib/interfaces   B. /etc/network
C. /usr/local/network   D. /etc/sysconfig/network-scripts

290. Which command can be used to define VAR as an environment variable so that programs running in subshells also see and use it?
A. echo   B. set   C. env   D. export

291. What would the command ssh-copy-id do?
A. Install private and public keys on a remote system   B. Install public key on a remote system
C. Install private key on a remote system   D. Copy public key to a different directory

292. What is the OpenSSH equivalent for the telnet command?
A. scp   B. openssh   C. ssh   D. sftp

293. Type the name of the TCP Wrappers daemon that controls access to the system via the /etc/hosts.allow and /etc/hosts.deny files.

_____

294. What is the use of the ssh-keygen command?
    A. To replace authentication keys   B. To copy authentication keys
    C. To delete authentication keys   D. To generate authentication keys

295. What is the name of the configuration file in Debian and derivatives that stores syslog rules?
    A. 50-default.conf   B. rsyslog.conf   C. syslog.conf   D. klogd.conf

296. Select TWO common encryption techniques.
    A. Symmetric   B. Cryptography   C. Secret key   D. Asymmetric

297. Which file in the /etc directory do we modify to enter NTP server names or IP addresses?
    A. ntp.sh   B. ntp.conf   C. ntpserver.conf   D. ntpclient.conf

298. Which log file stores authentication messages?
    A. /var/log/auth   B. /etc/log/secure   C. /var/log/secure   D. /etc/log/auth

299. Which THREE of the following are per-user shell startup files?
    A. /etc/bashrc   B. ~/.bashrc   C. ~/.bash_profile   D. ~/.profile

300. The groupmod and usermod commands may be used to perform the following. Select THREE.
    A. Modify group and user account attributes   B. Change GID and UID
    C. Set group and user passwords   D. Change group name and user name

301. What can we achieve by executing the command **ulimit -f 2048**?
    A. Set a minimum file size to 2MB for a user
    B. Set a maximum file size to 2MB for a user
    C. Set a maximum number of files to 2048 that a user can create
    D. Set a minimum number of files to 2048 that a user can create

302. What does the entry **hosts: dns [TRYAGAIN=return] files** mean in the /etc/nsswitch.conf file?
    A. Terminate a name lookup attempt even if DNS server is not busy
    B. Jump to the /etc/hosts file for lookup if DNS server is busy
    C. Terminate a name lookup attempt if DNS server is busy
    D. Continue to the hosts file for name lookup even if DNS server is busy

303. Write an SQL query to show only the count of records stored in a table called ex102t matching the name "Abraham".
    A. select * from ex102t where name='Abraham' count(*);
    B. select count(*) from ex102t where name='Abraham';
    C. select count(*) in ex102t where name='Abraham';
    D. select * from ex102t where name='Abraham';

304. How can we identify the files that are in use of running processes?
    A. With the help of the ps command   B. With the help of the pgrep command
    C. With the help of the fuser command   D. With the help of the lsof command

305. Which command can be used to print monitor settings, such as screen size, orientation, and reflection?
A. xrandr   B. xwininfo   C. display   D. xdpyinfo

306. Which of the following can be used to log a message to the default system log file?
A. write -i System Rebooted by $USER   B. log -i System Rebooted by $USER
C. logger -i System Rebooted by $USER   D. logger System Rebooted by $USER

307. Which command can be used to update the computer's hardware clock with the Linux system clock?
A. clock   B. date   C. time   D. hwclock

308. CUPS is not an implementation of the Internet Printing Protocol (IPP). True or False?

309. The selector field is divided into facility and priority in syslog configuration. What are their uses? Select TWO.
A. A facility represents process groups that generate messages
B. A priority identifies the severity associated with a facility
C. A priority represents process groups that generate messages
D. A facility identifies the severity associated with a facility

310. The setgid bit should/need not be enabled on TWO of the following.
A. Shared libraries   B. Executable files   C. Shell scripts   D. Directories

311. Which THREE statements are true about the arp command?
A. It can be used to ascertain a hardware address associated with an IP address
B. It can be used to determine duplicate MAC addresses active on the network
C. It may be used to identify duplicate IP addresses active on the network
D. It caches the information obtained in ARP cache

312. The OpenSSH private key must be shared with remote systems for user authentication. True or False?

313. Depending on the Linux distribution and version, which THREE commands can be used to change the system time zone to America/Toronto.
A. hostnamectl set-timezone America/Toronto
B. cp /usr/share/zoneinfo/America/Toronto /etc/localtime
C. ln -s /usr/share/zoneinfo/America/Toronto /etc/localtime
D. timedatectl set-timezone America/Toronto

314. Which entry can be placed in user2's crontable to run script2.sh at 5 minutes past 1 a.m. and 1 p.m. on every Tuesday and redirect the output to /tmp/script2.out file?
A. 5 1,13 * * 2 /home/user2/script2.sh > /tmp/script2.out
B. 5 1-13 * * 2 /home/user2/script2.sh > /tmp/script2.out
C. 5 1,13 * * * /home/user2/script2.sh > /tmp/script2.out
D. 1,13 5 * * 2 /home/user2/script2.sh > /tmp/script2.out

315. Which character appears just before the encrypted password in the /etc/shadow file to identify a locked user account?
A. ?   B. !   C. *   D. #

316. Which THREE statements are true about login/display manager programs?
   A. They are responsible for graphical user logins
   B. Unity and GNOME are two common login/display manager programs
   C. They start an appropriate desktop environment manager program for the user logging in.
   D. XDM, GDM, KDM, and LightDM are four common login/display manager programs

317. Toggle keys is an assistive technologies feature that sound an alert when keys such as NumLock and CapsLock are pressed. True or False?

318. Which THREE of the following can be used to search for directories with sticky bit on?
   A. find / -perm /o+t -type d   B. find / -perm -1000 -type d
   C. find / -type f -perm /o+t   D. find / -type d -perm /o+t

319. Which is the correct CIDR representation for an IP 192.168.30.40 using the default class C netmask?
   A. 192.168.30.40/16   B. 192.168.30.40/24   C. 192.168.30.40/32   D. 192.168.30.40/40

320. An MUA is used to read and write email messages. True or False?

321. Type the name of the service that runs after each system reboot and executes any missed cron and at jobs that were supposed to run during the time when the system was down.

_____

322. Depending on the Linux distribution and version, which TWO are valid configuration file names for turning network services on or off?
   A. /etc/inetd.conf   B. /etc/networkd.conf   C. /etc/network.conf   D. /etc/xinetd.conf

323. Which of the following can be used to establish a client/server netcat command connection on port 6000 on localhost? Select TWO answers, one to allow incoming connections and another to connect to it.
   A. nc -l 6000   B. nc localhost 6000   C. ncat 6000 -e   D. ncat 6000 127.0.0.1

324. It is highly recommended to enable suid-rights on shell scripts so that any user on the system can execute them successfully as and when required. True or False?

325. Which of the following is not a pre-defined environment variable?
   A. HOME   B. LOGNAME   C. NAME   D. TZ

326. What is the alias command used for?
   A. To create nick names for users   B. To create nick names for groups
   C. To create shortcuts to commands   D. To setup cron jobs

327. Which TWO of the following show the correct syntax to add a default route non-persistently?
   A. ifconfig route add default via 19.168.0.2 dev eth2   B. ip route add default via 19.168.0.2 dev eth2
   C. ip route add gw via 192.168.0.2 dev eth2   D. route add default gw 19.168.0.2 dev eth2

328. Which of the following would allow members of the group dba to run any administrative command on the system without being prompted for a password?
   A. %dba ALL=(ALL)   B. %dba ALL=(ALL) NOPASSWD: ALL
   C. dba ALL=(ALL)   D. dba ALL=(ALL) NOPASSWD: ALL

329. Log files are rotated based on a schedule. Which file stores the schedule and which command rotates the files?
   A. File: /etc/default/logrotate.conf, Command: rotate
   B. File: /etc/logrotate, Command: logrotate
   C. File: /etc/sysconfig/logrotate.conf, Command: logrotate
   D. File: /etc/logrotate.conf, Command: logrotate

330. Which THREE statements are true for command **date2 && hostname**?
   A. The && characters are list operators
   B. The && characters are used to perform a logical AND operation on given commands
   C. The hostname command will be executed and its result will be displayed
   D. There will be an error saying "date2 not found" when the above is executed

331. What would the command **cupsreject -r "prn1 is unavailable" prn1** do?
   A. Reject a submitted print job and return the message "prn1 is unavailable"
   B. Show the message "prn1 is unavailable" to the user and print a submitted job
   C. Disable the prn1 printer for good
   D. Return the message "prn1 is unavailable" to the user who attempts to submit a print request

332. The test command is used to perform tests in conditional statements. What would the -lt operation on integer values A and B, and -e operation on a file do?
   A. Test whether integer B is less than integer A, and whether a file exists
   B. Test whether integer A is less than integer B, and whether a file exists
   C. Test whether integer A is less than integer B, and whether a file is non-existent
   D. Test whether integer B is less than integer A, and whether a file is non-existent

333. Which of the following is not a valid environment variable in the output of the locale command?
   A. LANG   B. LC_MESSAGES   C. LC_NAME
   D. LC_ADDRESS   E. LC_DATE   F. LC_MEASUREMENT

334. What would the command **useradd -s /sbin/nologin user2** do?
   A. Add a user account called user2 who will be able to log in to the system once a day only
   B. Add a user account called user2 without login capability
   C. Create a user account called user2 with home directory called nologin created under /sbin directory
   D. Create a user account called user2 and copy per-user shell files from /sbin/nologin directory

335. What would the command **lpadmin -x prn1** do?
   A. Remove the prn1 printer   B. Add the prn1 printer
   C. Remove queued jobs from the printer   D. List print jobs queued on the prn1 printer

336. Write an SQL statement to delete all records stored from a database table called ex101t at Sno 2 and 7.
   A. delete from ex101t where Sno=2 or Sno=7
   B. delete from ex101t where Sno='2' or Sno='7';
   C. delete Sno='2' or 'Sno='7' from ex101t;
   D. select * from ex101t, delete where Sno='2' or 'Sno='7';

337. The behavior of a looping construct can be controlled via the following commands. Select THREE.
   A. break   B. sleep   C. continue   D. exit

338. What is the DNS resolver file name?
   A. /etc/dns.conf   B. /etc/nsswitch.conf   C. /etc/name.conf   D. /etc/resolv.conf

339. Which TWO of the following are the correct command syntaxes to run an at job on December 1, 2018 at 11:59 p.m.?
   A. at 11:59pm 12/1/18   B. at 11:59 1/12/18   C. at 23:59 12/1/18   D. at 23:59 1/12/18

340. The netcat (a.k.a. nc or ncat) command can be used to explore, monitor, and debug network connections. True or False?

341. Which of the following would list the contents of a user crontable?
   A. crontab -x   B. crontab -a   C. crontable -l   D. crontab -l

342. Depending on the Linux distribution and version, which TWO files store the time zone information in legible format?
   A. /etc/default/timezone   B. /etc/default/clock   C. /etc/sysconfig/clock   D. /etc/timezone

343. Which TWO of the following can be used instead of the command **find /usr -perm /2000 -type f**?
   A. find / -perm -g+s   B. find / -perm -g+s -type f
   C. find /usr -perm -g+s -type f   D. find /usr -type f -perm -g+s

344. The ping and ping6 commands send RARP packets to remote systems for testing network connectivity. True or False?

345. Which TWO of the following show the correct syntax to add an IP non-persistently to a network interface?
   A. ip add eth1 192.168.3.20/24 broadcast 192.168.3.255
   B. ifconfig eth1 192.168.3.20/24 broadcast 192.168.3.255
   C. ifconfig 192.168.3.20/24 broadcast 192.168.3.255 dev eth1
   D. ip a add 192.168.3.20/24 broadcast 192.168.3.255 dev eth1

346. Which of the following can be invoked to generate GnuPG keys?
   A. gpg2 -q --gen-key   B. gpg --show-keys --gen-key
   C. gpg2 --gen-key --list-keys   D. gpg2 --gen-key --show-keys

347. Which TWO of the following logging services are alternatives to the syslog service?
   A. syslogd-ng   B. rsyslog   C. syslog-ng   D. syslogd

348. The default network port that the syslog service use for its network operation is 514. True or False?

349. Which of the following can be used to view the current locale setting?
   A. echo $LANG   B. echo $LOCALE   C. echo $GLOBAL   D. echo $LC

350. Which TWO are valid IPv6 addresses?
   A. 192.168.3.25   B. fe80::a00:27ff:feae:f35b/64
   C. 140:add:34a:ab7:5d2:4ae:5de:c2   D. 1204:bab1:21d1:bb43:23a1:9bde:87df:bac9

351. The OpenSSH server configuration file is sshd_config. True or False?

352. UTF-8 and UTF-16 are character encoding schemes based on the unicode character set. True or False?

353. Which of the following commands can be used to examine, list, and set the locale setting on systems running systemd?
   A. locale-update   B. localectl   C. modlocale   D. locale-info

354. Why do we use the su command?
   A. To log out of the system   B. To shut down the system
   C. To switch user id   D. To display a list of logged in users

355. Which TWO commands can be used to display a user's current group memberships?
   A. groups   B. id   C. who   D. whoami

356. The command to submit a cron job is?
   A. cronfile   B. crontab   C. cron.allow   D. /usr/sbin/cron

357. A user password is case-insensitive. True or False?

358. Can a normal user change other users' passwords?
   A. Yes   B. No

359. Which command is used to change a user password?
   A. passwd   B. password   C. pass   D. chpasswd

360. Which command only displays a user's group memberships?
   A. id   B. newgrp   C. groups   D. usermod

361. What is the default location for user home directories?
   A. /export/home   B. /usr/home   C. /usr   D. /home

362. Which THREE of the following commands are used for user account management?
   A. useradd   B. usermod   C. adduser   D. userdel   E. deluser   F. moduser

363. What are the default permissions on the /etc/passwd file?
   A. 655   B. 666   C. 644   D. 640

364. What does the following crontab entry do?

   20 12 1-15 * * find / -name core -exec rm {} \;

   A. Runs the find command at 20:12 the first fifteen days of each month
   B. Runs the find command at 12:20 the first fifteen days of each month
   C. Runs the find command at 12:20 on the first and the fifteenth day of each month
   D. None of the above

365. What is the impact of using the -o option with the useradd command?
   A. Disallows the allocation of non-unique GIDs B. Allows the use of non-unique GIDs
   C. Disallows the allocation of non-unique UIDs D. Allows the use of non-unique UIDs

366. What is the name of the system-wide user initialization file for Bash shell users?
   A. /etc/profile   B. $HOME/profile   C. /etc/.profile   D. /etc/swprofile

367. Which of the following will create a user account called user5 with UID 1005, primary group dba, and
   secondary group linuxadm (assuming that dba and linuxadm groups already exist).
   A. useradd -u 1005 -g dba -G linuxadm user5   B. useradd -u 1005 -g dba,linuxadm user5
   C. useradd -u 1005 -g dba linuxadm user5   D. useradd -u 1005 -G dba linuxadm user5

368. Which option with the crontab command would allow you to modify your crontab file?
   A. -e   B. -a   C. -m   D. -r

369. What is the purpose of the cron daemon?
   A. To run scheduled jobs every hour   B. To run all scheduled jobs at their specified times
   C. To run all scheduled jobs simultaneously D. To run all scheduled jobs every hour

370. Type the name of the file in the /etc directory that stores the primary group for a user.
   _____

371. What happens when neither the cron.allow nor the cron.deny file exists?
   A. All users excluding root can schedule a job   B. All users including root can schedule a job
   C. No users excluding root can schedule a job   D. No users including root can schedule a job

372. Which is the log file for the cron daemon?
   A. cron has no log file   B. /var/log/crontab   C. /var/log/cron   D. /var/adm/cron

373. What would the following at command do if executed at 6pm?

   # at 11pm find / -name core -exec rm {} \;

   A. Executes the find command at 11pm next week   B. Executes the find command after 5 hours
   C. Executes the find command every night at 11pm D. All of the above

374. Which directory contains default user startup template files?
   A. /etc/skeleton   B. /etc/default/user   C. /etc/default   D. /etc/skel

375. What would **mailx user1 < $HOME/.bash_profile** do?
   A. Mail the contents of the sending user's .bash_profile file to user1
   B. Mail the sending user's .bash_profile file as an attachment to user1
   C. Mail user1's .bash_profile file from their home directory to the sending user
   D. Save an incoming email in user1's home directory as .bash_profile

376. To remove a user account called user1 along with home directory, which TWO of the following can
   you use?
   A. userdel user1   B. userdel -r user1   C. userdel user1 -r   D. userrem -r user1

Appendix D: Answers to Sample LX0-104/102-400 Quiz

1.	A	2.	False	3.	tzselect	4.	B	5.	D
6.	AC	7.	B	8.	True	9.	BD	10.	AD
11.	ACD	12.	CD	13.	D	14.	B	15.	A
16.	AC	17.	C	18.	CD	19.	C	20.	ABC
21.	BD	22.	D	23.	BC	24.	B	25.	AD
26.	B	27.	ABD	28.	A	29.	D	30.	B
31.	B	32.	True	33.	ABE	34.	C	35.	B
36.	B	37.	D	38.	C	39.	A	40.	B
41.	lightdm.conf	42.	A	43.	True	44.	C	45.	D
46.	/et/anacrontab	47.	ABD	48.	C	49.	D	50.	ACD
51.	255.255.0.0	52.	C	53.	/etc/at.deny	54.	True	55.	B
56.	A	57.	/etc/rsyslog.conf	58.	A	59.	B	60.	CD
61.	D	62.	ABD	63.	AC	64.	A	65.	B
66.	B	67.	22	68.	AD	69.	BC	70.	AD
71.	~/.ssh/id_rsa	72.	True	73.	C	74.	BC	75.	D
76.	BD	77.	D	78.	AD	79.	D	80.	True
81.	A	82.	fuser	83.	D	84.	False	85.	F
86.	journald.conf	87.	ABDE	88.	ABD	89.	C	90.	B
91.	B	92.	A	93.	D	94.	A	95.	389
96.	True	97.	C	98.	True	99.	BD	100.	A
101.	AC	102.	D	103.	D	104.	BC	105.	B
106.	False	107.	C	108.	A	109.	ABCD	110.	A
111.	ACD	112.	True	113.	B	114.	False	115.	B
116.	ABD	117.	D	118.	A	119.	A	120.	True
121.	BDE	122.	True	123.	B	124.	C	125.	B

126.	B	127.	groupmod	128.	D	129.	BD	130.	iconv
131.	True	132.	AD	133.	A	134.	C	135.	D
136.	B	137.	True	138.	False	139.	B	140.	CD
141.	C	142.	True	143.	B	144.	A	145.	D
146.	D	147.	BD	148.	ABD	149.	CD	150.	C
151.	lpr	152.	A	153.	B	154.	lpinfo	155.	ABCD
156.	AB	157.	BC	158.	B	159.	D	160.	ABC
161.	False	162.	C	163.	D	164.	True	165.	B
166.	AB	167.	C	168.	default route	169.	D	170.	AD
171.	C	172.	BD	173.	BC	174.	D	175.	AC
176.	CD	177.	A	178.	C	179.	ABC	180.	False
181.	B	182.	ABD	183.	True	184.	BD	185.	D
186.	ABEF	187.	BCD	188.	A	189.	C	190.	C
191.	B	192.	D	193.	B	194.	B	195.	A
196.	C	197.	ACEF	198.	sudoers	199.	AD	200.	A
201.	C	202.	ABC	203.	D	204.	A	205.	AB
206.	True	207.	False	208.	BD	209.	True	210.	ACD
211.	A	212.	D	213.	B	214.	xhost	215.	C
216.	True	217.	B	218.	True	219.	A	220.	AD
221.	D	222.	C	223.	B	224.	BC	225.	D
226.	AC	227.	A	228.	newgrp	229.	C	230.	False
231.	A	232.	B	233.	CD	234.	False	235.	B
236.	BE	237.	D	238.	A	239.	C	240.	D
241.	D	242.	True	243.	False	244.	B	245.	ABD
246.	CD	247.	ABDE	248.	B	249.	A	250.	ABD
251.	D	252.	AD	253.	C	254.	A	255.	B
256.	B	257.	True	258.	D	259.	B	260.	C
261.	C	262.	D	263.	ABC	264.	A	265.	A
266.	B	267.	ACD	268.	BC	269.	BD	270.	A
271.	False	272.	C	273.	Hierarchical	274.	D	275.	C
276.	BDE	277.	/etc/aliases	278.	A	279.	B	280.	AB

281.	F	282.	D	283.	BD	284. ssh_config	285.	CD
286.	A	287.	B	288.	C	289.	D	290.	D
291.	B	292.	C	293.	tcpd	294.	D	295.	A
296.	AD	297.	B	298.	C	299.	BCD	300.	ABD
301.	B	302.	C	303.	B	304.	D	305.	A
306.	C	307.	D	308.	False	309.	AB	310.	AC
311.	ACD	312.	False	313.	BCD	314.	A	315.	B
316.	ACD	317.	True	318.	ABD	319.	B	320.	True
321.	anacron	322.	AD	323.	AB	324.	False	325.	C
326.	C	327.	BD	328.	B	329.	D	330.	ABD
331.	A	332.	B	333.	E	334.	B	335.	A
336.	B	337.	ABC	338.	D	339.	AC	340.	True
341.	D	342.	CD	343.	CD	344.	False	345.	BD
346.	A	347.	BC	348.	True	349.	A	350.	BD
351.	True	352.	True	353.	B	354.	C	355.	AB
356.	B	357.	False	358.	B	359.	A	360.	C
361.	D	362.	ABD	363.	C	364.	B	365.	D
366.	A	367.	A	368.	A	369.	B	370.	passwd
371.	C	372.	C	373.	B	374.	D	375.	A
376.	BC								

Bibliography

The following websites, forums, and books were referenced in writing this book:

1. www.lpi.org
2. www.comptia.org
3. www.centos.org
4. www.redhat.com
5. www.ubuntu.com
6. www.debian.org
7. www.canonical.com
8. www.linux.org
9. www.opensource.org
10. www.oracle.com
11. www.virtualbox.org
12. www.gnome.org
13. www.chiark.greenend.org.uk/~sgtatham/putty/latest.html
14. www.afb.org
15. www.freedesktop.org
16. www.ibm.com
17. www.ietf.org
18. www.isc.org
19. www.linuxhq.com
20. www.ntp.org
21. www.openssh.org
22. www.pathname.com/fhs
23. www.postfix.org
24. www.sendmail.org
25. www.wikipedia.org
26. www.tldp.org
27. www.gnupg.org
28. RHCSA & RHCE Red Hat Enterprise Linux 7 by Asghar Ghori
29. Red Hat Certified System Administrator & Engineer for RHEL 6 by Asghar Ghori
30. Red Hat Certified Technician & Engineer for RHEL 5 by Asghar Ghori
31. HP-UX 11i v3 book by Asghar Ghori

Glossary

. (single dot)	Represents current directory
.. (double dots)	Represents parent directory of the current directory
Absolute mode	A method of allocating permissions to a file or directory
Absolute path	A pathname that begins with the forward slash (/) character
Accessibility options	Desktop accessibility tools and features for users with a hearing, speech, vision, or mobility impairment to help them interact with the operating system and applications
Access mode	See File permissions
Access rights	See File permissions
Algorithm	An ordered list of actions to accomplish a task, such as to generate a private/public keypair
Anaconda	An operating system installation program for Red Hat Enterprise Linux and its derivatives
Anacron	A service that runs scheduled jobs that were missed due to system shutdown
Archive	A file that contains one or more files in compressed or uncompressed form
Argument	A value passed to a command or program
ARP	(Address Resolution Protocol) A protocol used to determine a system's Ethernet address when its IP address is known
ASCII	(American Standard Code for Information Interchange) A set of characters used for text translation
Assistive technology	Any software or hardware, or a combination, that is used to provide assistance to impaired users in their interaction with the computer
Auditing	System and user activity record and analysis
Authentication	The process of identifying a user to a system
Authentication agent	A program that stores private keys and use them to authenticate users
Background process	A process that runs in the background and serves client requests
Backup	A process of saving data on an alternative media, such as a tape or another disk
Bash shell	A feature-rich common shell that is available in most Linux distributions
BIND	(Berkeley Internet Name Domain) A UC Berkeley implementation of DNS on Linux and UNIX. See Domain Name System.
BIOS	(Basic I/O System) Software code that sits in the computer's non-volatile memory and runs at system boot
Block	A collection of bytes of data transmitted as a single entity
Block special device file	A file associated with devices that transfer data randomly in blocks. Common examples are hard disk and optical drives.
Boot	A phased process of starting a computer
Bootloader	A program that finds and loads an operating system kernel
Braille display	An attachable computer device used by the blind to read the text displayed on the computer screen
Broadcast client	An NTP client that listens to time broadcasts to adjust its clock

Broadcast server	An NTP server that broadcasts time to NTP clients
Btrfs	(B-tree file system) An advanced fault-tolerant Linux file system that is based on the copy-on-write principle
Bus	Data communication path among devices in a computer system
Cache	A temporary storage area on the system where frequently accessed information is stored for quick future access
CentOS	(Community Enterprise Operating System) An unsponsored binary-compatible rebuild of Red Hat Enterprise Linux available for free
Character encoding	A scheme used to handle text transformation among a variety of locales.
Character special device file	A file associated with devices that transfer data serially, one character at a time. Common examples are hard disk, tape, and mouse.
Child directory	A directory one level below the current directory
Child process	A sub-process started by a process
CIDR	(Classless Inter-Domain Routing) A technique that is used to control the exhaustion of IPv4 addresses and the proliferation in the number of routing tables required to route IP traffic
Coldplug	Devices that require a complete shutdown of the system to be replaced or removed
Command	An instruction given to the system to perform a task
Command aliasing	A shell feature that allows the creation of command shortcuts
Command history	A shell feature that maintains a log of all commands executed at the command line
Command interpreter	See Shell
Command Line Argument	An argument passed to a command at the time of its invocation
Command line editing	A shell feature that allows editing of a command at the command line
Command prompt	The shell prompt where commands are typed for execution
Compression	The process of compressing files.
Conditionals	See Logical statement
Core	A core is a processor that shares the chip with another core. Multicore processor chips are common.
Crash	An abnormal system shutdown caused by an electrical outage, a kernel malfunction, etc.
CUPS	(Common UNIX Printing System) A standard printing system used on Linux and UNIX systems
Current directory	The present working directory for a user
Daemon	A server process that runs in the background and responds to client requests
Database	A structured collection of data containing facts and figures
DBMS	(DataBase Management System) A system that allows the storage, management, and manipulation of data stored in a database
Debian Linux	One of the earliest non-commercial Linux distributions from which many other Linux distributions/versions have forked
De-encapsulation	The reverse of encapsulation. See Encapsulation.
Default	Pre-defined values or settings that are automatically accepted by commands or programs

Default gateway	See Default route
Default permissions	Permissions assigned to a file at the time of its creation
Default route	A special network setting that is used by the system to send data packets to when no specific route to destination exists
Defunct process	See Zombie process
Desktop manager	Software such as GNOME and Unity that provide graphical environment for user interaction with the system
Device	A peripheral such as a printer, disk, mouse, keyboard, or an optical device
Device driver	Software that controls a hardware device
Device file	A special file that is used to access a hardware device on the system
Directory structure	A hierarchical Linux/UNIX directory tree
Disk-based file system	A file system created on a non-volatile storage device
Disk dumping	A process of duplicating an entire disk or a disk partition
Disk partitioning	A technique to partition a storage device for data storage
Display manager	A graphical program that presents a login screen for users to enter their credentials
DMA	(Direct Memory Access) A computer feature that allows hardware devices to access main system memory without the intervention of a processor
DNS	(Domain Name System) A common name resolution system used on corporate networks and the Internet
Domain	A group of computers configured to use a network service such as the DNS
Driver	See Device driver
Dynamic directory	A directory that contains log files, configuration files, temporary files, etc. that change often
Encapsulation	A process of forming a network packet through the seven OSI layers
Encryption	A method of scrambling information for privacy
Environment variable	A variable whose value is available in the current shell as well as any sub-shells that it spawns
EOF	An End Of File marker
Ethernet	A family of interface technologies designed for LAN communication
Export	A process of sharing a directory or file system over the network
Ext filesystem	A type of file system structure that has been around in Linux for years
Fedora	A Red Hat sponsored community project for collaborative enhancement of Red Hat Enterprise Linux
FHS	(Filesystem Hierarchy Standard) A standard that defines what, where, and how to store file and directory information
Fibre channel	A family of interface technologies designed for storage networking
File permissions	Read, write, execute or no permission assigned to a file or directory at the user, group or public level
File system	A detachable structure that is used to store files and directories
Filter	A command or program that is used to perform data transformation on the given input
FireWire	A bus interface standard for devices designed for very fast communication
Firmware	Code stored in flash memory to initialize the hardware and initiate the boot process
FTP	(File Transfer Protocol) A common protocol that is used for transfering files

Full path	See Absolute path
Function	A shell feature that allows the creation of sets of tasks that may be invoked individually
Gateway	A device that links two networks running completely different protocols
Gestures	A desktop environment feature that allows users with physical impairments to enter their login credentials using mouse gestures
GID	(Group ID) A numeric identifier assigned to a group
Globbing	A shell feature that allows the use of *, ?, and [] special characters in commands to perform an action on multiple files
GNOME	(GNU Network Object Model Environment) An intuitive graphical user environment
GNU	(GNU Not Unix) A project initiated to develop a completely free UNIX-like operating system
GnuPG	(GNU Privacy Guard) A technique to encrypt and sign email messages and files for privacy and confidentiality
GPL	(General Public License) It allows the use of software developed under the GNU project to be available for free to the public
GPT	(GUID Partition Table) A small disk partition on a UEFI system that stores disk partition information
Group	A collection of users with common file permission requirements
Group collaboration	A collection of users belonging to more than one groups to share files
GRUB Legacy	(GRand Unified Bootloader) A GNU bootloader program that supports multiboot functionality
GRUB2	A newer and enhanced version of GRUB Legacy
Guest	An operating system instance that runs in a virtual machine
GUI	(Graphical User Interface) An interface for graphical user interaction with the operating system
Home directory	A directory where a user lands upon successfully signing in
Hostname	A unique name assigned to a node on a network
Hotplug	Devices that can be replaced or removed while the system is operational
HTTP	(Hyper Text Transfer Protocol) Allows access to websites
HTTPS	(Secure cousin of HTTP) Allows access to secure websites
IMAP	(Internet Message Access Protocol) A client-side networking protocol used for email retrieval
init	The firstboot process on Linux systems using the older SysVinit initialization method
Initramfs	A read-only image of the root file system that is mounted at an early boot stage to load the required modules to support the loading and initialization of the kernel
Inode	An index node number holds a file's properties including permissions, size, and creation/modification time, as well as it contains a pointer to the disk location where the file's content are stored
Interface card	A hardware interface that allows a system to communicate to external devices
Internationalization	The ability of an operating system to accommodate linguistic, cultural, and time zone requirements of global user communities
Internet	A complex network of computers and routers
I/O redirection	A shell feature that allows getting input from a non-default location and sending output and error messages to non-default locations

IP address	A unique 32- or 128-bit software address assigned to a node on a network
ISO-8859	A series of 8-bit character sets to support European languages in operating systems and computer programs
ISO9660	A file system standard used for optical media, such as CD and DVD devices
IRQ	(Interrupt ReQuest) A signal sent by a device to the processor to request processing time
iSCSI	(Internet Small Computer System Interface) An IP-based storage networking protocol for sharing block storage on the network
Job scheduling	Scheduling and execution of commands, programs, or scripts in future
Job control	A shell feature that allows the switching (between background and foreground), suspending, and stopping of running jobs
Journal	A new way of capturing, viewing, and managing log files on Linux systems running systemd system initialization scheme
Journaling	A mechanism available in most file systems that provides the file systems the ability to recover quickly following a system crash
Kernel	Software piece that controls the entire system including all hardware and software
Label	A unique identifier that may be set on a file system to distinguish it from other file systems
LAN	(Local Area Network) A campus-wide network of computing devices
LDAP	(Lightweight Directory Access Protocol) A networking protocol that is used to retrieve information from an LDAP directory server
Link	A file or directory name that associates itself with an inode number
Link count	The number of file links
Linux	An open-source operating system
List operators	Shell operators that are used to separate two commands from each other
Load balancing	An architecture technique to allow any of many servers to serve a client request
Localization	The ability of an operating system to adapt itself to a specific language or culture
Local variable	A variable whose value is available only in the current shell
Logical statement	A conditional statement that is used in shell scripting for a command execution based on a logical decision
Logical volume	An LVM partition that holds a file system or swap
Logging	A process of capturing desired alerts and forwarding them to preconfigured locations
Login	A sequence of activities to identify a user to the system and to set environment for the user
Login directory	See Home directory
Login manager	See Display manager
Looping statement	A conditional statement that is used in shell scripting for a repetitive execution based on a logical decision
LVM	(Logical Volume Manager) A widely-used flexible disk-partitioning solution
MAC address	A unique 48-bit hardware address associated with a network interface
Mail forwarding	A mechanism to forward an incoming email to another email address
Major number	A number that points to a specific device driver
MariaDB	A relational DBMS, which forked from MySQL

Mass Storage Devices	Block devices, such as hard disk drives, solid state drives, and removable USB drives, that may be partitioned for a variety of usages. It also includes optical disc drives.
MBR	(Master Boot Record) A small region at the beginning of a disk that contains a bootloader program
MDA	(Mail Delivery Agent) A program that delivers email to recipient inboxes
Metacharacters	Characters that have a special meaning to the shell
Metadata	Structural information pertaining to a file, file system, software package, or other entity
Minor number	A unique number that identifies an individual device controlled by a specific device driver
Module	A device driver that is used to control a specific type of hardware device or a software component
Mounting	The process of attaching a file system to the Linux directory structure to make its files accessible
Mount point	A directory that is used to attach (mount) a file system to the Linux directory structure
MSA	(Mail Submission Agent) A program that submits email messages to a mail transfer agent.
MTA	(Mail Transfer Agent) A program that transports email messages from one system to another
MUA	(Mail User Agent) A mail client program that a user interacts with to read and compose email messages
Name resolution	A technique to determine IP address by its hostname
Name space	A hierarchical organization of DNS domains on the Internet
Netmask	See Subnet mask
Network	A configuration with two or more computers to share resources
Network interface	A network port that is used to connect a node to a network
Niceness	The ability of the system to determine the priority of a process
Nice value	See Niceness
Node	A device (a computer, printer, router, hub, switch, etc.) connected directly to a network interface and has a unique hostname and IP address
Node name	A unique name assigned to a network node
Nologin account	A special-purpose user account created for services, applications, and users that do not require login access to the system
NTP	(Network Time Protocol) A networking protocol that is used to synchronize system clocks with external time servers
NTP pool	A pool of NTP servers available from various providers to synchronize system clock with
Octal mode	A method of allocating permissions to files and directories
Octal numbering system	A 3-digit numbering system that represents values from 0 to 7
On-screen keyboard	A feature that presents a virtual keyboard on the computer screen particularly for people with typing issues
Open source	A software with source code available at no cost to the public under GNU GPL for copying, modification, and redistribution
OpenSSH	An open-source implementation of the secure shell service
Orphan process	An alive child process of a terminated parent process

OSI	(Open Systems Interconnection) A layered networking reference model that provides guidelines to networking equipment manufacturers to develop their products for multi-vendor interoperability
Owner	A user that creates a file, owns a file, or starts a process
Package	A set of necessary files and related metadata that make up a software application
Package database	A directory location that stores metadata for installed software packages
Package dependency	Additional software packages that are required for a successful installation of another package
Paging	The process of transferring data between memory and swap space
Parent directory	A directory one level above the current directory
Partition	A logical slice on a disk that is used to hold a file system or swap, or used as a raw device for certain applications
Password aging	A mechanism that delivers enhanced control on user passwords
Pattern matching	See Regular expression
PCI	(Peripheral Component Interconnect) A hardware interface adapter that is used to connect peripheral devices to the system
Peer-to-peer	A model which allows two computers, two applications, or two protocols to communicate with each other at the same level or layer
Physical volume	A whole hard disk or a disk partition that is initialized for use in LVM
PID	(Process ID) A numeric identifier assigned to a process at initiation by the kernel
Pipe	A shell features that allows sending output of one command as input to the next
POP	(Post Office Protocol) A client-side networking protocol used for email retrieval
Port	(Software) A number associated with a service. (Hardware) An interface to connect an external device to the computer. (Network) A random number appended to an IP address.
Port forwarding	A method of directing incoming network traffic to an alternative network port
Port tunneling	See Port forwarding
Positional parameter	See Command Line Argument
POST	(Power-On-Self-Test) A test that runs on the computer hardware at system startup
Postfix	A mail transfer agent used for transporting email messages across networks
PPID	(Parent process ID) The ID of a process that starts a child process
Primary prompt	The primary shell prompt where commands and programs are typed for execution
Print queue	A spooling location to hold submitted print jobs before they are sent to a printer for printing
Process	Any command, program, or daemon that runs on the system
Process state	One of many states in which a process is held during its lifecycle
Processor	A CPU chip, which may contain several cores
Protocol	A common language that two computers or applications understand for data exchange
Quota	A method for controlling the usage of a file system space based on the user or group requirement

RDBMS	(Relational DataBase Management System) A type of database whose organization is based on the relational model of data
Redirection	See I/O redirection
Regular expression	A string of characters commonly used in pattern matching or file globbing
ReiserFS	A type of file system
Relative path	A path to a file relative to the current user location in the directory hierarchy
Relay	A mail server configured to forward incoming mail to another mail server
Removable media	A medium, such as a USB or optical device, that may be attached to the system when needed
Repository	A network location to store software packages for downloading and installing
Rescue mode	A special Linux boot mode for fixing and recovering an unbootable system
Resolver	The client-side DNS functionality
RHEL	(Red Hat Enterprise Linux) A popular commercial Linux distribution
Root	See Superuser
Router	A device that routes data packets from one network to another
Routing	The process of choosing a path over which to send a data packet
Routing table	A location to store information about available routes
RPM	(Red Hat Package Manager) A software packaging file format that is used on RHEL and its clones for package installation and manipulation
Run control levels	Different levels of Linux operation available in SysVinit system initialization scheme
Runtime information	Live system information stored in /proc, /sys, and /dev, and updated automatically
SATA	(Serial Advanced Technology Attachment) A common hard disk interface that is used to connect block devices to the system
Scientific Linux	An unsponsored binary-compatible rebuild of Red Hat Enterprise Linux available for free
Screen magnifier	Software that enlarges the screen content for convenient viewing by visually impaired
Screen reader	Software that interfaces with a speech synthesizer or braille monitor to allow visually impaired to read the text displayed on the computer screen
Script	A text program written to perform a series of tasks
SCSI	(Small Computer System Interface) A hard disk interface that is used to connect block devices to the system
Search path	A list of directories where the system looks for the specified command
Secondary prompt	A shell prompt indicating that the command entered at the primary prompt is incomplete and needs more input in order to proceed with the command execution
Secure shell	A service that allows secure access to a system with encrypted data exchange
Security context	SELinux security attributes set on files, processes, users, ports, etc.
SELinux	(Security Enhanced Linux) An implementation of Mandatory Access Control architecture for enhanced and granular control on files, processes, users, ports, etc.
Server	(Hardware) A physical or virtual computer. (Software) A process or service daemon that serves client requests.

Setgid	(Set Group ID) A special permission bit that allows non-group owners to run a command with group owner's privileges. It also allows group members to have shared access to a directory.
Setuid	(Set User ID) A special permission bit that allows non-owners to run a command with file owner's privileges
Shadow password	A mechanism to store passwords and password aging data in a secure location
Shared library	Software code referenced by programs, commands, and applications for their successful execution
Shareable/non-shareable directory	A directory that may/may not be shared on the network due to the type of files they store
Shebang	A combination (#!) of the number sign and exclamation point characters specified at the beginning of a shell script to identify the script interpreter to be used for script execution
Shell	The Linux command interpreter that sits between a user and the kernel
Shell program	See Script
Shell script	See Script
Shell scripting	Writing programs for task automation
Signal	A software interrupt sent to a process to take an action, such as a graceful stop, an abrupt termination, or a restart
Single-user mode	An operating system state to perform maintenance tasks that cannot be otherwise carried out
Special characters	See Metacharacters
Special permissions	See Set group ID, Set user ID, and Sticky bit
SQL	(Structured Query Language) A computer language that is used for database management, query, and manipulation of data stored in the database
Standard error	A location to send error messages to
Standard input	A location to obtain input from
Standard output	A location to send output to
Static directory	A directory that contains non-changeable data, such as manual pages, library files, etc.
Stderr	See Standard error
Stdin	See Standard input
Stdout	See Standard output
Sticky bit	A special permission bit that disallows non-owners to erase files located in a public-writable directory
Sticky keys	A feature that allows users with difficulty pressing multiple keys at a time to use one finger for this operation
Stratum level	A categorization of NTP time sources based on their reliability and accuracy
String	A series of characters
Subnet	A smaller network space that is formed by dividing an IP address
Subnet mask	The segregation of network bits from node bits
Subnetting	The process of dividing an IP address into several smaller subnetworks
Sudo	A method of delegating a portion of privileged access to normal users
Superblock	A tiny portion in a file system that holds its critical information
Super-server	The master server program (xinetd/inetd) that is used to start services on the system
Superuser	A user with unlimited powers on the Linux system

Swap	An alternative disk or file system location set aside for paging
Switch	A physical or virtual network device that looks at the MAC address and switches the packet to the correct destination address based on the MAC address
Symbolic link	A shortcut created to point to a file or directory that exists somewhere on the system
Symbolic mode	A method of setting permissions on a file using non-decimal values
Symlink	See Symbolic link
System Administrator	A person with responsibility to install, configure, and manage Linux systems
System console	The main terminal screen on a Linux system to interact with OS installation and perform single-user and emergency mode operations, and where critical system messages are displayed
systemd	A method of system initialization and service management that has replaced both SysVinit and Upstart in newer Linux distribution versions
SysVinit	A method of system initialization used in older Linux distribution versions
Tab completion	A shell feature that allows command or file name completion by typing a partial name at the command prompt and then hitting the Tab key twice
Target	A logical collection of systemd units to achieve a desired state
TCP/IP	(Transmission Control Protocol / Internet Protocol) A stacked, standard suite of protocols for data communication
TCP Wrappers	An access control mechanism to allow (or disallow) hosts, networks, or domains to access (from accessing) one or more network services on the system
Tee	A shell feature that allows a user to send a command output to more than one destinations
Terminal	A window where commands are executed
Test conditions	Conditions used in logical and looping constructs for decision-making
Tilde substitution	A shell feature that allows the use of the tilde (~) character as a shortcut to a user's home directory
Time zone	A region of the globe that observes a uniform standard time
Tty	Refers to a terminal
Ubuntu Linux	A popular Linux distribution available for commercial and non-commercial uses
UEFI	(Unified Extensible Firmware Interface) Software code that is used in modern computers for pre-boot system management
UID	(User ID) A numeric identifier assigned to a user
Umask	A value used in calculating default access rights on files and directories
Unicode	An industry-standard character encoding system to handle the variances and provide a consistent mapping for every character to a unique number regardless of the language, program, or platform the character belongs to or is associated with
Unit	A systemd object that is used to handle service startups, socket creation, etc.
Unmounting	The process of dettaching a file system from the Linux directory structure to make its files inaccessible
Upstart	An event-based system initialization scheme that was used in some previous Linux distribution versions

USB	(Universal Serial Bus) A bus standard to connect peripheral devices to a computer
User limits	Controls that may be placed on certain user-accessible system resources to guarantee continuous execution of user processes
UUID	(Universally Unique IDentifier) A unique alphanumeric software identifier that is assigned to hardware and software objects, such as disks, logical partitions, file systems, swap areas, and PCI devices
Variable	A temporary storage of data in memory
VFAT	(Virtual File Allocation Table) A file system type based on the old MS-DOS FAT file system
Video card	A PC expansion card that converts electrical signals into visual signals for exhibiting on a display monitor
Virtual file system	A file system that is created in memory at system boot and destroyed at system shutdown automatically
Virtualization	A technology that allows a single physical computer to run several independent logical computers (called virtual machines) with complete isolation from one another
Virtual machine	A logical computer running on a virtualized physical computer
Volume group	A logical container that holds physical and logical volumes for file systems and swap
Web	A system of interlinked hypertext documents that is accessed over a network or the Internet via a web browser
Wildcard characters	See Metacharacters
Window manager	A program that controls the presentation, location, and adornment of windows on the desktop
X font server	A service that provides fonts to client systems to display the text properly
XFS	(X File System) A high-performance 64-bit extent-based journaling file system type
X server	A service that is used to manage the graphics and associated video hardware on the system
X Window System	A protocol that provides users with a graphical interface for system interaction
Zombie process	An abnormally-terminated child process with the parent process still waiting for a response from it

Index

.

.bash_history file, 96
.bash_logout file, 309
.bash_profile file, 309
.bashrc file, 309
.profile file, 309

/

/bin directory, 38
/boot/grub/grub.conf file, 161
/boot/grub/menu.lst file, 158
/boot/grub2/grub.cfg file, 162, 163
/dev directory, 38
/etc directory, 38
/etc/anacrontab file, 404
/etc/apt/sources.list file, 129
/etc/at.allow file, 399
/etc/at.deny file, 399
/etc/bash.bashrc file, 308
/etc/bashrc file, 308
/etc/cron.* directories, 404
/etc/cron.allow file, 399
/etc/default/grub file, 162, 166
/etc/default/locale file, 350
/etc/default/useradd file, 296
/etc/fstab file, 231
/etc/gdm/custom.conf file, 378
/etc/group file, 292
/etc/gshadow file, 293
/etc/hostname file, 321
/etc/hosts file, 332, 364
/etc/hosts.allow file, 412
/etc/hosts.deny file, 412
/etc/inittab file, 167
/etc/ld.so.conf file, 123
/etc/lightdm/lightdm.conf file, 380
/etc/locale.conf file, 350
/etc/localtime file, 352
/etc/login.defs file, 294, 296
/etc/logrotate.conf file, 409
/etc/network/interfaces file, 327
/etc/nsswitch.conf file, 364
/etc/ntp.conf file, 358
/etc/passwd file, 289
/etc/profile file, 308

/etc/protocols file, 324
/etc/redhat-release file, 100
/etc/resolv.conf file, 363
/etc/rsyslog.conf file, 406
/etc/services file, 341
/etc/shadow file, 291
/etc/skel directory, 295
/etc/ssh/ssh_config file, 424
/etc/ssh/sshd_config file, 424
/etc/sudoers file, 304
/etc/sysconfig/clock file, 352
/etc/sysconfig/desktop file, 378
/etc/sysconfig/i18n file, 350
/etc/sysconfig/network file, 321, 334
/etc/sysconfig/network-scripts directory, 326
/etc/syslog-ng/syslog-ng.conf file, 410
/etc/systemd/journald.conf file, 411
/etc/timezone file, 352
/etc/udev/udev.conf file, 196
/etc/X11/default-display-manager file, 378
/etc/X11/xdm/Xresources file, 378
/etc/X11/xorg.conf file, 373
/etc/xinetd.conf file, 341
/etc/yum.conf file, 143
/etc/yum.repos.d directory, 144
/lib directory, 39
/lib64 directory, 39
/mnt directory, 38
/proc directory, 38
/proc/cmdline file, 166, 199
/proc/cpuinfo file, 190
/proc/dma file, 188
/proc/interrupts file, 187
/proc/ioports file, 188
/proc/meminfo file, 250
/proc/modules file, 203
/proc/version file, 199
/root directory, 38
/sbin directory, 39
/sys directory, 38
/usr/bin directory, 38
/usr/lib directory, 39
/usr/lib64 directory, 39
/usr/sbin directory, 39
/var/log/boot.log file, 181
/var/log/cron file, 402
/var/log/dmesg file, 165, 181
/var/log/messages file, 182, 406
/var/log/secure file, 305, 413

/var/log/spooler file, 406
/var/log/syslog file, 182

A

accept command, 391
Accessibility, 382
  Assistive technologies, 382
    Keyboard navigation, 382
    Mouse cursors and gestures, 383
    Onscreen keyboard, 383
    Resolution adjustments, 383
    Screen magnifiers, 383
    Screen readers, 383
    Speech synthesizers, 383
    Visual and audible alerts, 383
  Configuring, 383
Accessing command prompt, 18
Address Resolution Protocol (ARP), 320
alias command, 94
anacron command, 405
apropos command, 30
apt vs. apt-get and apt-cache comparison, 135
apt-cache command, 129, 132
apt-get command, 129, 130
aptitude command, 129
Archiving tools, 26
ARP cache, 320
arp command, 320, 340
ASCII character set, 348
at command, 400

B

bg command, 114
BIND (See Domain Name System)
BIOS, 200
blkid command, 227
Block special device file (See File types)
Boot process, 155
  Firmware phase, 155
    BIOS initialization, 155
    UEFI initialization, 155
  GRUB phase, 156
    GRUB legacy, 157
    GRUB2, 162
  Initialization phase, 156
    Configuration directories, 169
    Firstboot process, 167
    init program, 156
    Initialization directories, 169
    Sequencer directories, 168
    SysVinit, 166
  Kernel phase, 156, 165
    Command line options, 166
  systemd

    Managing, 177
    Managing service units, 178
    Managing target units, 180
    Managing units, 177
    Overview, 174
    Target, 176
    Unit, 175
  Upstart, 157
  Upstart process, 167
  Viewing boot messages, 181
break command, 274
bunzip2 command, 25
bzip2 command, 25

C

cat command, 39, 41, 73
cd command, 21
chage command, 298
Character encoding, 347
Character special device file (See File types)
chgrp command, 51
chkconfig command, 171
chmod command, 48
chown command, 51
clear command, 24
Command Interpreter (See Shell)
Compression tools, 24
Computer hardware, 187
  BIOS, 200
  Communication channels, 187
    DMA, 188
    I/O port address, 188
    IRQ, 187
  Cores, 190
  D-Bus, 200
  Hotplug and coldplug, 196
  Mass storage, 192
    Hard disk drives, 192
      FireWire, 193
      IDE, 194
      PATA, 194
      SAS, 193
      SATA, 192
      SCSI, 193
      USB, 193
    Optical drives, 194
    Removable USB flash drives, 194
    Solid state drives, 194
  PCIe, 189
  Processor, 190
  Runtime information, 197
  udev, 196
  USB, 195
continue command, 274
cp command, 42

cpio command, 28
crontab command, 402
CUPS (See Printing)
cupsdisable command, 390
cupsenable command, 391
cut command, 73

D

Database
  DBMS, 275
  Defined, 275
  Foreign key, 276
  Managing and querying
    Creating database and table, 279
    Deleting records, 284
    Dropping table and database, 285
    Inserting records, 281
    Querying, 282
    Showing, 280
    Updating records, 284
  MariaDB shell, 278
  Relational, 275
  SQL, 276
date command, 352, 361
D-Bus, 174
dd command, 238
Debian packages
  APT, 129
    Cleaning cache, 132
    Displaying APT cache statistics, 134
    Displaying information, 133
    Downloading, 130
    Installing, 130
    Listing, 133
    Listing dependencies, 134
    Removing, 132
    Searching, 133
    Updating database, 131
    Upgrading, 131
    Using aptitude, 135
    Viewing unmet dependencies, 135
  Database, 125
  Dependency, 125
  Installing, 128
  Management tools, 125
  Naming, 124
  Overview, 124
  Purging, 128
  Querying, 126
  Reconfiguring, 128
  Removing, 128
  Repository, 129
  Verifying, 128
Default gateway (See Default route)
Default route, 333

df command, 227, 228, 232
dig command, 364
Disk partitioning
  GPT, 213
  Management tools, 214
    LVM
      Logical volume, 223
      Physical volume, 223
      Volume group, 223
    Using fdisk, 215
    Using gdisk, 219
    Using LVM, 222
      LVM commands, 224
    Using parted, 217
  MBR, 212
  UEFI, 212
dmesg command, 165
Domain Name System
  BIND, 362
  Domain, 362
  FQDN, 362
  Managing
    Lookup tools, 364
    Resolver configuration file, 363
    Resolver sources and order, 364
  Name space, 362
  Overview, 362
  Roles, 362
    DNS client, 363
    Primary or Master, 363
    Secondary or Slave, 363
dpkg command, 125
dpkg-reconfigure command, 352
du command, 227, 233

E

e2fsck command, 227, 239
e2label command, 227
echo command, 92, 260
edquota command, 246
egrep command, 85
Email
  Checking mail queue, 420
  Composing a message, 420
  How it works, 418
  Mail queue, 418
  Mailbox, 418
  Message parts, 417
  Overview, 417
  Protocols
    IMAP, 418
    POP, 418
    SMTP, 417
  Reading email, 420
  Redirecting user mail, 421

via .forward file, 421
via /etc/aliases file, 421
Sending and receiving, 419
Terms
MDA, 418
MSA, 418
MTA, 418
Postfix and sendmail, 419
MUA, 417
env command, 92
Ethernet address (See MAC address)
exec command, 266
expand command, 74

F

fdisk command, 193, 215
fg command, 114
fgrep command, 85
FHS (See File systems)
File permissions, 47
Access rights, 47
Classes, 47
Default, 50
Initial value, 50
Modes, 47
Modifying, 48
Using octal notation, 48
Using symbolic notation, 48
Special, 61
Finding directories with setgid bit on, 433
Finding directories with sticky bit on, 433
Finding files with setgid bit on, 433
Finding files with setuid bit on, 433
setgid (sgid) on directories, 63
setgid (sgid) on files, 62
setuid (suid), 61
Sticky bit, 63
Types, 47
File systems
/dev, 198
/proc, 199
/sys, 198
Benefits, 224
Common directories, 38
Debugging
Extended, 241
Defined, 224
Directory structure, 37
Extended file system with journal, 225
Filesystem Hierarchy Standard (FHS), 37
Label, 230
Managing, 227
Backing up MBR, 238
Commands, 227
Creating ext file system, 233

Creating vfat file system, 235
Creating xfs file system, 234
Determining UUID, 229
Disk dumping, 238
Dumping XFS metadata, 243
Labeling, 230
Mount options, 228
Mounting, 228
Mounting automatically, 231
Mounting manually, 234, 235, 236
Unmounting, 229
Monitoring, 232
Parent and child directories, 37
Quota
Defined, 244
Hard limit, 244
Managing
Activating at boot, 248
Activating quota support, 245
Commands, 244
Duplicating, 248
Enforcing, 245
Initializing, 245
Setting and viewing, 246
Reporting, 248
Soft limit, 244
Grace period, 247
Removable, 236
Mounting automatically, 238
Mounting manually, 237
Unmounting manually, 237
Repairing, 239
Extended, 239
XFS, 242
Tree, 37
Types, 224
Btrfs, 226
Extended, 225
Optical, 226
Reiser4, 226
ReiserFS, 226
VFAT, 226
XFS, 225
UUID, 229
File types, 45
Block special device files, 46, 198
Character special device files, 46
Directory files, 46
Executable files, 46
Raw device files, 198
Regular files, 45
Symbolic links, 46
Symlinks (See Symbolic links)
Files and directories
Copying, 42
Creating, 39

Displaying contents, 41
Moving and renaming, 43
Removing, 44
Shareable vs. non-shareable, 38
Static vs. dynamic, 38
Filters, 73
find command, 57, 432
Finding files, 56
Firstboot (See Boot process)
fmt command, 75
free command, 249
fuser command, 435

G

gdisk command, 219
getent command, 307, 366
GNU Linux, 3
GNU Privacy Guard
    Keyserver, 430
    Managing
        Commands, 428
        Encrypting files with signatures, 431
        Encrypting files without signatures, 431
        Exporting keys, 430
        Generating keys, 429
        Generating revocation certificate, 432
        Importing key, 431
        Listing keys, 430
        Sharing keys, 430
    Overview, 428
    Software package, 428
GNU Project, 3
GnuPG (See GNU Privacy Guard)
gpasswd command, 294
gpg command, 428
gpg2 command, 428
GPL, 3
GPT, 213
grep command, 83
groupadd command, 306
groupdel command, 306
groupmod command, 306
groups command, 23
grpconv command, 294
grpunconv command, 294
GRUB legacy, 157
    Autoboot timeout, 161
    Configuration file, 158
    Installing corrupted bootloader, 161
    Interacting, 159
GRUB2
    Configuration files, 162
    Interacting, 164
grub2-mkconfig command, 163
grub-install command, 161

grub-mkconfig command, 163
gunzip command, 25
gzip command, 24
gzip vs bzip2, 25

H

halt command, 171
Hardware address (See MAC address)
head command, 42
history command, 96
host command, 365
Hostname, 320
hostname command, 24, 321
hostnamectl command, 321
hwclock command, 352, 361

I

i18n (See Internationalization)
iconv command, 351
id command, 23
ifconfig command, 320, 321, 328
ifdown command, 326
init command, 168, 169
Installation
    Creating VM for CentOS, 6
    Creating VM for Ubuntu, 14
    Downloading CentOS, 6
    Downloading Ubuntu, 14
    Installing CentOS, 7
    Installing Ubuntu, 14
    LAB Setup, 5
Internationalization, 347
Internet services
    Client/server, 340
    Common services, 341
    Enabling and disabling, 342
    inetd/xinetd daemon, 341
    Overview, 340
    Super-server, 341
IP address, 321
ip command, 320, 321, 328

J

Job control, 113
Job scheduling
    Anacron, 404
    atd daemon, 400
    Controlling access, 399
    crond daemon, 402
    crontab file syntax, 402
    Logging, 400
    Overview, 399
    Using at, 400

Using crontab, 402
jobs command, 114
join command, 75
journalctl command, 411

K

Kernel
    Checking version, 202
    Command line options, 166
    Device drivers, 202
    Displaying module information, 204
    Listing modules, 203
    Loading a module, 204
    Modules, 202
    Unloading a module, 204
kill command, 111
killall command, 112

L

L10n (See Localization)
last command, 302
lastb command, 302
ldconfig command, 123
ldd command, 122
less command, 41
let command, 272
Link files, 52
    Copying vs. linking, 55
    Hard link, 53
    Symbolic link, 54
    Symlink (See Symbolic link)
Linux
    Command syntax, 19
    Common commands, 19
    Distributions
        CentOS, 4
        Debian, 4
        OpenSUSE, 4
        Oracle Linux, 4
        RHEL, 4
        Scientific Linux, 4
        SUSE
            SLES and SLED, 4
        Ubuntu, 4
List operators, 103
ln command, 54
locale command, 348
localectl command, 350
Localization, 347
    Changing encoding, 351
    Changing system-wide time zone, 352
    Displaying locale, 348
    Displaying time zone, 351
    Modifying per-user locale, 351

    Modifying system-wide locale, 350
    Setting per-user time zone, 354
    TZ variable, 354
locate command, 60
logger command, 407
Logical Volume Manager (See Disk partitioning)
logname command, 22
logrotate command, 409
lp command, 392
lpadmin command, 388
lpinfo command, 388
lpq command, 393
lpr command, 392
lprm command, 393
lpstat command, 388, 393
ls command, 20
lsblk command, 194, 213
lscpu command, 190
lsmod command, 203
lsof command, 433
lspci command, 189
lsusb command, 195
lvcreate command, 224
lvdisplay command, 224
lvextend command, 224
LVM (See Disk partitioning)
lvreduce command, 224
lvremove command, 224
lvs command, 223

M

MAC address, 320
mail command, 419, 420
mailq command, 419, 420
mailx command, 419
man command, 30
MBR, 212
mkdir command, 40
mke2fs command, 227
mkfs command, 227
mkfs.vfat command, 227
mkfs.xfs command, 227
mkswap command, 251
modinfo command, 204
modprobe command, 204
more command, 41
mount command, 227, 228
mv command, 43
mysql command, 279

N

nc command (See netcat command
ncat command (See netcat command)
netcat command, 337

netstat command, 337
Network Time Protocol
  Configurtaion file, 358
  Managing
    Checking status, 358
    Configuring client, 359
    Querying status, 358, 359
    Updating clock instantly, 360
  Mode of operation, 356
  ntpd daemon, 355
  Overview, 355
  Roles, 356
    Client, 356
    Peer, 356
    Primary server, 356
    Secondary server, 356
  Software packages, 357
  Stratum levels, 356
  Time sources, 355
    Internet-based, 355
    Radio/Atomic clock, 356
  Timeserver, 357
Networking
  Fundamentals, 315
    ARP, 320
    CIDR notation, 323
    Classes, 321
      Class A, 322
      Class B, 322
      Class C, 322
      Class D, 322
      Class E, 322
    Hardware address, 320
    Hostname, 320
    Hub, 317
    ICMP, 325
    IP address, 321
    IPv4 vs. IPv6, 326
    IPv6, 325
    NDP, 325
    Netmask, 323
    Packet, 318
    Ports, 324
    Protocol, 324
    Repeater, 317
    Route (See Routing)
    Router, 317
    Subnet mask, 323
    Subnetting, 322
    Switch, 317
    TCP, 324
    UDP, 324
  Network interfaces, 326
    Configuration file, 326
    Testing and debugging, 336
  OSI reference model, 316
    De-encapsulation, 318
    Encapsulation, 318
    Layer summary, 317
    Layers, 316
      Application, 316
      Data link, 317
      Network, 317
      Physical, 317
      Presentation, 317
      Session, 317
      Transport, 317
    Peer-to-peer, 319
  TCP/IP
    Layers, 319
    Overview, 319
newaliases command, 422
newgrp command, 294
nice command, 110
nl command, 76
nmap command, 339
nohup command, 113
nslookup command, 365
NTP (See Network Time Protocol)
ntpdate command, 360
ntpq command, 358, 359
ntpstat command, 358
ntsysv command, 173

O

od command, 75
Online help tools, 29
Open Source, vii, 3
OpenSSH
  Algorithms, 423
  Authentication agent, 426
  Configuring trusted login, 425
  Configuring trusted login with authentication
    agent, 426
  Copying securely, 427
  Encryption techniques, 423
  Overview, 422
  sshd daemon, 423
  System-wide client configuration file, 424
  System-wide server configuration file, 424
  Versions, 423
  X11 port tunneling, 427

P

parted command, 217
passwd command, 298
Password aging, 291
paste command, 76
Pattern matching, 83
pgrep command, 108

Physical address (See MAC address)
pidof command, 108
ping command, 336
Pipe (See Shell)
pkill command, 112
Ports, 324
poweroff command, 171
pr command, 77
printenv command, 92
Printing, 385
   Configuration
      Local, 386
      Network, 386
      Remote, 386
   Daemon
      cupsd, 385
      lpd, 385
   Directory hierarchy, 386
   Managing printers
      Accepting and rejecting, 391
      Enabling and disabling, 390
      Removing, 391
      Tools, 388
      Viewing status, 388
   Managing requests, 392
      Listing, 393
      Removing, 393
      Submitting, 392
      Tools, 392
   Managing Service
      Start and stop, 387
   Overview, 385
   Troubleshooting, 393
      Common fixes, 394
      Common symptoms, 394
Process
   Calling process, 104
   Child process, 104
   Daemon, 105
   Identifying PIDs using an open file, 435
   Job control, 113, 521
   Listing, 108
   Listing by ownership, 109
   Listing open files, 433
   Nice value, 109
   Niceness, 109
      Viewing, 109
   Parent process, 104
   PID, 104
   Signals, 111
   States, 108
   Terminating PIDs using an open file, 436
   Viewing with ps, 105
   Viewing with top, 106
Protocol, 324
ps command, 105

pvcreate command, 224
pvdisplay command, 224
pvremove command, 224
pvs command, 223
pwconv command, 294
pwd command, 21
pwunconv command, 294

Q

Quota (See File systems)
quotacheck command, 245
quotaoff command, 246
quotaon command, 245

R

rc levels
   Checking, 169
   Modifying default, 169
   Overview, 167
   Switching, 169
read command, 265
reboot command, 171
Redirection
   Defined, 100
   Error, 102
   Input, 100
      here document, 100
      here string, 101
   Output, 101
Regex (See Pattern matching)
Regular expressions (See Pattern matching)
reject command, 391
renice command, 110
repquota command, 248
rm command, 44
rmdir command, 45
Routing
   Adding, 334
      Default route, 335
      Static route, 334
   Default route, 333
   Overview, 332
   Routing table, 333
RPM
   Database, 138
   Dependency, 138
   Managing
      Extracting files, 143
      Freshening, 141
      Installing, 141
      Management tools, 138
      Querying, 139
      Removing, 142
      Upgrading, 141

Verifying, 141
Naming, 137
Overview, 137
Package, 137
rpm command, 138
rpm2cpio command, 143
Run control levels (See rc levels)

S

scp command, 423, 427
screen command, 114
Secure shell (See OpenSSH)
sed command, 78, 85
sendmail command, 420
seq command, 265
service command, 171
setquota command, 246
Shared libraries, 121
    Cache, 123
    Dependencies, 122
    LD_LIBRARY_PATH, 122, 123
    soname, 121
    Versions, 122
    vs. static libraries, 121
Shell
    Alias substitution, 94
    Bash, 91
    Child shell, 92
    Command history, 96
    Command substitution, 94
    Features, 91
    File globbing, 98
    Filename expansion, 98
    Internal and external commands, 91
    Invoking commands inside defined path, 97
    Invoking commands outside defined path, 98
    List operators, 103
    Modifying command prompt, 94
    Overview, 91
    Pipe, 102
    Variable substitution, 94
    Variables
        Environment, 92
        Local, 92
        Setting, 93
        Shell, 92
        Unsetting, 93
        Viewing, 93
    Wildcard characters, 45, 98
        Asterisk, 98
        Question mark, 99
        Square brackets, 99
Shell scripting
    Command line arguments, 263
    Defined, 259

Displaying system info, 259
Executing, 260
Generating number sequence, 265
Logical construct, 266
    Exit codes, 266
    Test conditions, 267
    Using if-then-elif-fi, 270
    Using if-then-else-fi, 269
    Using if-then-fi, 268
Looping construct, 271
    Controlling loop behavior, 274
    Test conditions, 272
    Using for-do-done, 272
    Using while-do-done, 273
Parsing command output, 262
Positional parameters, 263
Replacing current shell process, 266
setuid rights, 261
Shell parameter, 262
Special parameter, 262
Using environment variables, 262
Using function, 263
Writing interactive script, 265
shutdown command, 170
sleep command, 274
Socket, 174
sort command, 79
split command, 81
Split terminal, 114
ssh command, 423, 425
ssh-add command, 423
ssh-agent command, 423
ssh-copy-id command, 425, 426
ssh-keygen command, 424, 425, 426
startx command, 375
Static libraries, 121
su command, 62, 63, 303
Subnetting (See Networking)
sudo command, 303
Swap
    Activating, 251
    Commands, 251
    Deactivating, 251
    Defined, 249
    Demand paging, 249
    Determining usage, 249
swapoff command, 251
swapon command, 251
System logging
    Configuration file, 406
    journald, 411
        Configuration file, 411
    Logging, 182
    Logging custom messages, 407
    Overview, 405
    Rotating log files, 409

rsyslogd daemon, 405
syslog-ng, 410
systemd-journald daemon, 411
systemctl command, 177, 180

T

tail command, 42
tar command, 26
TCP Wrappers, 411
   Access control, 412
   tcpd daemon, 412
tee command, 103
telinit command, 168, 169
Time zone, 351
timeconfig command, 352
timedatectl command, 352, 360
top command, 106
touch command, 39
tr command, 82
tracepath command, 338
traceroute command, 338
tty command, 22
type command, 61
tzselect command, 354

U

udevadm command, 196
udevinfo command, 196
ulimit command, 305
umask command, 50
umount command, 227, 229
unalias command, 96
uname command, 23, 202, 321
unexpand command, 74
Unicode character set, 347
uniq command, 82
unxz command, 26
update-grub command, 163
update-locale command, 350
Upstart process (See Boot process)
uptime command, 22
useradd command, 295
userdel command, 296
usermod command, 295
Users and groups
   Authentication files
      /etc/group, 292
      /etc/gshadow, 293
      /etc/passwd, 289
      /etc/shadow, 291
   Displaying defaults, 296
   Doing as superuser, 303
   Getting entries, 307
   Managing groups

      Creating, 306
      Deleting, 306
      Modifying, 306
   Managing users
      Adding with custom values, 297
      Adding with default attributes, 296
      Adding with nologin access, 300
      Deleting, 296, 301
      Modifying, 295, 300
      Setting password aging, 298
   No-login account, 299
   Setting user limits, 305
   Shadow passwords, 294
   Startup files, 308
      Per-user, 309
      System-wide, 308
   Switching, 303
UTF-8 encoding scheme, 348

V

vgcreate command, 224
vgdisplay command, 224
vgextend command, 224
vgreduce command, 224
vgremove command, 224
vgs command, 223
vi editor, 69
   Changing, 71
   Copying, moving, and pasting, 71
   Deleting, 72
   Inserting, 70
   Modes, 69
      Command mode, 69
      Input mode, 69
      Last line mode, 69
   Navigating, 70
   Saving and quitting, 72
   Searching, 71
   Starting, 69
vim editor (See vi editor)
vmstat command, 250

W

w command, 302
wall command, 169
wc command, 83
whatis command, 31
whereis command, 61
which command, 61
who command, 301
whoami command, 22

X

X Window
  Changing default display manager, 378
  Customizing LightDM, 379
  Desktop managers, 377
  Display/Login managers, 375
  Overview, 371
  Rebuilding X server, 373
  Remote X, 380
  Server, 371
  Switching display manager on/off, 379
  Viewing configuration, 371
  Window managers, 378
  X font server, 375
xargs command, 59
xdpyinfo command, 372
xfs_admin command, 227
xfs_info command, 227
xfs_metadump command, 243
xfs_repair command, 225, 227, 242
xhost command, 380
xinit command, 375
Xorg command, 373

xrandr command, 371
xwininfo command, 372
xz command, 25

Y

yum
  Configuration file, 143
  Managing packages
    Displaying information, 149
    Downloading, 151
    Installing and updating, 148
    Listing, 146
    Listing dependencies, 147
    Listing providers, 147
    Reinstalling, 149
    Removing, 150
    Searching, 150
  Repository, 144
  Viewing repository, 146
yum command, 143, 145
yumdownloader command, 151

CPSIA information can be obtained
at www.ICGtesting.com
Printed in the USA
BVOW10s1211021117
499359BV00017B/662/P